# Lecture Notes in Computer Science    9569

Commenced Publication in 1973
Founding and Former Series Editors:
Gerhard Goos, Juris Hartmanis, and Jan van Leeuwen

## Editorial Board

More information about this series at http://www.springer.com/series/7410

Yun-Qing Shi · Hyoung Joong Kim
Fernando Pérez-González · Isao Echizen (Eds.)

# Digital-Forensics and Watermarking

14th International Workshop, IWDW 2015
Tokyo, Japan, October 7–10, 2015
Revised Selected Papers

 Springer

*Editors*
Yun-Qing Shi
NJIT
Newark, NJ
USA

Hyoung Joong Kim
Korea University
Seoul
Korea (Republic of)

Fernando Pérez-González
University of Vigo
Vigo
Spain

Isao Echizen
National Institute of Informatics
Tokyo
Japan

ISSN 0302-9743             ISSN 1611-3349   (electronic)
Lecture Notes in Computer Science
ISBN 978-3-319-31959-9     ISBN 978-3-319-31960-5   (eBook)
DOI 10.1007/978-3-319-31960-5

Library of Congress Control Number: 2016935957

LNCS Sublibrary: SL4 – Security and Cryptology

Printed on acid-free paper

This Springer imprint is published by Springer Nature
The registered company is Springer International Publishing AG Switzerland

# Preface

The International Workshop on Digital-Forensics and Watermarking 2015 (IWDW2015), the 14th IWDW, was held on Katsushika Campus of the Tokyo University of Sciences, located in the north-eastern part of Tokyo, Japan, during October 7–10, 2015. IWDW 2015, following the tradition of IWDW, aimed at providing a technical program covering the state-of-the-art theoretical and practical developments in the field of digital watermarking, steganography and steganalysis, forensics and antiforensics, and other multimedia-related security. From 54 submissions from 12 different countries and areas, the Technical Program Committee selected 35 papers (27 oral and eight poster presentations) for publication, including one paper for the best student paper award, and one for the best paper award. Besides these papers, the workshop featured two invited lectures titled "Advances on Video Forensics" and "Cyber Forensics: Key Trends and Opportunities" presented, respectively, by Dr. Alessandro Piva and Dr. Vrizlynn Thing; there was also a one-hour open discussion among all the participants.

We would like to thank all of the authors, reviewers, lecturers, and participants for their valuable contributions to IWDW2015. Our sincere gratitude also goes to all the members of Technical Program Committee, International Publicity Liaisons, and our local volunteers for their careful work and great efforts made in the wonderful organization of this workshop. We appreciate the generous support from the Tokyo University of Sciences. Finally, we hope that the readers will enjoy this volume and that it will provide inspiration and opportunities for future research.

February 2016

Yun-Qing Shi
Hyoung Joong Kim
Fernando Pérez-González
Isao Echizen

# Organization

## General Chairs

Kouichi Sakurai      Kyushu University, Japan
Choon Sik Park      Seoul Women's University, Korea

## Technical Program Chairs

Yun Q. Shi      New Jersey Institute of Technology, USA
Hyoung Joong Kim      Korea University, Korea
Fernando      University of Vigo, Spain
   Pérez-González

## Technical Program Committee

| | |
|---|---|
| Rainer Boehme | University of Münster, Germany |
| Lee-Ming Cheng | City University of Hong Kong, SAR China |
| Stelvio Cimato | University of Milan, Italy |
| Claude Delpha | University of Paris-SuD XI, France |
| Jana Dittmann | University of Magdeburg, Germany |
| Fangjun Huang | Sun Yet-sen University, China |
| Xinhao Jiang | Shanghai Jiao-Tong University, China |
| Xiangui Kang | Sun Yat-sen University, China |
| Mohan S. Kankanhalli | NUS, Singapore |
| Anja Keskinarkaus | University of Oulu, Finland |
| Minoru Kuribayashi | Kobe University, Japan |
| Chang-Tsun Li | University of Warwick, UK |
| Shenghong Li | Shanghai Jiaotong University, China |
| Feng Liu | Chinese Academy of Sciences, China |
| Zheming Lu | University of Zhejiang, China |
| Bing Ma | Shandong University of Political Science and Law, China |
| Jiang Qun Ni | Sun Yat-sen University, China |
| Michiharu Niimi | Kyushu Institute of Technology, Japan |
| Akira Nishimura | Tokyo University of Information Science, Japan |
| Alessandro Piva | University of Florence, Italy |
| Yong-Man Ro | KAIST, Korea |
| Vasiliy Sachnev | Catholic University, Korea |
| Andreas Westfeld | HTW Dresden, Germany |
| Xiaotian Wu | Sun Yat-sen University, China |
| Dawen Xu | Ningbo University of Technology, China |
| Diqun Yan | Ningbo University, China |

James C.N. Yang            NDHU, Taiwan
Rui Yang                   Sun Yet-sen University, China
Xinpeng Zhang             Shanghai University, China
Xianfeng Zhao             Chinese Academy of Sciences, China
Yao Zhao                  Beijing Jiao Tung University, China
Guopu Zhu                 Chinese Academy of Sciences, China

## International Publicity Liaisons

### Asia

Jiwu Huang                Shenzhen University, China
Alex Kot                  Nanyang Technological University, Singapore

### Europe

Anthony T.S. Ho           Surrey University, UK
Mauro Barni               Siena University, Italy

### America

Ton Kalker                DTS, USA
C.-C. Jay Kuo             University of Southern California, USA

## Organizing Chairs

Ryouichi Nishimura        National Institute of Information and Communications
                          Technology, Japan
Keiichi Iwamura           Tokyo University of Science, Japan
Isao Echizen              National Institute of Informatics, Japan

## Vice Organizing Chair

Hyunho Kang               Tokyo University of Science, Japan

## Organizing Committee

Masashi Unoki             Japan Advanced Institute of Science and Technology,
                          Japan
Michiharu Niimi           Kyushu Institute of Technology, Japan
Kazuhiro Kondo            Yamagata University, Japan
Hirohisa Hioki            Kyoto University, Japan
Tetsuya Kojima            National Institute of Technology, Tokyo College, Japan
Masaki Kawamura           Yamaguchi University, Japan
Minoru Kuribayashi        Okayama University, Japan
Akira Nishimura           Tokyo University of Information Science, Japan
Kitahiro Kaneda           Osaka Prefecture University, Japan
Motoi Iwata               Osaka Prefecture University, Japan
Yuji Suga                 Internet Initiative Japan Inc., Japan

# Abstracts of Invited Lectures

# Advances on Video Forensics

Alessandro Piva

Department of Information Engineering of the University of Florence
via S. Marta 3, 50139, Firenze, Italy
alessandro.piva@unifi.it

**Abstract.** When observing a visual content on a web site, often people do not realize that such media have undergone a long series of transformations before appearing in their current form. In particular, the authenticity of visual contents is often overestimated: just by looking around, it is evident that creating fake digital contents is very common today, since many commercial and open-source software allow to inexpert users editing images and videos in a few minutes. Multimedia forensics is a relatively new discipline that seeks to demonstrate the authenticity of a given multimedia content: the basic idea behind it is that any processing applied to a digital content leaves subtle traces, that can be analyzed to uncover the digital history of the object. A large part of the research activities in this field have been devoted to the analysis of still images. On the contrary, video forensics is still an emerging field, for several reasons: creating fake images is much easier than creating tampered videos; images are usually available in a few possible formats, while videos can be encoded with many different coders and, finally, videos usually undergo a stronger compression compared to images, making the forensic analysis more difficult. This contrasts with the fact that nowadays digital videos are probably used more than images, so their trustworthiness must be strengthened.

In this talk, the most useful traces that can be used for video processing detection, and the main forensic techniques that are based on them, will be described. Due to the ubiquitous diffusion of compressed videos, major focus will be given to traces relying on specific properties of the compression process.

**Keywords:** Multimedia forensics • Video forensics • Video integrity • Tampering detection

# Cyber Forensics: Key Trends and Opportunities

Vrizlynn Thing

Cyber Security & Intelligence, Institute for Infocomm Research,
Agency for Science, Technology and Research
1 Fusionopolis Way, #21-01, Connexis (South Tower), Singapore 138632
vriz@i2r.a-star.edu.sg

**Abstract.** Network prevalence and data asset digitalization enable higher productivity, enhanced communications and greater convenience. However, the borderless cyber space brings challenges to attribution in cyber forensics. Technological advancement in techniques directly or indirectly related to anti-forensics, such as big data, data manipulation/tampering/forgery, steganography and encryption, and perpetrators' sophistication and insiders' knowledge in conceiving novel and trickier fraud, scam, phishing and information theft, further exacerbate the problem.

This talk covers a discussion on how the fast paced advancement of technologies, and new attack means and techniques are leading to an ever-evolving cyber threat landscape and challenges in cyber forensics. Promising key focus areas in advanced cyber forensics research are presented and discussed in this talk.

**Keywords:** Digital forensics • Cyber threats • Anti-forensics • Cyber intelligence

# Contents

## Steganography and Steganalysis

## Digital Watermarking

# Digital Forensics

# Image Noise and Digital Image Forensics

Thibaut Julliand[1]([✉]), Vincent Nozick[2], and Hugues Talbot[1]

[1] Laboratoire d'Informatique Gaspard-Monge, Equipe A3SI, UMR 8049,
Université Paris-Est ESIEE, Paris, France
{thibault.julliand,hugues.talbot}@esiee.fr
[2] Laboratoire d'Informatique Gaspard-Monge, Equipe A3SI, UMR 8049,
Université Paris-Est Marne-la-Vallée, Paris, France
vincent.nozick@u-pem.fr

**Abstract.** Noise is an intrinsic specificity of all forms of imaging, and can be found in various forms in all domains of digital imagery. This paper offers an overall review of digital image noise, from its causes and models to the degradations it suffers along the image acquisition pipeline. We show that by the end of the pipeline, the noise may have widely different characteristics compared to the raw image, and consider the consequences in forensic and counter-forensic imagery.

**Keywords:** Noise · Digital forensics · Camera pipeline

## 1 Introduction

From the film grain of analogue cameras to the sensor noise of digital cameras, image noise has always been a concern in the history of image acquisition. Indeed, noise is an unwanted artefact that appears during the image capture process and can take various forms depending on the camera model and the lighting conditions during the image acquisition. For aesthetic reasons or for computer analysis clues, many studies have been concerned with suppressing this noise from the "original" signal. This interest is still an active research topic, particularly considering the increasing number of smartphones equipped with low quality sensors.

Since the noise problem is far from solved, some digital image forensics methods attempt to take advantage of this alteration of the signal to detect image forgeries. Some methods focus on the detection of local noise inconsistencies when some others attempt to identify the noise fingerprint of digital cameras.

The purpose of this paper is to outline the alterations of noise characteristics through the camera pipeline and the usual post-processing, in order to understand what kind of noise one can expect for image forensics purposes. This study first focuses on digital image noise characterisation and estimation. The next part deals with noise alteration during the image acquisition and processing pipeline. We distinguish the processing inherent to the camera pipeline from the usual post processing available on many software packages. Finally, we present some image forensics methods that fail when the image is corrupted with artificial noise.

© Springer International Publishing Switzerland 2016
Y.-Q. Shi et al. (Eds.): IWDW 2015, LNCS 9569, pp. 3–17, 2016.
DOI: 10.1007/978-3-319-31960-5_1

## 2   Digital Image Noise

Noise in digital images can come from various sources. Some are physical, linked to the nature of light and to optical artifacts, and some others are created during the conversion from electrical signal to digital data. As noise degrades the quality of an image, various models have been investigated to modelize the image noise for subsequent reduction or removal, at various steps of the image acquisition process.

### 2.1   Noise Sources

The main sources of noise can be divided into two main categories: the physical noise, linked to physics constraints like the corpuscular nature of light, and the hardware noise, linked to mechanical issues in the camera. Physical noise notably includes dark shot noise and photon shot noise [20]. The dark shot noise is created by electronic fluctuations caused by an accumulation of heat-generated electrons in the sensor. It is related to thermal noise, and can be reduced by cooling down the sensor. The photon shot noise, also called Poisson noise, is the one caused by the corpuscular nature of light: as photons arrive irregularly on the photosites, two adjacent pixels supposed to have a similar value can end up with different photon counts. As the name indicates, the photons follow a Poisson distribution. Its effect decreases proportionally to exposure time.

The hardware noise includes Fixed Pattern Noise (FPN), Photon Response Non Uniformity (PRNU) and quantification noise. PRNU and FPN are caused by imperfections in sensors. For the PRNU, the cause is mainly the inhomogeneity of silicon wafers and light variations in which individual sensor pixels convert light to electrical signals. It is most visible in pictures with a long exposure time and does not follow any particular statistical law. As for the FPN, it is caused by dark currents. Like photon shot noise, FPN tends to be reduced in long exposure images. Both of those effects increase with light intensity. While the FPN can be removed by substracting the dark frame, the PRNU is non-linear and as such is very hard to remove. Quantification noise is caused by the analogic-numeric converter. It is hard to quantify, because the process is non-linear, though there are some accepted models. More advanced analysis can be found in [5,29].

### 2.2   Noise Model

In the literature, the overall noise produced by a digital sensor is usually considered as a stationary white additive Gaussian noise. In [9], Faraji et al. justify the use of the Gaussian model for a specific interval of light intensity. However, this approach tends to overlook several noise components, even if we consider it in a global perspective. Jezierska et al. [15] present a more robust model which also considers a Poisson component. Both of those models take a high-level approach, trying to offer a simplified overall model. In [14], Irie et al. present another approach, which consists in modelising the noise step by step to get to a final formula. While this approach gives extremely precise results, it requires some specific data, such as the gain parameter for digital image enhancement, and thus cannot be used for blind modeling.

In the following parts of this paper, we adopt the Poisson-Gauss model from [15]. This model is applied to all the pixel $s$ of the image with:

$$I_s = \alpha Q_s + N_s \tag{1}$$

where $Q_s$ is analogous to a Poisson distribution $\mathcal{P}(u_s)$ of the "clean" signal $u_s$ and $\alpha \in \mathbb{R}$ is a scaling parameter corresponding to the strength of the Poisson component in the noise. $N_s$ is analogous to a Normal distribution $\mathcal{N}(c, \sigma^2)$ with mean $c \in \mathbb{R}$ and standard deviation $\sigma > 0$.

## 2.3 Noise Estimation and Denoising

Image denoising is a very active research field in the signal and image processing community. However, most existing denoising methods require noise parameters estimation before denoising. Hence, some noise parameters estimation studies have also been proposed. For accuracy purposes, the following overview presents the methods that can handle both Gaussian and Poisson noise.

Foi et al. [11] present such a method that identifies the Gaussian and the Poisson noise. However, this method is subject to an homogeneous image region search that discards a large part of the pixels of a natural image. Thus it may sometimes fail on small regions of the image where homogeneous parts are too small to be considered. Jezierska et al. [15] distinguish pixels that are more subject to Gaussian or Poisson noise from an iterative Expectation-Maximization process. Nevertheless, this method is extremely slow, and thus is impracticable for regular images. Colom and Buades [4] present a PCA noise decomposition approach which gets fast results and is efficient on post-CFA images.

It is important to note that the main purpose of noise estimators is to get a good noise estimation in order to denoise, but not really to get an accurate noise estimation. Thus, a possible approach for estimating the image noise may consist of first using one of the previously mentioned methods to roughly estimate the image noise, then to denoise the image and then subtracting the result from the original noised image. Among the large variety of denoising methods, the Non-Local Means, proposed by Buades et al. [2], performs well. However our tests show that the method lacks accuracy in highly textured zones. Moreover, this method only denoises the Gaussian noise component. Jezierska et al. [16] follows their previous work [15] and still suffers from time computation issue. Dabov et al. [6] introduce the so-called BM3D algorithm that performs a 3D collaborative filtering. This technique performs high-quality denoising for both homogeneous and textured regions, and denoises both the Gaussian and Poisson components.

In this paper, the noise estimation follows the latter approach and the noise estimation is computed from the provided noise image. The Poisson and Gaussian noise parameters are estimated from the difference image between the denoised image by BM3D and the original noised image. We first divide the pixel luminance range into $n$ equal intervals $\mathcal{I}_i$, $i \in [1, n]$. The pixels of the denoised

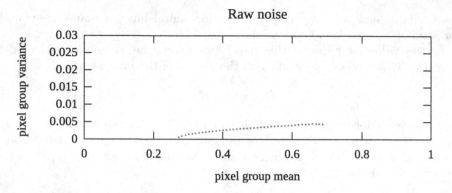

**Fig. 1.** Pixel group variances according to the group mean. Here, the (first) green channel of the raw image. This image does not use the full intensity range.

image with intensity in $\mathcal{I}_i$ are grouped together to compute a variance $\sigma_i$ of these pixels in the noise image and a mean value $m_i$ in the denoised image. As specified by [11], the noise that appear in the lower and higher pixel intensities is not reliable. Thus, these pixels are discarded from the noise estimation process. The plot of the variance as a function of the mean gives a line which slope corresponds to the Poisson noise parameters and the $y$-intercept corresponds to the Gaussian noise component. An example of this noise estimation is depicted in Fig. 1. The intervals $\mathcal{I}_i$ are referred to as *pixel groups* in the following Figures of the paper. In the case of a pure Gaussian noise, this line would be horizontal.

## 3    Noise Alterations Caused by Image Processing

### 3.1    Noise and Camera Pipeline

The camera pipeline often differs from one camera to the next, according to the sensor quality and the camera brand. Differences occur according to the processing steps and their ordering, however most pipelines include similar steps. A good description of these steps can be found in [18, Chaps. 1 and 3]. In this section, we focus on the processings that affect the noise, and show their impact on a raw image. The tests have been implemented using LibRaw [1] on a set of 15 raw images from various cameras. For clarity purposes, we selected one image (Fig. 2) of the set with representative results for the figures.

**Noise Reduction:** It is generally preferable to reduce noise as early as possible in the chain, before signal amplifier operations (notably color correction, gamma correction, edge enhancement and color filter array demosaicking). Some standard denoising methods employ wavelet denoising or Fake Before demosaicking De-noising (FBDD) on each of the four channels (R, G1, B, G2). Figure 3 shows how a light and a full FBDD affect the image noise.

**Fig. 2.** Input image used for the curves computation. *Courtesy of Michel Couprie.*

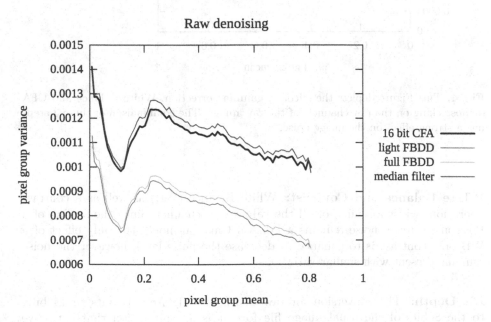

**Fig. 3.** Comparison of various denoising methods on raw images. For each image, color filter array demosaicking was performed after the denoising step.

**Color Filter Array:** The Color Filter Array (CFA) allows a single color to be acquired at each pixel. This means that the camera must interpolate the missing two color values at each pixel. This estimation process is known as demosaicking, and modifies the noise properties that could be found on a raw image. Many demosaicking methods also include edge detection or denoising, like Paliy et al. [22]. Therefore, the CFA can have a strong effect on the noise structure, as shown in Fig. 4, using adaptive homogeneity-directed (AHD) interpolation algorithms of *dcraw*.

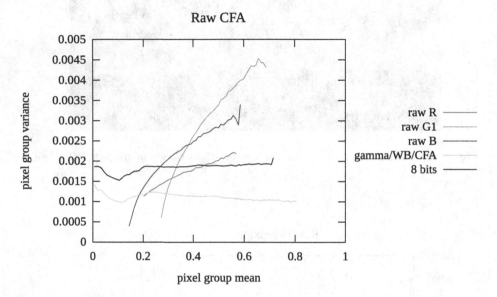

**Fig. 4.** This Figure depicts the effect of gamma correction, White Balance and CFA demosaicking on the raw channels of the raw image. The combinaison of these 3 steps has a strong effect on the image noise.

**White Balance and Contrast:** White Balance (WB) as well as a contrast operation is just a scaling of all the values of a channel. Since the scaling of a Poisson Gaussian noise remains a Poisson Gaussian noise, the only effect of a WB or a contrast is to enhance or decrease the noise level, however the noise remains present with similar variations.

**Bit Depth:** The conversion for raw depth, usually from 10 bits to 14 bits, to the 8 bits of the usual image file format is a compression that can have varying effects. Intuitively, we could expect noise levels to be reduced. However, we typically observed that the noise was either at the same level, or even higher, after quantification. There are several possible explanations for this phenomenon:

first, if the standard deviation is close enough to the conversion quantification step, results can be unpredictable. Second, the quantization actually removes most of the low standard deviation noise, which represents most of the noised pixels, and only leaves the noised pixels with high variations. As a consequence, the calculated standard deviation is much higher, even though the image may look less noisy. This phenomenon can be observed in Fig. 4.

**JPEG Compression:** JPEG is a lossy compression method with the lossy part predominantly in the high frequencies. Hence, it is not surprising that JPEG compression strongly affect the noise, as depicted in Fig. 5. However, our tests show that the global shape of the noise is conserved.

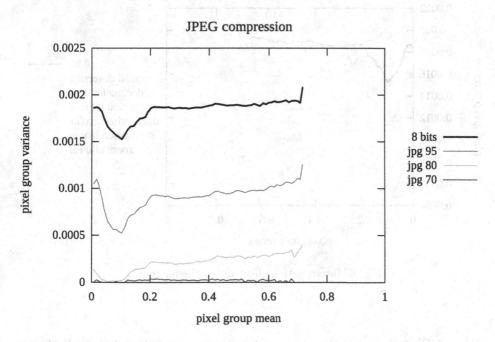

**Fig. 5.** JPEG compression effect on noise. The bold line is the uncompressed 8 bits image noise and the other curves correspond to the noise after a compression of 95, 80, 70 and 50.

## 3.2 "Legal" Image Enhancements

This section presents some usual image filters commonly used to enhance the visual image quality. These processes usually do not involve image forgery. The tests were performed on 8 bits digital images extracted from raw images without a denoising process or lossy compression, i.e. they still contain noise.

**Image Interpolation:** Image interpolation usually results from image resize, which is one of the most common image processing operation. Image interpolation can also occur for many other reasons, such as image rotation, image perspective transformations (e.g. stereoscopic rectification [21]), radial distortion and chromatic aberration correction, etc. The tests have been conducted with bilinear, bicubic, Lanczo and "area" interpolations for both decimation and zoom. The effect on noise is variable according to the interpolation method. The noise is always decreased but the global noise shape is globally conserved, as shown on Fig. 6.

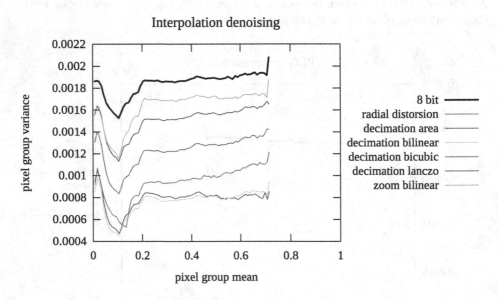

**Fig. 6.** Interpolation effect on the image noise.

**Others:** We tested some others images transformations with potential effects on images noise, without significant results. The image saturation process, where colors channels are be mixed together, does not significantly alter the noise. Brightness transformation will just translate the noise to higher pixel intensity levels. Contrast will increase or decrease the noise, but the noise shape remains the same. Image crop will just limit the image surface used for the noise estimation.

### 3.3    Noise and Strong Image Forgeries

This section aims at comparing image noise characteristics after a standard "legal" image enhancement and after a stronger image forgery. The questions are how far the transformed images are from the original in term of noise, and if the noise of a strong forgery still makes sens to study. In addition, we denoise the strongly falsified image and renoised it with a light artificial noise.

Figure 7 illustrates one of these experiments with the original image, this image with standard image processing (like non-linear histogram manipulations) and the initial image with strong forgeries. Figure 8 shows that both soft and strong image forgeries significantly impact the noise. More important, this figure demonstrates how an image with artificial noise may exhibit statistics similar to the initial image.

(a) Input image.

(b) image with "legal" modifications.

(c) image with strong forgery and virtual noise.

**Fig. 7.** (a): The input image used for the tests. (b): The input image with some "legal" transformations such resize, color enhancement, contrast, ... (c) Input image with a strong forgery. This image has been denoised and renoised with virtual noise. *Courtesy of Michel Couprie and Warren Miconi.*

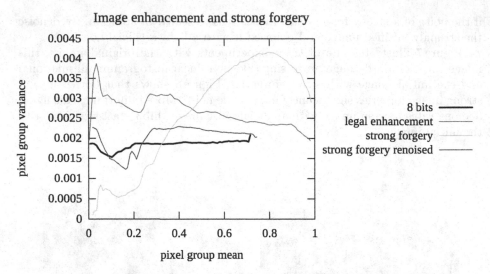

**Fig. 8.** Image noise curves for "legal" vs. strong image manipulation and for a renoised strong forgery (with an additional contrast modification).

## 4    Noise and Forensics Detection

This section outlines some digital forensic methods based on noise analysis.

**Noise Inconsistencies.** Mahdian and Saic [19] present a blind method to detect splicing from an image to the other by detecting the noise inconsistencies in the falsified image. The authors first perform a one-level wavelet analysis of the image and then divide the image into a grid to estimate the noise block per block. The authors use white Gaussian noise model. Finally, they merge blocks with similar noise estimation and generate a set of partitions with homogenous noise levels. Pan et al. [23] perform a similar image partition using the kurtosis values of natural images in band-pass filtered domains.

**The Device Sensor Fingerprint.** The device sensor fingerprint is a sensor pattern noise that can be extracted from the PRNU of a set of images from the same camera. Chen et al. [3], Fridrich [12] and many others like [17,25] use these fingerprints for device identification. Experiments reported in [3] show promising results even for JPEG compressed images down to a quality factor of 75.

**Computer Graphics.** Some image forgeries can include some Computer Graphics (CG) parts when splicing is not possible. These CG image areas may have unusual noise, or no noise. Dehnie et al. [7] look for traces of PRNU in the image and consider the areas with singular PRNU as forgeries.

**Color Forgery.** Hou et al. [13] detect hue modification by analysing the correlation of the PRNU from each color channel.

# 5 Adding Artificial Noise

Adding artificial noise can serve several purposes: used on artificial images, it can help to test noise models and algorithms. On natural images, it can be used as a kind of filter, to imprint an image with an old-fashioned grainy feel, or, sometimes, to camouflage an alteration. For our tests, we use the C++11 random number distributions to generate our Poisson and Gaussian distributions.

## 5.1 Artificial Images

Artificial images are ideal to test noise addition models, as they come free of any noise. We have used them to test and confirm the noise model proposed in Eq. (1) for raw images. They also allow to check the consistency of the noise model throughout various intensities and bit depth.

## 5.2 Natural Images

In the case of noise addition in natural images, the questions depend on the objective. If the noise addition is for a purely esthetical value, then the simple addition of a white Gaussian noise is enough. However, if the purpose is to cover other alterations, then a few parallel considerations have to be given thought. First, it is necessary to simulate some FPN, especially if there are several images coming from a single source being altered. Second, the added noise has to be coherent with the type of the image. The type of noise will be different, Gaussian for an 8-bit image and Poisson-Gaussian for a 16 bits one. In this second case, the noised value at pixel $s$ is obtained with $Q$ and $N$ from Eq. (1):

$$I_{noised_s} = \alpha Q_s \left( \frac{1}{\alpha} * I \right) + N_s$$

The last thing to consider is the necessity or not to denoise the image before adding noise. In the case of a splicing, for example, it is necessary to denoise beforehand: indeed, the spliced section may have different noise characteristics than the rest of the image, adding overall noise won't camouflage the difference. A preliminary denoising will help reduce this discrepancy.

# 6 Noise and Anti-Forensics

The objective of this section is to point out some forensics methods that fails to detect digital image forgeries if some artificial noise is added on the falsified images. Indeed, adding artificial noise may affect forgery detection method dealing with noise (Sect. 4) but also some methods where the pixel values distribution are important. On the following tests, artificial noise is added following the indications of Sect. 5, with a very light Gaussian noise with $\sigma = 2.5$, meaning that about 30 % of the pixels are not modified, due to quantization.

**Double JPEG Compression.** The double JPEG detection method introduced by Popescu and Farid [24] is based on an effect of the quantization step of the JPEG compression. Adding some noise on the falsified image will remove the quantization artefact and thus strongly decreases the double JPEG detection rate. Figure 9 shows the Fourier analysis of the first DCT coefficient for an image saved in JPEG, then saved again and finally artificially noised and saved in JPEG. The double JPEG artefact are much reduced, and so considerably more difficult to detect.

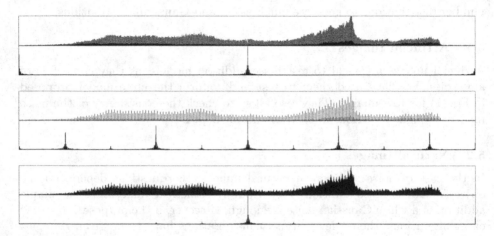

**Fig. 9.** These graphics correspond to single JPEG (top), double JPEG (middle), and double JPEG + artificial noise + JPEG (bottom). For each image, the upper part is the histogram of the first DCT coefficient and the lower part to its Fourier transform, where the peaks reveal a double JPEG.

**JPEG Ghost.** The jpeg Ghost method presented by Farid [10] is an extension of the double jpeg that handle local properties of the image. Surprisingly, the method is not altered by noise, unless it is implausibly high. Figure 10 shows the result of this method on a random image with the middle part previously saved in another jpeg quality than the overall image. Note that Stamm et al. [27] successfully disguise the JPEG compression history of an image by adding noise directly on its JPEG DCT coefficients. However, this process leaves slight image alterations that can be detected by [28]. Some recent methods can overcome this alterations issue [8].

**Histogram Based Methods.** Some histogram-based methods are used to detect global pixel intensity modifications, typically from Lookup-tables (LUT).

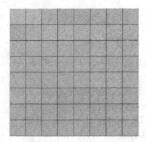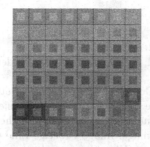

**Fig. 10.** JPEG ghost [10]: (Left) 64 levels on a random image. (Middle) the 64 levels on the random image where the middle square part is previously saved in another jpeg quality than the overall image. (Right) Same as middle, but with artificial noise before the last JPEG saving.

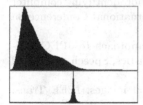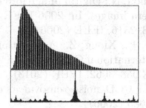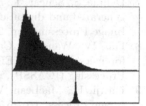

**Fig. 11.** These graphics correspond to an original image (left), a modified image by applying a LUT, here contrast and brightness (middle), and the middle image with artificial noise (right). For each graphic, the upper part is the histogram of green component of the image and the lower part to its Fourier transform, where the peaks reveal the LUT operation.

Stamm et al. [26] detects the residual peaks of the image histogram resulting from such transformation, by analysing the frequency spectrum of the histogram. Adding some noise on the modified image will strongly affect the LUT modification, as depicted in Fig. 11.

## 7   Conclusion

In this article, we have detailed the various sources and models of noise in digital images. Then we have explored a large panel of noise alterations, related to both the acquisition pipeline and the post-processing. We have shown how these alterations affect the quality and intensity of the noise, and study the precise impact of each of those alterations. A major observation we have made is that, by the time we get to a JPEG image, even a high-quality one, the noise is extremely different from its original form in the raw image and is strongly affected by the successive image processing operations. From a statistics point of view, it seems extremely challenging to use this final noise for forgeries detection. Finally, we have looked at the consequences for image forensics and anti-forensics based on noise analysis.

# References

1. LibRaw 0.17. Image decoder library (2015)
2. Buades, A., Coll, B., Morel, J.-M.: Non-local means denoising. Image Process. Line (2011)
3. Chen, M., Fridrich, J., Goljan, M., Lukáš, J.: Determining image origin and integrity using sensor noise. IEEE Trans. Inf. Forensics Secur. 3(1), 74–90 (2008)
4. Colom, M., Buades, A.: Analysis and extension of the PCA method, estimating a noise curve from a single image. Image Process. Line (2014)
5. Costantini, R., Susstrunk, S.: Virtual sensor design. In: Sensors and Camera Systems for Scientific, Industrial, and Digital Photography Applications V (2004)
6. Dabov, K., Foi, A., Katkovnik, V., Egiazarian, K.: Image denoising by sparse 3D transform-domain collaborative filtering. IEEE Trans. Image Process. 16(8), 2080–2095 (2007)
7. Dehnie, S., Sencar, T., Memon, N.: Digital image forensics for identifying computer generated and digital camera images. In: 2006 IEEE International Conference on Image Processing, pp. 2313–2316. IEEE (2006)
8. Fan, W., Wang, K., Cayre, F., Xiong, Z.: A variational approach to JPEG anti-forensics. In: 2013 IEEE International Conference on Acoustics, Speech and Signal Processing (ICASSP), pp. 3058–3062. IEEE (2013)
9. Faraji, H., MacLean, W.J.: CCD noise removal in digital images. IEEE Trans. Image Process. 15, 2676–2685 (2006)
10. Farid, H.: Exposing digital forgeries from JPEG ghosts. IEEE Trans. Inf. Forensics Secur. 4(1), 154–160 (2009)
11. Foi, A., Trimeche, M., Katkovnik, V., Egiazarian, K.: Practical Poissonian-Gaussian noise modeling and fitting for single image raw-data. IEEE Trans. Image Process. 17(10), 1737–1754 (2008)
12. Fridrich, J.: Digital image forensics using sensor noise. Signal Process. Mag. 26(2), 26–37 (2009)
13. Hou, J.-U., Jang, H.-U., Lee, H.-K.: Hue modification estimation using sensor pattern noise. In: 2014 IEEE International Conference on Image Processing (ICIP), pp. 5287–5291. IEEE (2014)
14. Irie, K., McKinnon, A.E., Unsworth, K., Woodhead, I.M.: A model for measurement of noise in CCD digital-video cameras. Meas. Sci. Technol. 19, 045207 (2008)
15. Jezierska, A., Chaux, C., Pesquet, J.-C., Talbot, H.: An EM approach for Poisson-Gaussian noise modeling. In: EUSIPCO, pp. 2244–2248, August 2011
16. Jezierska, A., Chouzenoux, E., Pesquet, J.-C., Talbot, H.: A primal-dual proximal splitting approach for restoring data corrupted with Poisson-Gaussian noise. In: IEEE International Conference on Acoustics, Speech and Signal Processing (ICASSP 2012), March 2012
17. Lawgaly, A., Khelifi, F., Bouridane, A.: Weighted averaging-based sensor pattern noise estimation for source camera identification. In: IEEE International Conference on Image Processing (ICIP 2014), pp. 5357–5361, October 2014
18. Lukac, R.: Single-Sensor Imaging: Methods and Applications for Digital Cameras. CRC Press, Boca Raton (2008)
19. Mahdian, B., Saic, S.: Using noise inconsistencies for blind image forensics. Image Vis. Comput. 27, 1497–1503 (2009)
20. Medkeff, J.: Using image calibration to reduce digital noise in images (2004)
21. Nozick, V.: Camera array image rectification and calibration for stereoscopic and autostereoscopic displays. Ann. Telecommun. 68(11), 581–596 (2013)

22. Paliy, D., Katkovnik, V., Bilcu, R., Alenius, S., Egiazarian, K.: Spatially adaptive color filter array interpolation for noiseless and noisy data. Int. J. Imaging Syst. Technol. **17**, 105–122 (2007)
23. Pan, X., Zhang, X., Lyu, S.: Exposing image splicing with inconsistent local noise variances. In: International Conference on Computation Photography (ICCP), pp. 1–10, April 2012
24. Popescu, A.C., Farid, H.: Statistical tools for digital forensics. In: Fridrich, J. (ed.) IH 2004. LNCS, vol. 3200, pp. 128–147. Springer, Heidelberg (2004)
25. Rosenfeld, K., Sencar, H.T.: A study of the robustness of PRNU-based camera identification. In: IS&T/SPIE Electronic Imaging, p. 72540M. International Society for Optics and Photonics (2009)
26. Stamm, M., Liu, K.J.R.: Blind forensics of contrast enhancement in digital images. In: 2008 15th IEEE International Conference on Image Processing, ICIP 2008, pp. 3112–3115. IEEE (2008)
27. Stamm, M.C., Tjoa, S.K., Lin, W.S., Liu, K.J.R.: Anti-forensics of JPEG compression. In: 2010 IEEE International Conference on Acoustics Speech and Signal Processing (ICASSP), pp. 1694–1697. IEEE (2010)
28. Valenzise, G., Nobile, V., Tagliasacchi, M., Tubaro, S.: Countering JPEG anti-forensics. In: 2011 18th IEEE International Conference on Image Processing (ICIP), pp. 1949–1952. IEEE (2011)
29. Vaseghi, S.V.: Advanced Digital Signal Processing and Noise Reduction. Wiley, New York (2008)

# Camera Source Identification with Limited Labeled Training Set

Yue Tan[1], Bo Wang[1(✉)], Ming Li[1], Yanqing Guo[1], Xiangwei Kong[1],
and Yunqing Shi[2]

[1] Dalian University of Technology, Dalian, Liaoning, China
yue985@mail.dlut.edu.cn, {bowang,mli,guoyq,kongxw}@dlut.edu.cn
[2] New Jersey Institute of Technology, Newark, NJ, USA
shi@njit.edu

**Abstract.** This paper investigates the problem of model-based camera source identification with limited labeled training samples. We consider the realistic scenario in which the number of labeled training samples is limited. Ensemble projection (EP) method is proposed by introducing prototype theory into semi-supervised learning. After constructing sub-sets of local binary patterns (LBP) features, several pre-classifiers are established for all labeled and unlabeled samples. According to the ranking of posterior probabilities, several prototype sets are constructed for the ensemble projection. Combining the outputs of all labeled samples from classifiers trained by prototype sets, a new feature vector is generated for camera source identification. Experimental results illustrate that the proposed EP method achieves a notable higher average accuracy than previous algorithms when labeled training samples is limited.

**Keywords:** Camera source identification · Limited labeled training samples · Ensemble projection · LBP features

## 1 Introduction

The advances of digital technologies, including low-cost digital cameras, sophisticated image editing software and internet techniques, bring us convenience, as well as a new issue and challenge with the integrity and authenticity of digital images. Developing reliable and accurate algorithms to verify the trust worthiness of digital images becomes an urgent need for law enforcement authorities, legal affairs, etc. Passive digital image forensics, which is considered as a promising solution of digital image authentication, has attracted more and more research interests. As an important branch, source camera identification focuses on the authentication of the originality of digital images and has significant potential in the applications of digital image forensics.

In recent years, various techniques have been proposed to solve the problem of source camera identification. These approaches can be categorized into two classes. The first one is tracing a unique intrinsic fingerprint of a specific device. Lukas *et al.* first utilized the photo response non-uniformity noise of

© Springer International Publishing Switzerland 2016
Y.-Q. Shi et al. (Eds.): IWDW 2015, LNCS 9569, pp. 18–27, 2016.
DOI: 10.1007/978-3-319-31960-5_2

imaging sensors as a device fingerprint for camera-based source identification [1]. Later on, a series of improved algorithms were proposed [2–7]. Another branch of image source identification is model-based source identification. A typical solution of model-based camera source identification is based on extracting multi-dimensional statistical characteristics for classification. For example, Swaminathan *et al.* [8] proposed a method for source camera identification by the estimation of CFA pattern and interpolation kernel, and gained an overall average accuracy of 90 % for 19 camera brands. Kharrazi *et al.* [9] proposed 34 features which can be categorized into three types: color features, image quality measurement (IQM), and high order wavelet characteristics (HOWS). They considered 16 models of cell-phone cam-eras. Then a classifier based on the features achieved an average accuracy of 88.02 %. Recently, Xu and Shi used the uniform gray-scale invariant local binary patterns (LBP) [10] and received an average classification accuracy of 98.0 % for 18 camera models from "Dresden Image Database".

In the previous works, a sufficient number of labeled training samples is indispensable to construct an accurate classifier. For example, a training set consisting of 150 images for each camera brand was used in [9]. And similarly in [10], the author used around 150 to 300 labeled images as training samples for each class. For camera model identification, it is possible to obtain enough labeled image samples to train a sophisticated classifier. While considering the time and manpower cost, collecting amount of labeled images as training set is usually not a simple task. For realistic scenario, reducing the labeled training samples meanwhile keeping the identification accuracies should be a practical and important problem for moving camera model identification from the laboratory into the real world. In this paper, we consider the realistic scenario in which the number of labeled training samples is limited. We propose to use prototype theory and ensemble projection method to achieve camera source identification with limited labeled training samples. Through constructing a series prototype set using LBP features, we obtain multiple sample sets. It means we include more information in training set from limited labeled samples. Ensemble learning features are proposed in our paper, and we use this feature to train SVM and identify the camera model source.

The rest of the paper is organized as follows. In Sect. 2, we introduce local binary patterns method for camera source identification. In Sect. 3, we proposed the EP method to solve the camera source identification with limited samples. In Sect. 4, experimental results demonstrate the efficiency of the proposed method. Finally, conclusions are drawn in Sect. 5.

## 2   Local Binary Patterns

The uniform gray-scale invariant local binary patterns [11] can be described by

$$LBP_{P,R} = \sum_{p=0}^{P-1} s(g_p - g_c)2^p \tag{1}$$

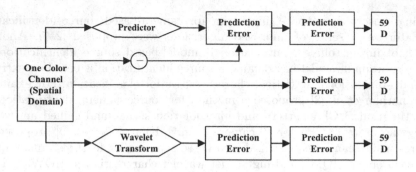

**Fig. 1.** Feature extraction framework for one color channel (Color figure online).

where $g_c$ represents a gray level of the center pixel, $g_p$, $p = 1, \ldots, P$, represent its neighbor pixels which are located on a circle with center at $g_c$ and a radius $R$. Then we can use the $P$ samples to calculation local binary pattern. In this paper, we set $P = 8$, $R = 1$. The function $s(x)$ can be defined as

$$s(x) = \begin{cases} 1, x \geq 0 \\ 0, x < 0 \end{cases} . \tag{2}$$

From Eqs. (1) and (2), we can calculate the gray-level difference between center pixel and its eight neighbors. The difference value $s$ between each couple point has totally $2^8 = 256$ patterns. In [10], the "uniform" local binary pattern and "non-uniform" local binary pattern were used, inspired by [11]. While "uniform" local binary pattern occupies majority of the total patterns, the authors only consider 58 "uniform" patterns and all of the "non-uniform" patterns are merged to one pattern. Thereby, the number of effective patterns is reduced from 256 to 59.

Finally, from each color channel, we extract LBP features from (i) original image, (ii) its prediction-error 2D array, and (iii) its $1^{st}$-level diagonal wavelet subband, resulting in a total of $59 \times 3 = 177$ features. Since red and blue color channels usually share the same image processing algorithms, only red and green channels are considered. Therefore, the final dimensions of the feature extracted from a color image is $177 \times 2 = 354$. The feature extraction framework is shown in Fig. 1.

## 3   Proposed Method

To our best knowledge, most of model-based camera source identification algorithms need large-scale labeled samples databases to sophisticatedly train a model and construct a classifier. Unfortunately, in many realistic cases, the labeled samples may be limited for model training but unlabeled samples are always sufficient. Our goal is to construct a reliable model for camera source identification with a rather limited number of labeled samples in conjunction with lots of unlabeled samples. Semi-supervised learning and ensemble learning

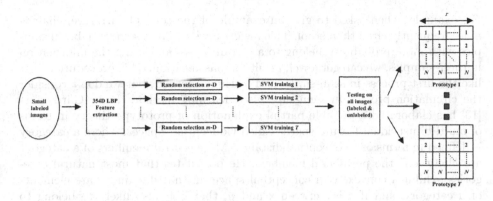

**Fig. 2.** Pipeline of constructing prototype set.

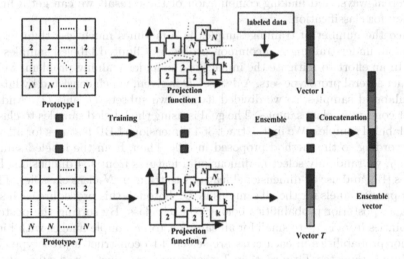

**Fig. 3.** Ensemble projection.

have been proposed to solve similar problem. However, the accuracy of classification is unsatisfactory when the number of the labeled samples is very low. To solve this problem, in this paper, we consider to construct a series of prototypes set by multiple random selected dimensional from LBP feature. And we propose a new ensemble projection algorithm to make combination of the information from all prototypes. The proposed method consists of two components, constructing prototype set and ensemble projection. The framework of these two steps are shown in Figs. 2 and 3.

## 3.1  Constructing Prototype Set

Eleanor Rosch's prototype theory [12] is a mode of graded categorization in cognitive science, where some members of a category are more central than others.

For example, when asked to give an example of the concept furniture, chair is more frequently cited than stool. This means if we can find some unlabeled samples with more probability belong to a certain class, and using the information in these samples, we can get a well result for classification. This procedure is just like the first process in semi-supervised learning method, but we don't consider the circulation process in semi-supervised learning method. Peter Gärdenfors [13] has elaborated a possible partial explanation of prototype theory in terms of multi-dimensional feature spaces called Conceptual Spaces, where a category is defined in terms of a conceptual distance. More central members of a category are "between" the peripheral members. He postulates that most natural categories exhibit a convexity in conceptual space, in that if $x$ and $y$ are elements of a category, and if $z$ is between x and $y$, then $z$ is also likely to belong to the category. According this, we believe if we can construct the projection set by different ways, and making combination of these result we can get a higher accuracy for classification.

Since the number of training samples is sometimes much less than feature dimension, under-training is a common problem in limited labeled samples scenario. In an effort to mitigate the impact of the under-training problem, we can construct several prototype sets. A dataset $D$ is given, which consisted by labeled and unlabeled samples, so we divided it into two subsets $D_l$ and $D_u$. And the dataset contain $N$-class samples. The goal is using the labeled samples to classify the unlabeled samples. We first extract 354 dimensions LBP features for all samples according to the method proposed in [10]. Then, from the labeled samples in set $D_l$, we randomly select $m$-dimensional features from 354 dimensions LBP features [10], and use $m$-dimensional features to train an $N$-class classifier. Then, we can predict labels for the all samples in $D$. Through this procedure each sample get an posterior probabilities belong to each class. By sorting the posterior probabilities from large to small for all samples, top $r$ sample images with higher posterior probabilities in each class are selected to construct a prototype. This procedure is repeated $T$ times, then $T$ prototypes are constructed subsequently, as shown in Fig. 2. In this figure, the "small" labeled images refer to the labeled samples is limited, and the $m$-D represents $m$-dimensional features.

The samples, which have equal probability of belonging to each class, may influence the classification accuracy. We named those ambiguous samples as noise samples. According to information theory, if an image has equal probability of belonging to each category, it has the largest entropy. The entropy can explicitly be written as:

$$H = -\sum_{i=1}^{N} p(c_i)\log_2 p(c_i) \tag{3}$$

where $p(c_i)$ represents the probability of belonging to $c_i$ class. So we can set a threshold value $e$ to exclude those samples from prototype set. If an image's entropy is less than the threshold $e$, it will be used for classifier training; otherwise, we consider it as a noise sample and ignore.

## 3.2   Ensemble Projection

Inspired by the ensemble learning [14], each prototype set, which represents partial classification information, can be seen as a new training set and $T$ classifiers could be trained. For each labeled image, we can obtain $T$ projection vectors from $T$ classifiers. Each projection vector is assembled by all of the posterior probabilities belong to N classes, and the dimension of projection vector is $N \times 1$. By combining all $T$ vectors, an $NT \times 1$ dimensional feature for a labeled image is obtained. For all labeled images, the feature vectors are extracted and then fed to SVM to construct a final classifier to identify the camera model, as shown in Fig. 3.

## 4   Experimental Studies

We carry out our experiments using "Dresden Image Dataset" used in [15]. In this dataset, 18 camera models (see Table 1) are employed and 350 JPEG images are captured by each camera model with varying settings. The LBP features used in our method are extracted in the central block with size of $512 \times 512$ and SVM classifier [16] is employed in our experiment. For comparison purpose, the LBP algorithm [10] is also evaluated.

**Table 1.** Dataset in Experiments.

| Camera model | Resolution | Abbr |
|---|---|---|
| Casio_EX_Z150 | $3264 \times 2448$ | CEZ |
| Kodak_M1063 | $3664 \times 2748$ | KM1 |
| Nikon_CoolPixS710 | $4352 \times 3264$ | NCP |
| Olympus_mju | $3648 \times 2736$ | OMJ |
| Panasonic_DMC | $3264 \times 2736$ | PDM |
| Praktica_DCZ5.9 | $2560 \times 1920$ | PDC |
| Nikon_D200 | $3872 \times 2592$ | ND1 |
| Ricoh_GX100 | $3648 \times 2736$ | RGX |
| FujiFilm_FinePixJ50 | $3264 \times 2448$ | FFP |
| Pentax_OptioA40 | $4000 \times 3000$ | POA |
| Rollei_RCP_7325X | $3072 \times 2304$ | RRC |
| Samsung_L74wide | $3072 \times 2304$ | SLW |
| Samsung_NV15 | $3648 \times 2736$ | SNV |
| Sony_DSC_H50 | $3456 \times 2592$ | SD1 |
| Sony_DSC_T77 | $3648 \times 2736$ | SD2 |
| Agfa_Sensor530s | $2560 \times 1920$ | AFS |
| Canon_Ixus70 | $3072 \times 2304$ | CI7 |
| Nikon_D70 | $3008 \times 2000$ | ND2 |

**Table 2.** Average comfusion matrix obtained by svm classification over 20 iterations.

| Average TP=90.2 | | Predicted | | | | | | | | | | | | | | | | |
|---|---|---|---|---|---|---|---|---|---|---|---|---|---|---|---|---|---|---|
| | | CEZ | KM1 | NCP | OMJ | PDM | PDC | ND1 | RGX | FFP | POA | RRC | SLM | SNY | SD1 | SD2 | AFS | CI7 | ND2 |
| Actual | CEZ | 87.7 | * | 1.3 | * | 2.3 | * | * | * | * | 3.7 | * | * | 3.0 | * | * | * | * | * |
| | KM1 | * | 90.0 | * | * | 1.3 | * | * | * | * | 1.3 | 1.0 | * | * | 4.0 | * | * | * | * |
| | NCP | * | * | 92.7 | * | * | 2.7 | * | * | * | 1.7 | * | * | * | * | * | * | 1.0 | * |
| | OMJ | * | * | * | 92.0 | * | * | * | * | * | * | * | 4.0 | 2.7 | * | * | * | * | * |
| | PDM | * | 1.3 | 1.0 | 1.0 | 90.0 | 2.3 | * | * | * | 1.0 | * | * | * | 1.3 | * | * | * | * |
| | PDC | * | * | * | * | 1.7 | 95.3 | * | * | * | * | * | * | 2.3 | * | * | * | * | * |
| | ND1 | * | * | * | * | 1.7 | 2.0 | 90.0 | * | * | * | 1.0 | 3.7 | * | * | * | 1.0 | * |
| | RGX | * | 5.0 | * | * | * | * | * | 85.0 | * | * | * | * | 1.0 | 4.3 | 2.7 | * | * | 1.0 |
| | FFP | * | * | * | * | * | 1.0 | * | * | 90.0 | * | 2.3 | * | 2.0 | * | * | * | * | 2.7 |
| | POA | * | * | * | 1.7 | * | * | * | * | * | 89.3 | 1.0 | * | * | * | * | 1.0 | * | 4.3 |
| | RRC | * | * | * | * | * | * | 2.7 | * | * | * | 92.3 | * | 2.0 | * | * | * | * | * |
| | SLM | * | * | 1.3 | * | * | * | * | * | * | * | 1.3 | 93.7 | 3.0 | * | * | * | * | * |
| | SNY | * | * | * | * | * | 4.0 | 1.0 | * | 1.0 | * | * | * | 89.0 | 1.0 | * | * | * | * |
| | SD1 | * | 1.3 | * | * | * | * | * | 6.7 | * | * | * | * | * | 88.7 | 2.3 | * | * | * |
| | SD2 | * | * | * | * | * | * | * | 2.0 | * | * | * | * | * | 9.0 | 88.0 | * | * | * |
| | AFS | * | * | * | * | * | * | * | * | * | 1.3 | 1.0 | * | * | * | 1.0 | 91.0 | * | 5.0 |
| | CI7 | 1.0 | * | * | * | 1.0 | * | * | * | * | * | * | * | 1.3 | * | * | * | 94.3 | * |
| | ND2 | * | * | * | * | * | * | 1.0 | 3.7 | * | 3.7 | * | * | * | 1.0 | * | 5.3 | * | 83.7 |

To prove the effectiveness of the method, the labeled images of each camera model are randomly selected from the image dataset, and the rest of images are considered as unlabeled and test samples. Experimental results are shown in Table 2, which give the average accuracy over 20 iterations. The asterisks in the table represent the classification probability below one percent. As demonstrated, our EP method achieves a highest accuracy of 95.3 % for Praktica_DCZ5.9 and a lowest accuracy of 83.7 % for Nikon D70. The overall average classification accuracy for 18 camera model is 90.2 %, when the number of labeled samples is $L = 50$, the number of prototype sets is $T=200$, and the number of the samples of each class in the prototype sets is $r = 50$.

Then, we attempt to evaluated the accuracy performance of the proposed algorithm, under different parameter $L$, $T$, $r$, condition. We first investigate the influence on parameter $L$, the numbers of labeled images, to the performance. We carry out experiment under the condition that the number of prototype sets is $T = 50$, and the number of samples of each class in the prototype sets is $r = 50$. As shown in Table 3, our EP method achieves average classification accuracy of 90.2 %, when the number of labeled samples is $L = 50$, while the LBP algorithm can only obtain the accuracy of 36.0 %. When the number of labeled samples decrease to an extremely low level $L = 10$, the classification accuracy of LBP algorithm is as low as 8.4 %, but our EP method can still maintain 74.5 %.

**Table 3.** Average accuracy of camera source identification with different number of labeled image samples.

| Algorithm | $L = 50$ | $L = 40$ | $L = 30$ | $L = 20$ | $L = 10$ |
|---|---|---|---|---|---|
| LBP | 36.0 % | 26.7 % | 29.3 % | 20.9 % | 8.4 % |
| **EP** | **90.2 %** | **88.3 %** | **85.0 %** | **82.6 %** | **74.5 %** |

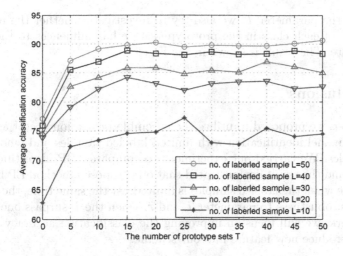

**Fig. 4.** Accuracy rate versus the number of prototype sets $T$.

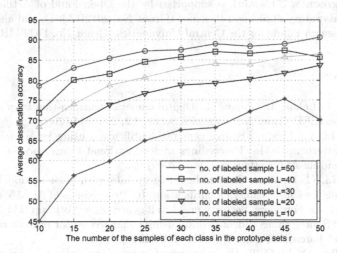

**Fig. 5.** Accuracy rate versus the number of the samples of each class in the prototype sets $r$.

The number of prototype sets $T$ is also an important parameter in our method. Figure 4 illustrates the average classification accuracy as a function of $T$. It can be observed that the accuracy can be always maintained at a level close to 90 % as long as $T$ is greater than 15, under the condition $L = 50$. And the number of labeled samples $L$ may influence the stability of performance. When the parameter $L$ drops down to 10, the stability decreases and the result presents a lot of volatility.

Besides the parameter $T$, we also try to investigate whether the number of the samples of each class in the prototype sets $r$ has influences to the average accuracy rate. The result is shown in the Fig. 5.

## 5   Conclusions

In this paper, we proposed to utilize the ensemble projection vector as features for camera model identification with limited labeled samples and amount unlabeled samples. We carried out experiment to compare LBP algorithm and EP algorithm, and the result demonstrated that our proposed method EP has better performance when the labeled samples is limited. At the same time, the proposed method has robustness to parameter $T$ and $r$, when the $L$ surpass one value. In a future work, we will focus on improving the classification accuracy rate, and consider introduce new feature into our scheme.

**Acknowledgments.** This work is supported by the Open Fund of Artificial Intelligence Key Laboratory of Sichuan Province (Grant No. 2012RZJ01), and also the Fundamental Research Funds for the Central Universities (Grant No. DUT14RC(3)103).

## References

1. Fridrich, J., Lukáš, J., Goljan, M.: Digital camera identifica-tion from sensor pattern noise. IEEE Trans. Inf. Forensics Secur. **12**, 205–214 (2006)
2. Yu, B., Hu, Y., Jian, C.: Source camera identification using large components of sensor pattern noise. In: Proceedings of International Conference on Computer Science and its Applications, pp. 1–5 (2009)
3. Hu, Y., Li, C.-T., Jian, C.: Building fingerprints with infor-mation from three color bands for source camera identification. In: Proceedings of ACM Workshop on Multimedia in Forensics, Security and Intelligence, New York, pp. 111–116 (2010)
4. Li, C.-T.: Source camera identification using enhanced sensor pattern noise. IEEE Trans. Inf. Forensics Secur. **5**(2), 280–287 (2010)
5. Hu, Y., Jian, C., Li, C.-T.: Using improved imaging sensor pattern noise for source camera identification. In: Proceedings of IEEE International Conference on Multimedia & Expo (ICME), Singapore, pp. 1481–1486 (2010)
6. Kang, X., Li, Y., Qu, Z.: Enhanced source camera identifi-cation performance with a camera reference phase sensor pattern noise. IEEE Trans. Inf. Forensics Secur. **7**(2), 393–402 (2012)
7. Fridrich, J.: Sensor defects in digital image forensic. In: Sencar, H.T., Memon, N. (eds.) Digital Image Forensics, pp. 179–218. Springer, New York (2013)
8. Swaminathan, A., Wu, M., Liu, K.J.R.: Nonintrusive com-ponent forensics of visual sensors using output images. IEEE Trans. Inf. Forensics Secur. **2**(1), 91–105 (2007)
9. Celiktutan, O., Sankur, B., Avcibas, I.: Blind identification of source cell-phone model. IEEE Trans. Inf. Forensics Secur. **3**(3), 553–566 (2008)
10. Xu, G., Shi, Y.Q.: Camera model identification using local binary patterns. In: Proceedings of IEEE International Conference on Multimedia & Expo (ICME), Melbourne, Australia, pp. 392–397 (2012)

11. Ojala, T., Pietikainen, M., Maenpaa, T.: Multiresolution gray-scale and rotation invariant texture classification with local binary patterns. IEEE Trans. Pattern Anal. Mach. Intell. **24**(7), 971–987 (2002)
12. Roach, E., Lloyd, B.B.: Cognition and Categorization, Mul-timedia Systems. Hillsdale, New Jersey (1978)
13. Gärdenfors, P.: Conceptual Spaces: The Geometry of Thought. England, London (2000)
14. Dai, D., Gool, L.V.: Ensemble projection for semi-surpervised image classification. In: Proceedings of IEEE International Conference on Computer Vision (ICCV), Sydney, Australia, pp. 2072–2079 (2013)
15. Gloe, T., Bohme, R.: The 'Dresden Image Database' for benchmarking digital image forensics. In: Proceedings of ACM Symposium on Applied Computing, Sierre, Switzerland, vol. 3(2–4) (2010)
16. Chang, C.C., Lin, C.J.: LIBSVM: a library for support vector machine. ACM Trans. Intell. Syst. Technol. N.Y. **2**(3), 27:1–27:27 (2011). Software, [Online]. Avaliable: http://www.cise.edu.tw/ cjlin/libsvm

# Detecting Video Forgery by Estimating Extrinsic Camera Parameters

Xianglei Hu[1]([✉]), Jiangqun Ni[1,2], and Runbiao Pan[1]

[1] Sun Yat-Sen University, Xingang Xi Road No. 135,
Guangzhou 510275, People's Republic of China
huxiangl@mail2.sysu.edu.cn, issjqni@mail.sysu.edu.cn
[2] State Key Laboratory of Information Security,
Institute of Information Engineering, Chinese Academy of Sciences, Beijing 100093,
People's Republic of China

**Abstract.** Nowadays, people can easily combine several videos into a fake one by means of matte painting to create visually convincing video contents. This raises the need to verify whether a video content is original or not. In this paper we propose a geometric technique to detect this kind of tampering in video sequences. In this technique, the extrinsic camera parameters, which describe positions and orientations of camera, are estimated from different regions in video frames. A statistical distribution model is then developed to characterize these parameters in tampering-free video and provides evidences of video forgery finally. The efficacy of the proposed method has been demonstrated by experiments on both authentic and tampered videos from websites.

**Keywords:** Forgery detection · Video forensics · Extrinsic camera parameter

## 1 Introduction

More and more techniques and software, such as Adobe After Effect and Corel Video Studio, provide to people the convenience of editing and altering videos. Among all the techniques, matte painting is one which can combine several video materials together, and it is widely used in movie effect area. However, by taking advantages of matte paining, people can also make fake videos for evil purposes. Since all the video materials components are real, it is not easy to extract obvious visual clues from the fake video (as in Fig. 1). To tackle this kind of problem, we propose a brand new digital forensic method to detect whether a video is authentic or faked by matte painting.

A lot of work have been done for different kinds of digital video forensics. Milani et al. outlined the video forensic technologies of different kinds of forgeries [1]. Wang and Farid successfully worked out the problem of interlaced and de-interlaced video [2]. Stamm et al. used the fingerprint model to detect the frame deleting/adding operations [3]. Hsu et al. used the temporal noise correlation to detect video forgery, however the model is sensitive to the quantization

© Springer International Publishing Switzerland 2016
Y.-Q. Shi et al. (Eds.): IWDW 2015, LNCS 9569, pp. 28–38, 2016.
DOI: 10.1007/978-3-319-31960-5_3

(a)

(b)

**Fig. 1.** A true (a) and fake (b) video are shown. The background region is replaced by another video clip and visual clues are hardly seen.

noise [4]. Chen and Fridrich used characteristics of the sensor noise to detect the tampering [5]. However, since lots of effects and recompression have been added to videos during the editing process, these methods can hardly detect the forgery implemented by Chroma key composition. Lighting [6], shadows [7] and reflections [8] are also used for forensics. But these content-based methods do not perform well under poor illumination conditions. The copy-move detecting techniques, such as [9], may not work properly because composites are not from the same source video. Thus, geometric methods are more suitable for the matte painting forensic task. Yao used perspective constraints to detect forgery [10]. Single-view metrology is the theoretical basis of that method, and ideal perspective effects and priori knowledge of objects are used to detect the forgery in images or videos. On the other hand, multi-view metrology based methods mainly focus on ways of detecting forgery by means of planar constraints [11–13]. However, these methods are applicable only when the fake contents are coplanar. To tackle more general matte painting problem in video, we propose a geometric technique using extrinsic camera parameters in this paper. This method implements multi-view metrology to estimate extrinsic camera parameters, and then we focus on investigating the differences of extrinsic parameters estimated from different regions in video frame. We find that regions can be characterized by the extrinsic parameters, and the difference of parameters can help to reveal the matte painting forgery. Experiments shows that our method is robust and efficient, even under the non-coplanar condition.

## 2  Extrinsic Camera Parameter Estimation

Extrinsic camera parameters are usually introduced to model the position and orientation of cameras. Currently, Structure from Motion (SfM) is one of the most popular methods to estimate extrinsic camera parameters from multi-view images [14,15]. Usually, for simplicity, a camera can be modeled as a pinhole camera. Let $p = [x, y]^T$ denote a 2D point in the image coordinate system. Similarly, $P = [X, Y, Z]^T$ denotes a 3D point in the world coordinate system. $p = [x, y, 1]^T$ and $P = [X, Y, Z, 1]^T$ denote the augmented vectors of them respectively.

In the pinhole camera model, a 3D real world point $P$ and its projection $p$ on the image plane satisfies:

$$sp = \mathbf{K} \begin{bmatrix} \mathbf{R} & \mathbf{t} \end{bmatrix} P \tag{1}$$

where $s$ is a scale factor; $\mathbf{K}$ is the intrinsic camera parameter matrix which carries the information such as the focal length, skewness and principal point of a camera; the extrinsic camera parameters, $\mathbf{t}$ and $\mathbf{R}$, represent the translation and rotation from the world coordinate to the image coordinate system. $\mathbf{t}$ is a $3 \times 1$ matrix and $\mathbf{R}$ is a $3 \times 3$ matrix:

$$\mathbf{t} = [T_x, T_y, T_z]^T \tag{2}$$

and

$$\mathbf{R} = \begin{bmatrix} r_{11} & r_{12} & r_{13} \\ r_{21} & r_{22} & r_{23} \\ r_{31} & r_{32} & r_{33} \end{bmatrix} \tag{3}$$

where

$$r_{11} = \cos\beta\cos\gamma, r_{12} = \sin\alpha\sin\beta\cos\gamma - \cos\alpha\sin\gamma$$
$$r_{13} = \cos\alpha\sin\beta\cos\gamma + \sin\alpha\sin\gamma$$
$$r_{21} = \cos\beta\sin\gamma, r_{22} = \sin\alpha\sin\beta\sin\gamma + \cos\alpha\cos\gamma$$
$$r_{23} = \cos\alpha\sin\beta\sin\gamma - \sin\alpha\cos\gamma$$
$$r_{31} = -\sin\beta, r_{32} = \sin\alpha\cos\beta$$
$$r_{33} = \cos\alpha\cos\beta$$

$\alpha$, $\beta$ and $\gamma$ are Euler angles representing three elementary rotations around $x, y, z-axis$ respectively. In this paper we use the rotation angle vector $\mathbf{r}$ instead of the rotation matrix in later sections:

$$\mathbf{r} = [\alpha, \beta, \gamma]^T. \tag{4}$$

When a camera moves in a scene and takes photos of the same object from different views, it is easy for us to find corresponding points of that same object in these photos. Let $p_1$ denote a point in image $\mathbf{I}_1$ and its corresponding point $p_2$ in image $\mathbf{I}_2$. $\mathbf{I}_1$ and $\mathbf{I}_2$ are images of the same object taken from different views. $p_1$ and $p_2$ satisfy the fundamental matrix constraint as follows:

$$p_2'^T \mathbf{F} p_1 = 0 \tag{5}$$

where $\mathbf{F}$ is the fundamental matrix which relates corresponding points in the stereo image pair:

$$\mathbf{F} = \mathbf{K_2}^{-T}\hat{\mathbf{T}}\mathbf{R}\mathbf{K_1}^{-1}, \hat{\mathbf{T}} = \begin{bmatrix} 0 & -T_z & T_y \\ T_z & 0 & -T_x \\ -T_y & T_x & 0 \end{bmatrix}.$$

Remarkably, if points in $\mathbf{I}_1$ and $\mathbf{I}_2$ are coplanar in the real world scene, the fundamental matrix constraint will degenerate to the planar constraint which is used in [11–13].

By matching enough corresponding points (at least 8 valid points for each pair) among multi-view images, we can solve the constraint problem and get the fundamental matrix $\mathbf{F}$ [16]. Given $\mathbf{F}$, we can further get $\mathbf{R}$ and $\mathbf{t}$ as well as $\mathbf{K}$. In this way, we can estimate successfully both intrinsic and extrinsic camera parameters. In [17], intrinsic parameters are applied to detect some kinds of video forgery in which the matte painting forgery is not included. Extra information, such as extrinsic parameters, is needed for such kind of forensic, and this paper focuses on how to explore the utility of extrinsic parameters.

## 3 Proposed Method

Our method is based on utilization of extrinsic camera parameters. Theoretically, in frames of authentic videos, all of the corresponding points should hold the same fundamental matrix constraint (5). Therefore, the same extrinsic camera parameters are supposed to be estimated from corresponding points in a authentic video. If we have extracted different extrinsic camera parameters from different image regions in the same video, it means the video has been tampered. In this way, the forgery in the video can be detected successively.

Steps of the proposed method are arranged as follows. Firstly, we divide each video frame into several different regions with masks. Secondly, we estimate extrinsic parameters from these regions respectively and calculate differences of the parameters. Thirdly, if the threshold is exceeded by the differences between a certain region and all other regions, this region will be considered as a fake one; otherwise, this region will be considered as an authentic one. Figure 2 shows the diagram of our proposed method.

### 3.1 Estimating Extrinsic Camera Parameters

There are many softwares for estimating the extrinsic camera parameter. Before estimating, we employ the SIFT algorithm to extract feature points [18] and RANSAC algorithm to match them [19]. Then we use the software VisualSFM [20,21] for estimation and bundle adjustment to refine the result [22].

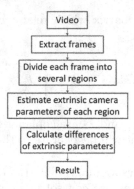

**Fig. 2.** Diagram of our proposed method

## 3.2  Detecting Forgeries with Extrinsic Camera Parameters

Even when applying the parameter estimation in a video without any tampering, it is difficult for us to get the exactly same result every time. Many factors, such as mismatched corresponding points, distortion of lens, will lead to the fluctuation of results.

Assuming elements in translation vector (2) and rotation angle vector (4) are independent and identically distributed(i.i.d) respectively, the translational and rotational differences between the estimated and the ground truth values should follow the zero mean Gaussian distribution, i.e.,

$$\mathbf{t}_{est} - \mathbf{t}_{truth} \sim N(\mathbf{0}, \sigma_t{}^2\mathbf{I}) \tag{6}$$

$$\mathbf{r}_{est} - \mathbf{r}_{truth} \sim N(\mathbf{0}, \sigma_r{}^2\mathbf{I}) \tag{7}$$

where $\mathbf{t}_{est}$ and $\mathbf{r}_{est}$ denote the estimated translation vector and rotation angle vector respectively, $\mathbf{t}_{truth}$ and $\mathbf{r}_{truth}$ are the ground truth vectors, $\mathbf{I}$ is the unit covariance matrix.

If we divide a video frame into $N$ regions and estimate the extrinsic parameter vectors for each region, we will get the translation vectors $\mathbf{t}_i$ from the $i$th region and $\mathbf{t}_j$ from the $j$th region. We define the translational difference between $\mathbf{t}_i$ and $\mathbf{t}_j$ as follows:

$$DT_{ij} = \frac{||\mathbf{t}_i - \mathbf{t}_j||^2}{\sigma_t{}^2} \tag{8}$$

where $i, j = 1, 2, ..., N$ and $i \neq j$; $||.||$ is the L2-norm of vector. Since the square of the L2-norm is equally the sum of squares, and meanwhile all elements of the vector are mutually independent Gaussian random variables, and thus the translational difference $DT_{ij}$ should follow the chi-squared distribution with 3 degrees of freedom (since the vector contains 3 elements):

$$DT_{ij} \sim \chi^2(3). \tag{9}$$

We define the rotational difference $DR_{ij}$ in the same way:

$$DR_{ij} = \frac{||\mathbf{r}_i - \mathbf{r}_j||^2}{\sigma_r^2} \tag{10}$$

$$DR_{ij} \sim \chi^2(3). \tag{11}$$

Usually the standard deviation factor is related to the ground truth parameters:

$$\sigma_t = k_t||\mathbf{t}_{truth}|| \tag{12}$$

$$\sigma_r = k_r||\mathbf{r}_{truth}|| \tag{13}$$

where $k_t$ is the total translation factor and $k_r$ is the total rotation factor.

With respect to the $i$th region, if the mean of $DT_{ij}$ and $DR_{ij}$ from all frames exceed the threshold, we can claim that the $i$th region is tampered. In this paper, the threshold is set 7.82 which comes from the $\chi^2$ value given the 0.05 p-value of the chi-squared distribution with 3 degrees of freedom, and it indicates that the probability that the object value exceeds 7.82 is less than 0.05.

## 4    Experiments

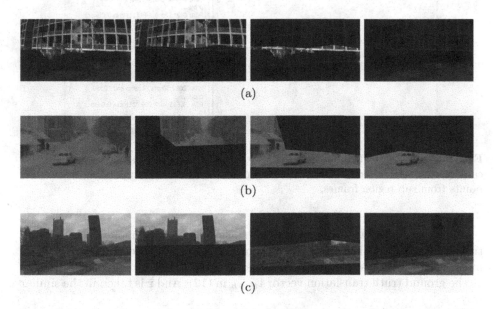

(a)

(b)

(c)

**Fig. 3.** Test videos from YouTube. The first column shows the first frames. Column 2 to 4 show the three divided regions. (a) and (b) are tampered videos. (c) is the true version of (a). Column 2 in (a) and (b) show the tampered regions.

### 4.1  Forensic Model Training

To estimate the total factor $k_t$ and $k_r$ in (12) and (13), we collect more than 50 true video clips, which are either taken by ourselves or downloaded from video-sharing websites. Then, more than 20 frames are extracted from each video. Next, we use Adobe Photoshop's mask tool to generate three new pictures from the original frame. Each new picture contains only one part information of the original frame, while the rest of the new picture contains nothing but black by setting RGB values to 0. The strategy which we run for segmenting frames, is that divide suspicious part from others as much as possible, and in the meantime, make sure each part contains enough feature points to keep VisualSFM work efficiently. So far, we get all triple-segmenting sub-region frame sequences resembling Fig. 3.

To extract the extrinsic camera parameters, the sub-region frame sequences are separately sent to VisualSFM. Afterward, we get extrinsic parameters, the position and orientation, of each sub-frame, as in Fig. 4.

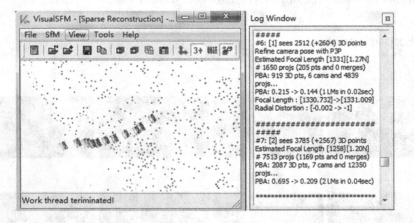

**Fig. 4.** Results provided by VisualSFM, the sequence of rectangles stand for the cameras taking different frames, while the points stand for corresponding feature 3D points from sub-region frames.

However, when we estimate the extrinsic camera parameters, the ground truth are always unknown. Thus, when evaluating our method, we take the mean value $\bar{t}$ of translation vectors extracted from different regions of all frames as the ground truth translation vector $t_{truth}$ in (12). And $\bar{r}$ is taken in the similar way.

After investigating the distribution of translational and rotational difference (as in Fig. 5), we find that 95 % of the difference values are less than 7.82 when $k_t = 1$ and $k_r = 0.5$. Thus, we take $k_t = 1$ and $k_r = 0.5$ in our later experiments.

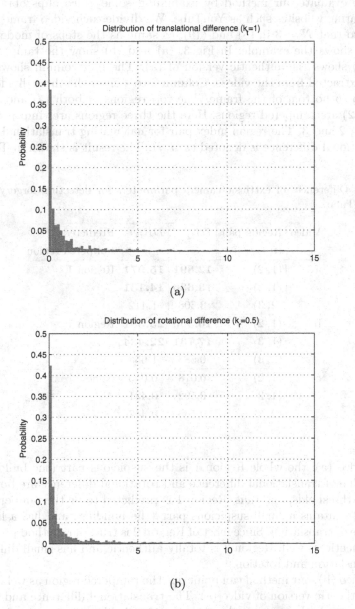

**Fig. 5.** Distribution of translational difference and rotational difference. The red dash line shows the $\chi^2$ distribution with 3 degrees of freedom. About 95 % of the difference values are less than 7.82.

## 4.2   Test of Fake Videos

Then we evaluate our method by examining some video clips obtained from video-sharing websites such as YouTube. We divide each video frame into three regions so that $N = 3$ in (8) and (10), as same as the steps of model training. Figure 3 shows the example. In Fig. 3, (a) and (b) show the tampered videos while (c) shows the authentic version of (a). The first column shows the first frames extracted from the videos. Column 2 to 4 show the three divided regions from top to bottom of the frame. The top regions of both (a) and (b) (as in Column 2) are tampered regions. Here the three regions are simply denoted as Region 1, 2 and 3. The region index pair for calculating translational difference and rotational difference is denoted as $(i, j)$. The result is shown in Table 1.

**Table 1.** Differences of extrinsic camera parameters for detecting forgery on videos from YouTube

| Video | Region pair $(i, j)$ | $D\bar{T}_{ij}$ | $D\bar{R}_{ij}$ | Predicted tampered region |
|---|---|---|---|---|
| a | (1, 2) | **12.891** | **15.971** | Region 1 |
|   | (1, 3) | **13.636** | **14.131** |   |
|   | (2, 3) | 3.508 | 1.412 |   |
| b | (1, 2) | **16.500** | **25.381** | Region 1 |
|   | (1, 3) | **17.731** | **22.434** |   |
|   | (2, 3) | 0.583 | 1.658 |   |
| c | (1, 2) | 0.078 | 0.055 | None |
|   | (1, 3) | 0.592 | 0.431 |   |
|   | (2, 3) | 0.765 | 0.447 |   |

In video (a), the whole Region 1 is the suspicious part (the building). The mean value of translational difference and rotational difference are both greater than the thresholds, and thus, Region 1 is predicted to be the tampered region. Region 2 contains a small suspicious part (the building) and has a little great difference of translation. Since most of Region 2 is true, our method predicts that it is authentic as well. Region 3 is totally authentic and has small differences of both translation and rotation.

In video (b), our method can point out the tampered region as well. Video (c) is the authentic version of video (a). The translational difference and rotational difference are both much smaller than the thresholds and no region is predicted fake.

Experiments of other test videos have the similar results. Our proposed method can detect fake regions by taking advantages of extrinsic camera parameters in videos.

# 5   Conclusion

We proposed a geometric method to detect forgery in video by means of extrinsic camera parameters. For a authentic video, no matter which frame region we use for camera parameter estimation, the estimated extrinsic parameters should not deviate much. Instead of purifying, we try to model the difference of extrinsic parameters in authentic videos so that we can distinguish the fake in a general way. With several real videos, we investigate the differences of extrinsic camera parameters extracted from different regions of the frame. We find that the translational difference and rotational difference follow the chi-squared distribution with 3 degrees of freedom. Then we choose the appropriate threshold for forensics from this distribution. Experiments on videos from video-sharing websites show the efficacy of our method.

**Acknowledgment.** The authors appreciate the supports received from National Natural Science Foundation of China (No. 61379156 and 60970145), the National Research Foundation for the Doctoral Program of Higher Education of China (No. 20120171110-037) and the Key Program of Natural Science Foundation of Guangdong (No. S2012020011114).

# References

1. Milani, S., Fontani, M., Bestagini, P., Barni, M., Piva, A., Tagliasacchi, M., Tubaro, S.: An overview on video forensics. APSIPA Trans. Sig. Inf. Process. **1**, e2 (2012). Cambridge Univ Press, Cambridge
2. Wang, W., Farid, H.: Exposing digital forgeries in interlaced and deinterlaced video. IEEE Trans. Inf. Forensics Secur. **2**(3), 438–449 (2007). IEEE Press, New York
3. Stamm, M.C., Lin, W.S., Liu, K.J.: Temporal forensics and anti-forensics for motion compensated video. IEEE Trans. Inf. Forensics Secur. **7**(4), 1315–1329 (2012). IEEE Press, New York
4. Hsu, C.C., Hung, T.Y., Lin, C.W., Hsu, C.T.: Video forgery detection using correlation of noise residue. In: 2008 IEEE 10th Workshop on In Multimedia Signal Processing, pp. 170–174. IEEE Press, New York(2008)
5. Chen, M., Fridrich, J., Goljan, M., Lukas, J.: Determining image origin and intergrity using sensor noise. IEEE Trans. Inf. Forensics Secur. **3**(1), 74–90 (2008). IEEE Press, New York
6. Johnson, M.K., Farid, H.: Exposing digital forgeries by detecting inconsistencies in lighting. In: Proceedings of the 7th Workshop on Multimedia and Security, pp. 1–10. ACM (2005)
7. Kee, E., O'Brien, J.F., Farid, H.: Exposing photo manipulation with inconsistent shadows. ACM Trans. Graph. **32**(4), 28 (2013). 1C-12. ACM
8. O'Brien, J.F., Farid, H.: Exposing photo manipulation with inconsistent reflections. ACM Trans. Graph. **31**(1), 4 (2012). 1C-11. ACM
9. Wang, W., Farid, H.: Exposing digital forgeries in video by detecting duplication. In: Proceedings of the 9th Workshop on Multimedia and Security, pp. 35–42. ACM (2007)
10. Yao, H., Wang, S.: Detecting image forgery using perspective constraints. Signal Process. Lett. **19**(3), 123–126 (2012). IEEE Press, New York

11. Wang, W., Farid, H.: Detecting Re-projected Video. Proceedings of International Workshop on Information Hiding. Springer, Heidelberg (2008)
12. Conotter, V., Boato, G., Farid, H.: Detecting photo manipulation on signs and billboards. In: 2010 17th IEEE International Conference on Image Processing, pp. 1741–1744. IEEE Press, New York (2010)
13. Zhang, W., Cao, X., Qu, Y., Hou, Y., Zhao, H., Zhang, C.: Detecting and extracting the photo composites using planar homography and graph cut. IEEE Trans. Inf. Forensics Secur. 5(3), 544–555 (2010). IEEE Press, New York
14. Zhang, Z.: Flexible camera calibration by viewing a plane from unknown orientations. In: Proceedings of the Seventh IEEE International Conference on Computer Vision, vol. 1, pp. 666–673 (2010)
15. Nister, D.: An efficient solution to the five-point relative pose problem. IEEE Trans. Pattern Anal. Mach. Intell. 26(6), 756–770 (2004). IEEE Press, New York
16. Hartley, R.: In defense of the eight-point algorithm. IEEE Trans. Pattern Anal. Mach. Intell. 19(6), 580–C593 (1997). IEEE Press, New York
17. Johnson, M.K., Farid, H.: Detecting photographic composites of people. In: Proceedings of International Workshop on Digital Watermarking, pp. 19–33. Springer, Heidelberg (2008)
18. Lowe, D.: Distinctive image features from scale-invariant keypoints. Int. J. Comput. Vis. 2(66), 91–110 (2004). Springer, Heidelberg
19. Fischler, M.A., Bolles, R.C.: Random sample consensus: A paradigm for model fitting with applications to image analysisand automated cartography. Commun. ACM 24(6), 381–395 (1981). ACM
20. Wu, C.: Towards linear-time incremental structure from motion. In: 2013 International Conference on 3D Vision-3DV 2013, pp. 127–134 (2013)
21. Wu, C.: VisualSFM: A Visual Structure from Motion System. http://ccwu.me/vsfm/
22. Wu, C., Agarwal, S., Curless, B., Seitz, S.M.: Multicore bundle adjustment. In: IEEE Conference on Computer Vision and Pattern Recognition, pp: 3057–3064. IEEE Press, New York (2011)

# Discriminating Between Computer-Generated Facial Images and Natural Ones Using Smoothness Property and Local Entropy

Huy H. Nguyen[1(✉)], Hoang-Quoc Nguyen-Son[2], Thuc D. Nguyen[1],
and Isao Echizen[3]

[1] VNUHCM - University of Science, Ho Chi Minh City, Vietnam
honghuy127@gmail.com, ndthuc@fit.hcmus.edu.vn
[2] SOKENDAI (The Graduate University for Advanced Studies), Kanagawa, Japan
nshquoc@nii.ac.jp
[3] National Institute of Informatics, Tokyo, Japan
iechizen@nii.ac.jp

**Abstract.** Discriminating between computer-generated images and natural ones is a crucial problem in digital image forensics. Facial images belong to a special case of this problem. Advances in technology have made it possible for computers to generate realistic multimedia contents that are very difficult to distinguish from non-computer generated contents. This could lead to undesired applications such as face spoofing to bypass authentication systems and distributing harmful unreal images or videos on social media. We have created a method for identifying computer-generated facial images that works effectively for both frontal and angled images. It can also be applied to extracted video frames. This method is based on smoothness property of the faces presented by edges and human skin's characteristic via local entropy. Experiments demonstrated that performance of the proposed method is better than that of state-of-the-art approaches.

**Keywords:** Facial image · Computer-generated image · Image forensics · Face spoofing

## 1 Introduction

Rapid developments in technology have led to major changes in the film and video game industries, particularly in the use of realistic graphics. For instance, it was virtually impossible to distinguish between the real Paul Walker and the computer-generated one in the film "The Fast and the Furious 7"[1]. The death of the actor during filming led the director to use previously recorded digital 3D

---

[1] http://www.techtimes.com/articles/42216/20150326/hollywood-studios-digitally-scanning-actors-bodies-archival.htm.

© Springer International Publishing Switzerland 2016
Y.-Q. Shi et al. (Eds.): IWDW 2015, LNCS 9569, pp. 39–50, 2016.
DOI: 10.1007/978-3-319-31960-5_4

scan data to reconstruct Mr. Walker's face for the unfinished scenes. Another example is Pro Evolution Soccer[2], a video game developed and published by Konami. Since the 2012 version, the images of the soccer players are rendered so realistically that they look almost like real people.

The identification of computer-generated facial images (and videos) has many applications. Detecting face spoofing is an example. Thanks to morphable model suggested by Blanz and Vetter [1], attackers can now reconstruct 3D images of a person's face from a single 2D frontal image. Unreal images and videos can be used to harm people or to gain political and/or economic advantage. For example, fake images or videos about aliens, disasters, statesmen, or businessmen can create confusion or change peoples' opinions. Social media such as Facebook, Twitter, Flickr, or YouTube is ideal environment to widespread them.

Facial images belong to a special class of images which includes faces of people. Discriminating between computer-generated facial images and natural ones is a specific case of the same problem on general images, which contain any kind of topics such as landscape, architecture, animals, or people. Facial images have some unique attributes of which some approaches for general images do not fully take advantage. These attributes could also degrade the performance of these approaches. In this paper, we focus on facial attributes to maximize the performance.

Our survey about facial images revealed that there are differences in the smoothness property of the faces and skin's characteristic between computer-generated and natural facial images. The smoothness property is reflected in the number of connected components given by an edge detection algorithm follows by morphological closing operation. Natural facial images tend to have more edges which connect to each other, meanwhile edges of computer-generated images are more discrete. Skin's characteristic can also be used in the form of the variation of local entropy. Natural images tend to have smaller variations of local entropy than computer-generated images.

The results of this survey led us to develop a novel method for discriminating between computer-generated facial images and natural ones. It is based on both smoothness property of the faces presented by edges and human skin's characteristic via local entropy. This method works for multi-stage facial images, including frontal and angled ones. For very realistic images, its accuracy is 71.25 %. For well-designed images in a well-known game, its accuracy is 91.23 %. The result is better than that of state-of-the-art methods [3, 4, 7, 8].

The rest of the paper is organized as follow: The related work is introduced in the next section. Continuing, the proposed method are presented with the overview and the two measurements. The experiments and their results are discussed in the evaluation section. The conclusions are drawn in the last section.

---

[2] https://pes.konami.com/.

## 2    Related Work

The discriminating between computer-generated images and natural ones topic focuses on two type of images: general images and facial ones. In addition, there are some approaches applying for videos.

### 2.1    Approaches for General Images

Peng et al. suggested a method for identifying computer-generated images based on the impact of filter array (CFA) interpolation on the photo response non-uniformity noise (PRNU) [10]. The differences of the PRNU correlations between computer-generated images and natural ones are used to discriminating them. The performance is limited by the quality of the noise, which is inferred from various types of filter (Bayer, RGBE, CYYM, etc.).

In other major study, Peng et al. suggested using the colors in images for discrimination [9]. They observed that the colors of natural images are typically more abundant than those of computer-generated ones. The colors are quantified via statistic features (such as histogram or relative frequency) and textural features (e.g. lacunarity, smoothness, entropy, consistency, and multi-fractal dimension). However, this method is not appropriate for facial images because such images have colors that are more balanced.

Lyu and Farid [8] proposed using the statistics of the first and higher-order wavelets. However, wavelet statistics are better suited for natural images than facial images due to the correlation of facial features. Khanna et al. utilized the noise made by digital cameras to efficiently classify not only computer-generated images and camera-produced images but also scanned images [7]. Conotter and Cordin developed a method for measuring the noises using wavelet transformation [3] that works well with both general and facial images. Unfortunately, noise is now being attached to computer-generated images to make them more realistic, and various technologies are now available for removing noise from digital images.

### 2.2    Approaches for Facial Images

There is only one method for identifying computer-generated facial images proposed by Dang-Nguyen et al. [4]. It is based on the finding that when creating a synthetic face, in most cases, only half of them are made and then duplicated to form a complete one. Post processing may be applied to make it more natural but usually does not change the geometric of the model. Human faces, on the other hand, are not perfectly symmetric. The more symmetric the face is, the high possibility it is generated by computer. The fact remains that symmetric property is detectable in only frontal facial images which limits the scope of this method.

## 2.3    Approaches for Videos

There are some methods for detecting computer-generated faces in video. In the one developed by Conotter et al. [2], the fluctuations in blood flow are used to distinguish computer-generated from actual faces. However, as the developers pointed out, this physiological signal can be easily simulated by computer to prevent detection. Another method is based on the assumption that facial expressions (such as happiness, sadness, surprise, fear, anger, and disgust) are important factors for recognizing actual faces [5]. A potentially useful characteristic of computer-generated videos is that they often contain repeatable patterns [6]. Unfortunately, these methods work only when there are multiple video frames; they cannot be used for a single image.

# 3    Proposed Method

## 3.1    Overview

Our proposed method has three phases, which is illustrated in Fig. 1

**Phase 1:** *Detect and extract face*
Face is detected and extracted from the input image by using Viola-Jones algorithm. The output is resized to $250 \times 250$ pixels to ensure that every image is treated equally and to reduce resource consumption. This size sufficiently preserves important patterns of the extracted faces. After that, an ellipse-shaped mask is used to filter out unnecessary parts such as background or hair, which is shown in Fig. 2. The major axis is in vertical direction with 375 pixels in length. The minor axis is in horizontal direction with 200 pixels in length. The intersection of the two axises is at the center of the image.

**Phase 2:** *Perform measurements*
With the facial image extracted in phase 1, edge-based measurement and entropy-based measurement are performed to obtain data for phase 3. Details about two measurements are presented in the next sections. Edge-base measurement component creates one feature and entropy-based measurement one generates four features for logistic regression.

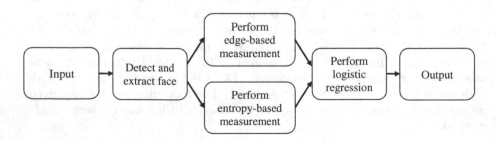

**Fig. 1.** Overview of proposed method

**Phase 3:** *Perform logistic regression*

Some well known machine learning algorithms such as logistic regression, support vector machine (SVM), and sequential minimal optimization (SMO) were evaluated to find the best candidate for the final phase. Logistic regression was chosen because of its best performance. The classification result is "computer-generated image" or "natural image."

**Fig. 2.** The ellipse-shaped mask

## 3.2   Edge-Based Measurement

This phase measures the smoothness of images based on the edge property. Natural images tend to have seamless and smooth connections among facial features and between these features than computer-generated images. This can be measured by the number of connected components obtained by edge detection algorithm. There are three steps in this measurement, which is presented in Fig. 3:

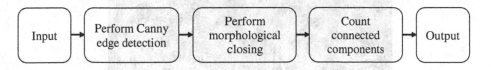

**Fig. 3.** Overview of edge-based measurement

**Step 1:** *Perform Canny edge detection*

Canny edge detection algorithm is employed because of its good performance.

The $5 \times 5$ Gaussian convolution kernel with $\sigma = 1.3$ is used to remove noise before edge detecting, shown by follows:

$$\frac{1}{159} \begin{bmatrix} 2 & 4 & 5 & 4 & 2 \\ 4 & 9 & 12 & 9 & 4 \\ 5 & 12 & 15 & 12 & 5 \\ 4 & 9 & 12 & 9 & 4 \\ 2 & 4 & 5 & 4 & 2 \end{bmatrix}$$

For Sobel operator, we use a pair of $3 \times 3$ convolution masks. The first mask $G_x$ estimates the intensity gradients of the image in the horizontal direction ($x$-direction) and the second mask $G_y$ estimates them in the vertical direction ($y$-direction), respectively shown as follows:

$$G_x = \begin{bmatrix} -1 & 0 & 1 \\ -2 & 0 & 2 \\ -1 & 0 & 1 \end{bmatrix} ; G_y = \begin{bmatrix} 1 & 2 & 1 \\ 0 & 0 & 0 \\ -1 & -2 & -1 \end{bmatrix}$$

The high and the low threshold used for filtering out some edge pixels caused by noise and color variation are respectively 0.01 and 0.004. We conducted experiment to make sure that these values are optimal, which is presented in evaluation section.

**Step 2:** *Perform morphological closing*
Morphological closing algorithm is used to fill gaps and to connect related edges together. The structuring element is a disk with 1 pixel radius. This step is significantly important to ensure that related features are connected to each other. Figure 4 illustrates the result of this step.

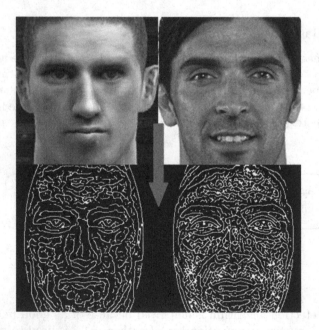

**Fig. 4.** After perform edge detection and morphological closing algorithm, the natural image on the right have more edges connected together than the computer-generated image on the left

**Step 3:** *Count connected components*
Connected components are determined and counted with 8-connected neighborhood, illustrated in Fig. 5. A stand-alone is a connected component. A group

| 0 | 1 | 0 | 0 | 0 | 0 | 0 | 0 | 0 | 3 |
|---|---|---|---|---|---|---|---|---|---|
| 0 | 1 | 0 | 0 | 0 | 0 | 0 | 0 | 3 | 0 |
| 0 | 0 | 1 | 0 | 0 | 0 | 0 | 0 | 3 | 0 |
| 0 | 0 | 1 | 0 | 0 | 0 | 0 | 0 | 3 | 0 |
| 1 | 1 | 1 | 1 | 1 | 0 | 0 | 3 | 0 | 0 |
| 0 | 0 | 1 | 0 | 0 | 0 | 0 | 0 | 0 | 0 |
| 0 | 0 | 0 | 1 | 0 | 0 | 2 | 2 | 2 | 2 |
| 0 | 0 | 0 | 0 | 1 | 0 | 0 | 0 | 0 | 0 |

**Fig. 5.** A matrix with three connected components. The component number one has two edges intersect

of edges connecting to each other is also a connected component. Breadth-first search or depth-first search could be employed in this phase.

### 3.3 Entropy-Based Measurement

This phase measures the variation of local entropy of skin areas in the input images. Based on observations and measurements on facial images, natural ones tend to have smaller variations of local entropy than computer-generated ones. There are three steps in this measurement, which is presented in Fig. 6:

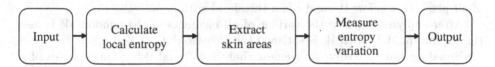

**Fig. 6.** Overview of entropy-based measurement

**Step 1:** *Calculate local entropy*
Input images are converted to gray-scale to calculate entropy value of the 9-by-9 neighborhood elements around the corresponding pixel. Symmetric padding is applied for pixels on the borders. Entropy values of the elements of the neighborhood is calculated as:

$$E = -\sum P \circ \log_2(P) \tag{1}$$

where $P$ is the distribution of the elements of the image.

**Step 2:** *Extract skin areas*
A mask is formed using the entropy matrix by being converted to black and white image with the threshold equal 0.8. Morphological closing algorithm is applied with the $9 \times 9$ matrix structuring element, follows by morphological filling holes algorithm. The skin areas of the entropy matrix is extracted by applying this mask. Figure 7 illustrates the result of this step.

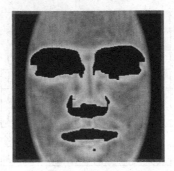

**Fig. 7.** Skin areas extracted from entropy matrix

**Step 3:** *Measure entropy variation*
A $5 \times 5$ window $W$ is moving along the extracted skin image from the left to the right and from the top to the bottom with step $S$ to perform normalization and measurement.

The measurement function is shown by follows:

$$W_{i,j} = \begin{cases} \overline{W} & \text{if } W_{i,j} < \epsilon. \\ W_{i,j}, & \text{otherwise.} \end{cases} \tag{2}$$

where $W_{i,j}$ is the intensity of the pixel at location $(i, j)$, $\overline{W}$ is the average intensity of all pixels in window $W$, and $\epsilon$ is a threshold with small value.

After applying Eq. 2, if the variant of all elements of the window $W$ is less than a threshold $T$, then $W$ is satisfied the threshold $T$.

Based on some surveys, we suggest that $S = 2$ and using four couples of $\epsilon$ and $T$:

$$(\epsilon, T) = (2, 2), (2, 4), (2, 8), (5, 5)$$

This step returns the proportion of satisfied windows and total windows. Windows which have all zero pixels are eliminated to improve the accuracy.

## 4 Evaluation

### 4.1 Datasets

The datasets were obtained from Dang-Nguyen et al. [4]. There are two datasets of facial images:

– Dataset 1 measures the ability of discriminating between very realistic images and natural images. 40 computer-generated were obtained from the CGSociety website[3] are almost undetectable by human. 40 counterpart natural images were obtained from a variety of sources. Figure 8 shows sample images from dataset 1.

---
[3] http://www.cgsociety.org/.

**Fig. 8.** Sample images from dataset 1. Images in top row were computer-generated; those in bottom row are natural

**Fig. 9.** Sample images from dataset 2. Images in top row were computer-generated; those in bottom row are natural

- Dataset 2 measure the ability of discriminating between computer-generated images rendered in a modern computer game and natural images. It contains 200 computer-generated images from Pro Evolution Soccer 2012[4] and 200 natural images of actual football players. Figure 9 shows sample images from dataset 2.

## 4.2   Threshold Values Evaluation

We evaluated the proposed edge-based measurement on training data of dataset 1 and dataset 2 with the high thresholds from 0.01 to 0.5. The distance between two adjacent thresholds is 0.05, except for the first one which is 0.04. The low threshold values are 40 % of the high threshold values. The output is classified using logistic regression. The result is illustrated in Fig. 10.

---

[4] http://www.pesfaces.co.uk.

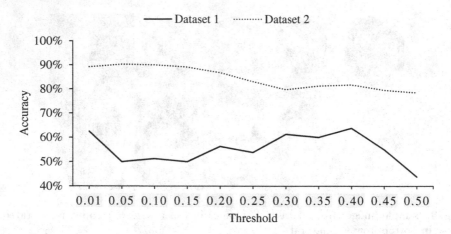

**Fig. 10.** Accuracy of edge-based measurement on dataset 1 and dataset 2

The high threshold 0.01 is chosen because it gives the best performance on both datasets. The corresponding low threshold is 0.004.

### 4.3   Experiments

We conducted three experiments: The first experiment is the proposed method with only edge-based measurement; the second is the one with only entropy-based measurement and the third is the full version of the proposed method. The result is shown in Table 1 in comparison with Dang Nguyen's approach [4], the best state-of-the-art one.

**Table 1.** Classification accuracy on dataset 1 and dataset 2

| Approach | Dataset 1 | Dataset 2 |
|---|---|---|
| Dang Nguyen's approach [4] | 67.50 % | 89.25 % |
| Edge-based measurement | 75.00 % | 84.20 % |
| Entropy-based measurement | 62.50 % | 89.20 % |
| Proposed approach | 71.75 % | 91.23 % |

The proposed approach with only edge-based measurement has very good performance on dataset 1 and the one with only entropy-based measurement has better performance on dataset 2. The full proposed approach, which contains the both measurements, has acceptable high performance on dataset 1 with 71.75 % in accuracy and the best performance on dataset 2 with 91.23 % in accuracy. This approach also outperforms Dang Nguyen's [4] and the three other approaches [3,7,8], which is illustrated in Fig. 11.

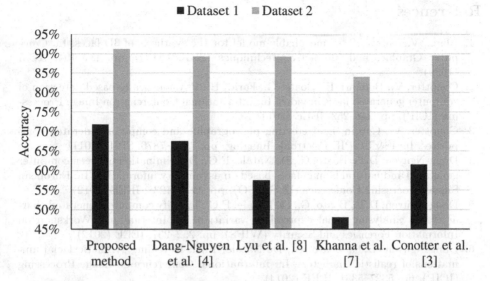

**Fig. 11.** Comparison of the proposed approach with four other methods using dataset 1 and 2

Images in dataset 1 are well-designed. The characteristic of the skin in this dataset is very similar to human skin. That explains why the performance of entropy-based measurement on dataset 1 is not high. Image resolution also affects edge property. An images with high resolution produces more edges than the same one with lower resolution. Many images in dataset 2, after being extracted faces, has low resolution. The size of the smallest image is $45 \times 45$ pixels. The performance of edge-based measurement is significantly influenced by this problem.

## 5    Conclusion

Our proposed method is an effective way to identify computer-generated facial images. It is based on two properties: the smoothness of the faces presented by edges and the characteristic of human skin via local entropy. Combining the strong points of two measurements, the method performs effectively on multi-stage images and could also be used for extracted video frames. Future work includes optimizing each phase of the proposed method. In particular, the thresholds need to be reevaluated and optimized automatically, and deep learning can be used instead of logistic regression.

**Acknowledgments.** We would like to thank Dr. Duc-Tien Dang-Nguyen in the Department of Information Engineering and Computer Science (DISI) of the University of Trento, Italy for providing the two datasets used for evaluation.

# References

1. Blanz, V., Vetter, T.: A morphable model for the synthesis of 3D faces. In: Computer Graphics and Interactive Techniques (SIGGRAPH), pp. 187–194. ACM (1999)
2. Conotter, V., Bodnari, E., Boato, G., Farid, H.: Physiologically-based detection of computer generated faces in video. In: International Conference on Image Processing (ICIP), pp. 248–252. IEEE (2014)
3. Conotter, V., Cordin, L.: Detecting photographic and computer generated composites. In: IS&T/SPIE Electronic Imaging, pp. 7870–7876. SPIE (2011)
4. Dang-Nguyen, D.T., Boato, G., De Natale, F.G.: Discrimination between computer generated and natural human faces based on asymmetry information. In: European Signal Processing Conference (EUSIPCO), pp. 1234–1238. IEEE (2012)
5. Dang-Nguyen, D.T., Boato, G., De Natale, F.G.: Identify computer generated characters by analysing facial expressions variation. In: International Workshop on Information Forensics and Security (WIFS), pp. 252–257. IEEE (2012)
6. Dang-Nguyen, D.T., Boato, G., De Natale, F.G.: Revealing synthetic facial animations of realistic characters. In: International Conference on Image Processing (ICIP), pp. 5327–5331. IEEE (2014)
7. Khanna, N., Chiu, G.C., Allebach, J.P., Delp, E.J.: Forensic techniques for classifying scanner, computer generated and digital camera images. In: Acoustics, Speech and Signal Processing (ICASSP), pp. 1653–1656. IEEE (2008)
8. Lyu, S., Farid, H.: How realistic is photorealistic? IEEE Trans. Signal Process. **53**(2), 845–850 (2005)
9. Peng, F., Li, J.T., Long, M.: Identification of natural images andcomputer-generated graphics based on statistical and textural features. J. Forensic Sci. **60**, 435–443 (2014)
10. Peng, F., Zhou, D.I.: Discriminating natural images and computer generated graphics based on the impact of CFA interpolation on the correlation of PRNU. Digit. Invest. **11**(2), 111–119 (2014)

# Multiple MP3 Compression Detection Based on the Statistical Properties of Scale Factors

Jinglei Zhou, Rangding Wang[✉], Chao Jin, and Diqun Yan

College of Information Science and Engineering, Ningbo University,
Ningbo 315211, China
wangrangding@nbu.edu.cn

**Abstract.** MP3 audio is one of the most popular audio formats, and it is easy to be tampered. By revealing the historical traces of the audio compression, it could be speculated effectively whether the suspicious MP3 audio has been tampered or not. Scale factor is an important parameter in MP3 encoding. In this paper, the variation law of the scale factor with various times of the compression is discovered by analyzing its statistical properties. The proposed method can be applied to detect multiple compression operations when the bit rates of the second and third compression are the same. The experimental results show that the proposed approach has good performance and higher accuracy with respect to the state-of-art.

**Keywords:** Scale factor · MP3 audio · Multiple compression detection

## 1 Introduction

Generally, most of the multimedia tampering operations occur with double or more compressions. Many approaches for detecting compression history have been proposed. A forensic method based on the statistical analysis of Benford-Fourier coefficients was proposed in [1]. Milani et al. [2] utilized the first digit features to detecting the multiple compressions of JPEG image. In his another work [3], a solution by using the statistics of DCT coefficients was designed for detecting multiple compressions of video sequences. Chu et al. [4] explored the fundamental limit of forensic ability by introducing an information theoretical framework for multimedia forensics.

Audio, as an important part of the multimedia information, attracts more and more researchers to work on solving the problem how to reveal its compression history. Since MP3 is the most popular audio format so far, nearly all audio compression detection methods were developed for it. Alessandro et al. [5] achieved the goal of detecting the real bit rate of MP3 audio by analyzing the power spectrum of audio under different bit rates. In [6], the proportion of the MDCT coefficients whose absolute values higher than the threshold was utilized as the detecting feature. Qiao et al. [7] proposed the method based on the small value of MDCT coefficients. Bianchi et al. [8, 9] estimated the double compressed audios by the characteristics of MDCT coefficient distribution histogram. Besides, the Huffman table index [10] and scale factor [11] were used for double compression detection. All the schemes above-mentioned, however, are suitable for detecting double compression.

© Springer International Publishing Switzerland 2016
Y.-Q. Shi et al. (Eds.): IWDW 2015, LNCS 9569, pp. 51–60, 2016.
DOI: 10.1007/978-3-319-31960-5_5

As described in [11], scale factor is an effective parameter for compression detection. The method in [11] has achieved good performance in detecting double compression at same bit rate. However, the detection results for multiple compression has not been given. To detect multiple compression, a novel method based on the scale factor is proposed in this paper. The features in this work are derived from the statistical properties of the two scale factor matrixes from the questionable MP3 audio and its recompressed version.

Multiple compression detection, however, is more difficult than double compression detection due to the following two reasons. Firstly, the change of MP3 parameters such as MDCT coefficients gets smaller as the number of compression times increases; Secondly, more cases of bit rates should be considered for multiple compression detection than for double compression detection. For simplicity, we assume that the bit rates of the second and third compressions are the same, and the number of compression times is up to three.

In the following, Sect. 2 briefly reviews the MP3 encoding and introduces the scale factors. Section 3 presents the feature extraction based on the characteristic of the scale factor. Experimental results are given in Sect. 4 and final conclusions are drawn in Sect. 5.

## 2   Preliminary Work

The block diagram of MP3 encoder is shown in Fig. 1, which is designed as a two-track structure. On the first track, the audio signal is split into 32 subbands with the analysis filterbank. The MDCT is performed in each subband, and 576 MDCT conferences are obtained for each frame. On the second track, the psychoacoustics model is used in the MP3 standard [12], which aims to ensure the added noise is unperceived by human ear. The audio signal after FFT is mapped to the critical band. Then the masking threshold in each partition is calculated by the frequency and energy of the corresponding audio signal.

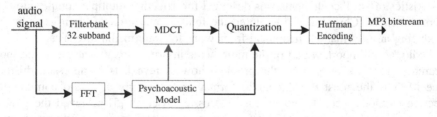

**Fig. 1.** Block diagram of MP3 encoding

Because the quantization and encoding processes of MP3 are operated based on the scale factor band, it needs to convert masking threshold from frequency band to scale factor band. In this transition, the audio signal is also divided into long or short blocks by the perceptual entropy which is derived from the signal's energy and the masking threshold. The 576 MDCT coefficients of the data in each long block are divided into

21 scale factor bands, and the coefficients of short block are divided into three successive bands, each of which consist of 12 scale factor subbands. After that, the corresponding minimum allowable distortion is calculated based on the masking threshold and the energy of each scale factor band.

Then the MDCT coefficients of each scale factor band are quantified and encoded through three loops, namely inter frame loop, outer loop and inner loop. The purpose of the inner loop is to adjust the quantization step length, which ensures that the quantified data size could satisfy the limited number of bits after Huffman coding. If the loop not satisfies the end condition [11], the inner loop would be restarted, and the absolute value of quantization step will be $-1$.

The outer loop calculates each scale factor's quantitative error which is caused by the inner loop, and then the loop determines whether the error of each subband is less than the minimum allowable distortion or not. Otherwise, it needs to amplify corresponding distortion subband, the corresponding scale factor value will be plus one. The amplified distortion subband will back into the inner loop until meet the requirements. So the increase of the scale factor value is equivalent to the decrease of quantization step absolute value indirectly [13].

As is mentioned above, the scale factor plays an important role in the process of compression. In addition, some studies [5] have found that the high frequency components show a trend of gradually decreasing with the increasing of compression times. Due to the energy of high frequency component is small, it needs to use bigger quantization step absolute value to preserve the accuracy of high frequency signal. After several times of compression, the high frequency component will be inevitably reduced and its energy is getting smaller. This leads to the increasing of quantization step absolute value and decreasing of the scale factor values. Therefore, the change of the scale factor in the different time compression process should be of great significance for detecting multiple MP3 compression.

## 3  Features Extraction

Due to long blocks arise more frequently than short blocks, the statistical characteristics of the scale factors in long block are studied in this work. Figure 2 shows the probability distribution of scale factors extracted from a single, double and triple compressed MP3 audio separately. Since the values of most scale factors are smaller than 8, the scale factors from 0 to 8 are counted in Fig. 2. From Fig. 2, it can be seen that the probability of the scale factor 0 is increasing with the number of compression growing, but the growth rate is gradually decreasing. Conversely, the probabilities of the rest scale factors are decreasing as the number of compression growing.

Before extracting the features, the MP3 audio $M_1$ decompressed into WAV audio $W$ as shown in Fig. 3. Then the WAV audio $W$ will be compressed to obtain a new MP3 audio $M_2$ with the same bit rate as the $M_1$. At last, the long block scale factor matrix $SF_1$ and $SF_2$ are separately extracted at the decoding process of MP3 audio $M_1$ and $M_2$.

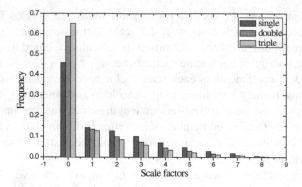

**Fig. 2.** The probability histogram of scale factor for a single, double and triple compressed MP3 audio (bit rate = 128 kbps)

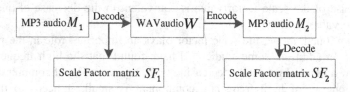

**Fig. 3.** Scale factor matrix extracting

$$SF_1 = \begin{bmatrix} sf_{1,1} & sf_{1,2} & \cdots & sf_{1,21} \\ sf_{2,1} & sf_{2,2} & \cdots & sf_{2,21} \\ \vdots & \vdots & \ddots & \vdots \\ sf_{w,1} & sf_{w,2} & \cdots & sf_{w,21} \end{bmatrix} \tag{1}$$

$$SF_2 = \begin{bmatrix} sf'_{1,1} & sf'_{1,2} & \cdots & sf'_{1,21} \\ sf'_{2,1} & sf'_{2,2} & \cdots & sf'_{2,21} \\ \vdots & \vdots & \ddots & \vdots \\ sf'_{w,,1} & sf'_{w,2} & \cdots & sf'_{w,21} \end{bmatrix} \tag{2}$$

$$w = \begin{cases} 2 \times I, \textit{for mono channel} \\ 4 \times I, \textit{for dual channel} \end{cases} \tag{3}$$

where, $I$ is the total number of frames.

Three feature sets are extracted after extracting scale factors. The average of the scale factor differences is extracted as a first feature for determining whether the MP3 audio is single compressed audio or not. Figure 2 shows that many scale factors are getting small with the increasing of compression number, so the average of the scale factor differences can effectively detect the number of compressions, as shown in Fig. 4. The averages of difference values are derived from the scale factor matrixes of

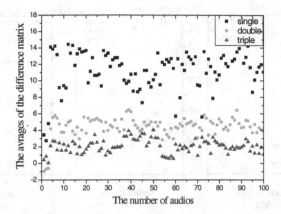

The number of audios

**Fig. 4.** The averages of scale factor difference for 100 single, double and triple compressed MP3 audios (bit rate = 128 kbps).

$M_1$ and $M_2$. The difference matrix $\Delta SF$ can be calculated as Eq. (4). The average of $\Delta SF$ can be denoted as Eq. (5), which is the first feature set.

$$\Delta SF = SF_1 - SF_2 = \begin{bmatrix} \Delta sf_{1,1} & \Delta sf_{1,2} & \cdots & \Delta sf_{1,21} \\ \Delta sf_{2,1} & \Delta sf_{2,2} & \cdots & \Delta sf_{2,21} \\ \vdots & \vdots & \ddots & \vdots \\ \Delta sf_{w,1} & \Delta sf_{w,2} & \cdots & \Delta sf_{w,21} \end{bmatrix} \tag{4}$$

$$\overline{\Delta SF} = \frac{1}{21 \times w} \sum_{i=1}^{w} \sum_{j=1}^{21} \Delta sf_{i,j} \tag{5}$$

where $i \in \{1, 2 \cdots, w\}, j \in \{1, 2 \cdots, 21\}$;

The statistical characteristics of probability for scale factors are calculated as the second feature set. This feature set is combined by three parts: the increment, the growth ratio and the differences of the growth ratio of probability for scale factors. The probability distribution vectors of scale factor 0 to 8 are separately extracted from the scale factor matrixes $SF_1$ and $SF_2$.

$$P_{SF_1} = [p_{SF_1}(0), p_{SF_1}(1) \cdots, p_{SF_1}(8)] \tag{6}$$

$$P_{SF_2} = [p_{SF_2}(0), p_{SF_2}(1) \cdots, p_{SF_2}(8)] \tag{7}$$

where $p_{SF_1}(k)$ and $p_{SF_2}(k)$ are the proportions of the scale factor $k$ in the matrix $SF_1$ and $SF_2$, respectively. And then the increment $\Delta p(k)$ and the growth ratio $r(k)$ of probability for scale factors are calculated as Eqs. (8) and (9). Finally, the differential growth ratio $\Delta r(n)$ is calculated based on the growth ratio, as shown in Eq. (10). Figure 5 shows the averages of the increment, the growth rate and the difference of growth rate for 539 single, double and triple compressed MP3 audios, respectively. From these figures, it can be seen that these three features in this set have obvious difference during various cases.

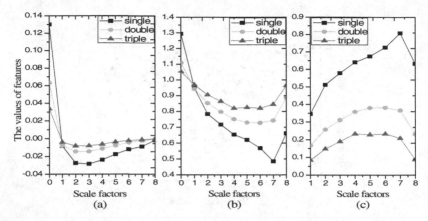

**Fig. 5.** The averages of the increment, the growth rate and the differential growth ratio for 539 single/double/triple compressed MP3 audios (bit rate = 128 kbps). (a) The increment features of scale factor 0 to 8; (b) The growth rate features of scale factor 0 to 8; (c) The differential growth ratio features of scale factor 1 to 8.

$$\Delta p(k) = p_{SF_2}(k) - p_{SF_1}(k), \quad k \in \{0, 1 \ldots, 8\} \tag{8}$$

$$r(k) = p_{SF_2}(k)/p_{SF_1}(k), \quad k \in \{0, 1 \ldots, 8\} \tag{9}$$

$$\Delta r(n) = r(0) - r(n), \quad n \in \{1, 2 \ldots, 8\} \tag{10}$$

The last feature set is the transition probabilities of scale factor matrix. As illustrated in Fig. 2, the probability of scale factor 0 is growing with the increasing of compression number, and the probabilities of other scale factors are decreasing. This phenomenon reveals that the scale factor 0 is transformed from other scale factors in the compression process. The averages of the transition probabilities of scale factor matrix for 539 single, double and triple compressed audios are calculated in Fig. 6. In this figure, it can be observed that some of these features can distinguish the three kinds of compressed MP3 audios. However, some of the transition probabilities have poor performance for deciding the compression times of MP3 audio. To ensure the validity of the algorithm and reduce the complexity of the features, the transition probabilities of scale factor 1, 2, 3, 4 and 5 to scale factor 0, 1, 2 and 3 are chosen as follows.

$$P = \begin{bmatrix} p_{1,0} & p_{1,1} & p_{1,2} & p_{1,3} \\ p_{2,0} & p_{2,1} & p_{2,2} & p_{2,3} \\ p_{3,0} & p_{3,1} & p_{3,2} & p_{3,3} \\ p_{4,0} & p_{4,1} & p_{4,2} & p_{4,3} \\ p_{5,0} & p_{5,1} & p_{5,2} & p_{5,3} \end{bmatrix} \tag{11}$$

where $p_{i,j} = \frac{\langle p_{SF_2}(j) | p_{SF_1}(i) \rangle}{p_{SF_1}(i)}$, $\langle p_{SF_2}(j) | p_{SF_1}(i) \rangle$ stands for the probability of scale factor $i$ in matrix $SF_1$ transforms to $j$ in matrix $SF_2$., and $p_{SF_1}(i)$ stands for the probability of scale factor $i$ in matrix $SF_1$.

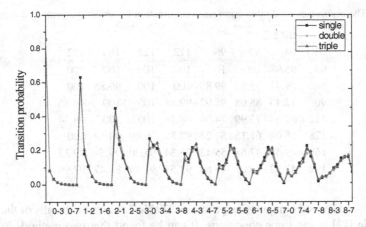

**Fig. 6.** The average of the transition probability of scale factor matrix for 539 single, double and triple compressed audios at 128 kbps. The value $i - j$ in x axis means that scale factor $i$ transformed to scale factor $j$.

## 4    Experimental Results and Discussions

539 uncompressed WAV audios are compressed by MP3 encoder (Lame 3.99.5) [14] at seven different bit rates (64, 80, 96, 112, 128, 160 and 192 kbps). So the 3773 single compressed MP3 audios which are denoted as $S$ are obtained. To get the second compressed MP3 audios, the MP3 audios $S$ are decompressed to get the WAV audio W1, and then recompress W1 at the seven different bit rates. The 26411 double compressed MP3 audios which are noted as $D$ are obtained. Then the MP3 audios $D$ are processed as the same step of $S$, the triple compressed MP3 audios $T$ are obtained. It should be noted that the bit rate used in third time should be the same as the second time.

The features with 47 dimensions are extracted from each sample in $S$, $D$ and $T$. The extracted features are normalized from $-1$ to 1 before training and testing by LIBSVM [15]. In experiment, 70 % samples are used for training, and the remaining 30 % samples are for testing. Every experiment repeats 10 times and the average is taken as the result.

This experiment is divided into two sections. The first part is double compression detection which is respectively used the proposed method and the method described in [11] at the same conditions. The second part is multiple compression detection. The goal of this experiment is to verify whether the proposed approach can identify the compression number or not.

### 4.1    Double Compression Detection

To testify the effectiveness of this approach for justifying the double compressed MP3 audio, $S$ and $D$ are chosen as the positive and negative samples separately. The experimental results are shown in Table 1, in which BR1 and BR2 stand for the bit

**Table 1.** The accuracies of double compression detection by using the proposed method (%)

| BR1 | BR2 | | | | | | |
|-----|-------|-------|-------|-------|-------|-------|-------|
|     | 64    | 80    | 96    | 112   | 128   | 160   | 192   |
| 64  | 95.98 | 100   | 100   | 100   | 100   | 100   | 100   |
| 80  | 79.41 | 95.98 | 99.85 | 100   | 100   | 99.85 | 100   |
| 96  | 72.45 | 88.08 | 98.92 | 99.84 | 100   | 100   | 99.85 |
| 112 | 62.54 | 73.99 | 74.30 | 98.14 | 100   | 100   | 99.54 |
| 128 | 56.04 | 61.15 | 64.24 | 92.88 | 99.69 | 99.69 | 100   |
| 160 | 49.54 | 47.68 | 55.42 | 93.34 | 95.20 | 99.54 | 99.23 |
| 192 | 47.52 | 49.07 | 49.69 | 92.57 | 91.49 | 89.47 | 97.99 |

rates at first and second compression processes. Table 2 shows the results of the method proposed in [11] at the same conditions. It can be found that two methods both have good performance when BR2 > BR1. Especially, the proposed method is superior to the method of [11] when BR1 ≥ BR2. For example, when BR1 = BR2 = 96 kbps, the accuracy of the proposed method can reach 98.92 % which is improved by 16.88 % compared to the approach in [11].

**Table 2.** The accuracies of double compression detection by using the method in [11] (%)

| BR1 | BR2 | | | | | | |
|-----|-------|-------|-------|-------|-------|-------|-------|
|     | 64    | 80    | 96    | 112   | 128   | 160   | 192   |
| 64  | 78.02 | 98.14 | 99.69 | 99.07 | 99.41 | 99.75 | 100   |
| 80  | 65.02 | 73.74 | 98.76 | 99.65 | 100   | 100   | 99.42 |
| 96  | 51.70 | 61.61 | 82.04 | 97.52 | 99.79 | 99.61 | 99.39 |
| 112 | 48.92 | 49.85 | 52.32 | 82.48 | 96.59 | 99.37 | 99.69 |
| 128 | 47.99 | 48.61 | 47.37 | 66.87 | 91.29 | 97.83 | 99.38 |
| 160 | 48.29 | 49.22 | 45.51 | 65.63 | 62.54 | 89.16 | 95.36 |
| 192 | 48.30 | 49.85 | 45.82 | 64.71 | 69.04 | 69.15 | 91.64 |

However, it can be seen that two methods cannot effectively detect the double compression when BR2 < BR1. As we know, every MP3 encoding is a kind of lossy compression which is irreversible. Especially under the low bit rate, the auditory quality of the audio will decline rapidly. So the MP3 audios transcoded from high bitrate to low bitrate is hard to be distinguished from the single compressed MP3 audio under low bitrate cases.

## 4.2 Multiple Compression Detection

In this experiment, $S$, $D$ and $T$ are united into the sample set for multiple compression detection. Experimental results are shown in Table 3, in which the BR3 stands for the third compression bit rate, and BR3 is equal to BR2. In Table 3, 86.49 % means the accuracy for detecting the single compressed MP3 audio with 96 kbps, the double compressed MP3 audio with 80 kbps and 96 kbps, and the triple compressed MP3

**Table 3.** The accuracies of multiple compression detection by using the proposed method (%)

| BR1 | BR2 = BR3 | | | | | | |
|-----|-------|-------|-------|-------|-------|-------|-------|
|     | 64    | 80    | 96    | 112   | 128   | 160   | 192   |
| 64  | 84.29 | 83.20 | 86.19 | 87.73 | 90.31 | 91.34 | 90.31 |
| 80  | 85.57 | 84.85 | 86.49 | 87.73 | 89.38 | 89.59 | 87.73 |
| 96  | 78.25 | 87.94 | 92.47 | 82.20 | 85.26 | 91.24 | 85.26 |
| 112 | 73.40 | 78.04 | 81.03 | 92.78 | 89.79 | 89.69 | 86.29 |
| 128 | 64.64 | 71.34 | 78.87 | 91.96 | 94.85 | 91.65 | 85.98 |
| 160 | 61.03 | 62.27 | 67.53 | 92.58 | 94.74 | 90.72 | 87.01 |
| 192 | 62.89 | 61.86 | 62.37 | 92.78 | 93.30 | 88.25 | 90.52 |

audio with 80 kbps, 96 kbps and 96 kbps. The experimental results show that the method can effectively detect the compression number of MP3 audio at the same bit rate used in the second and third compressions. Especially when BR1 ≤ BR2 = BR3, the detection rate can reach 94.85 %. Table 4 shows the results of multiple compression detection by using the method in [11] at the same conditions. It can be observed that the performance of the proposed method is better than the method [11] in the multiple compression detection, although both of two algorithms are based on the scale factors.

**Table 4.** The accuracies of multiple compression detection by using the method in [11] (%)

| BR1 | BR2 = BR3 | | | | | | |
|-----|-------|-------|-------|-------|-------|-------|-------|
|     | 64    | 80    | 96    | 112   | 128   | 160   | 192   |
| 64  | 67.01 | 66.19 | 72.16 | 72.58 | 74.85 | 77.53 | 74.23 |
| 80  | 55.26 | 60.62 | 74.85 | 68.25 | 72.99 | 75.46 | 71.56 |
| 96  | 55.88 | 55.67 | 77.73 | 77.32 | 72.78 | 77.11 | 73.40 |
| 112 | 49.07 | 50.36 | 65.15 | 74.02 | 80.21 | 69.28 | 69.69 |
| 128 | 50.72 | 50.52 | 55.26 | 60.21 | 82.89 | 68.25 | 67.22 |
| 160 | 48.66 | 45.57 | 53.40 | 55.05 | 61.86 | 75.46 | 72.58 |
| 192 | 47.01 | 41.24 | 53.81 | 53.42 | 66.39 | 62.27 | 76.29 |

## 5 Conclusions

This paper presents an approach for MP3 multiple compression, which relies on the statistical feature of scale factor matrix obtained from the decoding process of MP3. Then the experimental results imply that the algorithm can effectively detect the compression number of MP3 audio. But it has certain limitations in the work. For example, this work is limited in the condition that the bit rates used in the last two compression processes should be same, and the method is hard to detect whether the MP3 audio has been compressed more than three times. These mentioned issues will be explored in our future work.

**Acknowledgements.** This work is supported by the National Natural Science Foundation of China (Grant No. 61170137, 61300055, 61301247), Public Welfare Technology Application Research Project of Zhejiang Province (2015C33237), Zhejiang Provincial Natural Science Foundation of China (LY13F020013, LZ15F020002), Ningbo Natural Science Foundation (Grant No. 2013A610057), Ningbo University Fund (Grant No. XKXL1405, XKXL1420, XKXL1503), K.C. Wong Magna Fund in Ningbo University, and Chinese Government Scholarship (Grant No. 201508330278).

# References

1. Pasquini, C., Boato, G., et al.: Multiple JPEG compression detection by means of Benford-Fourier coefficients. In: IEEE International Workshop on Information Forensics and Security (WIFS), pp. 113–118, Atlanta, USA (2014)
2. Milani, S., Tagliasacchi, M., Tubaro, S.: Discriminating multiple JPEG compression using first digit features. In: IEEE International Conference on Acoustics, Speech, and Signal Processing, pp. 2253–2256, Kyoto, Japan (2012)
3. Milani, S., Bestagini, P., Tagliasacchi, M., Tubaro, S.: Multiple compression detection for video sequences. In: IEEE International Conference on Multimedia Signal Processing (MMSP), pp. 112–117, Banff, England (2012)
4. Chu, X., Chen, Y., Stamm, M.C., Liu, K.J.R.: Information theoretical limit of compression forensics. In: IEEE International Conference on Acoustics, Speech and Signal Processing (ICASSP), pp. 2689–2693, Florence, Italy (2014)
5. D'Alessandro, B., Shi, Y.Q.: MP3 bit rate quality detection through frequency spectrum analysis. In: Proceedings of the 11th ACM Workshop on Multimedia and Security, pp. 57–61, New York, USA (2009)
6. Liu, Q.Z., Sung, A.H., Qiao, M.Y.: Detection of double MP3 compression. Cogn. Comput. **2**(4), 291–296 (2010)
7. Qiao, M.Y., Sung, A.H., Liu, Q.Z.: Improved detection of MP3 double compression using content-independent features. In: Signal Processing, Communication and Computing (ICSPCC), pp. 1–4, Kun Ming, China (2013)
8. Bianchi, T., De Rosa, A., et al.: Detection and classification of double compressed MP3 audio tracks. In: Proceedings of the First ACM Workshop on Information Hiding and Multimedia Security, pp. 159–164, New York, USA (2013)
9. Bianchi, T., De Rosa, A., et al.: Detection and localization of double compression in MP3 audio tracks. EURASIP J. Inf. Secur. **10** (2014). http://jis.eurasipjournals.com/content/2014/1/10
10. Ma, P., Wang, R., Yan, D., Jin, C.: A Huffman table index based approach to detect double MP3 compression. In: Shi, Y.Q., Kim, H.-J., Pérez-González, F. (eds.) IWDW 2013. LNCS, vol. 8389, pp. 258–272. Springer, Heidelberg (2014)
11. Ma, P.F., Wang, R.D., Yan, D.Q., Jin, C.: Detecting double compression MP3 with the same bit-rate. J. Softw. **9**(10), 2522–2527 (2014)
12. Information technology - coding of moving pictures and associated audio for digital storage media up to about 1.5 mbit/s – part 3: audio. ISO/IEC International Standard IS 11172-3 (1993)
13. Gao, Z.H., Wei, G.: The core of technology of the broadband MP3 audio compression. Electroacoust. Technol. **9**(5), 9–13 (2000)
14. Lame MP3 Encoder. http://lame.sf.net
15. Chang, C.C., Lin, C.J.: LIBSVM: a library for support vector machines. ACM Trans. Intell. Syst. Technol. (TIST) **2**(3), 27 (2011)

# Detection of Double Compression for HEVC Videos Based on the Co-occurrence Matrix of DCT Coefficients

Meiling Huang, Rangding Wang[✉], Jian Xu, Dawen Xu, and Qian Li

College of Information Science and Engineering, Ningbo University,
Ningbo 315211, China
wangrangding@nbu.edu.cn

**Abstract.** Detection of double video compression can reveal partly the video processing history, which is considered to be an important auxiliary means used in video forensics. In this paper, by analyzing the distribution of quantized discrete cosine transform (DCT) coefficients, we propose a scheme to detect double HEVC videos compression under different quantization parameter (QP) values. Firstly, four $5 \times 5$ co-occurrence matrixes were derived from DCT coefficients along four directions respectively, i.e., horizontal, vertical, main diagonal and minor diagonal. Then other 9 high order statistics were constructed by each co-occurrence matrix. Finally, a 136 dimensions feature set constitutes all elements of $5 \times 5$ co-occurrence matrix and other 9 higher order statistics which was sent to support vector machine (SVM). It is used to identify whether video has been gone through double compression. Experiment results show the effectiveness of the algorithm.

**Keywords:** Video forensics · Detection of double compression · HEVC videos · Co-occurrence matrix · High order statistics · Support vector machine (SVM)

## 1 Introduction

With the rapid development of internet and the popularization of low-cost digital multimedia, a variety of digital multimedia information (video\audio\image) can be acquired easily and then be shared by people through social network. At the same time, the advent of powerful and easy-to-use digital multimedia editing software (Adobe Premier\Mokey) makes the digital multimedia information suffering from different kinds of modification. Most people manipulate the multimedia information to enrich their life, but some with ill intent sneak are engaged in illegal activities through modifying the multimedia information for their own interests [1]. For example, it will affect the judge making a correct judgement if the tampered videos are taken as evidences in court. Therefore, ascertaining the authenticity and integrity of the digital multimedia information is an urgent problem. Digital forensics techniques are in full swing currently.

Digital video forensic is an important field of the digital forensic techniques, it mainly divided into two categories, i.e., active [2] and passive digital video forensic

© Springer International Publishing Switzerland 2016
Y.-Q. Shi et al. (Eds.): IWDW 2015, LNCS 9569, pp. 61–71, 2016.
DOI: 10.1007/978-3-319-31960-5_6

techniques. Nowadays, more and more scholars pay their attention to passive forensics techniques, because the passive approaches only extract some intrinsic characteristics of video, rather than add information in advance. Generally, videos are stored and transmitted in compressed way due to the large amount of video data and strong correlation between data. But the tampering process for videos (frame deletion, frame insertion, the object removal and so on) needs to be worked on uncompressed domain. That is to say, a video forger should firstly decode the video streams into image sequences before dealing with the video contents, and then recode the tampered video in a compress way. Hence, double compression is a necessary condition in the video tampering process, and double compression detection plays an important role in revealing the tampering possibility.

Now the research on double JPEG compression detection is comparatively mature, which mainly includes three classical methods, e.g., DCT histogram [3], Benford law [4] and Markov transition probability [5]. But few studies have been done to detect double video compression. Wang and Farid [6] detected double MPEG-2 compression by examining the periodic artifacts in DCT histograms of I frames. In [7] and [8], the fitting result of the probability distribution of the first digit of non-zero quantized AC coefficients with Benford law is applied to detect double MPEG-2 compression. Jiang et al. [9] shows a method to detect double MPEG-4 video compression by modeling Markov transition probability matrix based on DCT coefficients. The probabilities of quantized non-zero AC coefficients ranged from $-10$ to 10 are treated as the features of double H.264 compression detection in [10].

HEVC video coding standard is the latest coding standard, which will has a big application prospect. The research of double compression detection for HEVC is very significant. Steganography and double compression have a trait in common, which can lead to the change of DCT coefficients directly or indirectly. Liu et al. [11] takes the co-occurrence matrix extracted from neighboring DCT coefficients of inter and intra-block as features for steganaysis. We are inspired to testing the effectiveness of statistics based on co-occurrence matrix for HEVC videos.

The rest of this paper is organized as follows. Section 2 briefly reviews the rounding error that is caused by the process of transformation and quantization for HEVC. In Sect. 3, we introduce the concept of co-occurrence matrix and apply it to double compression detection for HEVC by constructing some other related high order statistics. Section 4 shows how to implement the experiments, and also gives the detection results. The conclusions and feature work are summarized in Sect. 5.

## 2 Rounding Error in HEVC Compression Coding

Compared with the previous video compression coding standard, the traditional hybrid coding framework is still used for HEVC. However, HEVC gives up the concept of macroblock but introduces three basic units, i.e., coding unit (CU), prediction unit (PU) and transform unit (TU). The separation of three basic units makes the processes of prediction, transformation and entropy coding more flexibly [12].

During the process of HEVC video compression, residual signal is first obtained based on the prediction of neighborhood pixels. Then discrete cosine transform

(DCT) coefficients are achieved by which the prediction residual is coded using block transform. Finally, those DCT coefficients are quantized according to given QP value. CU is a root unit for HEVC compression, and a CU may be subdivided into one or multiple TUs of different size according to the residual properties. As shown in Eq. (1), it represents that residual pixels of a specific $N \times N$ TU are transformed into corresponding DCT coefficients in the frequency domain.

$$T_{mn} = C_m C_n \sum_{i=0}^{N-1} \sum_{j=0}^{N-1} X_{ij} \cos\frac{(2i+1)m\pi}{2N} \cos\frac{(2j+1)n\pi}{2N}, m, n = 0, 1, \ldots, N-1 \quad (1)$$

where $C_m = C_n = \begin{cases} \sqrt{\dfrac{1}{N}}, m, n = 0 \\ \sqrt{\dfrac{2}{N}}, else \end{cases}$ , $X_{ij}$ denotes the $i$ th row and $j$ th column residual

pixel in $N \times N$ TU, $T_{mn}$ indicates the $n$ th DCT coefficient in the $m$ th row of transform matrix.

The traditional scalar quantization is used to all of DCT coefficients in our work, DCT quantized coefficients are calculated by Eq. (2).

$$dct_{mn} = floor\left(\frac{T_{mn}}{Q_{step}} + f\right) \quad (2)$$

where $T_{mn}$ is DCT coefficient, $dct_{mn}$ marks the quantized DCT coefficient. The variable of round offset is $f$, $floor()$ represents a down integer function. $Q_{step}$ is the quantization step, which is related to quantization parameter (QP), the value of $Q_{step}$ is doubled if QP is increased by 6. For HEVC video compression coding, there are 52 quantization parameters which range from 0 to 51.

The above-mentioned Quantization process will produce a rounding error, which is the main resource of information loss and irreversible for the procedure of HEVC video compression. The distribution of DCT coefficients under different QP values is different on account of this error, and the second compression will retain part of evidences on the first compression. So the change of DCT coefficients can be used to characterize the difference between single compressed videos and double compressed videos.

## 3 The Proposed Scheme

### 3.1 Co-occurrence Matrix

The gray level co-occurrence matrix is the joint probability of pixel pairs with different direction and interval. It can reveal the distribution characteristics of the entire data and also illustrate the dependence well. On the basis of strong dependence between neighboring image data (such as pixels or coefficients), co-occurrence matrix is treated as a common method to depict the texture of an image in the early times. Now most researchers find that the stochastic modifications of image data during embedding secrets broken the strong dependence between adjacent data, which leads to the change of co-occurrence matrix. So co-occurrence matrix is successfully used in steganalysis. Suppose the size of coefficients matrix $C$ of an image is $M \times N$, the co-occurrence matrix of which can be defined as follows:

$$P_h(a,b) = \frac{\sum\limits_{x=1}^{M} \sum\limits_{y=1}^{N-d} \delta(C(x,y) = a, C(x,y+d) = b)}{M \times (N-d)} \tag{3}$$

$$P_v(a,b) = \frac{\sum\limits_{x=1}^{M-d} \sum\limits_{y=1}^{N} \delta(C(x,y) = a, C(x+d,y) = b)}{(M-d) \times N} \tag{4}$$

$$P_d(a,b) = \frac{\sum\limits_{x=1}^{M-d} \sum\limits_{y=1}^{N-d} \delta(C(x,y) = a, C(x+d,y+d) = b)}{(M-d) \times (N-d)} \tag{5}$$

$$P_m(a,b) = \frac{\sum\limits_{x=1+d}^{M} \sum\limits_{y=1}^{N-d} \delta(C(x,y) = a, C(x-d,y+d) = b)}{(M-d) \times (N-d)} \tag{6}$$

Where $\delta(X = a, Y = b) = \begin{cases} 1, X = a, Y = b \\ 0, \text{else} \end{cases}$, the parameter $d$ represents the distance of the selected adjacent element pairs, $P_h$, $P_v$, $P_d$, $P_m$ denote the co-occurrence matrix in horizontal, vertical, major diagonal and minor diagonal direction respectively, $P_h(a,b)$, $P_v(a,b)$, $P_d(a,b)$, $P_m(a,b)$ of which is corresponding to the frequency of adjacent coefficient pairs with values $(a,b)$.

## 3.2 Feature Extraction

As described in Sect. 2, it is investigated that DCT coefficients have been changed by comparing single compression video with double compression video. Therefore, DCT coefficients are regarded as basic feature to extract co-occurrence matrix and some other statistics in our proposed algorithm.

In HEVC standard, the size $64 \times 64$ of coding tree unit (CTU) is the basic processing unit to specify the decoding process. It is important to note that there is different TU size layout for different CTU. Each CTU has one or several kinds of TUs, and the size $L \times L$ of TUs can be chosen as $L = 32, 16, 8, 4$. In this paper, we first extract the quantized DCT coefficients in CTUs for given video and only take the coefficients in luminance component into account during the decoding process. Then all DCT coefficients of CTUs are arranged one after the other in a two-dimensional matrix $C$. We defines matrix $C$ which denotes all of DCT coefficients encoded $N$ frames:

$$C = \begin{pmatrix} C_1 \\ C_2 \\ \cdots \\ C_i \\ \cdots \\ C_q \end{pmatrix}, \; C_i = \begin{bmatrix} dct_{i,1,1} & dct_{i,1,2} & \cdots & dct_{i,1,64} \\ dct_{i,2,1} & dct_{i,2,2} & \cdots & dct_{i,2,64} \\ \vdots & \vdots & \ddots & \vdots \\ dct_{i,64,1} & dct_{i,64,2} & \cdots & dct_{i,64,64} \end{bmatrix}, \text{ in which } q \text{ is the number}$$

of CTU with $N$ frames, the value of $q$ changes with the resolution of given video. For example, $q = N \times \lceil \frac{416}{64} \rceil \times \lceil \frac{240}{64} \rceil = N \times 7 \times 4 = 28N$ if the resolution of video is $416 \times 240$. $\lceil X \rceil$ is a ceiling function. $C_i$ represents DCT coefficients of the $i$ th extracted CTU.

The neighboring DCT coefficients have a certain correlation more or less, but it will vary with compression times and quantization parameter. The co-occurrence matrix $P$ can well capture this subtle change, which is derived from DCT coefficients matrix according to the process introduced in Sect. 3.1. The size of matrix $P$ is related to the range of value in DCT coefficients matrix $C$, we should get an approximate matrix $C'$ by pre-processing $C$ to ensure a balance between preserving neighbor structure and the dimensions of matrix $P$. As far as we known, most of DCT coefficients are fallen into a small interval and obey the Laplace distribution with mean of 0 [13]. Further, according to our statistical analysis for HEVC videos, Fig. 1 shows that the probability of DCT coefficients in a fixed interval $[-4, 4]$ is about 99 % for different QP. Moreover, as indicated in Fig. 2, it can be seen that more and more nonzero values of quantized DCT coefficients are turned into zero with QP increasing. In addition, DCT coefficients are distributed symmetrically on the right and left sides of zero. From the above, we set a threshold $T = 4$ to truncate the matrix $C$, and then get the final approximate matrix $C'$ by taking the absolute value of truncated matrix.

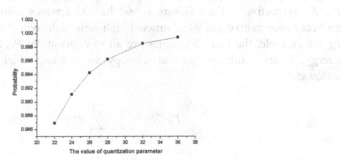

**Fig. 1.** The probability of DCT $\in [-4, 4]$

Co-occurrence matrix is separately modeled on matrix $C'$ in four different directions, so we can obtain four $5 \times 5$ joint probabilities matrixes. Like Fig. 3, example is cited to illustrate the difference of co-occurrence matrix $P_h$ between single and double compression video. It is important to note that the selection of distance parameter $d = 1$ is decided by experiments.

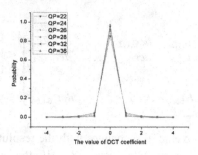

**Fig. 2.** The distribution of DCT coefficients

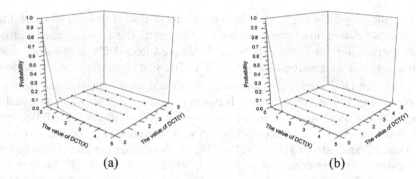

(a)                                      (b)

**Fig. 3.** The mean of co-occurrence matrix $P_h$ (d = 1) joint probabilities of 361 single compression videos and 361 double compression videos, in which (a) represents single compression videos for QP = 22, (b) denotes double compression videos for QP1 = 32, QP2 = 22.

In our proposed algorithm, we signed the four direction feature subsets as $F_h$, $F_v$, $F_d$, $F_m$ respectively. Each feature subset has 34 features containing 25 elements of co-occurrence matrix and 9 constructed high order statistics. Take horizontal direction $F_h$ for example, the first 25 features are all of elements in $P_h$, the rest features depict energy, inverse different moment, entropy and so on, which can be calculated as follows:

$$F_h(26) = \sum_{i=0}^{4} \sum_{j=0}^{4} P_h(i,j)^2 \tag{7}$$

$$F_h(27) = \max(P_h) \tag{8}$$

$$F_h(28) = \sum_{i=0}^{4} \sum_{j=0}^{4} \frac{P_h(i,j)}{1 + (i-j)^2} \tag{9}$$

$$F_h(29) = \sum_{i=0}^{4} \sum_{j=0}^{4} (i - mm)^2 \times P_h(i,j) \tag{10}$$

$$F_h(30) = -\sum_{i=0}^{4}\sum_{j=0}^{4} P_h(i,j) \times \log_2 P_h(i,j) \tag{11}$$

$$F_h(31) = -\sum_{i=0}^{4}\sum_{j=0}^{4} P_h(i,j) \times \log_2 \left(P_{hx}(i) \times P_{hy}(j)\right) \tag{12}$$

$$F_h(32) = -\sum_{i=0}^{4}\sum_{j=0}^{4} P_{hx}(i,j) \times P_{hy}(i,j) \times \log_2 \left(P_{hx}(i) \times P_{hy}(j)\right) \tag{13}$$

$$F_h(33) = -\sum_{i=0}^{4} P_{hx}(i) \times \log_2 P_{hx}(i) \tag{14}$$

$$F_h(34) = -\sum_{j=0}^{4} P_{hy}(j) \times \log_2 P_{hy}(j) \tag{15}$$

In which $P_{hx}(i) = \sum_{j=0}^{4} P_h(i,j)$, $P_{hy}(i) = \sum_{i=0}^{4} P_h(i,j)$, $mm = \frac{1}{T \times T}\sum_{i=0}^{4}\sum_{j=0}^{4} P_h(i,j)$, $P_h(i,j)$ denotes the $i$ th row and $j$ th column of matrix $P_h$.

## 4 Experiments and Discussion

### 4.1 The Establishment of Sample Library

In our experiments, thirty widely known YUV sequences are selected as source sequences, which contain six different resolutions, as shown in Table 1.

In order to increase sample quantity, we use the video editing package splitting each YUV sequences into several non-overlapped video clips. There are 361 video clips in total and each clip contains 30 frames in our experiments. For the sake of the video sample library consists of single-compressed and double-compressed video clips. All of 361 video clips (original standard YUV sequences) are first compressed with

**Table 1.** The selection of YUV sequences

| Resolution | YUV sequences |
|---|---|
| 416 × 240 | Basketballpass\Blowingbubbles\BQsquare\Flowervase_416 × 240\Mobisode2 |
| 832 × 480 | Basketballdrill\Basketballdrilltext\BQmall\Flowervase_832 × 480 |
| 1280 × 720 | Johnny\vidyo1\vidyo2\vidyo3 |
| 1920 × 1080 | BasketballDrive |
| 2560 × 1600 | Peopleonstreet\Traffic |
| 176 × 144 | akiyo\bridge_close\carphone\container\foreman_part\grandma\ hall\highway\miss_america\mother_daughter\news\salseman\silent |

QP. The value of QP is equal to 22, 24, 26, 28, 32 and 36. Then each compressed HEVC video streams is decoded and recoded with different quantization parameter QP, e.g., the second compressed QP is 24,26,28,32 and 36 if the first compressed QP is 22. We choose 361 single-compressed videos with QP2 and 361 double-compressed video with QP1 followed by $QP2(QP2 \neq QP1)$ as a group to model double compression detection under different QP. So 30 groups of datasets are generated in total. All the process of video compression coding is conducted in video coding reference software HM12.0, of which main configuration parameters are given in Table 2.

**Table 2.** Configuration parameters of HM12.0

| Parameters | Configuration |
|---|---|
| Frames to be encoded | 5 |
| Intra period | 1 |
| GOPsize | 1 |
| Scalinglist | 0 |

## 4.2 Experiments Results and Discussion

For each group, 361 single-compressed videos and 361 double-compressed videos are labeled as +1, −1 respectively. The extracted feature sets by dealing with normalization are sent to LIBSVM classifier [14]. For every group of dataset, the 50 % features are randomly selected for training a classification model, and the rest features are used for testing. For the LIBSVM classifier, Radial Basis Function (RBF) is chosen as the kernel function of svmtrain (•). And 5-fold cross-validation is performed to select the optimal parameters (Gamma and Cost) for the kernel. The entire experimental procedure is repeated for ten times. Every time the detection accuracy is calculated according to the Eq. (16). The average is treated as the final detection accuracy.

$$Accuracy = (TPR + TNR)/2 \tag{16}$$

where $TPR = TP/(TP + FN)$, $TNR = TN/(TN + FP)$, $TP$ represents the occurrence that a single compressed video is predicted as single compression, $FN$ denotes the incident that a single compressed video is classified as double compression, $TN$ shows the frequency that a double compressed video is predicted as double compression, $FP$ is the frequency that a double compressed video is classified as single compression.

In this paper, the necessity of adding the other high order statistics is illustrated by the detection results of experiments. We first take all the elements of co-occurrence matrix along four directions as effective 100 features to detect HEVC double compression. Table 3 gives the detection results. Further, as a result of high order statistics that can depict some detail information. So the construction of other high order statistics as described in Sect. 3.2 is also taken account into our method. That the extracted features of our method is the combination of co-occurrence matrix and high order statistics. The detection accuracies of our method is shown in Table 4. As can be seen from Tables 3 and 4, the combined feature set of our method can better distinguish the double compressed audio from the signal compressed audio.

**Table 3.** Detection accuracies of 100D co-occurrence features (%)

| QP1 | QP2 22 | 24 | 26 | 28 | 32 | 36 |
|---|---|---|---|---|---|---|
| 22 | – | 93.89 | 70.83 | 69.44 | 40.56 | 45.00 |
| 24 | 98.94 | – | 93.33 | 68.06 | 48.33 | 46.67 |
| 26 | 100.00 | 99.17 | – | 91.11 | 64.72 | 46.39 |
| 28 | 100.00 | 100.00 | 98.89 | – | 67.78 | 48.33 |
| 32 | 100.00 | 100.00 | 100.00 | 100.00 | – | 61.94 |
| 36 | 100.00 | 100.00 | 100.00 | 100.00 | 99.72 | – |

**Table 4.** Detection accuracies of our method (%)

| QP1 | QP2 22 | 24 | 26 | 28 | 32 | 36 |
|---|---|---|---|---|---|---|
| 22 | – | 93.61 | 70.28 | 69.72 | 45.56 | 43.06 |
| 24 | 98.33 | – | 93.06 | 69.44 | 56.39 | 43.61 |
| 26 | 100.00 | 99.17 | – | 90.28 | 64.44 | 47.50 |
| 28 | 100.00 | 100.00 | 99.44 | – | 72.22 | 48.89 |
| 32 | 100.00 | 100.00 | 100.00 | 100.00 | – | 62.78 |
| 36 | 100.00 | 100.00 | 100.00 | 100.00 | 100.00 | – |

Here, 'QP1' indicates the quantization parameter of single compression videos, 'QP2' means the quantization parameter of double compression videos by recompressing the single compression video with QP1. When 'QP1' and 'QP2' are 22 and 24 respectively, it denotes the detection accuracy of single-compressed videos with 24 and double-compressed videos with 22 followed by 24. The testing result located in the 3th row and the 3th column of Tables 3 and 4 are 93.89 % and 93.61 %.

To make a comparison with other method, the algorithm of double compression detection based on 162-D Markov statistics for MPEG-4 videos in [9] was applied to HEVC. The detection accuracies of literature [9] is provided in Table 5. The mean accuracies of our method and Ref. [9] are 82.26 % and 80.25 % respectively from Tables 4 and 5, i.e., our scheme outperforms Ref. [9]. In addition, a conclusion is summarized that the left bottom of these tables can achieve good classification ability,

**Table 5.** Detection accuracies of the method in Ref. [9] (%)

| QP1 | QP2 22 | 24 | 26 | 28 | 32 | 36 |
|---|---|---|---|---|---|---|
| 22 | – | 90.00 | 65.83 | 62.63 | 41.94 | 44.72 |
| 24 | 99.44 | – | 88.61 | 64.44 | 45.83 | 44.44 |
| 26 | 100.00 | 99.44 | – | 85.56 | 59.83 | 45.28 |
| 28 | 100.00 | 99.94 | 99.44 | – | 63.61 | 48.61 |
| 32 | 100.00 | 100.00 | 100.00 | 100.00 | – | 61.11 |
| 36 | 99.72 | 100.00 | 100.00 | 100.00 | 99.47 | – |

but the result of the upper triangle is not ideal. The bigger QP1, the deviation of DCT coefficient between single compressed videos and double compressed videos is more obvious. Because the first compression coding used higher QP1 will loss more unrecoverable details, which leave more clear evidences for the second compression coding to distinguish double compressed videos from single compressed videos. On the contrary, there is almost no information loss in the first compress coding used lower QP1. The distribution of DCT coefficient of single compressed videos are very close to double compressed videos, which leads to the decline of detection accuracies.

## 5    Conclusions and Future Work

In this paper, an effective method to detect double HEVC videos compression under different QP values was proposed. We have modeled a co-occurrence matrix based on DCT coefficient and constructed related high order statistic features to reveal the artifacts by double quantization errors. Experiment results show that the proposed algorithm performs well when the first quantization parameter QP1 is higher than the second quantization parameter QP2 for HEVC compression coding. Our future work will focus on how to detect double compression videos with the same quantization parameter, which is a blank so far.

**Acknowledgements.** This work is supported by the National Natural Science Foundation of China (Grant No. 61170137, 61300055, 61301247), Public Welfare Technology Application Research Project of Zhejiang Province (2015C33237), Zhejiang Provincial Natural Science Foundation of China (LY13F020013, LZ15F020002), Ningbo Natural Science Foundation (Grant No. 2013A610057), Open Fund of Zhejiang Provincial Top Key Discipline (xkx11405), Ningbo University Fund (Grant No. XKXL1405, XKXL1420) and K.C. Wong Magna Fund in Ningbo University.

## References

1. Yang, R., Luo, W., Huang, J.: Multimedia forensic. Sci. China Inf. Sci. **43**(12), 1654–1672 (2013)
2. Xu, D., Wang, R., Shi, Y.: Data hiding in encrypted H.264/AVC video streams by codeword substitution. IEEE Trans. Inf. Forensics Secur. **9**(4), 596–606 (2014)
3. Popescu, A.C., Farid, H.: Statistical tools for digital image forensics. In: Proceedings 6th International Workshop on Information Hiding, pp. 128–147, Toronto, Canada (2004)
4. Fu, D., Shi, Y., Su, W.: A generalized Benford's law for JPEG coefficients and its applications in image forensics. In: Proceedings of SPIE 6505, Security, Steganography and Watermarking of Multimedia Contents IX, 65051L, 27 Feb 2007
5. Chen, C., Shi, Y., Su, W.: A machine learning based scheme for double JPEG compression detection. In: Proceedings of International Conference on Pattern Recognition, pp. 1814–1817, Dec 2008
6. Wang, W., Farid, H.: Exposing digital forgeries in video by detecting double MPEG compression. In: Proceedings of the Multimedia and Security Workshop, pp. 37–47, Geneva, Switzerland, 26–27 Sept 2006

7. Chen, W., Shi, Y.Q.: Detection of double MPEG compression based on first digit statistics. In: Kim, H.-J., Katzenbeisser, S., Ho, A.T.S. (eds.) IWDW 2008. LNCS, vol. 5450, pp. 16–30. Springer, Heidelberg (2009)

8. Wang, W., Jiang, X., Sun, T.: Exposing double MPEG compression based on first digit features. J. Electron. Inf. Technol. **34**(12), 3046–3050 (2012)

9. Jiang, X., Wang, W., Sun, T., Shi, Y.: Detection of double compression in MPEG-4 videos based on markov statistics. IEEE Signal Process. Lett. **20**(5), 447–450 (2013)

10. Liao, D., Yang, R., Liu, H., Li, J., Huang, J.: Double H.264/AVC compression detection using quantized non-zero AC coefficients. In: Proceedings of SPIE International Society for Optical Engineering (Media Watermarking, Security, and Forensics), vol. 7880 (2011)

11. Liu, Q., Sung, A.H., Qiao, M.: Neighboring joint density-based JPEG steganalysis. ACM Trans. Intell. Syst. Technol. **2**(2), Article 16 (2011)

12. Sullivan, G.J., Ohm, J.R., Han, W.-J., Wiegand, T.: Overview of the high efficiency video coding (HEVC) standard. IEEE Trans. Circ. Syst. Video Technol. **12**(22), 1649–1668 (2012)

13. Lam, E.Y., Goodman, J.W.: A mathematical analysis of the DCT coefficient distributions for images. IEEE Trans. Image Process. **9**(10), 1661–1666 (2000)

14. Chang, C.-C., Lin, C.-J.: LIBSVM: a Library for Support Vector Machines. http://www.csie.ntu.edu.tw/~cjlin/libsvm/ (2001)

# An Advanced Texture Analysis Method for Image Sharpening Detection

Feng Ding[1(✉)], Weiqiang Dong[1], Guopu Zhu[2], and Yun-Qing Shi[1]

[1] Department of Electrical and Computer Engineering,
New Jersey Institute of Technology, Newark, NJ 07102, USA
{fd26,wd35,shi}@njit.edu
[2] Shenzhen Institutes of Advanced Technology,
Chinese Academy of Sciences, Shenzhen, Guangdong 518055, China
gp.zhu@siat.ac.cn

**Abstract.** Sharpening is a kind of basic yet widely utilized digital image processing techniques designed and utilized to pursue better image quality from human visual point of view. In image forensics it is required to detect this kind of operation. Huge progress has been made in this area in recent years. Overshoot artifact, as a unique phenomenon occurring on image edges after sharpening, is important in sharpening detection. In this paper, an advanced scheme for overshoot artifact determination is proposed to boost the detection performance in the case of mildor overshoot artifact-controlled sharpening, Several groups of experiments have been conducted to corroborate the new scheme possesses the best ability for blind sharpening detection regardless of the strength of overshoot artifact.

**Keywords:** Image forensics · Edge perpendicular binary code · Overshoot artifact · Sharpening detection

## 1 Introduction

Image, a medium reflects the natural information to human eyes is always considered to be a secured source. As an intuitionist source, besides the character of evidence in court, images also serve for many purposes in various medias such as in newspapers, magazines, television.

With the explosive advancement of digital technologies, digital images replace the traditional photo images. More and more techniques are created for the convenience of modern life, including the image editing techniques. Since ordinary people acquire the ability to tamper or even forge the digital images, the reliability of images serving as evidences is doubted [1]. In this situation, scientists start the image forensics [2,3] against the illegal or improper purpose of image forgery. Besides, especially for the requirements in court, all the possible manipulations need to be verified to protect the integrity of images.

Image sharpening [4] is a most widely used manipulation in digital image processing. People would like to obtain more detailed information from images

© Springer International Publishing Switzerland 2016
Y.-Q. Shi et al. (Eds.): IWDW 2015, LNCS 9569, pp. 72–82, 2016.
DOI: 10.1007/978-3-319-31960-5_7

via this manipulation. After sharpening, the contrast of image edges are enhanced to display clearer outlines of the content in images. Because sharpening is important and employed all over the world, it is necessary to detect this operation in image forensics.

Since the first detection approach proposed in 2009, more people and groups are getting involved in this area, and more papers are published. Cao *et al.* discovered the phenomenon of histogram abberation and proposed his first method for sharpening detection [5] in 2009. However, in [6], the authors also indicated this method may fail while facing the images with narrow shape histogram. Lately in his second work, by measuring the strength of overshoot artifact, Cao *et al.* exploited measuring the strength of overshoot artifact to surmount this drawback. By setting a proper threshold, Cao *et al.* can distinguish the sharpened images with a strong overshoot artifact. Then, in 2013, we found texture analysis is a more efficient way for sharpening detection. Hence, LBP [7,8], a simple but strong texture analysis tool [9,10] came to our mind. And the experimental results proved our point [11]. In the following year, inspired by our first work, a method named as Edge Perpendicular Binary Coding (EPBC) [12] was designed to specifically address the sharpening detection. Analyzing the overshoot artifact by a window with controlled length, this approach reaches the best detection ability comparing all the other published methods for a period. Although we have made great progress so far, there is still one more issue needs to be solved. That is, we have to admit all the above methods even the most recent one, are poor when detecting slightly sharpened images. However, in real world for most cases, only slightly sharpening are widely applied because strong sharpening also bring the defect of noises and distortions.

For the reasons above, in this paper, we propose an advanced scheme, Edge Perpendicular Ternary Coding (EPTC), to focus on boosting detection performance. We conduct plenty of experiments to compare the detection ability of these methods. The new scheme can achieve best performance among all the methods regardless of any circumstance.

The rest parts are organized as follows. In Sect. 2, we briefly introduce the overshoot artifact generated in image sharpening. Proposed detection method is described in Sect. 3. Experimental results are given and discussed in Sect. 4. Finally, in Sect. 5, conclusions are summarized.

## 2 Overshoot Artifact

Overshoot artifact also known as 'ringing artifact' can be considered as a specific texture that massively appears in sharpened images. Generally, after processed by all kinds of sharpening manipulations, overshoot artifact occurs on most of the edges in images. As the effect of sharpening, the edge pixels may have either a significant positive or negative gain in pixel values. Pixel value of sharpened pixels $P_s$ can be considered as the sum of original pixel value $P_i$ and overshoot artifact $O$.

$$P_s = P_i + O. \tag{1}$$

This phenomenon happening in images lead to a pleasant detail view for human eyes.

## 3  Proposed Method

In our previous works, differing from LBP, more than 5 pixels along the vertical direction to edge lines are adopted to discover the trace of overshoot artifact for sharpening detection. And EPBC has been verified as the best method among 3 proposed methods for sharpening detection in all kind of situations. However, especially for the weak sharpening strength and narrow sharpening range, the detection accuracy of EPBC remains in low levels of less than 85 % in extreme conditions. But in our daily life, these slightly sharpening manipulations are the most common cases because strong sharpening can also bring intense noises and distortion to digital images. So it is required to improve the detection ability in these cases.

In order to boost the performance of EPBC, the feature we extracted from images should be more efficient to distinguish the weakly sharpened edges from the other pixels. In slightly sharpened images, the overshoot artifact itself is weak. And sometimes, even the unsharpened images having certain amount of edge pixels with the similar structure of overshoot may be misjudged as slightly sharpened edges, which can confuse the machine to make wrong decisions. And image edges are not always in a straight direction, the edges with curves are also need to be considered. So, we propose a better scheme here to address these issues to enhance the detection ability. It is described in following steps.

(a) Edge detection

'Canny'[13] operator is the most intelligent method to detect accurate edges, and it is widely employed by many scientists in many papers. The 'Canny' operator can localize the pixels on the center of edges, and only mark edge once. For these properties, it is the most proper method for sharpening detection. Hence this time, we also used this method for edge detection to achieve quality performance. Because edge detection is only proper for the images with two dimensions, color images need to be converted to gray scale images before edge detection.

(b) Local edge area derivation

After revealing edge pixels, for each edge points as centre points, a rectangular window of size $1 \times N$ is set to be perpendicular to the edge lines. This window is defined as local area. Here, $N$ is an odd number larger than 1, meaning the amount of pixels we employed in the local area. In this paper, we take $N = 5$ for example, the pixels contained by local edge area can be denoted as $D = [P_0, P_1, P_2, P_3, P_4]$, and $P_2$ is the edge pixel which always located at the centre of each local edge area.

(c) Interpolation

As referred above, not all the edges are in straight directions, there may be edges appear as curves with different angles. For these situations, we find out the normal line of the edge point, and then interpolate certain pixels on both sides

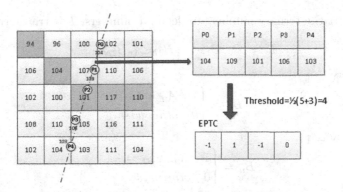

**Fig. 1.** Interpolation for edge with curve

of edge point in the vertical line to the normal line. By interpolation, even for these curves, we can still acquire a sequence of pixels that satisfy the definition of local edge area for feature extraction.

In Fig. 1, the line in yellow is the edge line, the interpolated pixels in dotted line denotes the local area we employed for feature extraction.

(d) Ternary coding

The main task of detection under slightly sharpening condition requires the coding method can differentiate the weak overshoot artifact from other points. Hence, we employ ternary coding method which can precisely distinguish the slightly sharpened edges.

With the local edge areas, we first need to derive a new sequence $C$ by computing the pixel value differences between neighbor pixels.

$$C = [P_0 - P_1, P_1 - P_2, \cdots, P_{N-2} - P_{N-1}]. \tag{2}$$

Differentiate from EPBC, here, we need to convert the set $C$ into a ternary set $T$ by

$$T = [A_0, A_1, \cdots, A_{N-2}], \tag{3}$$

where

$$A_n = f(P_n - P_{n+1}), \tag{4}$$

$$f(P_n - P_{n+1}) = \begin{cases} 1 & P_n - P_{n+1} > q \\ 0 & q \geq P_n - P_{n+1} \geq -q \\ -1 & P_n - P_{n+1} < -q, \end{cases} \tag{5}$$

Here, $q$ is a positive number and important threshold calculated in each local area. It is the average of the pixel value difference of all non-edge pixels in a local area. In a local area of length of 5, it is derived by

$$q = \frac{\sum_{i=0}^{i=(N-5)/2} \|P_i - P_{i+1}\| + \sum_{i=(N+1)/2}^{i=N-2} \|P_i - P_{i+1}\|}{(N-3)} \tag{6}$$

To convert the ternary numbers to decimal numbers, $T$ is transferred to $T'$

$$T' = [B_0, B_1, \cdots, B_{2N-4}, B_{2N-3}],\tag{7}$$

For $n < N - 1$

$$B_n = \begin{cases} 1 & A_n = 1 \\ 0 & otherwise \end{cases}\tag{8}$$

For $n \geq N - 1$

$$B_n = \begin{cases} 1 & A_{n-N+1} = -1 \\ 0 & otherwise \end{cases}\tag{9}$$

Then, a pattern number can be conveyed from $T'$ by

$$EPTC(T') = \sum_{n=0}^{n=2N-3} B_n \times 2^n.\tag{10}$$

Figure 2 indicates the general outline of the EPTC applied in sharpened image. The line in purple is a sample local edge area. When facing an overshoot artifact with a small gradient, ternary coding makes the machine easier to determine if the edge is slightly sharpened or just from a natural image. However, EPBC may fail to make the correct decision because this little difference of edges may be ignored when only applying binary patterns. From Figs. 2 and 3,

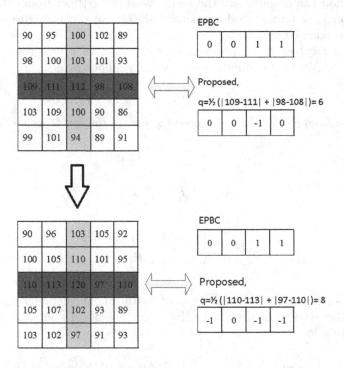

**Fig. 2.** EPTC applied in original and sharpened image

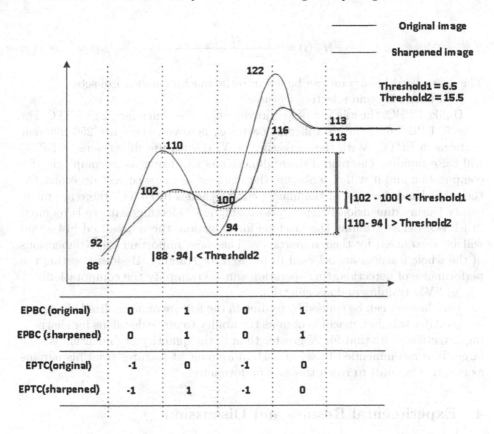

**Fig. 3.** Different coding methods applied on overshoot artifact

it can be observed that the EPBC pattern may not change in original image and slightly sharpened image, while EPTC can still distinguish them.

(e) Calculating histogram

For $N = 5$, there are 256 numbers for different patterns. Histogram can be derived from these numbers and the times each pattern appear in images.

$$H(i) = \sum_{T \in \triangle} \delta(EPTC(T) - i), \tag{11}$$

here, $\delta(x)$ denotes an impulse function that equals to one if $x = 0$, and zero otherwise, and $\triangle$ denotes the set of $T$ calculated from all of the local edge areas in the given image. It is well known that real images usually vary in contents and textures, this results in that the number of edge pixels detected by 'Canny' operator vary significantly for different images, and thus the histogram $H$ also change greatly due to the same reason. In order to make $H$ invariant to image contents and textures, we normalize the histogram $H$ by

$$H_N(i) = \frac{H(i)}{\sum_{i=0}^{i=4^{(N-1)}-1} H(i)}.$$  (12)

The normalized histogram can be fed into the machine as feature sets.

(f) Prioritizing and selecting features

Unlike EPBC, the amount of feature dimensions is much larger in EPTC. For $N = 5$, EPBC only has 16 different patterns, however, there are 256 different patterns in EPTC. With the increasing of $N$, the feature dimensions of EPTC will raise rapidly. The more feature dimensions will bring more complexity for computation and it will also obscure the machine to make correct decisions. On the other hand, because of the unique coding tactics in EPTC, there are many empty feature dimensions. Hence, prioritizing and selecting features is required in EPTC. Before training the machine for detection, the normalized histogram will be rearranged by their importance. The most important 20 % dimensions of the whole features are selected to be used for training. Besides boosting the performance of detection, this operation can also simplify the computation.

(g) SVM training and classification

The classifier can be trained by feeding in the feature of normalized histogram above. After training, machine obtains the ability to make decisions for sharpening detection. Note that for $N$ greater than 9, the quantity of dimension is very large. It is recommended to select certain amount of features from histograms as effective features to reach the best performance.

## 4   Experimental Results and Discussion

The image database we use here is the similar one from our last work. We collect 1000 images randomly from image data base UCID and NRCS respectively to form a test image base containing 2000 images. Images from both UCID and NRCS are gray scale image in BMP format. Images from UCID have the size of $384 \times 512$ while images from NRCS are $768 \times 512$.

And in the meaning of better comparison under more realistic cases, images are enhanced by USM method via the most widely used unsharp mask. This method features at generating an unsharp mask by Gaussian low-pass filter and then add the mask back to the original images to achieve sharpness. This algorithm features two coefficients $\sigma$ and $\lambda$. $\sigma$ controls the enhancement scale, at the meanwhile, $\lambda$ controls the enhancement strength. Comparison is made between two detection methods, our previously proposed method (EPBC) and the method proposed in this paper (EPTC). Different detection accuracy for the image database enhanced under various of coefficients pair are shown in Table 1.

Recall that the Gaussian filter-based USM method has two main parameters, i.e., $\sigma$ and $\lambda$, which control the sharpening range and strength, respectively. And the large $\sigma$ and $\lambda$ correspond to wide sharpening range and strong sharpening strength. In all our experiments, comparisons are only necessary between two sharpening detection methods, including our previously proposed EPBC and the

**Table 1.** Detection accuracy for USM sharpening when $N = 5$.

| Parameters of USM | EPTC N=5 | EPBC N=5 |
|---|---|---|
| $\sigma = 0.5, \lambda = 1$ | **94.51 %** | 86.74 % |
| $\sigma = 0.7, \lambda = 1$ | **95.42 %** | 88.04 % |
| $\sigma = 1, \lambda = 1$ | **96.35 %** | 91.90 % |
| $\sigma = 1.5, \lambda = 1$ | **96.74 %** | 93.53 % |
| $\sigma = 1, \lambda = 0.5$ | **94.73 %** | 86.52 % |
| $\sigma = 1, \lambda = 0.8$ | **95.22 %** | 90.03 % |
| $\sigma = 1, \lambda = 1.3$ | **97.40 %** | 93.34 % |
| $\sigma = 1, \lambda = 1.5$ | **98.18 %** | 95.07 % |
| $\sigma = 1.3, \lambda = 1.5$ | **98.69 %** | 96.50 % |

method proposed in this paper. Different length of edge area window sizes will be also considered later.

Table 1 shows the detection accuracy of EPTC and original EPBC [12]. The combination of sigma and lambda determines how the sharpened image looks like. While the values of sigma and lambda increase, it is more likely that the behavior of sharpening is visible.

In EPBC, the ideal window sizes of local edge area are specified as $N = 7$ and $N = 9$. However, larger window size such as $N = 9$, also increases the complexity of computation. Therefore, in this paper, the window sizes was selected as $N = 5$ and $N = 7$.

Apparently from the results in Table 1, it is proved that the proposed method has a better performance in assorted sets of sharpening range and sharpening strength. The detection accuracy of all cases have been improved. The most important case, when sigma and lambda is small (less than 0.7), EPTC makes a significant progress.

When $N = 5$, the detection accuracy of proposed method is higher than the original EPBC overall. It is more obvious when sigma and lambda have small values. Particularly, when $\sigma = 0.5$ or $\lambda = 0.5$, the detection accuracy of EPBC method is 8 % less than the proposed method. The better performance suggesting that the proposed method would be more efficient in weak sharpened images.

From Table 2, in the case $N = 7$, the detection accuracy of new method under all situations are over 95 %, which proves that the proposed method is satisfactorily stable. In the meantime, the original EPBC already has good performance in the strong sharpening case. however, when the sharpening strength is weak, the detection accuracy of EPBC may drop below 90 %. Considering the time cost for computation when $N = 9$, the higher detection accuracy of EPTC also suggest $N = 7$ reach the best balance between performance and computation complexity.

**Table 2.** Detection accuracy for USM sharpening when $N = 7$.

| Parameters of USM | EPTC N=7 | EPBC N=7 |
|---|---|---|
| $\sigma = 0.5, \lambda = 1$ | **95.42 %** | 88.74 % |
| $\sigma = 0.7, \lambda = 1$ | **96.13 %** | 91.20 % |
| $\sigma = 1, \lambda = 1$ | **97.90 %** | 95.53 % |
| $\sigma = 1.5, \lambda = 1$ | **98.30 %** | 96.55 % |
| $\sigma = 1, \lambda = 0.5$ | **95.52 %** | 89.32 % |
| $\sigma = 1, \lambda = 0.8$ | **96.36 %** | 94.13 % |
| $\sigma = 1, \lambda = 1.3$ | **98.14 %** | 96.48 % |
| $\sigma = 1, \lambda = 1.5$ | **98.97 %** | 97.34 % |
| $\sigma = 1.3, \lambda = 1.5$ | **99.11 %** | 97.70 % |

Furthermore, the robustness testing result of proposed method is shown in Tables 3 and 4. In these two experiments, sigma and lambda of USM is set as (1,1). At first, Guassian noise(sigma=3) is added to all the images. Table 4 shows that the proposed method still achieve a higher detection rate than the EPBC. In Table 3, accuracy of EPTC is averagely 3 % higher when against JPEG compression distortion.

The blind sharpening detection ability of our new proposed method on other USM manipulations is also evaluated. The image database with 2000 images are randomly separated into five subsets with 400 images respectively. Five different USM methods [4, 14–16] are utilized to match the subsets for sharpening purpose. After sharpening, all the subsets are mixed together for sharpening detection. The results are shown in Table 4.

The results authenticate the excellence of EPTC even with limited overshoot artifact. It can still reach a detection accuracy of 95 % which leads EPBC by 8 %.

**Table 3.** Detection accuracy under JPEG compression distortion.

| Quality factor | EPTC | EPBC |
|---|---|---|
| $Q = 80$ | **93.36 %** | 89.96 % |
| $Q = 60$ | **91.82 %** | 89.15 % |
| $Q = 40$ | **91.03 %** | 88.06 % |

**Table 4.** Detection accuracy under Gaussian noise distortion.

| Variance of noise | EPTC | EBPC |
|---|---|---|
| $\sigma_n = 3$ | **96.31 %** | 94.85 % |
| $\sigma_n = 1$ | **94.35 %** | 92.10 % |

**Table 5.** Detection accuracy on mixed sharpen images processed by five different USM methods.

|  | EPTC | EPBC |
|---|---|---|
| Detection accuracy | **96.14 %** | 92.53 % |

On the other hand, as a method relies on measuring overshoot artifact, Cao *et al.*'s method exposed the failure when facing the sharpening with overshoot control (Table 5).

From all the above experiments, it can be concluded that the performance of EPTC is outstanding among all methods. Regardless the strength of overshoot artifact, it is a trustworthy approach to detect all kinds of sharpening methods.

## 5  Conclusion

In this paper, a new method for universal sharpening detection is introduced. This new method is created to address the drawbacks for detection of slightly sharpened images. In order to optimize the detection ability, several novelties are introduced, First, a ternary coding method are used instead of binary coding. Second, for edge with curves, sub-pixels are interpolated for feature extraction. Third, during matchine training, feature selection is employed to both boost the detection performance and computation time. The experimental results validate the success of the new scheme.

**Acknowledgment.** The authors sincerely appreciate the help from Dr Gang Cao and Professor Yao Zhao for kindly offering the code of [6] for comparison.

## References

1. Lyu, S., Farid, H.: How realistic is photorealistic? IEEE Trans. Sig. Process. **53**(2), 845–850 (2005)
2. Farid, H.: Digital image forensics. Sci. Am. **298**(6), 66–71 (2008)
3. Fridrich, J.: Digital image forensics. IEEE Sig. Process. Mag. **26**(2), 26–37 (2009)
4. Gonzalez, R.C., Woods, R.E.: Digital Image Processing, 2nd edn. Prentice-Hall, Upper Saddle River (2002)
5. Cao, G., Zhao, Y., Ni, R.: Detection of image sharpening based on histogram aberration and ringing artifacts. In: IEEE International Conference on Multimedia and Expo, ICME 2009, pp. 1026–1029. IEEE (2009)
6. Cao, G., Zhao, Y., Ni, R., Kot, A.C.: Unsharp masking sharpening detection via overshoot artifacts analysis. IEEE Sig. Process. Lett. **18**(10), 603–606 (2011)
7. Ojala, T., Pietikäinen, M., Harwood, D.: A comparative study of texture measures with classification based on featured distributions. Pattern Recogn. **29**(1), 51–59 (1996)
8. Ojala, T., Pietikainen, M., Maenpaa, T.: Multiresolution gray-scale and rotation invariant texture classification with local binary patterns. IEEE Trans. Pattern Anal. Mach. Intell. **24**(7), 971–987 (2002)

9. Xu, G., Shi, Y.Q.: Camera model identification using local binary patterns. In: 2012 IEEE International Conference on Multimedia and Expo (ICME), pp. 392–397. IEEE (2012)

10. Li, Z., Ye, J., Shi, Y.Q.: Distinguishing computer graphics from photographic images using local binary patterns. In: Shi, Y.Q., Kim, H.-J., Pérez-González, F. (eds.) IWDW 2012. LNCS, vol. 7809, pp. 228–241. Springer, Heidelberg (2013)

11. Ding, F., Zhu, G., Shi, Y.: A novel method for detecting image sharpening based on local binary pattern. In: International Workshop on Digital Forensics and Watermaking, IWDW (2013)

12. Ding, F., Zhu, G., Yang, J., Xie, J., Shi, Y.Q.: Edge perpendicular binary coding for usm sharpening detection. IEEE Sig. Process. Lett. **22**(3), 327–331 (2015)

13. Canny, J.F.: Finding edges and lines in images. Massachusetts Institute of Technology Report 1 (1983)

14. Ramponi, G., Strobel, N.K., Mitra, S.K., Yu, T.H.: Nonlinear unsharp masking methods for image contrast enhancement. J. Electron. Imaging **5**(3), 353–366 (1996)

15. Polesel, A., Ramponi, G., Mathews, V.J.: Image enhancement via adaptive unsharp masking. IEEE Trans. Image Process. **9**(3), 505–510 (2000)

16. Lee, J.S.: Digital image enhancement and noise filtering by use of local statistics. IEEE Trans. Pattern Anal. Mach. Intell. **2**, 165–168 (1980)

# Source Camera Model Identification Using Features from Contaminated Sensor Noise

Amel Tuama[2,3]([✉]), Frederic Comby[2,3], and Marc Chaumont[1,2,3]

[1] Nîmes University, 30021 Nîmes Cedex 1, France
[2] Montpellier University, UMR 5506-LIRMM, Montpellier, France
amel.tuama@lirmm.fr
[3] CNRS, UMR 5506-LIRMM, 34392 Montpellier Cedex 5, France

**Abstract.** This paper presents a new approach of camera model identification. It is based on using the noise residual extracted from an image by applying a wavelet-based denoising filter in a machine learning framework. We refer to this noise residual as the polluted noise (POL-PRNU), because it contains a PRNU signal contaminated with other types of noise such as the image content. Our proposition consists of extracting high order statistics from POL-PRNU by computing co-occurrences matrix. Additionally, we enrich the set of features with those related to CFA demosaicing artifacts. These two sets of features feed a classifier to perform a camera model identification. The experimental results illustrate the fact that machine learning techniques with discriminant features are efficient for camera model identification purposes.

**Keywords:** Camera model identification · POL-PRNU · CFA · Co-occurrences matrix · Feature extraction · Rich model

## 1 Introduction

Source camera identification is one of the major interests in image forensics. It is the process of deciding which camera has been used to capture a particular image. The problem of establishing the origin of digital media obtained through an imaging device is important whenever digital content is presented and is used as evidence in the court. The general structure of a digital camera consists of lens system, filters, color filter array (CFA), imaging sensor, and digital image processor. The sensor is an array of rows and columns of photo-diode elements, or pixels. To produce a color image, a color filter array (CFA) is used in front of the sensor so that each pixel records the light intensity for a single color only. An interpolation algorithm is used to generate the missing colors values from adjacent pixels. All these elements can be used in extracting features in order to identify a camera device.

There are two families of methods for camera identification. The first one is based on producing a model, for example a PRNU, and then compute the correlation between a given image and the model of a specified camera. The second one is based on features extraction on a machine learning approach.

© Springer International Publishing Switzerland 2016
Y.-Q. Shi et al. (Eds.): IWDW 2015, LNCS 9569, pp. 83–93, 2016.
DOI: 10.1007/978-3-319-31960-5_8

From the first family of camera identification methods, a reliable one for identifying source camera based on sensor pattern noise is proposed by Lukas et al. [1]. Due to imperfections in sensor manufacturing process, the Photo Response Non-Uniformity (PRNU) is a major source of pattern noise. This makes the PRNU a natural feature for uniquely identifying sensors.

Choi et al. [2] proposed to use the lens radial distortion as a fingerprint to identify source camera model. Each camera model expresses a unique radial distortion pattern that helps to identify it.

Dirik et al. [3] proposed the device identification from sensor dust in digital single lens reflex cameras (DSLR). This problem arises due to the dust particles attracted to the sensor. When the interchangeable lens is removed, a dust pattern is created in front of the imaging sensor. Sensor dust patterns are used as artifacts on the captured images to identify the camera device.

On the other hand, we have the second family of camera identification methods related to features extraction and machine learning. Bayram et al. [4] explored the CFA interpolation process to determine the correlation structure presented in each color band which can be used for image classification. The main assumption is that the interpolation algorithm and the design of the CFA filter pattern of each manufacturer (or even each camera model) are somewhat different from others, which will result in distinguishable correlation structures in the captured images.

Kharrazi et al. [5] identified a set of 34 image features that can be used to uniquely classify a camera model. The proposed features are color features, Image Quality Metrics (IQM), and wavelet domain statistics. Celiktutan et al. [6] used a set of binary similarity measures and a set of Image Quality Metrics to identify the source cell-phone.

Our approach is a mix of the two families of methods since we use a polluted PRNU in a machine learning framework. The polluted PRNU, that we called POL-PRNU, is the sensor noise but also some residual linked to the content of the image. In our approach, extracting the polluted PRNU from a single image leads to an easy way to extract statistics from an image (co-occurrences and color features from polluted PRNU). Indeed, the set of images used to train the classifier will be lightly scattered thus limiting the overfitting effect. Additionally we propose to use a bigger set of features (compared to the classical machine learning approaches) in order to better describe the statistics.

This paper is structured as follows. Section 2 explains the classical approach to compute PRNU. Section 3 presents all the details of our approach, from POL-PRNU extraction to the features computed from co-occurrences and CFA interpolation. In Sect. 4, we describe the experiments, the results, and the database used for experiments. Finally, we conclude in Sect. 5.

## 2   Preliminaries

Camera sensor consists of a large number of photo detectors called pixels which convert photons to electrons. Each pixel in a digital camera's sensor records the

**Fig. 1.** Sample image and its residual noise

amount of incident light that strikes it. Slight imperfections in manufacturing introduce small amounts of noise in the recorded image.

This noise is spatially varying and consistent over the time and can therefore be used for forensic purposes. It has a stochastic nature and is unique for each sensor. This makes it an ideal candidate for forensic applications, such as camera identification [7].

Generally, most PRNU-based image forensic techniques extract the residual noise from image by subtracting the denoised version of the image from the image itself as in Eq. (1):

$$N = I - F(I), \tag{1}$$

where $I$ is the image, $F(I)$ is the denoised image, and $F$ is a denoised filter. Wavelet based denoising filter is recommended and it is used in most cases because it provides the least amount of traces of the scene [7].

In order to extract the PRNU of a camera, multiple images are averaged. At least 50 images are used to calculate the reference pattern $K_c$ [7] of a known camera $C$ as in Eq. (2).

$$K_c = \frac{\sum_{i=1}^{n}(N_i I_i)}{\sum_{i=1}^{n} I_i^2}. \tag{2}$$

A common approach to perform a comparison is to compute the Normalized Cross-Correlation which measures the similarity between the reference pattern $K_c$ and the estimated noise $N$ of an image under test which is of unknown source [7]. Normalized Cross-Correlation is defined as:

$$\rho(N, K_c) = \frac{(N - \overline{N}).(K_c - \overline{K_c})}{\|N - \overline{N}\|.\|K_c - \overline{K_c}\|}. \tag{3}$$

Where $\overline{N}$ and $\overline{K_c}$ are the means of $N$ and $K_c$, respectively.

By applying Eq. (1) on an image $I$, we obtain the residual noise. The residual noise is a sum of different noise. One of them is the sensor pattern noise PRNU. Other types of noise, such as image content, may pollute the PRNU and are part of the residual noise given in Eq. (1). An example is provided in Fig. 1 shows an image and its residual noise which contains some clear parts of the scene.

In this paper, we will consider only the residual noise and call it polluted PRNU (POL-PRNU). This POL-PRNU will then be used for extracting discriminant features. In a machine learning framework, the polluted PRNU is beneficial for the learning process. Indeed, the set of images for a given camera better fill the space and make the obtained cloud in the feature space more spread. Finally, this paper shows that extracting features of high dimension achieves very good results even if the learning database is small.

## 3    Proposed Method

Camera model identification approach based on machine learning is used to classify the camera based on discriminant features extracted from images. In our approach we extract the features directly from what we called the POL-PRNU. The scheme presented in Fig. 2 shows the functional diagram of our proposal. In general, the image is decomposed into its three color channels (r, g, b) considering the central $1024 \times 1024$ pixel image block. The POL-PRNU of the image is obtained by subtracting from the original image its filtered version by a wavelet denoising filter. Two sets of features are extracted from POL-PRNU for classification. The following two sub-sections describe the theoretical aspects of the major parts of our approach.

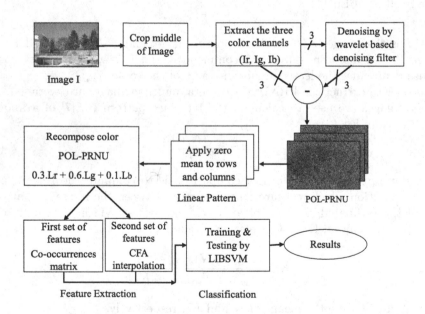

**Fig. 2.** The proposed system framework

## 3.1  POL-PRNU Extraction

First of all after decomposing the image into its three color channels, the central block $1024 \times 1024$ is extracted. Using a small block from the original size reduces the computational complexity, and speeds up the matching process. In [10], the authors prove that the false-positive rate FPR decreases as the size of the image block is greater, which reaches the minimum when the block size is $1024 \times 1024$ pixels.

Our POL-PRNU $N$ is extracted by subtracting the denoised version of the image from the image itself $I$ [1] as in Eq. (1). For the denoising process, a wavelet based denoising filter, $F(I)$, is used based on a Wiener filtering of each wavelet sub-band for each channel as in [1].

In order to suppress all artifacts introduced by color interpolation and JPEG compression, a periodic signal of pattern noise, called the linear pattern $L$, is extracted by subtracting the average row (respectively average column) from each row (respectively column) of $N$ from each color channel separately [7]. This leads to the three linear patterns corresponding to each color channel, noted $L_r$ for red channel, $L_g$ for the green channel, and $L_b$ for the blue channel.

Finally, the three linear patterns are combined into one pattern, noted L by using the conversion formula from RGB to gray-scale as in Eq. 4. Extracting the features from the recombined linear patterns will be more reliable due to the fact that the three linear patterns are highly correlated and provide a compact information for the classifier [7].

$$L = 0.3.L_r + 0.6.L_g + 0.1.L_b. \tag{4}$$

## 3.2  Description of Features

**Co-occurrences Matrix.** The promising aspects of rich models approach [11] can be adapted to extract co-occurrences of a POL-PRNU image. Rich models can play a potential role to provide a good model for forensics applications, especially, in forgery detection and localization [12,13].

Indeed co-occurrences are a very good way to describe the statistics of some data owning neighborhood relations, which is the case for POL-PRNU images. Calculating the co-occurrences of the POL-PRNU allows a reduction of the dimension and gives a good representation of the statistical properties of fingerprint. The co-occurrences feature vector is made of joint probability distributions of neighboring residual samples. In our case, the residual is the POL-PRNU image which is explained in Sect. 3.1. We use four-dimensional co-occurrences matrices formed by groups of four horizontally and vertically adjacent residual samples after they were quantized and truncated as follows:

$$R \leftarrow trunc_T(round(L/q)), \tag{5}$$

where $trunc_T$ is a function to minimize the residual range with $T \in \{-T, ..., T\}$, $round(x)$ gives the nearest integer value of $x$, L is the linear pattern of the POL-PRNU given in Eq. (4), and $q \in \{1, 1.5, 2\}$ is the quantization step.

The final co-occurrences matrix will be constructed from horizontal and vertical co-occurrences of four consecutive values from $R$ of Eq. (5). The horizontal co-occurrence matrix $C_d^h$ is computed as follows:

$$C_d^h = \frac{1}{Z} \left| \{(i,j) \mid R_{i,j} = d_1, R_{i,j+1} = d_2, R_{i,j+2} = d_3, R_{i,j+3} = d_4\} \right|, \tag{6}$$

where $Z$ is the normalization factor, with $R_{i,j} \in \mathbb{N}$ is the coefficient from the matrix $R$ at position $(i,j) \in \{1,...,n\}^2$, $d = (d1,...,d4) \in \{-T,...,T\}^4$ with $T = 2$.

Equivalently, we can compute the vertical co-occurrences matrix.

**Color Dependencies.** The underlying assumption is that, the CFA interpolation algorithms leave correlations across adjacent pixels of an image. In digital cameras, the color filter array is placed before sensor to produce the colored image. The CFA is usually periodic and forms a certain pattern. The missing color components are interpolated using existing neighbor color components. The CFA pattern and the way of colors interpolation are important characteristics of the camera model and can be used in the camera identification process [4].

In this section we will describe the features extracted from the $L_r$, $L_g$, and $L_b$ by computing local dependencies or periodicity among neighboring samples. The normalized cross-correlation is computed between the estimated linear pattern from POL-PRNU of color channels and their shifted version as in [14]. For each color channel pair $(C1, C2)$, $C1, C2 \in \{L_r, L_g, L_b\}$ and shift $\triangle_1 \in \{0,...,3\}$, $\triangle_2 \in \{0,...,3\}$. The normalized cross correlation between two matrices is defined as:

$$\rho(C1, C2, \triangle) = \frac{\sum_{i,j}(C1_{i,j} - \overline{C1})(C2_{i-\triangle_1,j-\triangle_2} - \overline{C2})}{\sqrt{\sum_{i,j}(C1_{i,j} - \overline{C1})^2 \sum_{i,j}(C2_{i-\triangle_1,j-\triangle_2} - \overline{C2})^2}}, \tag{7}$$

where $\rho$ is the normalized cross correlation, $\triangle = [\triangle_1 \ \triangle_2]^T$ is the 2D shift, $\overline{C1}$ and $\overline{C2}$ are sample means calculated from matrices $C1$ and $C2$ respectively. This step results in 96 features which are the result of six combinations of color channels by $4 \times 4$ shifts of $\triangle_1$ and $\triangle_2$.

### 3.3  Classification

A Support Vector Machine (SVM) constructs a hyperplane, or a set of hyperplanes, in a high dimensional space which can be used for classification. The effectiveness of the SVM depends on the selection of kernel function, and the kernel's parameters [18].

Using a kernel function provides a single point for the separation among classes. The radial basis function (RBF), which is commonly used, maps samples into a higher dimensional space that can handle the case when the relation between class labels and attributes is nonlinear.

Projecting into high-dimensional spaces can be problematic due to the so-called curse of dimensionality. As the number of variables under consideration increases, the number of possible solutions also increases exponentially. The result is that the boundary between the classes is very specific to the examples in the training data set. The classifier has to handle the overfitting problem, so as it has to manage the curse of dimensionality [15].

In our case, the training and testing sets have 100 instances each, and the number of features is 10860 which is considered much larger than the number of instances. Here, we have to proceed the learning process with a small data base and a large dimension. Thus, the overfitting and the curse of dimensionality problem may occurs.

Fortunately, when the SVM uses the cross validation procedure, the cost parameter that controls the over/under-fitting phenomenon, is set to a value that allows a better handling of the curse of dimensionality problem and then, can prevent the overfitting problem. A cross validation procedure splits the original training data into one or more training subsets. More precisely, the v-fold cross validation divides the training set into v subsets of equal size, v-1 subsets are used for training and the rest subset is left for testing.

## 4   Experimental Results

### 4.1   Data Acquisition

The Dresden Image Database is designed to fill the needs for digital image forensics applications by providing a useful resource for investigating camera-based image forensic methods [16]. It provides 16,000 authentic digital full-resolution natural images in the JPEG format, and of 1,500 uncompressed raw images. It covers different camera settings, environments and specific scenes, facilitate rigorous analyses of manufacturer, model or device dependent characteristics and their relation to other influencing factors. In our experiments 14 different camera models were used, as outlined in Table 1. A set of 100 images for the training and an another one of 100 images for the test are used from Dresden database for each camera model. As a result 1400 images for training and 1400 images for testing were used from 14 camera model which are randomly selected.

### 4.2   Experimental Protocol

Since each color channel is denoised separately, an image is decomposed into its three color channels (R, G, B). It is recommended that when image blocks are used in forensic investigation, they should be taken from the image center before POL-PRNU extraction stage. This will reduce false positive rate [10]. The images from the training and testing sets are cropped to obtain the $1024 \times 1024$ central images. The essential step is to extract POL-PRNU from all images by applying wavelet denoising filter on the original image. This step then followed by subtracting the denoised image from original as explained in Sect. 3.1.

Two sets of features are extracted from linear pattern of POL-PRNU of each image. The first set is the co-occurrences matrix which consists of 10764

**Table 1.** Models used from Dresden database

| Abbreviations | Brand | Model | Resolution |
|---|---|---|---|
| (A1) | Agfa Photo | DC-733s | 3072 × 2304 |
| (A2) | Agfa Photo | DC-830i | 3264 × 2448 |
| (A3) | Agfa Photo | Sensor 530s | 4032 × 3024 |
| (C1) | Canon | Ixus 55 | 2592 × 1944 |
| (F1) | Fujifilm | FinePix J50 | 3264 × 2448 |
| (K1) | Kodak | M1063 | 3664 × 2748 |
| (N1) | Nikon | D200 Lens A/B | 3872 × 2592 |
| (O1) | Olympus | M1050SW | 3648 × 2736 |
| (Pa1) | Panasonic | DMC-FZ50 | 3648 × 2736 |
| (Pr1) | Praktica | DCZ 5.9 | 2560 × 1920 |
| (Sa1) | Samsung | L74wide | 3072 × 2304 |
| (Sa2) | Samsung | NV15 | 3648 × 2736 |
| (So1) | Sony | DSC-H50 | 3456 × 2592 |
| (So2) | Sony | DSC-W170 | 3648 × 2736 |

features of different statistical relationships among neighboring pixels. While the second set consists of 96 features from normalized cross correlation between POL-PRNU and its shifted versions to get the CFA interpolation dependencies among neighbor pixels. See Sect. 3.2 for the two feature sets. This resulting in 10860 as a total number of features.

For the feature normalization step, we used the method of min-max scaling for both training and testing sets. In this approach, the features will be re-scaled, to a specific range [0,1]. This will avoid attributes in the greater numeric ranges dominating those in the smaller ranges. For the classification, LIBSVM package was used [17] with the Radial Basis Function (RBF) and v-fold cross validation scheme. Although SVM is a binary classification model, LIBSVM package performs multi-classification by using one-versus-rest (OVR) approach.

We used the kernel parameter $\gamma = 2^{-7}$ and cost parameter $C = 4096$ for the SVM after examining a grid search over a range of values. For $\gamma \in \{2^3, 2^2, 2^1, ..., 2^{-15}\}$ and $C \in \{2^{15}, 2^{14}, 2^{13}, ..., 2^{-5}\}$ as is recommended in [18]. The training and testing sets consisted of 100 images each for each camera model. The method was implemented under core$i$7 processor with memory of 16 gega bytes. For the computation cost, the feature extraction process took few seconds for each image, while the training process took 30 mins.

Filler et al. [14] proposed a method for camera model identification which aims to classify camera models using some features. We have implemented this method for comparison purposes on the same set of images from Dresden database. The later method [14] proposed features are concerning statistical moments, cross correlation between color channels, block covariance, and cross

**Table 2.** Confusion matrix of the proposed method for the fourteen camera models, the symbol '-' refers to the values less than 1 %.

| Camera model | A1 | A2 | A3 | C1 | F1 | K1 | N1 | O1 | Pa1 | Pr1 | Sa1 | Sa2 | So1 | So2 |
|---|---|---|---|---|---|---|---|---|---|---|---|---|---|---|
| A1 | 96.93 | - | 1.0 | - | - | - | - | - | 1.32 | - | - | - | - | - |
| A2 | 1.53 | 97.92 | - | - | - | - | - | - | - | - | - | - | - | - |
| A3 | - | - | 98.93 | - | - | - | - | - | - | - | - | - | - | - |
| C1 | - | - | - | 99.57 | - | - | - | - | - | - | - | - | - | - |
| F1 | - | - | - | - | 98.57 | - | 1.33 | - | - | - | - | - | - | - |
| K1 | - | 1.29 | - | - | - | 98.21 | - | - | - | - | - | - | - | - |
| N1 | - | - | - | - | - | - | 99.07 | - | - | - | - | - | - | - |
| O1 | - | - | - | - | - | - | - | 98.93 | - | - | - | - | - | - |
| Pa1 | - | - | - | - | - | - | - | - | 99 | - | - | - | - | - |
| Pr1 | - | - | - | 1.37 | - | - | - | - | - | 97.79 | - | - | - | - |
| Sa1 | - | - | - | - | - | - | - | - | - | - | 99.91 | - | - | - |
| Sa2 | - | - | - | - | - | - | - | - | - | - | 2.20 | 97.57 | - | - |
| So1 | 1.51 | - | 1.01 | - | - | - | - | - | - | - | - | - | 93 | 4.36 |
| So2 | - | - | - | - | - | - | - | - | - | 2.83 | - | - | 3.3 | 93.94 |

correlation of the linear pattern. The images are cropped to $1024 \times 1024$. We did not perform the step of reducing feature space.

### 4.3 Results and Discussion

A comparison is performed between our method and three other experiments. From the proposed method, we take the first set of features (the co-occurrences matrix) and perform it alone. The experiment resulted in 96.91 % as an identification accuracy. This proves the potential role of the statistical features represented by co-occurrences matrix.

The second experiment is performed by taking the set of CFA interpolation features alone from our proposed method. It gave a result of 86.93 % of accuracy. This is considered acceptable but not enough, and still less than the result of the first experiment of the co-occurrences computed on the POL-PRNU.

The method presented in [14] is tested under a similar conditions as discussed in Sect. 4.2. This method only achieved 88.23 % as an average identification accuracy. This low result may be explained by the use of probabilities of first order.

Back to our method, we gathered the two sets of proposed features. By combining the co-occurrences computed on the linear pattern from Eq. 4 and the CFA features, we gain almost 1 % accuracy. The computation of the co-occurrences on the linear pattern is the most important features and the addition of CFA features allows to improve the efficiency. Our method achieved an average accuracy of 97.81 %. We can see from the Table 2 that some of the models are identified with a very high accuracy. For example, Samsung-L74wide, and Canon-Ixus55 achieve 99.91 %, and 99.57 % respectively. Also, most of the other camera models do so, except for the Sony-DSC-H50, and Sony-DSC-W170. They achieve

**Table 3.** Overall average identification rates for all the tested algorithms.

| Camera identification method | Result (%) |
|---|---|
| CFA | 86.93 |
| Co-occurrences | 96.91 |
| Compared method in [14] | 88.23 |
| Proposed method | 97.81 |

the lowest rates of 93 %, and 93.94 % respectively, and this is, maybe, PRNU structure is very close between the two cameras.

Table 3 shows all the mentioned comparisons with their accuracy rates. Finally, we conclude that our method always performs better than the compared method. This is due to the strength of the descriptive features of the co-occurrences, and the additional interesting features of CFA interpolation characteristics.

## 5   Conclusion

This paper proposes an algorithm for identifying camera sources combining techniques based on sensor pattern noise and machine learning. The algorithm is mainly composed of extracting two sets of features from the noise residual POL-PRNU. The first set is the co-occurrences matrix. The second set is the color dependencies from normalized cross correlation of the three color channels and their shifted versions. These sets of features served as input to the SVM which is used as a classifier. The effectiveness of the method for source camera model identification, was tested on a set of images from the Dresden data-base.

The results illustrate the efficiency of the proposed method since it provides an identification rate of 97.81 %. Compared to Filler's method [14], we increase the identification rate by 9.58 % since it only achieved 88.23 % of identification on the same data set.

One problem related to the PRNU correlation based methods is their weak detection rate if geometrical transformations such as, cropping or scaling, have been performed. The direct detection will not succeed because of the desynchronization introduced by additional distortion [9].

Our future work include enhancing the proposed method to a better classification accuracy by improving the former feature set, and considering the problem of the geometrical transformations. Adding an unknown class will also be one of the perspectives, as an additional class, to handle models which are not in the training set.

# References

1. Lukas, J., Fridrich, J., Goljan, M.: Digital camera identification from sensor pattern noise. IEEE Trans. Inf. Forensics Secur. 1(2), 205–214 (2006)
2. Choi, S., Lam, E.Y., Wong, K.K.Y.: Source camera identification using footprints from lens aberration. In: Proceedings of the SPIE, vol. 6069, San Jose, CA, p. 60690J60690J8 (2006)
3. Dirik, A.E., Sencar, H.T., Memon, N.: Source camera identification based on sensor dust characteristics. In: IEEE Workshop on Signal Processing Applications for Public Security and Forensics, SAFE 2007, Washington, USA, 11–13 April 2007
4. Bayram, S., Sencar, H.T., Memon, N.: Improvements on source camera model identification based on CFA interpolation. In: International Conference on Digital Forensics, Orlando, FL (2006)
5. Kharrazi, M., Sencar, H.T., Memon, N.: Blind source camera identification. In: 2004 International Conference on Image Processing, ICIP 2004, vol. 1, pp. 709–712, October 2004
6. Celiktutan, O., Sankur, B., Avcibas, I.: Blind identification of source cell-phone model. IEEE Trans. Inf. Forensics Secur. 3(3), 553–566 (2008)
7. Fridrich, J.: Digital image forensic using sensor noise. IEEE Signal Process. Mag. 26(2), 26–37 (2009)
8. Goljan, M., Fridrich, J.: Estimation of lens distortion correction from single images. In: Proceedings of the SPIE, Electronic Imaging, MediaWatermarking, Security, and Forensics, San Francisco, CA, 26 February 2014
9. Goljan, M., Fridrich, J.: Camera identification from cropped and scaled images. In: Proceedings of the SPIE, Electronic Imaging, Forensics, Security, Steganography, and Watermarking of Multimedia Contents X, San Jose, CA, 26–31 January 2008
10. Li, C.-T., Satta, R.: Empirical investigation into the correlation between vignetting effect and the quality of sensor pattern noise. IET Comput. Vis. 6, 560–566 (2012)
11. Fridrich, J., Kodovsky, J.: Rich models for steganalysis of digital images. IEEE Trans. Inf. Forensics Secur. 7(3), 868–882 (2012)
12. Qiu, X., Li, H., Luo, W., Huang, J.: A universal image forensic strategy based on steganalytic model. In: Proceedings of the 2nd ACM Workshop on Information Hiding and Multimedia Security IHMMSec, Salzburg, Austria, pp. 165–170 (2014)
13. Cozzolino, D., Gragnaniello, D., Verdoliva, L.: Image forgery detection through residual-based local descriptors and block-matching. In: IEEE International Conference on Image Processing (ICIP), Paris, France, pp. 5297–5301, October 2014
14. Filler, T., Fridrich, J., Goljan, M.: Using sensor pattern noise for camera model identification. In: Proceedings of the 15th IEEE International Conference on Image Processing ICIP, San Diego, California, 12–15 October, pp. 1296–1299 (2008)
15. Bengio, Y., Delalleau, O., Le Roux, N.: The curse of dimensionality for local kernel machines, Technical report 1258, Département d'informatique et recherche opérationnelle, Université de Montréal (2005)
16. Gloe, T., Böhme, R.: The dresden image database for benchmarking digital image forensics. In: Proceedings of the ACM Symposium on Applied Computing, SAC 2010, New York, NY, USA, pp. 1584–1590 (2010)
17. Chang, C.-C., Lin, C.-J.: Libsvm: a library for support vector machines. ACM Trans. Intell. Syst. Technol. (TIST) 2(3), 27:127:27 (2011). Software available at http://www.csie.ntu.edu.tw/cjlin/libsvm
18. Hsu, C.-W., Chang, C.-C., Lin, C.-J.: A practical guide to support vector classification, Technical report, Department of Computer Science, National Taiwan University (2003). http://www.csie.ntu.edu.tw/~cjlin/papers/guide/guide.pdf

# Inter-frame Forgery Detection
# for Static-Background Video Based
# on MVP Consistency

Zhenzhen Zhang$^{(\boxtimes)}$, Jianjun Hou, Zhaohong Li, and Dongdong Li

School of Electronic and Information Engineering, Beijing Jiaotong University,
Beijing 100044, China
{11111053,houjj,zhhli2,14120011}@bjtu.edu.cn

**Abstract.** Frame deletion and duplication are common inter-frame tampering methods in digital videos. In this paper, an efficient forensic method based on motion vector pyramid (MVP) and its variation factor (VF) is proposed to detect frame deletion and duplication in videos with static background. This method is composed of two parts: feature extraction and discontinuity point detection. In the stage of feature extraction, each frame of the video is transformed to grayscale image firstly. Then, motion vector pyramid (MVP) sequence and its corresponding variation factor (VF) are calculated for every two adjacent frames. In the stage of discontinuity point detection, forgery type is identified and tampering point is localized by performing modified generalized ESD test. Experimental results show that the proposed method is efficient at forgery identification and localization. Compared with other existing methods on inter-frame forgery detection, our proposed method is more generic.

**Keywords:** Video forensics · Inter-frame forgery · Motion vector · Image pyramid · Static background

## 1 Introduction

Digital videos have been one of the most popular forms of multimedia in our daily lives. For instance, statistics show that around 100 h of video are uploaded to YouTube website every minute [1]. Meanwhile, powerful and user-friendly digital video editing tools such as Adobe Premiere [2] have been developed and used to manipulate the video content. Therefore, the integrity and authenticity of digital video contents cannot be taken for granted, especially when they serve as judicial evidence in court for instance. Although it is more time-consuming and challenging to tamper with videos than still images, growth in the cases of video tampering has made a real impact on the society [3]. As digital video editing techniques become more and more sophisticated, forensic tools against video forgeries are highly desired. One possible solution is to pre-embed authentication information into digital videos, such as embedding watermarks during video-capturing process. But watermarking techniques have not been widely adopted in

© Springer International Publishing Switzerland 2016
Y.-Q. Shi et al. (Eds.): IWDW 2015, LNCS 9569, pp. 94–106, 2016.
DOI: 10.1007/978-3-319-31960-5_9

consumer-level video recording devices. Without actively embedding information in advance, authentication process has to rely solely on the analysis of traces left by tampering. We call such kind of process passive video forensics.

Passive digital video forensics has been an active research field over the past few years. Based on research focuses, video forensics has four major branches: video source identification, copy-paste detection, double compression analysis and inter-frame forgery detection.

Video source identification aims to detect the information of the device that used to capture the given video. Chen et al. [4] extended photo-response non-uniformity (PRNU) as sensor fingerprint for digital camcorder identification, which was first proposed to identify digital cameras. Yahaya et al. [5] proposed conditional probabilities (CP) of DCT coefficients and their neighbors as video camera identification features. They improved their approach by reducing the number of CP features from 72 frame-based features to 15 in [6].

Copy-paste detection and double compression analysis are the other two focuses and have gained more discussion in recent years. For copy-paste detection methods, according to [7], we can classify it into two categories: pixel-based and camera-based. Pixel-based approaches detect tampered regions at pixel level. Camera-based approaches exploit camera inherent artifact such as photon shot noise [8] to identify abnormal regions. As the essential operation when falsifying digital videos is double compression, the analysis of compression history of a given video can be used to reveal that it may have been tampered [9,10].

In the aspect of inter-frame forgery, there are two kinds of forensic techniques. One is related to video codec, which using artifacts introduced by coding standards, e.g. MPEG-x, H.264. For example, Wang et al. [11] proposed to detect frame deletion forgery for MPEG2 videos by using the periodicity of mean prediction error of P frame which is caused by re-ordering of GOP when re-encoding the frame-deleted forgery. Stamm et al. [12] developed a theoretical model for inter-frame forgery detection and improved the detection technique proposed in [11] by using the model. Gironi et al. [13] proposed a method which is applicable even when different codecs are used for the first and second compression.

The other one is independent of video codec, which transform the compressed video into image sequence. Meanwhile, it is our focus in this paper. Chao et al. [14] decompressed the given video into frame sequences and calculated the optical flow between adjacent frames. The basic idea is that the optical flow for original videos is continuous, while the consistency would be broken for tampered videos. Zhang et al. [15] also transformed the given video into image sequences and exposed inter-frame forgery by using the consistency of quotients of correlation coefficients between LBP (Local Binary Patterns) coded frames. The shortcoming of above mentioned methods is that the falsified videos were generated by random manipulation which left visible traces in forgeries. In contrast, Wu et al. [16] manually created a delicate tampered video set which consists of both moving background and static background. Among the delicate video set, the tampered videos with static background, e.g., videos of elevator scenes left less visible traces, and are more difficult for eyes to observe, therefore in this paper, we focus on the detection of this kind of delicate forgeries for videos with static scenes. Wu et al. [16] proposed an efficient algorithm to detect inter-frame forgeries based on velocity field consistency. However, the proposed method cannot determine the manipulated location at frame level, and the data set with static background only contains 10 videos, and a larger video set are needed to evaluate the algorithm.

In this paper, we extend the video set by combining static-background video set of Wu et al. [16] and those of Wang et al. [17], and propose an efficient method for inter-frame forgery detection based on the consistency of MVP. The main procedures of the proposed algorithm are: (1) calculate MVP between adjacent frames of a video, (2) modify the extracted MVP feature by reducing the periodic effect caused by MVP calculation process and releasing the extremely small MVP, (3) calculate the variation factor (VF) sequence, (4) detect and locate the discontinuity points by using modified Generalized ESD test [18]. Experimental results show that the proposed algorithm can not only determine the forgery type efficiently, but also determine the manipulated location precisely at frame level.

The rest of the paper is arranged as follows. In next section, the proposed features and their feasibility are introduced. Section 3 gives a detailed description of the proposed identification algorithm. Experimental results are illustrated in Sect. 4 and Sect. 5 concludes the paper.

## 2   MVP Analysis for Video Forgery Detection

Motion vector measures the displacement between an anchor block and its corresponding prediction block, and is commonly used by video codec in compression domain. For static-background video sequence, one characteristic is that adjacent frames are of high similarity. Suppose that we define one frame as anchor frame, and its previous one as prediction frame, the sum of motion vectors of the whole anchor frame would be small because of the similarity of the two frames. However, the sum would be enlarged if inter-frame forgery operation occurs between these two frames, even though the forgery operation is delicate and leaves few obvious traces. Motivated by this consideration, we bring in motion vector to detect inter-frame forgeries in temporal domain. Furthermore, Gaussian pyramid was adopted when calculating Lucas-Kanade optical flow in [14] with the aim of obtaining more accurate instantaneous speed of pixels. With the consideration of obtaining more precise motion vector, we combine the motion vector and Gaussian pyramid and obtain our feature - motion vector pyramid abbreviated as MVP. The following section will demonstrate the extraction of MVP in detail.

### 2.1   MVP Extraction in the Video

Given a video, the first step of MVP extraction is decompressing it into image sequence and transforming them into grayscale images. After that, MVP are calculated between every two consecutive frames. The major steps are as follows:

1. Construct Gaussian pyramid for the adjacent two frames. Take $k^{th}$, ($k = 1, 2, \cdots, L-1$) frame and $(k+1)^{th}$ frame for example, where $L$ denote the total number of frames in the video. As shown in Fig. 1, the left column represents the Gaussian pyramid of $k^{th}$ frame, and the right column represents that of $((k+1)^{th}$ frame. At the bottom of the pyramid are the two original frames. The upper layers are obtained by blurring their immediate lower-layer frames, and down-sampling the blurred frames by a factor of 2 both horizontally and vertically.

**Fig. 1.** Gaussian pyramid of $k$ frame and $(k+1)$ frame

2. Calculate the motion vectors in both X and Y dimensions of each layer from top to bottom. Figure 2 shows the calculation of motion vectors for one anchor block, the process of which is similar to what common video encoders perform. The first step is dividing the $i^{th}$ layer of the $(k + 1)^{th}$ frame into non-overlapping $4 \times 4$ blocks. For each of these anchor block, find the best prediction block within the search window in the $k^{th}$ frame (the size of the search window we used is $32 \times 32$). The prediction block which has the minimum sum of prediction error is regarded as the best prediction block, and its corresponding displacements in X and Y directions are chosen as motion vectors of the anchor block. Note that before calculating the motion vectors between $k^{th}$ and $(k + 1)^{th}$ frames in $(i + 1)^{th}$ layer, the $k^{th}$ frame should be interpolated according to the motion vectors obtained in $i^{th}$ layer.

3. Calculate the MVP sequences. Expand motion vectors of each layer in both X and Y directions to the same size of its lower layer, and then add them to the motion vectors of their lower layers. After that, smooth the sum of these two layers. Repeat these operations until bottom layer is reached. Finally, the final sum, i.e., the MVP between $k^{th}$ frame and $(k + 1)^{th}$ frame is obtained. Let $MVP(i, j, k)_x$ and $MVP(i, j, k)_y$ denote MVP at $(i, j)$ location of $k^{th}$ frame in X and Y directions, respectively. In this paper, we only take the sum of amplitude of MVP into consideration:

$$MVP(k) = \sum_i \sum_j \sqrt{MVP(i, j, k)_x^2 + MVP(i, j, k)_y^2} \qquad (1)$$

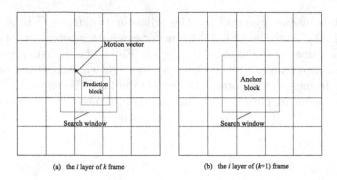

(a) the *i* layer of *k* frame        (b) the *i* layer of (*k*+1) frame

**Fig. 2.** Calculation of motion vector

4. Reduce the periodic effect caused by MVP calculation process. Firstly, we review some background of encoding a video. When encoding a video sequence, such as MPEG-x and H.264 encoder, the sequence is segmented into sets of frames named 'group of pictures' (GOP). In each GOP, I frames are encoded independently and without any other predication frames. P frames and B frames are predicted with respect to the initial I frame either directly or indirectly. The fact that the prediction process does not occur across GOPs result in larger difference between the last frame of one GOP and the first I frame of the next GOP. Then we combine the background with MVP calculation. When we calculate the MVP between the last frame of one GOP and the first I frame of the next GOP, take Fig. 3 as an example, the last P frame of GOP1 will be used as the prediction frame of the first I frame of GOP2. As a result, a larger MVP will be emerged at this location. The circumstance happens periodically with a period $T$ equal to the number of frames within one GOP. As the location where larger MVP occurs is considered as suspicious manipulated position, we suppress the MVP at the periodic location in order to reduce false alarm rate. Therefore, we get $MVP'$ after reducing periodic effect, shown as Eq. 2, where $N = 0, 1, \cdots, M$, and $M = floor((L-1)/T)$.

$$MVP'(k) = \begin{cases} 0.8 \times MVP(k), & \text{if } k = N \times T \\ MVP(k), & \text{if } otherwise \end{cases} \tag{2}$$

5. Release the extremely small $MVP'$. According to Wu et al. [16], camera coding error leads to similarity of two adjacent frames, which further leads to extremely small $MVP'$. The reason to release the extremely small $MVP'$ is that the extremely small $MVP'$ will lead to big variation factor $VF$ which is defined in the following step, and will further lead to false alarm. Here, the extremely small $MVP'$ is replaced with the average value of its five neighbors. Then we get the new sequence, shown as Eq. 3, where $MVP''$ indicates the sequence after releasing the extremely small $MVP'$.

$$\{MVP''(k) \mid k = 1, 2, \cdots, L-1\} \tag{3}$$

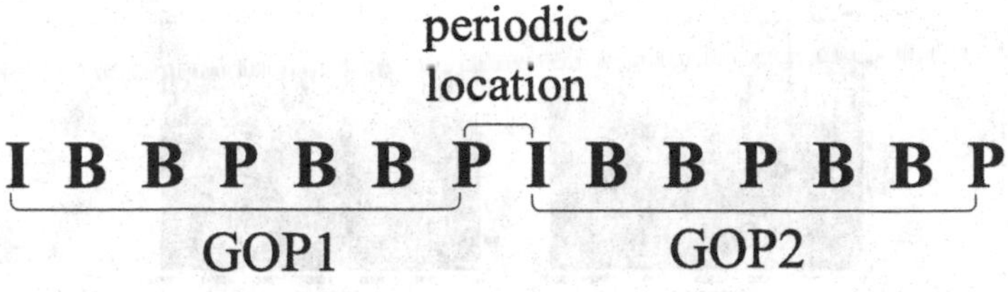

periodic
location

**I B B P B B P I B B P B B P**

GOP1                  GOP2

**Fig. 3.** Illustration of period effect

6. Suppress the influence of video content variation. For a video with moving foreground, the $MVP''(k)$ of this part will be increased, which may result in false alarm. To reduce this kind of phenomenon, we propose to use variation factor $VF$ to represent the relative changes of $MVP''(k)$ sequence:

$$VF(k) = \frac{MVP''(k)}{MVP''(k-1)} + \frac{MVP''(k)}{MVP''(k+1)} \qquad (4)$$

As a result, the discontinuity point introduced by inter-frame forgery will be highlighted in the variation factor sequence $\{VF(k) \mid k = 2, 3, \cdots, L-2\}$.

### 2.2 Traces in Variation Factor Sequence

In this paper, we take into consideration two types of inter-frame forgery, frame deletion and frame duplication. Note that we focus on meaningful forgeries detection. Figure 4 shows an example of meaningful frame deletion. Frames between (a) and (d) are deleted to cover two men walking out of the elevator. After the deletion operation, few obvious traces would be left in the forgery video.

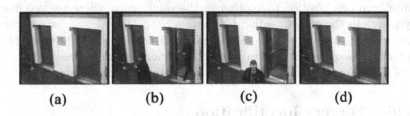

(a)                    (b)                    (c)                    (d)

**Fig. 4.** An example of meaningful frame deletion

Our basic idea is that $VF$ sequences of original videos are approximately consistent, while abnormal points could be detected on inter-frame falsified videos. Figure 5 illustrates the $MVP$ sequence and its corresponding $VF$ sequence of a given video.

From Fig. 5, we can see that the $VF$ sequence of original video is approximately continuous and without obvious discontinuity points. As for frame-deleted video, because of the deletion process, two originally non-adjacent frames

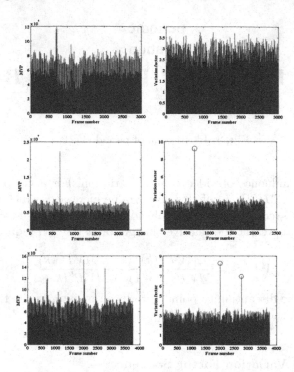

**Fig. 5.** The $MVP$ sequence (left) and its corresponding variation factor sequence (right) of a given video. The first row is for original video, the second row is for frame-deleted video, and the third row is for frame-duplicated video.

become neighbors, which results in a discontinuity point in the corresponding $VF$ sequence. While for frame-duplicated video processed by copy-pasting a set of frames from one position to another in the same video, there are two discontinuity points in the corresponding $VF$ sequence.

Furthermore, localization of tampered frame is possible. Suppose the $k^{th}$ position of $VF$ sequence is determined as the abnormal point, then the $(k+2)^{th}$ frame of the video sequence will be the tampered frame according to Sect. 2.1.

## 3   Video Forgery Identification

According to Sect. 2, discontinuity points indicate the occurrence of inter-frame forgery operation. In this section, we firstly extract discontinuity points in $VF$ sequence by using the modified generalized ESD test and then identify the type of forgery.

### 3.1   Extraction of Discontinuity Points

Generalized ESD test is known as an outliers-detection method for random variable which follows approximately normal distribution. Since $VF$ sequence is approximately normally distributed, generalized ESD test is suitable for discontinuity-points extraction of $VF$ sequence.

There are two significant parameters in the test, the maximum number of outliers $r$ and significance level $\alpha$. Since there are at most two discontinuity points in the $VF$ sequence, according to Sect. 2, we define $r = 2$. The decision threshold in the test is denoted as $\lambda_i (i = 1, 2, \cdots, r)$. In this paper, we also modified it as Wu et al. [16] does:

$$\lambda_i' = TS \times \frac{t_{(p,n-i+1)} \times (n-i)}{\sqrt{(n-i-1+t_{n-i-1}^2) \times n - i + 1}}, i = 1, 2, \cdots, r \qquad (5)$$

$$p = 1 - \frac{\alpha}{2 \times (n-i+1)} \qquad (6)$$

where $n$ denotes the number of samples in the dataset, $t_{(p,n-i+1)}$ represents the $p^{th}$ percentile of a $t$ distribution with $(n-i+1)$ degrees of freedom and $TS$ is our fine-tuned coefficient. As we consider two types of inter-frame forgeries, we define $TS_{del}$ and $TS_{dup}$ as fine-tuned coefficient for deletion detection and duplication detection, respectively, which will be important parameters in the following identification algorithm. Note that the $TS$ in the generalized ESD test is $TS = 1$, here we define it as our fine-tuned coefficient.

## 3.2   Identification Algorithm

After extraction of discontinuity points of $VF$ sequence according to Sect. 3.1, identification process shown in Fig. 6 is carried out. The process consists of two stages.

In stage one, frame-duplicated forgery is detected. Take the $TS_{dup}$ as fine-tuned coefficient in generalized ESD test and extract the corresponding discontinuity points of $VF$ sequence. Let $N_{dup}$ denotes the number of discontinuity points. If $N_{dup} = 2$, the given video is taken as suspicious duplication forgery. For the frame-duplicated forgery, there exist similar sets of frames in the video. Hence we define the $MVP$ sequence between the two discontinuity points as target subsequence. Then compare the target subsequence with the whole $MVP$ sequence. If the correlation coefficient denoted as $Corr$ between two subsequences is larger than the threshold $T_{cor}$, the given video is authenticated as frame-duplicated forgery. Note that in order to reduce false alarm of judging an original video as a duplicated one, we ignore the target subsequence with the length less than $s$. Since we only consider meaningful forgeries in this paper, and subsequence with implausible short length won't be meaningful.

In stage 2, frame-deleted forgery is detected. Similar to stage 1, take the $TS_{del}$ as fine-tuned coefficient in generalized ESD test and extract the corresponding discontinuity points of $VF$ sequence. Let $N_{del}$ denotes the number of discontinuity points. If $N_{del} \geqslant 1$, the given video is authenticated as frame-deleted forgery. Otherwise, the given video is authenticated as original video.

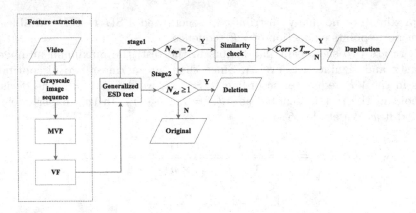

**Fig. 6.** Flowchart of identification algorithm

# 4    Experimental Results

## 4.1    Video Dataset

In this paper, the static-background video dataset on which we test our proposed algorithm is the combination of the static-background video datasets from [16,17]. The combined dataset is consisted of 30 original videos, 30 corresponding frame-deleted videos, and 30 frame-duplicated videos. All the falsified videos are delicately built, without obvious traces left in the video. Each original video contains about 3000 frames with resolution $720 \times 576$. Both the original video and tampered video are MPEG-2 encoded with same parameters. The encoding parameters of video dataset from [16] are: GOP structure IBBPBBPBBPBB, vbr coding with Qscale $= 2$. Those parameters of video dataset from [17] are: GOP size is 12 and without B frames, cbr coding with 5.0 Kbps.

## 4.2    Results and Analysis

We empirically set the parameters of the proposed method as follows: maximum number of outliers is $r = 2$, significance level is $\alpha = 0.05$; fine-tuned coefficients for duplication and deletion detection are $TS_{dup} = 0.8, TS_{del} = 1.4$; the minimum subsequence length is $s = 100$.

**Identification Accuracy and Location Accuracy on the Dataset of Reference** [16]. An efficient method to detect inter-frame forgery based on the consistency of velocity field was proposed in Ref. [16]. Since Ref. [16] only include ten static-background videos, we enlarged the video dataset by combining the static-background videos included in Ref. [17], and compared these three features. In this section, we illustrate the performance of the three features on the static-background video dataset of Ref. [16]. For fair comparison, we applied the identification algorithm proposed in this paper to the three features respectively and optimized parameters for each feature. The best similarity thresholds for the proposed feature, velocity field in Ref. [16] and optical flow in Ref. [17] are $T_{cor} = 0.76$, $T_{cor} = 0.85$ and $T_{cor} = 0.85$, respectively. Furthermore, the fine-tuned coefficient for deletion detection of Ref. [16] is $TS_{del} = 1.2$.

Identification accuracies are presented in Table 1. From Table 1, we can see that the optical flow feature proposed in Ref. [17] performs best among the three features for identifying frame-deleted forgeries. However, for identifying original videos, its identification accuracy is only 30 %, which is pretty low. The proposed feature and velocity field feature proposed in Ref. [16] have same accuracy for identifying frame-deleted forgeries. Reference [16] is better at identifying frame-duplicated forgeries, while the accuracy of the proposed feature is 10 % higher than the method proposed in Ref. [16] for identifying original videos.

**Table 1.** Identification accuracy of the three features on Ref. [16]'s dataset (%). $u/v/w$ denotes the accuracy of the proposed feature ($u$), Ref. [16] ($v$), and Ref. [17] ($w$), respectively.

| Video type | Original | Deletion | Duplication |
|---|---|---|---|
| Original | 100/90/30 | 0/0/70 | 0/0/0 |
| Deletion | 0/10/0 | 90/90/100 | 10/0/0 |
| Duplication | 0/0/0 | 20/30/20 | 80/90/80 |

**Table 2.** Location accuracy of the three features on Ref. [16]'s dataset (%). $u/v/w$ denotes the accuracy of the proposed feature ($u$), Ref. [16] ($v$), and Ref. [17] ($w$), respectively.

| Forgery type | Deletion | Duplication |
|---|---|---|
| Accuracy | 100/100/90 | 100/100/100 |

Location accuracies of the three features are shown in Table 2. The proposed MVP feature and velocity field feature proposed in Ref. [16] can locate tampering point more precisely than optical flow feature proposed in Ref. [17], though its location accuracy is as high as 90 %. Furthermore, the tampering points determined by Ref. [16] can only be in a range of three frames, not at specific frame. In contrast, the proposed method can accurately report the exact frame of the tampering point, according to Sect. 2.2.

**Identification Accuracy and Location Accuracy on the Combined Dataset.** In order to test the generality of the three features, in this part, we enlarged the static-background video dataset of Ref. [16] by combining the static-background videos included in Ref. [17], and compared these three features. Same as the above experiments, we applied the identification algorithm proposed in this paper to the three features respectively and optimized parameters for each feature. The best similarity thresholds for the proposed feature, velocity field in Ref. [16] and optical flow in Ref. [17] are $T_{cor} = 0.71, T_{cor} = 0.85$ and $T_{cor} = 0.9$, respectively. Furthermore, the fine-tuned coefficient for deletion detection of Ref. [16] is $TS_{del} = 1.2$. Table 3 illustrates identification accuracies of the three features on the combined video dataset.

**Table 3.** Identification accuracy of the three features on the combined dataset (%). $u/v/w$ denotes the accuracy of the proposed feature ($u$), Ref. [16] ($v$), and Ref. [17] ($w$), respectively.

| Video type | Original | Deletion | Duplication |
|---|---|---|---|
| Original | 93.33/96.77/70 | 3.33/3.33/30 | 3.33/0/0 |
| Deletion | 13.33/70/16.67 | 80/30/83.33 | 6.67/0/0 |
| Duplication | 6.67/66.67/6.67 | 23.33/3.33/13.33 | 70/30/80 |

As shown in Table 3, the accuracies of the proposed method are 93.33 %, 80 %, 70 % for identifying original video, frame-deleted forgeries and frame-duplicated forgeries, respectively; while the corresponding accuracies of Ref. [16] are 96.67 %, 30 %, and 30 %, respectively. Though Ref. [16] is better at identifying original videos, its accuracy for detection of frame deletion and frame duplication is pretty low compared with the proposed method. Therefore, we can conclude that the proposed method is more generic than Ref. [16].

Also as shown in Table 3, the accuracies of Ref. [17] are 70 %, 83.33 %, 80 % for identifying original video, frame-deleted forgeries and frame-duplicated forgeries, respectively. Reference [17] is better at identifying frame-deleted forgeries and frame-duplicated forgeries, while the proposed method performs much better at identifying original videos, with accuracy 23.33 % higher than Ref. [17].

As for location accuracy shown in Table 4, Ref. [17] performs better at duplication localization, while the proposed method is better at deletion location. Though the proposed method performs slightly worse than Ref. [16], the lowest

**Table 4.** Location accuracy of the three features on the combined dataset (%). ($m/n$) indicates $m$ of $n$ locations are accurate.

| Accuracy | Deletion | Duplication |
|---|---|---|
| Proposed | 23/24 | 40/42 |
| Ref. [16] | 9/9 | 18/18 |
| Ref. [17] | 22/25 | 47/48 |

accuracy of 95.24 % (40/42) is still acceptable. The main drawback of method proposed in Ref. [16] is that it cannot localize tampering point at specified frame according to illustrations in the above section.

## 5    Conclusion

In this paper, a new algorithm for detecting delicately built inter-frame forgeries with static background is proposed. The basic idea is that there exist discontinuity points in the $VF$ sequence of inter-frame forgeries. By using the modified generalized ESD test, the forgery type can be identified, and the tamper point can be localized precisely. Experimental results show the efficiency of the proposed method. Our future work will focus on increasing the identification accuracy for detecting frame-duplicated forgeries and testing the robustness of proposed method over videos re-encoded with different coding standards.

**Acknowledgement.** We would like to thank Yuxing Wu and Dr. Tanfeng Sun from Shanghai Jiao Tong University for their kindness by providing us with their database and codes. We also appreciate Guanshuo Xu for his help and kindly suggestions. The first author was supported by the Fundamental Research Funds for the Central Universities (W13JB00070) and (W15JB00280), and SRF for ROCS, SEM (W15C300020).

## References

1. http://www.youtube.com/yt/press/statistics.html
2. http://www.adobe.com/products/premiere.html
3. Wang, W.H., Farid, H.: Exposing digital forgeries in video by detecting duplication. In: MM & Sec 2007, pp. 35–42 (2007)
4. Chen, M., Fridrich, J., Goljan, M., Lukàš, J.: Source digital camcorder identification using sensor photo response non-uniformity. In: Electronic Imaging 2007, International Society for Optics and Photonics (2007)
5. Yahaya, S., Ho, A.T.S., Wahab, A.A.: Advanced video camera identification using conditional probability features. In: IET Conference on Image Processing, pp. 1–5 (2012)
6. Yahaya, S., Ho, A.T.S., Li, S.J.: Improving Conditional Probability Based Camera Source Identification
7. Cheng-Shian, L., Jyh-Jong, T.: A passive approach for effective detection and localization of region-level video forgery with spatio-temporal coherence analysis. Digital Invest. Int. J. Digit. Forensics Incident Response 11(2), 120–140 (2014)
8. Kobayashi, M., Okabe, T., Sato, Y.: Detecting forgery from static-scene video based on inconsistency in noise level functions. IEEE Trans. Inf. Forensics Secur. 5(4), 883–892 (2010)
9. Chen, W., Shi, Y.Q.: Detection of double mpeg compression based on first digit statistics. In: Kim, H.-J., Katzenbeisser, S., Ho, A.T.S. (eds.) IWDW 2008. LNCS, vol. 5450, pp. 16–30. Springer, Heidelberg (2009)
10. Milani, S., Bestagini, P., Tagliasacchi, M., Tubaro, S.: Multiple compression detection for video sequences. In: 2012 IEEE 14th International Workshop on Multimedia Signal Processing, pp. 112–117 (2012)

11. Wang, W.H., Farid, H.: Exposing digital forgeries in video by detecting double MPEG compression. In: Proceedings of the 8th ACM Workshop on Multimedia and Security, pp. 37–47 (2006)
12. Stamm, M.C., Lin, W.S., Liu, K.J.R.: Temporal forensics and anti-forensics for motion compensated video. IEEE Trans. Inf. Forensics Secur. $7(4)$, 1315–1329 (2012)
13. Gironi, A., Fontani, M., Bianchi, T., Piva, A., Barni, M.: A video forensic technique for detecting frame deletion and insertion. In: 2014 IEEE International Conference on Acoustics, Speech and Signal Processing (ICASSP), pp. 6226–6230 (2014)
14. Chao, J., Jiang, X., Sun, T.: A novel video inter-frame forgery model detection scheme based on optical flow consistency. In: Shi, Y.Q., Kim, H.-J., Pérez-González, F. (eds.) IWDW 2012. LNCS, vol. 7809, pp. 267–281. Springer, Heidelberg (2013)
15. Zhang, Z.Z., Hou, J.J., Ma, Q.L., Li, Z.H.: Efficient video frame insertion and deletion detection based on inconsistency of correlations between local binary pattern coded frames. Secur. Commun. Netw. $8(2)$, 311–320 (2015)
16. Wu, Y.X., Jiang, X.H., Sun, T.F., Wang, W.: Exposing video inter-frame forgery based on velocity field consistency. In: 2014 IEEE International Conference on, Acoustics, Speech and Signal Processing (ICASSP), pp. 2674–2678 (2014)
17. Wang, W., Jiang, X., Wang, S., Wan, M., Sun, T.: Identifying Video Forgery Process Using Optical Flow. In: Shi, Y.Q., Kim, H.-J., Pérez-González, F. (eds.) IWDW 2013. LNCS, vol. 8389, pp. 244–257. Springer, Heidelberg (2014)
18. Iglewicz, B., Hoaglin, D.C.: How to Detect and Handle Outliers, vol. 16. ASQC Quality Press, Milwaukee (1993)

# An Effective Detection Method Based on Physical Traits of Recaptured Images on LCD Screens

Ruihan Li, Rongrong Ni[✉], and Yao Zhao

Institute of Information Science and Beijing Key Laboratory of Advanced Information Science
and Network Technology, Beijing Jiaotong University, Beijing 100044, China
{rrni,yzhao}@bjtu.edu.cn

**Abstract.** The detection of recaptured images plays a particular role in public
security forensics. Although researches achieve some progress, low quality of
image samples and long time consuming for feature extraction are still prominent
problems. From the analysis to the photography process, we present two effective
features for distinguishing high-resolution and high-quality recaptured images
from LCD screens. One feature is the block effect and blurriness effect caused by
JPEG compression, and the other feature is screen effect described by wavelet
decomposition with aliasing-enhancement preprocessing. Experiments show that
the proposed scheme obtains outstanding performances, which is fast and has
higher discriminative accuracy.

**Keywords:** Recaptured images · Block effect · Blurriness effect · Aliasing-
enhancement preprocessing · Wavelet decomposition

## 1 Introduction

With the fast updating of image acquisition devices and image editing software, the
abnormal images increasingly emerges in the real world. 'Seeing Is Believing' is not
always right in some conditions. Image tampering or forgery is increasingly becoming
a common phenomenon, which causes people's suspect to the authenticity of images.
For example, some news media speculate and seek profits by means of forged images,
which are created by editing software like Adobe Photoshop. It will lead people to
misunderstand the truth and bring bad influences on the social justice and equality. There
are various ways of images tampering, in which recapture is drawing public attention.

Recapture is a new measure of image tampering. Recaptured images are images
captured again from medium on which the original images display. The recapture
processing is shown in Fig. 1. The forgery events involving recaptured images have
occurred in recent years. For example, in the event of South China Tiger, a recaptured
tiger image by means of a painting tiger was released to announce the existence of the
wild South China Tiger, which caused lies flying in China. Moreover, the threat of
recapture also occurs in the bio-metric authentication. For instance, payment based on
face recognition technology presented by Alibaba Corporation aroused a commotion.
Single facial recognition payment technology has great limitations because of

© Springer International Publishing Switzerland 2016
Y.-Q. Shi et al. (Eds.): IWDW 2015, LNCS 9569, pp. 107–116, 2016.
DOI: 10.1007/978-3-319-31960-5_10

reproducibility of human face. The recaptured facial image is one of reproduction and can successfully pass the authentication system. Apart from face authentication, similar threats exist in many other types of biometric authentication, such as fingerprint and iris. Nowadays, many forensic algorithms can identify the forged images synthetizing from different devices. But after they are shown on LCD and reshot, the detection algorithms could fail because the recaptured images are really captured by the identical camera. Therefore, recapture detection is of significance, which can provide public property safety, judicial proof, access rights protection, etc.

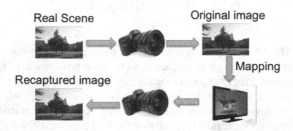

**Fig. 1.** The diagram of the recapture process

In the research field of recapture detection, researchers have presented various schemes aiming at different types of images, such as recaptured images printed on papers or shown on LCD screens. In recent researches, the original or recaptured images were discriminated based on the statistical feature difference in spatial or transform domain. For recaptured printed images, Ng et al. [1] built a general physical model using a series of physical properties which included image background information, spectrum distribution and gradient, color histogram, etc. The experiments show that to some extent the proposed physical features work well in images from smart phones. Ng's work is of great significance to recaptured images detection. However, some problems still exist, such as poor visual quality and low discriminating accuracy. For recaptured images shown on LCD screens, Cao and Alex [2] identified recaptured images using multiple statistical features, which were described by LBP operator, multi-scale wavelet statistics and color features. A complete recaptured flow based on LCD screen was also proposed. Their methods greatly improve the image discrimination accuracy, but consume more time due to the feature extraction for high-resolution images. From the viewpoint of the noise and double JPEG compression, Yin and Fang [3] studied the character of the noise in images firstly, which was obtained by using the denoising algorithm of wavelet threshold. Secondly, they utilized Mode Based First Digital Features (MBFDF) to study the distribution character of the first effective digit of DCT coefficients. In 2015, Thongkamwitoon et al. [4] thought aliasing and blurriness are scene dependent features and presented an algorithm based on learned edge blurriness. Firstly, two dictionaries were separately trained from the line spread profiles of selected edges of single captured and recaptured images by K-SVD approach; secondly, a SVM classifier was built using dictionary approximation errors and the mean edge spread width from the training images. The experimental results show that the algorithm can get an excellent effect by low dimension feature.

To handle the detection problem of high quality recaptured images, we present two features based on the physical characteristics of recaptured images. The characteristics stem from the physical mechanism of the LCD screen and the camera in the image generation process. On one hand, the effect of block and blurriness is analyzed for JPEG images. The original and recaptured images go through different times of compression. Moreover, each compression can bring loss of detail information to some extent. Therefore, we first study the difference of block and blurriness effect in the original and recaptured images, which is effective to distinguish the two kinds of images. One the other hand, the mechanism difference between LCD screen and camera exists in the process of recapture. The unmatched frequency of screen and camera leads to interference in the recaptured images, which is a significant trace to differ the two kinds of images. So another feature is proposed to extract the information of interference and reflect the variation of statistic characteristics. The experiment results show that the algorithm is effective for recapture forensics. In this paper, the organization of the rest is as follows. Section 2 describes the block effect and blurriness based on JPEG compression, and wavelet decomposition method with preprocessing; Sect. 3 includes the experimental results and analysis; conclusions are given in Sect. 4.

## 2 Effective Features and Analysis

### 2.1 The Block Effect and Blurriness Induced by JPEG Compression

#### 2.1.1 Analysis of Recapture Effects

JPEG is a common lossy compression method which is adopted by majority of image acquisition equipments in daily life. Generally, images captured by the camera are saved in JPEG format. As we know, the process of recapturing an image is as follows: firstly, an original image is shown on the medium; secondly, the scene shown on the medium is captured by a camera. The recaptured image looks similar as the original one, but it undergoes twice lossy compression. Influences brought by twice JPEG compression are helpful to identify the recaptured images. According to the principle of JPEG compression, an image goes through block partition, DCT transform, quantization and entropy coding, etc. Furthermore, the quantization of image blocks is conducted independently. Discontinuity will exhibit along the image blocks' boundary, which is called block effect. The degree of discontinuity is different due to different compression times. Moreover, the image compression generally causes much more losses in high frequency than in low frequency due to the structure of quantization table. Different times of compression can lead to different degree of high frequency loss, and high frequency component is related to the detail information of the image. Intuitive feeling is that the image is not clear or become indistinct, which is called blurriness effect. Compared with the original images, the recaptured images undergo twice JPEG compression and result in prominent block effect and blurriness effect. The proper feature description is effective to distinguish the recaptured from the original.

### 2.1.2   The Block Effect and Blurriness Effect

Suppose pixel value of grayscale image as $x(m, n)$, where $m \in [1, M]$, $n \in [1, N]$, $M, N$ represent numbers of row and column in the image matrix, respectively. $d_h(m, n)$ represents the deviation of adjacent pixels along horizontal direction from right to left, in a similar way, $d_v(m, n)$ represents the vertical deviation between adjacent pixels from bottom to top.

$$d_h(m, n) = x(m, n + 1) - x(m, n), \quad n \in [1, N - 1] \tag{1}$$

$$d_v(m, n) = x(m + 1, n) - x(m, n), \quad m \in [1, M - 1] \tag{2}$$

As mentioned above, the quantization is independently conducted block-wise in the JPEG compression. The boundaries of adjacent blocks are discontinuous in the spatial domain. Because of different compression process of the original and the recaptured images, the bouncing degree of pixel values along the block boundaries will differ. The horizontal variation, given in Eq. (3), is represented by the mean deviation of the adjacent pixels located at the vertical block boundaries. In the same way, the vertical variation shown in Eq. (4) is represented by the mean deviation of the adjacent pixels located at the horizontal block boundaries. The two variables capture the bouncing characteristic of pixels at adjacent blocks' boundaries, so Eq. (5) represents the discontinuity feature of the blocks in the whole image.

$$B_h = \frac{1}{M(\lfloor N/8 \rfloor - 1)} \sum_{i=1}^{M} \sum_{j=1}^{\lfloor N/8 \rfloor - 1} |d_h(i, 8j)| \tag{3}$$

$$B_v = \frac{1}{N(\lfloor M/8 \rfloor - 1)} \sum_{j=1}^{N} \sum_{i=1}^{\lfloor M/8 \rfloor - 1} |d_v(8i, j)| \tag{4}$$

$$B = \frac{B_h + B_v}{2} \tag{5}$$

Moreover, when images undergo the JPEG compression, the high frequency information will inevitably be lost, which influences the clarity of images. With the growth of compression times, the loss degree of high frequency information will increase and the sharpness of images will decrease more seriously as well. Due to the original and the recaptured images are compressed by different times, they can be told apart by evaluating the image blurriness. The correlation among pixels can reflect the blurriness of images. On one hand, the average deviations among adjacent pixels within blocks can be utilized to represent the correlation of images. Equations (6) and (7) represent the horizontal and vertical average deviation, respectively. Then, the mean of these two variables is used as a feature to describe the blurriness of images.

$$A_h = \frac{1}{7} \left[ \frac{8}{M(N - 1)} \sum_{i=1}^{M} \sum_{j=1}^{N-1} |d_h(i, j)| - B_h \right] \tag{6}$$

$$A_v = \frac{1}{7}\left[\frac{8}{N(M-1)}\sum_{i=1}^{N}\sum_{j=1}^{M-1}|d_v(i,j)| - B_v\right] \tag{7}$$

$$A = \frac{A_h + A_v}{2} \tag{8}$$

On the other hand, the zero-crossing rates of deviations are introduced to express the correlation of images. Zero-crossing (ZC) means that neighboring values have the different sign. Equation (10) [5] represents the horizontal zero-crossing rate, and the vertical one is obtained in a similar way. To some extent, the mean of the two variables reflects the correlation of pixels and can be used to distinguish recaptured images.

$$z_h(m, n) = \begin{cases} 1 & horizontal\ ZC\ at\ d_h(m, n) \\ 0 & otherwise \end{cases} \tag{9}$$

$$Z_h = \frac{1}{M(N-2)}\sum_{i=1}^{M}\sum_{j=1}^{N-2}z_h(m, n) \tag{10}$$

$$Z = \frac{Z_h + Z_v}{2} \tag{11}$$

The color space $YC_bC_r$ is selected to acquire the image feature vector. $B$, $A$ and $Z$ are calculated in each channel of $YC_bC_r$. The final feature vector is defined as Block_Blur_$YC_bC_r$, which is constructed by $[B_1, A_1, Z_1, B_2, A_2, Z_2, B_3, A_3, Z_3]$. The subscripts 1, 2, 3 represent the channel Y, $C_b$, and $C_r$, respectively.

## 2.2  Wavelet Decomposition with Aliasing-Enhancement Preprocessing

### 2.2.1  Emphasis of Aliasing and Interference

In this paper, the recaptured images are reproduction of original images shown on LCD screens. Because of the different physical characteristic of LCD screens and cameras, the subtle differences exist in the original images and the recaptured ones. However, as shown in Fig. 2, the difference cannot be discovered by human naked eyes. The reason is the color of images and the outside illumination introduced in recaptured process conceal the difference. To reveal the distinction, the preprocessing is introduced to emphasize the aliasing and interference phenomenon before the feature extraction.

The preprocessing consists of three steps, as shown in Fig. 3. Firstly, Gamma correction is utilized to achieve nonlinear grayscale adjustment by Eq. (12)

$$I_r = I^\gamma, \gamma \in [0, 1] \tag{12}$$

Secondly, differential Gaussian filtering (DOG) is used to reduce the high-frequency components and retain the low-frequency components at the same time.

Finally, to limit the obtained values within a certain range, the equalization is selected to adjust the peak value according to Eqs. (13)–(15) [6].

$$I'(x, y) = \frac{I_r(x, y)}{(mean(|I(x, y)|^{\alpha}))^{1/\alpha}} \tag{13}$$

$$I''(x, y) = \frac{I'(x, y)}{(mean(\min(\tau, |I'(x, y)|)^{\alpha}))^{1/\alpha}} \tag{14}$$

$$I_p(x, y) = \tau * \tanh(I''(x, y)) \tag{15}$$

**Fig. 2.** The left column corresponds to recaptured image samples, and the right column corresponds to original image samples

**Fig. 3.** Flow chart for emphasis of aliasing and interference

### 2.2.2 Multi-scale Wavelet Decomposition of Preprocessed Images

When recaptured images go through the aliasing-enhancement preprocessing, the output images exhibit great differences from the original images' outputs, as shown in Fig. 4. Texture of the preprocessed recaptured images presents the property of aliasing, on the contrary, texture of the preprocessed original images is relatively clear with keeping the outline of the original content. Naturally, the texture of the output images contains the valuable information, which is essential to recapture detection.

**Fig. 4.** The first column is the original and recaptured grayscale image, among them the first two rows are original grayscale images, the last two rows are recaptured grayscale images; the first and the third rows are the original and the corresponding recaptured image, the second and the fourth line rows are another original and the corresponding recaptured image. The second column is preprocessed images with binarization.

Driven by the observation, wavelet decomposition method is selected to decompose output images into multi-scales and multi-directions sub-bands. In this paper, the 2-D quadrature mirror filter is used in wavelet decomposition process. Compared with the preprocessed original image, the acquired sub-bands of the preprocessed recaptured image contain more regular interference information, which leads to different statistics for the original images and the recaptured images. Then, mean and standard deviation of coefficients in each sub-band are used as the features, which can measure the variation of the sub-bands.

If three-level wavelet decomposition is conducted, the image is transformed to wavelet domain with 9 sub-bands, referring to 3 scales and 3 directions. Finally, the mean and standard deviation of each decomposed sub-band are calculated. Thus, the dimension number of feature vector of an image is $3 * 3 * 2 = 18$. The feature is denoted as Pre_wavelet.

After feature extraction and construction, the feature vector is input in the SVM classifier to identify the recaptured images.

# 3    Experimental Results

## 3.1    Database Construction

To evaluate the effectiveness of the proposed algorithms for high resolution images, an image database $DB_1$ consisting of 636 original and 636 recaptured images is constructed by using Nikon D600 and Canon EOS 500D. In the database, the images include different scenes, such as buildings, persons, materials, scenery, etc.

In order to obtain satisfied recapture images, 160 high-quality original images are selected for recapturing. The numbers of the acquired images from the LCD screen is 320, which are separately shot by two Single Lens Reflex cameras. The recapture process is conducted indoors with ordinary incandescent light bulb and the used cameras are setting in automatic mode. To verify universality of the proposed algorithms, 316 recaptured images provided by other research team [3] are added to build the database.

## 3.2    Experiment 1

The experiments are conducted on PC with configuration of i5 quad-core processors. The pattern classification is carried out with the help of toolbox of LIBSVM [8], and the selected kernel function is radial basis kernel function (RBF). Here, 636 original images are selected as negative samples and 636 recaptured images are selected as positive samples in the experiment. The proportion between the training and the testing is 5:1, that is, the 5/6 of all the images are used training model and the remainder 1/6 is used as testing. To ensure the objectivity of distinguishing result, the quantities of training and testing images are always consistent. Then, the cross-validations are carried out ten times to get the average value.

The feature vector consists of the block and blurriness effect, and the wavelet based on preprocessing. The results of the experiment are displayed in Table 1. As is shown, the overall accuracy (ACC) is 98.32 %, and the time consuming is shorter. TPR means the ratio of accurate detection for recapture images, and TNR is the ratio of accurate detection for original images.

**Table 1.** The experimental test results (%) (in DB$_1$)

| Method | ACC | TPR | TNR | Time |
|---|---|---|---|---|
| LBP [2] | 98.11 | 97.83 | 98.39 | ≈180.0 s |
| Block_Blur_YCbCr | 95.28 | 93.61 | 96.96 | ≈8.0 s |
| Pre_Wavlet | 96.44 | 96.75 | 96.12 | ≈1.5 s |
| Block_Blur_YCbCr + Pre_Wavlet | 98.32 | 97.48 | 99.16 | ≈9.5 s |

### 3.3 Experiment 2

To further verify the effectiveness of the proposed algorithm in the high-quality (HQ) and high-resolution (HR) images, we utilize 3000 images provided in [2] to implement the second experiment. The number of original images and the number of recaptured images are both 1500. The experimental environment setting is the same as the first. The results of experiment 2 show significant advantages as listed in Table 2. The overall accuracy is 98.95 %, which illustrates that the proposed algorithms can also achieve better performance in HQ-HR recaptured images detection.

Compared with the experiment 1, the overall accuracy of the experiment 2 is more superior. Moreover, the quality and resolution of the recapture images in experiment 2 is higher than that in DB$_1$. Therefore, the proposed algorithms are more suitable for detecting HQ-HR recaptured images.

Not only in terms of the feature' dimensionality but also in terms of the discrimination accuracy can the proposed method be dominant to some extent.

**Table 2.** The experimental test results (%) (in DB provided by [2])

| Method | ACC | TPR | TNR | Time |
|---|---|---|---|---|
| Block_Blur_YCbCr | 97.07 | 98.5 | 95.63 | ≈8.0 s |
| Pre_Wavlet | 96.33 | 96.2 | 96.47 | ≈1.5 s |
| Block_Blur_YCbCr + Pre_Wavlet | 98.95 | 99.27 | 98.63 | ≈9.5 s |

## 4    Conclusions

In this paper, a detection method of high-quality (HQ) recaptured images based on physical characteristics is proposed. Two features are presented to effectively describe the recapture phenomenon. One feature is the block effect and blurriness effect, and the other feature is screen aliasing effect described by wavelet decomposition with aliasing-enhancement preprocessing. The combined feature is better for detecting HQ recaptured images. The lower dimension of feature vector and the less time consumption are our superiorities. However, there are also some disadvantages. At first, because of the limit of conditions, the scale of the image database is not large enough, resulting to the validation of the method universality is not comprehensive enough; Secondly, the proposed method has not yet developed into practical application software.

**Acknowledgement.** This work was supported in part by 973 Program (2011CB302204), National NSF of China (61332012, 61272355), PCSIRT (IRT 201206), Fundamental Research Funds for the Central Universities (2015JBZ002), Open Projects Program of NLPR (201306309).

# References

1. Yu, H., Ng, T.T., Sun, Q.: Recaptured photo detection using specularity distribution. In: 15th IEEE International Conference on ICIP 2008. IEEE, pp. 3140–3143 (2008)
2. Cao, H., Alex, K.: Identification of recaptured photographs on LCD screens. In: 2010 IEEE International Conference on Acoustics Speech and Signal Processing (ICASSP), pp. 1790–1793. IEEE (2010)
3. Yin, J., Fang, Y.M.: Digital image forensics for photographic copying. In: IS&T/SPIE Electronic Imaging. International Society for Optics and Photonics, pp. 83030F–83030F-7 (2012)
4. Thongkamwitoon, T., Muammar, H., Dragotti, P.L.: An image recapture detection algorithm based on learning dictionaries of edge profiles. IEEE Trans. Inf. Forensics Secur. 953–968 (2015)
5. Zhou, W., Hamid, R.S., Alan, C.B.: No-reference perceptual quality assessment of JPEG compressed images. 2002 International Conference on Image Processing, Proceedings, vol. 1, pp. I-477–I-480. IEEE (2002)
6. Tan, X.Y., Triggs, B.: Enhanced local texture feature sets for face recognition under difficult lighting conditions. IEEE Trans. Image Process. 168–182 (2010)
7. Lyu, S., Farid, H.: How realistic is photorealistic? IEEE Trans. Signal Process. **53**(2), 845–850 (2005)
8. Chang, C.C., Lin, C.J.: LIBSVM - a library for support vector machines. http://www.csie.ntu.edu.tw/cjlin/libsvm

# Steganography and Steganalysis

# Video Steganalysis Based on Intra Prediction Mode Calibration

Yanbin Zhao, Hong Zhang, Yun Cao[✉], Peipei Wang,
and Xianfeng Zhao

State Key Laboratory of Information Security,
Institute of Information Engineering, Chinese Academy of Sciences,
Beijing 100093, People's Republic of China
{zhaoyanbin, zhanghong, caoyun,
wangpeipei, zhaoxianfeng}@iie.ac.cn

**Abstract.** Currently, some H.264 video steganographic algorithms based on intra prediction mode (IPM) have been proposed. By modulating IPMs over blocks during the intra-coding process, they achieve low computational complexity, considerable capacity and high security. Up to now, there is no existing steganalytic methods found for effective detection. However, we have observed that the existing IPM-based steganography usually modifies IPMs with non-optimal selection rules which violate the encoding principles. By exploiting these weaknesses, we propose a calibration-based video steganalytic scheme, which extracts IPM calibration (IPMC) features to detect IPM-based steganography. The proposed features are of a very low dimension and sensitive to the presences of non-optimal IPMs. Particularly, calibration parameters are directly obtained from the video stream. Therefore, we avoid estimating erroneous calibration parameters which can lead to the decline of detection performance. Experimental results demonstrate that the proposed IPMC features can be used to effectively detect the IPM modulations even at a low embedding rate, and the IPMC makes the new steganalytic scheme outperform the existing ones.

**Keywords:** Video steganalysis · H.264 · Intra prediction mode (IPM) · Calibration

## 1 Introduction

Modern steganography is used for covert communication by hiding messages into innocent-looking digital media objects (e.g. image, text and video). Statistical and perceptual characteristics of embedded file, known as stego-object, should be similar to those of original unaltered carrier, known as cover-object. On the other hand, to cope with the abuse of steganography, steganalysis, which aims at detecting the present of hidden data, has also attracted wide attention.

Digital video is provided with more inherent advantages than other cover object. Video steganography can easily achieve a large capacity with slight modification. According to the embedding domain, video steganography is classified into two categories. Spatial domain directly embeds data in pixels. By the fact that the vast majority

© Springer International Publishing Switzerland 2016
Y.-Q. Shi et al. (Eds.): IWDW 2015, LNCS 9569, pp. 119–133, 2016.
DOI: 10.1007/978-3-319-31960-5_11

of videos are stored in compression format, spatial domain steganography is not practical. The second type of video steganography hides secret messages into compressed domain. These algorithms modify motion vectors [1, 2], quantized DCT coefficients [3, 4], variable length codes [5, 6], or prediction modes [7–10].

In the intra-coding process of H.264, video steganography can be implemented by modulating the intra prediction modes (IPMs). Currently, some IPM-based steganographic algorithms have appeared. These algorithms have low computational complexity, considerable steganographic capacity and extremely high concealment. Typical IPM-based steganography shared some common features, i.e., basic principle of existing IPM-based steganography is to replace optimal with suboptimal IPM according to pre-agreed mapping rules to achieve the embedding. Hu et al. [7] proposed a video steganographic algorithm based on IPM, which exploited the intra $4 \times 4$ prediction modes (I4PM). Data hiding was implemented by modulating the intra prediction modes of qualified intra $4 \times 4$ luminance blocks. In the hiding process, one-bit information was mapped to a selectable I4PM and the prediction mode shall be optimal or suboptimal at utmost degree after modification. A similar approach was proposed by Xu et al. [8] where macroblocks were selectively chosen based on a chaotic sequence and most probable prediction mode was manipulated to embed information. Yang et al. [9] optimized Hu's algorithm, introduced matrix coding technology, at most one IPM needs to be modified for embedding 2bits information. Bouchama et al. [10] divided 9 prediction modes into four groups according to the prediction direction of I4PM, and designed the steganography which modified the prediction modes within the same group. This algorithm ensured both visual quality and steganographic capacity of the video.

However, according to our investigation, there was no existing steganalysis that can effectively detect IPM-based steganography. The only targeted steganalytic method that we found was proposed by Li et al. [11]. Li believed that there was inherent correlation between intra $4 \times 4$ blocks of one $16 \times 16$ macroblock. Embedding operation would change these inherent correlations. According to that observation, Li designed a set of statistical features based on Markov chain to quantify these correlations. Although Li carried on a relatively rational model, his assumption was relatively idealized, while the detection performance was not ideal.

In this paper, we propose a steganalytic scheme against the IPM-based video steganography. During the intra-coding process, in order to ensure the quality of the compressed video while minimizing the size of bit stream, H.264 encoder prefer to choose the best intra prediction mode. Therefore, the IPMs in the cover video are usually optimal under specific encoding control algorithm. However, the IPMs of modified blocks in stego video are very likely to be non-optimal. If we decompress a stego video into spatial domain and reselect IPMs with no embedding involved, modified IPMs would be apt to revert to prior optimal value. According to this observation, we propose IPM calibration (IPMC) features for the detection of IPM-based steganography. The proposed features are of a very low dimension and sensitive to the presences of non-optimal IPMs.

The rest of the paper is organized as follows: In Sect. 2, the intra prediction process is briefly introduced, and general model of IPM-based steganography is offered. In Sect. 3, the principle of IPMC is illustrated, and our proposed steganalytic scheme is described in detailed manner. In Sect. 4, comparative experiments are conducted to show the performance of our IPMC features. In the end, conclusion and future work are given in Sect. 5.

# 2 Preliminaries

## 2.1 Intra Prediction Process in H.264

In H.264, the types of IPM contain intra_4 × 4, intra_16 × 16, intra_chroma and I_PCM [12]. Intra 4 × 4 prediction mode (I4PM) is mainly used for characterizing the video frame details. Human eyes are less sensitive to noise in detail areas rather than in smooth areas, suggesting I4PM is more suitable for embedding. Actually, only I4PM is chosen for embedding in existing IPM-based steganographic algorithms.

As Fig. 1 shows that a~p are 4 × 4 block pixels to be predicted, and reference pixels A ~ M are boundary pixels of adjacent blocks which have already been encoded. 9 I4PMs are supported by H.264 encoder for 4 × 4 luminance block prediction as shown in Fig. 2. According to different prediction modes (based on prediction direction), the weighting calculation of reference pixels A ~ M is carried out in order to get pixels a~p. For example, (A + B + C + D + I + J + K + L)/8 is used to calculate all a~p pixels in prediction mode 2 (DC mode).

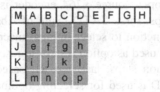

**Fig. 1.** 4 × 4 luminance block to be prediction

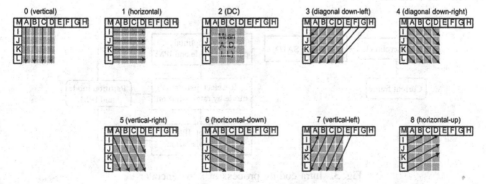

**Fig. 2.** Intra 4 × 4 prediction modes

In order to ensure coding efficiency and minimizing the encoding bit rate, encoder will choose an optimal prediction mode. H.264 encoder is recommended to use the coding control model based on Lagrangian optimization algorithm to achieve the choice of optimal prediction mode. Compared to the previous coding standards, the encoding performance has improved greatly. However, the computational complexity is also much higher than the previous coding standards. We record $k$ 4 × 4 pixel blocks as $S = (S_1, \ldots, S_k)$ where $S_i(1 \leq i \leq k)$ represent the $i^{th}$ block. Each block chooses a prediction mode $I_i \in M$ from prediction mode set $M = (M_1, \ldots, M_9)$ for intra coding. The optimal prediction mode should ensure cost function $J(S, I|QP, \lambda)$ reach the minimum value, H.264 recommended rate-distortion (RD) cost function is defined as:

$$J(S, I|QP, \lambda) = SSD(S, I|QP) + \lambda \times R(S, I|QP) \tag{1}$$

$QP$ is the quantization parameter, $\lambda$ is Lagrange multiplier for mode decision and $R$ is the required number of bits to encode the block. SSD is the sum of squared differences between the reconstructed ($S_{REC}$) and the original ($S$) block pixels given by formula (2):

$$SSD = \sum_{(x,y) \in A} |S(x, y) - S_{REC}(x, y)|^2 \tag{2}$$

$A$ represents current block. $(x, y)$ is the pixel coordinates. SSD is used to describe the coding distortion.

However, the computational complexity of RD cost function is quite high. In practical, encoding control algorithm is usually optimized to ensure the coding speed. The intra coding process of open source x264 encoder is shown as Fig. 3, and the dotted portion is optional steps. First, SATD (Sum of Absolute Transformed Differences) [13] is used as cost function to select optimal macroblock partition mode and IPM. RD cost function can be used as optional steps to reselect optimal partition mode and IPM. In the three selection steps, last two RD-based steps are optional. With default parameters, only SATD is used for selecting optimal IPM. The computational complexity of SATD is much lower than that of RD, and video quality is also guaranteed while minimizing the video bit stream. The calculation formula of SATD is defined as follows:

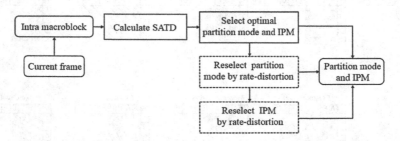

**Fig. 3.** Intra coding process of x264 encoder

$$SATD = \sum_{(x,y)\in A} |H(S(x,y) - S_{REC}(x,y))| \qquad (3)$$

$H(\cdot)$ represents the Hadamard transform. In practical applications, to ensure coding efficiency, generally only SATD is used for IPM selection.

## 2.2 Modeling of IPM-Based Steganography

As already mentioned, existing IPM-based steganographic algorithms only choose I4PM for embedding. Therefore, the following IPM specially refers to I4PM. Figure 4 describes the general embedding process of existing IPM-based steganography.

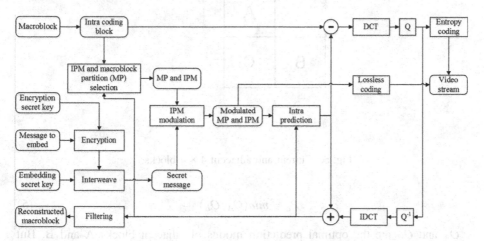

**Fig. 4.** Flow chart of IPM-based steganography

After macroblock partition (MP) and IPM selection, optimal MP and IPM are obtained. The 4 × 4 blocks are chosen to be the candidate embedding blocks. Then modulate IPM according to the secret message which is encrypted and interweaved. The subsequent steps are same as original H.264 encoding process.

IPM-based steganography usually divided 9 I4PM into two groups. One represent secret message 0, and another group represent secret message 1. Some IPM-based steganography [8–10] uses more sophisticated mapping method to expand capacity and enhance concealment. Steganography operation can be generally expressed as follows:

$$\tilde{P}_k = (P_k + \alpha_k \cdot \omega_k) \qquad (4)$$

$\tilde{P}_k \in [1,9]$ denotes IPM after embedding and $P_k \in [1,9]$ indicates the original IPM of block $k$. $\omega_k \in [-8,8]$ represents the noise introduced by embedding process, which makes the IPM of stego video deviated from the original IPM. $\alpha_k \in \{0,1\}$ determines whether a block will be used to embedding. Overall, the basic principle of existing IPM-based steganography is using suboptimal IPM replace optimal according to pre-agreed mapping rules to achieve the embedding. The distortion introduced by embedding mainly caused by the quantization of substantial residuals. The distortion is very weak while the video bit rate is not particularly low, and even can be ignored when the bit rate is sufficiently high.

Not all $4 \times 4$ blocks are suitable for embedding. To compress the prediction modes bits more efficiently, predictive coding is utilized. As shown in Fig. 5, for each current $4 \times 4$ block C, the most probable prediction mode $P_c$ can be established from the adjacent upper (A) and left (B) blocks as following formula:

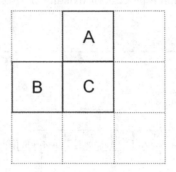

**Fig. 5.** Current and adjacent $4 \times 4$ blocks

$$P_c = min(O_A, O_B) \tag{5}$$

$O_A$ and $O_B$ are the optimal prediction modes of adjacent blocks A and B. But blocks A or B is not available in some cases. If either of them is not available (such as not coded in intra $4 \times 4$ mode or C is a boundary block), $P_c$ will be set to 2 (DC mode).

For each current block, encoder will assign an identifier *Pre*. *Pre* will be set to 1 when $O_C$ (optimal prediction mode of block C) is equal to $P_c$, at this time, only one bit is require to store the prediction mode. Otherwise, *Pre* is set to 0 and $O_C$ will be indicated by following formula:

$$O_C = \begin{cases} O_C & O_C \leq P_c \\ O_C - 1 & O_C > P_c \end{cases} \tag{6}$$

When *Pre* = 1, the prediction mode of current block will not be stored in code stream. For this reason, all the existing IPM-based steganography have ignored these blocks which *Pre* = 1 when embedding. There are other criteria for choosing embedding blocks. Such as Hu et al. [7] determines the candidate embedding blocks according to embedding templates which were generated by embedding secret key.

During the intra-coding process, H.264 encoder will comprehensively consider to select the best IPM. Therefore, the IPMs in cover video are usually optimal under specific encoding control algorithm. However, existing IPM-based steganography uses suboptimal IPMs to replace the optimal ones under the same encoding control algorithm. Thus, we can detect whether a video is stego if only we can judging whether the IPM is optimal.

## 3  Proposed Steganalytic Scheme

### 3.1  Intra Prediction Mode Calibration

It well known that Calibration [14] serves as an image steganalytic method with the aim to construct an estimation of the cover based on the stego image and draw steganalytic features from the differences between them. Cao et al. [15] introduced calibration technique into video steganalytic field, and used it for the detection of motion vector-based steganography.

In this paper, calibration technique is applied to perform video steganalysis against IPM-based steganography. In our scheme, calibration is performed based on single $4 \times 4$ block in order to maintain the consistency of macroblock, and each one is decompressed and compressed again. During the second compression, reselecting of IPM and saving of relevant information are made for later extraction of features. IPMs in cover video will remain unchanged after calibration at utmost degree. But altered IPMs are very likely to revert to their prior optimal value in stego video, implying that several IPMs will change. Therefore, steganalysis can be achieved by distinguishing the differences of IPMs before and after calibration. This new calibration scheme is named as IPM calibration (IPMC). According to the demonstration in Fig. 6, IPMC is carried out in the following 8 steps:

**Step1:** Pick out an I frame from video stream.
**Step2:** Pick out a $4 \times 4$ block from I frame. If identifier $Pre = 1$, skip this block.
**Step3:** Save original IPM of current $4 \times 4$ block.
**Step4:** Obtain the quantization parameter of current $4 \times 4$ block.
**Step5:** Decompress current $4 \times 4$ block into pixel data.
**Step6:** Reselect the IPM of current $4 \times 4$ block, traverse all 9 IPMs and calculate the corresponding SATD. IPMs and corresponding STAD constitute calibrated IPM-SATD set (CISS) ordered by SATD. The SATD of original IPM can be estimated from CISS.
**Step7:** Back to step2 until the end of the frame.
**Step8:** Back to step1 until the end of the video.

In Cao's [15] calibration scheme, there is a problem that the calibration parameters are difficult to be matched, leading to dramatic decline of detection performance. But this problem has been avoided in our IPMC, because the consistency of macroblock partition modes has been maintained and other calibration parameters can be obtained directly from original video stream. Main calibration parameter is quantization parameter $QP$, being similar to quantization factor in image calibration [16]. In particular, H.264 compression standard enables each macroblock to apply an individual $QP$. Thus we need to set $QP$ for each $4 \times 4$ block (directly reuse the original $QP$).

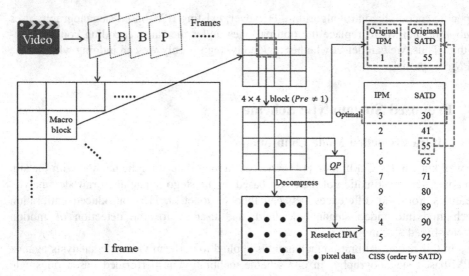

**Fig. 6.** IPM-based calibration process

Because SATD cost function has similar functions as RD, the calibration based on SATD is still effective to the embedding encoder based on RD cost function. The experimental section will demonstrate this point.

## 3.2    The Proposed IPMC Features

We can take the reference from Fig. 6 when reading this section, which will help us understand the meaning of the variables in formulas. Based on IPMC, we propose IPMC features, which can be classified into two sets.

The first feature set, i.e., the IPM shift probability feature set, indicates the probability of optimal calibrated IPM deviating from original IPM. The first feature set is calculated by

$$F_x^k = \frac{\sum_{l=1}^{L_k} \delta(I_l, \tilde{I}_{l,x})}{L_k} \tag{7}$$

In (7), $x \in [1, 9]$ is the features index of first feature set, and $k$ is the frame index. $L_k$ is the number of $4 \times 4$ blocks which participate in the calibration. $I_l \in [1, 9]$ is the original IPM, $\tilde{I}_{l,x} \in [1, 9]$ is the $x^{th}$ IPM in CISS of a $4 \times 4$ block $l$ and

$$\delta(I_l, \tilde{I}_{l,x}) = \begin{cases} 1 & I_l = \tilde{I}_{l,x} \\ 0 & I_l \neq \tilde{I}_{l,x} \end{cases} \tag{8}$$

Figure 7 contrasts the first feature sets of cover and stego video. Bouchama's [10] algorithm was used for embedding. 1 Mb/s and 0.2 Mb/s video bit rate are both considered. As we can see, most probability falls on the first feature in cover video,

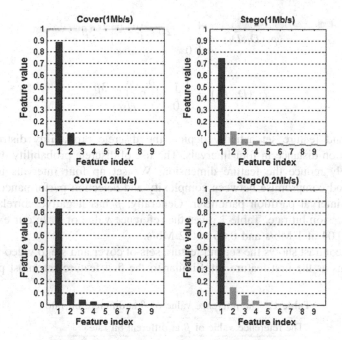

**Fig. 7.** First feature set of cover and stego video

implying most calibrated IPMs are consistent with the original IPM. But in stego video, more probability disperses to other features (red tagging).

The second feature set, called the SATD shift distance feature set, indicates the SATD deviation distance after calibration. The deviation of SATD may be caused by IPM-based steganography noise or compression distortion. Compression distortion only introduces small SATD deviation and almost approaches 0 when bit rate is high enough. However, SATD deviation caused by IPM-based steganography noise will be much higher. Thus, we design the second feature set to improve the detection performance. Second feature set will be calculated by

$$F_{9+y}^k = \frac{\sum_{l=1}^{L_k} \varphi_y(D_l, \tilde{D}_l)}{L_k} \qquad (9)$$

In (9), $y \in [1, 4]$ is the features index of second feature set, and $D_l$ is the original SATD. $\tilde{D}_l$ is the optimal SATD after calibration and

$$\varphi_1(D_l, \tilde{D}_l) = \begin{cases} 1 & \left|\frac{D_l - \tilde{D}_l}{\tilde{D}_l}\right| \leq \beta \\ 0 & else \end{cases} \qquad (10)$$

$$\varphi_2(D_l, \tilde{D}_l) = \begin{cases} 1 & \beta < \left|\frac{D_l - \tilde{D}_l}{\tilde{D}_l}\right| \leq 2\beta \\ 0 & else \end{cases} \qquad (11)$$

$$\varphi_3\left(D_l, \tilde{D}_l\right) = \begin{cases} 1 & 2\beta < \left|\frac{D_l - \tilde{D}_l}{\tilde{D}_l}\right| \leq 3\beta \\ 0 & else \end{cases} \tag{12}$$

$$\varphi_4\left(D_l, \tilde{D}_l\right) = \begin{cases} 1 & \left|\frac{D_l - \tilde{D}_l}{\tilde{D}_l}\right| > 3\beta \\ 0 & else \end{cases} \tag{13}$$

The second feature set actually depicts the discrete probability distribution of SATD deviation distance in four intervals. The use of discrete probability distribution can effectively reduce the feature dimension. We set up four intervals to make a relatively good compromise between complexity and detection performance.

$\beta$ is the interval partition parameter. Generally, $\beta$ has negative correlation with video compression bit rate. Table 1 gives the reference value of $\beta$. In our experiment, we set $\beta$ to 0.04 at 1 Mb/s and 0.06 at 0.2 Mb/s.

Figure 8 contrast shows the second feature sets of cover and stego video with same test conditions as the first feature set. Similar to the first feature set, most probability

**Table 1.** The reference value of $\beta$ at different bit rate

| The reference value of $\beta$ at different bit rate | | | | | | |
|---|---|---|---|---|---|---|
| Bit rate(Mb/s) | 0.1 | 0.2 | 0.5 | 1.0 | 2.0 | >2.0 |
| $\beta$ | | 0.08 | 0.06 | 0.05 | 0.04 | 0.03 | 0.025 |

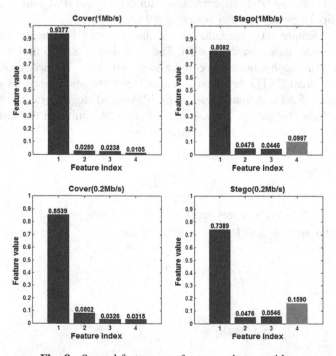

**Fig. 8.** Second feature set of cover and stego video

falls on the first feature in cover video which indicates the SATD deviation distance is small. The SATD deviation distance in stego video increases significantly, and more probability falls on the fourth feature (red tagging).

Comparative tests denote that IPMC features well distinguish the stego and cover videos. The total dimension of IPMC features is $9 + 4 = 13$. Having gotten IPMC features, the support vector machine (SVM) [17] is implemented for training and classification, and we choose polynomial kernel as the kernel function.

Video bit rate is the main factor affecting the result of classification, which means we need to train different models according to the video bit rate of testing set. During classification, a similar bit rate model is to be matched for better classification performance.

## 4 Experiments

### 4.1 Experimental Setup

*(1) Test Sequences*: A database of 30 CIF videos in the 4:2:0 YUV format is used for experiments. We randomly intercept 500 consecutive frames from each video as one experimental sequence. Then each experimental sequence is divided into 100-frame subsequences and the total number of subsequences sums up to 150.

*(2) Steganographic Methods*: To evaluate the effectiveness of the proposed features, two typical IPM steganalytic schemes, i.e. Yang's [9] and Bouchama's [10] are leveraged to produce stego video sets and referred to as Tar1 and Tar2. These two methods are implemented by open source encoder x264. The embedding strength is measured by corrupted prediction modes rate (CPMR), which indicates the average modification rate of available I4 × 4 prediction modes ($Pre = 1$). In Yang's method, matrix coding was used. In every three IPMs, at most one (modification probability is 1/2) needs to be modified for embedding 2 bits information. Therefore the maximum CPMR is $1/2 × 1/3 = 1/6$ (4/24). In Bouchama's method, the maximum CPMR is 8/16.

*(3) Video Compression Configuration*: All experimental samples are compressed by open source x264 encoder to create the class of cover. At the same time, with a given steganographic method, all videos are subjected to compression and embedding with different CPMR to build the class of stego. Video bit rate contains 1 Mb/s and 0.2 Mb/s.

*(4) IPM Steganalytic Features*: Besides our IPMC features, PMC and TPMC (Truncated PMC) features are also tested. The dimension of original PMC features, proposed by Li et al. [11], is up to 9801. In order to reduce the complexity, Li truncated the first 200 most important features as TPMC features.

*(5) The Experimental Groups:* The first group is represented by G1, which is close to the actual scenarios. Randomly selecting 100 video subsequences for training, the rest 50 video subsequences were used for classification. The experiment was repeated 10 times to calculate the average detection performance. Besides, we choose SATD as the cost function when building test sequences. The second group is represented by G2.

Most experimental setting is the same as G1, but only Tar2 was tested and RD was adopted to reselect IPM during encoding. G2 is designed to verify that the our calibration scheme is still valid to the RD-based embedding encoder.

## 4.2    Performance Results

We adopt true positive rate (TP) and true negative rate (TN) to evaluate detection performance. TP is the occurrence that a stego video is classified as stego, and TN is the occurrence that a cover video is classified as cover.

Table 2 shows the detection performance of PMC, TPMC and our IPMC features for G1. The optimal results are displayed in bold. Figure 9 shows the comparison of TP in Table 2 in the form of a graph. In almost all test conditions, our IPMC features perform much better than PMC and TPMC features, and the higher the bit rate, the more significant the advantage. Particularly, when CPMR is 4/24 (For Tar1 and 1 Mb/s), TP of IPMC is up to 97.3 %, but the PMC and TPMC's TP are only 71.2 % and 67.3 %. TN of our IPMC is higher than 95 %, but that of PMC and TPMC is only about 75 %. Bit rate has some influences on the test results of IPMC features, and the detection performance is slightly decreased at lower bit rate. This is because more quantization noise will be introduced at a lower bit rate, but the decrease is not significant, which indicates IPMC features have robustness to the decline of bit rate. The overall performance of TPMC is lower than the PMC, especially when the CPMR is relatively high.

**Table 2.** Detection performance comparison within PMC, TPMC and our IPMC for G1

| Steganography methods | Bit rate (Mb/s) | CPMR | PMC features | | TPMC features | | IPMC features | |
|---|---|---|---|---|---|---|---|---|
| | | | TP (%) | TN (%) | TP (%) | TN (%) | TP (%) | TN (%) |
| **Tar1** | **1.0** | 1/24 | 51.0 | 75.8 | 50.0 | 73.5 | **77.1** | **98.6** |
| | | 2/24 | 62.1 | | 59.3 | | **90.6** | |
| | | 3/24 | 67.8 | | 63.1 | | **94.1** | |
| | | 4/24 | 71.2 | | 67.3 | | **97.3** | |
| | **0.2** | 1/24 | 48.1 | 74.9 | 51.0 | 74.2 | **75.4** | **95.5** |
| | | 2/24 | 61.9 | | 60.0 | | **89.1** | |
| | | 3/24 | 68.1 | | 62.4 | | **93.6** | |
| | | 4/24 | 73.3 | | 64.7 | | **96.2** | |
| **Tar2** | **1.0** | 1/16 | 56.0 | 75.8 | 52.0 | 73.5 | **84.5** | **98.6** |
| | | 2/16 | 61.0 | | 59.1 | | **87.1** | |
| | | 4/16 | 77.3 | | 66.0 | | **91.3** | |
| | | 8/16 | 89.3 | | 76.7 | | **99.6** | |
| | **0.2** | 1/16 | 55.6 | 74.9 | 51.3 | 74.2 | **82.1** | **95.5** |
| | | 2/16 | 59.2 | | 56.9 | | **85.1** | |
| | | 4/16 | 78.1 | | 69.7 | | **90.6** | |
| | | 8/16 | 89.1 | | 77.2 | | **96.5** | |
| **Feature dimension** | | | 9801 | | 200 | | **13** | |

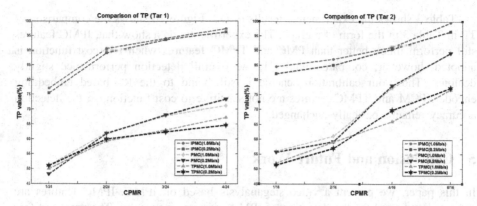

**Fig. 9.** The comparison of TP for G1

**Table 3.** Detection performance comparison within PMC, TPMC and our IPMC for G2

| Steganography methods | Bit rate (Mb/s) | CPMR | PMC features | | TPMC features | | IPMC features | |
|---|---|---|---|---|---|---|---|---|
| | | | TP (%) | TN (%) | TP (%) | TN (%) | TP (%) | TN (%) |
| Tar2 | 1.0 | 1/16 | 55.0 | 75.5 | 52.3 | 73.6 | **80.1** | 94.6 |
| | | 2/16 | 61.1 | | 60.1 | | **87.3** | |
| | | 4/16 | 73.4 | | 66.3 | | **88.3** | |
| | | 8/16 | 89.7 | | 75.9 | | **91.1** | |
| | 0.2 | 1/16 | 57.6 | 74.4 | 52.1 | 74.9 | **73.2** | 91.5 |
| | | 2/16 | 59.4 | | 57.1 | | **86.2** | |
| | | 4/16 | 78.7 | | 70.3 | | **87.1** | |
| | | 8/16 | 90.1 | | 76.9 | | **91.5** | |
| **Feature dimension** | | | 9801 | | 200 | | 13 | |

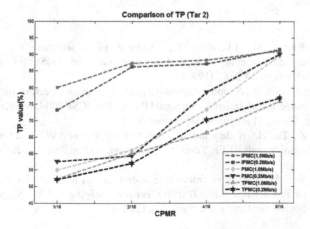

**Fig. 10.** The comparison of TP for G2

Table 3 shows the experimental results of G2. Figure 10 shows the comparison of TP in Table 3 in the form of a graph. The experimental data show that, IPMC features still perform much better than PMC and TPMC features when RD cost function is adopted, however, compared with G1, the overall detection performance slightly declines. Thus, our calibration scheme is still valid to the RD-based embedding encoder. PCM and TPMC features are not sensitive to cost function, so the detection accuracy remains basically unchanged.

## 5    Conclusion and Future Work

In this paper, we present a video steganalysis based on IPMC. IPMC features are extracted and used for the detection of IPM-based steganography. The proposed features are of a very low dimension and sensitive to the presences of non-optimal IPMs. Moreover, calibration parameters are obtained directly from the video stream. Therefore, we avoid estimating erroneous calibration parameters which can lead to the decline of the detection performance. Experimental results show that proposed IPMC features are sensitive to IPM-based steganography even at low embedding rate, and outperform other existing steganalytic methods.

As shown in experimental results, the detection performance dropped when RD cost function was adopted to reselect IPM during encoding. In the future work, we would like to blend RD and SATD during the calibration process to improve the performance of IPMC features. Moreover, adaptive steganalysis has become a trend, so we also will try to improve the adaptability of our IPMC features. Possible schemes include higher-order features and adaptive feature extraction/selection techniques.

**Acknowledgement.** This work was supported by the NSFC under 61170281 and 61303259, and the Strategic Priority Research Program of Chinese Academy of Sciences under XDA06030600.

## References

1. Jordan, F., Kutter, M., Ebrahimi, T.: Proposal of a watermarking technique for hiding/retrieving data in compressed and decompressed video. ISO/IEC Doc. JTC1/SC 29/QWG 11 MPEG 97/M 2281 (1997)
2. Liu, Z., Liang, H., Niu, X.: A robust video watermarking in motion vectors. In: Proceedings of the 2004 7th International Conference on Signal Processing, ICSP 2004, vol. 3, pp. 2358–2361. IEEE, Beijing, China, 31 August–4 September 2004
3. Ma, X., Li, Z., Tu, H.: A data hiding algorithm for H.264/AVC video stream without intra-frame distortion drift. IEEE Trans. Circuits Syst. Video Technol. **20**(10), 1320–1330 (2010)
4. Neufeld, A., Ker, A.: A study of embedding operation and locations for steganography in H.264 video. In: Proceedings of IS&T/SPIE Electronic Imaging, vol. 8665, pp. 86650J:1–14. International Society for Optics and Photonics (2013)

5. Lu, C., Chen, J., Fan, K.: Real-time frame-dependent video watermarking in VLC domain. Sig. Process. Image Commun. **20**(7), 624–642 (2005)
6. Seo, Y., Choi, H., Lee, C.: Low-complexity watermarking based on entropy coding in H.264/AVC. IEICE Trans. Fundam. Electron. Commun. Comput. Sci. **91**(8), 2130–2137 (2008)
7. Hu, Y., Zhang, C., Su, Y.: Information hiding based on intra prediction modes for H.264/AVC. In: Proceedings of 2007 IEEE International Conference on Multimedia and Expo, ICME 2007, pp. 1231–1234. IEEE, Beijing China, 2–5 July 2007
8. Xu, D., Wang, R., Wang, J.: Prediction mode modulated data-hiding algorithm for H.264/AVC. J. Real-Time Image Proc. **7**(4), 205–214 (2012)
9. Yang, G., Li, J., He, Y.: An information hiding algorithm based on intra-prediction modes and matrix coding for H.264/AVC Video stream. Int. J. Electron. Commun. **65**(4), 331–337 (2011)
10. Bouchama, S., Hamami, L., Aliane, H.: H.264/AVC data hiding based on intra prediction modes for real-time application. In: Proceedings of the World Congress on Engineering and Computer Science, vol. 1, pp. 655–658 (2012)
11. Li, S., Deng, H., Tian, H.: Steganalytic of prediction mode modulated data-hiding algorithms in H.264/AVC video stream. Ann. Telecommun. (annales des télécommunications) **69**(7–8), 461–473 (2014)
12. Wiegand, T., Sullivan, G.J., Bjontegaard, G., Luthra, A.: Overview of the H.264/AVC video coding standard. IEEE Trans. Circuits Syst. Video Technol. **13**(7), 560–576 (2003)
13. Kim, J., Jeong, J.: Fast intra mode decision algorithm using the sum of absolute transformed differences. In: Proceedings of 2011 International Conference on Digital Image Computing: Techniques and Applications, DICTA 2011, pp. 655–659. IEEE (2011)
14. Fridrich, J., Kodovsky, J.: Rich models for steganalytic of digital images. IEEE Trans. Inf. Forensics Secur. **7**(3), 868–882 (2011)
15. Cao, Y., Zhao, X., Feng, D.: Video Steganalysis exploiting motion vector reversion-based features. Sig. Process. Lett. **19**(1), 35–38 (2012). IEEE
16. Pevny, T., Fridrich, J.: Detection of double-compression in JPEG images for applications in steganography. IEEE Trans. Inf. Forensics Secur. **3**(2), 247–258 (2008)
17. Chang, C., Lin, C.: LIBSVM: a library for support vector machines. ACM Trans. Intell. Syst. Technol. (TIST) **2**(3), 27 (2011)

# Feature Selection for High Dimensional Steganalysis

Yanping Tan[1], Fangjun Huang[1(✉)], and Jiwu Huang[2]

[1] School of Information Science and Technology, Sun Yat-Sen University,
Guangzhou 510006, China
huangfj@mail.sysu.edu.cn
[2] College of Information Engineering, Shenzhen University,
Shenzhen 518060, China

**Abstract.** In today's digital image steganalysis, the dimensionality of the feature vector is relatively high. This may result in much redundancy and high computational complexity. In this paper, a novel feature selection method is proposed from a new perspective. The main idea of our proposed feature selection method is that the element in the extracted feature vector should consistently increase or decrease with the increase of embedding rate for a given steganographic scheme. Various experimental results tested on 10000 grayscale images demonstrate that our feature selection method can reduce the dimensionality of the high dimensional feature vector efficiently, and meanwhile the detection accuracy can be well preserved.

**Keywords:** Steganalysis · Steganography · Dimensionality reduction · Feature selection

## 1 Introduction

Steganography is the art and science of concealing secret messages [11]. Currently, adaptive embedding is one of the major research directions. Some spatial domain adaptive steganographic schemes have been proposed in recent years, such as WOW (Wavelet Obtained Weights) [5] and EAMR (Edge adaptive image steganography based on LSB matching revisited algorithm) [8]. The basic idea of adaptive steganographic schemes is to preferentially modify some elements (pixels/coefficients) in complex textural regions that are difficult to model, and keep the elements in the smooth regions unchanged. Generally, adaptive steganographic schemes are more secure than non-adaptive steganography, such as LSB (Least Significant Bit) based [2,10] algorithms, especially when the embedding rate is high.

In order to accurately detect adaptive steganographic schemes in the spatial domain, the higher and higher dimensional feature representation of image is required in steganalysis. For example, the dimensionality of the feature vector extracted by SRM (Spatial Rich Model) [4] is higher than thirty thousand. Although the high dimensional feature vector may perform better in detecting secret messages, some limitations may exist in practical applications because

© Springer International Publishing Switzerland 2016
Y.-Q. Shi et al. (Eds.): IWDW 2015, LNCS 9569, pp. 134–144, 2016.
DOI: 10.1007/978-3-319-31960-5_12

of the high computational complexity. Thus proper dimensionality reduction for the high dimensional feature vector is necessary. In this paper, according to some specific characteristics in the field of steganography/steganalysis, a novel feature selection method is proposed. For the ease of explanation, the elements in the feature vector are called features in the following. The main idea of our proposed novel feature selection method is that the values of effective feature (belonging to the high dimensional feature vector) should consistently increase or decrease with the increase of embedding rate, and thus the feature that does not have this characteristic should be removed from the original high dimensional feature vector. Various experimental results demonstrate that the dimensionality of the high dimensional feature vector can be reduced efficiently via using our proposed new feature selection method, and meanwhile the detection accuracy of the corresponding steganalytic algorithm can be well preserved.

The rest of this paper is arranged as follows. Section 2 provides a brief description of three high dimensional steganalytic algorithms. The characteristic of stego images with different embedding rates are described in Sect. 3. Our new feature selection method is proposed in Sect. 4. The experimental results are shown in Sect. 5 and we draw the conclusion in Sect. 6.

## 2   Overview of Three High Dimensional Steganalytic Algorithms

In this section, we give a brief overview of three high dimensional steganalytic algorithms, i.e., Spatial Rich Model (SRM) [4], maxSRM [3] and maxSRMd2 [3], which are used for testing our proposed feature selection method.

### 2.1   SRM

In order to capture a large number of different types of dependencies among neighboring pixels, the SRM model is formed by merging multiple diverse and smaller submodels to produce a better detection result. There are mainly three steps for explaining how to form the SRM submodels.

(1) Computing residuals: The submodels are formed from noise residuals, $R = R_{ij} \in R^{n1 \times n2}$, computed using high-pass filters of the following form:

$$R_{ij} = \widehat{X_{ij}}(N_{ij}) - cX_{ij}, \tag{1}$$

where $c \in \mathbb{N}$ is the residual order, the $\mathbb{N}$ represents the set of all integers. $X_{ij}$ represents pixel values located at $(i, j)$ of 8-bits grayscale cover images. $N_{ij}$ is a local neighborhood of pixel $X_{ij}, X_{ij} \notin N_{ij}$, and $\widehat{(X_{ij})}(.)$ is a predictor of $cX_{ij}$ defined on $N_{ij}$. The set $\{X_{ij} + N_{ij}\}$ is called the support of the residual.

(2) Truncation and quantization: Each submodel is formed from a quantized and truncated version of the residual:

$$R_{ij} \leftarrow trunc_T(round(\frac{R_{ij}}{q})), \tag{2}$$

where $q > 0$ is a quantization step. The operation of rounding to an integer is denoted by $round(x)$. The truncation function with threshold $T > 0$ is defined for any $x \in \mathbb{R}$ as $trunc_T(x) = x$ for $x \in [-T, T]$ and $trunc_T(x) = T sign(x)$ otherwise. The symbol $\mathbb{R}$ is used to represent the set of all real numbers.

(3) Co-occurrences: Submodels will be constructed from horizontal and vertical co-occurrences of four consecutive residual samples processed using (2) with $T = 2$. Formally, each co-occurrence matrix $C$ is a four-dimensional array indexed with $d = (d_1, d_2, d_3, d_4) \in T_4 \triangleq \{-T, \ldots, T\}^4$. The $d^{th}$ element of the horizontal co-occurrence for residual $R = (R_{ij})$ is formally defined as the normalized number of groups of four neighboring residual samples with values equal to $d_1, d_2, d_3, d_4$:

$$C_d^{(h)} = \frac{1}{Z} |\{(R_{ij}, R_{i,j+1}, R_{i,j+2}, R_{i,j+3}) | R_{i,j+k-1} = d_k, k = 1, \ldots, 4\}|, \tag{3}$$

where $Z$ is the normalization factor ensuring that $\sum_{d \in T_4} C_d^{(h)} = 1$. The vertical co-occurrence, $C^{(v)}$, is defined analogically (please refer to [4] for more details). For a finite set $\chi$, the $|\chi|$ denotes the number of its elements.

## 2.2    maxSRM

The maxSRM is a variant of the SRM (Spatial Rich Model), and it is built in the same manner as the SRM, but the process of forming the co-occurrence matrices is modified to consider the embedding change probabilities $\widehat{\beta}_{ij}$ estimated from the analyzed image. The SRM uses the 4D co-occurrences, where 4D arrays are defined as

$$C_{d_0 d_1 d_2 d_3} = \sum_{i,j=1}^{n_1, n_2 - 3} \left[ \widehat{\beta}_{ij} = d_k, \forall k = 0, \ldots, 3 \right], \tag{4}$$

This is an example of a horizontal co-occurrence. The $(i, j)$ denotes the location of pixel in the image.

In maxSRM, this definition is modified to

$$\tilde{C}_{d_0 d_1 d_2 d_3} = \sum_{i,j=1}^{n_1, n_2 - 3} \max_{k=0, \ldots, 3} \widehat{\beta_{i,j+k}} \left[ \widehat{\beta}_{ij} = d_k, \forall k = 0, \ldots, 3 \right], \tag{5}$$

That is, instead of adding a 1 to the corresponding co-occurrence bin, the maximum of the embedding change probabilities taken across the four residuals will be added. The rest of the process of forming the SRM stays the same, including the symmetrization by sign and direction and merging into SRM submodels.

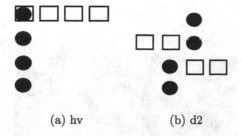

(a) hv          (b) d2

**Fig. 1.** Two types of co-occurrence scan direction

### 2.3 maxSRMd2

Both the original SRM and maxSRM use horizontal and vertical scans (see the case (a) in Fig. 1). However, the version of the maxSRM with all co-occurrence scan directions is replaced with the oblique direction 'd2' (see the case (b) in Fig. 1), and this version of the rich model is called the maxSRMd2.

In principle, the three high dimensional steganalytic algorithms are similar in the process of catching distortions, and they are frequently used to detect the existence of secret messages in the spatial images. The feature vectors extracted by the three steganalytic algorithms all have the dimension of 34671.

## 3  The Characteristic of Stego Images with Different Embedding Rates

For any steganographic scheme, the detectable distortions that may be introduced to the carrier image will increase with the increase of embedding rate, which may also influence the value of extracted features. Some experimental results corresponding to the steganographic scheme WOW are illustrated in Fig. 2. The cover image is shown in Figs. 2(a) and (b–e) show the positions of those pixels changed by using the WOW algorithm with different embedding rates. The white points indicate that in these positions the pixels have been modified after embedding secret messages.

From Fig. 2, it is observed that even if embedding rates are different, the modifications are in the same area generally. As seen in Fig. 2, most of the modifications are made in the edge areas and those smooth areas are kept unchanged, such as the region in the sky. However, with the increase of embedding rate, the difference between the cover and stego images will be more clearly visible. As we all know, the features in steganalysis are extracted to discriminate the difference between cover and stego images. In general, the value of each effective feature should consistently increase or decrease with the increase of embedding rate. Some examples are shown in Table 1.

The values of three features (i.e., $1^{th}$, $4^{th}$ and $27^{th}$) extracted by SRM from an image with different embedding rates are shown in Table 1. It is observed from Table 1 that values of the $1^{th}$ ($27^{th}$) feature consistently decrease (increase) with

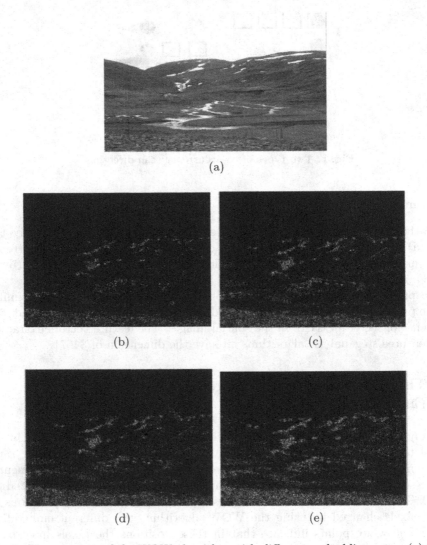

**Fig. 2.** Stego images of the WOW algorithm with different embedding rates. (a) The cover image. (b) The stego image with the embedding rate of 0.1 bpp(bits per pixel). (c) The stego image with the embedding rate of 0.2 bpp. (d) The stego image with the embedding rate of 0.3 bpp. (e) The stego image with the embedding rate of 0.4 bpp.

the increase of embedding rate. Whereas for the $4^{th}$ feature, it may decrease or increase randomly with the increase of embedding rate. According to our opinion, these kinds of features (e.g., $1^{th}$ and $27^{th}$) may be effective and should be selected in the steganalytic process. However, those kinds of features (e.g., $4^{th}$) may confuse the classifier and can be excluded from the high dimensional feature vector in the steganalytic process.

**Table 1.** Values of the same feature with different embedding rates

| Embedding rates | Feature values | | |
|---|---|---|---|
| | The $1^{th}$ feature | The $4^{th}$ feature | The $27^{th}$ feature |
| cover | 0.2672 | 0.0515 | 0.0196 |
| 0.1 bpp | 0.2670 | 0.0515 | 0.0199 |
| 0.2 bpp | 0.2664 | 0.0516 | 0.0205 |
| 0.3 bpp | 0.2661 | 0.0514 | 0.0207 |
| 0.4 bpp | 0.2660 | 0.0517 | 0.0219 |

# 4   Proposed Feature Selection Method

Based on the characteristic described in Table 1, the detailed realization of our proposed feature selection method in the experiments is given in the following. Assume that $f_{i,j}^{\beta}\ (1 \leq i \leq M, 1 \leq j \leq N, \beta \geq 0)$ denotes the value of $j^{th}$ feature of the $i^{th}$ image with the embedding rate $\beta$, where $M$ denotes the number of images in the image set, $N$ denotes the total number of features extracted from the $i^{th}$ image, and $j$ denotes the $j^{th}$ feature extracted from the $i^{th}$ image. The parameter $\beta$ represents the embedding rate. In this paper, we have selected $\beta$ as 0.1, 0.2, 0.3 and 0.4 in all our testing, that is, the embedding rate is 0.1 bits per pixel (bpp), 0.2 bpp, 0.3 bpp and 0.4 bpp, respectively. Note that $\beta = 0$ represents that the embedding rate is 0 bpp. The $A_{i,j}^{\beta}$ is defined as

$$A_{i,j}^{\beta} = \begin{cases} 1, if(f_{i,j}^{\beta} - f_{i,j}^{0}) > 0 \\ 0, otherwise \end{cases} \quad (1 \leq i \leq M, 1 \leq j \leq N, \beta > 0), \quad (6)$$

where the $f_{i,j}^{0}$ represents the value of the $j^{th}$ feature extracted from the $i^{th}$ cover image, and the $f_{i,j}^{\beta}$ denotes the value of the $j^{th}$ feature extracted from the $i^{th}$ stego image with the embedding rate $\beta$. Then the $S_{j}^{\beta}$ is defined as

$$S_{j}^{\beta} = \sum_{i=1}^{i=M} A_{i,j}^{\beta} \quad (1 \leq j \leq N, \beta > 0), \quad (7)$$

In Eq. (7), for a given embedding rate $\beta$, if the value of $S_{j}^{\beta}$ is a big value (e.g., nearly the value $M$), it represents that for most of the images in the testing image data set the value of $j^{th}$ feature may increase with the increase of embedding rate. On the contrary, if the value of $S_{j}^{\beta}$ is a small value (e.g., nearly the value of 0), it represents that for most of the images in the testing image data set the value of $j^{th}$ feature may decrease with the increase of embedding rate. In both of these two cases, the $j^{th}$ feature is considered as an effective feature. However, if the value of $S_{j}^{\beta}$ is around $M/2$, it represents that for about half of the images in testing image data set the value of $j^{th}$ feature may increase whereas for the remaining half of the images in testing image data set the value of $j^{th}$ feature may decrease with the increase of embedding rate. In this case, the $j^{th}$ is considered as the non-effective feature and should be excluded from the original high dimensional feature vector. Thus, in our proposed method, the extracted feature may be selected as an effective feature in these two cases.

In the first case, the extracted feature from the original high dimensional feature vector must satisfy the following two conditions.

(1) For any given embedding rate, e.g., $\beta_1, \ldots, \beta_k$ ($k \in \mathbb{N}$), the following inequality Eq. (8) must be satisfied.

$$M \times (1 - P/2) \leq S_j^{\{\beta_1, \beta_2, \ldots, \beta_k\}} \leq M \qquad (1 \leq j \leq N, k \in \mathbb{N}), \qquad (8)$$

where $P\,(0 < P < 1)$ is a control parameter which is used to control the number of features that may be excluded from the original high dimensional feature vector. Generally, we can select $P = 0.7 \sim 0.9$, which means that for most of the images in the testing image data set, and the value of the $j^{th}$ feature may increase with the increase of embedding rate.

(2) For any embedding rate, e.g., for different embedding rates $\beta_1$ and $\beta_2$, if $\beta_1 < \beta_2$, then $S_j^{\beta_1} < S_j^{\beta_2}$ must be satisfied. In the same way, when there are $k$ embedding rates, such as $\beta_1, \ldots, \beta_k$ ($k \in \mathbb{N}$), if $\beta_1 < \beta_2 < \cdots < \beta_k$, the inequality $S_j^{\beta_1} < S_j^{\beta_2} < \cdots < S_j^{\beta_k}$ must be satisfied.

In the same way, in the second case the extracted feature from the original high dimensional feature vector must satisfy the following feature two conditions.

(1) For any given embedding rate, e.g., $\beta_1, \ldots, \beta_k$ ($k \in \mathbb{N}$), the following inequality Eq. (9) must be satisfied.

$$0 < S_j^{\{\beta_1, \beta_2, \ldots, \beta_k\}} \leq P \times \left\lfloor \frac{M}{2} \right\rfloor \qquad (1 \leq j \leq N). \qquad (9)$$

where for any value of $M$, the largest integer smaller than or equal to $M$ is $\lfloor M \rfloor$. Similarly, we can choose $P = 0.7 \sim 0.9$ in general, which means that for most of images in the testing image data set, and the value of $j^{th}$ feature may decrease with the increase of embedding rate.

(2) For any embedding rate, e.g., for different embedding rates $\beta_1$ and $\beta_2$, if $\beta_1 < \beta_2$, then $S_j^{\beta_1} > S_j^{\beta_2}$ must be satisfied. In the same way, when there are $k$ embedding rates, such as $\beta_1, \ldots, \beta_k$ ($k \in \mathbb{N}$), if $\beta_1 < \beta_2 < \cdots < \beta_k$, the inequality $S_j^{\beta_1} > S_j^{\beta_2} > \cdots > S_j^{\beta_k}$ must be satisfied.

## 5    Experimental Results

In this paper, all experimental results are obtained on BOSSbase ver. 1.01 [1], which consists of 10000 gray-scale cover images with the size $512 \times 512$. Four different embedding rates, i.e., 0.1 bpp, 0.2 bpp, 0.3 bpp and 0.4 bpp, are selected in our testing. The ensemble classifier [7] is used for classification. We randomly select 5000 images for training and the remaining 5000 images are used for testing. In the training process, the effective features are selected according to

**Table 2.** Features dimension and $E_{OOB}$ for four different embedding rates, i.e., 0.1 bpp, 0.2 bpp, 0.3 bpp and 0.4 bpp. 'Original' denotes the feature vector without undergoing feature selection.

| Embedding rates | | | Steganography | | |
|---|---|---|---|---|---|
| | | | WOW | HUGO | S-UNIWARD |
| 0.1 | Original | Dimension | 34671 | 34671 | 34671 |
| | | $E_{OOB}$ | 0.3958 | 0.3780 | 0.4020 |
| | P = 0.9 | Dimension | 16598 | 14248 | 16896 |
| | | $E_{OOB}$ | 0.3660 | 0.3735 | 0.4008 |
| | P = 0.8 | Dimension | 9507 | 7830 | 9906 |
| | | $E_{OOB}$ | 0.4094 | 0.3804 | 0.4045 |
| | P = 0.7 | Dimension | 4947 | 3835 | 5250 |
| | | $E_{OOB}$ | 0.4105 | 0.3959 | 0.4082 |
| 0.2 | Original | Dimension | 34671 | 34671 | 34671 |
| | | $E_{OOB}$ | 0.3202 | 0.2576 | 0.3209 |
| | P = 0.9 | Dimension | 16598 | 14248 | 16896 |
| | | $E_{OOB}$ | 0.3245 | 0.2656 | 0.3239 |
| | P = 0.8 | Dimension | 9507 | 7830 | 9906 |
| | | $E_{OOB}$ | 0.3255 | 0.2703 | 0.3258 |
| | P = 0.7 | Dimension | 4947 | 3835 | 5250 |
| | | $E_{OOB}$ | 0.3379 | 0.2804 | 0.3311 |
| 0.3 | Original | Dimension | 34671 | 34671 | 34671 |
| | | $E_{OOB}$ | 0.2560 | 0.1880 | 0.2600 |
| | P = 0.9 | Dimension | 16598 | 14248 | 16896 |
| | | $E_{OOB}$ | 0.2579 | 0.1904 | 0.2619 |
| | P = 0.8 | Dimension | 9507 | 7830 | 9906 |
| | | $E_{OOB}$ | 0.2584 | 0.1952 | 0.2616 |
| | P = 0.7 | Dimension | 4947 | 3835 | 5250 |
| | | $E_{OOB}$ | 0.2703 | 0.2097 | 0.2697 |
| 0.4 | Original | Dimension | 34671 | 34671 | 34671 |
| | | $E_{OOB}$ | 0.2105 | 0.1318 | 0.2085 |
| | P = 0.9 | Dimension | 16598 | 14248 | 16896 |
| | | $E_{OOB}$ | 0.2109 | 0.1315 | 0.2090 |
| | P = 0.8 | Dimension | 9507 | 7830 | 9906 |
| | | $E_{OOB}$ | 0.2116 | 0.1382 | 0.2166 |
| | P = 0.7 | Dimension | 4947 | 3835 | 5250 |
| | | $E_{OOB}$ | 0.2201 | 0.1490 | 0.2197 |

the control parameter $P$ ($P$ is selected as 0.9, 0.8 or 0.7 in our testing) and a series of classifiers can be obtained. Then these obtained classifiers are used for testing.

## 5.1   Experiment #1

The efficiency of our proposed feature selection method for dimensionality reduction regarding to the steganalytic algorithm (SRM) is shown in the Table 2. In this case, three steganographic schemes, i.e., WOW [5], HUGO [9] and S-UNIWARD [6] and four different embedding rates, i.e., 0.1 bpp, 0.2 bpp, 0.3 bpp, 0.4 bpp are tested.

**Table 3.** Features dimension and $E_{OOB}$ for three high dimensional steganalytic algorithms and three steganographic schemes with the embedding rate of 0.4 bpp.

| Steganalysis | | | Steganography | | |
|---|---|---|---|---|---|
| | | | WOW | HUGO | S-UNIWARD |
| SRM | Original | Dimension | 34671 | 34671 | 34671 |
| | | $E_{OOB}$ | 0.2105 | 0.1318 | 0.2085 |
| | P = 0.9 | Dimension | 16598 | 14248 | 16896 |
| | | $E_{OOB}$ | 0.2109 | 0.1315 | 0.2090 |
| | P = 0.8 | Dimension | 9507 | 7830 | 9906 |
| | | $E_{OOB}$ | 0.2116 | 0.1382 | 0.2166 |
| | P = 0.7 | Dimension | 4947 | 3835 | 5250 |
| | | $E_{OOB}$ | 0.2201 | 0.1490 | 0.2197 |
| maxSRM | Original | Dimension | 34671 | 34671 | 34671 |
| | | $E_{OOB}$ | 0.2080 | 0.1310 | 0.2063 |
| | P = 0.9 | Dimension | 16598 | 14248 | 16896 |
| | | $E_{OOB}$ | 0.2107 | 0.1345 | 0.2084 |
| | P = 0.8 | Dimension | 9507 | 7830 | 9906 |
| | | $E_{OOB}$ | 0.2117 | 0.1405 | 0.2129 |
| | P = 0.7 | Dimension | 4947 | 3835 | 5250 |
| | | $E_{OOB}$ | 0.2187 | 0.1480 | 0.2155 |
| maxSRMd2 | Original | Dimension | 34671 | 34671 | 34671 |
| | | $E_{OOB}$ | 0.1993 | 0.1295 | 0.1995 |
| | P = 0.9 | Dimension | 17797 | 14346 | 18248 |
| | | $E_{OOB}$ | 0.2012 | 0.1334 | 0.2012 |
| | P = 0.8 | Dimension | 8352 | 6290 | 9826 |
| | | $E_{OOB}$ | 0.2026 | 0.1386 | 0.2053 |
| | P = 0.7 | Dimension | 3244 | 2670 | 3639 |
| | | $E_{OOB}$ | 0.2110 | 0.1430 | 0.2133 |

From the Table 2, it is obvious that the dimensionality of the original high dimensional feature vector (dimension of 34671) can be reduced efficiently by using our proposed feature selection method. For example, when the steganographic scheme is selected as the WOW algorithm and the embedding rate is 0.4 bpp, the testing error $E_{OOB}$ is 0.2105 with the feature dimension of 34671. However, when $P = 0.7$, the testing error is 0.2116 with the feature dimension of 9507 by using our feature selection method (please refer to the Table 2 for more details).

### 5.2   Experiment #2

The efficiency of our feature reduction method regarding to three different high dimensional steganalytic algorithms, i.e., SRM [4], maxSRM [3] and maxSRMd2 [3] is shown in the Table 3. In this case, three different adaptive steganographic schemes, i.e., WOW, HUGO and S-UNIWARD and one embedding rate, i.e., 0.4 bpp, are tested.

From the Table 3, it is obvious that our proposed feature selection method can be applied to various high dimensional steganalytic algorithms for dimensionality reduction. For example, when the steganographic scheme is HUGO with the embedding rate 0.4 bpp and the steganalytic algorithm is maxSRMd2, the original feature dimension of 34671 can be reduced to 2670, namely the dimension is reduced by more than ten times. However, the testing error almost keeps the same as before (please refer to the Table 3 for more details).

## 6   Conclusions

In this paper, we firstly point out that the element in the extracted feature vector should consistently increase or decrease with the increase of embedding rate for a given steganographic scheme. Moreover, this new finding can be utilized to achieve the dimensionality reduction for various steganalytic algorithms with high dimensional feature vector. The realization of our feature selection method can not only eliminate the redundancy in the high dimensional feature vector, but may also improve the overall classification efficiency. We will further optimize our proposed feature selection method and extend it to other pattern classification fields, not limit to the field of image steganalysis.

**Acknowledgment.** This work was partially supported by the 973 Program of China (2011CB302204), the National Natural Science Foundation of China (61173147, U1135001, 61332012), and Shenzhen R&D Program (GJHZ20140418191518323).

## References

1. Bas, P., Filler, T., Pevný, T.: Break our steganographic system: the ins and outs of organizing BOSS. In: Filler, T., Pevný, T., Craver, S., Ker, A. (eds.) IH 2011. LNCS, vol. 6958, pp. 59–70. Springer, Heidelberg (2011)

2. Chan, C.-K., Cheng, L.-M.: Hiding data in images by simple lsb substitution. Pattern Recogn. **37**(3), 469–474 (2004)
3. Denemark, T., Sedighi, V., Holub, V., Cogranne, R., Fridrich, J.: Selection-channel-aware rich model for steganalysis of digital images. In: 2015 National Conference on Parallel Computing Technologies (PARCOMPTECH), pp. 48–53. IEEE (2015)
4. Fridrich, J., Kodovský, J.: Rich models for steganalysis of digital images. IEEE Trans. Inf. Forensics Secur. **7**(3), 868–882 (2012)
5. Holub, V., Fridrich, J.: Designing steganographic distortion using directional filters. In: 2012 IEEE International Workshop on Information Forensics and Security (WIFS), pp. 234–239. IEEE (2012)
6. Holub, V., Fridrich, J., Denemark, T.: Universal distortion function for steganography in an arbitrary domain. EURASIP J. Inf. Secur. **2014**(1), 1–13 (2014)
7. Kodovský, J., Fridrich, J., Holub, V.: Ensemble classifiers for steganalysis of digital media. IEEE Trans. Inf. Forensics Secur. **7**(2), 432–444 (2012)
8. Luo, W., Huang, F., Huang, J.: Edge adaptive image steganography based on lsb matching revisited. IEEE Trans. Inf. Forensics Secur. **5**(2), 201–214 (2010)
9. Pevný, T., Filler, T., Bas, P.: Using high-dimensional image models to perform highly undetectable steganography. In: Böhme, R., Fong, P.W.L., Safavi-Naini, R. (eds.) IH 2010. LNCS, vol. 6387, pp. 161–177. Springer, Heidelberg (2010)
10. Wang, R.-Z., Lin, C.-F., Lin, J.-C.: Image hiding by optimal lsb substitution and genetic algorithm. Pattern Recogn. **34**(3), 671–683 (2001)
11. Zhang, X., Wang, S.: Steganography using multiple-base notational system and human vision sensitivity. IEEE Signal Process. Lett. **12**(1), 67–70 (2005)

# Synthetic Speech Detection and Audio Steganography in VoIP Scenarios

Daniele Capolupo[1] and Fabrizio d'Amore[2(✉)]

[1] Enterprise Engineering Department, University of Tor Vergata, Rome, Italy
danielecapolupo@outlook.it
[2] Department of Computer, Control, and Management Engineering,
Sapienza University of Rome, Rome, Italy
damore@dis.uniroma1.it

**Abstract.** The distinction between synthetic and human voice uses the techniques of the current biometric voice recognition systems, which prevent that a person's voice, no matter if with good or bad intentions, can be confused with someone else's. Steganography gives the possibility to hide in a file without a particular value (usually audio, video or image files) a hidden message in such a way as to not rise suspicion to any external observer. This article suggests two methods, applicable in a VoIP hypothetical scenario, which allow us to distinguish a synthetic speech from a human voice, and to insert within the Comfort Noise a text message generated in the pauses of a voice conversation. The first method takes up the studies already carried out for the Modulation Features related to the temporal analysis of the speech signals, while the second one proposes a technique that derives from the Direct Sequence Spread Spectrum, which consists in distributing the signal energy to hide on a wider band transmission.

Due to space limits, this paper is only an extended abstract. The full version will contain further details on our research.

**Keywords:** Synthetic detection · Modulation · Temporal feature · Steganography · Information hiding · Speech signal covert communication · Data embedding · Spread spectrum · Signal processing

## 1 Introduction

This paper was developed starting from the hypothesis that automatic systems generate conversations using a synthetic voice, whose breaks, where a comfort noise is usually inserted, contain text messages, to be sent to a specific recipient through a VoIP phone call. The idea of the scenario is to use the artifice of the synthetic voice as a tool to confuse a hypothetical observer, thus giving the

This work has been partially supported by the TENACE PRIN Project (no. 20103P34XC) funded by the Italian Ministry of Education, University and Research.

© Springer International Publishing Switzerland 2016
Y.-Q. Shi et al. (Eds.): IWDW 2015, LNCS 9569, pp. 145–159, 2016.
DOI: 10.1007/978-3-319-31960-5_13

possibility to transmit hidden messages from one point to another without the risk of being caught. In this scenario there are two important phases: first, the recognition of a synthetic voice from the human one, taking as object of analysis a VoIP conversation intercepted and rebuilt; second, the introduction of the steganographic method, which could be used in VoIp conversations, but in our case it will be applied directly to audio files of conversations.

In [2] a biometric voice verification system was initially proposed. The development of such systems implies very deep studies for safety purposes, to prevent that false identities are exchanged for real ones [9,13]. To prevent a false identity to be mistaken for a real one, the current safety studies start with the discrimination of a human voice from a synthetic one. This work uses techniques of vocal signals and aims at illustrating two new algorithms (MelFCC and MagM) able to recognize human voices. Our research was inspired by the apporoach in [12], where techniques for voice verification/conversion were introduced. Usually, in these techniques the voice signal is not input to directly the system that performs the processing of the voice, but it is first transformed into a more compact and meaningful representation [12], that allows to obtain a set of properties named "features" [10], that use the well-know Mel scale [8], which approximates the human auditory system response. The Mel-Frequency Cepstral Coefficients (MFCCs) are coefficients that collectively make up the Mel-Frequency Cepstrum (MFC), which are a short-term representation of power spectrum of a voice signal. A cepstrum is the result of taking the Inverse Fourier transform (IFT) of the logarithm of the estimated spectrum of a signal and the power cepstrum in particular finds applications in the analysis of human speech [1]. The MFCCs (Mel Frequency Cepstral Coefficients [1,8]) are calculated for each single frame without knowing the next frame (frame by frame), therefore, it is very difficult to capture the correlations between frames, or the temporal characteristics. On the other hand, the frame-based operation in the process of synthesizing voice can introduce temporal artifacts [11]. In order to consider the subsequent frame dependence and therefore capture temporal artifacts generated by synthetic voice, modulation properties were used to develop another algorithm for extraction of features, together with the implementation of an additional technique that is able to discriminate the human voice from synthetic one, named Magnitude Modulation. The modulation features, derived from the amplitude spectrum, carry a long term temporal voice information and therefore, are able to detect temporal artifacts due to the frame by frame processing in synthesizing voice signal [3,4,7]. The modulation features were used to capture the audio frame change in order to recognize the synthesized voice. In our study, to carry out discrimination, were produced two identical versions (length and vocabulary used) by two different voice conversations, one containing the human voice, the other with a synthesized voice. Each conversation was divided into parts of equal length and each of them has been subjected to the analysis of algorithms implemented. Similar partitioning was performed on individual conversations after have been transmitted through a VoIP phone call, whose client used G. 711 codec.

In many VoIP telephony services, a signal called Comfort Noise (CN) is introduced into the conversation breaks. The presence of this signal allows partners to have the feeling that the line remains on, even during long or above average breaks. This signal is typically generated directly to the terminals, but, at the source side, you can insert a hidden signal that contains a text message $M$, which, as such, is recognized as a network communication activities and therefore encoded as if it were a voice, tricking monitoring system, located downstream from the recipient, mistaking for CN. Since the direct insertion of a text message, appropriately converted to a digital signal within the CN, would produce a peak clearly visible with a simple frequency signal analysis, this work proposes a steganographic technique, known in signal-processing as Direct Sequence Spread Spectrum (DSSS). The DSSS allows to distribute the same earlier information (energy of the converted text message) on a wider transmission bandwidth, thus eliminating the peak emerged from the frequency analysis of the background noise. This process does not change the overall power of the signal, which must be sufficiently higher than noise to allow reconstruction at the nodes, because the decrease in average spectral power density (dBm/Hz) is compensated by the enlargement of the bandwidth [5,6].

## 2 Synthetic Voice Detection

Some methods to recognize the synthetic voice from the human voice work at frame level, i.e. splitting the signal into segments and lead, in the first instance, separate analysis on them. Some of these techniques are focused on the study of the characteristics of the signal amplitude such as the MFCC (Mel Frequency Cepstral Coefficient), others, such as the MGDCC (Modified Group Delay Cepstral Coefficients), exploit some properties of the phase of the signal (and, therefore, its group delay). Both MFCC and MGDCC do not allow to derive correlations between different frames as well as the temporal characteristics of the extracted features. MM methods (Magnitude Modulation) and PM (Phase Modulation) are respectively based on previous MFCC and MGDCC, but they introduce additional processing that make possible to engage the temporal relations between different frames, projecting features in an analysis of medium-long term. This work used exclusively structured analytic methods of signal amplitude, i.e. the MFCC and MM.

### 2.1 MFCC (Mel-Frequency Cepstral Coefficients)

To derive the MFCC coefficients of a given signal it is necessary to process it by the analysis of Short Time Fourier Transform (STFT), assuming that the signal is quasi-stationary within a short period (for example a 25 ms window).

The STFT of a signal voice $x(n)$ is as follows:

$$X(\omega) = |X(\omega)|e^{i\Phi(\omega)} = X_{real}(\omega) + iX_{imaginary}(\omega)$$

where $|X(\omega)|$ is the magnitude spectrum, $\Phi(\omega)$ is the phase spectrum and $i = \sqrt{-1}$. We note that $X(\omega)$ has two parts: real part

$$X_{real}(\omega) = \sqrt{(X_{real}(\omega))^2 + (X_{imaginary}(\omega))^2}$$

and imaginary part

$$X_{imaginary}(\omega) = \arctan(\frac{X_{imaginary}(\omega)}{X_{real}(\omega)})$$

The power spectrum is defined to be $|X(\omega)|^2$.

Before running the STFT, and then derive the MFCCs, we must preprocess the speech signal and divide it into separate windows. The pre-processing consists in:

1. The speech signal is divided into overlapping segments of equal size with duration of 25 ms, called frames, with a percentage of overlap between consecutive frames of 50 %.
2. Each frame is multiplied by a "window function," in our case we used the Hamming window function needed to mitigate the effect that would create, in the subsequent extraction of features, if you used a finite-size segment, thinning the edges which lie at the beginning and end of each frame and avoiding ghostly artifacts.

After terminated the pre-processing, the Mel-Frequency Cepstral Coefficients are obtained for each frame window using the following steps:

1. Apply the FFT (Fast Fourier Transform) to compute for each frame the spectrum $X(\omega)$ of $x(n)$.
2. Compute the power spectrum $(|X(\omega)|)^2$.
3. Process the Filter-Bank Energies (FBE) applying the Mel frequency filter-bank to the power spectrum $(|X(\omega)|)^2$.
4. Apply the Discrete Cosine Transform (DCT) to access the scale of the FBE and enable us so to calculate the MFCCs.

## Features Extraction from MFCC

1. The signal is decomposed into frames consisting of $n$ points with $m$ shift points.
2. For each frame the above analysis described is conduct to obtain $c$ Mel coefficients.
3. From the $c$ Mel coefficients, new coefficients are derived, defined by the two following functions "DELTA" and "DELTA-DELTA":

DELTA. Consider a vector $x$ of $K$ elements

$$x(0), x(1), \ldots, x(K-1)$$

The DELTA is the function $\delta_{x,N}$ defined as follows:

$$\delta_{x,N}(k) = \begin{cases} x(k) & k \in \{-1,\ldots,N\} \cup \{K-N,\ldots,K\} \\ \frac{\sum_{i=1}^{N} i(x(k+i)-x(k-i))}{2\sum_{i=1}^{N} i^2} & k \in \{N,N+1,\ldots,K-N\} \end{cases}$$

DELTA-DELTA. Once defined $\delta_{x,N}$, the DELTA-DELTA is defined as follows:

$$\delta\delta_{x,N}(k) = \begin{cases} \delta_{x,N}(x(k)) & k \in \{-1,\ldots,N\} \cup \{K-N,\ldots,K\} \\ \frac{\sum_{i=1}^{N} i(\delta_{x,N}(x(k+i))-\delta_{x,N}(x(k-i)))}{2\sum_{i=1}^{N} i^2} & k \in \{N,N+1,\ldots,K-N\} \end{cases}$$

Notice that $\delta\delta_{x,N}(k) = \delta_{x,N}(\delta_{x,N}(k))$. The coefficients computed through DELTA and DELTA-DELTA are known as the "differential" and the "acceleration" coefficients, respectively. Because the voice seems to contain dynamic information that is distributed over time and because the MFCC feature vectors only describe the power spectral envelope of a single frame, the DELTA coefficients allow to calculate the trajectories of the MFCC coefficient over time. The DELTA-DELTA coefficients are calculated in a similar way, but this time starting from DELTA and not from the MFCC static coefficients.
4. For each frame is obtained a vector of length $3c$.

If $N$ is the number of frames where the signal has been split, connecting the $N$ vectors of length $3c$, we get a super vector of length $3cN$. The variance of this super vector is the feature of the signal under test.

## 2.2  Magnitude Modulation (MM)

The modulation features, obtained from amplitude spectrum, contain information on long-term temporal features of voice signal, and therefore are able to detect temporal artifacts due to the frame by frame processing in synthesizing voice signal. The modulation features were thus used to capture frame variations for synthesized voice.

## Features Extraction from Magnitude Modulation (MM)

1. Divides the signal into frames, consisting of $n_{FFT}$ points with $m_{FFT}$ shift samples.
2. Defines a "segment" consisting of $n$ consecutive frames of the type described in Sect. 1, with $m$ frame shift. The value of $n$ must be sufficiently large to allow the capture of temporal information.
3. From the spectrum of each frame gets $c$ coefficients of the filtered banks by Mel scale ($c$ Mel-scale filter-bank coefficients). It defines "path filter-bank" the $n$ points set of the same coefficient of Mel.
4. Applies a MVN (Unitary Mean Zero Variance) for each trajectory of filterbank to normalize the average and variance from zero to one.
5. For each normalized trajectory, calculates the power density spectrum, calculated with a different number of FFT points ($nS$) (considering only the positive frequencies and therefore consists of $\frac{nS}{2}$ points).

6. For the current window, gets an array that consists of $c$ rows and $\frac{nS}{2}$ columns, vector given by concatenating of the $c$ rows and $\frac{nS}{2}$ coefficients.
7. Due to the large size and to the high correlation of the spectral modulation, derived from different trajectories of filter-bank, it is necessary to reduce the size by applying a Principal Component Analysis (PCA) method. For each window, it is calculated the maximum PCA variance among the possible $c$ (the PCA is applied considering as variables the Mel's coefficients and the frames as observations).

At the end of the above described process, if $K$ is the number of windows where the signal has been devided, we get $K$ variances. In this experimental work we used as feature of the signal the average (arithmetic mean) of the $K$ maximum variances.

## 2.3    Experiments and Results

The study covers the extraction of the features related to the conversation files (syntetic and human), which were divided in 17 and 16 parts. The features to extract are 33 for the audio signal with human voice and 33 for the audio signal with synthetic voice. Each of the $2N$ files available ($N = 33$ human and $N = 33$ synthetic) were submitted to MelFCC (Mel Frequency Cepstral Coefficients) and MagM (Modulation Magnitude) analysis. To evaluate the performance of the two methods, the study adopts the EER (Error Equal Rate). The EER is the error rate that results when the percentage of the human voice is incorrectly classified as a synthetic one and it is equal to the percentage of synthetic voice incorrectly classified as a human voice. The two parameters considered were the FAR (False Acceptance Rate) and FRR (False Rejection Rate). The FAR, specifies how often the system is tricked, i.e. when a synthetic voice gets wrongly perceived as a human voice. The FRR, specifies the frequency with which the system fails to indicate that a human voice is truly human. Lower is the EER value, better will be the performance. In order to calculate the variance of the trajectories produced by the models between the different signals (synthetic and human) there was produced a simulation with the two methods of analysis proposed (MelFCC and MagM).

Each point on the blue curve corresponds to a feature of one of the 33 parts of 2 human conversation files. Similarly, each point of the green curve is given from the feature derived from the 33 parts of 2 synthetic conversation files. The curves shown in Fig. 1 are the result of an experimental standardization process, whose steps will be described in detail. This work is based on the assumption that events logging of digital files, can be characterized, from a statistical point of view, in such a way that the features associated with human speech, as well as those relating to synthesized conversations, are determinations of a variable of a stationary and ergodic random process.

We consider three random variables: $r$, which is extracted from the $R(t)$ process, associated with the "real signal" $E_r$, with expected value $m_r$; variable $s$, that is extracted from process $S(t)$ concerning the event "synthetic signal" $E_s$,

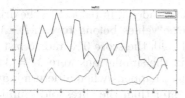 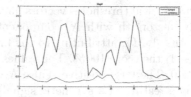

**Fig. 1.** MelFCC and MagM graphs curves (Color figure online).

with expected value $m_s$; variable $x$, extracted from the process $X(t)$, associated with the event "signal" $E_x$ given by the union event "real signal" with the event "synthetic signal" ($E_x = E_r \cup E_s$). We adopt the following assumptions:

1. Variable $r$ has $N$ determinations in a $R$ set of equally probable values.
2. Variable $s$ has $N$ determinations in a set $S$ of equally probable values.
3. Variable $x$ has $2N$ determinations in a set $X$ of equally probable values (as of $R$ and $S$), where the first $N$ determinations belong to set $R$ and the determinations by the $(N+1)$-th to the $2N$-th belong to set $S$.
4. Both $R(t)$ and $S(t)$ are stationary and ergodic (then $X(t)$ is the same).

The expected value of the random variable $x$ is

$$E(x) = \sum_{i=1}^{2N} \frac{1}{2N} x_i = \sum_{i=1}^{N} \frac{x_i}{2N} + \sum_{i=N+1}^{2N} \frac{x_i}{2N} = \frac{m_r}{2} + \frac{m_s}{2} = m_x$$

that is given by the arithmetic mean of the two expected values $m_r$ and $m_s$.

Thus, proceeding to a experimental normalization, as depicted in Fig. 2, if $x$ is the vector of the $2N$ determinations of the random cumulative variable $x$, taking away $m_x$ to each of $2N$ determinations (or features), it gets a new random variable with expected value zero. In order to make it with single variance, simply compute the variance of the new random variable $(x - m_x)$ and split each of the new $2N$ for this determination. As shown in Fig. 2, the straight line parallel to $x$-axis through the origin is a little "watershed" between the features of human signals and those of the synthetic conversations.

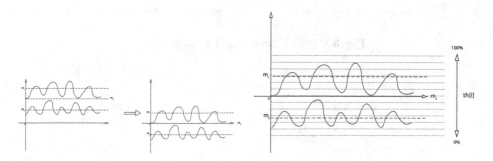

**Fig. 2.** Experimental normalization of random variable $x$.

Symmetrical thresholds vectors have been considered in respect to the origin, namely vectors th with $N_t$ components, whose values belong to $\{-M, -M + 1, \ldots, M - 1, M\}$, attributing to the first cell th[0] the score 0 % and to last cell th[$N_t - 1$] the score 100 %. The values used in the simulations were $M = 3$ and $N_t = 240$. The false positive (False Acceptance) happens when a determination (that is a feature of a synthetic signal) is greater than the threshold. Similarly the false negative FR (False Rejection) happens when a value of $r$ (in other words, a feature of a real signal) is less than the threshold.

We denote by Fr the vector of false negative FRR (False Rejection Rate), with $N_t$ length, and by Fa the vector of false positives FAR (False Acceptance Rate). For each threshold value th[$i$], Fr(th[$i$]) is the number of points on the curve of real signals that are under the threshold, divided by $N$, while the Fa(th[$i$]) is the number of points on the curve synthetic signals which are above the threshold, divided by $N$. The Fr curve increases with the value of th[$i$], while Fa decreases. There will be a th[$j$] threshold value for which Fr(th[$j$]) = Fr(th[$j$]) = EER (Equal Error Rate).

## 2.4 VoIP Conversations Analysis with MelFCC and MagM Algorithms

Also in this case the study proceeded by applying the algorithms MelFCC and MagM to human voice files and to synthesized voice files, obtained through a VoIP connection. The following figures report the obtained results and show there is not a substantial difference in the operation of the algorithms we used. EER curves for both algorithms demonstrate that it is possible to discriminate a human voice from a synthetic one, even for VoIP conversations, confirming the greater goodness (more value the EER) of MagM algorithm than the MelFCC (Figs. 3, 4 and 5). In Table 1 we can observe EER values obtained from the simulations.

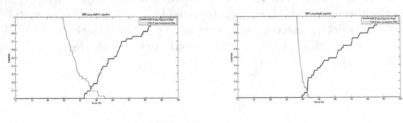

**Fig. 3.** MelFCC and MagM EER graphs.

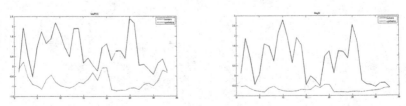

**Fig. 4.** MelFCC and MagM VoIP graphs curves.

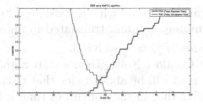
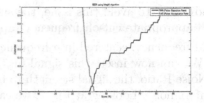

**Fig. 5.** MelFCC and MagM EER VoIP graphs

**Table 1.** EER Values

|         | No-VoIP | VoIP   |
|---------|---------|--------|
| MelFCC  | 0.1212  | 0.1515 |
| MagM    | 0.0606  | 0.0758 |

## 3 Steganography: Direct Sequence Spread Spectrum

In Fig. 6 we have a representation, both in time and frequency domain, of a 50 ms duration Comfort Noise signal, sampled at 32 KHz and estimated spectrum of 4096 FFT points. Supposing to have a bits sequence, derived from a text encoding, as a message $M$ to be transmitted. Each character is encoded with $n_B$ bits (for example 8 in ASCII). A message of a length of $n_C$ characters, will produce a $n_C n_B$ bits length message to be transmitted. Consider for example these possible initial 18 bits, obtained by encoding some text characters: 01111000, 11010111, and 11. $T_b$ is the bit time. With reference to the sampling rate of 32 kHz, it follows that a single bit corresponds to $n_{\text{samplePerBit}} = T_b f_s$ samples. Setting the interval bit to 32 ms and having sampling rate like 32 kHz we get a $n_{\text{samplePerBit}}$ of 1024 samples. Therefore, the previous 18-bit sequence will be used in a window of a 576 ms time and composed of 18432 samples. A signal of this type will never be transmitted because its drastic changes in amplitude will produce very large high frequency components, thus requiring a very large transmission

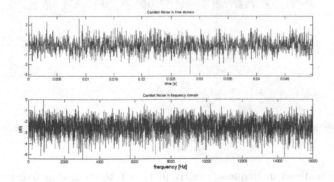

**Fig. 6.** Comfort noise in time and frequency domains.

bandwidth. To avoid this issue, the signal can be filtered with a low-pass filter with appropriate cut-off frequency (approximately $\frac{0.5}{T_b}$) and translated in audio band frequency, centered in a frequency carrier of $f_c = \frac{f_s}{4} = 8\,\text{KHz}$.

We can now insert this signal inside the Comfort Noise, then a 3dB Signal to Noise Ratio, the signal strength to be inserted will be about twice that of the comfort noise. Looking at Fig. 7, we can realize that in the domain of time it is pretty hard to note an anomaly, but in the frequency domain we notice a visible peak frequency.

In order to improve this method, and inspired by papers [5,6], we introduce a technique called Spread Spectrum, which allows to eliminate the peak that previously emerged of about 16 dB from the background noise. For example, Fig. 8 shows two signals with associated power equal to about −44 dBm (40 nW), but having respectively (in blue), power physics average spectral density, of about $\frac{-71\,dBm}{Hz}$ ($\frac{79.5\,pW}{Hz}$), for a band of 500 Hz, and that wider (green) power physics average spectral density of about $\frac{-86\,dBm}{Hz}$ ($\frac{2.5\,pW}{Hz}$), for a 16 KHz band.

Figure 8 shows that if we decrease the power spectral density, we can get results by widening the bandwidth, thus, if the signal carries a binary message, also a considerable increase in throughput, i.e. reduction of bit time $T_b$. In order to broaden the signal bandwidth, without increasing the bit transmission speed (therefore decreasing $T_b$) we must multiply the signal, each bit time $T_b$, for another signal, named Spreading, that for simplicity is always the same for each bit interval (but in theory it could be used an algorithm to modify it) consisting of a number $S_f$ (Spreading factor) of bits not carrying any information, because they are repeated periodically, each of which has a chip time durability $T_c = T_b/S_f$. It follows that the number of samples for each interval ($T_c$) chips will be a $S_f$-th for each bit interval ($T_b$). According to the general principle presented, we decided to multiply the signal, each bit time $T_b = 32\,\text{ms}$, for a Pseudo Noise sequence of spreading, to ensure a more evenly distributed spectrum in the

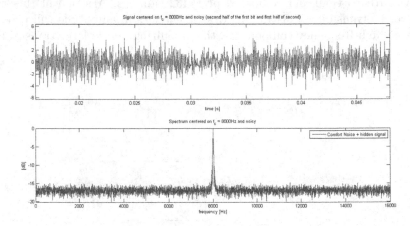

**Fig. 7.** Signal centered in frequency 8KHz in time (above) and in frequency (below) domains.

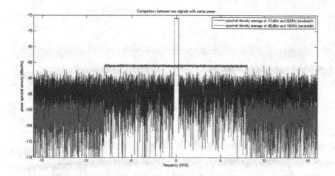

**Fig. 8.** Comparison between two signals with same power (Color figure online).

existence band. Using a spreading sequences of this type, spectrum will be as flat as possible. Selecting a spreading factor $S_f = 256$, the chip time of PN sequence (which will multiply the signal bit time for bit time) will be $T_c = \frac{T_b}{S_f}$, i.e. $32 \cdot 10^{-3}/256 = 125\,\mu s$.

Therefore we have again a difficult distinction in the time domain, but this time the distinction will be difficult even in the frequency domain, since there will no longer be the presence of a carrier wave with a peak spectral density that emerges from the depths of about 16 dB. In Fig. 9 we can observe a comparison between the first and the second technique of steganography.

The last comparison locates the only critical point of the technique previously presented. In the first technique we did a simple analysis of the signal density spectrum to detect an anomaly, but the Spread Spectrum technique can be noticed just by considering the signal power density spectrum to the second power. Indeed, although it is difficult to see any trace of the modulated signal in occult way, if we look at the spectrum in Fig. 10, we can notice the presence of a spectral density peak at $f = f_c = 8\,KHz$ and two other equally spaced peaks from $f_c$.

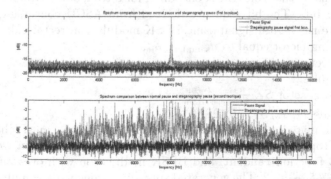

**Fig. 9.** Spectrum comparisons between normal and steganography pause.

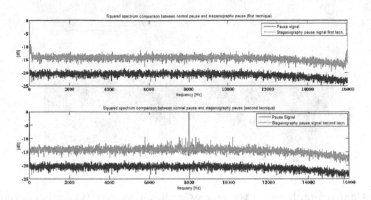

**Fig. 10.** Squared spectrum comparisons between normal and steganography pause.

## 3.1   Application and Results

To implement the steganography algorithm, the 33 synthetic files were examined to identify the files with long pauses. From the examination 3 files were chosen, and then the study applied the steganography algorithm, getting the same results for each one. The text message that was transmitted and subsequently recovered was "Rome22May," indicating a place and a day of the week, to simulate the will of sending occult logistic and temporal informations.

1. Pre-processing phase
   Used variables:
   - Hiddentext = "Rome22May" 9 characters
   - Number of samples for bit $n_{\mathrm{SampleForBit}} = 136$
   - Frequency sampling $f_s = 22050\,\mathrm{Hz}$
   - Bit time $T_b$, $n_{\mathrm{SampleForBit}}/f_s = 0.0062\,\mathrm{s}$
   - Number of samples for chip $n_{\mathrm{SampleForChip}} = 2$

   After identifying the time period containing the longest pause and inserted the comfort noise signal within all pauses, the hiding message has been converted to bits by using the 8 bit ASCII encoding, for a total of 9 characters of 8 bits, namely 72 bits. The bit sequence derived from ASCII conversion was used to generate the digital signal using BPSK modulation, rectangular filter and oversampling factor equal to $n_{\mathrm{samplePerBit}}$.

2. Spread Spectrum phase
   Used variables:
   - SpreadingFactor $S_f$, $\frac{n_{\mathrm{SampleForBit}}}{n_{\mathrm{SampleForChip}}} = 68$
   - Chip time $T_c$, $T_b/S_f = 9.12 \cdot 10^{-5}$

   Once modulated, the spreading binary sequence must have good spectral properties, looking like a white noise. For this reason we used the MATLAB function randint, and BPSK modulation with oversampling factor of $\frac{n_{\mathrm{SamplePerBit}}}{S_f} = 2$. The generated spreading sequence was multiplied with the previously generated digital signal, for each bit time. In order to reduce the bandwidth occupation, a 256-th order minimum phase filter (FIR) was applied, low-pass with $\frac{f_c}{2} = 2$ cut-off frequency, where $f_c = \frac{1}{T_c} = 2$, $T_c = $ chip time equal to $\frac{T_b}{S_f}$. The spreading signal was filtered and used to modulate a carrier frequency $f_p$ and summed to the comfort noise signal to be inserted into the pause of the audio file selected (see Fig. 11).

3. De-Spreading phase

The De-Spreading phase requires that the recipient is aware of the following parameters:

- startSample and stopSample of the signal audio received.
- $n_{\text{SamplePerChip}}$ value and SpreadingFactor value.
- $f_p$ carrier frequency where the signal was modulated.
- Spreading/De-Spreading sequence, composed by $S_f$ binary symbols.

From the audio signal received, containing the hidden text message, the portion in question was extracted for the process of steganography, and restored in the base-band. This is obtained by multiplying the signal by $\cos(2\pi f_p t)$ and applying a lowpass filter to remove the $2f_p$ replication. The BPSK signal with a binary frequency equal to $f_c = f_b S_f$, has been demodulated exploiting the small oversampling factor equal to 2, to get a signal with an antipodal levels signal 1, and $-1$. The reconstruction of the spreading binary signal was obtained by applying the sign function $(1 - \text{sign}())/2$, which passes from the antipodal levels 1 and $-1$ to the logic levels 0 and 1. The bits sequence that we got, equal to 9792 bit ($N_b \times n_{\text{SamplePerBit}}$), was organized in an array of $N_b$ rows by $n_{\text{SamplePerBit}}$ columns. Each row corresponds to one bit of the ASCII encoded text message which has been sent. To get the despreading bit sequence we carried a series of mathematical operations, applying the XOR function, between the received bits and the spreading bits sequence. The generic $r$ line of the despreading matrix, is given by $\text{XOR}(c, s)$, where $c$ is a binary string of $n_{\text{SamplePerBit}}$ bit, all equals the ASCII encoding bits of the case, and $s$ is the binary version of spreading sequence. Because the receiver knows $s$, she will compute $\text{XOR}(\text{XOR}(c, s), s) = \text{XOR}(c, \text{XOR}(s, s)) = \text{XOR}(c, z) = c$, where $z = 00 \cdots 0$.

After the despreading process, for each bit of the binary ASCII sequence of the transmitted text, $n_{\text{SamplePerBit}}$ bits were obtained, which should be all equal to each other and equal to the original text bits transmitted. In the case that something was received incorrectly, the error can be recovered as long as at least $n_{\text{SamplePerBit}}/2 + 1$ are properly received. To recover the 72 bits of the ASCII encoding text transmitted we proceeded to conduct a review with a majority decision for every 136-bit sequence ($\frac{9792}{136} = 72$), which is equal to the value we used for $n_{\text{SamplePerBit}}$.

The process of recovering the transmitted text was completed by applying the function that transforms the binary sequence obtained into 8-bit ASCII characters, from which was derived the information "Rome22May," which was been transmitted in covert mode.

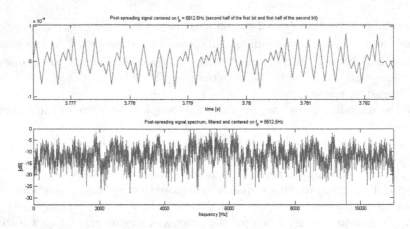

**Fig. 11.** Post-spreading signal centered on 5512.5Hz in time (above) and frequency (below) domains.

## 4   Conclusions

This work showed the feasibility of the initial scenario assumptions, concerning the transmission using steganography techniques of hidden messages through VoIP calls and the use of a synthetic voice audio signals. In that regard, the Mel Frequency Cepstral Coefficient (MelFCC) algorithm and the Magnitude Modulation (MagM) algorithms have been developed, based on the analysis of the voice detection techniques proposed in the literature, to discriminate a human voice audio signal from a synthetic voice audio signal. The results showed that these algorithms have basically the same behavior, whether applied to the original file, synthetic or human, whether transmitted through a VoIP phone call. The steganography algorithm proposed, based on the application of the technique called "Spread Spectrum," has allowed us to confirm that we can hide a text within the comfort noise introduced in the pauses (as normally happens in a telephone call) of an audio file.

## References

1. Bogert, B.P., Healy, M.J.R., Tukey, J.W.: The frequency analysis of time series for echoes: cepstrum, pseudo-autocovariance, cross-cepstrum, and saphe cracking. In: Rosenblatt, M. (ed.) Proceedings of Symposium Time Series Analysis, pp. 209–243. Wiley, New York (1963)
2. Campbell, J.P.: Speaker recognition: a tutorial. Proc. IEEE **85**(9), 1437–1462 (1997)
3. Kingsbury, B., Morgan, N., Greenberg, S.: Robust speech recognition using the modulation spectrogram. Speech Commun. **25**(1–3), 117–132 (1998)
4. Kinnunen, T., Lee, K.A., Li, H.: Dimension reduction of the modulation spectrogram for speaker verification. In: Odyssey, p. 30. ISCA (2008)

5. Nugraha, R.: Implementation of direct sequence spread spectrum steganography on audio data. In: 2011 International Conference on Electrical Engineering and Informatics (ICEEI), pp. 1–6, July 2011

6. Rupanshi, Preeti, V.: Vandana: Audio steganography by direct sequence spread spectrum. Int. J. Comput. Trends Tech. (IJCTT), Published Seventh Sense Res Group **13**, 83–86 (2014)

7. Sam, S., Xiao, X., Besacier, L., Castelli, E., Li, H., Siong, C.E.: Speech modulation features for robust nonnative speech accent detection. In: INTERSPEECH, pp. 2417–2420. ISCA (2011)

8. Stevens, S.S., Volkmann, J., Newman, E.B.: A scale for the measurement of the psychological magnitude pitch. J. Acoust. Soc. America **8**(3), 185–190 (1937)

9. Stylianou, Y., Cappe, O., Moulines, E.: Continuous probabilistic transform for voice conversion. IEEE Trans. Speech Audio Process. **6**(2), 131–142 (1998)

10. Wolf, J.J.: Efficient acoustic parameters for speaker recognition. J. Acoust. Soc. America **51**(6B), 2044–2056 (1972)

11. Wu, Z., Siong, C.E., Li, H.: Detecting converted speech and natural speech for anti-spoofing attack in speaker recognition. In: INTERSPEECH, pp. 1700–1703. ISCA (2012)

12. Wu, Z., Xiao, X., Chng, E., Li, H.: Synthetic speech detection using temporal modulation feature. In: ICASSP, pp. 7234–7238. IEEE (2013)

13. Yamagishi, J., Kobayashi, T., Nakano, Y., Ogata, K., Isogai, J.: Analysis of speaker adaptation algorithms for HMM-based speech synthesis and a constrained smaplr adaptation algorithm. IEEE Trans. Audio Speech Lang. Process. **17**(1), 66–83 (2009)

# Digital Watermarking

# Fingerprinting for Broadcast Content Distribution System

Minoru Kuribayashi$^{(\boxtimes)}$

Graduate School of Natural Science and Technology, Okayama University,
3-1-1 Tsushima-naka, Kita-ku, Okayama 700-8530, Japan
kminoru@okayama-u.ac.jp

**Abstract.** The objective of traitor tracing technique is to enable a broadcaster to identify illegal users from secret keys issued to them. In a broadcast encryption scheme, although a broadcaster can identify a traitor when a secret key is leaked, the decrypted copy is not protected from illegal distribution. In the fingerprinting scheme, a broadcaster can trace illegal users from a pirated copy because each user purchases the copy watermarked by his own fingerprint. However, the transaction to distribute the copy is one-to-one. In this paper, we have proposed a broadcast-type fingerprinting scheme such that only authorized users who have own decryption key can obtain the fingerprinted copy.

## 1 Introduction

Due to the spread of computer networks, multimedia content such as music, images, movies, etc. can be broadcasted in an easy and cheap way. However, they also facilitate the illegal distribution of the copies. In order to prevent the illegal distribution or illegal reception, cryptographic techniques and watermarking techniques have been investigated.

Broadcast encryption schemes define methods for encrypting content so that only privileged users can recover the content from broadcasted data. It provides a convenient way to distribute content to users over an insecure broadcast channel, which allows a broadcaster to deliver information to dynamically changing sets of users. The first idea of the broadcast encryption is introduced in [5], and a traceability from the distinct key issued to each user is developed in [4]. The exclusion of a subset of users from receiving information could be required due to lack of payment, subscription of expiration date, or leak of the key. In the broadcast encryption, a broadcaster can enforce conditional access by selectively encrypting content so that only the privileged users can decrypt it. However, the employment of the broadcast encryption scheme introduces a certain system overhead, and it is impossible to protect against illegal distribution of the decrypted content.

In many applications, there is a time bound associated with each access control policy so that a users is assigned to a certain class for just a period of time. The user's key need to be updated periodically to keep his right for the access.

© Springer International Publishing Switzerland 2016
Y.-Q. Shi et al. (Eds.): IWDW 2015, LNCS 9569, pp. 163–175, 2016.
DOI: 10.1007/978-3-319-31960-5_14

In a tree structured environment, time-bound hierarchical key management schemes [1,15] have been proposed for secure broadcasting applications. However, the scheme presented in [15] is insecure against collusion attacks, and the scheme [1] requires a tamper resistant device for the security reason.

A simple solution to trace the rebroadcasting source is to embed a fingerprint of each user's identity information and to trace it by examining the fingerprint in the rebroadcasted content. Dynamic traitor tracing scheme [6,9] allows a broadcaster to trace traitors with a little sacrifice of bandwidth. The basic idea is to break time into consecutive intervals and modify the watermarking strategy of the system in each interval using the rebroadcasted content. After observing the rebroadcast for long enough time, one or more traitors can be traced. However, the method is completely ineffective against delayed rebroadcast attack such that the traitors rebroadcast the content with some delay. Sequential traitor tracing scheme [10] improves the dynamic scheme so that the channel feedback is only used for tracing, not for allocation of marks to users. Although the sequential scheme can trace traitors from broadcasted content, a broadcaster cannot prove the fact to an arbiter. Because he knows the content finally distributed to a user, he may attempt to frame an innocent user by distributing it by himself. Therefore, an asymmetric property is required so that only the user can know the fingerprinted content being decrypted from broadcasted ciphertext.

Fingerprinting scheme enables a merchant to identify the buyer of illegally distributed multimedia content by providing each buyer with a slightly different ones. And the asymmetric property is achieved by using several cryptographic techniques. Regretfully, the existing fingerprinting schemes [3,7,8,12] are only applicable for one-to-one transaction.

In this paper, we present a new broadcasting system with asymmetric property and traitor tracing capability from both decryption keys and distributed content. The basic idea is to introduce a time-bound key management scheme into a fingerprinting scheme so that a user key issued at a trusted center is available within a certain expiration date. The expiration date is hierarchically designed to the secret information issued to each user. As a result, each user receives the content with his fingerprint without increasing both the computational costs and the amount of transmission data required for the broadcaster to broadcast the content. Furthermore, the asymmetric property is achieved by ingeniously managing the keys issued to each user. In our system, once an illegal copy is detected, a traitor must pay the compensation for all content during a period $TW$ even if he bought a license to receive the content during the time $T_2$ from $T_1$ that is within the period $TW$. Such a risk may effectively work for the prevention of illegal distribution.

## 2    Preliminaries

Our proposed scheme is to apply the time-bound key management scheme combined with fingerprinting scheme for the construction of content distribution system. In this section, we review the broadcast encryption scheme and point out the potential problems. Then, the summary of time-bound key management scheme is described, and the applied fingerprinting protocol based on a key management is shown.

## 2.1  Broadcast Encryption

Broadcast encryption scheme enables a broadcaster to send information securely to a group of receivers excluding specified receivers called revoked receivers over a broadcast channel. One of the main applications of this technology is digital rights management of copyrighted content. In this scheme, only privileged receivers who have collect receiver keys can retrieve session keys to encrypt or decrypt the content. If these receiver keys are stolen or exposed, these keys are revoked from the system by adaptively designing the broadcasting ciphertexts.

Broadcast encryption schemes were first formalized by Fiat and Naor [5], and the traceability was introduced in [4], which enables a broadcaster to identify a traitor from illegally distributed keys. In the broadcast encryption scheme, the data to be broadcasted is composed of two ciphertexts: one is the encrypted session-encrypting key (SEK) which is considered as a header information, and the other is the encrypted content using SEK. The decryption of the SEK is possible for only privileged users who have their own receiver keys, which are called key-encrypting key (KEK). Because KEK of each user is distinct, the owner of KEK is identified.

The main goal is to construct efficient schemes that can revoke a set of users with only small size of both the header information and the decryption keys while the private decryption keys issued to users are fixed [11]. However, the broadcast encryption schemes contain two difficult problems. Once the broadcasted content is delivered to legitimate users, the broadcaster cannot prevent the users from distributing the illegal copy. In addition, since the revocation is governed by the supplier, he must know each user's decryption key. Under such a situation, he cannot prove to someone else that the leaked decryption key is come from a traitor even if he actually finds it, because he may distribute the key by himself to frame a legitimate user.

## 2.2  Time-Bound Key Management

The idea of time-bound key services is to construct a key in such a way that it is automatically activated and deactivated, and the expiration date is freely chosen by a user. On a broadcast system, the transition of privileged users may be done rapidly. In applications such as pay-TV, it is desirable to broadcast content with low and constant complexities independent on the transition of users. Now suppose that each user key has its expiration date. Then, a broadcaster need not to adjust his broadcast system to the transition of users even if users illegally distribute their keys because such keys become useless after expiration date, which decreases the key management costs. What a broadcaster should do is the monitoring of networks to detect the illegal distribution.

A formal model of the time-bound key management scheme is summarized by means of probabilistic polynomial-time algorithms.

**Definition 1.** *The time-bound key management is a quadruple of polynomial-time algorithms (*Init*,* KeyGen*,* KeyEnc*,* KeyDec*) such that:*

- Init *is an algorithm used by a broadcaster to set up parameters of the system. It takes an integer seed that makes the behavior of the other algorithms.*
- KeyGen *is an algorithm to compute a user key with expiration date. The date is designed by a broadcaster using parameters generated from seed.*
- KeyEnc *is an algorithm by a broadcaster to generate an encryption key. It takes a current time and parameters generated from seed, and outputs a current key, which is assumed as a session-encryption key similar to the broadcast encryption scheme.*
- KeyDec *is an algorithm by a user to generate a decryption key. It takes a user key and a current time, and outputs the key that will be the same one as the encryption key during the expiration date, otherwise outputs $\perp$ which is not available for decryption.*

In the time-bound key management scheme, a master key $K_{\{0,\infty\}}$ that is owned by a broadcaster can be used for the generation every piece of keys, and user keys $K_{\{T_1,T_2\}}$ is only available to generate the piece of keys as long as the time $T_2$ from $T_1$. For example, at a time $T_c$, a user can obtain the current key $K_{T_c}$ if $T_1 \leq T_c \leq T_2$. Public information in the time-bound key management scheme is dependent on the construction.

## 2.3   Fingerprinting

Fingerprinting technique can prevent a user from executing illegal redistribution of digital content by enabling a merchant to identify the original buyer of the redistributed copy. The technique is classified into two schemes. One is the method to produce the fingerprint, and the other is the protocol to embed the fingerprint in digital content. In the fingerprinting technique, each user purchases the content containing his own fingerprint, and hence each content is slightly different. If users collect some of them, they may try to find the difference and try to delete/change the embedded information. In order to withstand such an attack, the former scheme makes an approach by generating specific codes such as c-secure code [2], anti-collusion code (ACC) [14], and Tardos code [13]. On the other hand, a cryptographic protocol for trade between a buyer and a merchant is considered in the latter scheme. If both the buyer and the merchant obtain fingerprinted content in the protocol, the merchant cannot claim that an illegal copy is distributed from the buyer even if the buyer's fingerprint is extracted. Because the merchant can distribute it by himself in order to frame an innocent buyer. So it is desirable that only a buyer can obtain his own fingerprinted content in the protocol, such a protocol is called asymmetric fingerprinting protocol [12]. It is worthy to mention that the employment of Tardos code in the asymmetric protocol is studied in [3].

The basic idea for realizing the asymmetric protocol is to exploit the homomorphic property of public-key cryptosystem that enables a merchant to embed an encrypted fingerprint in an encrypted content. Since the ciphertext is computed using a buyer's encryption key, only the buyer can decrypt it; hence, only he can obtain the fingerprinted content. Although the homomorphic property is effective for constructing asymmetric fingerprinting, there are problems in its low enciphering rate and heavy computational costs. In [7], the enciphering rate is improved by packing several bits in one ciphertext while the computational costs are remained considerably high.

In [8], an efficient asymmetric fingerprinting protocol has been proposed by introducing the management of the enciphering keys for symmetric cryptosystem.

**Definition 2.** *The asymmetric fingerprinting protocol is a quintuple of polynomial-time algorithms (*KeyGen, Reg, Protocol, Tracing, Trial*), performed by three parties, buyer, merchant, and trusted center.*

- KeyGen *is an algorithm used by a merchant to generate a key table. The table is registered at a trusted center.*
- Reg *is an algorithm used by a trusted center to issue a secret key and registration proof for a new buyer.*
- Protocol *is an algorithm both by a buyer and a merchant. The buyer inputs the secret key, identity and registration proof, and the merchant inputs content to the algorithm. Then, the buyer obtains the content which contain his identity, and the merchant obtains a valid record of the transaction.*
- Tracing *is an algorithm that takes as input an illegal copy, and it outputs a certain buyer's identity.*
- Trial *is an algorithm that takes as input an illegal copy, the buyer's identity, and the record of transaction. The algorithm is to be public in order not to be disputed by both a traitor and a merchant.*

In Reg, a trusted center issues a buyer $t$ with a partial sequence $key_t$ such that each element of the sequence is selected based on the buyer's identity,

$$w_t = \{w_{t,j} | 0 \leq j \leq L - 1\}, \tag{1}$$

from each two elements of the whole sequence $k_{t,j}, (0 \leq j \leq 2L - 1)$ which is an extended sequence $g(k_t)$ using a function $g(\cdot)$ and a key $k_t$ listed in a key table.

$$key_t = \{key_{t,j} | 0 \leq j \leq L - 1\}, \tag{2}$$

where

$$key_{t,j} = \begin{cases} k_{t,2j} & (w_{t,j} = 0) \\ k_{t,2j+1} & (w_{t,j} = 1). \end{cases} \tag{3}$$

Considering the security, the function $g(\cdot)$ must achieve the following two requirements

**G1:** For a given $k_{t,j}$, no information about $k_{t,j'}, (j \neq j')$ is leaked.
**G2:** For a given $g(k_t)$, no information about $g(k'_t), (t \neq t')$ is leaked.

Although the merchant shares the whole sequence with the center, he cannot extract the buyer's key sequence from the whole one.

In `Protocol`, the transaction begins when a buyer makes a request to a merchant. We assume that the buyer purchases content $X = \{X_j | 0 \le j \le L - 1\}$. First, the buyer proves that he is a legitimate user by showing a proof of registration issued at a trusted center. Then, the merchant generates two ciphertexts for each packet $X_j, (0 \le j \le L - 1)$ as follows:

1. Two kinds of packets $X_j^{(0)}$ and $X_j^{(1)}$ are calculated for one packet $X_j$ by embedding information bit "0" and "1", respectively.
2. Both the packets $X_j^{(0)}$ and $X_j^{(1)}$ are compressed.
3. An information string that guarantees the success of the decryption is attached to each compressed packet.
4. The compressed packets with information strings are encrypted based on the symmetric cryptosystem. Following this, $k_{t,2j}$ is used for the compressed packet of $X_j^{(0)}$ and $k_{t,2j+1}$ are for that of $X_j^{(1)}$. The produced ciphertexts are denoted by $c_j^{(0)}$ and $c_j^{(1)}$, respectively.
5. The order of two ciphertexts is rearranged by a permutation function $\sigma_j\left(c_j^{(0)}, c_j^{(1)}\right)$.

The buyer decrypts parts of the ciphertexts $\sigma_j\left(c_j^{(0)}, c_j^{(1)}\right)$, $(0 \le j \le L - 1)$, and decompresses the compressed files. Since the buyer's key $key_{t,j}$ is a proper decryption key for one of two ciphertexts $c_j^{(0)}$ and $c_j^{(1)}$, one of two marked packets $X_j^{(0)}$ and $X_j^{(1)}$ is obtained. Here, $key_{t,j}$ is selected based on Eq. (3), and hence what the buyer decrypts from $\sigma_j\left(c_j^{(0)}, c_j^{(1)}\right)$ is $X_j^{(w_j)}$. Therefore, the fingerprinted content can be obtained.

$$X^{(w_t)} = \{X_j^{(w_{t,j})} | w_{t,j} \in \{0,1\}, 0 \le j \le L - 1\} \tag{4}$$

In the protocol, before trade between a buyer and a merchant, the merchant can previously produce the marked packets and compress them, which enables the reduction of both the computational costs for the encryption and the amount of data for transmission. So only the enciphering operation is performed by a merchant during the on-line protocol, and hence real-time operation may be possible.

The above fingerprinting protocol is only available for one to one transaction because of the following reason. If it is expanded for broadcast-type content distribution system, the user key should be issued before broadcasting and should be used more than one time (In a broadcast encryption scheme, only one decryption key is issued for each user until it is revoked). Since the decrypted contents contain a same fingerprint corresponding to the key, a traitor may be framed by a broadcaster for other redistributions which is not responsible for his illegal action. Therefore, a fingerprinting protocol should be performed with one-time secret key of a buyer; hence it is difficult to apply the protocol for broadcasting system.

# 3   Proposed Broadcasting System

In this section, we present a new broadcasting system with the tracing capability from both decryption keys and distributed content. In our system, content is broadcasted in such a way that only authorized users who have own decryption key can obtain the content with distinct fingerprint.

## 3.1   Model

We have four types of parties: broadcaster, users, trusted center, and arbiter who should be convinced in trials. Technically, the role of the arbiter should not be restricted, i.e., it should be possible to convince anyone as long as they know a specific public information.

**Definition 3.** *The proposed broadcasting system is composed of seven polynomial time algorithms* (KeyGen, Reg, Purchase, Broadcast, Reception, Tracing, Trial).

- KeyGen *is an algorithm used by a broadcaster to generate a key table. The key table is registered at a trusted center.*
- Reg *is an algorithm used by a trusted center to issue a secret key* $key_t$ *to a user t using a master key* $k_s$ *and the user's identity* $w_t$. *Then, registration proof is also issued.*
- Purchase *is an algorithm for a user to buy a time-bound decryption key* $K_{\{T_1, T_2\}}$ *from a trusted center, which is designed an expiration date* $T_2$ *from* $T_1$. *The purchase record is stored at the center.*
- Broadcast *is an algorithm used by a broadcaster to calculate the packets from content and to broadcast them.*
- Reception *is an algorithm by users to receive fingerprinted content from a broadcast channel.*
- Tracing *is an algorithm that takes as input an illegal copy, and it outputs a certain user's identity.*
- Trial *is an algorithm that takes as input an illegal copy, the user's identity, and the record of purchase. The algorithm is to be public in order not to be disputed by both a traitor and a broadcaster.*

Since each user obtains the content with distinct fingerprint, a traitor can be traced from redistributed content if the fingerprint is extracted correctly. Then, a broadcaster gets to know the user's fingerprint; hence, he can identify the traitor. It is noted that once the fingerprint is leaked, the broadcaster may try to frame the same traitor for other content. In order to avoid such a multiple accusation, it is desirable to use the fingerprint information only one-time. However, it is difficult in our scenario of broadcasting system. Therefore, we introduce a time-bound viewing system for each broadcast channel like TV channel such that a user pays for each series of content broadcasted via a specified channel.

**Definition 4.** *The expiration date of secret key* $key_t$ *is TW that includes the period* $T_2$ *from* $T_1$.

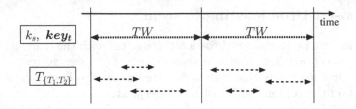

**Fig. 1.** An example of expiration date of keys. The expiration date of time-bound key $T_{\{T_1,T_2\}}$ can be designed freely as long as it is within the period $TW$.

During a time $TW$, each user key $\boldsymbol{key}_t$ is generated from the same master key $k_s$ listed in a table, and $\boldsymbol{key}_t$ is only available for one broadcast channel. Under such a condition, a broadcaster can encrypt content using one master key $k_s$ for multiple users during the period, and the user key $\boldsymbol{key}_t$ is used for the decryption of each packet of content broadcasted at the corresponding channel. For the revocation of the receiver set, the time-bound key is jointly applied for the generation of decryption key at each time combined with $\boldsymbol{key}_t$. Based on the above definitions, the information issued to each user is designed two kinds of expiration date. In a period $TW$, a session-encryption key is generated from a same key $k_s$ combined with each time-bound key $T_{\{T_1,T_2\}}$ which expiration date is within $TW$ depicted in Fig. 1.

Once a fingerprint is detected from an illegal copy, the user specified from the fingerprint is accused for the illegal action. In our scheme, the accusation covers all content broadcasted during the period $TW$, because the content contains a same fingerprint because the user key $\boldsymbol{key}_t$ is generated by following the operation Reg in the fingerprinting described in the previous section.

## 3.2  Construction

The proposed broadcast system is based on the following ideas. A broadcaster commits secret information to a trusted center, and the center partially gives the information to each user in a registration. By managing the expiration date of those information adaptively, each user can receive the content that contain his own fingerprint from a broadcasted channel during a specified period. In our system, two kinds of secret keys are used, and each expiration date is designed adaptively considering the amount of information to be transmitted to users.

KeyGen: A broadcaster generates master keys $K_{\{0,\infty\}}$ and $k_s, (s = 1, 2, \cdots)$ for time-bound key and content encryption key, respectively. They are all committed to a trusted center. Each piece of time-bound key is for the encryption of a session-encryption key which is partially used for the encryption of content to be broadcasted.

Reg: When a user $t$ makes an entry to the system, the center assigns a fingerprint information $\boldsymbol{w}_t = \{w_{t,j} | 0 \leq j \leq L - 1\}$, and then using a current master key $k_s$, the center generates an extended sequence $g(k_s) = \{k_{s,j} | 0 \leq j \leq$

$2L-1\}$ in order to produce the user's key sequence $\textbf{\textit{key}}_t = \{key_{t,j}|0 \le j \le l_i-1\}$;

$$key_{t,j} = \begin{cases} k_{s,2j} & (w_{t,j} = 0) \\ k_{s,2j-1} & (w_{t,j} = 1) \end{cases} \tag{5}$$

Note that the key sequence $\textbf{\textit{key}}_t$ can be used only in a period $TW$. After the period, the user must registers at the system again. Then, considering the security, the fingerprint $\textbf{\textit{w}}_t$ is changed each time and is not revealed to the user.

**Purchase:** The center sells a time-bound key $K_{\{T_1,T_2\}}$ that is only available for a period $\{T_1, \ldots, T_2\}$, where the period does not exceed the expiration date $TW$. The record of purchase is stored at the center.

**Broadcast:** We assume that the current time is $T_c$ which is within $TW$. The broadcaster generates an extended sequence $g(k_s)$ using a master key $k_s$, and calculates an encryption key sequence $\textbf{\textit{k}}_s^\star = \{k_{s,j}^\star | 0 \le j \le 2L-1\}$ using a current time-bound key $K_{T_c}$, where the expiration date of $k_s$ is $TW$ and only the user key $\textbf{\textit{key}}_t$ generated from $k_s$ is available to receive the broadcasted content.

First, current encryption keys for the distribution of content $\textbf{\textit{X}}$ using symmetric cryptosystem are generated as follows:

1. Extract a current time-bound key $K_{T_c}$ from $K_{\{0,\infty\}}$.
2. Calculate each piece of key sequence using a one-way function $f(\cdot)$.

$$k_{s,j}^\star = f(k_{s,j}, K_{T_c}), \ (0 \le j \le 2L - 1) \tag{6}$$

In this operation, each key sequence $k_{s,j}$ is modified by $K_{T_c}$ for the encryption of the content to be distributed at a time $T_c$. Note that $k_{s,j}^\star$ and $K_{T_c}$ are regarded as SEK and KEK, respectively.

For each packet $X_j, (0 \le j \le L-1)$, the supplier calculates its ciphertext $\sigma_j(c_j^{(0)}, c_j^{(1)}), (0 \le j \le L-1)$ using the key sequence $k_{s,j}^\star, (0 \le j \le 2L-1)$ based on the same operations as that of **Protocol** in fingerprinting described in the previous section. The broadcasted ciphertext from the broadcaster is composed of several packets as follows.

$$C_{T_c} = head||\sigma_0(c_0^{(0)}, c_0^{(1)})|| \cdots ||\sigma_{L-1}(c_{L-1}^{(0)}, c_{L-1}^{(1)}) \tag{7}$$

where $head$ is a header information file contains synchronization time and $||$ means concatenation. Note that the size of $head$ is constant and is completely independent from both content and a number of users.

**Reception:** The time-bound key $K_{\{T_1,T_2\}}$ issued to a user is designed according to the user's request and a user key sequence $\textbf{\textit{key}}_t$ is also issued at the center. Using those information, the user receives a ciphertext $C_{T_c}$ from a broadcast channel to obtain the content $\textbf{\textit{X}}$. A session-encryption key is required for the decryption of the ciphertext, which can be generated by modifying $\textbf{\textit{key}}_t$ using $K_{\{T_1,T_2\}}$ as long as the time-bound key is not expired. It is noted that the user's SEK contains a partial information of the supplier's SEK as the user key $\textbf{\textit{key}}_t$ is a partial sequence of $g(k_s)$. The user's SEK is generated as follows:

1. Extract the information about the received ciphertext from the header file *head*.
2. Synchronize the time-bound key with the time $T_c$ described in *head* and $K_{T_c}$ is calculated if $T_1 \leq T_c \leq T_2$.
3. Calculate each piece of key sequence using the user's key sequence $\boldsymbol{key}_t$.

$$key_{s,j}^{*} = f(key_{t,j}, K_{T_c}), \tag{8}$$

The user decrypts parts of the ciphertexts $\sigma_j(c_j^{(0)}, c_j^{(1)})$, $(0 \leq j \leq L-1)$, and decompresses the compressed files. Finally the fingerprinted content can be obtained.

$$\boldsymbol{X}^{(\boldsymbol{w}_t)} = \{X_j^{(w_{t,j})} | w_{t,j} \in \{0,1\}, 0 \leq j \leq L-1\} \tag{9}$$

**Tracing:** When an illegal copy $\boldsymbol{X}^{(\boldsymbol{w}_t)}$ is found, the broadcaster try to extract the fingerprint $\boldsymbol{w}_t$ from it. Such an operation is easily performed by comparing each packet with two candidates $X_j^{(0)}$ and $X_j^{(1)}$.

1. Partition the illegally distributed content $\hat{X}$ into each packet $\hat{X}_j$.
2. For each packet $\hat{X}_j$, determine one of two packet $X_j^{(0)}$ and $X_j^{(1)}$; if $X_j^{(0)}$ is similar to $\hat{X}_j$, then $\hat{w}_{t,j} = 0$, otherwise $\hat{w}_{t,j} = 1$.

**Trial:** The broadcaster submits the illegal copy and the detected fingerprint $\boldsymbol{w}_t$ to an arbiter. Then, the arbiter asks for the center to identify the corresponding user, and requests the record of the purchase to judge. If the identified user really purchase the content, the arbiter determines the user is a traitor, otherwise he determines the broadcaster is trying to frame an innocent user.

In the above construction, the information gap between a broadcaster and a user is important similar to the fingerprinting protocol in [8]. Hence the secret information with respect to each party and the public information are summarized in Table 1.

**Table 1.** The secret information with respect to each party and the public information.

| | |
|---|---|
| Broadcaster | $k_s$, $K_{\{0,\infty\}}$ |
| User | $\boldsymbol{key}_t$, $K_{\{T_1,T_2\}}$ |
| Trusted center | $k_s$, $K_{\{0,\infty\}}$, $\boldsymbol{w}_t$, $\boldsymbol{key}_t$ |
| Public information | $f()$, $g()$ |

## 4    Considerations

In this section, we discuss about the traceability and the security of our construction. Although a traitor tracing scheme can identify traitors from decryption keys issued to the users, our scheme can trace both from the decryption keys and broadcasted content.

## 4.1 Traceability

We have showed the procedure to identify a traitor from the broadcasted content in the above construction. Here, we consider the traceability from the secret information issued to each user at `registration` and `purchase` protocol because the traceability is achieved in conventional traitor tracing schemes and broadcast encryption schemes.

The user key sequence $key_t$ contains the information about a fingerprint $w_t$. Because in our setting, $key_{s,j}$ is selected from one of $k_{s,2j}$ and $k_{s,2j+1}$ based on $w_{t,j}$, hence the sequence $key_t$ semantically indicates the fingerprint $w_t$. On the other hand, a time-bound key $K_{\{T_1,T_2\}}$ does not contain any information related to a user.

In our construction, the received content from a broadcast channel during the period $TW$ contains potentially the same fingerprint for a user. Namely, the fingerprint $w_t$ is used multiple times. Although it may cause a multiple accusation for one fingerprint, such a drawback will not be a problem from the following reason. For a legitimate user, the fingerprint is never leaked as the fingerprinted content are only stored in his storage. On the other hand, a hostile user may try to redistribute the content at a risk of tracking. Once an illegal copy is detected, the user must pay the compensation for all content during the period $TW$ even if he bought a license to receive the content during the period $T_2$ from $T_1$. Such a risk may effectively work for the prevention of illegal distribution.

In a real market, a user has a membership with an expiration date when he joins a system to get a service. For example, on a video rental service, a user can rent a video for one week if he is the member of the shop which membership is usually one year. Such a system can be achieved by applying our scheme because of two kinds of expiration date.

## 4.2 Security

In our construction, it is necessary to obtain a session-encryption key on a current time $T_c$ that is contained in *head* to decrypt a ciphertext $C_{T_c}$. For a user, the session-encryption key is calculated using a one-way function $f()$ from $key_t$ and $K_{\{T_1,T_2\}}$ as long as the they are not expired. The one-way function modifies a plain user key $key_t$ to a current session-encryption key $key_t^*$ using a current time-bound key $K_{T_c}$. Therefore, for a given time $T_c$, $(T_c < T_1$ or $T_2 < T_c)$, it is difficult for a user to obtain a proper session-encryption key $key_t^*$ from $key_t$ and $K_{\{T_1,T_2\}}$.

A user key $key_t$ is generated from $g(k_s)$ by interleaving one of $k_{s,2i}$ and $k_{s,2i+1}$ for $0 \leq i \leq L - 1$. In this operation, a part of the information about $g(k_s)$ is revealed to the user, but the remain one is kept secret if the two requirements G1 and G2 are achieved. A time-bound key $K_{\{T_1,T_2\}}$ contains no information related to $g(k_s)$ as it is only used for the modification of $key_t$ to $key_t^*$ in order to decrypt a ciphertext $C_{T_c}$. Even if some users collect their user keys, the secrecy of $g(k_s)$ will be kept because of the use of collusion resistant code such as c-secure code, ACC, and Tardos code.

In this paper, a time-bound key management scheme is applied for the construction of the system. It does not mean only such a scheme is available. Any broadcast encryption scheme is also applicable if a set of decryption keys is issued to each user. For example, the decryption keys are set in line with time sequence and use each one of them in the arranged order. If each key is discarded after a predefined period, simple time-bound keys are able to be generated from a certain successive set of the keys.

## 5   Conclusion

In this paper, we proposed a new traitor tracing technique that enables a broadcaster to retrieve traitors from broadcasted content. In order to distribute fingerprinted content to each user, the time-bound key management technique and asymmetric fingerprinting based on the key management are applied. In our system, a broadcaster can identify a traitor from both the decryption key issued to each specified user and the content such that each user obtained from a broadcast channel. Such a system is based on the ingenious key management of a trusted center with introducing an expiration date. Since the broadcaster need not to generate the ciphertext adaptively for a set of users, the computational complexity does not increase with respect to the number of users. Since the asymmetric property in the distribution of fingerprinted content is achieved, the repudiation of the traitor may not be possible.

## References

1. Bertino, E., Shang, N., Wagstaff Jr., S.S.: An efficient time-bound hierarchical key management scheme for secure broadcasting. IEEE Trans. Dependable Secure Comput. **5**(2), 65–70 (2008)
2. Boneh, D., Shaw, J.: Collusion-secure fingerprinting for digital data. IEEE Trans. Inform. Theory **44**(5), 1897–1905 (1998)
3. Charpentier, A., Fontaine, C., Furon, T., Cox, I.: An asymmetric fingerprinting scheme based on Tardos codes. In: Filler, T., Pevný, T., Craver, S., Ker, A. (eds.) IH 2011. LNCS, vol. 6958, pp. 43–58. Springer, Heidelberg (2011)
4. Chor, B., Fiat, A., Naor, M., Pinkas, B.: Trating traitors. IEEE Trans. Inform. Theory **46**(3), 893–910 (2000)
5. Fiat, A., Naor, M.: Broadcast encryption. In: Stinson, D.R. (ed.) CRYPTO 1993. LNCS, vol. 773, pp. 480–491. Springer, Heidelberg (1994)
6. Fiat, A., Tassa, T.: Dynamic traitor tracing. J. Cryptology **14**, 211–223 (2001)
7. Kuribayashi, M., Tanaka, H.: Fingerprinting protocol for images based on additive homomorphic property. IEEE Trans. Image Process. **14**(12), 2129–2139 (2005)
8. Kuribayashi, M., Tanaka, H.: Fingerprinting protocol for on-line trade using information gap between buyer and merchant. IEICE Trans. Fundam. **E89–A**(10), 1108–1115 (2006)
9. Laarhoven, T.: Dynamic Tardos traitor tracing schemes. IEEE Trans. Inform. Theory **59**(7), 4230–4242 (2013)
10. Naini, R.S., Wang, Y.: Sequential trating traitors. IEEE Trans. Inform. Theory **49**(5), 1319–1326 (2003)

11. Naor, D., Naor, M., Lotspiech, J.: Revocation and tracing schemes for stateless receivers. In: Kilian, J. (ed.) CRYPTO 2001. LNCS, vol. 2139, pp. 41–62. Springer, Heidelberg (2001)
12. Pfitzmann, B., Schunter, M.: Asymmetric fingerprinting. In: Maurer, U.M. (ed.) EUROCRYPT 1996. LNCS, vol. 1070, pp. 84–95. Springer, Heidelberg (1996)
13. Tardos, G.: Optimal probabilistic fingerprint codes. J. ACM **55**(2), 1–24 (2008)
14. Trappe, W., Wu, M., Wong, Z.J., Liu, K.J.R.: Anti-collusion fingerprinting for multimedia. IEEE Trans. Signal Process. **51**(4), 804–821 (2003)
15. Tzeng, W.G.: A time-bound cryptographic key assignment scheme for access control in a hierarchy. IEEE Trans. Knowl. Data Eng. **14**(1), 182–188 (2002)

# Image Watermarking Based on Reflectance Modification

Piyanart Chotikawanid[✉] and Thumrongrat Amornraksa

Multimedia Communication Laboratory, Computer Engineering Department,
Faculty of Engineering, King Mongkut's University of Technology Thonburi,
Bangkok, Thailand
piyanart.cho@gmail.com, t_amornraksa@cpe.kmutt.ac.th

**Abstract.** This paper proposes a spatial image watermarking method based on the modification of reflectance component of a color image. In the proposed method, the reflectance component is extracted from the $YCbCr$ color space of the host image pixels, and used to carry a binary watermark image with the same size. Each embedded bit is blindly achieved based on the estimation of original watermarking component from the $3 \times 3$ watermarked components. The performance of the proposed method in terms of quality of watermarked image and accuracy of extracted watermark is evaluated and presented. Its robustness against image processing operations at various strengths is also evaluated and compared with the previous method.

**Keywords:** Data hiding · Digital image watermarking · Reflectance component

## 1 Introduction

With limitless communications in social networks, digital images can be easily shared, copied and distributed to anyone without permission from the real owner. Due to characteristics of digital media, it is infeasible to distinguish an illegal made copy from the original one. This problem may discourage ones from producing and sharing their work to the public. To solve this problem, a method called digital image watermarking is invented and used to hide some information within an original image before releasing it to the public. Technically, the method embeds secret information called "watermark" into a digital image called "host" in such a way that the embedded watermark should be invisible to an observer, reliable for future recovery and robust against image processing operations. Moreover, the embedded watermark should exist within a new made copy of that watermarked image, so that the watermark inside can later be recovered and used to verify the real owner of such image. In practice, a decent image watermarking method should be very effective against attempts to destroy or remove the watermark inside. In fact, it should be robust against all possible noises and attacks introduced unintentionally and/or intentionally [1].

Basically, image watermarking can be divided into two main groups based on its working domain, i.e. frequency domain and spatial domain. In the frequency domain based method, transformation of image pixels is used to acquire some proper components for embedding a watermark, so that the embedded watermark can naturally survive

© Springer International Publishing Switzerland 2016
Y.-Q. Shi et al. (Eds.): IWDW 2015, LNCS 9569, pp. 176–190, 2016.
DOI: 10.1007/978-3-319-31960-5_15

most common image compression schemes, such as JPEG and JPEG2000. Examples of image watermarking methods in frequency domain are [2–5], where the discrete wavelet transform (DWT) and the discrete cosine transform (DCT) were used for image transformation. For the spatial domain based method, the processes of watermark embedding and extracting are performed by modifying the host image pixels directly, so that the embedded watermark can naturally survive most geometrical attacks, such as rotation, scaling, and translation (RST). Apart from *RGB* (red-green-blue) color space, the modification of image pixels can be performed in various color spaces, such as in, *YCbCr* (luminance-chroma blue-chroma red) [6] and *HSV* (hue-saturation-value) [7]. An interesting spatial image watermarking method based on amplitude modulation was proposed in 1998 by *Kutter et al.* [8]. The method embedded a watermark bit into an image pixel by modifying the blue color channel of that pixel using either additive or subtractive depending on the watermark bit, and proportional to the luminance of the embedding pixel. The blue channel was selected to be modified because it is the one that human eye is least sensitive to. The blue image pixels were modified by using either additive or subtractive depending on the watermark bit, and proportional to the luminance of the embedding pixel. The watermark extraction was blindly achieved by using a prediction technique based on a linear combination of pixel values in a cross-shape neighborhood around the embedded pixels. The predicted original pixel value was then subtracted from the watermarked one to obtain the extracted watermark bit. Apart from several types of geometrical attacks, this method was proved to be robust against the most widely used compression standard, i.e. JPEG. To improve the performance of the watermarking method, *Amornraksa and Janthawongwilai* [9] proposed three different techniques to enhance its watermark extraction accuracy, i.e. by adjusting the pattern of watermark bits around the embedding pixels, modifying the strength of embedding watermark in according with the nearby luminance, and using a new technique for predicting the original image pixel from its the surrounding watermarked image pixels. They demonstrated how to embed a binary watermark image (logo) having the same size as the host color image as well. However, in some particular types of images having high variation of image pixel values, inaccurate prediction of original image pixel still existed.

In 2009, *Lai and Wu* [10] proposed the image watermarking method based on multiscale block matching which solved the problem of high variation in image pixel values. That is, by comparing the standard deviation of the $3 \times 3$ pixel block with a predefined threshold to determine if the center pixel in that block is suitable for watermark embedding. With the watermark positions map sent from the embedder to the detector, the watermark extraction was simply achieved by differentiating between the embedded pixel value and the average of its neighbors. *Miao et al.* [11] proposed the image descriptor based semi-blind watermarking for depth-image-based rendering (DIBR) 3D images, where the spread spectrum based technique was used for the watermark embedding. In the watermark extraction, image descriptor extracted from the 2-view input color images was used for resynchronization purpose. *He et al.* [12] proposed an image watermarking method based on histogram modification. The watermark was embedded by modifying the number of the gray samples of the image histogram, where every three consecutive bins was divided into a group for embedding one-bit watermark. Each watermark bit was extracted through calculating and judging the relationship of those three successive bins. Although the above three methods achieved a high accuracy of extracted watermark, it lost an ability of embedding a binary watermark image having the same size as the host image.

Recently, in 2014, *Abdallah et al.* proposed the homomorphic image watermarking with a singular value decomposition algorithm [13], which was developed from the previous SVD-based watermarking method proposed by *Ruizhen and Tieniu* [14]. Accordingly, the method embedded the watermark with the SVD algorithm in the reflectance component after applying the homomorphic transform to the $Y$ color channel of a host color image. The reflectance component was selected to be modified because it contains most of the image features having low energy, so that watermark embedded in this component will be invisible to an observer. Although the method was exposed to be robust against several types of image processing based attacks, too many parameters were needed for the watermark detection, i.e. the $U$ and $V$ matrices of the watermarked component, the $S$ matric of the watermark image, the scale factor that controls the strength of the watermark, and the secret key. Apart from its inconvenience for a practical use, due to the size and space required to keep those parameters, it was demonstrated by *Ping and Kan* that the SVD based watermarking algorithm is fundamentally flawed in that the extracted watermark is not the embedded watermark but determined by the reference watermark, resulting in the false positive detection rate with a probability of one [15]. That is, any reference watermark that is being searched for in an arbitrary image can be found.

In this paper, we propose a spatial image watermarking method based on the modification of reflectance component of a color image. The proposed method is blind, so that the watermark extraction can be achieved with the same secret key used in the embedding process only. Sets of experiments are conducted to verify the performance of our method. The next section describes background of reflectance component in a color image and the process of acquiring this component from an image. Details of the proposed watermarking method on reflectance component are presented in Sect. 3. In Sect. 4, the experimental setting is given, and the results are shown and discussed. The conclusion is drawn in Sect. 5.

## 2 Background on Reflectance Component

According to [16], an image, $I$, is assumed to consist of two multiplicative components: illumination and reflectance. Illumination component, $L$, represents the amount of light falling on the image while the reflectance component, $R$, represents the amount of light reflected by the image,

$$I(i,j) = L(i,j)R(i,j), \tag{1}$$

Typically, both illumination and reflectance components can be characterized by slow spatial variations, and sudden change in spatial variations, particularly at the junctions of dissimilar objects, respectively, so that most of the image details lie in the reflectance component, while the illumination component is approximately constant [17]. These characteristics lead to associating the low frequencies of the natural logarithm of an image with illumination and the high frequencies with reflectance. In order to separate the reflectance component from the image, we first perform the natural logarithm on the image pixel values, in order to convert the multiplication relationship between the two components to the addition one,

$$ln(I(i,j)) = ln(L(i,j)R(i,j) = ln(L(i,j)) + ln(R(i,j)), \qquad (2)$$

and then apply a spatial low pass filter to the result to obtain the natural logarithm of illumination component. The natural logarithm of reflectance component is finally obtained by subtracting the result of the low pass filter from the result of the logarithmic function, see Fig. 1.

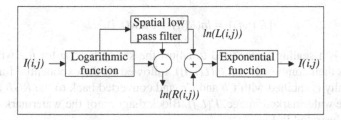

**Fig. 1.**  Block diagram of the reflectance component separation process

From the figure, the original image can be reconstructed by performing the natural exponential function on the combination of natural logarithm of both illumination and reflectance components. Note that, for convenience, the natural logarithm of illumination component, $ln(L(i,j))$, will be called "illumination component" from now on. Also, in this paper, a spatial Gaussian filter was used as a low pass filter, and the Gaussian probability distribution function is given by

$$f(i,j) = e^{\frac{-(i^2+j^2)}{2\sigma^2}}, \qquad (3)$$

where $i$ and $j$ is the distance from the origin in the horizontal and vertical axis, respectively. $\sigma$ is the standard deviation of the zero mean Gaussian distribution.

## 3   Proposed Watermarking Method

The proposed method consists of two processes; watermark embedding and watermark extraction. In the embedding process, a host color image, $I$, in the *RGB* color space is first converted into the *YCbCr* color space using the formula below.

$$\begin{bmatrix} Y \\ Cb \\ Cr \end{bmatrix} = \begin{bmatrix} 0.257 & 0.504 & 0.098 \\ -0.148 & -0.291 & 0.439 \\ 0.439 & -0.368 & -0.071 \end{bmatrix} \begin{bmatrix} R \\ G \\ B \end{bmatrix} + \begin{bmatrix} 16 \\ 128 \\ 128 \end{bmatrix} \qquad (4)$$

The separation of reflectance component is then performed on the $Y$ color channel to obtain the watermarking component. Note that the value of $\sigma$ in the Gaussian filter is determined from the standard deviation of all pixel values within the input image. Next, a binary watermark image $I_w \in \{0,1\}$, with the same size as $I$ is created. All bits within $I_w$ are then permuted by using Gaussian distribution to disperse bits 0s and 1s, and the result is XORed with a pseudo-random bit stream generated from a key-based bits generator. After XORing, bits 0s are converted into $-1$, so that the watermark to be embedded become as $w(i,j) \in \{-1,1\}$. The watermark embedding operation is performed by modifying the reflectance component, $ln(R(i,j))$, of $I$ in a line scan fashion, left to right and top to bottom in accordance with $w(i, j)$ and watermark strength, $s$. The watermarked component, $ln(R'(i, j))$, can be represented by

$$ln\big(R^{'}(i,j)\big) = ln(R(i,j)) + s.w(i,j), \tag{5}$$

where $s$ is a scaling factor used to adjust the strength of $w$ for the whole image. $ln(R'(i, j))$ is then combined with $ln(L(i, j))$, followed by the exponential function. The result is finally combined with $Cb$ and $Cr$, and converted back to the $RGB$ color space to obtain the watermarked image, $I'(i, j)$. Block diagram of the watermark embedding process is illustrated in Fig. 2.

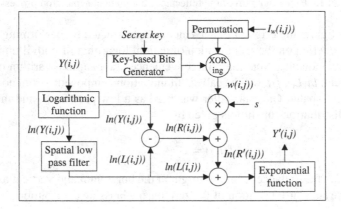

**Fig. 2.** Block diagram of the proposed watermark embedding process

In the watermark extraction process, the reflectance component is extracted from the watermarked image the same way as performed in the watermark embedding. Since the embedded watermark is a noise-like signal added to the original image, a noise removal technique called averaging filter is applied to the watermarked image to predict the original image. With the assumption that the reflectance component values are close within a small image area, the prediction of the original reflectance component, $ln(R''(i, j))$, can be estimated from $ln(R'(i, j))$ and its eight surrounding components, as given by

$$ln\big(R^{''}(i,j)\big) = \frac{1}{9}\Big[\sum\nolimits_{m=-1}^{1}\sum\nolimits_{n=-1}^{1} ln\big(R^{'}(i+m,j+n)\big)\Big]. \tag{6}$$

The extracted watermark $w'(i, j)$ is then obtained as a result of the subtraction between $ln(R'(i, j))$ and $ln(R''(i, j))$.

$$w'(i,j) = \ln\left(R'(i,j)\right) - \ln\left(R''(i,j)\right) \tag{7}$$

Since $w'(i, j)$ can be either positive or negative, its sign is used to estimate the value of $w(i, j)$. That is, if $w'(i, j)$ is positive (or negative), $w'(i, j)$ is estimated as 1 (or −1, respectively). Finally, the bits −1s of $w'(i, j)$ is converted into 0, and the result is XORed with the same bit stream, as used in the embedding process and then re-permuted to obtain the extracted watermark image $I'_w(i, j) \in \{0,1\}$. Block diagram of the watermark extraction process is illustrated in Fig. 3.

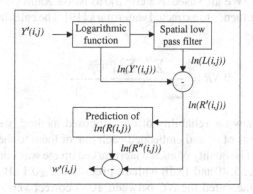

**Fig. 3.** Block diagram of the proposed watermark extraction process

## 4   Experimental Setting and Results

In the experiments, six standard 256 × 256 pixels color images having different characteristics were used as the original images, i.e. 'airplane', 'lena', 'baboon', 'peppers', 'house' and 'jellybeans'. A 256 × 256 pixels binary image containing a human face was used as a watermark. An objective quality measure that matches the human visual system (HVS) properties called the weighted peak signal-to-noise ratio (wPSNR) was used for evaluating the quality of watermarked image. wPSNR is a variation of PSNR that uses weights for perceptually different image areas based on the visibility of noise in flat image areas is higher than that in textures and edges [18]. The calculation of wPSNR is given by

$$wPSNR = \frac{255\sqrt{3MN}}{\sqrt{\sum_{k=1}^{3}\sum_{i=1}^{M}\sum_{j=1}^{N}\left[NVF(I'(k,i,j) - I(k,i,j)\right]^2}}, \tag{8}$$

where $k$, $M$ and $N$ are the image plane, the numbers of row and column in the images, respectively. NVF is the noise visibility function which characterizes the local texture of an image and varies between 0 and 1, where 1 is for flat areas and 0 is for highly textured areas. After the watermark is extracted, its quality may be judged directly from the intelligibility of its content, due to the recognizable patterns inside the watermark image. However, for performance comparison purpose, numeric quality measures e.g. Normalized Correlation (*NC*), Bit Error Rate (*BER*) were considered. In this paper, a numeric quality measure called Normalized Correlation (*NC*) was used. The calculation of *NC* is given by

$$NC = \frac{\sum_{i=1}^{M} \sum_{j=1}^{N} I_w(i,j) I_{w'}(i,j)}{\sqrt{\sum_{i=1}^{M} \sum_{j=1}^{N} I_w(i,j)^2} \sqrt{\sum_{i=1}^{M} \sum_{j=1}^{N} I_{w'}(i,j)^2}} \tag{9}$$

Note that the maximum value of *NC* is 1. A higher *NC* value indicates a more accurate extracted watermark. We also used Watermark to Noise Ratio (*WNR*) to demonstrate an amount of noise influence to extracted watermark [19]. The calculation of *WNR* shows is given by

$$WNR = \frac{\sum_{i=1}^{M} \sum_{j=1}^{N} w_{i,j}^2}{\sum_{i=1}^{M} \sum_{j=1}^{N} (w_{i,j} - w'_{i,j})^2} \tag{10}$$

First of all, to show the reliability of our proposed method, we randomly created 1000 different versions of *w*, and embedded each one of them to the host images using the same secret key. The quality of each watermarked image was controlled to reach the *wPSNR* of 20, 25, 30, 35, 40 and 45 dB with the precision of ±0.1 dB. Then, we extracted the watermark and measured the *NC* between 1000 correct versions of *w* and 1000 incorrect versions of *w*. Figure 4 shows an example of the resultant *NC* obtained from the test image 'jellybeans' at *wPSNR* of 35 dB.

Obviously form the figure, the corrected embedded watermark could be reliably separated from the incorrect ones. From the tests, the highest *NC* value obtained from incorrect watermark versions in all test images was 0.489. The value was used as a threshold to identify the existence of corrected watermark. That is, if the extracted watermark has

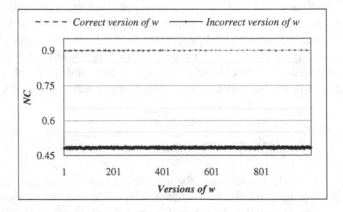

**Fig. 4.** Performance in terms of *NC* from 1000 different versions of watermark from the test image 'jellybeans' at 35 dB

the *NC* value of 0.49 or less, that watermark may be considered as an invalid watermark. Table 1 shows the highest *wPSNR* for each test image from the proposed watermarking method that gave the maximum *NC*. From the table, the highest *wPSNR* of 14.4 dB, on average, gave the maximum *NC* value of 0.97. Note that the highest value of *NC* that our method could achieve individually was 0.99, not 1. This is mainly because in the original reflectance component prediction step, all surrounding components around coordinate *(i, j)* were used in the calculation. Thus the prediction of *ln(R(i, j))* within a small area, i.e. 3 × 3 block, could be disturbed by its surrounding watermarked components. However, in practice, as long as the patterns contained within the extracted watermark are still recognizable, the resultant *NC* may not be of that great concern.

**Table 1.**  The highest *wPSNR* that gave the maximum *NC*

| Image | 'lena' | 'peppers' | 'baboon' | 'house' | 'airplane' | 'jellybeans' |
|---|---|---|---|---|---|---|
| *wPSNR* (dB) | 13.9 | 13.1 | 14.4 | 16.4 | 13.0 | 15.5 |
| *NC* | 0.99 | 0.99 | 0.85 | 0.99 | 0.99 | 0.99 |

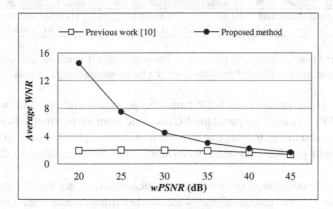

**Fig. 5.**  Performance comparison in terms of average *WNR* at various *wPSNR* values

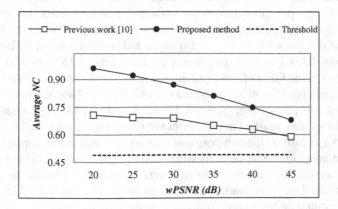

**Fig. 6.**  Performance comparison in terms of average *NC* at various *wPSNR* values

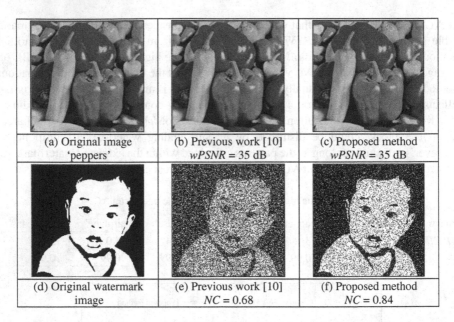

| (a) Original image 'peppers' | (b) Previous work [10] *wPSNR* = 35 dB | (c) Proposed method *wPSNR* = 35 dB |
|---|---|---|
| (d) Original watermark image | (e) Previous work [10] *NC* = 0.68 | (f) Proposed method *NC* = 0.84 |

**Fig. 7.** (a)–(c) Original image 'peppers' and its watermarked versions and (d)–(f) Original watermark image and its extracted versions from the two watermarking methods

Figure 5 shows the average *WNR* from the proposed and previous work [10] at various *wPSNRs*. We also compared the *NC* obtained from the two methods at equivalent *wPSNRs*, as shown in Fig. 6. Note that the previous method [10] was used in comparison because it could provide equivalent watermark embedding capacity to the proposed method.

As shown in both figures, our method was measurably better than the previous one. Figure 7 shows some results of the watermarked images and their corresponding extracted watermark from the two watermarking methods at *wPSNR* of 35 ± 0.1 dB.

We evaluated the robustness of the embedded watermark against different types of image processing operations at various strengths, and compared the results to the previous method [10]. Eight types of operations were used: JPEG compression standard at image qualities from 100 to 50 %, zero mean additive Gaussian distributed noise at variances from 0.0001 to 0.05, brightness enhancement at 15 % to 100 %, contrast adjustment by scaling factors from 1 to 2, image rescaling at various scaling factors from 0.25 to 2, cropping at 5 %–50 %, rotation at 0.1 to 0.8°, and image sharpening at various factors from 0.2 to 1.2, see Figs. 8, 9, 10, 11, 12, 13, 14 and 15, respectively. Note that the *wPSNR* of all watermarked images from the two comparing method was controlled to achieve 35 ± 0.1 dB. In the cropping and rotating operations, the cropped parts of the watermarked images were replaced by white color pixels. Also, we did not perform the watermark resynchronization by using an image registration technique as described in [10]. We extracted the watermark directly from the attacked watermarked image with the aims of evaluating the true performance of the two watermarking methods when watermark resynchronization loss occurred.

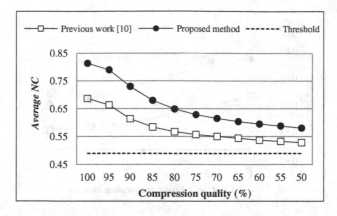

**Fig. 8.** JPEG compression standard at various image qualities

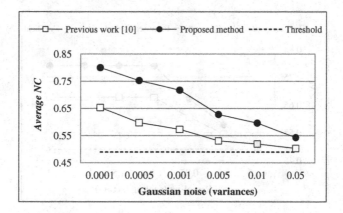

**Fig. 9.** Zero mean Gaussian noise at various variances

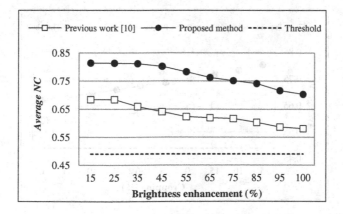

**Fig. 10.** Brightness enhancement at various percentages

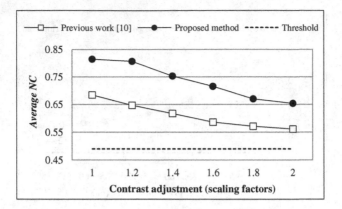

**Fig. 11.** Contrast adjustment at various scaling factors

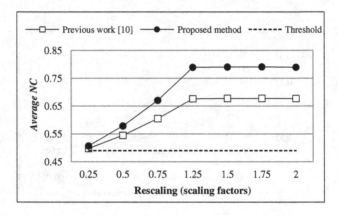

**Fig. 12.** Rescaling at various scaling factors

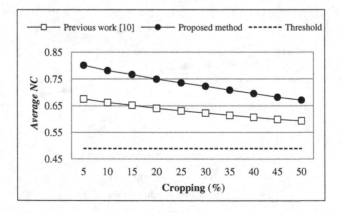

**Fig. 13.** Cropping at various percentages

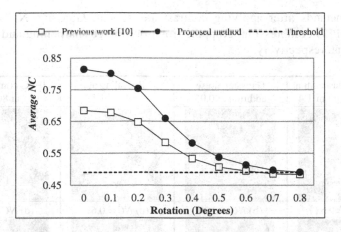

**Fig. 14.** Rotation at various degrees in clockwise direction

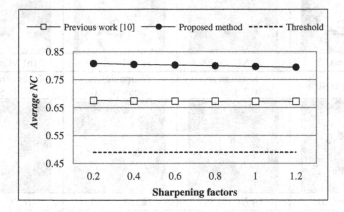

**Fig. 15.** Image sharpening at various sharpening factors

From Fig. 14, the embedded watermarks from both methods could survive the rotation attack at a small angle, i.e. less than 0.6°. In practice, we may survive this type of attack by using a watermark resynchronization mechanism. Noting that strength of image sharpening attack gave small effects on the accuracy of the entire extracted watermark, see Fig. 15. This is because most of watermark energy did not settle on the edge information. Figure 16 shows some example of from the two methods after contrast adjustment at scaling factor of 1.4, zero mean Gaussian noise addition at variance of 0.05, rescaling ratio of 1.5, JPEG compression at 80 % quality, image cropping at 40 %, rotation at 0.3° in clockwise direction, sharpening at factor of 0.6, and brightness enhancement of 55%, see (a)–(p), respectively. Differences in visual quality of the extracted watermarks from the two methods were undetectable with the naked eye, although the average *NC* obtained from the new method was higher. Figure 16(a)–(p) shows some improved results of our proposed methods after applying contrast adjustment, Guassian Noise addition, rescaling, JPEG compression, cropping, rotation, image sharpening and brightness enhancement, respectively.

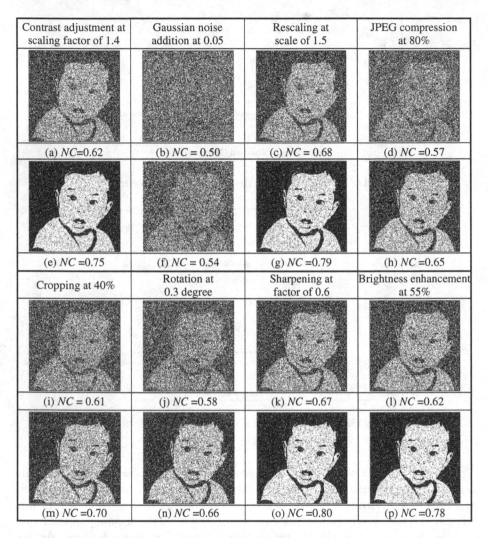

| Contrast adjustment at scaling factor of 1.4 | Gaussian noise addition at 0.05 | Rescaling at scale of 1.5 | JPEG compression at 80% |
|---|---|---|---|
| (a) *NC*=0.62 | (b) *NC* = 0.50 | (c) *NC* = 0.68 | (d) *NC* =0.57 |
| (e) *NC* =0.75 | (f) *NC* = 0.54 | (g) *NC* =0.79 | (h) *NC* =0.65 |
| Cropping at 40% | Rotation at 0.3 degree | Sharpening at factor of 0.6 | Brightness enhancement at 55% |
| (i) *NC* = 0.61 | (j) *NC* =0.58 | (k) *NC* =0.67 | (l) *NC* =0.62 |
| (m) *NC* =0.70 | (n) *NC* =0.66 | (o) *NC* =0.80 | (p) *NC* =0.78 |

**Fig. 16.** (a)–(d) and (i)–(l) Extracted watermark from the previous work [10], (e)–(h) and (m)–(p) from the proposed method

We also evaluated the robustness of the embedded watermark using Stirmark benchmark (Version 4) [20]. Four types of attacks were applied to the image 'peppers' at *wPSNR* of 35 dB, i.e. left rotated by 0.5° and cropped to 99 %, left rotated by 0.25° and scaled with ratio of 0.98, affine transform type 6 (general), and affine transform type 3 (shearing in y-axis). Figure 17 shows the robustness comparison between the two methods against the four types of attacks from Stirmark.

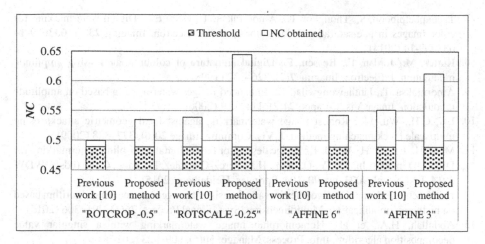

**Fig. 17.** Robustness comparison against some attacks from Stirmark

## 5  Conclusion

This paper has presented the new image watermarking method based on the modification of the reflectance component of a color image. The proposed method was experimentally shown to provide a reliable watermark extraction. Its performance in terms of average *NC* and *WNR* at equivalent quality of watermarked image was higher than the previous method [10], even under various attacks. Our proposed method can be effectively applied to a gray scale image as well.

**Acknowledgments.** The authors would like to thank Prince of Songkla University for partially supporting this research through a Ph.D. scholarship. We would also like to thank the reviewers for their fruitful comments and Miss Kharittha Thongkor for her help in coding.

## References

1. Shin, F.Y.: Digital Watermarking and Steganography: Fundamental and Techniques. CRC Press, Boca Raton (2007)
2. Peijia, Z., Jiwu, H.: Discrete wavelet transform and data expansion reduction in homomorphic encrypted domain. IEEE Trans. Image Process. **22**(6), 2455–2468 (2013)
3. Thongkor, K., Mettripun, N., Pramoun, T., Amornraksa, T.: Image watermarking based on DWT coefficients modification for social networking services. In: Proceedings of ECTI-CON 2013, Krabi, Thailand, 15–17 May 2013
4. Qianli, Y., Cai, Y.: A digital image watermarking algorithm based on discrete wavelet transform and discrete cosine transform. In: Proceedings of ITME 2012, Hokkaido, Japan, 3–5 August 2012
5. San, L.J., Bo, L.: Self-recognized image protection technique that resists large-scale cropping. IEEE Trans. Multimedia **21**(1), 60–73 (2014)
6. Mettripun, N., Amornraksa, T., Delp, E.J.: Robust image watermarking based on luminance modification. J. Electron. Imaging **22**(3), 033009-1–033009-15 (2013)

7. Tachaphetpiboon, S., Thongkor, K., Amornraksa, T., Delp, E.J.: Digital watermarking for color images in hue-saturation-value color space. J. Electron. Imaging **23**(3), 033009-1–033009-14 (2014)
8. Kutter, M., Jordan, F., Bossen, F.: Digital signature of colour images using amplitude modulation. J. Electron. Imaging **7**(2), 326–332 (1998)
9. Amornraksa, T., Janthawongwilai, K.: Enhanced images watermarking based on amplitude modulation. Image Vis. Comput. **24**(2), 111–119 (2006)
10. Lai, C.H., Wu, J.L.: Robust image watermarking against local geometric attacks using multiscale block matching method. J. Vis. Commun. Image **20**(6), 377–388 (2009)
11. Miao, H., Lin, Y.-H., Wu, J.-L.: Image descriptor based digital semi-blind watermarking for DIBR 3D images. In: Shi, Y.-Q., Kim, H.J., Pérez-González, F., Yang, C.-N. (eds.) IWDW 2014. LNCS, vol. 9023, pp. 90–104. Springer, Heidelberg (2015)
12. He, X., Zhu, T., Yang, G.: A geometrical attack resistant image watermarking algorithm based on histogram modification. Multidimension. Syst. Signal Process. **26**(1), 291–306 (2015)
13. Abdallah, H.A., et al.: Homomorphic image watermarking with a singular value decomposition algorithm. Info. Process. Manage. **50**(6), 909–923 (2014)
14. Ruizhen, L., Tieniu, T.: An SVD-based watermarking scheme for protecting rightful ownership. IEEE Trans. Multimedia **4**(1), 121–128 (2002)
15. Ping, Z.X., Kan, L.: Comments on An SVD-based watermarking scheme for protecting rightful ownership. IEEE Trans. Multimedia **7**(3), 593–594 (2005)
16. Gonzalez, R.C., Woods, R.E.: Digital image processing, 3rd edn. Prentice Hall Inc., New Jersey (2010)
17. Fathi, E., et al.: Image Encryption: A Communication perspective. CRC Press, Boca Raton (2013)
18. Boato, G., Conotter, V., De Natale, F.G.B.: GA-based robustness evaluation method for digital image watermarking. In: Shi, Y.Q., Kim, H.-J., Katzenbeisser, S. (eds.) IWDW 2007. LNCS, vol. 5041, pp. 294–307. Springer, Heidelberg (2008)
19. Tsai, F.-M., Hsue, W.-L.: Image watermarking based on various discrete fractional fourier transforms. In: Shi, Y.-Q., Kim, H.J., Pérez-González, F., Yang, C.-N. (eds.) IWDW 2014. LNCS, vol. 9023, pp. 135–144. Springer, Heidelberg (2015)
20. Petitcolas, F.A.P.: Watermarking schemes evaluation. IEEE Signal Process. **17**(5), 58–64 (2000)

# Digital Video Watermark Optimization for Detecting Replicated Two-Dimensional Barcodes

Takeru Maehara[1], Ryo Ikeda[2], and Satoshi Ono[1(✉)]

[1] Department of Information Science and Biomedical Engineering,
Graduate School of Science and Engineering, Kagoshima University,
1-21-40 Korimoto, Kagoshima 890-0065, Japan
{sc110071,ono}@ibe.kagoshima-u.ac.jp
[2] Technical Division, Graduate School of Science and Engineering,
Kagoshima University, 1-21-40 Korimoto, Kagoshima 890-0065, Japan
ikeda@ibe.kagoshima-u.ac.jp

**Abstract.** Two-dimensional barcodes (2D codes) have become common as an authentification way of e-tickets and e-coupons. However, easy replication by using other mobile phone camera is apprehended. This paper proposes a method for detecting copied 2D code by a semi-fragile digital video watermark which can be destroyed by replication. Compared to digital image watermarking, it is more difficult to copy 2D code in which the time-varying watermark is embedded without destroying the watermark. In the proposed method, the video watermarking scheme is optimized to maximize the difference of the watermark extraction degree between valid and replicated 2D code videos. The optimization is performed using a novel self-adaptive differential evolution algorithm with actual mobile devices rather than simulation. Experimental results have shown that the proposed method successfully designs a video watermarking scheme which allows authenticity determination of 2D codes displayed on mobile device screen.

**Keywords:** Semi-fragile video watermark · Pseudo three-dimensional discrete cosine transform · Replication detection · Two-dimensional barcode · Watermark optimization

## 1 Introduction

The use of 2D codes displayed on mobile phone screens has become increasingly common as a paperless verification, e.g., "Passbook" by Apple and "Mobile AMC Application" by All Nippon Airways. The deployment of 2D code has been accelerated by mobile phone applications offered by mobile phone manufacturers, operating system developers, and airline companies. However, easy replication by capturing it with other mobile phone camera is apprehended.

Ono et al. have proposed a method for detecting copied 2D code by *semi-fragile* image watermarking based on Discrete Wavelet Transform (DWT) [11].

© Springer International Publishing Switzerland 2016
Y.-Q. Shi et al. (Eds.): IWDW 2015, LNCS 9569, pp. 191–205, 2016.
DOI: 10.1007/978-3-319-31960-5_16

The watermark can be extracted from genuine 2D codes because replication with mobile phone camera destroys the watermark. The appropriate semi-fragileness is brought by evolutionary multi-objective optimization with multiple real mobile phones for solution evaluation.

Making use of the properties of mobile phone screens, this paper proposes a method for copy detection of 2D code with time-varying image watermark. Utilizing both time and spatial frequency allows to embedding the watermark with lower image resolution than image watermark, resulting in relaxing decoder hardware requirement. Though there is apprehension of long capturing time when extracting watermark, it only takes less than 0.2 s to capture the video watermark whose time period is 8 frames and that is displayed on 60 Hz LCD. The capturing time is sufficiently short compared to the time to hold the mobile device to a barcode reader.

Video watermarks are widely investigated to protect the copyrights of digital videos. Nakamura et al. proposed a DCT-based method for video watermarking, in which watermark is embedded into DC components in order not to be destroyed by rephotographing [10]. Anqiang et al. proposed a robust watermarking scheme based on 3D-DWT, in which the video sequence is segmented into shots and two level 3D-DWT is performed for adaptive embedding [1]. Although many robust and fragile watermarking methods have been proposed, little attention has been paid to semi-fragile video watermarking [2,9,15].

To design a video watermark with appropriate semi-fragileness, this paper proposes a video watermark design method that optimizes a subband set for watermark embedding and watermarking strength levels. The proposed method models the video watermarking design problem as a continuous optimization problem, and adopts Adaptive Differential Evolution with an optional external archive (JADE) [16] to find sufficiently optimal solution. The proposed method uses Pseudo 3D Discrete Cosine Transform (P3D-DCT) [7] for reducing computational cost with keeping watermarking performance. Experimental results have shown that the proposed method is promising for 2D code copy detection.

## 2  The Proposed Method

### 2.1  Key Idea

The key ideas of the proposed method are as follows:

- **A still cover image for video watermark:** Making use of the properties of mobile phone screens, the proposed method embeds a video watermark to a still cover image. The watermarked 2D code video looks like a still 2D code image but involves small perturbation of image patterns. Malicious users who misunderstand the watermarked 2D code as a still image would try to replicate it by capturing a still image of the code, which cannot copy the video watermark. Although capturing a video of the 2D code might copy the video watermark, it is difficult to properly preserve the watermark during the replication due to the gap of video frame frequency between a camera and a screen.

Furthermore, in general, the captured video is compressed according to video coding formats such as MPEG since the data amount is quite large, which damages the embedded video watermark with high possibility. Authoritative 2D code videos are uncompressed because they are played by an exclusive mobile phone application software.

– **Utilizing Adaptive DE with Optional External Archive (JADE):** We utilize a stochastic global optimization algorithm to optimize the watermarking method. This is because the problem properties are unknown, though middle frequency subband should be selected to achieve appropriate semi-fragileness; for instance, whether a unique subband would be sufficient, or a set of subbands might produce a good effect.

   Adaptive DE with an optional external archive (JADE) is a popular SADE algorithm proposed by Zhang *et al.* [16]. JADE utilizes a new mutation strategy DE/current-to-$p$best with an optional external archive and adaptively updating control parameters.

– **Evaluating potential solutions on real mobile phones:** A camera-captured 2D code image displayed on a screen is affected by both the displaying and photographing systems. The copied image is degraded not merely by Gaussian blurring but also by distortion, moire patterns, false color, dark current noise, and similar factors. Blurring is contributed by physical phenomena such the optical transfer functions (OTFs) of the screen, the lens set, and the image sensor. Because factors such as blurring, distortion, moire, and noise are not easily incorporated into copy process models, recaptured images of replicated 2D codes are difficult to obtain by simulation. Therefore, the proposed method captures movies of original and maliciously copied 2D codes from real mobile phones.

– **Pseudo three-dimensional discrete cosine transform:** Although JADE finds sufficiently good solutions, the optimization requires much processing time. For instance, in previous work [8], optimizing a still watermarking method requires 50,000 times solution evaluation. Evaluating a video watermarking method requires longer time than a still watermarking method because both the processing times of capturing watermarked video and frequency transformation are longer than those of still watermarking.

   Therefore, to suppress the increase of the processing time while maintaining semi-fragileness, the proposed method adopts Pseudo three-dimensional DCT (P3D-DCT) to embed a video watermark. The computational complexity of P3D-DCT is $O(n^4)$, whereas general 3D DCT requires $O(n^6)$.

## 2.2   Watermarking Method

In the proposed method, a cover image is decomposed by P3D-DCT, and a watermark is embedded to the selected subbands. The strength levels of the watermark for each subband and region are determined according to the optimized scheme. In a color cover image, the watermark is embedded using only the luminance component (Fig. 1).

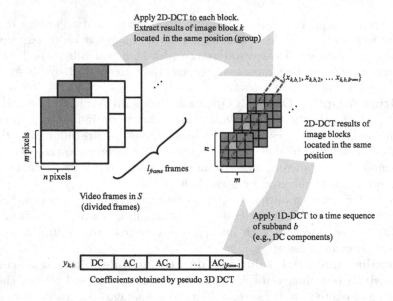

**Fig. 1.** Pseudo 3D-DCT in the proposed method.

The cover image used in this research is a 2D code composed of dark and bright cells, or modules, arranged in a grid pattern. Different from general 2D code, which uses a rectangular one module, the 2D code in this study adopts a circular module, which includes high-frequency components in all directions and not merely horizontal and vertical directions. 2D code decoding is independent of module shape (apart from specific module patterns such as finder patterns, alignment patterns, and timing patterns in QR code), because the code is read by sampling the module center: the sampling points are globally estimated by the specific module patterns such as finder patterns in QR code, rather than being locally estimated from the module shape.

A watermark in the proposed method is represented as a binary sequence. A valid barcode and illegally replicated barcode can be distinguished by the watermark knowledge provided by a combination of public and confidential keys. The public key is calculated from the embedded information of the cover 2D code and the confidential key in a decoder. The public key may also be stored in the filler code of the cover 2D code.

The proposed method optimizes a set of subbands to which the watermark is embedded and the embedding strength of each subband. As the designed watermarking scheme is unaffected by the module patterns of the cover 2D code image, it is accessible to all 2D code with similar module resolution and different information to be stored. That is, the watermarking scheme does not require re-optimization every time a 2D code used as a cover image is generated.

When a 2D code with a semi-fragile watermark is used as a ticket or a coupon, the cover 2D code is decoded independently of watermark extraction. If the appropriate watermark is extracted, then the 2D code is regarded as a genuine code. Otherwise, it is considered to be a replicate because the copy process destroys the embedded watermark.

A 2D code in which the watermark is embedded by the optimized watermarking scheme is compatible with a general 2D code, which is a cover 2D code before watermarking. For example, a watermarked QR code can be decoded by general QR code readers, though existing hardware/software barcode readers must update themselves to verify the existence of the watermark.

**Watermarking Process.** The watermarking algorithm of the proposed method utilizing P3D-DCT is as follows:

**Step 0 (preparation):** Let $S$ be a cover video with the size of $w_S \times h_S$, and $l_{frame}$ be a time period (frames) of a video watermark. A watermark is embedded to the all $n \times m$ size *image blocks* of the cover image, though it can also be embedded to any region of the cover image. $l_{frame}$ image blocks located on the same position in all frames is mentioned as *a group*; totally, $N_G = \frac{w_S}{n} \times \frac{h_S}{m}$ groups exist in a video. Let $B = \{B_1, B_2, \ldots, B_{N_G}\}$ be an embedded watermark code that is a binary sequence with length of $N_G$. Each watermark bit is embedded into a group.

**Step 1 (preprocessing):** Generate cover video $S$ involving $l_{frame}$ frames of the same cover image, and divide each frame image into $n \times m$ size image blocks. Perform Step 2 through 5 for all image blocks.

**Step 2 (apply 2D-DCT in P3D-DCT):** Apply 2D-DCT for all image blocks in all frames.

**Step 3 (apply 1D-DCT in P3D-DCT):** Apply 1D-DCT to a sequence $s_{k,b,1}, s_{k,b,2}, \ldots, s_{k,b,l_{frame}}$ which is 2D-DCT coefficients of subband $b$ in image block group $k$, and transform the value sequence into 1D-DCT domain. Let the obtained sequence comprising DC value and AC values of 1D-DCT be $y_{k,b}$.

**Step 4 (embed the watermark):** Embed a watermark according to the following equation:

$$y'_{k,b,t+1} = Q(y_{k,b,t+1}, \alpha_{B_k,t}) \quad (t = 1, \ldots, l_{frame} - 1) \qquad (1)$$

where $t$ denotes subband ID obtained by 1D-DCT, $B_k$ is a watermark bit embedded to image block group $k$, and $\alpha_{B_k} = \{\alpha_{B_k,1}, \alpha_{B_k,2}, \ldots, \alpha_{B_k,l_{frame}-1}\}$ is a constant binary sequence where $\alpha_1$ has the opposite bit sequence of $\alpha_0$. Watermark is embedded to AC components of 1D-DCT $y_{k,b,2}, y_{k,b,3}, \ldots, y_{k,b,l_{frame}}$ rather than DC component $y_{k,b,1}$ because embedding the watermark into $y_{k,b,1}$ gives rise to serious video image quality deterioration. $Q(\cdot)$ is a quantization function of Quantization Index Modulation (QIM) [3] as follows:

$$Q(y_{k,b,t+1}, \alpha) = L_b \times round\left(\frac{y_{k,b,t+1} - \alpha \times \frac{L_b}{2}}{L_b}\right) + \alpha \times \frac{L_b}{2} \qquad (2)$$

where $L_b$ is a watermarking strength. The watermark bit $B_k$ can be embedded to more than one subband in the same group.

**Step 5 (apply inverse P3D-DCT):** Apply inverse 1D DCT to reconstruct 2D-DCT coefficients on the frames, and apply inverse 2D DCT to reconstruct the watermarked frame images that form watermarked video $Y$.

**Watermark Extraction Process.** The watermark extraction process begins by capturing the watermarked video by a camera or a barcode reader. Then, the extraction proceeds through three steps, as described below:

**Step 1 (preprocessing):** Locate the watermarked 2D code region in the captured video and extract the 2D code region. The trimmed and scaled 2D code video is denoted as $Y^{captured}$. Divide each of the frame image in $Y^{captured}$ into $n \times m$ size image blocks in all frames. Perform Steps 2 and 3 for all image blocks.

**Step 2 (apply P3D-DCT):** Apply 2D-DCT for all the image blocks in all frames of $Y^{captured}$, and then apply 1D-DCT for all the subbands used for watermarking of each group. The obtained 1D-DCT coefficient in subband $b$ of group $k$ is mentioned as $y_{k,b}^{captured}$.

**Step 3 (extract watermark):** Watermark bit candidate $B_{k,b}^{captured}$ is extracted from 1D-DCT coefficients of each subband $b$ used for watermarking, and extracted watermark bit $B_k^{captured}$ is determined under majority rule as follows:

$$B_k^{captured} = \begin{cases} 0 & \text{if } \dfrac{\sum_{b \in \mathcal{B}} B_{k,b}^{captured}}{|\mathcal{B}|} < 0.5 \\ 1 & \text{otherwise} \end{cases} \tag{3}$$

where $\mathcal{B}$ denotes a set of subbands used for watermarking. Watermark bit candidate $B_{k,b}^{captured}$ is calculated by the following equation:

$$B_{k,b}^{captured} = \underset{BIT \in \{0,1\}}{\arg\max} \; corr(\alpha_{BIT}, \beta_{k,b}) \tag{4}$$

where $corr(\cdot)$ denotes a correlation function, and $\beta_{k,b} = \{\beta_{k,b,1}, \beta_{k,b,2}, \ldots, \beta_{k,b,l_{frame}-1}\}$ is a bit sequence defined by the following equation:

$$\beta_{k,b,t} = \underset{BIT \in \{0,1\}}{\arg\min} \left| y_{k,b,t+1}^{captured} - Q(y_{k,b,t+1}^{captured}, BIT) \right| \; (t = 1, \ldots, l_{frame} - 1) \tag{5}$$

## 2.3   Formulation

**Design Variables.** The proposed method embeds a watermark into subband coefficients obtained by P3D-DCT. The subband sets into which the watermark is embedded and watermarking strength levels are targets for optimization, and regarded as *a watermarking scheme*. The proposed method designs a unified watermarking scheme for all image blocks, though different watermarking scheme for image block can be simultaneously designed. Design variable $x_b$ corresponding to subband $b$ has a real value ranging from 0 to 1, and determines whether $b$ is used to embed a watermark and the watermarking strength for $b$. That is, if $x_b$ is below 0.5, $b$ is not used for watermarking, otherwise the watermark is embedded to $b$ with strength of $L_b = 2 \times (x_b - 0.5) \times L_{max}$ where $L_{max}$ is the maximum watermarking strength level. This dispenses the need to assign separate variables to subband selection and strength adjustment. It also allows the proposed method to naturally select 50 % (on average) of the subbands when randomly generating a potential solution.

The objective function $f(\cdot)$ of the semi-fragile video watermark optimization is the difference in the bit correct ratios (BCRs) [4,6] between the watermarks extracted from a valid and a replicated 2D codes:

$$f(\boldsymbol{x}) = \text{BCR}(\boldsymbol{B}, \boldsymbol{B}^{vld}) - \max\left(\text{BCR}(\boldsymbol{B}, \boldsymbol{B}^{rpl}), 0.5\right) - P(Y^{vld}) \qquad (6)$$

where $\boldsymbol{x}$ denotes a potential solution (watermarking scheme candidate), $\boldsymbol{B}^{vld}$ and $\boldsymbol{B}^{rpl}$ are watermark bit sequences extracted from the valid and replicated 2D code videos. The second term of Eq. (6) aims to avoid overfitting; although BCR value of replicated 2D code would not be less than 0.5 on average, BCR value of replicated 2D code decreases below 0.5 when overfitting arises, which inappropriately raises the objective function value. $P(\cdot)$ is a penalty function related to the decodability of the cover 2D code:

$$P(Y^{vld}) = \text{ECR}(Y^{vld}) \times P_{max} \qquad (7)$$

where ECR denotes error correction ratio which is required to decode the cover 2D code, e.g., Reed-Solomon error correction [12] is performed and ECR is calculated when using QR code as a cover 2D code. In the case that the cover 2D code cannot be decoded, $ECR = 1$.

## 2.4   Process Flow and Optimization Algorithm

Figure 2 shows the whole optimization process flow of the proposed method. The proposed method adopts JADE [16] to optimize watermarking scheme. JADE is one of the most popular self-adaptive differential evolution algorithms [5,13], which dynamically adjusts control parameters, scale factor and crossover rate. The following is algorithm of JADE.

**Step 1 (initialization):** Let a potential solution $i$ in generation $g$ be vector $\boldsymbol{x}_{i,g} = \{x_{i,g,1}, x_{i,g,2}, \ldots x_{i,g,D}\}$, and $SF_i$ ($0 < SF_i \leq 1$) and $CR_i$ ($0 \leq CR_i \leq 1$) be scale factor and crossover rate of $i$, respectively. $D$ is the number of dimensions of this optimization problem, i.e., $D = m \times n$. Let generation $g = 0$. Initialize all $N_P$ vectors (potential solutions) $\boldsymbol{x}_{i,g}(i = 1, 2, \ldots, N_P)$ in the population, i.e., values of design variables are determined by random.

**Step 2 (evaluation):** Calculate objective function $f(\boldsymbol{x}_{i,g})$ of all vectors in the population using real mobile devices as described in Sect. 2.5.

**Step 3 (update control parameters):** Update $SF_i$ and $CR_i$ by the following equations:

$$SF_i = randc_i(\mu_{SF}, 0.1) \qquad (8)$$

$$\mu_{SF} = (1 - c) \cdot \mu_{SF} + c \cdot mean_L(S_{SF}) \qquad (9)$$

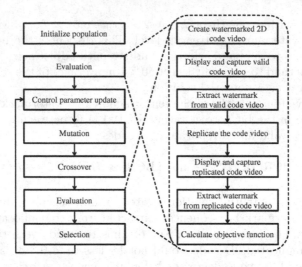

**Fig. 2.** Optimization process flow of the proposed method.

$$mean_L(S_{SF}) = \frac{\sum_{SF \in S_{SF}} SF^2}{\sum_{SF \in S_{SF}} SF} \tag{10}$$

$$CR_i = randn_i(\mu_{CR}, 0.1) \tag{11}$$

$$\mu_{CR} = (1 - c) \cdot \mu_{CR} + c \cdot mean_A(S_{CR}) \tag{12}$$

where $S_{SF}$ and $S_{CR}$ denotes sets of $SF$ and $CR$ values which are all successful scale factors and crossover rates at generation $g$, respectively. $randc_i$ indicates the Cauchy distribution, $mean_L$ denotes Lehmer mean, $randn_i$ does Gaussian distribution, and $mean_A$ denotes the arithmetic mean. As shown the above equations, $SF_i$ and $CR_i$ are updated according to success values of $SF$ and $CR$, Cauthy and Gaussian distributions.

**Step 4 (mutation):** JADE utilizes a strategy called current-to-$p$best, where a base vector is selected from the top $p\%$ of the current population by random. $p$ affects the balance between search exploitation and exploration; small $p$ behaves more greedy [14]. In mutation, calculate difference vector $v_{i,g}$ by the following equation:

$$v_{i,g} = x_{i,g} + SF_i(x^p_{best,g} - x_{i,g}) + SF_i(x_{r1,g} - \tilde{x}_{r2,g}) \tag{13}$$

**Step 5 (crossover):** After mutation, crossover is applied to generate a trial vector $u_{i,g}$. In binomial crossover, $u_{i,g}$ is generated as follows,

$$u_{j,i,g} = \begin{cases} v_{j.i,g} & \text{if } rand_{j,i} \le CR_i \, or \, j = j_{rand} \\ x_{j,i,g} & \text{otherwise} \end{cases} \tag{14}$$

where $u_{j,i,g}$ is $j$-th dimensional component of $u_{i,g}$, $rand_{j,i}$ is a uniform random number with the range of $[0, 1]$, and $j_{rand}$ is a randomly selected dimension.

**Step 6 (evaluation and selection):** Calculate objective function value $f(u_{i,g})$ of the trial vector $u_{i,g}$, and then $u_{i,q}$ is compared with the target vector $x_{i,g}$. Higher one survives to next generation as $x_{i,g+1}$.

## 2.5  System Configuration

To optimize the semi-fragile video watermarking scheme for 2D codes displayed on mobile phone screens, we implement an evaluation system as shown in Figs. 3 and 4. Replication in this system is performed under ideal replication conditions; the two mobile phones used to display and capture the 2D code are set to be focused rather than distorted, and moire patterning is reduced, and the phones are affixed to prevent blurring by camera shake. Furthermore, to avoid the effect of video compression, the replicated watermarked video is displayed by preview mode, which works as a kind of pass-through mode without compression.

In solution evaluation, valid and replicated 2D code videos are displayed and captured in turn. A valid code is displayed by mobile phone $MP_2$ and decoded by the decoder, while a replicated code is generated by two mobile phones $MP_1$ and $MP_2$; the valid code video is displayed on $MP_1$'s screen, and $MP_2$ captures it and displays the captured (replicated) 2D code video. Namely, $MP_2$ alternately displays a valid and a replicated 2D codes.

The valid watermarking extraction process performs by $MP_2$ and the decoder evaluates the robustness of the watermark sufficiently to overcome the noise caused by one cycle of DAD conversions (photographing) via the mobile phone screen and a camera. Moreover, the replication process by $MP_1$, $MP_2$, and the decoder evaluates the fragileness of the watermark sufficiently to be destroyed by two cycles of DAD conversions (rephotographing) between $MP_1$ and $MP_2$ and between $MP_2$ and the decoder.

# 3  Evaluation

## 3.1  Experimental Setup

To verify the effectiveness of the proposed method, experiments with a mobile phone model (Samsung Galaxy S6 SC-04E) was performed, which has a camera (13 megapixels resolution) and a screen (5.0 in $1,920 \times 1,080$ pixels EL (Super AMOLED)). A CCD camera (Pointgrey FLEA3 FL3-U3-88S2C-C, $4,096 \times 2,160$ pixels resolution) and a lens (FUJIFILM DV3.4x3.8SA-1) were used as a barcode decoder for decoding cover 2D code and extracting watermark. All solvers run on a computer (CPU: Intel(R)Core(TM) i7-4770 (3.40 GHz), Mem.: 16 GB, GPU: NVIDIA GeForce GTX780 Ti (876 MHz, 2,880 shader cores, 3 GB mem.)). The cover 2D code image used in the experiment comprises white and blue-purple circular-shaped modules as shown in Fig. 5, while general 2D code which comprises black and white rectangles. The resolution of cover 2D code was $256 \times 256$ pixels, and the actual size of the code on mobile phone screen was 17 mm.

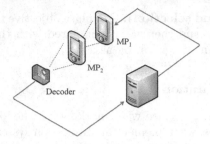

**Fig. 3.** System structure.

**Fig. 4.** Implemented system.

The cover 2D codes displayed on mobile phone screens were captured by the decoder camera with the resolution of almost 704 pixels per side. Other parameters for P3D-DCT were configured as follows: $l_{frame} = 8$, $(m, n) = (8, 8)$[1], and $L_{max} = 200$. $\alpha_0$ and $\alpha_1$ were set to $\{1, 0, 1, 1, 1, 0, 0\}$ and $\{0, 1, 0, 0, 0, 1, 1\}$, respectively. Population size, maximum generation, and $p$ in JADE were set to 30, 120, and 0.05, respectively.

## 3.2  Experimental Results

Figure 6 shows the transition of the objective function value of the best potential solution in the population averaged over three independent runs. Figure 6 demonstrates that a robust watermark that was extracted even from the replicated 2D code video was undesirably generated at the earlier stage of the search. Finally the proposed method found the solution whose objective function value was almost 0.4.

---

[1] Values of $m$ and $n$ were determined by referring to JPEG compression.

**Fig. 5.** Cover 2D code.

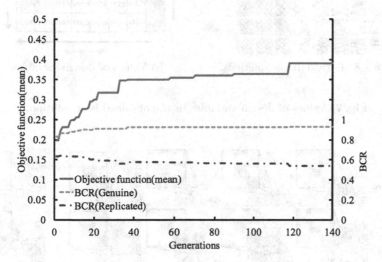

**Fig. 6.** Objective function transitions of the best solution.

The values of design variables in the obtained best solution are shown in Fig. 7, which correspond to basis functions of 2D-DCT and red values indicate subbands used for watermarking. In addition, Fig. 8 shows watermarked video frames in the original digital video, captured videos of valid and replicated 2D codes. Figure 7 demonstrates that the best solution embeds the watermark into many subbands ranging from low frequency to high frequency subbands. The combination of these selected subbands generate sparse peak patterns in bright module region as shown in frames 1 and 4 of the original video, which properly preserved in the captured video frames of the valid code but disappeared in replicated code.

Figure 9 shows the error distributions of extracted watermark by the best solution, where white rectangles indicate the image blocks involving a watermark extraction error. No apparent deviation could be seen in both results of valid and replicated 2D codes.

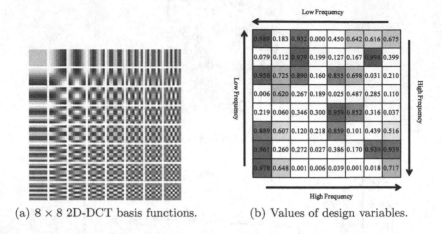

(a) 8 × 8 2D-DCT basis functions.    (b) Values of design variables.

**Fig. 7.** Values of design variables in the obtained best solution.

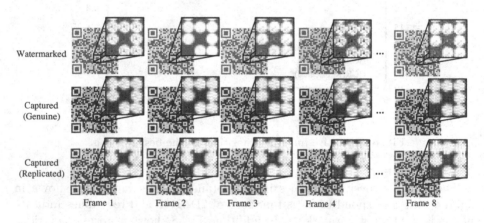

**Fig. 8.** Watermarked video frames by the best solution.

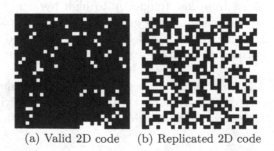

(a) Valid 2D code    (b) Replicated 2D code

**Fig. 9.** Distribution of watermark extraction error.

### 3.3    Discussions

The objective function value of almost 0.4 of the obtained best solution indicates that a simple thresholding in BCR can easily divide valid and replicated 2D codes. However, the designed watermarking scheme embeds the watermark to many subbands. Figure 10 shows watermark extraction accuracy for each subband averaged over the all image block group. It is thought that lower frequency subbands are suitable for robust watermark, and vice versa. However, Fig. 10 demonstrates that horizontal high, vertical low (top right part) and horizontal low, vertical high (bottom left part) frequency subbands were quite effective for semi-fragile watermark; the watermark embedded those subbands could not destroyed by one cycle DAD conversion and destroyed by two cycle conversions.

As described in Sect. 2.5, the replication process in the experiment operated in favor for replication because replicated video was not compressed. Therefore, in practical situations, it would be harder to preserve the video watermark during replication.

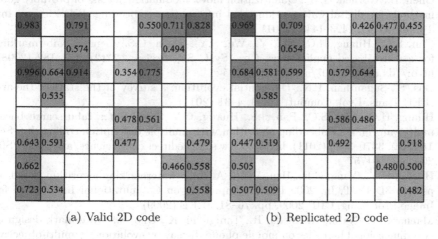

(a) Valid 2D code                    (b) Replicated 2D code

**Fig. 10.** Accuracy for each subband.

## 4    Conclusions

This paper proposes a method for optimizing video watermark for a 2D code displayed on a mobile phone screen. The proposed method designs semi-fragile video watermark for replication detection of the 2D code, which is more difficult to replicate than still image watermark. Experimental results have shown that the proposed method successfully designed a semi-fragile video watermark allowing us to detect replication since there was almost 40 % of BCR difference between original and replicated 2D codes.

In future, we plan to utilize robust optimization techniques to avoid over-fitting and design simpler watermarking scheme with keeping its appropriate semi-fragileness.

**Acknowledgements.** Part of this work was supported by SCOPE of MIC, and JSPS KAKENHI Grant Number 15H02758. The authors also would like to thank A-T Communications, Co., LTD., and DENSO WAVE Inc.

# References

1. Anqiang, L., Jing, L.: A novel scheme for robust video watermark in the 3D-DWT domain. In: 2007 The First International Symposium on Data, Privacy, and E-Commerce, ISDPE 2007, pp. 514–516. IEEE (2007)
2. Chen, A.H.L., Chyu, C.C.: A memetic algorithm for maximizing net present value in resource-constrained project scheduling problem. In: Proceedings of IEEE World Congress on Computational Intelligence, pp. 2401–2408 (2008)
3. Chen, B., Wornell, G.W.: Quantization index modulation: a class of provably good methods for digital watermarking and information embedding. IEEE Trans. Inf. Theory **47**(4), 1423–1443 (2001)
4. Chu, S.C., Huang, H.C., Shi, Y., Wu, S.Y., Shieh, C.S.: Genetic watermarking for zerotree-based applications. Circ. Syst. Sig. Process. **27**(2), 171–182 (2008). http://dx.org/10.1007/s00034-008-9025-z
5. Das, S., Suganthan, P.N.: Differential evolution: a survey of the state-of-the-art. IEEE Trans. Evol. Comput. **15**(1), 4–31 (2011)
6. Huang, H.C., Chu, S.C., Pan, J.S., Huang, C.Y., Liao, B.Y.: Tabu search based multi-watermarks embedding algorithm with multiple description coding. Inf. Sci. **181**(16), 3379–3396 (2011). http://www.sciencedirect.com/science/article/pii/S0020025511001757
7. Huang, H.Y., Yang, C.H., Hsu, W.H.: A video watermarking algorithm based on pseudo 3D DCT. In: 2009 IEEE Symposium on Computational Intelligence for Image Processing, CIIP 2009, pp. 76–81. IEEE (2009)
8. Maehara, T., Nakai, K., Ikeda, R., Taniguchi, K., Ono, S.: Watermark design of two-dimensional barcodes on mobile phone display by evolutionary multi-objective optimization. In: Proceedings of Joint 7th International Conference on Soft Computing and Intelligent Systems and 15th International Symposium on Advanced Intelligent Systems, pp. 149–154 (2014)
9. Mitrea, M., Hasnaoui, M.: Semi-fragile watermarking between theory and practice. In: Proceedings of the Romanian Academy, pp. 328–327, October 2013. https://hal.archives-ouvertes.fr/hal-00941082
10. Nakamura, H., Gohshi, S., Fujii, R., Ito, H., Suzuki, M., Takai, S., Tani, Y.: A digital watermark that survives after re-shooting the images displayed on a CRT screen. J. Inst. Image Inf. Telev. Eng. **60**(11), 1778–1788 (2006)
11. Ono, S., Maehara, T., Nakai, K., Ikeda, R., Taniguchi, K.: Semi-fragile watermark design for detecting illegal two-dimensional barcodes by evolutionary multi-objective optimization. In: Proceedings of Genetic and Evolutionary Computation Conference (GECCO) (Companion), pp. 175–176 (2014)
12. Reed, I.S., Solomon, G.: Polynomial codes over certain finite fields. J. Soc. Ind. Appl. Math. **8**(2), 300–304 (1960). http://www.jstor.org/stable/2098968

13. Storn, R., Price, K.: Differential evolution a simple and efficient heuristic for global optimization over continuous spaces. J. Global Optim. **11**, 341–359 (1997). http://dl.acm.org/citation.cfm?id=596061.596146

14. Tanabe, R., Fukunaga, A.: Success-history based parameter adaptation for differential evolution. In: 2013 IEEE Congress on Evolutionary Computation (CEC), pp. 71–78, June 2013

15. Thiemert, S., Sahbi, H., Steinebach, M.: Using entropy for image and video authentication watermarks. In: Proceedings of the SPIE 6072, Security, Steganography, and Watermarking of Multimedia Contents VIII. No. 607218 (2006). http://dx.org/10.1117/12.643053

16. Zhang, J., Sanderson, A.: JADE: adaptive differential evolution with optional external archive. IEEE Trans. Evol. Comput. **13**(5), 945–958 (2009)

# An Authentication and Recovery Scheme for Digital Speech Signal Based on DWT

Jing Wang, Zhenghui Liu[✉], Junjie He, and Chuanda Qi

College of Mathematics and Information Science, Xinyang Normal University,
Xinyang 464000, China
{wangjing_cosy, zhenghui.liu, hejj99}@163.com,
qichuanda@sina.com

**Abstract.** A tamper recovery scheme for speech signal based on digital watermark is proposed. In this paper, a compression method based on discrete wavelet transform is discussed, and one block-based embedding method for speech signal is explored. Firstly, speech signal is framed, scrambled and segmented. Secondly, frame number is embedded into the first two segments. The compressed signal of each frame after being scrambled is embedded into other two segments by using the block-based method. Attacked frames can be located by frame number. If watermarked speech is attacked, compressed signals are extracted to perform tamper recovery. Performance analyses indicate that the scheme proposed not only improves the accuracy of tamper localization and the security, but also has the ability of tamper recovery.

**Keywords:** Digital watermark · Tamper recovery · Speech compression · Desynchronization attack

## 1 Introduction

It is easy to edit, attack and forge digital speech signal, with the increasingly rich of editing tools. The expressed meaning of attacked signal is different to the original one. If recipient regards the attacked signal is an authentic one and acts according to the requirements, it may cause serious consequences. Fortunately, the forensic technology based on digital watermarking [1–4] gives a method to authenticate the integrity of speech signal.

For digital speech signals, most of the results are focused on speaker recognition and identification [5–8]. However for content authentication and recovery schemes, the results are rarely [9–11]. In daily life, if the instruction of one speech signal is an urgent task and the signal is attacked, maybe the greatest wish is to reconstruct the attacked signal for users, to acquire the expressed meaning of the original speech. Currently, there has been a considerable amount of work on authentication and recovery for digital images [12–15]. It's a pity that, the schemes for speech signal are very rarely [16].

For tamper recovery schemes, the first step is to locate the attacked signal precisely. The tamper location method used commonly is based on synchronization code. While,

© Springer International Publishing Switzerland 2016
Y.-Q. Shi et al. (Eds.): IWDW 2015, LNCS 9569, pp. 206–219, 2016.
DOI: 10.1007/978-3-319-31960-5_17

with regard to the recovery schemes, there are some shortcomings for the method [17–19]. (1) There is a potential security threat analyzed in [20]. (2) For the schemes, the content between two neighboring synchronization codes is regarded as the watermarked signal. As to the content, the forensics is not investigated. So, it can locate the watermarked signal only, but not locate the signal attacked. (3) For the short-time stationarity of speech signals, there are some segments, from which the synchronization codes can be extracted correctly, but not only one. That is, it can locate the watermarked signal roughly not precisely.

Considering the background and motivation above, a tamper recovery scheme is proposed. The compression method for speech signal based on discrete wavelet transform (DWT) is analyzed, and the block-based embedding method is explored. For the scheme, speech signal is framed, and all samples of each frame are scrambled and segmented. The compressed signal of each frame is scrambled before embedding. Frame number is embedded into the first and second segment, respectively. And the compressed signal is embedded into other two segments. In the paper, attacked frames are located precisely, and reconstructed by the compressed signals extracted from other frames. Theoretical analysis and experimental evaluation demonstrate that the scheme proposed is robust against desynchronization attacks, and has the ability of tamper location and recovery.

The organization of this paper is as follows. Section 2 describes the theoretical foundation. Section 3 describes the tamper recovery scheme. Section 4 analyzes the performance of the scheme theoretically and experimentally, which demonstrates that the scheme is effective. Finally, we summarize the conclusion in Sect. 5.

## 2 Theoretical Foundation

### 2.1 Signal Compression

In this paper, original speech signal is compressed firstly, and the compressed signal as watermark is embedded. Suppose that the original speech signal is denoted by $A$, and the compression steps are as follow.

**Step 1:** $A$ is cut into $P$ frames, and the length of each frame is $N$. The $i$-th frame is denoted by $A_i$.

**Step 2:** The sampling frequency is dropped from $f$ to $f_r$, where $f$ and $f_r$ denote the sampling frequency of $A$ before and after re-sampling. The signal re-sampled is denoted by $S$.

**Step 3:** $S$ is cut into $P$ frames, and the $i$-th frame is denoted by $S_i$. The length of $S_i$ is $N \cdot f_r/f$.

**Step 4:** $D$-level DWT is performed on $S_i$, and the wavelet coefficients $F_i^D$, $G_i^D, G_i^{D-1}, \ldots, G_i^1$ can be obtained, where $F_i^D$ is the approximate coefficient, and $G_i^D, G_i^{D-1}, \ldots, G_i^1$ are the detail coefficients from 1 to $D$-level.

In this paper, $F_i^D$ is regarded as the compressed signal, which is as watermark and used to tamper recovery. The recovery method is as follow. ① The value of $G_i^D, G_i^{D-1}, \ldots, G_i^1$ are reset to 0. ② $D$-level inverse DWT is performed on

$F_i^D, G_i^D, G_i^{D-1}, \ldots, G_i^1$. ③ Re-sample the signal using sampling frequency $f$ to obtain the reconstructed signal.

In order to clearly illustrate the compression and recovery method proposed, an example is given in the following. One speech signal is selected randomly as the test signal. It is 16-bit quantified mono signal and sampled at 44.1 kHz. Figure 1(a) shows one segment of the signal, and the length is 960. Firstly, the signal is re-sampled and subjected to 3-level DWT, and the re-sampling frequency $f_r$ is 14.7 kHz. Then the coefficients $F^3$, $D^3$, $D^2$ and $D^1$ are obtained. $F^3$ is regarded as the compressed signal and the length of it is 40. Secondly, the values of $D^3$, $D^2$ and $D^1$ are reset to 0. And 3-level inverse DWT is performed on $F^3$, $D^3$, $D^2$ and $D^1$. The signal obtained is shown in Fig. 1(b). Lastly, re-sample the signal obtained (shown in Fig. 1(b)) with the sampling frequency $f$ 44.1 kHz. The result is shown in Fig. 1(c), which is the recovered signal.

Based on the results shown in Fig. 1, it can be seen that the recovered signal is close to the original one, which indicates that the recovery method is feasible.

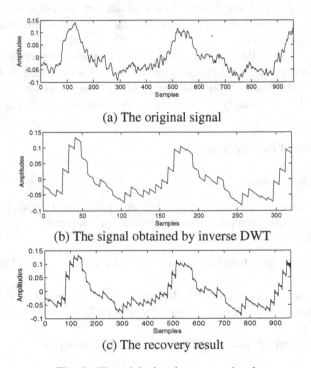

(a) The original signal

(b) The signal obtained by inverse DWT

(c) The recovery result

**Fig. 1.** The original and recovery signal

## 2.2   Embedding Strategy

For the scheme proposed, the compressed signals are scrambled before embedding, aiming to make the compressed signal of one frame is embedded into other frame. The strategy is shown in Fig. 2.

In Fig. 2, $A_i$ denotes the $i$-th frame of the speech signal, $F_i^D$ denotes the compressed signal of $i$-th frame, and $\hat{F}_i^D$ denotes the $i$-th compressed signal after being scrambled. For the proposed scheme, $\hat{F}_i^D$ is the signal that will be embedded into the $i$-th frame $A_i$.

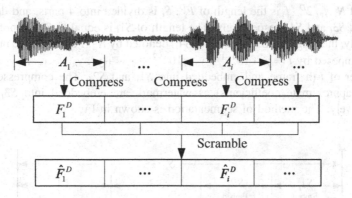

**Fig. 2.** Scrambling the compressed signal

# 3   The Recovery Scheme Based on Digital Watermark

The tamper recovery scheme is described as follow, and the original speech signal is denoted by $A = \{a_l | 1 \leq l \leq L\}$, where $a_l$ represents the $l$-th sample, and $L$ is the length of the signal.

## 3.1   Preprocessing

**Step 1:** The signal $A$ is cut into $P$ frames. The $i$-th frame is denoted by $A_i = \{a_{i,j} | 1 \leq j \leq N\}$, $1 \leq i \leq P$, $N = L/P$, $a_{i,j}$ is the $j$-th sample of $A_i$.

**Step 2:** For each frame $A_i$, it is compressed and the signal obtained is denoted by $F_i^D$, $1 \leq i \leq P$. Then $F_i^D$ $(1 \leq i \leq P)$ is scrambled using chaotic address index sequence as follows.

Denote $X = \{x_i | i = 1, 2, \ldots, P\}$ as the pseudo-random sequence, where $x_i$ can be obtained by the Logistic chaotic mapping shown in Eq. (1).

$$x_{i+1} = \mu x_i (1 - x_i), \quad x_0 = k, \quad 3.5699 \leq \mu \leq 4 \tag{1}$$

where $k$ is the initial value as key of the system. The elements of $X$ are sorted in ascending order shown in Eq. (2), where $h(i)$ is the address index of the sorted chaotic sequence.

$$x_{h(i)} = \text{ascend}(x_i), \quad i = 1, 2, \cdots P \tag{2}$$

Denote $\hat{F}_i^D$ as that after being scrambled, $\hat{F}_i^D = F_{h(i)}^D$, $1 \leq i \leq P$.

**Step 3:** The samples of $A_i$ are scrambled using the same method above, which is denoted by $S_i$, $S_i = \{s_{i,j}, 1 \leq j \leq N\}$, where $s_{i,j} = a_{i,h(j)}, j = 1, 2, \cdots N$.

**Step 4:** Denote $\hat{F}_i^D = \{\hat{F}_{i,t}^D, 1 \leq t \leq N \cdot f_r/2^D \cdot f\}$, where $\hat{F}_{i,t}^D$ is as the $t$-th value of $\hat{F}_i^D$, and $N \cdot f_r/2^D \cdot f$ is the length of $\hat{F}_i^D$. $S_i$ is divided into 4 parts, and denoted by $S1_i$, $S2_i$, $S3_i$ and $S4_i$, respectively. The length of $S1_i$ is equal to $S2_i$, denoted by $N_1$. Similarly, the length of $S3_i$ is equal to $S4_i$, denoted by $N_2$. For the frame number $i$, it is decomposed by $i = y_n \cdot 10^{n-1} + y_{n-1}10^{n-2} + \cdots + y_1$. $y_n, y_{n-1}, \ldots, y_1$ are as the identifier of $i$-th frame and embedded into $S1_i$ and $S2_i$. The compressed signals (DWT approximate coefficients) as watermark are embedded into $S3_i$ and $S4_i$, respectively. The method of segmentation is shown in Fig. 3.

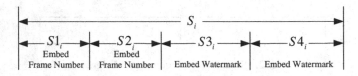

**Fig. 3.** Segmentation method

## 3.2   Watermark Embedding

### 3.2.1   Embed Frame Number

Embed $y_n, y_{n-1}, \ldots, y_1$ into $S1_i$ and $S2_i$, respectively. Denote $S1_i = \{s1_1, s1_2, \cdots s1_{N_1}\}$. $y_n$ is embedded into the first 3 consecutive samples of $S1_i$, $s1_1, s1_2, s1_3$. The embedding method is described as follows.

**Step 1:** Denote $z_m = \lfloor |100 \cdot s1_m| \rfloor \bmod 10$, where $\lfloor \cdot \rfloor$ returns the largest integer less than the original value, $1 \leq m \leq 3$, and $v_m = sign(s1_m)$. If $s1_m \geq 0$, $v_m = 0$. If $s1_m < 0$, $v_m = 1$. It's worth noting that, if $z_m = 0$, set $z_m = 1$, $1 \leq m \leq 3$. Calculate $V = f(z_1, z_2, z_3, v_1, v_2, v_3)$ according to the Eq. (3).

$$f(z_1, z_2, z_3, v_1, v_2, v_3) = [(v_1 + v_2 + v_3 + z_1) \times 1 + z_2 \times 2 + z_3 \times 3] \bmod 10 \qquad (3)$$

If $y_n = V$, $z_1$, $z_2$ and $z_3$ are not need to be quantified.

If $y_n \neq V$, quantify $z_1$, $z_2$ or $z_3$, to make $y_n = V$, under the condition that the original values are as close as possible to that after being quantified.

The quantitative method is $z_1 \pm 1$, $z_2 \pm 1$ or $z_3 \pm 1$. Using the quantified values substitute $z_1$, $z_2$ and $z_3$, to embed $y_n$. For example, if $s1_1 = 0.5692$, $s1_2 = -0.3817$, $s1_3 = 0.3271$ and $y_n = 2$, it's got that $z_1 = 6$, $z_2 = 8$, $z_3 = 2$, $v_1 = 0$, $v_2 = 1$, $v_3 = 0$, Based on the Eq. (3), $V = 9$. In order to make $V = y_n$, $z_3' = z_3 + 1$. $z_3'$ is the value after being quantified.

**Step 2:** Using the method, $y_n, y_{n-1}, \ldots, y_1$ are embedded into $S1_i$ and $S2_i$, respectively.

The quantified signal is denoted by $W1_i$ and $W2_i$. To make the illustrate clear, an example is given in Table 1, $i = 272 \Leftrightarrow (2, 7, 2)$, and $n = 3$.

**Table 1.** Example of quantifying method

| Samples | | $V$ | | Quantified | |
|---|---|---|---|---|---|
| $sl_1$ | 0.5692 | 9 | $y_3 = 2$ | $sl_1$ | 0.5692 |
| $sl_2$ | −0.3817 | | | $sl_2$ | −0.3817 |
| $sl_3$ | 0.3271 | | | $sl_3$ | 0.3$\underline{3}$71 |
| $sl_4$ | −0.4128 | 2 | $y_2 = 7$ | $sl_4$ | −0.4128 |
| $sl_5$ | −0.6534 | | | $sl_5$ | −0.6$\underline{6}$34 |
| $sl_6$ | 0.2326 | | | $sl_6$ | 0.2$\underline{4}$26 |
| $sl_7$ | 0.1125 | 1 | $y_1 = 2$ | $sl_7$ | 0.1$\underline{2}$25 |
| $sl_8$ | 0.3278 | | | $sl_8$ | 0.3278 |
| $sl_9$ | −0.4569 | | | $sl_9$ | −0.4569 |

### 3.2.2 Embed Compressed Signal

Embed $\hat{F}_i^D = \left\{ \hat{F}_{i,t}^D, 1 \leq t \leq N \cdot f_r / 2^D \cdot f \right\}$ into $S3_i$ and $S4_i$ by using the block-based method, and denote $S3_i = \{s3_1, s3_2, \cdots s3_{N_2}\}$.

In this paper, each coefficient, containing sign ("+" or "−") and five numbers are embedded. For $\hat{F}_{i,1}^D \in \hat{F}_i^D$, the first coefficient, $c_{i,1}^1 = \left\lfloor \left| \hat{F}_{i,1}^D \right| \right\rfloor \bmod 10$, $c_{i,1}^2 = \left\lfloor \left| 10 \cdot \hat{F}_{i,1}^D \right| \right\rfloor \bmod 10$, $c_{i,1}^3 = \left\lfloor \left| 100 \cdot \hat{F}_{i,1}^D \right| \right\rfloor \bmod 10$, $c_{i,1}^4 = \left\lfloor \left| 1000 \cdot \hat{F}_{i,1}^D \right| \right\rfloor \bmod 10$ and $c_{i,1}^5 = \left\lfloor \left| 10000 \cdot \hat{F}_{i,1}^D \right| \right\rfloor \bmod 10$ are the five numbers of $c_{i,1}$. For example, if $\hat{F}_{i,1}^D = 1.3628$, sign is "+", and the five numbers are 1, 3, 6, 2 and 8. They are embedded into the first 6 consecutive samples of $S3_i(s3_1, s3_2, \ldots, s3_6)$.

The 6 samples are partitioned into 6 blocks. The first block is composed by $\lfloor |10 \cdot s3_1| \rfloor$, $\lfloor |10 \cdot s3_2| \rfloor$, $\lfloor |10 \cdot s3_3| \rfloor$ and the sign of $s3_1$, $s3_2$ $s3_3$. The second is composed by $\lfloor |10 \cdot s3_4| \rfloor$, $\lfloor |10 \cdot s3_5| \rfloor$, $\lfloor |10 \cdot s3_6| \rfloor$ and the sign of $s3_4$, $s3_5$ $s3_6$. Similarly, other four blocks can be obtained. In this paper, "+" is mapped to 0, and "−" is mapped to 1. As an example, 6 samples are selected, and the partition result is shown in Table 2. Based on the partition, the embedding method is as follows.

**Table 2.** The partition result

| 6 samples | $B_1$ | | $B_2$ | | $B_3$ | | $B_4$ | | $B_5$ | | $B_6$ | |
|---|---|---|---|---|---|---|---|---|---|---|---|---|
| −0.3125 | 1 | 3 | | | 1 | 1 | | | 1 | 2 | | |
| −0.2191 | 1 | 2 | | | 1 | 1 | | | 1 | 9 | | |
| 0.1567 | 0 | 1 | | | 0 | 5 | | | 0 | 6 | | |
| 0.2237 | | | 0 | 2 | | | 0 | 2 | | | 0 | 3 |
| −0.5123 | | | 1 | 5 | | | 1 | 1 | | | 1 | 2 |
| 0.6318 | | | 0 | 6 | | | 0 | 3 | | | 0 | 1 |

**Step 1:** Embed the sign of $\hat{F}_{i,1}^D$, "+" or "−", into $B_1$.

Denote $z'_m = \lfloor |10 \cdot s3_m| \rfloor \bmod 10$, and $v'_m = sign(s3_m)$, $1 \leq m \leq 3$. The sum of 6 values in $B_1$ is denoted by $T$. If $0 \leq \hat{F}_{i,1}^D$, and $T \bmod 2 = 1$, quantify $z'_1$, $z'_2$ or $z'_3$, to make $T \bmod 2 = 0$ and embed the sign "+", such as $z'_1 + 1$ or $z'_1 - 1$. If $\hat{F}_{i,1}^D < 0$, and $T \bmod 2 = 0$, quantify $z'_1$, $z'_2$ or $z'_3$, to make $T \bmod 2 = 1$ and embed the sign "−". For other conditions, $z'_1$, $z'_2$ and $z'_3$ remain the same without modification

**Step 2:** Denote $z'_m = \lfloor |10 \cdot s3_m| \rfloor \bmod 10$, and $v'_m = sign(s3_m)$, $4 \leq m \leq 6$. For the values, $V$ can be obtained based on the Eq. (3). By using the frame number embedding method, $c_{i,1}^1$ is embedded by quantifying $z'_4$, $z'_5$ and $z'_6$.

**Table 3.** The embedding method for $\hat{F}_{i,1}^D = -1.3551$

| 6 samples | $B_1 \rightarrow B'_1$ ("−") | | $B_3 \rightarrow B'_3$ $(c_{i,1}^2)$ | | $B_5 \rightarrow B'_5$ $(c_{i,1}^4)$ | | Samples quantified |
|---|---|---|---|---|---|---|---|
| −0.3125 | 3 | 3 | 1 | 1 | 2 | 2 | −0.3125 |
| −0.2191 | 2 | 3 | 1 | 1 | 9 | 8 | −0.3181 |
| 0.1567 | 1 | 1 | 5 | 6 | 6 | 5 | 0.1657 |
| | $B_2 \rightarrow B'_2$ $(c_{i,1}^1)$ | | $B_4 \rightarrow B'_4$ $(c_{i,1}^3)$ | | $B_6 \rightarrow B'_6$ $(c_{i,1}^5)$ | | |
| 0.2237 | 2 | 2 | 2 | 3 | 3 | 3 | 0.2337 |
| −0.5123 | 5 | 5 | 1 | 1 | 2 | 2 | −0.5123 |
| 0.6318 | 6 | 6 | 3 | 3 | 1 | 1 | 0.6318 |

**Step 3:** Similarly, $c_{i,1}^2$, $c_{i,1}^3$, $c_{i,1}^4$ and $c_{i,1}^5$ are embedded into the blocks of $B_3$, $B_4$, $B_5$ and $B_6$. Suppose that $\hat{F}_{i,1}^D = -1.3556$, the quantitative method is show in Table 3, in which $B'_l$, $1 \leq l \leq 6$ represents the corresponding values after being quantified.

**Step 4:** According to the steps 1–3 above, $\hat{F}_{i,t}^D$, $1 \leq t \leq N \cdot f_r / 2^D \cdot f$ is embedded into $S3_i$ and $S4_i$, respectively.

For $S3_i$ and $S4_i$, the signals after being quantified are denoted by $W3_i$ and $W4_i$. $W1_i$, $W2_i$, $W3_i$ and $W4_i$ are concatenated, then inverse scrambling is performed on the signal, to obtain the watermarked signal of the $i$-th frame. The process of watermark embedding is shown in Fig. 4.

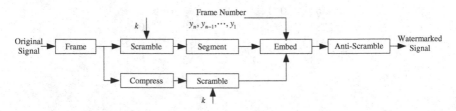

**Fig. 4.** The process of watermark embedding

## 3.3 Content Authentication and Tamper Recovery

Denote $A'$ as the watermarked speech signal.

(1) $A'$ is cut into $P$ frames, and the samples of each frame are scrambled. The $i$-th frame after being scrambled is denoted by $S'_i$. $S1'_i$, $S2'_i$, $S3'_i$ and $S4'_i$ are the 4 segments of $S'_i$. The length of $S1'_i$ and $S2'_i$ is $N_1$, the length of $S3'_i$ and $S4'_i$ is $N_2$.
(2) Extract frame number from $S1'_i$ and $S2'_i$.

**Step 1:** Denoted $S1'_i = \left\{ s1'_1, s1'_2, \cdots, s1'_{N_1} \right\}$, based on Eq. (4), $y'_n$ can be extracted from $s1'_1$, $s1'_2$ and $s1'_3$. Similarly, $y'_{n-1}, \cdots y'_1$ can be extracted from other samples of $S1'_i$. Denote $n'_i = y'_n \times 10^{n-1} + y'_{n-1} \times 10^{n-2} + \cdots + y'_1$, which is the frame number extracted.
**Step 2:** Extract frame number from $S2'_i$ by using same method. And the number extracted is denoted $n^*_i$.

(3) Extract the compressed signal from $S3'_i$ and $S4'_i$, based on the block-based method shown in Tables 2 and 3. Take the first one coefficient extracted from $S3'_i$ as an example, and the coefficients are denoted by $c'_{i,1}$.

**Step 1:** Extract the sign of $c'_{i,1}$ from the values in $B_1$, according to Eq. (4), in which $T'$ represents the sum of values in $B_1$.

$$U = T' \bmod 2 \tag{4}$$

If $U = 0$, it indicates that the sign of $c'_{i,1}$ is "+". If $U = 1$, it indicates that the sign of $c'_{i,1}$ is "−".

**Step 2:** According to the values in $B_2$, $c1'_{i,1} = \left\lfloor \left| c'_{i,1} \right| \right\rfloor$ can be obtained by using the Eq. (3). Similarly, $c2'_{i,1} = \left\lfloor \left| 10 \cdot c'_{i,1} \right| \right\rfloor \bmod 10$, $c3'_{i,1} = \left\lfloor \left| 100 \cdot c'_{i,1} \right| \right\rfloor \bmod 10$, $c4'_{i,1} = \left\lfloor \left| 1000 \cdot c'_{i,1} \right| \right\rfloor \bmod 10$, $c5'_{i,1} = \left\lfloor \left| 10000 \cdot c'_{i,1} \right| \right\rfloor \bmod 10$ can be extracted. And $c'_{i,1}$ can be constructed by Eq. (5).

$$c'_{i,1} = sign \times \left( c1'_{i,1} + \frac{c2'_{i,1}}{10} + \frac{c3'_{i,1}}{100} + \frac{c4'_{i,1}}{1000} + \frac{c5'_{i,1}}{10000} \right) \tag{5}$$

**Step 3:** By using the same method, other coefficients are extracted from $S3'_i$ and $S4'_i$, denoted by $c'_{i,j}$ and $c^*_{i,j}$, respectively, $1 \leq j \leq N \cdot f_r / 2^D \cdot f$.

(4) Content authentication

If $n'_i = n^*_i$, and $c'_{i,j} = c^*_{i,j}$, $1 \leq j \leq N \cdot f_r / 2^D \cdot f$, the $i$-th frame is regarded to be intact. Otherwise, $n'_i \neq n^*_i$ or $c'_{i,j} = c^*_{i,j}$, it indicates that the $i$-th frame has been tampered, and the tamper recovery is performed by the following Sect. (5). The method of content authentication is shown in Fig. 5.

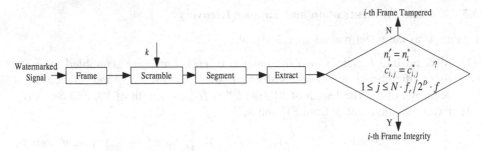

**Fig. 5.** The process of content authentication

**(5)\* Tamper recovery**

Suppose that the frames of 1-th to $i$-th are all intact and the next $N$ successive samples are attacked, the tamper recovery method is as follow.

**Step 1:** Move and authenticate the next $N$ successive samples, until the samples can be authenticated successfully. Then extract the frame number, denoted by $i'$. The content between $i$-th and $i'$-th frame is regarded as the attacked frame, and the method is shown in Fig. 6.

**Step 2:** Find the embedding position of compressed signal corresponding to attacked frame, according to the address index of the sorted chaotic sequence, in Eq. (2).

**Step 3:** Extract the compressed signal, and reset the value of detail coefficients to 0, to perform $D$-level inverse DWT. The recovered signal can be got by re-sampling with the sampling frequency $f$.

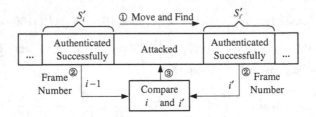

**Fig. 6.** The tamper location method

## 4  Performance Analysis and Experimental Results

In the following, the performance of the recovery scheme proposed in this paper is evaluated. 60 speech signals are recorded by Sony PCM-100, and divided into 4 types, denoted by Type 1, Type 2, Type 3 and Type 4, respectively. Type 1 is recorded in a quiet room, which represents that recorded in a quiet closed space; Type 2 is recorded in a noisy room, which represents that recorded in a noisy closed space. Type 3 is recorded in an open field, and Type 4 is recorded in a noisy station. They are WAVE format 16-bit quantified mono signals, sampled at 44.1 kHz. The parameters used in the scheme are set as follows, the length of test speech $L = 144000$, containing 20 frames, that is $P = 20$, the length of each frame $N = 7200$; the sampling frequency $f = 44100$, and that after being re-sampled $f_r = 22050$, the order of DWT $D = 3$, $N_1 = 9, n = 10$, $k = 0.68$. Based on the values above, we can get that the length of $F_i^D$ (the DWT approximate coefficient) is 450, that is $N \cdot f_r / 2^D \cdot f = 450$.

## 4.1    Inaudibility

In the paper, the inaudibility of 4 types watermarked speech signal is tested based on subjective difference grades (SDG) and objective difference grades (ODG), and the values of SDG and ODG are listed in Table 4. SDG values are obtained from 15 listeners, and ODG values are acquired by using the PEAQ system. Based on the test results, it can be seen that the watermark embedding method proposed has a good inaudibility. The meaning of the scores in SDG and ODG are shown in [20].

**Table 4.** The SDG and ODG values of different types watermarked signal

| Watermarked signal | SDG | ODG |
|---|---|---|
| Type 1 | −0.4836 | −0.624 |
| Type 2 | −0.5267 | −0.738 |
| Type 3 | −0.4651 | −0.615 |
| Type 4 | −0.4132 | −0.697 |

## 4.2    Security and Ability of Tamper Location

For some watermark schemes, watermark embedded is based on public features. From the analysis in [20], we get that the schemes have safety problems.

In this paper, samples of each frame are scrambled before embedding. Frame number and watermark are embedded into the scrambled samples. Watermarked signal is obtained by inverse scrambling after embedding. That is watermarked samples are randomly throughout the whole speech signal. So, for attackers, the features used to embed watermark are secret and it's difficult to get the embedding position to perform attack without the key. If one frame is attacked, it can be detected with high probability $1 - 1/2 \cdot 10^{n+5Q}$, where $Q = N \cdot f_r / 2^D \cdot f$. So, the scheme improves the security of watermark system.

In addition, one code (a integer number) is embedded into samples as few as possible (three samples), to locate the attacked frames precisely. Based on the parameters selected, the probability of false tamper location is $1/2 \cdot 10^{n+5Q}$, which is approximate to zero. So, the method can tamper location precisely.

### 4.3   Tamper Recovery Results

In this section, tamper recovery result is given. Due to spaces constraints, the result for deletion attack is shown only, and for other attack, the result is the same. One watermarked speech signal is selected and shown in Fig. 7(a). Figure 7(b) shows the watermarked signal after being scrambled for each frame. The detailed steps, attack, tamper location and tamper recovery are given, aiming to make the method of tamper location and recovery explicitly.

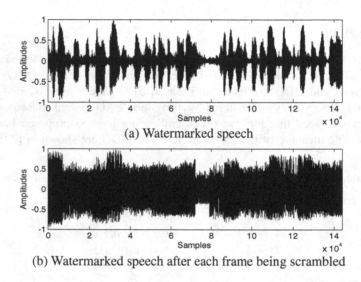

(a) Watermarked speech

(b) Watermarked speech after each frame being scrambled

**Fig. 7.**  Watermarked speech and the scrambled signal

**Step 1:** The samples 72001-th to 82000-th of the watermarked signal are selected and deleted, shown in Fig. 8(a).
**Step 2:** For the attacked signal, each frame is scrambled and authenticated from the first frame, until that the $N$ successive samples cannot pass authentication. The authentication result for the intact frames is shown in Fig. 8(b).
**Step 3:** Move and scramble next $N$ successive samples, until the samples can pass authentication. The result is shown in Fig. 8(c). Then extract the frame number, which is the next frame number that can be authenticated successfully.
**Step 4:** The attacked frames can be identified by the difference between the back and ahead frame number that can be authenticated successfully. The tamper location result is shown in Fig. 8(d), in which $TL = 0$ indicates that the corresponding frame is intact.
**Step 5:** Based on the scrambling method, find the frames that can extract DWT approximate coefficients of the attacked frames. In this paper, the DWT approximate coefficients of the attacked frame, 11-th and 12-th, are embedded into the 17-th and 5-th frame, respectively. Extract the compressed signals from 17-th and 5-th frame, to reconstruct the attacked signals. The tamper recovery result is shown in Fig. 8(e).

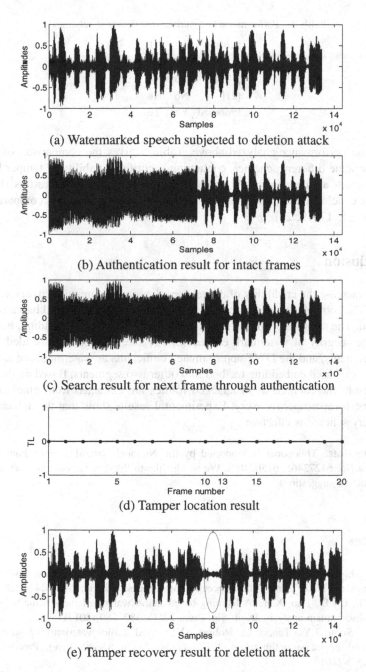

(a) Watermarked speech subjected to deletion attack

(b) Authentication result for intact frames

(c) Search result for next frame through authentication

(d) Tamper location result

(e) Tamper recovery result for deletion attack

**Fig. 8.** Watermarked signal subjected to deletion attack and the tamper recovery result

**Table 5.** Performance comparison for different schemes

| Scheme | AI | AII |
|---|---|---|
| [1] | No | Yes |
| [17–19] | No | No |
| [21] | No | No |
| Proposed | Yes | Yes |

Based on performance analyzed above, Table 5 gives the comparison of various abilities for some different schemes, containing security and ability of tamper location precisely, which are denoted by AI and AII, respectively. From the results shown in Table 5, we concluded that, the scheme proposed has many advantages comparing with the schemes [1, 17–19, 21].

## 5  Conclusion

In order to increase the credibility of digital speech signal, a tamper recovery scheme is proposed. The compression and reconstructed method for speech signal based on DWT is discussed. The samples of speech signal are scrambled before embedding, in order to improve the security of watermark embedding. Frame number is embedded into the first two segments, and the DWT approximate coefficients as watermark are embedded by using block-based embedding method into other two segments. Based on the tamper location result, the coefficients of attacked frames are extracted from other authentic frames to perform tamper recovery. Experimental results show that the authentication and recovery scheme is effective.

**Acknowledgments.** This paper is supported by the National Natural Science Foundation of China (Grant No. 61272465, 61502409). We would like to thank the anonymous reviewers for their constructive suggestions.

## References

1. Pun, C.M., Yuan, X.C.: Robust segments detector for de-synchronization resilient audio watermarking. IEEE Trans. Audio Speech Lang. Process. **21**(11), 2412–2424 (2013)
2. Peng, H., Li, B., Luo, X.H.: A learning-based audio watermarking scheme using kernel Fisher discriminant analysis. Digit. Sig. Proc. **23**(1), 382–389 (2013)
3. Lei, B., Soon, I.Y., Tan, E.L.: Robust SVD-based audio watermarking scheme with differential evolution optimization. IEEE Trans. Audio Speech Lang. Process. **21**(11), 2368–2378 (2013)
4. Akhaee, M.A., Kalantari, N.K., Marvasti, F.: Robust audio and speech satermarking using Gaussian and Laplacian modeling. Sig. Process. **90**(8), 2487–2497 (2010)
5. Herbig, T., Gerl, F., Minker, W.: Self-learning speaker identification for enhanced speech recognition. Comput. Speech Lang. **26**(3), 210–227 (2012)

6. Khan, L.A., Baig, M.S., Youssef, A.M.: Speaker recognition from encrypted VoIP communications. Digital Invest. **7**(1–2), 65–73 (2010)
7. Navarathna, R., Dean, D., Sridharan, S.: Multiple cameras for audio-visual speech recognition in an automotive environment. Comput. Speech Lang. **27**(4), 911–927 (2013)
8. Sahidullah, M., Saha, G.: Design, analysis and experimental evaluation of block based transformation in MFCC computation for speaker recognition. Speech Commun. **54**(4), 543–565 (2012)
9. Park, C., Thapa, M.D., Wang, G.N.: Speech authentication system using digital watermarking and pattern recovery. Pattern Recogn. Lett. **28**(8), 931–938 (2007)
10. Chen, O.T.C., Liu, C.H.: Content-dependent watermarking scheme in compressed speech with identifying manner and location of attacks. IEEE Trans. Audio Speech Lang. Process. **15**(5), 1605–1616 (2007)
11. Yuan, S., Huss, S.A.: Audio watermarking algorithm for real-time speech integrity and authentication. In: Proceedings of the 2004 Workshop on Multimedia and Security, pp. 220–226 (2004)
12. Chamlawi, R., Khan, A., Usman, I.: Authentication and recovery of images using multiple watermarks. Comput. Electr. Eng. **36**(3), 578–584 (2010)
13. Lee, T.Y., Lin, S.D.: Dual watermark for image tamper detection and recovery. Pattern Recogn. **41**(11), 3497–3506 (2008)
14. Li, C.L., Wang, Y.H., Ma, B., Zhang, Z.X.: Tamper detection and self-recovery of biometric images using salient region-based authentication watermarking scheme. Comput. Stan. Interfaces **34**(4), 367–379 (2012)
15. Roldan, L.R., Hernandez, M.C., Miyatake, M.N., Meana, H.P., Kurkoski, B.: Watermarking-based image authentication with recovery capability using halftoning technique. Sig. Process. Image Commun. **28**(1), 69–83 (2013)
16. Fakhr, M.W.: Sparse watermark embedding and recovery using compressed sensing framework for audio signals. In: Proceedings of International Conference on Cyber-Enabled Distributed Computing and Knowledge Discover, pp. 535–539 (2012)
17. Vivekananda, B.K., Indranil, S., Abhijit, D.: A new audio watermarking scheme based on singular value decomposition and quantization. Circuits Syst. Sig. Process. **30**(5), 915–927 (2011)
18. Lei, B.Y., Soon, I.Y., Li, Z.: Blind and robust audio watermarking scheme based on SVD-DCT. Sig. Process. **91**(8), 1973–1984 (2011)
19. Wang, X.Y., Ma, T.X., Niu, P.P.: A pseudo-Zernike moments based audio watermarking scheme robust against desynchronization attacks. Comput. Electr. Eng. **37**(4), 425–443 (2011)
20. Liu, Z.H., Wang, H.X.: A novel speech content authentication algorithm based on Bessel-Fourier moments. Digital Sig. Process. **24**, 197–208 (2014)
21. Wang, Y., Wu, S.Q., Huang, J.W.: Audio watermarking scheme robust against desynchronization based on the dyadic wavelet transform. J. Adv. Sig. Process. **2010**(13), 1–17 (2010)

# Enrichment of Visual Appearance
# of Aesthetic QR Code

Minoru Kuribayashi[1(✉)] and Masakatu Morii[2]

[1] Graduate School of Natural Science and Technology, Okayama University,
3-1-1 Tsushima-naka, Kita-ku, Okayama 700-8530, Japan
kminoru@okayama-u.ac.jp
[2] Graduate School of Engineering, Kobe University, 1-1 Rokkodai-cho,
Nada-ku, Kobe, Hyogo 657-8501, Japan

**Abstract.** Quick Response (QR) code is a two dimensional barcode widely used in many applications. Similar to a visible watermarking technique, the visual appearance can be modified to display an image while a standard QR code reader can decode the data contained in such a QR code. In this paper, we consider the characteristic of images to be displayed on a QR code, and propose an effective method to produce a visually better aesthetic QR code without sacrificing its error correcting capability. We also investigate the shape of modules to represent the image to be displayed and consider the trade-off between the visual quality and its readability.

## 1 Introduction

QR code is a two-dimensional code consisting of black and white square modules. It is originally developed by Denso Wave[1] as an effective way for accessing digital data by forming a machine-readable format. It can carry more information than conventional barcodes and can be read very quickly by software equipped in smart phones. The QR code has become a popular tool for advertising by companies as it enables customers to easily access to their websites.

### 1.1 Background

A standard QR code contains only black and white square modules and its appearance is noisy looks. There are many approaches for producing aesthetic QR codes by displaying images on a QR code. For a given message and an image, it is desirable to automatically generates such a QR code because manually designed barcodes are too expensive. It is also required for the aesthetic QR codes to be readable by standardized decoders. The conventional approaches satisfying these requirements can be categorized into four classes.

The first class globally transforms an input image, and superimposes it on part of the QR code [5–7]. It modifies several modules of an original QR code

---

[1] http://www.qrcode.com/en/.

© Springer International Publishing Switzerland 2016
Y.-Q. Shi et al. (Eds.): IWDW 2015, LNCS 9569, pp. 220–231, 2016.
DOI: 10.1007/978-3-319-31960-5_18

within a possible error correcting capability to display a small logo image. The drawback is that it sacrifices the readability of original QR codes and the displayable size is limited to be small. The second class modifies the size and color of modules according to the pixel of image. Visualead[2] and LogoQ[3] keep a concentric region of modules untouched and uniformly blend the neighboring regions with pixels of an image preserving the original contrast. The third class changes the padding modules to display an image on the QR code [8,9]. The possible area on which the image is displayed is restricted due to the standardized structure of QR code. A free software of the QR-JAM MAKER[4] is open to be public. The main restriction is the systematic encoding of Reed-Solomon (RS) code [4]. The fourth class employs the non-systematic encoding of RS code which allows us to select the displaying position without sacrificing the error correcting capability [3]. However, the conventional method reduces the resolution of the image due to the limitation of the number of modules.

Some other works studied the combination of the above classes and image processing techniques to effectively enhance the visual quality. Chu et al. [1] applied the half-toning technique for displaying image to produce an aesthetic QR code. Fang et al. [2] considered the sampling process and error correction to optimize the generation procedure by modeling the procedure as the watermark embedding problem. Zhang et al. [10] proposed two-stage approach that is a combination of module-based and pixel-based embeddings. Even though these methods can enhance the visual quality, they try to reduce the noise-like appearance at the center of image by using error correcting capability or shape of modules. The basic white/black patterns at the important region of an image are not removed in a literature.

## 1.2   Our Contribution

In this paper, we focus on the following two tendencies for generic images. (1) The outer end of an image is less important than the center region. (2) The noisy region of an image is less sensitive to the modification of pixels because most watermarking techniques avoid flat regions for embedding. Based upon these tendencies, we propose a weighting function to determine the positions for non-systematic encoding. On the non-systematic encoding of RS codeword, the positions of information symbols can be freely selected among all positions including the parity check symbols [4]. By fixing the first some positions for representing a data to be contained, we control the positions of the other information symbols according to the calculated weights. As the results, we can generate visually better aesthetic QR codes than the conventional ones [3] while its numerical measurement is slightly degraded. The conventional method randomly generates several RS codewords using the non-systematic encoding and determines the best one under the constraint such that the hamming distance with the

---

[2] http://www.visualead.com.

[3] http://logoq.net.

[4] http://staff.aist.go.jp/hagiwara.hagiwara/qrjam/index.html.

original pixel values of an image becomes minimum. On the other hand, the proposed method mainly focuses on the visual appearance as the constraint.

We also investigate the module which represents the image to be displayed. Because the number of modules in a QR code is relatively small, the resolution of an image should be scaled down in order to adjust the QR code. To increase the resolution, we propose sub-modules that express each module with a matrix description. Using some examples of such sub-modules, we measure the trade-off between the readability and visual quality of generated QR code.

## 2    Preliminaries

### 2.1    Overview of QR Code

QR code basically consists of black modules arranged in a square pattern on a white background. The module represented by black or white pattern is the minimum component of a QR code and each module is assigned a single bit value. The size of QR code is determined by a version number from 1 to 40. The number of modules representing an encoded data in a QR code of version $v$ is $(17 + 4v) \times (17 + 4v)$. The QR code has function patterns in order for a reader to identify the position in which an encoded data is involved. The patterns are composed of three main parts; finder pattern, alignment pattern, and timing pattern.

The QR code uses the RS code for error correction which capability is classified into 4 levels: L, M, Q, and H in the increasing order. Each error correction level can correct symbols up to about 7 %, 15 %, 25 % and 30 % to all symbols of the QR code. Because of the characteristic of the RS code, each symbol of the codeword is composed of 8 bits, and it is arranged by neighboring 8 modules in a QR code. Considering a dirt on a QR code, the symbols of the codeword are arranged not in a successive order, but in an interleaved one.

Given the version number and the error correction level, the number of codewords and their constructions expressed by $(n, k, d)$ are uniquely determined in a QR code, where $n$, $k$, and $d$ mean the code length, the number of information symbols, and the minimum distance satisfying $d = n - k + 1$. For instance, 5L or less QR codes are composed of a single codeword, while 5M or more QR codes are composed of two or more codewords and their symbol positions at the QR code is set by an interleaved order. The code length $n$ is increased with the version number, while $k$ is decreased with the error correction level.

Since each symbol of the codeword is composed of 8 bits, at most $8k$ bits ($k$ bytes) are represented by a single codeword. If the amount of information to be embedded is less than the capacity, padding symbols are attached with the information symbols. The padding symbols have no information, so it can be changed freely. The remaining $n - k$ symbols are called parity symbols in a RS code, and its redundancy contributes on an error correcting capability. In the systematic encoding, the parity symbols are derived uniquely from the information symbols.

Considering the readability by optical camera devices, the number of black and white modules should be balanced in the QR code. There are eight mask patterns that changes the bits according to their coordinates in order to make the QR code easier to read. At the encoding, each element of a selected mask pattern is XORed with a current module.

## 2.2   Non-Systematic Encoding Method

Let $\boldsymbol{\delta} = (\delta_1, \delta_2, \ldots, \delta_k)$ be information symbols of length $k$, Then, the parity symbols $\boldsymbol{p} = (p_1, p_2, \ldots, p_{n-k})$ is calculated from $\boldsymbol{\delta}$ using a systematic encoding function $enc()$, and the generated codeword $\boldsymbol{c}$ is represented by

$$\boldsymbol{c} = enc(\boldsymbol{\delta}) = (c_1, c_2, \ldots, c_n) \tag{1}$$

$$= (\delta_1, \delta_2, \ldots, \delta_k, p_1, p_2, \ldots p_{n-k}). \tag{2}$$

Notice that the information symbols $\boldsymbol{\delta}$ are arranged in the first $k$ symbols of its codeword $\boldsymbol{c}$. Such positions of symbols are fixed in a QR code. The information symbols $\boldsymbol{\delta}$ can be decoded by performing a decoder $dec()$ from a distorted codeword $\boldsymbol{c}^*$ if the bit errors are within an error correcting capability. In general, if a non-systematic encoding is performed, the information symbols cannot be separated from the symbols of codeword.

When the encoding function is modified, it is possible to obtain a non-systematic encoding function for RS code. The RS code is known that a codeword encoded by the non-systematic encoding is one of the codewords encoded by a systematic encoding. In addition, it is possible to fix arbitrary $k$ symbols of the codeword $\boldsymbol{c}'$ encoded by the non-systematic encoding, and to calculate the remain $n - k$ symbols using the non-systematic encoding function.

Let $\mathcal{C}$ be the group of all RS codewords generated by $enc()$, namely, $\forall \boldsymbol{c} \in \mathcal{C}$. Then, the codewords $\boldsymbol{c}'$ encoded by the non-systematic encoding satisfies $\forall \boldsymbol{c}' \in \mathcal{C}$. Thus, we can obtain certain information symbols from $dec(\boldsymbol{c}')$. If no error is occurred, the first $k$ symbols of the codeword $\boldsymbol{c}'$ is the decoded information symbols. For a given index $\boldsymbol{\theta} = (\theta_1, \theta_2, \ldots, \theta_k)$, the $k$ symbols of the codeword $\boldsymbol{c}'$ is represented by

$$c'_{\theta_i} = \delta_i, \ (1 \leq i \leq k), \tag{3}$$

where $1 \leq \theta_i \leq n$ and $\theta_i \neq \theta_j$ for $i \neq j$. The other $n - k$ symbols are calculated according to these $k$ symbols using the non-systematic encoding function.

It is clear that QR codes encoded by the non-systematic encoding also can be read with common QR code readers. Suppose that the first $\hat{k}(< k)$ symbols are used to represent a data to be encoded and the remain $k - \hat{k}$ symbols are regarded as padding symbols. In such a case, it is possible to use the following index.

$$\boldsymbol{\theta}_{\hat{k}} = (1, 2, \ldots, \hat{k}, \theta_{\hat{k}+1}, \ldots, \theta_k) \tag{4}$$

It means that there are $C(n - \hat{k}, k - \hat{k})$ candidates for the index $\boldsymbol{\theta}_{\hat{k}}$, where $C(a, b)$ stands for the number of $b$-combinations from a given set of $a$ elements. In short, we can freely select the positions for padding symbols within the range $[\hat{k}+1, n]$ at the codeword. When the amount of encoding data is small, the designable area becomes large in the method. If a QR code has $m$ codewords whose information symbols are $k_t$, $(1 \leq t \leq m)$ bytes, and the size of the information symbols is $\sigma$ bytes, then the size of designable area is $(\sum_{t=1}^{m} k_t) - \sigma$ bytes.

### 2.3   Conventional Method

In [3], a non-systematic encoding of RS code is introduced for producing aesthetic QR codes. Without loss of generality, the data to be embedded is composed of $\sigma$ bytes and it is partitioned into $m$ segments of length $\hat{k}_t$, $(1 \leq t \leq m)$, namely $\sum_{t=1}^{m} \hat{k}_t = \sigma$. For each segment, the RS codeword $c'_t$ is calculated by a non-systematic encoding using a certain index $\theta_{\hat{k}_t}$.

First, each pixel of an image is regarded as each module of ideal QR code. However, the pixels of an image may not be coincident with the binary represented RS codewords. Allowing some errors, we generates several RS codewords by changing $\theta_{\hat{k}_t}$ and choose the best one whose hamming distance becomes minimum. The procedure to make aesthetic QR codes is described as follows.

**Step 1.** Assign pixels of an image to modules of a QR code, and binarize the modules with the threshold determined by the average of all RGB values.

**Step 2.** Operate a predetermined masking pattern to the binary matrix, and replace $\sigma$ symbols of the masked image with information symbols, which are never changed in the following steps.

**Step 3.** Partition the masked image into $m$ sequences which are corresponding to the RS codewords placed on the QR code in an interleaved order. We denote the $m$ sequences by $\alpha_t$, $(1 \leq t \leq m)$.

**Step 4.** For $1 \leq t \leq m$, find the best RS codeword $\ddot{c}'_t$, whose Hamming distance from $\alpha_t$ becomes minimum, by changing the index $\theta_{\hat{k}_t}$.

**Step 5.** Replace the best RS codeword $\ddot{c}'_t$ with $\alpha_t$ for $1 \leq t \leq m$.

**Step 6.** Operate the predetermined masking pattern again to cancel the masking operation at step2.

There are $C(n - \hat{k}_t, k_t - \hat{k}_t)$ candidates for the index $\theta_{\hat{k}_t}$ for $(1 \leq t \leq m)$. It is computationally difficult to check all candidates for the search in Step 4. Therefore, the index $\theta_{\hat{k}_t}$ are randomly selected and the trial is bounded to $N$ times.

## 3   Proposed Weighting Method

In the conventional method, the index $\theta_{\hat{k}_t}$ is randomly generated without any strategies. Considering the characteristics of an image to be displayed, we propose an effective method to classify perceptually important regions with the others.

## 3.1   Weighting Function

It is widely recognized that noisy regions of an image are less sensitive to modification than flat regions. For instance, watermark signal is usually embedded into edges of an image in order to control the perceptual degradation. It is also reasonable to assume that the center region of an image is much more important than its surroundings. Based upon the characteristics, we calculate weights for modules.

Suppose that an image is square size with $L \times L$ pixels and each pixel is represented by RGB color components. Using a certain conversion algorithm equipped at a QR code reader, a binary matrix $B_{i,j}$, $(1 \le i, j \le 17 + 4v)$ is calculated from the input image for the given version $v$ of QR code. In our method, the following algorithm is used as the conversion.

**Step 1.** The scale of the input image is changed to be the same size of the given version $v$ of QR code.

**Step 2.** The RGB color components are translated into YUV color components, and the luminance(Y) components $Y_{i,j}$, $(1 \le i, j \le 17 + 4v)$ are obtained.

**Step 3.** The average $\bar{Y}$ of the values at its center square, which size is the quarter of the original image size, is calculated.

$$\bar{Y} = \frac{4}{L^2} \sum_{i=\frac{L}{4}}^{\frac{3L}{4}} \sum_{j=\frac{L}{4}}^{\frac{3L}{4}} Y_{i,j} \tag{5}$$

**Step 4.** The binary matrix $B_{i,j}$ is determined by the following rule:

$$B_{i,j} = \begin{cases} 1 & \text{if } Y_{i,j} > \bar{Y} \\ 0 & \text{otherwise} \end{cases} \tag{6}$$

Next, the Laplacian filter $LF()$ is operated to the matrix $B_{i,j}$, which discrete convolution kernel is given by

$$\begin{bmatrix} -1 & -1 & -1 \\ -1 & 8 & -1 \\ -1 & -1 & -1 \end{bmatrix}.$$

The weight matrix $W_{i,j}$ is calculated as.

$$W_{i,j} = |LF(B_{i,j})|, \tag{7}$$

where $|a|$ returns the absolute value of $a$. It is noticed that $0 \le W_{i,j} \le 8$ because $B_{i,j} \in \{0,1\}$. At the $\gamma$-th outer end of the matrix for $0 \le \gamma \le 7$, if $W_{i,j} < 8 - \gamma$, then the value is replaced as $W_{i,j} = 8 - \gamma$.

At the Step 3 in the conventional method, the sequences $\alpha_t$ are extracted from the binary matrix $B_{i,j}$. According to the positions for symbols of RS codewords, the weight sequences $w_t$ for the $t$-th sequence $\alpha_t$ is selected from the weight matrix $W_{i,j}$ at the same coordinate. Here, it is remarkable that the symbols of RS codeword are not binary. In a QR code, each symbol is represented

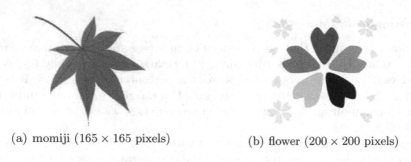

(a) momiji (165 × 165 pixels)          (b) flower (200 × 200 pixels)

**Fig. 1.** Original images for displaying on a QR code.

by 8-bit modules, and is placed on a certain neighboring modules which positions depend on the version $v$. Considering such neighboring positions and their values $\boldsymbol{w_t}$, the index $\theta_{\hat{k}_t}$ is determined to mainly select flat regions at the center of QR code for the assignment of information symbols as many as possible. It is worth-mentioning that the modules at noisy regions and the outer end of the QR code are tend to be the parity symbols of RS codeword, and their values may be different from $\boldsymbol{\alpha_t}$. By changing the index $\theta_{\hat{k}_t}$ under the constraint of such a rule, the best codewords $\acute{\boldsymbol{c}}'_t$ are determined in the proposed method.

After the determination of RS codewords $\acute{\boldsymbol{c}}'_t$, each module of QR code is modified according to the original RGB color components in order not to change the color balance. Let $\beta_{i,j}$, $(1 \leq i,j \leq 17 + 4v)$ be the binary represented RS codewords placed on the matrix of QR code. It is noted that $\beta_{i,j}$ must satisfy the black and white function patterns at the corresponding positions. We finally generate a QR code involving a given image as follows.

If $\beta_{i,j} = 1$, then

$$Y'_{i,j} = \begin{cases} Y_{i,j} & \text{if } Y_{i,j} > \bar{Y} + \epsilon \\ \bar{Y}_{i,j} + \epsilon & \text{otherwise} \end{cases}, \tag{8}$$

otherwise,

$$Y'_{i,j} = \begin{cases} Y_{i,j} & \text{if } Y_{i,j} < \bar{Y} - \epsilon \\ \bar{Y}_{i,j} - \epsilon & \text{otherwise} \end{cases}, \tag{9}$$

where $\epsilon$ is a threshold for ensuring the readability. The RGB color components are translated from the modified luminance components $\boldsymbol{Y'}$ as well as the original U and V components, and the color QR code is finally obtained.

## 3.2   Comparison of Performance

For the evaluation of visual quality, we implement three algorithms, systematic encoding, conventional method [3], and proposed method, for generating RS codeword using a same conversion algorithm. The systematic encoding is the third class of method that changes the padding modules to display an image on the QR code such as QR-JAM and [8,9]. We use two RGB color images of

**Table 1.** Comparison of Hamming distance.

| image | Level | Sys | Conv. [3] | Prop |
|-------|-------|-----|-----------|------|
| momiji | L | 283 | 217 | 225 |
| | M | 558 | 392 | 412 |
| flower | L | 260 | 210 | 226 |
| | M | 494 | 400 | 410 |

different size, which are shown in Fig. 1. The conversion algorithm translates the RGB color space into the YUV space, and the binary matrix $B_{i,j}$ is calculated only from the luminance(Y) components after modifying its resolution into the size of QR code with a given version $v$.

Figures 2 and 3 show the generated QR codes of version 10 with error correction level L and M. The threshold for the conversion algorithm is fixed by $\epsilon = 64$. The embedded data is the URL: www.iwdw2015.tokyo, which is represented by 18 bytes. The QR code of version 10 composed of $57 \times 57$ modules, and the maximum number of information symbols for level L and M is 274 and 216 bytes, respectively. Because the number of padding symbols is 256 and 198 bytes, respectively for level L and M, it is possible to display an image at the center of QR code for the systematic encoding method. However, the left side of the QR code looks like random patterns because they are determined by the RS encoding function. The number of trials is $N = 1000$ in this experiment both for the conventional and proposed methods, and the best RS codewords are determined which hamming distance becomes minimum. Table 1 shows the total hamming distances of generated QR code. It is noticed that the conventional method is better than the proposed method in terms of this measurement. However, the visual appearance of the proposed method is better as observed from Figs. 2 and 3. As the proposed method keeps perceptually important regions unchanged introducing a weight matrix $W_{i,j}$, the modules which are different from the original color are appeared mainly at the outer edge and noisy regions. From these results, we can say that the weighting function effectively works to improve the visual quality of aesthetic QR code.

## 4    Enrichment of Visual Quality

Although the visual quality is improved by the introduction of weight matrix at the encoding of RS codeword, the low resolution of the displayed image still degrades its benefit. One simple method to increase the resolution is to use higher version of QR code. However, the higher the version of QR code becomes, the more difficult to read by an optical device. In addition, most modules becomes padding modules which is a waste of space. In this section, we propose a method to increase the resolution by a factor of 3.

Our idea is to assign $3 \times 3$ sub-modules for each module except for the finder pattern modules placed at corners of QR code. At the proposed method

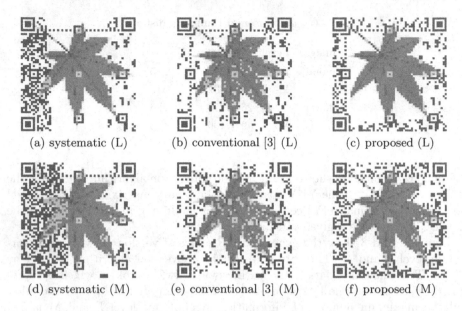

(a) systematic (L)    (b) conventional [3] (L)    (c) proposed (L)

(d) systematic (M)    (e) conventional [3] (M)    (f) proposed (M)

**Fig. 2.** Comparison of the visual appearance of aesthetic QR code of version 10 for an image "momoji", where (L) and (M) stand for the error correction level.

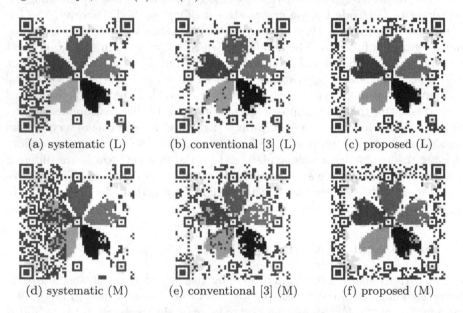

(a) systematic (L)    (b) conventional [3] (L)    (c) proposed (L)

(d) systematic (M)    (e) conventional [3] (M)    (f) proposed (M)

**Fig. 3.** Comparison of the visual appearance of QR code of version 10 for an image "flower", where (L) and (M) stand for the error correction level.

explained in Sect. 3, the resolution of input image is scaled down to adjust the size $(17 + 4v) \times (17 + 4v)$ of QR code for a given version $v$. We use the size $3(17 + 4v) \times 3(17 + 4v)$ to represent the input image on the QR code.

It is possible to only change the center of $3 \times 3$ sub-modules if necessary to generate the aesthetic QR code because most of QR code readers check the center region of the modules to determine black/white. However, the readability becomes much lower. On the other hand, if Eqs. (8) and (9) are directly applied to the sub-modules, the visual quality is still low. In order to investigate a good balance between the readability and visual quality, we examine some types of sub-module representation method. Some typical examples are given by the following four module types $M_1$ to $M_4$ for calculating the sub-modules' values.

$$M_1 = \left\{ \begin{bmatrix} 1\,1\,1 \\ 1\,1\,1 \\ 1\,1\,1 \end{bmatrix}, \begin{bmatrix} 1\,1\,1 \\ 1\,1\,1 \\ 1\,1\,1 \end{bmatrix} \right\}, \qquad M_2 = \left\{ \begin{bmatrix} 0\,0\,0 \\ 0\,1\,0 \\ 0\,0\,0 \end{bmatrix}, \begin{bmatrix} 1\,1\,1 \\ 1\,1\,1 \\ 1\,1\,1 \end{bmatrix} \right\}$$

$$M_3 = \left\{ \begin{bmatrix} 0\,0\,0 \\ 0\,1\,0 \\ 0\,0\,0 \end{bmatrix}, \begin{bmatrix} 0\,1\,0 \\ 1\,1\,1 \\ 0\,1\,0 \end{bmatrix} \right\}, \qquad M_4 = \left\{ \begin{bmatrix} 0\,0\,0 \\ 0\,1\,0 \\ 0\,0\,0 \end{bmatrix}, \begin{bmatrix} 0\,0\,0 \\ 0\,1\,0 \\ 0\,0\,0 \end{bmatrix} \right\}$$

The left matrix is used for the modules satisfying $B_{i,j} = \beta_{i,j}$, where "1" stands for the sub-module that is modified according to Eqs. (8) and (9), and "0" is the sub-module that uses the original luminance value $Y_{i,j}$. The right matrix is the modules that become $B_{i,j} \neq \beta_{i,j}$.

It is remarkable that only one center sub-module is modified for module types $M_2$, $M_3$, and $M_4$ if $B_{i,j} = \beta_{i,j}$. The modules satisfying $B_{i,j} = \beta_{i,j}$ are mainly flat regions, which are selected as information symbols of RS codewords in order not to be modified by the non-systematic encoding. Thus, these module types manage to preserve the original pixel values at flat regions as many as possible. As the result, the visual appearance of the displayed image becomes very close to

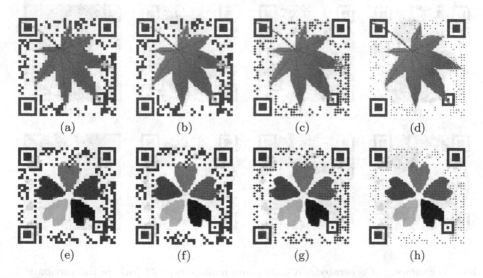

(a)　　　　　(b)　　　　　(c)　　　　　(d)

(e)　　　　　(f)　　　　　(g)　　　　　(h)

**Fig. 4.** Hi-resolution of QR code of version 5 with error correction level L, where the module types are $M_1$:(a)(e), $M_2$:(b)(f), $M_3$:(c)(g), and $M_4$:(d)(h).

the original image. It is worthy to mention that the readability of such modules is not seriously degraded in our experiments when $M_2$ and $M_3$ types are employed.

Figure 4 shows the generated QR code using four module types, where the version of QR code is 5 and error correction level is L. Generally, the optical device is sensitive to external noise including LCD display's performance, scaling factor, brightness, printing quality and so on. Because of the difficulty to measure the performance under a fair environment, we give some obtained features for the above four module types. When the type $M_4$ is used, it is extremely difficult to read the data, which examples are shown in Fig. 4 (d) and (h). The readability of type $M_3$ is not seriously decreased from that of $M_1$ though its visual quality is much better as observed from Fig. 4 (c) and (g). In some cases, a QR code reader takes much time to read the data from the QR code with error correction level is L because of its failure at the decoding of the RS codeword.

When higher error correction level is employed, the readability can be improved, but it also increases the number of different modules in a QR code. Figure 5 shows some examples of the other images using error correction level L and M and module type $M_3$. When a gray image is displayed on a QR code, it is easy to read because the sensitivity to the environmental changes is much lower than a color image. For instance, the images shown in Figs. 5 (a)(e) are easy to read compared with images (b) and (f). Considering the visual quality, the noisy image like Figs. 5 (c) and (g) are much suitable because the difference of modules are less irritating. For a portrait image like Figs. 5 (d) and (g), the visual quality is preserved even if the resolution is less than the original image.

From the above results, it is difficult to determine the best module type because of its dependency on an environment. Nevertheless, the proposed

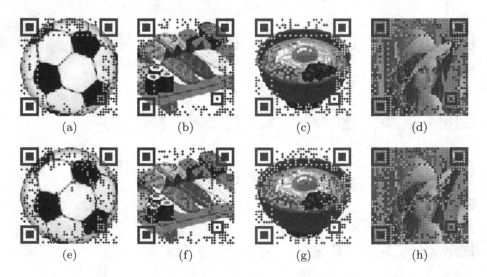

| (a) | (b) | (c) | (d) |

| (e) | (f) | (g) | (h) |

**Fig. 5.** Examples of generated QR code using module type $M_3$, where the version is 5 and the error correction level is L and M for (a)-(d) and (e)-(h), respectively.

weighting method has a strong merit compared with some conventional methods including the non-systematic method [3] as confirmed at Sect. 3.

## 5    Concluding Remarks

In this paper, we investigate the aesthetic QR code by displaying a color image. In general, the outer end of an image is less important than its center region. It is also common that the changes at noisy region are less sensitive than the flat region. Based on these characteristics, we proposed a weighting function to control the symbols of RS codeword at the flat and center regions of an image. For the improvement of the resolution of displayed image, we also proposed some module types and investigated the readability as well as the visual quality.

There is a trade-off between the readability and the visual quality, and hence, we cannot say which module type is the best. The employment of better module types and the comprehensive evaluation of performance are left for our future work. Because the readability is sensitive to several factors including noise, displayed device, printing quality, displayed scale, and so on, the selection of good parameters may be dependent on the applied environment, but it is worthy for investigation.

## References

1. Chu, H.K., Chang, C.S., Lee, R.R., Mitra, N.J.: Halftone QR codes. ACM Trans. Graph. **32**(6), 217:1–217:8 (2013)
2. Fang, C., Zhang, C., Chang, E.E.: An optimization model for aesthetic two-dimensional barcodes. In: Gurrin, C., Hopfgartner, F., Hurst, W., Johansen, H., Lee, H., O'Connor, N. (eds.) MMM 2014, Part I. LNCS, vol. 8325, pp. 278–290. Springer, Heidelberg (2014)
3. Fujita, K., Kuribayashi, M., Morii, M.: Expansion of image displayable area in design QR code and its applications. In: Proceedings of FIT 2011. pp. 517–5520 (2011)
4. Lin, S., Costello, D.J.: Error Control Coding, 2nd edn. Prentice-Hall Inc, Upper Saddle River, NJ, USA (2004)
5. Ono, S., Morinaga, K., Nakayama, S.: Two-dimensional barcode decoration based on real-coded genetic algorithm. In: Proceedings of CEC 2008. pp. 1068–1073 (2008)
6. Ono, S., Nakayama, S.: A system for decorating QR code with facial image based on interactive evolutionary computation and case-based reasoning. In: Proceedings of NaBIC 2010.pp. 401–406 (2010)
7. Samretwit, D., Wakahara, T.: Measurement of reading characteristics of multiplexed image in QR code. In: Proceedings of INCoS 2011. pp. 552–557 (2011)
8. Wakahara, T., Yamamoto, T.: Image processing of 2-Dimensional barcode. In: Proceedings of NBiS 2011. pp. 484–490 (2011)
9. Wakahara, T., Yamamoto, T., Ochi, H.: Image processing of dotted picture in the QR code of cellular phone. In: Proceedings of 3PGCIC 2010. pp. 454–458 (2010)
10. Zhang, Y., Deng, S., Liu, Z., Wang, Y.: Aesthetic QR codes based on two-stage image blending. In: He, X., Luo, S., Tao, D., Xu, C., Yang, J., Hasan, M.A. (eds.) MMM 2015, Part II. LNCS, vol. 8936, pp. 183–194. Springer, Heidelberg (2015)

# Nondestructive Readout of Copyright Information Embedded in Objects Fabricated with 3-D Printers

Piyarat Silapasuphakornwong[1], Masahiro Suzuki[1(✉)], Hiroshi Unno[1], Hideyuki Torii[1], Kazutake Uehira[1], and Youichi Takashima[2]

[1] Kanagawa Institute of Technology, Atsugi, Japan
silpiyarat@gmail.com, msuzuki@ctr.kanagawa-it.ac.jp,
{unno,torii,uehira}@nw.kanagawa-it.ac.jp
[2] NTT Service Evolution Laboratories, Yokosuka, Japan
takashima.youichi@lab.ntt.co.jp

**Abstract.** We studied a technique to protect the copyrights of digital data for 3-D printers to prevent illegal products from being fabricated with 3-D printers, which has become a serious economic problem. We previously proposed a technique that could be used to check whether illegal acts had been committed by embedding copyright information inside real objects fabricated with 3-D printers by forming fine cavities inside them and nondestructively reading the information out. We demonstrated that the proposed technique was feasible in practice. We examined a new method of nondestructive readout in this study by using thermographic movie files where the binary images of individual frames were summarized to amplify the signals of the cavity patterns and demonstrated the feasibility of automatic readout with 100 % accuracy in reading out embedded information.

**Keywords:** 3-D printer · Digital fabrication · Copyright protection · Thermography

## 1 Introduction

Three-dimensional printers have extensively been used in household manufacturing and techniques to protect copyrights are essential. Anyone can currently easily produce finished products by using their home 3-D printers. Customers may also prefer to create products that have high-end quality at low cost. Many people expect that such features of 3-D printers will change the ways in which manufacturing and physical distribution are carried out. However, this also means that pirated products can very easily be manufactured that have quality equivalent to that of regular versions. As the market for digital fabrication is certain to expand rapidly in the near future, it is clear that the piracy problem with 3-D fabrication will also become more serious. Thus, technologies to protect against piracy, such as technology to protect the copyrights of digital data for 3-D printers, are required so that the business of digital fabrication, such as that using 3-D printers, can grow.

© Springer International Publishing Switzerland 2016
Y.-Q. Shi et al. (Eds.): IWDW 2015, LNCS 9569, pp. 232–238, 2016.
DOI: 10.1007/978-3-319-31960-5_19

Various techniques of protecting the copyrights of digital content have been studied thus far, including those for 3-D objects [1–3]. However, conventional technologies cannot be applied to protect digital content for 3-D printers because the final products here are real objects produced by consumers and the copyright of digital content should be checked from real objects after they have been produced, while conventional copyright protection of digital content is checked from digital data.

Since it is essential to check the copyright of digital content from real objects, we have proposed techniques where copyright information was embedded inside real objects fabricated with 3-D printers by structuring the inside cavities of objects. Moreover, we have proposed a technique that can nondestructively read out the embedded information from inside real objects by using thermography [4–7]. The basic concept underlying the techniques we have proposed is the same as that for conventional watermarking techniques, but it differs in that copyright information is embedded inside the real objects.

We experimentally demonstrated the feasibility of our proposed techniques in a previous study. We propose a new method in this study in which we use thermographic videos to read out copyright information, which is a technique that enables automatic processing in reading out embedded information.

## 2    Copyright Protection Technique Using Information Embedded in Inside of Physical Objects

Our proposed techniques can be used to check illegally produced real objects in which copyright information is concealed by nondestructively reading out embedded information using thermography. When the digital data for printing a 3-D model is created, the copyright information is contained in it so that when a real object is fabricated with a 3-D printer, it contains fine structures inside it that express the copyright information. These fine structures can be seen from outside the object. These internal fine structures are detected nondestructively and the copyright information can be read out. As such fine structures inside the object work as a kind of watermark, this technique effectively protects the copyright of digital data for 3-D printers.

Fine structures can be formed by making fine domains using materials whose physical characteristics differ from those of other regions inside the object. We can detect fine structures inside objects by using this difference in physical characteristics.

We formed fine cavities as fine structures in a previous study. Copyright information was represented by the characteristics of these fine cavities. Information was encoded in binary code and if there were cavities in predetermined positions, they were represented as ones or otherwise expressed as zeros.

We used a method of thermography to nondestructively read out information. If fine cavities are formed near an object's surface, the temperatures of the surface area above the cavities become higher than those in other surface areas when the surface is heated because the cavities block thermal diffusion from the surface to inside the object because of the far lower thermal conductivity of the cavity regions than that of the other regions.

Therefore, we can detect cavities inside the object from the thermal image of the surface that we can obtain with thermography.

We used still thermographic images in reading out the patterns of cavities in previous studies [4–7]. We found that heat irregularly spread out through the samples. It was difficult to capture only one image at certain times that could completely read out all embedded code. The technique we propose in this paper uses video processing to solve this problem. We recorded thermographic videos of a sample while heating and cooling it and we found that the code for the embedded cavities appeared and disappeared as partial areas over time. Therefore, if we could identify the codes in individual partial areas over time and then sum up all the images together, we could improve our technique of reading out information so that it became more effective.

## 3    Methodology

We embedded the information code patterns, represented by the fine structures, and read out the embedded code by recording thermographic videos. Patterns of fine structures were formed inside the object as a group of small cavities. After heating ceased, we recorded thermographic videos to measure the surface temperature distribution until the temperature had cooled down to the original temperature before heating. Finally, we used image processing techniques to detect the patterns of the cavities.

The sample, which was used in this experiment, was fabricated by using a fused deposition modeling 3-D printer with polylactic acid (PLA) plastic filament. The sample was prepared as a hard opaque black cuboid with a size of $5 \times 5 \times 1$ cm (width $\times$ length $\times$ height). The pattern for the cavities is outlined in Fig. 1. The cavities were formed 1 mm under the surface. Figure 2 outlines the setup for the heating and video recording system that we used in this experiment. Two halogen lamps (maximum output of 500 W) were positioned on opposite sides to heat the sample. A thermal imaging camera (Testo 875) was placed in front of the sample to record the video and measure the distribution of surface temperature. The resolution of the recorded video was $160 \times 120$ pixels.

A video clip was recorded from when heating started until the sample was cooled down to room temperature (RT) in the process of image processing. The images were captured from the video in each frame. Background images were selected from when heating stopped to when the sample was cooled down and under condition:

$$G = \frac{1}{\sqrt{2\pi}\sigma} e^{-\frac{1}{2}\left(\frac{I-Bg}{\sigma}\right)^2} \approx \sigma 10^{-3} \pm 0.002 \tag{1}$$

where $G$ is the index to select a suitable background scene ($Bg$), $I$ is the original current image scene, and $\sigma$ is the standard deviation of $I$ or constant value (this value in the experiment was set at 15 as the best result). Note that the best registered background image should have the $G$ index in this interval, $\sigma 10^{-3} \pm 0.002$.

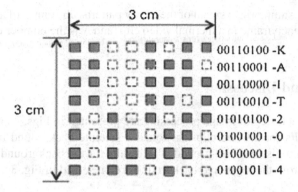

**Fig. 1.** A cavities pattern schematic of ASCII code as "KAIT2014". The gray square is where there is a cavity in the predetermined position; the white dotted line box indicates that there is no void in place. 0 represent as the cavity position and 1 is a cavity predetermined position. The size of each cavity as a $2 \times 2 \times 2$ mm, the spacing between the cavity it was 2 mm.

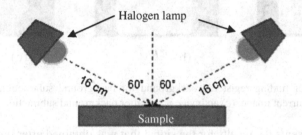

**Fig. 2.** A schematic of heating and recording system; two halogen lamps were placed far from the sample with 16 cm distance and set as 60° to the incident angle.

The background image that was obtained contained the profile of luminance that referred to the ambient temperature when the sample began to be heated. It was used as the ground truth for each thermal video clip.

After that, the gray values in each image frame were subtracted from the registered background image to only segment regions that had temperatures higher than that in the ground truth. Then, small differences in illumination between surrounding areas and cavity patterns were compared to create binary images. If there were no differences, the value was set to zero and it was set to one if the region of interest (ROI) was a cavity. Binary images of cavity patterns in individual frames were obtained after processing. Finally, all binary images were summarized as all the video length to more clearly amplify the signal from cavities, as seen in Eq. (2). The cavity pattern in the proposed approach could be clearly detected as the pattern in Fig. 1.

$$S = \sum_{n=1}^{N} h_n \tag{2}$$

Here, $S$ is the summarized signal of the cavity patterns all frames of a video, $h$ is the binary signal of each frame in a thermal video clip, and $N$ is the number of all frames in a video clip.

## 4    Results and Discussion

The results for each step of image processing are presented in Figs. 3 and 4. Figure 3a has sample results for a video clip that found a suitable background image in frame number 123 as a registered background. The results for the background subtraction of a current scene from the registered background are presented in Fig. 3c.

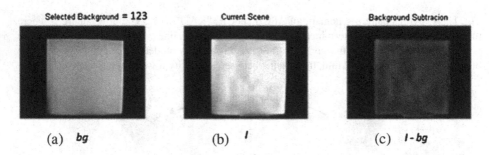

(a) *bg*    (b) *I*    (c) *I - bg*

**Fig. 3.** Results of finding registered background for background subtraction; (a) registered background, (b) current image, (c) an image result after background subtraction.

Figure 4 presents the results for the signal that was obtained after processing when heating stopped after 1, 50, 100, 150, 200, and 300 frames. The first row has the original image of each frame. The second row has the signal for the cavity pattern after processing in each frame and the percentage of accuracy in recognition. The third row has the signal for the cavity pattern after processing with our proposed method that summarizes all frames of the video and compares the percentage of accuracy in recognition for each period. The binary images of the cavity patterns reveal white and black squares as a result. The white squares indicate that cavities were detected, and the black squares indicate that no cavities were detected.

The results indicate that the cavity pattern could be detected correctly as the accuracy was 100 % in the final image, but only in frame number 50, when we processed the pattern in each frame. However, when the images were processed with all images summed up together, i.e., the summed image from 150 frames and after, accuracy was 100 % in all the results. Therefore, these results demonstrated the efficiency of the technique we propose.

The cavity pattern could be correctly detected using video and automated readout of data was possible. Conventional methods use still images for accurate detection by visual inspection. However, it was possible to accurately detect cavity patterns even without such visual inspection. Generating and adding different images has contributed greatly to protect the copyrights of digital data for 3-D printers. It will be necessary in the future to extensively investigate conditions to establish more robust reading methods.

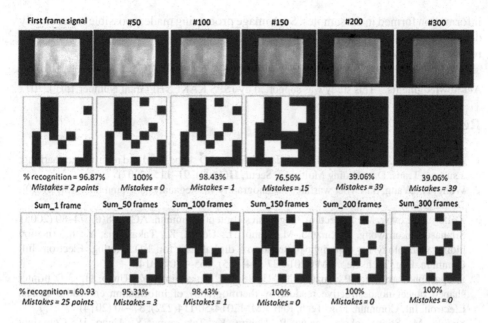

**Fig. 4.** Comparison between the method that process image in each period and our proposed techniques that process signal by summarized all image from video clip. First row, the original image at frame number (from left to right) 1, 50, 100, 150, 200, 300, respectively; Second row, the binarized image of cavities pattern signal at each frame processing and their percentage of recognition; Third row, the binarized image of summarized cavities pattern signal since the first to current image processing and their percentage of recognition; white squares means that a cavity is detected, and black squares means to no-cavities detection.

## 5  Conclusion

Nondestructive readout by using thermography to reveal copyright information that was concealed in real objects and examined with the new method using video was proposed in this paper. Samples that had fine structures as cavities inside them were heated. After heating was stopped, thermographic videos were captured to measure the surface temperature distribution until samples were cooled to the original temperature. These videos were processed by image processing to find the cavity patterns inside the samples. First, a suitable image for processing for registration as a background image for these video clips was found during the period of heating until heating stopped. Then, different images between the registered background image and the images of individual frames after heating had stopped, up until samples had cooled to the original temperature, were calculated. Then, targets with only small differences in images were compared with surrounding areas to find the cavity pattern signal in the current image. The binary images that were obtained conformed to the rules that zeros meant no cavities and ones meant cavities. Finally, all the binary images were summarized to more clearly amplify the cavity pattern signal. Then, the final signal was generated to decode the embedded information formed in the samples. Such image processing made it possible to accurately detect cavities in the patterns. These results demonstrated the feasibility of automated readout of data with thermographic videos.

**Acknowledgments.**  This study was supported by JSPS KAKENHI Grant Number 15H02707.

# References

1. Alface, P.R., Macq, B.: From 3D mesh data hiding to 3D shape blind and robust watermarking: a survey. Trans. Data Hiding Multimed. Secur. **II**(4499), 91–115 (2007)
2. Wang, H., Wang, S.: Cyber warfare: steganography vs. steganalysis. Commun. ACM **47**(10), 76–82 (2004)
3. Koller, D., Levoy, M.: Protecting 3D graphics content. Commun. ACM **48**(6), 74–80 (2005)
4. Silapasuphakornwong, P., Suzuki, M., Unno, H., Uehira, K., Takashima, Y.: Information hiding technology for copyright protection of digital data for 3-D printing. Electron. Inf. Commun. Eng. Tech. Rep. EMM2014-37 **114**(115), 265–270 (2014)
5. Silapasuphakornwong, P., Suzuki, M., Uehira, K., Takashima, Y., Unno, H.: 3-D printer shaped object nondestructive readout by thermography of information embedded inside. Electron. Inf. Commun. Eng. Tech. Rep. EMM2014-50 **114**(222), 37–40 (2014)
6. Suzuki, M., Silapasuphakornwong, P., Uehira, K., Takashima, Y., Unno, H.: Copyright protection technology of digital data for the 3-D printer. In: Cryptography and Information Security Symposium Proceedings, Kitakyushu, Fukuoka Prefecture, 1B2-1, January 2015
7. Suzuki, M., Silapasuphakornwong, P., Uehira, K., Unno, H., Takashima, Y.: Copyright protection for 3-D printing by embedding information inside real fabricated objects. In: Proceedings of VISIGRAPP 2015, pp. 1–6 (2015)

# Blind Watermarking Based on Adaptive Lattice Quantization Index Modulation

Bingwen Feng[1], Wei Lu[1(✉)], Wei Sun[1], Zhuoqian Liang[2], and Juan Liu[3]

[1] School of Information Science and Technology, Sun Yat-sen University,
Guangzhou 510006, China
bingwfeng@gmail.com, {luwei3,sunwei}@mail.sysu.edu.cn
[2] Department of Computer Science, Jinan University, Guangzhou 510632, China
tliangzq@jnu.edu.cn
[3] Department of Mathematics, Jinan University, Guangzhou 510632, China
liujuan@jnu.edu.cn

**Abstract.** Lattice Quantization Index Modulation (LQIM) is an important tool in blind watermarking. Traditional compensative LQIM can only handle the global tradeoff between fidelity and robustness. To adapt the embedding strength to the local perceptual characteristics of the host signal, this paper proposes an adaptive LQIM scheme. The adaptive encoder minimizes the embedding distortion in the term of weighted-mean-squared error (wMSE) while maintaining the robustness at an acceptable level. The weight value associated with each signal element can be set according to certain perceptual measurement and is not required at the decoder. Experimental results demonstrate the superiority of the proposed scheme. Compared with the compensative LQIM, the proposed adaptive LQIM provides better fidelity without the loss of robustness.

**Keywords:** Blind watermarking · Robustness · Perceptual distortion · Weighted-Mean-Squared Error (wMSE) · Adaptive Lattice Quantization Index Modulation (adaptive LQIM)

## 1 Introduction

Digital watermarking is a technique related to copyright notification and content verification for audio, video, images, and so on. Robustness and imperceptibility are necessary for effective watermarking algorithms. The embedding must cause no serious perceptual degradation. Meanwhile, the embedded watermark must survive against common attacks. A good design needs to carefully handle the tradeoff between these two requirements.

Watermarking algorithms can be broadly categorized into two types [1]: Spread Spectrum (SS) codes [2–4] and Quantization Index Modulation (QIM) codes [5,6]. As blind approaches, the latter have been widely used in practical watermarking approaches. Chen and Wornell [5] presented a construction of high-dimensional QIM, that is, the sparse QIM, to embed one message bit in a

© Springer International Publishing Switzerland 2016
Y.-Q. Shi et al. (Eds.): IWDW 2015, LNCS 9569, pp. 239–249, 2016.
DOI: 10.1007/978-3-319-31960-5_20

$L$-length host vector. Another implementation referred as the Lattice QIM (LQIM) employed the $L$-dimensional nested lattices to embed one codeword [1,5]. The number of codewords is usually larger than 2, indicating that more than one message bits can be embedded into each host vector. Based on these QIM codes, practical QIM algorithms such as the angle QIM [6] and logarithmic QIM [7] have also been proposed.

Higher-dimensional quantization usually achieves better performance [8]. Further, empirical results have also supported that the performance of QIM codes improves with increasing the dimensionality [9]. Inspired by this, we are devoted to studying the high-dimensional QIM, especially the LQIM. However, one cannot afford using arbitrary high-dimensional lattices due to the quantization expensive. Therefore, in this paper, we only examine three lattices, that is, A2, D4 and E8, since they perform good in the corresponding dimensional spaces [10]. The practical code constructions suggested in [1] can be employed for a higher dimensionality.

The tradeoff between fidelity and robustness can be improved by adapting the watermark strength to the local perceptual characteristics of the host signal. This technique has been frequently used in SS-based watermarking, where the local embedding strength can be determined by, for example, the Watson Distance [11], the Just Noticeable Difference (JND) [12], and the Structural SIMilarity index (SSIM) [13]. The compensation factor used in the compensative QIM can also handle the global embedding distortion [5]. However, there are little methods controlling the local embedding strength in QIM-based watermarking. Some schemes try to change the quantization step to match the local host signal [11,14]. However, all the quantization steps have to be known at the decoder. Though they are estimable for particular host, it is difficult to extend the suggested estimation methods to universal cases, which limits their application in practice.

In this paper, a blind watermarking based on adaptive LQIM is proposed by adopting the concept of adaptive distortion compensation. In contrast to the compensative LQIM in [1] and [5], the distortion compensation on each element of the host vector can be individually adjusted according to the corresponding weight value, which can be assigned by using certain perceptual distortion measurement. The decoder does not need the weight values assigned in the embedding phase. Compared with the original compensative LQIM, the proposed adaptive LQIM provides better fidelity without the loss of robustness. In addition, the decoder of adaptive LQIM is blind and formed as simply as that in compensative LQIM.

## 2   Nested Lattice and LQIM

A $L$-dimensional lattice $\Lambda$ is defined as a collection of vectors that are integral combinations of the $L$ basis vectors $\mathbf{g}_1, \mathbf{g}_2, \cdots, \mathbf{g}_L$ in $\mathbb{R}^L$. Or equivalently,

$$\Lambda \triangleq \{\mathbf{b} = \mathbf{v}G, \mathbf{v} \in \mathbb{Z}^L\} \tag{1}$$

where $\mathbf{b}$ and $\mathbf{v}$ are row vectors of size $1 \times L$, and the $L \times L$ size generator matrix $G$ is composed of $\mathbf{g}_1, \mathbf{g}_2, \cdots, \mathbf{g}_L$ as its row vectors.

There are several constructions for nested lattices. Herein we employ the self-similar construction [15]: given $L$-dimensional lattice $\Lambda_c$, the fine lattice $\Lambda_f$ is computed with

$$\Lambda_f = \Lambda_c/p \tag{2}$$

where $p$ is a positive integer. The construed two lattices are nested, which means

$$\Lambda_f = \bigcup_{m=1}^{\rho} (\Lambda_c + \mathbf{d}_m) \tag{3}$$

for the coset leaders $\mathbf{d}_m \in \mathbb{R}^L$ [16]. Lattice $\Lambda_f$ and its coarser sublattice $\Lambda_c$ are referred as fine and coarse lattices, respectively [16]. $\rho$ represents the number of coset leaders, also known as the nesting ratio, which can be calculated by

$$\rho = p^L \tag{4}$$

The Mean-Squared Error (MSE) quantizer $Q_\Lambda$ associated with lattice $\Lambda$ is defined by

$$Q_\Lambda(\mathbf{x}) = \mathbf{b}, \text{ if } \mathbf{x} \in \mathcal{V}_\Lambda(\mathbf{b}) \tag{5}$$

where $\mathcal{V}_\Lambda(\mathbf{b})$ denotes the Voronoi region of the lattice point $\mathbf{b} \in \Lambda$ [10]. The quantization radius of the quantizer, which is equal to the packing radius of $\Lambda_c$ $r_{c,\text{pack}}$ [10], requires being scaled in order to gain a reasonable robustness.

Let $\mathbf{x}$, $\mathbf{y}$, and $\hat{\mathbf{y}}$ denote the host, watermarked, and received signal vectors, respectively. A type of compensative LQIM watermarks the host vector with message symbol $m$ using [17]

$$\mathbf{y} = E_{\text{cmp}}(\mathbf{x}, m, \alpha) \triangleq \mathbf{x} + \alpha\left(Q_\Lambda(\mathbf{x} - \mathbf{d}_m) + \mathbf{d}_m - \mathbf{x}\right) \tag{6}$$

where $\mathbf{d}_m$ is the coset leader corresponding to message $m$. $\alpha \in [0,1]$ is called the compensation factor, which is used to control the global tradeoff between robustness and imperceptibility. Setting $\alpha = 1$ provides the best robustness whereas reducing $\alpha$ weakens robustness for the purpose of improving the signal fidelity.

It should be noted that this compensative LQIM is different from those in [1,5,9]. However, the encoders defined there requires the prior knowledge of channel attack to optimize $\alpha$. We consider the blind situation and thus employ the encoder defined in Eq. (6). Equation (6) can be rewritten as

$$\mathbf{y} = \mathbf{x} + (E_{\text{cmp}}(\mathbf{x}, m, 1) - \mathbf{x}) A \tag{7}$$

where $A = \alpha \times I$, $I$ is an $L \times L$ identity matrix. This indicates that compensative LQIM reduces all the embedding distortions by a fixed scale. Compensative LQIM is originally designed with respect to MSE criterion [2,18]. However, rather than MSE, we know that the correct choice of the distortion measurement should be premised on the signal type [12,13,19]. Furthermore, different local image contents allow different embedding strengths, which cannot be simply handled by a scalar $\alpha$. In view of this, we extend the compensative LQIM to adaptive LQIM by using a generalized compensation factor $A$, whose elements are set according to local image contents.

# 3   Adaptive LQIM

## 3.1   Perceptual Measurement

Many distortion measurements can be formed as weighted norms, such as Watson Distance [11], JND-DIST [12], weighted-PSNR [19]. In view of this, the weighted norm is employed here to measure the perceptual distortion. For simplicity, we only consider the weighted-MSE (wMSE) and show the optimization of adaptive LQIM with respect to this measurement. The proposal can be easily extended to measurements in terms of other weighted norms. The wMSE between the quantized and original signals, i.e., $\mathbf{y}$ and $\mathbf{x}$, can be defined as

$$\Phi(\mathbf{y}, \mathbf{x}) \triangleq (\mathbf{y} - \mathbf{x})W(\mathbf{y} - \mathbf{x})^T \triangleq \sum_{i=1}^{L} w_i(y_i - x_i)^2 \qquad (8)$$

where $x_i$ and $y_i$ are $i$-th elements $\mathbf{x}$ and $\mathbf{y}$, respectively. $w_i$ is the $i$-th diagonal element of the $L \times L$ sized diagonal matrix $W$. $w_i$ represents the weight associated with $x_i$, which can be set according to certain human perceptual system-based measurement.

## 3.2   Adaptive Encoder

Imperceptibility and robustness of watermarking should be well satisfied simultaneously. A tradeoff of these two requirements can be achieved by imposing an appropriate self-noise to the quantized signal. The self-noise in compensative LQIM is in the form of compensation interferences determined by compensation factor $\alpha$. In contrast to that, we straightforwardly define the self-noise as

$$\Omega(\mathbf{y}) = \|E_{\mathrm{cmp}}(\mathbf{x}, m, 1) - \mathbf{y}\| \qquad (9)$$

where $E_{\mathrm{cmp}}(\mathbf{x}, m, 1)$ embeds the watermark with no compensation interference and watermarked vector $\mathbf{y}$ may contain a self-noise.

In practice, the self-noise should not be too large so that the watermark can resist an aliased attacker's noise with certain strength, while the perceptual distortion should be as small as possible to maintain the image quality. We denote the maximum self-noise as $\bar{\Omega}$. Then, the adaptive encoder requires finding the watermarked vector that minimizes the perceptual distortion meanwhile satisfying the constraint $\Omega(\mathbf{y}) \leq \bar{\Omega}$, that is,

$$\underset{\mathbf{y}}{\arg\min} \, \Phi(\mathbf{y}, \mathbf{x}) \qquad (10)$$

$$\text{s.t.} \quad \Omega(\mathbf{y}) \leq \bar{\Omega}$$

This optimization problem can be solved by a Lagrangian method. Define the Lagrangian function as

$$\mathcal{L}(\mathbf{y}, \lambda) \triangleq \Phi(\mathbf{y}, \mathbf{x}) - \lambda(\bar{\Omega} - \Omega(\mathbf{y})) \qquad (11)$$

Then, at the solution of Eq. (10), there is a non-negative scalar $\lambda$ such that

$$\nabla_{\mathbf{y}} \mathcal{L}(\mathbf{y}, \lambda) = 0 \tag{12}$$

By combining Eq. (12) with the complementary condition $\lambda(\bar{\Omega} - \Omega(\mathbf{y})) = 0$, we can solve $\lambda$, which is the negative real solution of

$$(E_{\text{cmp}}(\mathbf{x}, m, 1) - \mathbf{x})(W(\lambda I - W)^{-1})^2 (E_{\text{cmp}}(\mathbf{x}, m, 1) - \mathbf{x})^T = \bar{\Omega}^2 \tag{13}$$

and $\mathbf{y}$, which is formed as

$$\mathbf{y} = \mathbf{x} + (E_{\text{cmp}}(\mathbf{x}, m, 1) - \mathbf{x}) \left( I - \frac{1}{\lambda} W \right)^{-1} \tag{14}$$

It can be observed that we get an expression similar to Eq. (7), except that the compensation factor is now with the value as $A = (I - \frac{1}{\lambda}W)^{-1}$.

Note that Eq. (13) only has solutions when $\bar{\Omega} > 0$. In the case $\bar{\Omega} = 0$, since no compensation is allowed, the solution of Eq. (10) can be obtained by using Eq. (6) with $\alpha = 1$. Furthermore, if $\bar{\Omega} \geq \|E_{\text{cmp}}(\mathbf{x}, m, 1) - \mathbf{x}\|$, the host vector has already satisfied the constraint and thus no change is in need. In summary, the adaptive encoder $E_A(\mathbf{x}, m, W, \bar{\Omega})$ is constructed as same as Eq. (7) with the compensation factor satisfies

$$A = \begin{cases} 0 & \text{if } \bar{\Omega} \geq \|E_{\text{cmp}}(\mathbf{x}, m, 1) - \mathbf{x}\| \\ I & \text{if } \bar{\Omega} = 0 \\ (I - \frac{1}{\lambda}W)^{-1} & \text{otherwise} \end{cases} \tag{15}$$

### 3.3   MSE Decoder

Similar to the compensative LQIM defined in Eq. (6), adaptive LQIM does not change the lattice quantizer. Given self-noise $\Omega(\mathbf{y})$, the received signal will lie in a sphere of radius $\Omega(\mathbf{y}) + \sqrt{L}\sigma_n$, $\sigma_n$ is the standard deviation of the noise, centered at $E_{\text{cmp}}(\mathbf{x}, m, 1)$, which is as same as that in the compensative LQIM. As a result, the received vector $\hat{\mathbf{x}}$ obtained by $E_A$ can also be extracted by the MSE detector used in compensative LQIM, which is written as

$$\hat{m} = D_{\text{mse}}(\hat{\mathbf{y}}) \triangleq \arg\min_{1 \leq m \leq \rho} \|Q_\Lambda(\hat{\mathbf{y}} - \mathbf{d}_m) - \hat{\mathbf{y}} + \mathbf{d}_m\| \tag{16}$$

## 4   Experimental Result

### 4.1   Comparison on Gaussian Channel

Firstly, we evaluate the proposed adaptive LQIM by comparing it with the compensative LQIM defined in Eq. (6) on Additive White Gaussian Noise (AWGN) channel. These two methods are compared on various dimensionality by successively using A2, D4, and E8 lattices. The number in each lattice name indicates the dimensionality of that lattice. All these lattices are with the same quantization radius as $r_{c,pack} = 0.5$. For each lattice, the self-similar construction [15] with radius ratio $r_{c,pack}/r_{f,pack} = 2$ is chosen to construct the nested lattices, yielding the nesting ratio as $\rho = 2^L$, where $L$ denotes the lattice dimensionality. As a result, the number of codewords is also equal to $2^L$.

The perceptual performance of both methods are measured by wMSE. Since the weights of wMSE vary among different signal and it seems difficult to evaluate all the possible values, our experiments are conducted on a generalized situation: all the host vectors are assumed to be associated with the same weight matrix $W$, which is defined in certain weight profile. We speak of a weight profile with exponent $d$ if the $i$-th element of weight vector $\mathbf{w}$ is set as $w_i = i^d$. It can be observed that $E_A$ reduces to $E_{cmp}$ in the case of weight profile with $d = 0$. Therefore, only profiles with $d \geq 1$ are taken into account.

Consider an artificial Gaussian signal in the AWGN channel. Robustness can be quantified by the Signal-to-Noise Ratio (SNR) [1], which is defined as the ratio between the squared minimum distance between quantizers and the total interference energy from both distortion-compensation and channel interferences. The energy from distortion-compensation interference in compensation LQIM is formed as mean($\frac{1}{L}(1-\alpha)^2\|E_{DC}(\mathbf{x}_k, m_k, 1) - \mathbf{x}_k\|^2$). Therefore, its SNR can be calculated as

$$\text{SNR}_{cmp} = \frac{4r_{f,pack}^2}{\frac{(1-\alpha)^2}{L} \times \underset{k}{\text{mean}}(\|E_{DC}(\mathbf{x}_k, m_k, 1) - \mathbf{x}_k\|^2) + \sigma_n^2} \tag{17}$$

where $\sigma_n^2$ denotes the variance of the channel noise. For adaptive LQIM, except for the first case of Eq. (15), the adaptive encoder introduces a self-noise equal to $\bar{\Omega}$ by optimizing the compensation factor $A$. Therefore, its SNR can be roughly computed by

$$\text{SNR}_A = \frac{4r_{f,pack}^2}{\frac{1}{L} \times \underset{k}{\text{mean}}(\bar{\Omega}_k^2) + \sigma_n^2} \tag{18}$$

From Eqs. (17) and (18) it can be observed that, when the maximum self-noise associated with the $k$-th vector is set as

$$\bar{\Omega}_k = (1-\alpha)\|E_{cmp}(\mathbf{x}_k, m_k, 1) - \mathbf{x}_k\| \tag{19}$$

adaptive LQIM and compensative LQIM are with the same SNR and thus present similar robustness (Note that Eq. (18) becomes exact with this setting since the first case of Eq. (15) will never happen in this case). In view of this, we maintain the two schemes at the same robustness level and compare their perceptual distortions.

Let the host signal $\mathbf{X}$ be a sequence of i.i.d. $N(0, 100)$ random variables. Different schemes use the same 512 host vectors to send the same watermark sequence $\mathbf{m} \in \{0, \ldots, 2^L\}^{512}$. The comparison results averaged over 50 runs with 50 different pseudorandom sequences as host and watermarks are reported in Figs. 1, 2, and 3, where the factor $\alpha$ is used to control the distortion compensation in both schemes (note that $\alpha$ is used to calculate $\bar{\Omega}$, which subsequently

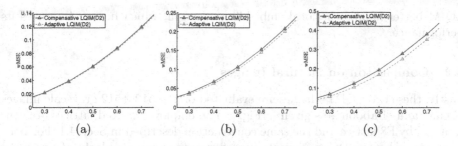

**Fig. 1.** Comparison of perceptual distortions on A2 lattice in the cases of weight profiles with : (a) $d = 1$, (b) $d = 2$, and (c) $d = 3$.

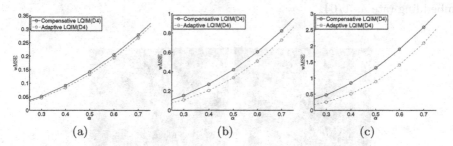

**Fig. 2.** Comparison of perceptual distortions on D4 lattice in the cases of weight profiles with : (a) $d = 1$, (b) $d = 2$, and (c) $d = 3$.

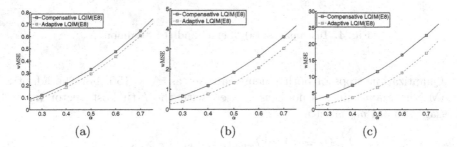

**Fig. 3.** Comparison of perceptual distortions on E8 lattice in the cases of weight profiles with : (a) $d = 1$, (b) $d = 2$, and (c) $d = 3$.

controls distortion compensation of adaptive LQIM). It can be observed that the reduction of perceptual distortion gained by adaptive LQIM is enhanced with increasing the order of weight profiles, indicating that A-LQIM is more suitable for the weights that vary in a large range. Additionally, A-LQIM reduces the perceptual distortion more significantly when increasing the lattice dimensionality.

It should be noted that $\bar{\Omega}$ are adjusted to make adaptive LQIM present similar robustness as compensative LQIM in the above experiments. In practice, however, it can be set according to the host signal. This makes adaptive

LQIM better handle the local embedding strength, which further improves its performance.

## 4.2 Comparison on Natural Images

Lastly, these two LQIM schemes are evaluated on the $512 \times 512$ grayscale images "Lena" and "Baboon", as given in Fig. 4. The employed nested lattices are constructed by E8 lattice and the same construction described in Sect. 4.1. For both compared schemes, DC coefficients from 8 successive image blocks of size $8 \times 8$ are extracted as a host vector to embed one message symbol $m \in \{0, \ldots, 2^L\}$. As a result, 8 message bits can be embedded into each host vector, yielding an embedding rate as $1/64$.

(a)                                    (b)

**Fig. 4.** Test images: (a) "Lena" and (b) "Baboon".

Quantization steps of both schemes are set as $\Delta = 150$. For the adaptive LQIM, the maximum self-noise associated with the $k$-th host vector $\mathbf{x}_k$ and message symbol $m_k$ is set as

$$\bar{\Omega}_k = 0.4 \times \| E_{\text{cmp}}(\mathbf{x}_k, m_k, 1) - \mathbf{x}_k \| \tag{20}$$

The weight value associated with the DC coefficient of the $k$-th block (denoted as $B_k$) is set as $w_k = 1/\phi$ where $\phi$ is calculated by

$$\max \phi \tag{21}$$

$$\text{s.t.} \quad \min\{\text{SSIM}(X, X + \frac{\phi}{8}C)\} \leq 0.99$$

where $X$ represents the test image, $\text{SSIM}(X, Y)$ computes the SSIM map between images $X$ and $Y$, and $C$ is defined as

$$C(m, n) = \begin{cases} 1, \text{ if } C(m, n) \in B_k; \\ 0, \text{ otherwise.} \end{cases}$$

Table 1. Comparison of PSNRs and MSSIMs

|                  | Lena  |       | Baboon |       |
|------------------|-------|-------|--------|-------|
|                  | PSNR  | MSSIM | PSNR   | MSSIM |
| Compensative LQIM | 41.63 | 0.9815 | 41.80 | 0.9927 |
| Adaptive LQIM    | 41.36 | 0.9815 | 41.47 | 0.9927 |

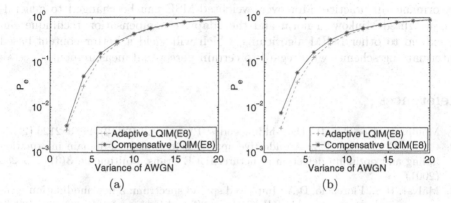

(a)                                     (b)

**Fig. 5.** Robustness Comparison on images: (a) "Lena" and (b) "Baboon".

Peak Signal-to-Noise Ratio (PSNR) and Mean Structural SIMilarity (MSSIM) [13] are employed as perceptual distortion measurements. Factor $\alpha$ used in the compensative LQIM is adjusted so that the watermarked images obtained by both schemes are of the similar MSSIM values. Table 1 lists the perceptual comparison result.

The robustness performance is measured by the error probability $P_e$, defined as [1]

$$P_e = \frac{1}{\rho} \sum_{1 \leq m \leq \rho} \Pr\{\hat{m} \neq m \mid m \text{ send}\} \tag{22}$$

Robustness comparison in the present of AWGN attack is shown in Fig. 5. It can be observed that the proposed scheme provides higher robustness. Similar results can be obtained when changing SSIM to other perceptual distortion measurement, especially those in the form of weighted norm.

## 5  Conclusion

In this paper, we proposed an adaptive LQIM algorithm to embed one codeword in each host vector. Unlike other QIM-based approaches, the weighted-MSE is employed to constrain the embedding distortion. By adapting the weight value to specified perceptual distortion measurement, a better tradeoff between fidelity and robustness with respect to certain signal channel can be achieved. The proposed scheme is blind. The employed weight values are not required in the decoding phase. Experimental results have demonstrated the superiority of the proposed scheme compared with other blind watermarking schemes. It should be noted that the proposed scheme is somewhat different from the parallel-Gaussian watermarking [20], since the number of subchannel is infinite and the decoder does not need to know which subchannel each signal element belongs to. In our experiment, all the perceptual distortions have been assumed to be identical for the sake of simplicity. However, they can be adaptively adjust to gain a better performance in practice. Moreover, weighted-MSE can be changed to generalized weighted-Minkowski norm and the adaptive compensation technique can be extend to other LQIM algorithms, which will yield a better content-based watermarking schemes with regard to certain perceptual measurement.

# References

1. Moulin, P., KoeTter, R.: Data-hiding codes. Proc. IEEE **93**(12), 2083–2126 (2005)
2. Cheng, Q., Huang, T.S.: An additive approach to transform-domain information hiding and optimum detection structure. IEEE Trans. Multimedia **3**(3), 273–284 (2001)
3. Malvar, H.S., Florêncio, D.A.: Improved spread spectrum: a new modulation technique for robust watermarking. IEEE Trans. Signal Process. **51**(4), 898–905 (2003)
4. Huang, X., Zhang, B.: Statistically robust detection of multiplicative spread-spectrum watermarks. IEEE Trans. Inf. Forensics Secur. **2**(1), 1–13 (2007)
5. Chen, B., Wornell, G.W.: Quantization index modulation: a class of provably good methods for digital watermarking and information embedding. IEEE Trans. Inf. Theory **47**(4), 1423–1443 (2001)
6. Ourique, F., Licks, V., Jordan, R., Pérez-González, F.: Angle QIM: a novel watermark embedding scheme robust against amplitude scaling distortions. In: Proceedings of the IEEE International Conference on Acoustics, Speech, and Signal Processing, ICASSP 2005, vol. 2, pp. ii/797–ii/800. IEEE (2005)
7. Kalantari, N.K., Ahadi, S.M.: A logarithmic quantization index modulation for perceptually better data hiding. IEEE Trans. Image Process. **19**(6), 1504–1517 (2010)
8. Erez, U., Litsyn, S., Zamir, R.: Lattices which are good for (almost) everything. IEEE Trans. Inf. Theory **51**(10), 3401–3416 (2005)
9. Bardyn, D., Dooms, A., Dams, T., Schelkens, P.: Comparative study of wavelet based lattice QIM techniques and robustness against AWGN and JPEG attacks. In: Ho, A.T.S., Shi, Y.Q., Kim, H.J., Barni, M. (eds.) IWDW 2009. LNCS, vol. 5703, pp. 39–53. Springer, Heidelberg (2009)
10. Sloane, N.J., Conway, J., et al.: Sphere packings, lattices and groups, vol. 290. Springer (1999)
11. Li, Q., Cox, I.J.: Using perceptual models to improve fidelity and provide resistance to valumetric scaling for quantization index modulation watermarking. IEEE Trans. Inf. Forensics Secur. **2**(2), 127–139 (2007)
12. Wang, C., Ni, J., Huang, J.: An informed watermarking scheme using hidden Markov model in the wavelet domain. IEEE Trans. Inf. Forensics Secur. **7**(3), 853–867 (2012)
13. Wang, Z., Bovik, A.C.: Image quality assessment: from error visibility to structural similarity. IEEE Trans. Image Process. **13**(4), 1–14 (2004)

14. Liu, N., Subbalakshmi, K.P.: Nonuniform quantizer design for image data hiding. In: International Conference on Image Processing, vol. 4, pp. 2179–2182. IEEE (2004)
15. Forney Jr., G.D.: Multidimensional constellations. ii. voronoi constellations. IEEE J. Sel. Areas Commun. **7**(6), 941–958 (1989)
16. Zamir, R., (Shitz), S.S., Erez, U.: Nested linear/lattice codes for structured multi-terminal binning. IEEE Trans. Inf. Theory **48**(6), 1250–1276 (2002)
17. Perez-Freire, L., Perez-Gonzalez, F., Furon, T., Comesana, P.: Security of lattice-based data hiding against the known message attack. IEEE Trans. Inf. Forensics Secur. **1**(4), 593–610 (2006)
18. Zamir, R., Feder, M.: On lattice quantization noise. IEEE Trans. Inf. Theory **42**(4), 1152–1159 (1996)
19. Abdel-Aziz, B., Chouinard, J.-Y.: On perceptual quality of watermarked images – an experimental approach. In: Kalker, T., Cox, I., Ro, Y.M. (eds.) IWDW 2003. LNCS, vol. 2939, pp. 277–288. Springer, Heidelberg (2004)
20. Moulin, P., Mihcak, M.K.: The parallel-gaussian watermarking game. IEEE Trans. Inf. Theory **50**(2), 272–289 (2004)

# Self-Embedding Watermarking Scheme Based on MDS Codes

Dongmei Niu[1,2(✉)], Hongxia Wang[1], Minquan Cheng[1], and Linna Zhou[3]

[1] Southwest Jiaotong University, Chengdu, 610031, China
niudongmei2007@163.com, hxwang@home.swjtu.edu.cn
[2] Southwest University of Science and Technology, Mianyang 621010, China
[3] University of International Relations, Beijing 100091, China

**Abstract.** This paper proposes a self-embedding watermarking scheme based on Maximum Distance Separable (MDS) codes. The watermark is comprised of the reference-bits and the authentication-bits. The reference-bits is generated by encoding the principal content of all the image blocks. The encoding matrix is derived from the generator matrix of selected systematic MDS code. Based on this encoding method, the reference-bits embedded in an image block will be shared by all the image blocks. Therefore our scheme realize a new reference share mechanism and is immune to the tampering coincidence and the reference waste. Moreover, the maximal tampering rate can be analyzed from the error resilience of the MDS code. On the receiver side, the tampered image blocks can be located by the embedded authentication-bits. As long as the tampering rate is not larger than the maximal tampering rate, the principal content of the tampered image blocks can be recovered perfectly. The restoration is deterministic and the quality of recovered content is constant. Our experimental results demonstrate that the proposed method outperforms the recently state-of-the-art works.

**Keywords:** Self-embedding · Image authentication · Fragile watermarking · MDS codes · Cauchy matrix

## 1 Introduction

Self-embedding watermarking scheme has been proposed in [1] for detecting the tampered image regions and recovering the tampered content. In most self-embedding watermarking schemes, the original image will be divided into blocks. In addition to the authentication-bits for detecting the tampered image blocks, the reference-bits for recovering the tampered image blocks is embedded in the image [2]. The reference-bits is usually the representative information of the host image blocks such as the prime DCT coefficients, the MSB of all pixels in the image block, and the vector quantization values. In some schemes, for example in [1, 3–6], the reference-bits of an image block is usually embedded into another different image block. Usually a block-mapping is needed to determine the embedding position. This method will inevitably lead to the problems of tampering coincidence and the reference waste [7]. In some schemes [8–11], the reference-bits will be duplicated and embedding in the image for many times to reduce

© Springer International Publishing Switzerland 2016
Y.-Q. Shi et al. (Eds.): IWDW 2015, LNCS 9569, pp. 250–258, 2016.
DOI: 10.1007/978-3-319-31960-5_21

the probability of the tampering coincidence, while the cost of reference waste will increase accordingly.

In [12, 13], a reference-sharing mechanism is proposed to avoid the tampering coincidence and the reference waste problems. In the schemes, the reference-bits embedded in an image block is generated by encoding the principal content in different blocks and shared by these blocks for content restoration, which can achieve good recovery performance even higher tampered rate. This thought is also reflected in the other schemes [14–16]. In [17], the content reconstruction problem is modeled as a communication over an erasure channel. The reference information blocks are generated by encoding the reference symbols blocks of all the image blocks based on Random Linear Fountain (RLF) codes. So, the reference information block embedded in an image block will be shared by all the image blocks, which allows for working with higher tampering rates than other self-embedding schemes with the same rate of reference information per image block. To resolve the problems of the tampering coincidence and reference waste, both [13, 17] adopted the reference-sharing method based on different spreading mechanism. However, the tampered image blocks can only be recovered perfectly with a great probability by using the methods in [13, 17]. In this paper, we propose a deterministic self-embedding watermarking scheme based on MDS codes. As long as the tampering rate is not larger than the maximal tampering rate, the restoration will be perfect absolutely.

## 2    Watermark Embedding Procedure

Similar to the common self-embedding schemes, the watermark data of the proposed scheme is made up of two parts: the reference-bits and the authentication-bits. In the watermark embedding procedure, we first select a suitable MDS code, then encode the 5 most significant bits (MSB) of all pixels in the image blocks by using the MDS code to generate the reference-bits. The authentication-bits is the hash-bits determined by both the MSB of the image block and the reference-bits. The reference-bits and the hash-bits will replace the 3 least significant bits (LSB) of all pixels in the image block.

### 2.1    Reference-Bits Generation

Assume the original image is divided into blocks sized $8 \times 8$ pixels. The number of the blocks is denoted as $K$. For each image block, we collect the 5 MSB of all pixels in the block to form a column vector. There will be $K$ vectors in total. We denote them as $(D_1, D_2, \ldots, D_K)$. The length of each vector is 320. The reference-bits vectors will be generated by encoding the vectors based on MDS code and embedded as part of watermark into the 3LSB planes of the image block. We use 160 bits to store the reference-bits. So, the length of the reference-bits vector is 160. The ratio of the length of the reference-bits vector to the length of MSB vector is denoted as $R$. The value of $R$ will determine which MDS code will be used.

Here $R = 1/2$, we will calculate the reference-bits vectors based on the systematic $(3K, 2K)$-MDS code over the finite field. First, we divide $D_i (i = 1, 2, \ldots, K)$ into 2 shorter vectors $D_{i1}$, $D_{i2}$. There will be $2K$ shorter vectors in total. Then, we encode the $2K$ shorter vectors base on the $(3K, 2K)$-MDS code in the following way:

$$(C_1, C_2, \ldots, C_K) = (D_{11}, D_{12}, D_{21}, D_{22}, \ldots, D_{K1}, D_{K2}) A_{2K \times K}, \tag{1}$$

where $A$ is the $2K$ rows and $K$ columns matrix and $(I|A)$ is the generator matrix of the systematic $(3K, 2K)$-MDS code over the finite field. The calculation will be done over the finite field. For this purpose, $D_{ij}(i = 1, \ldots, K, j = 1, 2)$ will be transformed to an $n$-dimensional column vector in the finite field. For example, $D_{11}$ is transformed to $(d_{11}, d_{21}, \ldots, d_{n1})^T$. So, we can rewrite (1) as,

$$(C_1, C_2, \ldots, C_K) = \begin{bmatrix} d_{11} & d_{12} & \cdots & d_{1,2K} \\ d_{21} & d_{22} & \cdots & d_{2,2K} \\ \vdots & \vdots & \cdots & \vdots \\ d_{n1} & d_{n2} & \cdots & d_{n,2K} \end{bmatrix} A_{2K \times K}. \tag{2}$$

From (2), we can see that $C_i$ ($i = 1, \ldots, K$) is an $n$-dimensional column vector in the finite field. Finally, we transform $C_i$ ($i = 1, \ldots, K$) to binary vector. The transformed binary vectors are denoted as $(R_1, R_2, \ldots, R_K)$, which are the reference-bits vectors.

From (1) it can be seen that $C_i$ ($i = 1, \ldots, K$) is the linear combination of all the MSB vectors. That means $C_i$ ($i = 1, \ldots, K$) or the reference-bits vector $R_i$ ($i = 1, \ldots, K$) carries the information of all the image blocks. The reference-bits vector $R_i$ will be shared as the recovery information by all the image blocks. So, a new reference share mechanism is realized based on the MDS codes.

## 2.2   Authentication-Bits Generation

For the $i$th ($i = 1, \ldots, K$) image block, the MSB vector $D_i$ and the reference-bits $R_i$ are connected and then fed into a hash function to generate the 32 hash bits vector $H_i$. The vectors $\{H_1, H_2, \ldots, H_K\}$ is the authentication-bits which will be embedded into the 3LSB of all pixels in the image block as a part of the watermark. In our experiment, we use the MD5 function, the output is shortened by exclusive disjunction on neighboring bit pairs to generate the required length hash bits.

## 2.3   Watermark-Bits Embedding

For the $i$th ($i = 1, \ldots, K$) image block, the 160 reference-bits $R_i$ and the 32 authentication-bits $H_i$ are connected and permuted based upon the secret key to generate the 192 watermark bits $W_i$, which will be used to replace the 3LSB of all pixels in the $i$th image block. After all the image blocks have been processed, the watermarked image is produced. The entire procedure of watermark embedding can be sketched in the Fig. 1.

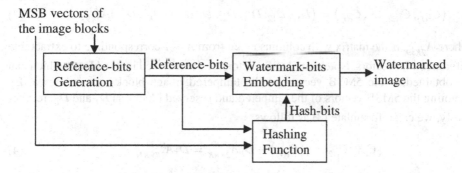

**Fig. 1.** The procedure of watermark embedding

# 3   Tampering Detection and Content Recovery Procedures

On the receiver side, the received image will be divided into blocks with the same size as the original image. One can identify if the image block is tampered or not and locate the tampered image blocks by the authentication data. The ratio between the number of tampered image blocks and the number of all blocks is called as the tampering rate, the maximal tampering rate is the upper bound of the tampering rate. As long as the tampering rate is not larger than the maximal tampering rate, the representative data of the tampered image blocks can be recovered perfectly. In our work, the maximal tampering rate can be easily derived based on the superior error-correcting characteristics of the MDS codes, which will be discussed in detail in Sect. 3.3.

## 3.1   Tampered Blocks Detection

For the $i$th image block, the watermark bits is extracted from the redundant space, scrambled inversely using the same secret key and decomposed into two parts: the reference-bits vector $R_i$ and the hash-bits vector $H_i$. If the recalculated hash value of the 5MSB vector $D_i$ and the extracted reference-bits differs from the extracted hash value, the $i$th image block is judged to be "tampered", that is, some content in the image block has been modified. Otherwise, we say it is a "reserved" [13]. As long as the tampering rate is not larger than the maximal tampering rate, we can perfectly recover the failed 5MSB of the tampered image blocks by the decoding method of the systematic MDS codes. The decoding procedure can be illustrated as follows.

## 3.2   Content Recovery

After identifying the tampered image blocks, we extract the reference-bits vectors blocks from the reserved image blocks. Suppose the number of reserved image blocks is $r$. So, we can extract $r$ reference-bits vectors, which are denoted as $(C_{e(1)}, C_{e(2)}, \ldots, C_{e(r)})$. Then we can rewrite (1) as,

$$\left(C_{e(1)}, C_{e(2)}, \ldots, C_{e(r)}\right) = \left(D_{11}, D_{12}, D_{21}, D_{22}, D_{2,2}, \ldots, D_{K1}, D_{K2}\right)A_{2K\times K}^{(E)}, \tag{3}$$

where $A_{2K\times K}^{(E)}$ is the matrix with columns taken from $A_{2K\times K}$ corresponding to extractable reference-bits vectors. Note that 5MSB vectors of the reserved image blocks which can be obtained, while 5MSB vectors of the tampered image blocks are unknown. By denoting the 5MSB vectors of the tampered and reserved blocks as $D_T$ and $D_R$, respectively, we can reformulate (3) as follows,

$$\left(C_{e(1)}, C_{e(2)}, \ldots, C_{e(r)}\right) - D_R A_{2K\times K}^{(E,R)} = D_T A_{2K\times K}^{(E,T)}, \tag{4}$$

where $A_{2K\times K}^{(E,R)}$ and $A_{2K\times K}^{(E,T)}$ are matrices whose rows are those in $A_{2K\times K}^{(E)}$ corresponding to the 5MSB vectors in $D_R$ and $D_T$, respectively. In (4), the left side and matrix $A_{2K\times K}^{(E,T)}$ are known, and our purpose is to find the $D_T$. Denote the length of $D_T$ as $n_T$ so that the size of $A_{2K\times K}^{(E,T)}$ is $n_T \times r$. We will solve the $n_T$ unknowns according to the $r$ equations over the finite field. Actually, it can be demonstrated that if the tampering rate is not larger than the maximal tampering rate, there will be $n_T \le r$. This implies that the number of equations is more than the number of the unknowns. We can rewrite (4) as,

$$(C_{e(1)}, C_{e(2)}, \ldots, C_{e(n_T)}) - D_R A_{2K\times K}^{(E,R,n_T)} = D_T A_{2K\times K}^{(E,T,n_T)} \tag{5}$$

where $A_{2K\times K}^{(E,T,n_T)}$ is the $n_T \times n_T$ matrix whose columns are the first $n_T$ columns of the matrix $A_{2K\times K}^{(E,T)}$, $A_{2K\times K}^{(E,R,n_T)}$ is the first $n_T$ columns of the matrix $A_{2K\times K}^{(E,R)}$. In the left side of (5), $(C_{e(1)}, C_{e(2)}, \ldots, C_{e(n_T)})$ is the first $n_T$ data block of $(C_{e(1)}, C_{e(2)}, \ldots, C_{e(r)})$. It is noticeable that the matrix $A_{2K\times K}^{(E,T,n_T)}$ is the square submatrix of $A$. So, $A_{2K\times K}^{(E,T,n_T)}$ will be nonsingular because $(I|A)$ is the generator matrix of systematic MDS. Therefore, the Eq. (5) has an unique solution. We can solve the Eq. (5) over the finite field to retrieve the original values of $D_T$. That implies we can retrieve the original values of $(D_{11}, D_{12}, D_{21}, D_{22}, \ldots, D_{K1}, D_{K2})$. So, we can recover the $K$ MSB vectors $(D_1, D_2, \ldots, D_K)$.

The recovered MSB vectors can be used to reconstruct the tampered image blocks. Provided that the tampering rate is not larger than the maximal tampering rate, the quality of the reconstructed image areas will be constant. That is the quality of the reconstructed content does not degrade with the tampering area increasing.

### 3.3 Analysis of the Maximal Tampering Rate

From the previous analysis, we generate the $K$ reference-bits vectors by encoding the $2K$ shorter vectors based on the systematic $(3K, 2K)$-MDS code. We know that the $(3K, 2K)$-MDS code is capable of being resilient to arbitrary $K$ failures. That is, the system can recover arbitrary $K$ failures happening in the $K$ reference-bits vectors and the $2K$ shorter vectors. But it need to be noted that if an image block is identified as a tampered block, there will be 2 shorter vectors and 1 reference-bits vector is identified as the failed data blocks. This means there will be 3 failures happening. So, the proposed scheme can only recover arbitrary $K/3$ image blocks failures. There are $K$ image blocks in total. Therefore, the maximal tampering rate of our scheme is 1/3.

## 4    Experimental Results and Comparisons

8-bit gray scale image Lake sized $512 \times 512$ is used as the host. The number of image blocks $K = 2^{12}$. To produce the reference data blocks we need a systematic $(3 \times 2^{12}, 2 \times 2^{12})$-MDS code. Assume its generator matrix is $(I|A)$, $A$ is an $2^{13} \times 2^{12}$ matrix. Here we generate the matrix $A$ by constructing the $2^{13} \times 2^{12}$ Cauchy matrix over $G(2^{16})$. The 5MSB vector of each image block is divided into two short vectors size of 160 bits. So there are $2^{13}$ shorter vectors in total. Each vector will be represented as a column vector of 10 elements in the finite field $G(2^{16})$. Then we calculate the $2^{12}$ reference-bits vectors according to (2). Each reference data block will be a column vector of 10 elements in the finite field $G(2^{16})$ and can be transformed into a binary vector of length 160 bits.

(a)                           (b)

**Fig. 2.** (a) Original image Lake. (b) Watermarked image Lake produced by $R = 1/2$.

Figure 2(a) gives the Lake image. Figure 2(b) give the watermarked Lake in the experiment. The values of PSNR due to watermark embedding are 37.9 dB. Figure 3 shows three tampered versions of watermarked Lake with different tampering rates, and their corresponding identification and restoration results in the first experiments. We can see when the tampering rate $\alpha = 9.8\,\%$, 21.83 % and 32.69 %, all tampered blocks are located correctly. The tampered blocks are represented by the extreme white. The original MSB of tampered blocks are recovered without any error. In the three cases, PSNR values in the restored area are all 40.7 dB when regarding original image as reference. The quality of the recovered content does not degrade with the growth of tampering rate. Here, just like the method used in [13], forcing the first and second LSB as 0 and the third LSB as 1. The experiment demonstrate than if the ratio $R = 1/2$, the proposed scheme can perfectly recover the representative data of the tampered image blocks as long as the tampering rate is not larger than 1/3.

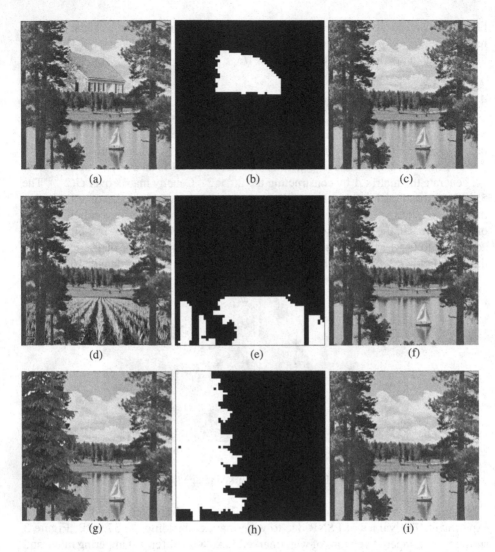

**Fig. 3.** (a) Tampered Lake with $\alpha = 9.8$ %. (b) Tampered blocks identification result of (a). (c) Restored version of (a). (d) Tampered Lake with $\alpha = 21.83$ %. (e) Tampered blocks identification result of (d). (f) Restored version of (d). (g) Tampered Lake with $\alpha = 32.69$ %. (h) Tampered blocks identification result of (g). (i) Restored version of (g).

Finally, we compares the restoration capability of the proposed scheme in the experiment with the methods in [13, 17]. The experimental parameters of the three methods is the same. The performance comparison is made by three main evaluation indexes: the watermarked image quality, the maximal tampering rate and the restored image quality. All the three methods exploit 3 LSB watermark embedding. Therefore, the PSNR due to watermarking embedding is identical and equals 37.9 dB. The reference-bits vectors are all 160 bits and generated by encoding the 5MSB of all pixels in the $8 \times 8$ image blocks. When the tampering rate is not larger than the maximal tampering rate, all the three methods can recover the 5MSB vectors of the tampered image blocks. PSNR values in restored area is identical and equals 40.7 dB when regarding original image as reference. But the maximal tampering rate of our proposed method is 33 % which is better than 24 %, the maximal tampering rate of the method in [13] and equals to that of the method in [17]. However, the biggest advantage of the proposed method is our encoding matrix is derived from the generator matrix of the systematic MDS code. The property of the MDS code can promise the restoration can be successful absolutely, but the encoding matrix applied in the methods in [13, 17] are random matrix. The random matrix can only promise the restoration could be successful with a great probability. So, the proposed method offers a deterministic self-embedding scheme which has the same performance comparing to the method in [17], while increasing the maximal tampering rate comparing to the method in [13].

## 5 Conclusions

This paper proposed a self-embedding watermarking scheme based on MDS codes. The scheme realizes a new reference sharing mechanism to resist the tampering coincidence and the reference waste. Based on our model, the maximal tampering rate can be derived from the error resilience of MDS code. As long as the tampering rate is not larger than the maximal tampering rate, the representative data of the tampered image blocks can be recovered absolutely. The quality of the recovered content is constant. Our theoretical analysis and experimental results demonstrate that the proposed method outperforms the recently state-of-the-art works.

**Acknowledgements.** This work is supported in part by the National Natural Science Foundation of China (NSFC) (Nos. 61170226, 61170175), and is supported in part by Guangxi Natural Science Foundation under Grant No. 2013GXNSFCA019001.

## References

1. Fridrich, J., Goljan, M.: Images with self-correcting capabilities. In: Proceeding of IEEE International Conference on Image Processing, pp. 792–796 (1999)
2. Korus, P., Dziech, A.: Adaptive self-embedding scheme with controlled reconstruction performance. IEEE Trans. Inf. Forensics Secur. 9(2), 1134–1147 (2014)
3. Yang, C.W., Shen, J.J.: Recover the tampered image based on VQ indexing. Signal Process. 90(1), 331–343 (2010)
4. Huo, Y., He, H., Chen, F.: Alterable capacity fragile watermarking scheme with restoration capability. Opt. Commun. 285(7), 1759–1766 (2012)
5. Qin, C., Chang, C.-C., Chen, P.-Y.: Self-embedding fragile water-marking with restoration capability based on adaptive bit allocation mechanism. Signal Process. 92(4), 1137–1150 (2012)
6. He, H., Chen, F., Tai, H.M., Kalker, T., Zhang, J.: Performance analysis of a block-neighborhood-based self-recovery fragile watermarking scheme. IEEE Trans. Inf. Forensics Secur. 7(1), 185–196 (2012)

7. Zhang, X., Qian, Z., Ren, Y., Feng, G.: Watermarking with flexible self-recovery quality based on compressive sensing and compositive reconstruction. IEEE Trans. Inf. Forensics Secur. **6**(4), 1223–1232 (2011)
8. Lee, T.Y., Lin, S.: Dual watermark for image tampering detection and recovery. Pattern Recogn. **41**(11), 3497–3506 (2008)
9. Li, C., Wang, Y., Ma, B., Zhang, Z.: A novel self-recovery fragile watermarking scheme based on dual-redundant-ring structure. Comput. Electr. Eng. **37**(6), 927–940 (2011)
10. Qin, C., Chang, C.C., Hsu, T.J.: Effective fragile watermarking for image authentication with high-quality recovery capability. KSII Trans. Internet Inf. Syst. **7**(11), 2941–2956 (2013)
11. Qin, C., Chang, C.C., Chen, K.N.: Adaptive self-recovery for tampered images based on VQ indexing and inpainting. Signal Process. **93**(4), 933–946 (2013)
12. Zhang, X., Wang, S., Feng, S.G.: Fragile watermarking scheme with extensive content restoration capability. In: Proceeding of International Workshop Digital Watermark, pp. 268–278 (2009)
13. Zhang, X., Wang, S., Qian, Z., Feng, G.: Reference sharing mechanism for watermark self-embedding. IEEE Trans. Image Process. **20**(2), 485–495 (2011)
14. Zhang, X., Wang, S.: Fragile watermarking with error free restoration capability. IEEE Trans. Multimedia **10**(8), 1490–1499 (2008)
15. Zhang, X., Wang, S.: Fragile watermarking scheme using a hierarchical mechanism. Signal Process. **89**(4), 675–679 (2009)
16. Qian, Z., Feng, G., Zhang, X., Wang, S.: Image self-embedding with high-quality restoration capability. Digit. Signal Process. **21**(2), 278–286 (2011)
17. Korus, P., Dziech, A.: Efficient method for content reconstruction with self-embedding. IEEE Trans. Image Process. **22**(3), 1134–1147 (2013)
18. MacWilliams, F.J., Sloane, N.J.A.: The Theory of Error Correcting Codes. North-Holland, Amsterdam (1977)

# Watermarking Method Using Concatenated Code for Scaling and Rotation Attacks

Nobuhiro Hirata and Masaki Kawamura[✉]

Graduate School of Science and Engineering, Yamaguchi University,
1677-1 Yoshida, Yamaguchi-shi, Yamaguchi 753-8512, Japan
kawamura@sci.yamaguchi-u.ac.jp

**Abstract.** We proposed a watermarking method using a concatenated code and evaluated the method on the basis of IHC evaluation criteria. The criteria include JPEG compression, clipping, scaling, and rotation as attacks. For the robustness of messages, we introduced concatenated code, since it has a high error corrective ability to decode messages against JPEG compression. When a region is cropped from a stego-image, the position of watermarks might be unclear. Therefore, markers or synchronization codes were embedded into the stego-image. Since scaling causes pixel loss, and rotation causes distortion, watermarks were embedded into minified images. Quantization index modulation was used for embedding and extracting the watermarks without the original images. As a result, our method was evaluated on the basis of highest image quality and could achieve an average peak signal-to-noise ratio of 36.250 dB. Moreover, our method was evaluated on the basis of highest tolerance and could achieve an average compression ratio of 2.633 % without errors.

**Keywords:** Digital watermarking · Concatenated code · BCH code · LDPC code · Information Hiding Criteria

## 1 Introduction

Digital watermarking techniques are techniques for embedding marks into digital contents such as still images, movies, and music. An image embedded with watermarks is called a stego-image. The stego-image may be degraded by compression, format conversion, clipping, scaling, or rotation. However, it should still be possible to decode watermarks from such a degraded image. To do so, one should embed watermarks strongly or use error correcting codes. However, the image quality of the stego-image should be preserved as much as possible. When watermarks are strongly embedded, visual effects may be worse. When using error correcting codes, the codeword length of embedded information increases in bit-length, possibly resulting in image quality degradation. In other words, there is trade-off between image quality and robustness for watermarks.

Tolerance and image quality assessments are defined by the Information Hiding Criteria (IHC) [1] committee. These criteria define that image quality

© Springer International Publishing Switzerland 2016
Y.-Q. Shi et al. (Eds.): IWDW 2015, LNCS 9569, pp. 259–270, 2016.
DOI: 10.1007/978-3-319-31960-5_22

is measured by peak signal-to-noise ratio (PSNR) and PSNR should be over 30 dB. The criteria also define attacks on stego-images. The attacks are performed using JPEG compression, clipping, scaling, and rotation. Due to JPEG compression, the watermarks are also damaged. In cropped stego-images, the watermarks are desynchronized. That is, the positions of watermarks become unclear. Geometric attacks such as scaling and rotation may make watermarks undetectable since coordinate axes are changed.

A method using both low density parity check (LDPC) [2–4] and repetition codes against JPEG compression and clipping was proposed [5]. The LDPC code could encode messages by using a low density parity check matrix, and had great capabilities for correcting errors. In their method [5], a watermark was generated from a message by using LDPC code, and it was repeatedly embedded into an image. To decode a message from the distorted image, errors of extracted watermarks could be roughly corrected by majority voting. Moreover, by using LDPC code, almost all errors could be corrected. Due to tolerance against JPEG compression, watermarks were embedded into 2D discrete cosine transform (DCT) coefficients. The watermarks were embedded by using Quantization Index Modulation (QIM) [6], which could extract watermarks without access to an original image. In order to synchronize watermarks, markers or synchronization codes were also embedded into the image.

On the basis of their method [5], we propose a method that has not only JPEG compression and clipping but also tolerance against scaling and rotation. Some pixels are lost in a minified image. If a part of a watermark is on lost pixels, the watermark cannot be extracted correctly. When a stego-image is magnified, errors in extracted watermarks are small. Therefore, we propose a method in which the original image is minified in advance before embedding the watermarks. We call this process pre-reduction.

Rotation of a stego-image causes pixels to become unaligned. Therefore, pixel values change. Since the chance of an alignment error at a nearby rotation center is smaller than one far from the center, a smaller image is better for watermarking. Therefore, pre-reduction is effective. Moreover, we also introduce concatenated code [7,8] since a lot of errors are induced by scaling and rotation attacks. Concatenated code has great capabilities for correcting errors by using two different error correcting codes. They are used in communication channels. In European digital terrestrial broadcasts [8], a concatenated code with BCH [9,10] and LDPC codes is in practical use. The BCH code is robust over random errors and can correct within a given number of errors. The LDPC code is a stochastic code and can roughly correct a large number of errors. Therefore, many errors are reduced to a few errors by LDPC code, and then the residual errors are corrected by BCH code.

Let us define the terminologies used in this paper. The meaning of the word 'watermark' in the IHC evaluation criteria [1] includes both the message and the embedded information. The message is the information to be sent, and the embedded information is the encoded message. In this paper, since we use error correcting codes, we distinguish between the message and the embedded information. Moreover, we call the embedded information a watermark. Therefore, message length, i.e., the amount of watermark information described in the IHC, is 200 bits. Note that we use column vector notation for the watermark and codewords instead of row vector notation, which is usually used in code theory.

This paper is organized as follows. Section 2 describes the proposed method. Results from computer simulations are described in Sect. 3. We conclude the paper in Sect. 4.

## 2 Proposed Method

In the IHC evaluation criteria, the size of an original image is $4608 \times 3456$ pixels. Message length, i.e., the amount of watermark information, is 200 bits. Attacks on stego-images are performed using JPEG compression, clipping, scaling, and rotation. Ten HDTV-size areas, i.e., $1920 \times 1080$ pixels, are cropped from each stego-image, and then the original message is decoded from the clipping rectangle. The scaling factor and rotation angle are known in the current criteria. Therefore, we will decode messages from restored images by using inverse transformation.

### 2.1 Embedding Process

Figure 1 shows the encoding and embedding processes. In the beginning, the original image is minified in advance before embedding the watermarks due to tolerance against scaling and rotation. Since the IHC evaluation criteria assumes that scaling ratios are $70, 90, 110$, and $130\%$, we selected the smallest ratio $70\%$. Therefore, the $Y$ component of the $70\%$ minified YUV image is divided into $167 \times 93$ block segments as shown in Fig. 2. Moreover, each segment is divided into $8 \times 8$ pixel blocks. Each block is transformed by using a 2D discrete cosine transform (DCT). Due to JPEG compression, watermarks and markers will be embedded into a low frequency by using Quantization Index Modulation (QIM). Each bit of a watermark is embedded into a fixed position in the DCT domain since there is no information about embedded positions in the cropped regions [11]. We also selected the $(1, 1)$ position in the DCT domain for embedding.

Various synchronization codes or markers are embedded with watermarks in order to synchronize them against a clipping attack [12,13]. The markers are embedded in the grid pattern as shown in Fig. 2. The value of each marker is one.

After embedding the markers, watermarks are embedded in the watermarked area as shown in Fig. 2. Due to different attacks, watermarks are extracted with errors. Therefore, to decode messages from the extracted watermarks, we introduce a concatenated code with BCH [9,10] and LDPC [8] codes. As shown in Fig. 3, a message is encoded by BCH code in the outer encoder, and then the encoded message, i.e., the outer codeword, is encoded by LDPC code in the inner encoder. We obtain an inner codeword as a watermark.

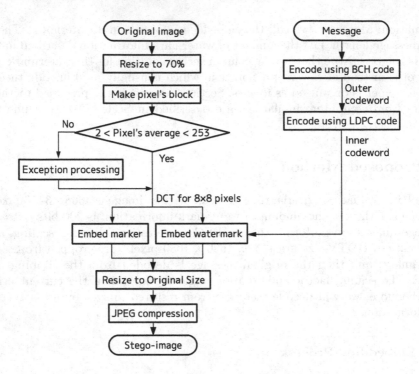

**Fig. 1.** Encoding and embedding process. Message is encoded by concatenated code with BCH and LDPC codes. Markers and watermarks are embedded into DCT domain of minified image. Image is rescaled to original size and is compressed by JPEG compression.

For more detail, by BCH code, a $K$ bit message $\boldsymbol{\xi}$ is encoded to an outer codeword,

$$c^{\text{out}} = \left( \boldsymbol{\xi}^{\top} \left( \boldsymbol{p}^{\text{BCH}} \right)^{\top} \right)^{\top}, \tag{1}$$

where $\boldsymbol{p}^{\text{BCH}}$ is a parity bit in BCH code, $\xi_i \in \{0,1\}, i = 1, 2, \cdots, K$, $c_j^{\text{out}} \in \{0,1\}, j = 1, 2, \cdots, N_{\text{BCH}}$, $p_j^{\text{BCH}} \in \{0,1\}, j = 1, 2, \cdots, N_{\text{BCH}} - K$, and $N_{\text{BCH}}$ is the codeword length of $c^{\text{out}}$. By LDPC code, the outer codeword $c^{\text{out}}$ is encoded to an inner codeword,

$$c^{\text{in}} = \left( \left( c^{\text{out}} \right)^{\top} \left( \boldsymbol{p}^{\text{LDPC}} \right)^{\top} \right)^{\top}, \tag{2}$$

where $\boldsymbol{p}^{\text{LDPC}}$ is a parity bit in LDPC code, $c_k^{\text{in}} \in \{0,1\}, k = 1, 2, \cdots, N_{\text{LDPC}}$, $p_k^{\text{LDPC}} \in \{0,1\}, k = 1, 2, \cdots, N_{\text{LDPC}} - N_{\text{BCH}}$, and $N_{\text{LDPC}}$ is the codeword length of $c^{\text{in}}$. The watermark $\boldsymbol{w}$ consists of the inner codeword $c^{\text{in}}$ and check bit $\boldsymbol{s}$, that is, $\boldsymbol{w} = \left[ \boldsymbol{s}^{\top} \left( c^{\text{in}} \right)^{\top} \right]^{\top}$. The check bit $\boldsymbol{s}$ is used for measuring errors in extracted watermarks during the decoding process. Let the length of the check

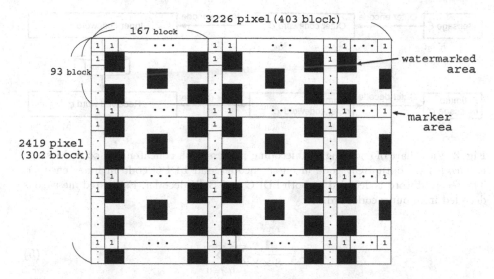

**Fig. 2.** Layout of watermarked and marker areas in segment within minified image. Segment consists of $167 \times 93$ blocks. There are five watermarked areas (black) in the segment. Top and right side blocks are marker area. Value of each marker is one. Parts of watermarks are embedded in segments furthest left or at bottom.

bit be $B$ bits. Therefore, $B + N_{\mathrm{LDPC}}$ bit watermark is embedded to watermarked areas. There are five watermarked areas in a segment, as shown in Fig. 2. Each watermarked area is a square of length $\ell$ on a side, where

$$\ell = \left\lceil \sqrt{B + N_{\mathrm{LDPC}}} \right\rceil, \tag{3}$$

where $\lceil x \rceil$ stands for the ceiling function, which returns the smallest integer greater than $x$.

QIM is used for embedding watermarks and markers. When a bit of a watermark or marker, $w \in \{0, 1\}$, is embedded, the modified DCT coefficient $C'$ is given by

$$C' = 2\Delta \left( \left\lfloor \frac{C}{2\Delta} - \frac{w}{2} + 0.5 \right\rfloor + \frac{w}{2} \right), \tag{4}$$

where $C$ is the original DCT coefficient and $\Delta$ is the quantization step size. The size $\Delta$ is shared by both the encoder and decoder. $\lfloor x \rfloor$ stands for the floor function, which returns the largest integer not greater than $x$.

We note that there is an exception. When the pixel value is near 255, i.e., it is colored white, the pixel values after embedding watermarks or markers might be over 255. Therefore, we introduce an exception in processing for the following condition. Let a pixel value in a block be $P_{ij}, i = 0, 1, \cdots, 7, j = 0, 1, \cdots, 7$. When the average over the pixel values in a block,

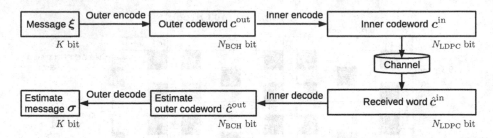

**Fig. 3.** Flowchart of encoding and decoding process with concatenated code. Message is encoded by both BCH code in outer encoder and LDPC code in inner encoder. The received word is decoded by both LDPC and BCH decoder. Estimated message is decoded from outer codeword.

$$
\text{AVE} = \frac{1}{8 \times 8} \sum_{i=0}^{7} \sum_{j=0}^{7} P_{ij}, \tag{5}
$$

is near 255 or 0, all pixel values in the block are modified to

$$
\tilde{P}_{ij} = \begin{cases} P_{ij} - 5 \,, \text{AVE} \geq 253 \\ P_{ij} + 5 \,, \text{AVE} \leq 2 \\ P_{ij} \quad\ \,, \text{others} \end{cases} . \tag{6}
$$

## 2.2    Extraction Process

Figure 4 shows the decoding process from a $1920 \times 1080$ pixel cropped image. First, the cropped image is resized to 70 % of its size. There are $8 \times 8$ candidates for watermark areas. The resized image is divided into $8 \times 8$ pixel blocks. All blocks are transformed to a frequency domain by 2D DCT. To synchronize the area, embedded markers are detected from the resized image. Since the value of all the markers is one, the position which gives the largest summation of marker candidates in rows and columns will be the marker position. When the marker position is detected, the blocks in the segment are swapped as shown in Fig. 5. The marker row and column are arranged to the top and left, respectively.

After synchronization, watermarks are extracted from the watermark area by QIM. Let the value of a DCT coefficient be $\widehat{C}$. The extracted value of a watermark $w$ is given by

$$
w = \left\lfloor \frac{|\widehat{C}|}{\Delta} + 0.5 \right\rfloor \bmod 2. \tag{7}
$$

There are five watermarked areas in a segment. From each area, $B + N_{\text{LDPC}}$ bit watermark $\widetilde{\boldsymbol{w}}$ is extracted. The $\mu$-th watermark $\widetilde{\boldsymbol{w}}^{\mu} = \left( (\widetilde{\boldsymbol{s}}^{\mu})^{\top} \ \left( \widetilde{\boldsymbol{c}}_{\mu}^{\text{in}} \right)^{\top} \right)^{\top}$ consists of extracted check bit $\widetilde{\boldsymbol{s}}^{\mu}$ and extracted inner codeword $\widetilde{\boldsymbol{c}}_{\mu}^{\text{in}}$. Since there

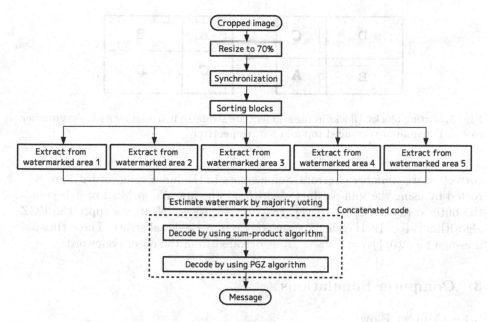

**Fig. 4.** Decoding process. By extracting marker candidates, marker area is detected from DCT coefficient of minified images. After synchronization, watermarks are extracted from five watermarked areas, and then estimated message is decoded from watermarks.

are some errors in the extracted watermarks, the reliability of each watermark, $\alpha_\mu$, is calculated from $B$ bit of check bit $\widetilde{s}^\mu$. The $\mu$-th reliability for the check bit $\widetilde{s}^\mu$ is given by

$$\alpha_\mu = \frac{1}{B} \sum_{j=1}^{B} \widetilde{s}_j^\mu, \ \mu = 1, 2, \cdots, 5. \tag{8}$$

Using the reliability, the estimated inner codeword $\widehat{c}^{\mathrm{in}}$ is calculated by weighted majority voting using the five watermarks $\widetilde{c}_\mu^{\mathrm{in}}$. Now, due to weighted majority voting, the extracted inner codeword $\widetilde{c}_{\mu,k}^{\mathrm{in}} \in \{0,1\}$ is converted to $\widetilde{y}_k^\mu \in \{1,-1\}, k = 1, 2, \cdots, N_{\mathrm{LDPC}}$. The estimated codeword $\widehat{y}_k \in \{1,-1\}$ is given by

$$\widehat{y}_k = \mathrm{sgn}\left(\sum_{\mu=1}^{5} \alpha_\mu \widetilde{y}_k^\mu\right), \tag{9}$$

where the function $\mathrm{sgn}(x)$ is defined by

$$\mathrm{sgn}(x) = \begin{cases} +1, & x \geq 0 \\ -1, & x < 0 \end{cases}, \tag{10}$$

and is then converted to the estimated inner codeword $\widehat{c}_k^{\mathrm{in}} \in \{0,1\}$. The sum-product algorithm [4] is a stochastic algorithm for LDPC code, and can roughly

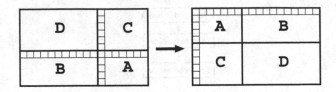

**Fig. 5.** Sorting blocks. Blocks in the segment are swapped in a manner such that marker row and column are arranged top and left, respectively.

correct a large number of errors. Some errors in the inner codeword $\widehat{c}^{\text{in}}$ are corrected by using the sum-product algorithm. The first $N_{\text{BCH}}$ MSB of it becomes the outer codeword $\widehat{c}_j^{\text{out}} \in \{0, 1\}, j = 1, 2, \cdots, N_{\text{BCH}}$. Next, we apply the PGZ algorithm [14] of BCH code to completely remove residual errors. The estimated message $\sigma_i \in \{0, 1\}, i = 1, 2, \cdots, K$ is decoded from the outer codeword.

## 3   Computer Simulations

### 3.1   Contest Flow

We evaluated our proposed method with computer simulations in accordance with IHC evaluation criteria [1]. The message length is $K = 200$ bit. Ten initial values to generate messages and six test images are given by the IHC Committee. Figure 6 shows the IHC standard images. The size of each image is $4608 \times 3456$ pixels. The default evaluation procedure is summarized as follows.

1. Generated watermarks are embedded into original images.
2. For image encoding, the first JPEG compression is executed. The file size should be less than 1/15 the original size.
3. For preliminary compression, the second JPEG compression is executed. The file size should be less than 1/25 the original size. To preserve the same compression ratio, the quality factor (QF) used here is stored. The peak signal to noise ratio (PSNR) should be higher than 30 dB. Image quality is also evaluated by MSSIM [15].
4. One of the additional attacks, scaling, rotation, or their combination, is applied to the images. Scaling ratios are $s = \{70, 90, 110, 130\,\%\}$, rotation angular degrees are $\theta = \{3, 6, 9, 12°\}$, and their combination is $(s, \theta) = \{(90, 3), (90, 9), (110, 3), (110, 9)\}$. They should be checked for the evaluation. These used parameters are known to the decoder.
5. The attacked images are compressed by using the same QF as used for the preliminary compression.
6. The attacked images are normalized to the original size and direction by using the parameters $s$ and $\theta$.
7. For each normalized image, ten $1920 \times 1080$ rectangular regions are cropped from the image.

No. 1          No. 2          No. 3

No. 4          No. 5          No. 6

**Fig. 6.** IHC standard images

8. Watermarks are extracted from a rectangular region, and then the $K = 200$ bit message is estimated from the watermarks. The correctness of the estimated message is measured by the bit error rate (BER).

There are two competition categories: *highest tolerance* and *highest image quality*.

– Highest tolerance
The bit error rate for the estimated message must be BER = 0. Those who can achieve the highest compression ratio for the six images win the award for highest tolerance.
– Highest image quality
The BER for each stego-image must be less than or equal to 1.0 %, and at worst the BER should be equal to or less than 2.0 %. Those who can achieve the highest average PSNR for all images win the award for highest image quality.

## 3.2   Results

We describe our parameters used for the evaluations. The original message $\xi$ is encoded to the outer codeword $c^{\text{out}}$ by BCH code. The $\tilde{K} = 207$ bit message is encoded with the outer codeword. Since the original message length is $K = 200$ bit, 7 bits are padded with zero. The codeword length becomes $N_{\text{BCH}} = 255$ bit when the minimal Hamming distance is at least $d = 6$. The outer codeword $c^{\text{out}}$ with the $N_{\text{BCH}} = 255$ bit is encoded with the inner codeword $c^{\text{in}}$ by LDPC code.

**Table 1.** Average compression ratio, PSNR, and MSSIM

|  | Compression ratio [%] | | PSNR [dB] | | MSSIM | |
|---|---|---|---|---|---|---|
|  | 1st coding | 2nd coding | 1st coding | 2nd coding | 1st coding | 2nd coding |
| Average | 6.535 | 3.967 | 37.854 | 36.250 | 0.954 | 0.933 |

**Table 2.** Average error rate for ten HDTV-size areas with additional attacks (%)

|  | Position | | | | | | | | | |
|---|---|---|---|---|---|---|---|---|---|---|
|  | 1 | 2 | 3 | 4 | 5 | 6 | 7 | 8 | 9 | 10 |
| No attack | 0 | 0 | 0 | 0 | 0 | 0 | 0 | 0 | 0 | 0 |
| Scaling | 0 | 0 | 0 | 0 | 0 | 0 | 0 | 0 | 0 | 0 |
| Rotation | 0 | 0 | 0 | 0 | 0 | 0 | 0 | 0 | 0 | 0 |
| Combination | 0 | 0 | 0 | 0 | 0 | 0 | 0 | 0 | 0 | 0 |
| Average | 0 | 0 | 0 | 0 | 0 | 0 | 0 | 0 | 0 | 0 |

The inner codeword length becomes $N_{\mathrm{LDPC}} = 1012$ bit. We used a parity-check matrix with a column weight of 3 and a row weight of 4. The length of the check bit is $B = 25$ bit. Therefore, the length of a watermark is 1037 bits, and the length of the watermarked area on a side is $\ell = 33$. The watermarks are embedded into the images by QIM with step size $\Delta = 40$.

We evaluated our method on the basis of highest image quality. Table 1 shows the average compression ratio, PSNR, and MSSIM for the six IHC standard images. The values in the 1st coding stand for values after the first JPEG compression. After the second JPEG compression, the average compression ratio achieved less than 4.0 %. For image quality, PSNR was 36.250 dB, which was over the criterion value of 30 dB. Also, MSSIM was 0.933. The BERs for each attack are shown in Table 2. There are ten rectangular regions. The values are the BERs for the ten regions. 'No attack' means that only JPEG compressions are executed twice. No scaling or rotation is applied. 'Scaling' or 'Rotation' mean that either scaling or rotation is applied for the additional attack. 'Combination' means that both scaling and rotation are applied. Our method could achieve zero errors for all attacks.

Next, we evaluated our method on the basis of highest tolerance. Under the conditions in which the bit error rate is BER = 0 and image quality PSNR is over 30 dB, stego-images were compressed to be as small as possible. Table 3 shows the average compression ratio, image quality PSNR, and MSSIM for the highest tolerance. Note that PSNR is over 30 dB. The compression ratios for all images are 2.771 % (1/35) for No. 1, 3.316 % (1/30) for No. 2, 1.800 % (1/55) for No. 3, 1.296 % (1/75) for No. 4, 3.323 % (1/30) for No. 5, and 3.294 % (1/30) for No. 6. Our method has robustness for JPEG compression.

**Table 3.** Average compression ratio, PSNR, and MSSIM for the Highest Tolerance

|  | Compression ratio[%] | | PSNR[dB] | | MSSIM | |
|---|---|---|---|---|---|---|
|  | 1st coding | 2nd coding | 1st coding | 2nd coding | 1st coding | 2nd coding |
| Image 1 | 6.608 | 2.771 | 37.523 | 33.304 | 0.961 | 0.907 |
| Image 2 | 6.492 | 3.316 | 36.473 | 34.683 | 0.952 | 0.925 |
| Image 3 | 6.634 | 1.800 | 38.267 | 34.127 | 0.955 | 0.891 |
| Image 4 | 6.309 | 1.296 | 39.666 | 35.066 | 0.949 | 0.870 |
| Image 5 | 6.554 | 3.323 | 38.553 | 36.805 | 0.953 | 0.931 |
| Image 6 | 6.628 | 3.294 | 36.638 | 33.577 | 0.956 | 0.913 |
| Average | 6.538 | 2.633 | 37.853 | 34.594 | 0.954 | 0.906 |

## 4    Conclusion

We proposed a method which achieves a zero bit error rate against scaling, rotation, and their combination. Scaling causes pixel loss, and rotation causes distortion. Therefore, watermarks might be extracted incorrectly due to these attacks. In our method, the original images are minified to 70 % of the size of the original ones in advance. Nevertheless, we introduced both concatenated code and majority voting in preparation for the occurrence of errors. For the concatenated code, BCH and LDPC codes are used as outer and inner codes, respectively. The layout for watermark and marker areas in a segment is our original, and it affects the performance of BER. As a result, our method achieved BER = 0 for all attacks, and the average PSNR was 36.250 dB when the compression ratio was 1/25.

**Acknowledgments.** This work was supported by JSPS KAKENHI Grant Number 25330028 and was partially supported by the Cooperative Research Project, RIEC in Tohoku University. The computer simulations were carried out on PC clusters at Yamaguchi University.

## References

1. Information hiding and its criteria for evaluation, IEICE. http://www.ieice.org/iss/emm/ihc/en/
2. Gallager, R.G.: Low-density parity-check codes. IRE Trans. Inf. Theory **IT–8**(1), 21–28 (1962)
3. MacKay, D.J.C.: Good error-correcting codes based on very sparse matrices. IEEE Trans. Inform. Theory **45**, 399–431 (1999)
4. Wadayama, T.: A coded nodulation scheme based on low density parity check codes. IEICE Trans. Fundam. **E84–A**(10), 2523–2527 (2001)
5. Hirata, N., Kawamura, M.: Digital watermarking method using LDPC code for clipped image. In: Proceedings of the 1st International Workshop on Information Hiding and its Criteria for Evaluation, IWIHC2014, pp. 25–30 (2014)

6. Chen, B., Wornell, G.W.: Quantization index modulation: a class of provably good methods for digital watermarking and information embedding. IEEE Trans. Inf. Theory **47**(4), 1423–1443 (2001)
7. Forney Jr., G.D.: Concatenated Codes. MIT Press, Cambridge (1966)
8. ETSI EN 302 755, V1.3.1, Digital Video Broadcasting (DVB); Frame structure channel coding and modulation for a second generation digital terrestrial television broadcasting system (2012)
9. Hocquenghem, A.: Codes correcteurs d'Erreurs. Chiffres **2**, 147–156 (1959)
10. Bose, R.C., Ray-Chaudhuri, D.K.: On a class of error correcting binary group codes. Inf. Control **3**(1), 68–79 (1960)
11. Yamamoto, T., Kawamura, M.: Method of spread spectrum watermarking using quantization index modulation for cropped images. IEICE Trans. Inf. Syst. **E98–D**(7), 1306–1315 (2015)
12. Fang, Y., Huang, J., Wu, S.: CDMA-based watermarking resisting to cropping. In: Proceedings of 2004 International Symposium on Circuits and Systems, ISCAS 2004, vol. 2, pp. 25–28 (2004)
13. Hakka, M., Kuribayashi, M., Morii, M.: DCT-OFDM based watermarking scheme robust against clipping attack, IEICE Technical report, vol. 113, no. 291, pp. 107–112 (2013). (in Japanese)
14. Srinivasan, M., Sarwate, D.V.: Malfunction in the Peterson-Gorenstein-Zierler decoder. IEEE Trans. Inf. Theory **40**(5), 1649–1653 (1994)
15. Wang, Z., Bovik, A.C., Sheikh, H.R., Simoncelli, E.P.: Image quality assessment: from error visibility to structural similarity. IEEE Trans. Image Process. **13**(4), 600–612 (2004)

# DCT-OFDM Based Watermarking Scheme Robust Against Clipping, Rotation, and Scaling Attacks

Hiroaki Ogawa[1]([⊠]), Minoru Kuribayashi[2], Motoi Iwata[1], and Koichi Kise[1]

[1] Graduate School of Engineering, Osaka Prefecture University, 1-1 Gakuencho,
Naka, Sakai, Osaka 599-8531, Japan
ogawa@m.cs.osakafu-u.ac.jp, {iwata,kise}@cs.osakafu-u.ac.jp
[2] Graduate School of Natural Science and Technology, Okayama University, 3-1-1,
Tsushima-naka, Kita-ku, Okayama 700-8530, Japan
kminoru@okayama-u.ac.jp

**Abstract.** The digital watermark is used for copyright protection, and the methods should have the robustness against various attacks such as JPEG compression, clipping, rotation, and scaling attacks. Based on the DCT-OFDM based watermarking method presented at IWIHC2014, we propose a method enhancing the performance in this paper. There are two ideas in the proposed method. One idea is to reduce the computational costs required for the synchronization recovery. The other idea is to encode watermark information by error correcting code and to decode it by maximum likelihood algorithm. As the result, our method has high robustness against the IHC evaluation criteria with less degradation of quality and less computational costs.

**Keywords:** JPEG compression · Clipping attack · Synchronization signal · Rotation attack · Scaling attack · Convolutional code

## 1 Introduction

Because of the recent development of digital technology, multimedia content such as image, video and audio has become familiar, and has been distributed over the Internet through several web services. On the other hand, copyright infringement such as unauthorized copying and unauthorized distribution of digital content has become a problem. Digital watermark is one of the means to protect the copyright of digital content. It enables us to embed additional information into multimedia content without seriously degrading its perceptual quality. For the copyright protection of multimedia content, digital watermarking methods should have the robustness against various attacks such as JPEG compression, clipping, rotation, and scaling attacks. Even though there are famous benchmark tools such as stirmark [1,2], we should evaluate watermarking method in terms of quality, robustness, and capacity. The IHC (Information Hiding Criteria) Committee developed standard evaluation criteria [3].

© Springer International Publishing Switzerland 2016
Y.-Q. Shi et al. (Eds.): IWDW 2015, LNCS 9569, pp. 271–284, 2016.
DOI: 10.1007/978-3-319-31960-5_23

Hakka et al. [4] have proposed a digital watermarking method based on the OFDM (Orthogonal Frequency Divisible Multiple) technique to satisfy the IHC evaluation criteria with less degradation of image quality. The Hakka's method won the 2nd highest image quality of the watermark competition held in IWIHC2014. In the Hakka's method, watermark is embedded into low-frequency component to improve the robustness against JPEG compression by employing the QIM method [12] to the DCT-OFDM modulated signal. Considering the robustness against clipping attack, the watermark is repetitively embedded for partitioned blocks of an image. At the detection, however, the recovery of the synchronization is required to find a correct block position. Thus, synchronization signal is embedded in each block that is designed not to interfere with the watermark. The synchronization procedure in the Hakka's method were regretfully checking all possible positions by detecting the synchronization signal in a certain block size. Since the block size is very large and several blocks with the size must be transformed by DCT. Therefore, the synchronization procedure is quite time-consuming. Furthermore, the large size of the quantization step in QIM is required to improve the robustness against JPEG compression.

In this paper, we first propose an efficient synchronization method to reduce the computational complexity at the synchronization recovery. Because of the characteristics of the embedding method, the synchronization signal can be detected not only at the exact position, but also at the neighborings of the position. Because of this characteristic, the Hakka's method checks all candidate positions and calculates their center. We focus on the false-positive detection of the synchronization which is controlled into sufficiently small, and propose a hierarchical detection procedure. First, we check the synchronization position in a raster-scan order. Once a position is detected, then only its neighborings are checked. In addition, the pattern matching with the original synchronization sequence is performed in hierarchical steps in order to reduce the number of heavy computations like full-domain DCT operations. Next, we encode watermark information by an error correcting code to improve the robustness. Because we forgive a few errors at the synchronization recovery process, the error correcting code is only applied to the watermark. According to the experiments, the proposed method meets the requirements of the watermark competition organized by the IHC committee.

## 2    Conventional Method

In this section, we present a watermarking system including the embedding, the recovery of synchronization, and the detection algorithms on the basis of the Hakka's method.

### 2.1    The QIM Variant to DCT-OFDM Based Watermarking Scheme

In conventional spread spectrum watermarking schemes [5], statistically quasi-orthogonal sequences are used as secret carriers to embed watermark information in a spread form. However, the mutual interferences among SS sequences as well as the host signal degrade the performance. Even though the ISS(improved spread spectrum) operation [6] can remove the host interference, the interference among SS sequences are difficult to control because they are basically composed of random variables.

Hakka et al. introduced the idea of OFDM at the modulation of watermark information to completely remove the mutual interference [4]. It effectively employs DCT basic vectors as orthogonal sequences combined with a PN(Pseudo-random number) sequence such as M-sequence [7]. It calculates the sequence $d = \{d_0, d_1, \ldots, d_{L-1}\}$ from a host signal $x$, which is selected from frequency components of a host image according to a secret key.

$$d = \text{DCT}(\rho \otimes x) \tag{1}$$

where $\rho = \{\rho_0, \rho_1, \ldots, \rho_{L-1}\}, \rho_t \in \{\pm 1\}$ is a PN sequence generated by a secret key, $\otimes$ is the multiplication of each element of the sequence, and DCT() is a function of discrete cosine transform. Watermark information $\omega = \{\omega_0, \omega_1, \ldots, \omega_{\hat{k}-1}\}, \omega_t \in \{0, 1\}$ is embedded into the sequence $d'$ as follows:

$$D_t = \left\lfloor \frac{d_t + \frac{\delta_\omega}{2}}{\delta_\omega} \right\rfloor \ (0 \leq t < k), \tag{2}$$

$$d'_t = \begin{cases} \delta_\omega D_t & \text{if } D_t \bmod 2 = w_t \\ \delta_\omega D_t - \frac{\delta_\omega}{2} & \text{if } D_t \geq 0 \cap D_t \bmod 2 \neq w_t \\ \delta_\omega D_t + \frac{\delta_\omega}{2} & \text{otherwise} \end{cases} \tag{3}$$

where $\delta_\omega$ is a quantization step for embedding the watermark $\omega$. It is possible to obtain the sequence from a watermarked host data, namely, the operation is invertible. By performing the following inverse operation, the watermarked data $x'$ is obtained:

$$x' = \text{IDCT}(\rho \otimes d'). \tag{4}$$

A watermarked image can be calculated by replacing the host signal $x$ with the watermarked signal $x'$. The watermark is embedded by QIM. It is noticed that the above quantizing operation classifies the host signal whether its value is positive or negative. Because the host signal in the method expected to be Gaussian with zero mean, the probability density function is symmetric centering on 0. Considering the property, the embedding operation is slightly different from the original QIM method.

At the detection, the host data $\tilde{x}$ is extracted from the watermarked image and then, calculate $\tilde{d}$ as follows.

$$\tilde{d} = \text{DCT}(\rho \otimes \tilde{x}) \tag{5}$$

The elements $\tilde{D}_t$ is generated by $\tilde{d}_t$ using an embedding strength $\delta_\omega$ as follows.

$$\tilde{D}_t = \left\lfloor \frac{\tilde{d}_t + \frac{\delta_\omega}{2}}{\delta_\omega} + 0.5 \right\rfloor, \ (0 \leq t < k), \tag{6}$$

From the elements $\tilde{D}_t$, the watermark bit $\tilde{w}_t$ can be detected:

$$\tilde{w}_t = \tilde{D}_t \bmod 2 \tag{7}$$

## 2.2 Synchronization Recovery

A synchronization sequence $s = \{s_0, s_1, \ldots, s_{\hat{k}-1}\}$, $s_t \in \{0,1\}$ is embedded to recover the synchronization loss from a clipped image.

Suppose that a sequence $\tilde{s}$ is extracted from a clipped image using a certain coordinate in the following operation. Starting from the coordinate, the clipped image is divided into blocks of $N \times N$ pixels. Similar to the detection process of watermark information, each piece of synchronization sequence is extracted from each blocks using the quantization step $\delta_s$. If the hamming distance $d_H(\tilde{s}, s)$ is less than a threshold $e$, the point is a correct synchronization position. Otherwise, we must return the procedure to generate the blocks after shifting from the starting point. The same process has to be repeated by shifting to horizontal and vertical directions until determining the correct synchronization point $(X, Y)$. Then, the correct synchronization point $(X, Y)$ could be located within the range $0 \leq X, Y < N$. Here, some synchronization points may be detected around the correct synchronization point because the synchronization signal is mainly embedded into the low- and middle-frequency components in a spread form. If some synchronization points are detected, the correct synchronization point $(X, Y)$ is calculated by

$$(X, Y) = \left( \frac{X_{min} + X_{max}}{2}, \frac{Y_{min} + Y_{max}}{2} \right) \tag{8}$$

where $X_{min}$ and $Y_{min}$, respectively, stand for the smallest coordinates in detected $X$ and $Y$, and $X_{max}$ and $X_{max}$ for the biggest ones. The center point among them is determined as the correct synchronization point.

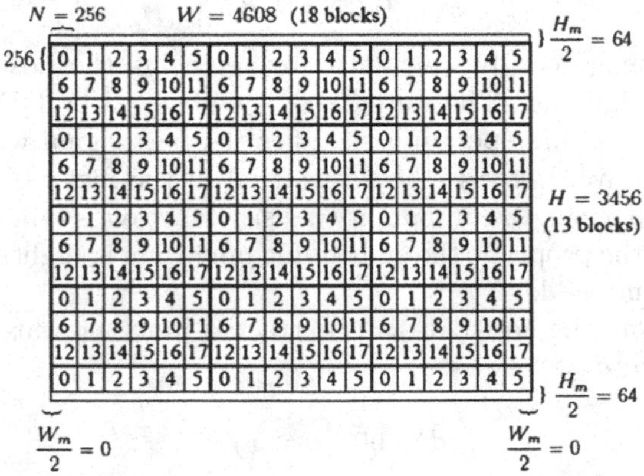

**Fig. 1.** Partitioning into blocks when $H = 3456$, $W = 4608$, $N = 256$, and $r = 18$.

## 2.3    Embedding

The luminance components of an original image ($W \times H$ pixels, YUV422 format) is divided into $n$ blocks of $N \times N$ pixels. If $H$ and $W$ cannot be divided by $N$, we must allow some margin at the edge of image frame. Let $W_m = W \bmod N$ be the margin of the horizontal direction and $H_m = H \bmod N$ be that of the vertical direction. Then, each half of them is located at the edge of the image frame. Watermark information $\boldsymbol{\omega}$ is divided into $r$ pieces, and each piece $\tilde{\boldsymbol{w}}_i$ is embedded into each block along with a synchronization sequence. In total, $n(k/r + \hat{k})$ bits are embedded in an image. At least $r$ blocks with $N \times N$ pixels are required for detecting the watermark information $\boldsymbol{\omega}$. In order to adjust the image specified by the IHC evaluation criteria ver.4 [3], an image is partitioned into blocks with a certain margin at the outer end of an image. Figure 1 shows the detailed parameters for partitioning blocks. We prepare for $r$ sub-sequences $\boldsymbol{s}_i$, $(0 \leq i \leq r - 1)$ with length $\hat{k}$. Each sub-sequence $\boldsymbol{s}_i$ corresponds one-to-one with each piece of partitioned watermark information. Similar to the watermark information $\boldsymbol{\omega}$ embedded by using Eqs. (2) and (3), the synchronization sequence $\boldsymbol{s}_i$ is also embedded by using these equations and a quantization step $\delta_s$. Thus the sub-sequence $\boldsymbol{s}$ is composed of $r$ sub-sequences $\boldsymbol{s}_i$:

$$s = s_0||s_1|| \cdots ||s_{r-1}, \tag{9}$$

where $||$ stands for a concatenation.

## 2.4    Detection

Suppose that a watermarked image is clipped by attackers and its size is $W_c \times H_c$ pixels. At the detection, the luminance components of the image is divided into blocks of $N \times N$ pixels. The synchronization sequence is extracted from the blocks using the method explained in Sect. 2.2. It is noticed that the extracted sequence is not always the original synchronization sequence. In addition, the partitioned position is not known at the detector side because there are $r$ candidates for the order of partitioned sequences. Thus, we have to extract $r$ pieces of sub-sequences from neighboring $r$ blocks which position is specified in Fig. 1, and to check $r$ types of concatenated sub-sequences using the pieces. The false-detection probability seems to be large. In [4], the probability is controlled to be sufficiently small by mathematically calculating the probability for a given parameters $r$, $N$, and $\hat{k}$. For instance, the probability is less than $1.72 \times 10^{-6}$ when $r = 18$, $N = 256$, and $\hat{k} = 3$. After the recovery of synchronization, each piece $\tilde{\boldsymbol{w}}_i$ of watermark information is also extracted. The watermark $\tilde{\boldsymbol{\omega}}$ is composed of the sequences $\tilde{\boldsymbol{\omega}}_i$, $(0 \leq i \leq r - 1)$ as follows.

$$\tilde{\omega} = \tilde{\omega}_0||\tilde{\omega}_1|| \cdots ||\tilde{\omega}_{r-1} \tag{10}$$

# 3   Proposed Method

## 3.1   Hierarchical Synchronization Recovery

In the Hakka's method, we must search all possible coordinates by checking the extracted synchronization signal. The signal is divided into $r$ segments in order to adjust $r$ kinds of partitioned blocks. Because of the exhaustive search, the method is computationally extremely expensive.

It is also reported in [4] that the synchronization sequence can be detected not only from the actual position, but also its neighborings. In the proposed method, we first attempts to check possible coordinates in a raster scan order. Once we detect the synchronization sequence at a certain position, only its neighborings are intensively searched. Figure 2 shows the searching area and possible positions at which the synchronization signal is detected. Since the synchronization recovery procedure checks the positions in a raster scan order from the left upper position, the first position at which the synchronization signal is detected must be the coordinate $(X_f, Y_f)$ illustrated in Fig. 2. Therefore, once we find one synchronization point, the neighborings shown in a square of $v \times v$ pixels are intensively checked in the proposed method. The detailed procedure is summarized as follows:

**Step1.** We set the upper left corner point of an clipped image($W_c \times H_c$ pixels) as the starting point $(0, 0)$ and divide into blocks of $N \times N$ pixels.

**Step2.** For each block, the luminance components are transformed by 2-dimentional DCT with the size $N \times N$, and the host signal $\tilde{x}_i$ is extracted from the low- and middle-frequency components according to a secret key.

**Step3.** The sequence $\tilde{d}_i$ is extracted from the block as follows.

$$\tilde{d} = \text{DCT}(\rho \otimes \tilde{x}) \tag{11}$$

**Step4.** The elements $\tilde{D}_{i,t}(0 \leq i \leq r - 1, 0 \leq t \leq L - 1)$ is generated from $\tilde{d}_{i,t}$ and the embedding strength $\delta_s$ as follows.

$$\tilde{D}_{i,t} = \left\lfloor \frac{\tilde{d}_{i,t} + \frac{\delta_s}{2}}{\delta_s} + 0.5 \right\rfloor \tag{12}$$

From the elements $\tilde{D}_{i,t}$, we detect the synchronization signal $\tilde{s}_{i,t}$.

$$\tilde{s}_{i,t} = \tilde{D}_{i,t} \bmod 2 \tag{13}$$

**Step5.** We do above procedures for all $r$ blocks, and we compare the $r$ sequences $\tilde{s}_i$ and the synchronization signal $s$. If the sum of $r$ hamming distances $d_H(\tilde{s}_i, s)$ for the $r$ sequences $\tilde{s}_i$ is less than a threshold $e$, we regard the point as a correct synchronization position.

**Step6.** If the sum of hamming distance is more than a threshold $e$, we return to Step1 and shift the current position one pixel to the next position.

**Step7.** Once we detect the synchronization signal at a certain position $(X_f, Y_f)$, we check only its neighborings, where the searching area is shown in Fig. 2.

**Step8.** If $m$ pieces of synchronization points are detected, the correct synchronization point $(\acute{X}, \acute{Y})$ is calculated by

$$(\acute{X}, \acute{Y}) = \left( \frac{\sum X_p}{m}, \frac{\sum Y_p}{m} \right) \tag{14}$$

where $X_p$ and $Y_p$, respectively, stand for the $m$ vertical and horizontal coordinates of synchronization points.

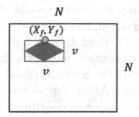

**Fig. 2.** Illustration of searching area of $v \times v$ pixels from the firstly detected synchronization position $(X_f, Y_f)$. The shaded area in a diamond shape is the coordinates at which the synchronization signal is correctly detected.

It must be mentioned that the hamming distance $d_H(\tilde{s}, s)$ is calculated for all extracted pieces of sequence considering the $r$ candidates for the order of partitioned sequences. Here, it is noticed that the computationally heavy full-domain DCT operation with the size $N \times N$ must be performed for $r$ times to extract $r$ pieces of sequences for each coordinate in the above procedure. In order to reduce the computations as many as possible, we proposed a hierarchical method for matching the synchronization sequence. For simplicity, we suppose the conditions such that the parameters for partitioning blocks are given in Fig. 1 for the IHC standard images. Namely, $r = 18$ and the $6 \times 3$ blocks are minimum unit for extracting watermark information as well as the synchronization sequence. By introducing three thresholds $e_1$, $e_2$, and $e_3$, we check the synchronization sequence by three steps, where these thresholds satisfy $e_1 \leq e_2 \leq e_3$. At the first step, $r/3$ sub-sequences are extracted and are checked if their concatenated sequence is coincident with the part of synchronization sequence. At this step, the decision is done using a low threshold $e_1$ to reduce the amount of computations. Only when the first step is passed, the second step is performed. Similar to the strategy at the first step, we use a low threshold $e_2$ for the decision at this step. At the final step, the final threshold $e_3$ is used. The proposed hierarchical method performs the following operations instead of the above Step 5 and Step 6.

**Step I.** From the first row of $r/3$ blocks, 6 pieces of sub-sequences are extracted, and the hamming distance is checked using possible candidates of combinations. If the hamming distance is less than the first threshold $e_1$, then go to

Step II; otherwise, quit and go to Step I shifting the current position one pixel to the next position.

**Step II.** From the second row, $r/3$ additional pieces of sub-sequences are extracted, and the sum of their hamming distance is checked. If the distance is less than the second threshold $e_2$, then go to Step III; otherwise, go to Step I accordingly.

**Step III.** Finally, $r = 18$ pieces of sub-sequences are checked if the total hamming distance does not exceed the third threshold $e_3$, we regard the position as the synchronization point.

In most cases, the hamming distance exceeds the threshold $e_1$ at Step I. Compared with the Hakka's method, the required computations for performing 2-dimentional DCT becomes $1/3$. Even if Step I is accidentally passed, Step II also restricts the increase of computational costs. By adaptively setting three threshold, it is possible to control the computational costs with less degradation of the synchronization capability. According to the search of coordinate in the raster scan order, the expected number of coordinates for check is $N^2/2$ because the candidates are $N \times N$ positions. In most blocks, the required computations in the proposed method become $1/3$ from the original method. Therefore, the computational costs of the proposed method is roughly estimated to be reduced by a factor of $1/6$. In the proposed method, the synchronization signal is checked in three steps. At each step, $r/3$ blocks are examined in a same time. It is possible to examine block-by-block to further reduce the number of blocks for checking in the synchronization process. However, the number of conditional branches may be increase as the side-effect. Considering the simplicity, we employ the three-step procedure in the proposed method.

## 3.2    Enhancement of Robustness

One simple method to improve the robustness against attacks is to enlarge the QIM step size, but it sacrifices the image quality. Because of the large size of the original image, the effects caused by rotation attacks are different at the clipped location. In addition, some local area are sensitive to the scaling attack, and a few errors are appeared at the detected watermark information from such area. It is observed from our preliminary experiments under the IHC evaluation criteria ver.4 that some positions are more sensitive to attacks than others. It implies that we should enlarge the QIM step size only for those sensitive positions in order to control the image quality as high as possible. However, it seems much complicated to adaptively determine a suitable QIM step size considering the local sensitivity. We try to improve the robustness not to increase the step size, but to employ an error correcting code. The Viterbi decoding [8] can be applied for the Convolutional code [9] even if a coding rate of $1/2$ and the code length is about 400 from the standpoint of calculation amount. The LDPC code [10] is also conceivable, and is employed in [11] under the assumption such that the noisy channel is regarded as a binary symmetric channel with a certain estimated error probability. In this paper, we regard the Maximum Likelihood decoding as important, the convolutional code is employed in our method. The detailed embedding and detecting procedures with convolutional code is summarized as follow:

## Embedding

**Step1.** The watermark $\omega$ is encoded as convolution code $\Omega$.
**Step2.** An original image partitioned into blocks of $N \times N$ pixels.
**Step3.** The sequence $d_i$ is calculated by performing DCT to the sequence $x_i$ extracted from the $i$-th block after multiplying the PN sequence $\rho$ like Eq. (1).
**Step4.** Each partitioned convolution code $\Omega$ as well as each partitioned synchronization signal $s_i$ are embedded into each sequence $d_i$ using Eqs. (2) and (3).
**Step5.** The sequence $x'_i$ is calculated using the PN sequence $\rho$ to the sequence calculated from $d'_i$ as follows.

$$x'_i = \text{IDCT}(\rho \otimes d'_i) \tag{15}$$

**Step6.** We can obtain the watermarked image by replacing with the sequence $d'_i$

## Detection

**Step1.** Detect a synchronization point using the method in Sect. 3.1.
**Step2.** The elements $\tilde{D}_{i,t}$ is calculated by $\tilde{d}_{i,t}$ and an embedding strength $\delta_w$ as follows.

$$\tilde{D}_{i,t} = \left\lfloor \frac{\tilde{d}_{i,t} + \frac{\delta_w}{2}}{\delta_\omega} + 0.5 \right\rfloor, \ (0 \leq t < k/r). \tag{16}$$

Then, partitioned codeword $\tilde{\Omega}_{i,t}$ is extracted by:

$$\tilde{\Omega}_{i,t} = \tilde{D}_{i,t} \bmod 2 \tag{17}$$

**Step3.** The sequence $\tilde{\Omega}$ is generated from the sequences $\tilde{\Omega}_i$, $(0 \leq i \leq r - 1)$ like Eq. (10).
**Step4.** By performing the Viterbi algorithm, the watermark $\tilde{w}$ is decoded from $\tilde{\Omega}$.

## 4   Simulation

### 4.1   Simulation Conditions

We use the six IHC standard images [3] in order to evaluate the performance of proposed method by computer simulation. In this simulation, we use a convolutional code of constraint length 7, code rate of 1/2. The IHC committee determined the evaluation criteria ver.4 [3] as follows.

**Table 1.** Cropping positions.

| Position | $(x_1, y_1)$ | $(x_2, y_2)$ | $(x_3, y_3)$ | $(x_4, y_4)$ |
|----------|--------------|--------------|--------------|--------------|
| 1  | (16, 16)     | (1935, 16)   | (1935, 1095) | (16, 1095)   |
| 2  | (1500, 16)   | (3419, 16)   | (3419, 1095) | (1500, 1095) |
| 3  | (2617, 16)   | (4536, 16)   | (4536, 1095) | (2617, 1095) |
| 4  | (16, 770)    | (1935, 770)  | (1935, 1849) | (16, 1849)   |
| 5  | (1500, 770)  | (3419, 770)  | (3419, 1849) | (1500, 1849) |
| 6  | (2617, 770)  | (4536, 770)  | (4536, 1849) | (2617, 1849) |
| 7  | (1344, 768)  | (3263, 768)  | (3263, 1847) | (1344, 1847) |
| 8  | (16, 1520)   | (1935, 1520) | (1935, 2599) | (16, 2599)   |
| 9  | (1500, 1520) | (3419, 1520) | (3419, 2599) | (1500, 2599) |
| 10 | (2617, 1520) | (4536, 1520) | (4536, 2599) | (2617, 2599) |

- **JPEG Compression.** The compressing-decompressing cycle should be performed twice. The file size should less than $1/15$ the original size after the first compression, and the decompressed images should be compressed on the second compression. After the second compression, the files size should be less than $1/25$ the original size.
- **Clipping Attack.** Ten HDTV-size ($1920 \times 1080$) images should be cropped from each decompressed $4608 \times 3456$ image. The vertices of these cropped images are listed in Table 1. The watermark embedded in each cropped image should be detectable.
- **Scaling and Rotation Attack.** Scaling $s = \{70, 90, 110, 130\,\%\}$, Rotation $\theta = \{3, 6, 9, 12°\}$, and their combination $(s, \theta) = \{(90, 3),(90, 9),(110, 3),(110, 9)\}$ should be checked for the evaluation.
- **Watermark Information.** The amount of watermark information to be embedded is 200 bits. The information should be generated by using eight ordered maximal length sequences (M-sequences). Each polynomial should be generated in the form $x^8 + x^4 + x^5 + x^2 + 1$. The initial values should be given as follows:

$$a_7 x^7 + a_6 x^6 + a_5 x^5 + a_4 x^4 + a_3 x^3 + a_2 x^2 + a_1 x + a_0 \rightarrow (a_7, a_6, a_5, a_4, a_3, a_2, a_1, a_0) \tag{18}$$

1.(1,0,1,0,1,0,1,0)   2.(1,0,1,0,1,0,1,1)   3.(1,0,1,1,1,0,1,0)
4.(1,1,1,0,1,0,1,0)   5.(1,0,1,0,1,0,0,0)   6.(1,0,1,0,0,0,1,0)
7.(1,0,0,0,1,0,1,0)   8.(0,0,1,0,1,0,1,0)   9.(1,1,1,1,1,0,1,0)
10.(1,0,1,0,1,1,1,0)

- **Parameters of the simulation.** Table 2 shows the parameters in the simulation. We select $L$ samples extracted from the low- and middle-frequency components for robustness against JPEG compression. The watermark information is generated according to the evaluation criteria determined by IHC Committee. The $k = 200$ bits watermark information is encoded in the convlutional code of length $K = 400$.

**Table 2.** Parameters in the experiment.

| | |
|---|---|
| original image ($W \times H$) | ($4608 \times 3456$) |
| clipped image ($W_c \times H_c$) | ($1920 \times 1080$) |
| block size $N$ | $N = 256$ |
| sequence length $L$ | $L = 512$ |
| watermark information bits $k$ | $k = 200$ |
| length of codeword $K$ | $K = 400$ |
| synchronization signal bits $\hat{k}$ | $\hat{k} = 3$ |
| synchronization number $r$ | $r = 18$ |
| threshold ($e_1, e_2, e_3$) | ($2, 2, 3$) |
| size of searching area $v$ | $v = 9$ |

**Table 3.** Average compression ratio, PSNR value, and MSSIM value for the Highest Tolerance.

| | Compression ratio | | PSNR[dB] | | MSSIM | |
|---|---|---|---|---|---|---|
| | 1st coding | 2nd coding | 1st coding | 2nd coding | 1st coding | 2nd coding |
| img1 | 0.06467 | 0.00917 | 41.1443 | 30.5158 | 0.96749 | 0.92801 |
| img2 | 0.06657 | 0.00894 | 42.0431 | 30.7011 | 0.96010 | 0.92969 |
| img3 | 0.06611 | 0.00956 | 42.7092 | 32.1111 | 0.95255 | 0.92011 |
| img4 | 0.06420 | 0.00857 | 43.0889 | 33.8732 | 0.90213 | 0.87120 |
| img5 | 0.06548 | 0.00891 | 42.6435 | 30.5903 | 0.95909 | 0.93982 |
| img6 | 0.06515 | 0.00939 | 41.5366 | 31.5816 | 0.97182 | 0.94309 |
| Average | 0.06536 | 0.00909 | 42.1949 | 31.5622 | 0.95220 | 0.92199 |

## 4.2  Simulation Results

Table 3 shows the maximum compression ratio under the distortion constraint of the PSNR value more than 30 [dB]. The embedded watermark information is correctly detected from 10 clipped images as shown in Table 4. The results indicated that the proposed method can tolerate for double JPEG compression which compression ratio is less than 0.00909 ($<1/110$) in average, combined with rotation attack, scaling attack, and clipping attack. The proposed method is improved compared with the Hakka's method (0.0163 $<1/60$).

Table 5 shows the PSNR and MSSIM between the original image and the watermarked image after double JPEG compression which second compression rate is less than 1/25, rotation attack, and scaling attack. The embedded watermark information is correctly detected from 10 clipped images as shown in Table 6. The results indicated that the average PSNR value is approximately 40.65 [dB] when the proposed method tolerated, rotation attack, scaling attack, and clipping attack as well as the double JPEG compression with less than 1/25 ratio.

**Table 4.** Average error rate for ten HDTV-size areas with additional attacks for the Highest Tolerance.

|  | Position | | | | | | | | | |
|---|---|---|---|---|---|---|---|---|---|---|
|  | 1 | 2 | 3 | 4 | 5 | 6 | 7 | 8 | 9 | 10 |
| No attack | 0 | 0 | 0 | 0 | 0 | 0 | 0 | 0 | 0 | 0 |
| Scaling | 0 | 0 | 0 | 0 | 0 | 0 | 0 | 0 | 0 | 0 |
| Rotation | 0 | 0 | 0 | 0 | 0 | 0 | 0 | 0 | 0 | 0 |
| Combination | 0 | 0 | 0 | 0 | 0 | 0 | 0 | 0 | 0 | 0 |
| Average | 0 | 0 | 0 | 0 | 0 | 0 | 0 | 0 | 0 | 0 |

**Table 5.** Average compression ratio, PSNR value, and MSSIM value for the Highest Image Quality.

|  | Compression ratio | | PSNR[dB] | | MSSIM | |
|---|---|---|---|---|---|---|
|  | 1st coding | 2nd coding | 1st coding | 2nd coding | 1st coding | 2nd coding |
| img1 | 0.06467 | 0.03455 | 40.7956 | 39.3712 | 0.99659 | 0.99426 |
| img2 | 0.06716 | 0.03647 | 42.0553 | 40.9162 | 0.99638 | 0.99531 |
| img3 | 0.06608 | 0.03456 | 42.7318 | 41.1635 | 0.99592 | 0.99333 |
| img4 | 0.06419 | 0.03174 | 43.0546 | 41.6658 | 0.99399 | 0.98939 |
| img5 | 0.06546 | 0.03327 | 42.6493 | 41.2025 | 0.99686 | 0.99520 |
| img6 | 0.06513 | 0.03569 | 41.5265 | 39.5678 | 0.99681 | 0.99552 |
| Average | 0.06545 | 0.03438 | 42.1949 | 40.6478 | 0.99609 | 0.99384 |

**Table 6.** Average error rate for ten HDTV-size areas with additional attacks for the Highest Image Quality.

|  | Position | | | | | | | | | |
|---|---|---|---|---|---|---|---|---|---|---|
|  | 1 | 2 | 3 | 4 | 5 | 6 | 7 | 8 | 9 | 10 |
| No attack | 0 | 0 | 0 | 0 | 0 | 0 | 0 | 0 | 0 | 0 |
| Scaling | 0 | 0 | 0 | 0 | 0 | 0 | 0 | 0 | 0 | 0 |
| Rotation | 0 | 0 | 0 | 0 | 0 | 0 | 0 | 0 | 0 | 0 |
| Combination | 0 | 0 | 0 | 0 | 0 | 0 | 0 | 0 | 0 | 0 |
| Average | 0 | 0 | 0 | 0 | 0 | 0 | 0 | 0 | 0 | 0 |

### 4.3    Consideration

In order to control the distortion-robustness behavior, the employment of error correcting code actually improves the sensitivities at some local weak regions. Even if higher QIM step size is used instead of the use of error correcting code, some errors are detected at some bits of extracted watermark information. Therefore, we can say that the encoding by a convolutional code effectively

**Table 7.** Average computational costs of synchronization recovery (sec).

|         | Hakka's method | Proposed method |
|---------|----------------|-----------------|
| Image1  | 11914.33       | 1212.51         |
| Image2  | 11606.38       | 1189.25         |
| Image3  | 12098.92       | 1251.23         |
| Image4  | 12281.60       | 1192.32         |
| Image5  | 11871.03       | 1165.97         |
| Image6  | 13788.68       | 1472.90         |
| Average | 12260.15       | 1247.33         |

enhances the performance of the DCT-OFDM based watermarking method. We also observed the following interesting feature. At the selection of a quality factor of JPEG algorithm satisfying the compression rate subjected by the IHC evaluation criteria, we got better PSNR value using lower quality factors that can compress much more in some cases. The main reason may come from the embedding algorithm such that the size of partitioned block is not equal to that of JPEG algorithm. Namely, $256 \times 256$ pixels is used for our method while $8 \times 8$ pixels for JPEG algorithm. This mismatch of the block size may cause such an interesting feature. The detailed analysis is left for our future work.

Table 7 shows the computational costs required for the synchronization recovery. The time consumption is evaluated on a computer (Intel Xeon(R) E5 4627 v2 (3.3 GHz) and 512-GB RAM). It is observed from the table that the computational costs of our method become approximately 1/10 from the original method. As mentioned in Sect. 3.1, the computational costs of the proposed method is expected to be reduced by a factor of 1/6 in a rough estimation. We expected to a factor of 1/6 at Sect. 3.1, but we got a different result. The reason comes from the clipping positions specified in the IHC evaluation criteria such that most of the positions are located in the first 1/3 area of blocks with $N \times N$ pixels. Therefore, more computational costs are reduced under this experimental condition than expected.

## 5    Conclusion

We employed an error correcting code to enhance the robustness against combination of some attacks such as JPEG compression, clipping, rotation, and scaling attacks. In order to reduce the computational costs at the synchronization recovery, we proposed a hierarchical searching method which checks only for the neighborings of one detected position. From computer simulation, it was revealed that the performance of our method satisfied the evaluation criteria determined by the IHC committee. We also discovers an interesting feature about the robustness against JPEG compression. The mismatch of the partitioning of blocks may change the quality measurement evaluated by PSNR. The detailed analysis of the relationship between the quality factor and the PSNR value is left for our future work.

# References

1. Petitcolas, F.A.P., Anderson, R.J., Kuhn, M.G.: Attacks on copyright marking systems. In: Aucsmith, D. (ed.) IH 98. LNCS, vol. 1525, pp. 219–239. Springer, Heidelberg (1998)
2. Petitcolas, F.A.P.: Watermarking schemes evaluation. IEEE Trans. Signal Process. **17**(5), 58–64 (2000)
3. IHC Committee. IHC Evaluation Criteria and Competition. http://www.ieice.org/iss/emm/ihc/IHC_criteriaVer4.pdf
4. Hakka, M., Kuribayashi, M., Morii, M.: DCT-OFDM based watermarking scheme robust against clipping attack. In: Proceedings of IWIHC 2014, pp. 18–24 (2014)
5. Cox, I., Kilian, J., Leighton, F., Shamson, T.: Secure spreadspectrum watermarking for multimedia. IEEE Trans. Image Process. **6**(12), 1673–1687 (1997)
6. Malvar, H.S., Florêncio, D.A.F.: Improved spreadspectrum: a new modulation technique for robust watermarking. IEEE Trans. Signal Process. **51**(4), 898–905 (2003)
7. Maximal, R.G.: Recursive sequences with 3-valued recursivecross-correlation functions. IEEE Trans. Inf. Theor. **14**(3), 154–156 (1968)
8. Viterbi, A.J.: Error bounds for convolutional codes and an asymptotically optimum decoding algorithm. IEEE Trans. Inf. Theor. **13**(2), 260–269 (1967)
9. Siozaki, A.: Basis of Information and Coding Theory. Ohmsha, Ltd. (2011)
10. Gallager, R.G.: Low Density Parity Check Codes. M.I.T. Press, Cambridge (1963)
11. Hirata, N., Kawamura, M.: Digital watermarking method using LDPC code for clipped image. In: Proceedings of IWIHC 2014, pp. 25–30. ACM (2014)
12. Chen, B., Wornell, G.W.: Quantization index modulation: aclass of provably good methods for digital watermarking and information embedding. IEEE Trans. Inf. Theor. **47**(4), 1423–1443 (2001)

# Robust Imperceptible Video Watermarking for MPEG Compression and DA-AD Conversion Using Visual Masking

Sang-Keun Ji, Wook-Hyung Kim, Han-Ul Jang, Seung-Min Mun,
and Heung-Kyu Lee(✉)

School of Computing, Korea Advanced Institute of Science and Technology,
Daejeon, Republic of Korea
{skji,whkim,hanulj,smmun,hklee}@mmc.kaist.ac.kr

**Abstract.** In this paper, we propose a robust and invisible video watermarking scheme. To ensure robustness against various non-hostile disturbances which can occur during the distribution of digital content, the proposed system selects certain blocks using a robust and imperceptible block selection scheme and watermarks are embedded into these blocks using spread-spectrum watermarking in DCT domain. In addition, visual masking is applied to the watermarking embedding process for high invisibility. Our system is designed to extract 16 bits data in any 15-second interval. Experimental results show that the proposed system offers high invisibility and that it is robust against MPEG-4 compression and DA-AD conversion.

**Keywords:** Video watermarking · Video compression · DA-AD conversion · Visual masking

## 1 Introduction

Digital watermarking is a technique to embed an imperceptible message in the digital cover works such as audio, or video, etc. This watermarking scheme is mainly used for copyright protection [1]. The main properties of digital watermarking are robustness, imperceptibility, and payload.

There are various non-hostile disturbances that threaten to degrade the robustness of digital video. These include such as noise addition, compression, and digital/analogue - analogue/digital (DA-AD) conversion [2]. The latter, in particularly, can have such strong effect that it makes other copyright protection techniques, such as digital rights management (DRM), ineffective. Moreover, digital video watermarking should be robust to DA-AD conversion because if it is not, copy-protected videos could easily be duplicated using analogue means [3].

There have been proposals for robust watermarking schemes against DA-AD conversion attack in several papers. Lubin et al. created a watermark pattern at very low frequency and embedded the pattern in both space and time domains

© Springer International Publishing Switzerland 2016
Y.-Q. Shi et al. (Eds.): IWDW 2015, LNCS 9569, pp. 285–298, 2016.
DOI: 10.1007/978-3-319-31960-5_24

satisfying fidelity, robustness, and security [4]. Lee et al. designed a robust water-marking method where the watermark pattern was low-pass filtered because low frequency is less influenced by common signal processing, especially by DA-AD conversion [5].

Imperceptibility is one of the main goals of digital watermarking and it means that the embedded watermark creates insignificant changes to the cover work which cannot be perceived by human visual system (HVS). Generally, high imperceptibility is required to provide high quality watermarked content.

Niu et al. proposed visual-saliency-based watermarking to provide high imperceptibility [8]. Visual saliency indicates the degree and location to which human visual attention is most attracted [6]. Kim et al. designed a digital video watermarking scheme using an HVS masking function for high robustness and high invisibility [9]. Kutter et al. presented a watermarking method where the blue channel was the watermark embedding domain [10]. They employed the characteristic that human eyes are least sensitive to the blue channel.

In this paper, we propose a video watermarking system with high impercep-tibility and robustness against MPEG-4 compression and DA-AD conversion. In order to satisfy these requirements, our system selects significantly imper-ceptible blocks using a robust and imperceptible block selection method, and a watermark is embedded into these blocks using spread-spectrum watermarking in DCT domain. For robustness against MPEG-4 compression and DA-AD con-version, the watermark should be strongly embedded, though this can decrease the degree of invisibility. Therefore, visual masking is applied to watermarked blocks for high invisibility and a watermark is only embedded in the blue chan-nel of RGB channel because human eyes are less sensitive to changes in the blue channel [10]. In the proposed system, the changes caused by the water-mark are not noticeable by human eyes because the robust and imperceptible block selection scheme along with visual masking were applied to ensure good invisibility.

The rest of the paper is organized as follows. In Sect. 2, The proposed water-marking system is described. In Sect. 3, the experimental setup and results are shown and Sect. 4 concludes.

## 2    Proposed Method

The overall process of the proposed method consists of watermarking embedding and extraction process as shown in Figs. 3 and 5. Watermarking embedding process consists of visual masking, the robust and imperceptible block selection, data encoding and watermark embedding.

### 2.1    Visual Masking

Generally, there is a trade-off between the robustness and the imperceptibility of watermarking. In the embedding process, the stronger the watermark, the less imperceptible the watermarked content, and vice versa. However, the strength

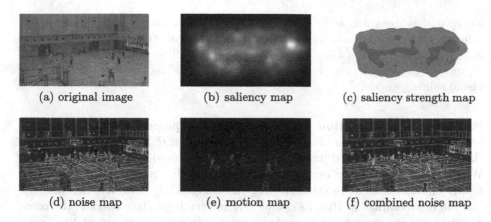

| (a) original image | (b) saliency map | (c) saliency strength map |

| (d) noise map | (e) motion map | (f) combined noise map |

**Fig. 1.** Examples of Visual Masking

of the watermark can be maintained and imperceptibility can be increased if HVS is used. Watermarks are normally not embedded at low frequencies because changes at a low frequency are significantly more visible than those done at a high frequency. Thus, visual masking is utilized to embed high-strength watermarks in less perceptible areas, while low-strength watermarks are embedded in more perceptible areas. We describe the visual masking schemes used to improve the watermarking performance of the proposed method in this section.

**Visual Saliency Model.** There are various approaches which can be used to model human visual characteristics, as human visual characteristics are highly complex. Particularly, the visual saliency model (VSM) is a scheme employing the area which are highly attractive to human visual attention. The visual saliency model creates a saliency map using features such as color, intensity, and orientation. In this paper, we create a visual saliency map using Graph-Based Visual Saliency (GBVS), as proposed by Harel et al. [7]. GBVS is a simple and biologically plausible bottom-up visual saliency model which uses a graph-based random walk to reflect human visual characteristics.

The process of applying GBVS is as follows. First, the saliency map of a frame is calculated using GBVS. The saliency map tends to be concentrated in a particular range, as shown in Fig. 1(b). For the human visual system in the saliency map, segmentation depending on the distribution of the values on the map is important as opposed to the values themselves. For the segmentation of the saliency map, the cumulative distribution function (CDF) of the saliency map is calculated, and the saliency strength map is then computed considering the CDF, as shown below:

$$
\alpha_{x,y}^{vsm} = \begin{cases} \alpha_1, & F(p_{x,y}) < 0.5 \\ \alpha_2, & 0.5 \le F(p_{x,y}) < 0.8 \\ \alpha_3, & 0.8 \le F(p_{x,y}) \end{cases} \tag{1}
$$

where $p_{x,y}$ is the value at $(x,y)$ of the saliency map, and $F$ is the CDF of the saliency map. $\alpha_1$, $\alpha_2$, and $\alpha_3$ are the watermark strength constants, and $\alpha_{x,y}^{vsm}$ is the value at $(x,y)$ of the saliency strength map. The saliency strength map represents the weight map in the watermark embedding process based on the visual saliency model.

**Noise Visibility Function.** Voloshynovskiy et al. proposed the HVS function based on the computation of a noise visibility function (NVF) that characterizes the properties of the local image by identifying textured and edge regions [11]. Watermarks are strongly embedded at less attractive regions, while they are lightly embedded at more attractive regions using NVF. However, this method has the disadvantage in that its complexity is very high. To overcome the complexity problem, our system computes a noise map using a simplified NVF with a 2-D linear separable filter with low complexity as proposed by Kim et al. [9].

In addition to this, human eyes are less attracted to moving objects such as driving cars. Thus, a motion map is computed using the differences between video frames based on the time domain, as shown in Fig. 1(e). Then, a binary motion map is calculated considering a predefined threshold. For example, the binary motion value of $(x,y)$ is set to 1 when the motion value of $(x,y)$ is higher than the threshold; otherwise, the value is set to 0. As shown in Fig. 1(f), a noise map and a binary motion map are finally combined to increase the both watermark embedding regions and strength. A combined noise map is used as the weight map in the same manner as a saliency strength map. To use these maps as the weight map, the values of the saliency strength map and the combined noise map are normalized so that they are between 0 and 1.

## 2.2   Robust and Imperceptible Block Selection

In the proposed method, the watermark is embedded by means of visual masking, as described above. However, visual masking has a limitation in that the watermark extraction accuracy is seriously low when the masking value is too low. For example, the masking value is very low at an area of high attention and a flat area, and this causes the watermark signal to be weak. Therefore, a robust and imperceptible block selection scheme is proposed to overcome this limitation of visual masking. The scheme employs the blocks with the highest masking values to improve the degree of imperceptibility and minimize the data loss caused by compression.

The selection process of a robust and imperceptible block is as follows. First, an image is divided into blocks and a NVF map is calculated at every block. Then, $m$ blocks with the highest intensity of a noise map are selected. A saliency strength map is calculated at $m$ blocks and $k$ blocks with the highest strength are selected, where $k$ is the number of necessary blocks to embed watermarks, with $k$ being smaller than $m$. These selected blocks are more imperceptible than other blocks because visual masking is applied. Moreover, these blocks are more robust against the data loss as compared to other blocks because the watermark strength of the selected blocks is higher than that of the other blocks.

An example of the correlation of the blocks in uncompressed and compressed videos is in Fig. 2. In this example, the frame was divided into 16 blocks, and the watermarked video explained in Sect. 3.1 is compressed by MPEG-4 part10 (H.264) with 1,200 Kbps. Red dots represent 5 blocks with the highest strength using a robust and imperceptible block selection method, and blue dots represent 5 blocks with the lowest strength. As shown in Fig. 2, blocks with the highest strength tend to have a higher correlation compared to other blocks.

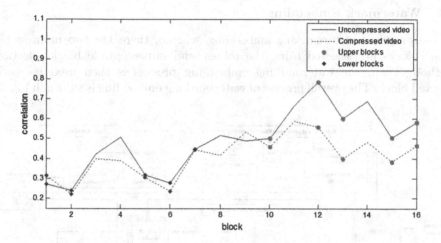

**Fig. 2.** An example of the correlation of the blocks (Colour figure online)

The watermark accuracy and robustness increase when $k$ increases; however, the imperceptibility decreases. In contrast, the watermark accuracy and robustness decrease when $k$ is low. Therefore, we experimentally determined the number of necessary blocks and obtained high robustness and high imperceptibility.

## 2.3   Data Encoding

In the proposed system, watermark patterns are designed to represent 16 bits data. To this end, two sets, $X$ and $Y$, of pseudo-random sequences are used as the watermark. Each set is composed of $256 (= 2^8)$ pseudo-random sequences to represent 8 bits data, as expressed by the following equation.

$$X = \{X_0, X_1, X_2, ..., X_{255}\},$$
$$Y = \{Y_0, Y_1, Y_2, ..., Y_{255}\}. \tag{2}$$

To represent 16 bits data, the sequences $X_i$ and $Y_j$ are selected from $\boldsymbol{X}$ and $\boldsymbol{Y}$. Here, $X_i$ represents the upper 8 bits data and $Y_j$ represents the lower 8 bits data. By attaching them, two pseudo-random sequences can present 16 bits data. For example, if the data is $0x00FF$, then $X_i$ corresponds to a sequence representing $0x00$ from $\boldsymbol{X}$ and $Y_j$ corresponds to a sequence representing $0xFF$ from $\boldsymbol{Y}$. Each pseudo-random sequence of $X_i$ and $Y_j$ is an $N$-length pseudo-random sequence, as determined by the equation below.

$$X_i = \{x_{i1}, x_{i2}, ..., x_{iN}\},$$
$$Y_j = \{y_{j1}, y_{j2}, ..., y_{jN}\}. \tag{3}$$

## 2.4   Watermark Embedding

In the proposed watermarking embedding scheme, there are two main steps. First, blocks are selected using the robust and imperceptible block selection method. Then, the watermarking embedding process is then used for each selected block. The overall process of watermarking embedding is shown in Fig. 3.

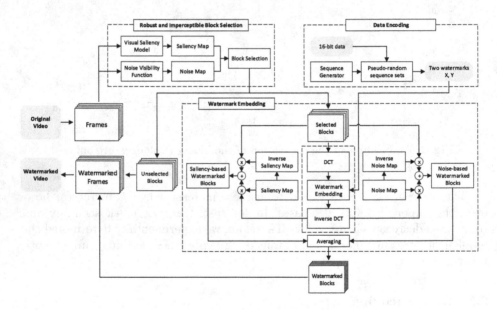

**Fig. 3.** Watermark embedding process

First, the blocks which are used for watermark embedding are selected by means of robust and imperceptible block selection for invisibility. Then, two pseudo-random sequences $X_i$ and $Y_j$ are embedded into each half of the selected blocks. In the proposed method, the selected blocks are sorted according to visual masking values, and the sequence $X_i$ is embedded into odd-ordered blocks, with $Y_j$ embedded into even-ordered block.

For each of the selected blocks, the watermark embedding precess is performed as follows. First, spread-spectrum watermarking in the DCT domain [12] is used for robustness. In each block, the discrete cosine transform is calculated and the vector $V$ having coefficients of length $N$ is extracted from a fixed point. A pseudo-random sequence is then embedded into the vector $V$ via the following equation:

$$v'_i = v_i + \alpha |v_i| w_i, \quad (0 \leq i \leq N) \tag{4}$$

where $V_i = \{v_1, v_2, ..., v_n\}$ is the vector of the original coefficients and $V'_i = \{v'_1, v'_2, ..., v'_n\}$ is the vector of the watermarked coefficients. $\alpha$ is the strength of the watermark signal. $W = \{w_1, w_2, ..., w_n\}$ is a pseudo-random sequence from $X$ or $Y$ in the selected block. In the DCT domain, coefficients of length $N$ are selected from the mid-frequency coefficients for robustness of compression and for good visual quality. After embedding a sequence, inverse DCT is performed and the watermarked block $B'$ is obtained. An example of a watermarked frame is in Fig. 4. In Fig. 4, the number of blocks is 16 and the number of selected blocks k is 6, a sequence $X_i$ is embedded into blocks with red line, and a sequence $Y_j$ is embedded into blocks with blue line. White regions of left-top corner indicates watermark embedding regions for each block.

**Fig. 4.** An example of watermark embedding in selected blocks (Colour figure online)

Finally, visual masking is applied to the watermarked blocks to enhance the invisibility. The visual masking method is

$$B_s = I_s * B' + (1 - I_s) * B,$$
$$B_n = I_n * B' + (1 - I_n) * B, \tag{5}$$
$$B_w = (B_s + B_n)/2$$

where $B$ denotes the original block of the selected block and $B'$ is the watermarked block of the selected block. In addition $I_s$ and $I_n$ represent the value of the saliency map and the combined noise map, respectively. The bigger these values are, the stronger the watermarks are embedded. Finally, the masked watermarked block $B_w$ is the average of $B_s$ and $B_n$. Masking using a combined noise map can achieve high transparency, but it incurs a large amount of information loss, which can decrease the robustness. In contrast, masking using a saliency strength map inserts the watermark more strongly compared to the use of a combined noise map. Therefore, masking is better when these two characteristics are balanced by averaging. This embedding process is repeated in each selected block. A frame is then reconstructed by combining the selected blocks $B_w$ and the unselected blocks, and this process is repeated for each frame.

The proposed method selects the blocks in which to embed watermarks, and it provides higher imperceptibility than a method which uses all of the blocks. The watermarks are embedded strongly to prevent any decreases in the robustness; however, the traces are imperceptible due to visual masking. Also, watermark losses are minimized because blocks with low masking values are excluded. Therefore, the proposed method achieves high robustness and high imperceptibility.

## 2.5    Watermark Extraction

The watermark extraction process is shown in Fig. 5. First, a frame is divided into blocks and the DCT coefficients of each block are calculated. Then, an $N$-length vector $V^*$ is extracted from the DCT coefficients at a fixed point. During the watermark extraction process, a correlation is used to determine whether a watermark is embedded or not. The correlation is computed between vector $V^*$ and all sequences from the two sequence sets $X$ and $Y$ via the following equation:

$$z = \frac{W \cdot V^*}{N} = \frac{1}{N} \sum_{i=1}^{N} w_i \cdot v_i^*. \tag{6}$$

where $z$ is the correlation value and $W$ is a pseudo-random sequence from $X$ and $Y$.

By comparing the correlation $z$ and the threshold, the presence or absence of the watermark $W$ is determined. The threshold is calculated as

$$T = \frac{1}{15 \cdot N} \sum_{i=1}^{N} |v_i^*|. \tag{7}$$

The threshold is determined by experimental results to minimize a false-positive rate.

After correlation computation of each block, the existence of a watermark is determined by the following watermark extraction rule. The result of watermark extraction of a frame is calculated using the extraction results of all blocks in a frame. The watermark extraction rule of a frame is as follows.

---

**Rule 1.** Watermark extraction rule of a frame

---

**if** (The total number of detected blocks != 2)
    **then** Watermarks are not detected
**else** (The total number of detected blocks == 2)
    **if** two watermarks are in the same set of watermark
        **then** Watermarks are not detected
    **else** (one is in the set of $X$ and the other is in the set of $Y$)
        **then** Watermarks are detected
    **end**
**end**

---

For example, if sequences that are over the threshold are $X_{10}, X_{20}, Y_{128}$, it means that a watermark is not detected. Also, if sequences that are over the threshold are $Y_{48}, Y_{241}$, it describes that a watermark is not detected. In contrast, if sequences that are over the threshold are $X_{149}, Y_{214}$, it means that a watermark is detected. In this way, the watermark extraction rule of a frame is applied to each frame.

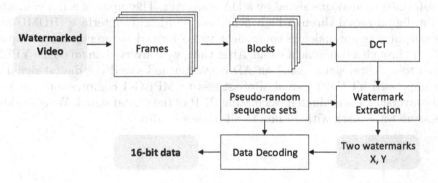

**Fig. 5.** Watermark extraction process

# 3   Experimental Results

## 3.1   Experimental Environment

**Experimental Setup.** We simulated our method using the sample video set IWIHC provided, as shown in Fig. 7. (display resolution: $1920 \times 1080$, 30 frames per seconds, 30 s, 12 Gbps, 8bits depth uncompressed AVI files) The proposed watermarking algorithm was implemented in the MATLAB R2013a environment, and a computer of Intel i7-4770K (3.50 GHz) with 16 GB main memory was used to evaluate the performance. We used 'Fosmon HDMI to component video (YPbPr) / VGA & SPDIF output converter box' that supports $1280 \times 720$ resolution as a digital-to-analogue (DA) converter and 'skyHD captureX HDMI' that supports real-time full high definition (FHD) recording as an analogue-to-digital (AD) converter. The important point is that the video after DA-AD conversion has different resolution from that of the original video since the maximum resolution of a DA converter is $1280 \times 720$.

The number of a robust-and-imperceptible block $k$ and the number of the selected block in a noise map $m$ were experimentally set to 6 and 8 respectively. $\alpha_1$, $\alpha_2$ and $\alpha_3$ used in Sect. 2.1 were set to 0.7, 0.6 and 0.5. Also, 25,000 coefficients represented by $N$ in Sect. 2.3 were selected at the fixed location in the DCT domain. The determined coefficients were robust to scaling caused by DA-AD conversion because the coefficients were used at middle frequency. The experiments were implemented to test the visual quality and robustness. We used peak signal-to-noise ratio (PSNR) and structural similarity (SSIM) [13] to evaluate imperceptibility, and we used bit error rate (BER) to evaluate the watermarking performance.

The proposed watermarking scheme is designed to have robustness to MPEG-4 compression and DA-AD conversion. The overall process of experiments is as shown in Fig. 6. First, we embedded watermarks into videos using the proposed watermark embedder and compressed the watermarked video using MPEG-4 part10 (H.264) codec that FFmpeg provided. Then, the compressed video was transformed to analogue signal by a DA converter. The input of a DA converter was a digital signal through high definition multimedia interface (HDMI) and the output was an analogue component video formed by analogue color space YPbPr through a component cable. After that, we converted an analogue YPbPr signal to a digital signal using an AD converter and saved the digital signal as uncompressed YUV422 format. Robustness to MPEG-4 compression and DA-AD conversion was evaluated calculating BER of the digital signal. We embedded the same watermark with 16 bits to all frames in 15 s.

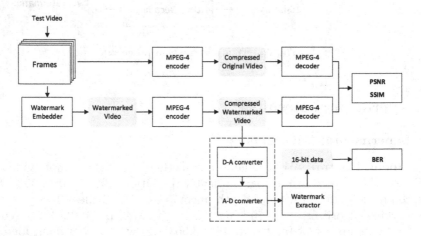

**Fig. 6.** Test process in the proposed watermarking system

**Fig. 7.** Compressed original images (first row), and compressed watermarked videos for $\alpha = 0.4$ (second row) (bit rate = 12,000Kbps, compressibility = 1/100)

## 3.2 Image Quality

We performed experiments to determine the relation between the robustness and an image quality in the proposed watermark embedding algorithm by changing various watermark strengths $\alpha$.

To evaluate image quality, the following process was performed, as shown in Fig. 6. The watermarked video and the original video were compressed with the same bit rate by using the MPEG-4 part 10 (H.264) codec. In this paper, the size of the compressed bit stream were set to have 1/100 of the original bit stream. After that, two compressed video were decompressed and the luminance channel $Y$ was calculated from the RGB channel according to the following equation.

$$Y = 0.7152G + 0.0722B + 0.2126R \tag{8}$$

Then, the PSNR and SSIM were calculated for each pair of luminance channels.

Because the original video has a bit rate of 12 Gbps, the watermarked video was compressed to have a bit rate of 12 Mbps, which is 1/100 of the bit rate of the original video. Also, the BER(Bit Error Rate) was calculated to represent the relation between image quality and the robustness to compression. For exact data extraction without errors, BER should be zero during the watermark extraction process. We consider the results having a non-zero BER as a failure in watermark extraction.

Table 1 shows the PSNR, SSIM, and BER results at various watermark strengths $\alpha$ for MPEG4 compression with 12,000Kbps. As results, there is no bit error if $\alpha$ is larger than or equal to 0.3. When the watermark is robust to MPEG-4 compression with a 12,000Kbps bit rate, the minimum of an average PSNR is 43.92dB and the minimum of an average SSIM is 0.9965. In the case of the 'Walk2' video, there is a great deal of data loss in MPEG-4 compression and the PSNR and SSIM are lower than for other videos because the textured and edge regions are larger than those of other videos. Also, the experiment shows that there is little change in the PSNR and SSIM with increasing $\alpha$ because of using a robust and imperceptible block selection method.

**Table 1.** Test Result at various watermark strength $\alpha$ for MPEG-4 with 12,000 Kbps

| WM strength $\alpha$ | | 0.2 | 0.3 | 0.4 | 0.5 | 0.6 | 0.7 | 1.0 | 1.5 |
|---|---|---|---|---|---|---|---|---|---|
| Basketball | PSNR(dB) | 46.69 | 46.63 | 46.57 | 46.50 | 46.43 | 46.35 | 46.11 | 45.64 |
| | SSIM | 0.9977 | 0.9977 | 0.9976 | 0.9976 | 0.9976 | 0.9975 | 0.9974 | 0.9972 |
| | BER | 0.00 | 0.00 | 0.00 | 0.00 | 0.00 | 0.00 | 0.00 | 0.00 |
| Lego | PSNR(dB) | 43.72 | 43.67 | 43.63 | 43.60 | 43.54 | 43.49 | 43.30 | 42.93 |
| | SSIM | 0.9961 | 0.9960 | 0.9960 | 0.9960 | 0.9959 | 0.9959 | 0.9957 | 0.9955 |
| | BER | 0.00 | 0.00 | 0.00 | 0.00 | 0.00 | 0.00 | 0.00 | 0.00 |
| Library | PSNR(dB) | 43.76 | 43.72 | 43.68 | 43.63 | 43.57 | 43.50 | 43.22 | 42.67 |
| | SSIM | 0.9965 | 0.9965 | 0.9964 | 0.9964 | 0.9964 | 0.9963 | 0.9962 | 0.9958 |
| | BER | × | 0.00 | 0.00 | 0.00 | 0.00 | 0.00 | 0.00 | 0.00 |
| Walk1 | PSNR(dB) | 46.52 | 46.44 | 46.33 | 46.22 | 46.10 | 45.98 | 45.52 | 44.64 |
| | SSIM | 0.9982 | 0.9982 | 0.9981 | 0.9981 | 0.9981 | 0.9980 | 0.9978 | 0.9975 |
| | BER | 0.00 | 0.00 | 0.00 | 0.00 | 0.00 | 0.00 | 0.00 | 0.00 |
| Walk2 | PSNR(dB) | 39.17 | 39.11 | 38.99 | 38.83 | 38.70 | 38.53 | 37.94 | 37.16 |
| | SSIM | 0.9942 | 0.9941 | 0.9940 | 0.9938 | 0.9936 | 0.9934 | 0.9926 | 0.9911 |
| | BER | × | 0.00 | 0.00 | 0.00 | 0.00 | 0.00 | 0.00 | 0.00 |
| average | PSNR(dB) | 43.97 | 43.92 | 43.84 | 43.75 | 43.67 | 43.57 | 43.22 | 42.61 |
| | SSIM | 0.9965 | 0.9965 | 0.9964 | 0.9964 | 0.9963 | 0.9962 | 0.9959 | 0.9954 |
| | BER | × | 0.00 | 0.00 | 0.00 | 0.00 | 0.00 | 0.00 | 0.00 |

× : watermark is not detected

### 3.3    Robustness

To protect the copyrights of the digital HDTV contents, a watermarking scheme should be robust to various attacks such as compression and DA-AD conversion. Also, during DA-AD conversion, the scaling of frames inevitably occurs. In the proposed watermarking embedding algorithm, we select middle-low frequencies to embed the watermark and the watermarked is embedded the fixed points of DCT coefficients. Therefore, the proposed method is robust to attacks that eliminate high frequencies, such as compression and scaling.

In this paper, the watermarking system is designed to extract 16 bits data within any 15-seconds period of video. In order to achieve this requirement, two watermarks should be extracted within any 7.5 s in the proposed method. If two watermarks are not extracted within 7.5 s, we consider that the watermark is not detected.

An experiment was performed to evaluate the robustness to compression and DA-AD conversion at various watermark strength $\alpha$ while decreasing the bit rate in compression. We selected $\alpha = 0.3, 0.7, 1.5$ to determine the relation between the bit rate and $\alpha$. Tables 2, 3 and 4 show the BER in various bit rates with fixed $\alpha$. When $\alpha = 0.3$, the embedded data is not extracted except for a 1,200Kbps bit rate. When $\alpha = 1.5$, the embedded data is exactly extracted within 1/1000 compressibility. Also, we determined that there is little change in the PSNR and SSIMS as $\alpha$ is increased.

**Table 2.** Robustness test results for $\alpha = 0.3$ (PSNR 43.92 dB, SSIM 0.9965)

| Bit rate | | 12,000 | 8,000 | 6,000 | 3,000 | 1,500 | 1,200 |
|---|---|---|---|---|---|---|---|
| Compressibility | | 1/100 | 1/150 | 1/200 | 1/400 | 1/800 | 1/1000 |
| Basketball | BER | 0.000 | 0.000 | 0.000 | 0.000 | × | × |
| Lego | BER | 0.000 | 0.000 | 0.000 | × | × | × |
| Library | BER | 0.000 | 0.000 | × | × | × | × |
| Walk1 | BER | 0.000 | 0.000 | 0.000 | 0.000 | 0.000 | × |
| Walk2 | BER | 0.000 | × | × | × | × | × |
| Average | BER | 0.000 | × | × | × | × | × |

× : watermark is not detected

**Table 3.** Robustness test results for $\alpha = 0.7$ (PSNR 43.57 dB, SSIM 0.9962)

| Bit rate | | 12,000 | 8,000 | 6,000 | 3,000 | 1,500 | 1,200 |
|---|---|---|---|---|---|---|---|
| Compressibility | | 1/100 | 1/150 | 1/200 | 1/400 | 1/800 | 1/1000 |
| Basketball | BER | 0.000 | 0.000 | 0.000 | 0.000 | 0.000 | 0.000 |
| Lego | BER | 0.000 | 0.000 | 0.000 | 0.000 | 0.000 | × |
| Library | BER | 0.000 | 0.000 | 0.000 | 0.000 | × | × |
| Walk1 | BER | 0.000 | 0.000 | 0.000 | 0.000 | 0.000 | 0.000 |
| Walk2 | BER | 0.000 | 0.000 | 0.000 | 0.000 | 0.000 | × |
| Average | BER | 0.000 | 0.000 | 0.000 | 0.000 | × | × |

× : watermark is not detected

**Table 4.** Robustness test results for $\alpha = 1.5$ (PSNR 42.61 dB, SSIM 0.9954)

| Bit rate | | 12,000 | 8,000 | 6,000 | 3,000 | 1,500 | 1,200 |
|---|---|---|---|---|---|---|---|
| Compressibility | | 1/100 | 1/150 | 1/200 | 1/400 | 1/800 | 1/1000 |
| Basketball | BER | 0.000 | 0.000 | 0.000 | 0.000 | 0.000 | 0.000 |
| Lego | BER | 0.000 | 0.000 | 0.000 | 0.000 | 0.000 | 0.000 |
| Library | BER | 0.000 | 0.000 | 0.000 | 0.000 | 0.000 | 0.000 |
| Walk1 | BER | 0.000 | 0.000 | 0.000 | 0.000 | 0.000 | 0.000 |
| Walk2 | BER | 0.000 | 0.000 | 0.000 | 0.000 | 0.000 | 0.000 |
| Average | BER | 0.000 | 0.000 | 0.000 | 0.000 | 0.000 | 0.000 |

× : watermark is not detected

# 4  Conclusion

This paper has proposed a watermarking system to be robust to MPEG-4 compression and DA-AD conversion with high transparency. The watermarking system employs a robust-and-imperceptible block selection method we propose and a spread spectrum watermarking method in DCT domain. Also, we apply a visual masking method that fuses a saliency map based on visual saliency model and a noise map based on a noise visibility function. As a result, the proposed scheme has high imperceptibility. The experimental results show robustness to compression and DA-AD conversion as well as high imperceptibility with high PSNR and SSIM. Also, the results indicate that the proposed watermarking system extracts 16 bits data in every 15 s. However, the proposed method has a disadvantage that it is weak to geometrical attacks because it uses spread spectrum watermarking based on DCT domain. Therefore, the improvement to be robust to geometrical attacks should be needed.

**Acknowledgements.** This research project was supported by Ministry of Culture, Sports and Tourism (MCST) and from Korea Copyright Commission in 2015.

# References

1. Cox, I., Miller, M., Bloom, J., Fridrich, J., Kalker, T.: Digital Watermarking and Steganography. Morgan Kaufmann (2007)
2. Doërr, G., Dugelay, J.-L.: A guide tour of video watermarking. Sig. Process. Image Commun. **18**(4), 263–282 (2003)
3. Diehl, E., Furon, T.: Watermark: closing the analog hole. In: 2003 IEEE International Conference on Consumer Electronics, pp. 52–53 (2003)
4. Lubin, J., Bloom, J.A., Cheng, H.: Robust content-dependent high-fidelity watermark for tracking in digital cinema. In: SPIE 2003, pp. 536–545 (2003)
5. Lee, M.J., Kim, K.S., Lee, H.Y., Oh, T.W., Suh, Y.H., Lee, H.K.: Robust watermark detection against D-A/A-D conversion for digital cinema using local autocorrelation function. Proceedings of International Conference on Image Processing, pp. 425–428 (2008)
6. Itti, L., Koch, C., Niebur, E.: A model of saliency-based visual attention for rapid scene analysis. IEEE Trans. Pattern Anal. Mach. Intell. **20**(11), 1254–1259 (1998)
7. Harel, J., Koch, C., Perona, P.: Graph-based visual saliency. In: Advances in Neural Information Processing Systems, pp. 545–552 (2006)
8. Niu, Y., Kyan, M., Ma, L., Beghdadi, A., Krishnan, S.: A visual saliency modulated just noticeable distortion profile for image watermarking. In: European Signal Processing Conference, pp. 2039–2043 (2011)
9. Kim, K.S., Lee, H.Y., Im, D.H., Lee, H.K.: Practical, real-time, and robust watermarking on the spatial domain for high-definition video contents. In: IEICE Transactions on Information and Systems, vol. E91-D, no. 5, pp. 1359–1368 (2008)
10. Kutter, M., Jordan, F., Bossen, F.: Digital watermarking of color images using amplitude modulation. J. Electron. Imaging **3022**, 518–526 (1998)
11. Voloshynovskiy, S., Herrigel, A., Baumgaertner, N., Pun, T.: A stochastic approach to content adaptive digital image watermarking. In: Pfitzmann, A. (ed.) IH 1999. LNCS, vol. 1768, pp. 211–236. Springer, Heidelberg (2000)
12. Barni, M., Bartolini, F., Cappellini, V., Piva, A.: A DCT-domain system for robust image watermarking. Sig. Proc. **66**, 357–372 (1998)
13. Wang, Z., Bovik, A.C., Sheikh, H.R., Simoncelli, E.P.: Image quality assessment: from error visibility to structural similarity. IEEE Trans. Image Process. **13**(4), 600–612 (2004)

# Detection of Frequency-Scale Modification Using Robust Audio Watermarking Based on Amplitude Modulation

Akira Nishimura[✉]

Department of Informatics, Faculty of Informatics,
Tokyo University of Information Sciences,
4–1 Onaridai, Wakaba, Chiba, Chiba 265-8501, Japan
akira@rsch.tuis.ac.jp

**Abstract.** An audio watermarking system based on amplitude modulation (AM) is tested under the evaluation criteria proposed by the Information Hiding Criteria committee. Sinusoidal AMs at relatively low modulation frequencies, which are applied in opposite phase to neighboring subband signals, are used as the carrier of embedded information and for synchronization of the data frame. In contrast to previous methods, the detection of frame synchronization is conducted by compensating the frequency scale from −6 to +6 % in 1 % steps in the time-frequency domain for the attack of frequency-scale modification. The maximum amplitude of AM collected from the subband group for synchronization is observed at the frequency-scale compensation that corresponds to the amount of frequency-scale modification. The results of a computer simulation showed that the quality degradation caused by the watermarking was tolerable and that the detectability of the watermark under mandatory attack tests (simulated DA/AD conversion and MP3 coding) and optional attack tests (bandpass filtering, tandem MP3 coding, MPEG4AAC coding, a single echo addition, and ±4 % frequency-scale modification) was sufficiently maintained.

**Keywords:** Objective audio quality · Bit error rate · Perceptual coding · Subband coding · Audio coding · Frequency-scale modification

## 1 Introduction

### 1.1 Previous Works

A watermarking system based on subband coding using amplitude modulation (AM) has been proposed [10]. In this method, sinusoidal amplitude modulations (SAMs) at relatively low modulation frequencies, applied in opposite phase to neighboring subband signals, are used as the carrier of embedded information and for synchronization of data frames. The embedded information is encoded in the form of relative phase differences between the amplitude modulations applied to several groups of subband signals.

© Springer International Publishing Switzerland 2016
Y.-Q. Shi et al. (Eds.): IWDW 2015, LNCS 9569, pp. 299–311, 2016.
DOI: 10.1007/978-3-319-31960-5_25

In addition to the conventional method, optimal tuning of the values of the embedding parameters and improvements to the decision algorithm of AM depth by considering perceptual modulation masking were implemented [11]. A computer simulation to test the robustness and objective sound quality of stego audio according to the IHC evaluation criteria version 3 [3] revealed that the quality degradation caused by the watermarking was tolerable and that sufficient detectability of watermarking was maintained under mandatory attacks (simulated DA/AD conversion and MP3 coding) and optional attacks (bandpass filtering, tandem MP3 coding, and MPEG4AAC coding). Moreover, performance in terms of both robustness and objective sound quality was superior to the previous method [10].

However, the AM-based watermarking system is sensitive to frequency-scale modifications and time-scale modifications, i.e., geometric attacks. A frequency-scale modification causes mismatches in the center frequencies between subbands of embedding and extraction because the bandwidths of the subbands are constant over the center frequencies. It causes overlaps between adjacent subbands of the opposite AM phase and contradicts the depth of AM. Tolerances to the frequency-scale modification are $\pm 0.6\%$ for the 172-Hz bandwidth of the subband [9] and $\pm 0.2\%$ for the 86-Hz bandwidth [10].

Several audio watermarking technologies based on amplitude modifications to subband signals have been proposed [6,7,12]. These technologies are robust against frequency-scale and time-scale modifications to stego audio to some extent because the bandwidths of the subbands are proportional to the logarithmic frequency scale [6,12]. The tolerances of these methods to frequency-scale modifications range from $\pm 2$ to $\pm 4\%$. In addition to the logarithmic frequency bandwidth, active searching by changing the alignment of the frequency scale to $\pm 6\%$ in the watermark detection stage has been shown to be effective against attack of the excessive ($\pm 10\%$) frequency-scale modification [7].

## 1.2    Aims

To extract payload data from stego audio to which frequency-scale modification has been applied, the frame synchronization algorithm in the detection stage is modified to search for the amount of frequency-scale modification by compensating the frequency scale. The compensation of the frequency scale of the subbands can estimate the amount of frequency-scale modification and achieve extraction of the AM envelope. The system is evaluated according to the criteria proposed by the Information Hiding Criteria (IHC) committee [4] in terms of bit error rate (BER) and objective difference grade (ODG) of stego audio. In addition to the optional attacks that are satisfied by the previous AM-based watermarking system [11], optional attacks of a single echo addition, frequency-scale modification, and Gaussian noise addition are tested.

# 2   Audio Watermarking Based on Amplitude Modulation

The fundamentals of the algorithm for embedding and decoding are available in the literature [10]. Additionally, parameter tuning and improvements to the decision algorithm of AM depth by considering perceptual modulation masking are available in the literature [11]. The following subsections briefly describe the algorithm for embedding, decoding, frame synchronization [10], and controlling watermarking intensity [11]. The subsequent subsection describes the newly added algorithm for frequency-scale compensation in the frame synchronization at the beginning of the detection stage to estimate the amount of frequency modification.

## 2.1   Basic Embedding and Decoding Method

At the beginning of the embedding process, a host signal is filtered by a filter bank of equal bandwidths. For low-frequency bands, SAMs at relatively low modulation frequencies are applied in opposite phase to neighboring subband signals. Higher-frequency bands of the host signal, those above the highpass cutoff frequency, are not watermarked. A higher high-pass cutoff frequency results in greater robustness of the watermarking system; however, note that the high-frequency region can be eliminated or replicated (for example, using the technique of spectral band replication in MPEG4 AAC) without significant perceptual degradation. SAMs are used as the carrier of the embedded information. A key defined by a known pseudo-random number generator classifies $n$ subband pairs into $k$ subband groups. Embedded information is encoded by phase-shift keying (PSK), defined as the phase differences between SAMs applied to the first (pilot) subband group and each of the other groups. A 4-PSK encodes 2-bits of information to every $\pi/2$ phase difference. Multiple watermark embedding is achieved by simultaneously applying different modulation frequencies. Inverting the relative phase of the SAMs between successive data frames for the pilot subband group achieves frame synchronization of the data frames, which is described in Sect. 2.2.

Figure 1 presents a block diagram of the detection process for the $i$th subband group. At the beginning of the extraction process, a stego signal $X(t)$ ($t = 0, 1, 2, ..., T_p - 1$) is split into $2n$ subband signals using the equal-bandwidth filter bank used in the embedding process, where $T_p$ is the length of the frame period. The filtering process is performed by calculating amplitude spectra from a 7/8-overlapped running discrete Fourier transform (DFT) of length $T_f$.

$$E(f, \tau) = \text{abs}\big(\text{DFT}(X(t + \tau T_f/8))\big), (0 \leq t < T_f, f = 0, 1, 2, ..., T_f/2) \quad (1)$$

where abs denotes absolute value and $\tau$ is the index number of the overlapped DFT process for the observation period of the stego signal. $E(f, \tau)$ is a matrix of the amplitude spectra indexed by the discrete frequency $f$ and discrete time $\tau$. The temporal amplitude envelopes of the $m$th subband signal $E_m(\tau)(m = 1, 2, ..., 2n)$ can be derived by

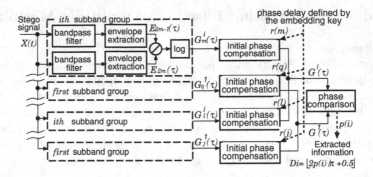

**Fig. 1.** Block diagram of watermark detection for the $i$th subband group.

$$E_m(\tau) = \sum_{f=f_{ml}}^{f_{mh}} E(f,\tau), \tag{2}$$

where $f_{ml}$ is the lowest frequency index and $f_{mh}$ is the highest frequency index of the $m$th subband.

Extraction of the SAM waveform $G_m(\tau)$ from the watermarked signal is performed by calculating the logarithmic ratio of the amplitude envelopes extracted from neighboring subband signals (Eq. (3)).

$$G_m(\tau) = \log \frac{E_{2m}(\tau)}{E_{2m-1}(\tau)}. \tag{3}$$

The synchronized addition of the SAM waveforms extracted from the same subband group with modulation phase $r(m)$ compensation emphasizes the SAM waveform. Consequently, the modulation depth during the embedding process can be kept small. The initial phase difference between the first and $i$th subband groups, that is, the embedded information, is obtained by comparing the phase angles of the DFT spectra calculated from $G^1(\tau)$ and $G^i(\tau)$.

## 2.2  Frame Synchronization

Prior to decoding the phase-shift keying data, the starting point of the embedded data frame must be detected. A rectangular temporal window of the data frame of length $T = \lfloor 8T_p/T_f \rfloor$ is iteratively applied to the modulation waveform $G^1(\tau)$ extracted from the first (pilot) subband group. Equation (4) defines a vector $\mathbf{R}_u$, where the starting point at the window is denoted by $u$. Then, $F(u)$ is derived by subtracting the synchronized sum of the modulation waveforms in the odd-order windows from the synchronized sum of the modulation waveforms in the even-order windows.

$$\mathbf{R}_u = \{G^1(u), G^1(u+1), ..., G^1(u+T-1)\} \tag{4}$$

$$F(u) - \sum_{v=0} \mathbf{R}_{u+2vT} - \sum_{v=0} \mathbf{R}_{u+(2v+1)T} \tag{5}$$

The Fourier amplitude of $F(u)$ corresponding to the modulation frequency $f$, denoted by $\text{AMP}_f(F(u))$, exhibits a maximum when the position of the window completely overlaps with the position of the frame. Consequently, the starting point of data frame $y$ is given by

$$y = \underset{u}{\text{argmax}} \; \text{AMP}_f(F(u)). \tag{6}$$

The present implementation utilizes a stego signal length of $10T$ to calculate $F(u)$.

## 2.3   Decision Process of Watermarking Intensity

The intensity of a watermark, that is, the depth of the SAM $A(m)$ for the $m$th subband pair, is determined relative to the inherent logarithmic ratio of the subband amplitude envelopes of the host signal in every decision period $T_g$. Figure 2 shows schematic diagram of watermarking intensity decision process.

First, watermark extraction processing is conducted for the host signal with no watermarking to obtain the amplitude $M_0(m)$ of the inherent logarithmic ratio of the amplitude envelopes of neighboring subband signals. The watermarking intensity is determined by considering the AM depth that realizes $M_0(m)$ as $0\,\text{dB}$.

Let the amplitude modulation depth at the modulation frequency given to the subband pair be $x_0(m)$ when it realizes a logarithmic modulation amplitude ratio of $M_0(m)$. Let the amplitude of the direct current component of the amplitude envelope extracted from the $(2m-1)$th subband be $a$ times larger than that of the $2m$th subband. If the amplitude of the direct current component of the AM observed from both subbands is assumed to be constant during the modulation period, the valley of the AM envelope of the $(2m-1)$th subband is expressed using $x_0(m)$ as follows:

$$D - M_0(m) = \log \frac{a(1 - x_0(m))}{1 + x_0(m)}, \tag{7}$$

where $D = \log a$. Additionally, the peak of the AM envelope is expressed as

$$D + M_0(m) = \log \frac{a(1 + x_0(m))}{1 - x_0(m)}. \tag{8}$$

Then, $x_0(m)$ is expressed in terms of $M_0(m)$ as follows:

$$x_0(m) = (\exp(M_0(m)) - 1)/(\exp(M_0(m)) + 1). \tag{9}$$

The watermarking intensity for the $m$th subband pair is determined by the AM depth $A(m)$ and is expressed relative to $x_0(m)$ in dB in the form of $20 \log_{10}(A(m)/x_0(m))$.

To reduce the audibility of AM in components of relatively high intensity, the AM depth for subband pairs that exhibit a large level difference is controlled. If the level difference $\Delta L$ between the subband pair exceeds 20 dB, then the AM depth for the subband of the higher level is multiplied by $1 - 0.2\log(10^{\Delta L/20})$ and that of the lower level is multiplied by $1 + 0.2\log(10^{\Delta L/20})$. These multiplications of AM depth maintain the same extracted AM depth while suppressing the audibility of watermarking for higher-level components. The threshold of the level difference of 20 dB was chosen such that the higher-level components sufficiently mask the lower-level components to which a large AM is applied. The threshold of the level difference and the additional AM depth were determined by performing preliminary listening tests on the audibility of watermarking.

$T_g$ was equal to the length of the data frame period. Moreover, the maximum modulation depth was limited to 0.7.

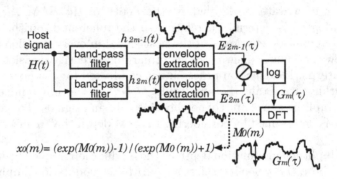

**Fig. 2.** Schematic diagram of watermarking intensity decision process. DFT indicates the discrete Fourier transform.

The empirical parameter values for embedding, which are used in the current study, are shown in Table 1. The watermarking intensity was 8 dB in a previous study [11], whereas it is 6 dB in the current study. Since the host signals recommended by the IHC evaluation criteria version 4 were revised to exclude the segments with an amplitude of zero, the watermarking intensity can be smaller to achieve sufficient robustness and objective sound quality.

The bit rate of a payload in the IHC evaluation criteria is required to be 6 bps, corresponding to 90 bits of payload in each 15 s signal frame, which is divided into three data frames of 5 s each in the embedding stage, while the current embedding bit rate is 7.2 bps. The frame synchronization method described in Sect. 2.2 achieves 5 s data frame synchronization. The IHC evaluation criteria ver. 4 require 180-bit payload extraction from the second and third signal frames. Therefore, 18 bits of synchronization code, which is determined by the secret key, and 90 bits of payload are embedded into each 15 s signal frame. Then, the extracted synchronization codes are compared with the embedded synchronization codes to detect the second and third signal frames. It is established at

**Table 1.** Embedding conditions and parameters. Note that these values are identical for the embedding of all host signals.

| Parameters | Values [11] |
|---|---|
| Sampling freq | 44100 Hz |
| High-pass cutoff freq | 11025 Hz |
| Length of frequency analysis $T_f$ | 1024 |
| Subband pairs $n$ | 64 |
| Subband groups $k$ | 4 |
| Mod. frequencies | 2, 5, 9 Hz |
| Data frame period | 5 s |
| Watermarking intensity | 6 dB |
| Bit rate per channel | 3.6 bps |

the signal frames that exhibit the minimum difference between embedded and extracted synchronization codes.

## 2.4 Modulation Masking Among Frequency Bands

This section describes improvements to the inaudibility of AM and to robustness in the previous study [11]. The basic idea is to reduce the AM depth for subbands that exhibit strong intensity while increasing the AM depth for subbands of lower intensity.

The power level of the $m$th subband pair $P(m)$ is calculated for every period $T_g$. The following process is iterated by changing the target subband pair from that of the highest power to that exhibiting a power of $-50$ dB relative to the highest power.

The AM depth for the $r$th subband pair $A(r)$ and the target subband pair $A(m)$ are modified according to the power level difference $\Delta P = P(m) - P(r)$. If the center frequency of the $r$th subband pair is higher than that of the $m$th subband pair, then their frequency separation is within 1.5 ERB$_\text{N}$-number scale [8] (the ERB$_\text{N}$-number scale corresponds to the ERB rate in [2]), and if $\Delta P$ is larger than 10 dB, then $A(m)$ is modified to $A(m)(1 - \Delta P/400)$ and $A(r)$ is modified to $A(r)(1 + \Delta P/100)$. If the center frequency of the $r$th subband pair is lower than that of the $m$th subband pair, then their frequency separation is within 0.5 ERB$_\text{N}$-number scale, and if $\Delta P$ is larger than 15 dB, then $A(m)$ is modified to $A(m)(1 - \Delta P/500)$ and $A(r)$ is modified to $A(r)(1 + \Delta P/100)$. Note that the above algorithm is identical for the embedding of all host signals.

The above algorithm and parameter values are intuitively determined based on the results of objective sound quality measurements, not on auditory theory or human perception. There is no quantitative study on the effects of frequency separation and level difference on perceptual modulation detection in specific frequency components.

## 2.5    Frequency-Scale Compensation

A frequency-scale modification to the stego signal causes mismatches in the frequencies between subbands of embedding and extraction because the bandwidths of the subbands are constant in all frequency ranges. It causes overlaps between adjacent subbands of opposite AM phase and contradicts the depth of AM. In this section, active searching by compensating the frequency scale from −6.0 to +6.0 % in 1.0 % steps in the frame synchronization stage is proposed.

When the attack of frequency-scale modification is applied to the stego signal, the frequency scale should be compensated before frame synchronization and extraction. Equation (2), which calculates the amplitude envelope of the subband, is rewritten to apply $q$-% frequency-scale compensation as follows:

$$r = \frac{100 + q}{100},$$    (10)

$$E_m(\tau) = \sum_{f=\text{round}(rf_{ml})}^{\text{round}(rf_{mh})} E(f, \tau).$$    (11)

The estimation of the amount of frequency-scale modification using frequency-scale compensation at the frame synchronization stage is confirmed by the simulated attack of frequency-scale modification to the stego signal (SQAM No. 27). The embedding conditions of the simulation are identical to the IHC evaluation criteria.

In the frame synchronization stage, the Fourier amplitude of $F(u)$ corresponding to the modulation frequency $f$, denoted by $\text{AMP}_f(F(u))$, exhibits a maximum when the position of the window completely overlaps with the position of the frame. This maximum AM amplitude is utilized to predict the amount of frequency-scale modification. Figure 3 shows the resulting maximum AM amplitude obtained from a frequency-scale compensation of $q\%$ at the frame synchronization stage as a function of frequency-scale modification from 3.4 to 4.6 % to the stego signal. Figure 3 shows that the maximum AM amplitude is observed when the ratio of frequency-scale compensation corresponds to the ratio of frequency-scale modification. Thus, active searching using frequency-scale compensation is effective for estimating the amount of frequency-scale modification.

Figure 4 shows the effects of the frequency-scale compensation compared with the conventional method [11]. It shows the averaged BERs (%) across 100 simulation runs of the attack of frequency-scale modification from −1.5 % to +1.5 % in 0.025 % steps. The simulation conditions were the same as those described in Sect. 3.2. The results of no compensation, that is, the conventional payload detection [11], and of −1 % and +1 % frequency-scale compensations at the detection process are compared. The tolerance of the BERs obtained from the no compensation condition is acceptable among frequency-scale modification of ±0.5 %. By contrast, the BERs obtained from frequency-scale compensation of ±1% outperform the conventional results obtained from the attack of frequency-scale modification of ±1 and ±0.75%.

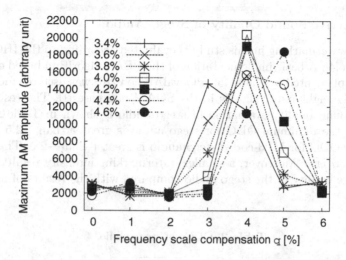

**Fig. 3.** Maximum AM amplitude obtained from frequency-scale compensation at the frame synchronization stage as a function of frequency-scale modification to the stego signal (SQAM No. 27). The simulated range of frequency-scale modification attack is from 3.4 to 4.6 %.

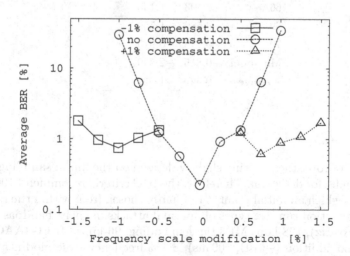

**Fig. 4.** Averaged BERs (%) across 100 simulation runs of the attack of frequency-scale modification from −1.5 % to +1.5 % in 0.025 % steps. The simulation conditions were the same as those described in Sect. 3.2. The results of −1 % and +1 % frequency-scale compensations and of no compensation at the detection process were compared.

# 3 Evaluation

## 3.1 Objective Sound Quality of Stego Audio

The audio watermarking in this study is evaluated according to the IHC evaluation criteria [4]. A basic implementation of the PEAQ algorithm based on ITU-R BS.1387 implemented by Kabal [5] (PQevalAudio v2r0) was used to calculate the ODGs of the eight music signals in the SQAM database [1]. The result of the objective sound quality evaluation of stego audio is shown in Table 2. Table 2 shows that the minimum ODG for stego audio is greater than −2.5 and that the average ODG for MP3-coded stego audio is greater than −2.0. These values satisfy the criteria. Moreover, a smaller watermarking intensity results in a better objective quality of the stego audio compared with the results of a previous study [11].

Table 2. ODGs of stego audio.

| Track | Stego | MP3 coded stego |
|---|---|---|
| 27 | −0.632 | −1.475 |
| 32 | −0.519 | −2.349 |
| 35 | −0.815 | −1.480 |
| 40 | −0.645 | −2.275 |
| 65 | −0.749 | −2.030 |
| 66 | −0.403 | −1.136 |
| 69 | −0.583 | −1.559 |
| 70 | −0.443 | −0.915 |
| Minimum | −0.815 | −2.349 |
| Average | −0.599 | −1.652 |

## 3.2 Robustness

The results of robustness testing slightly depend on the initial sampling point of the stego audio for detection. Therefore, the IHC criteria recommend 100 simulation runs in which an initial point is randomly chosen from within the initial 15 s for each simulation run. Six types of optional attacks, namely, bandpass filtering (100 Hz — 6 kHz), 128-kbps MP3 tandem coding, 96-kbps MPEG4AAC coding, a single echo addition (−6 dB, 100 ms), ±4 % frequency-scale modification, and Gaussian noise addition, are tested.

    If the amount of frequency-scale compensation corresponds to the amount of frequency-scale modification applied to the stego signal, the best BER performance is obtained. However, the amount of frequency shift of the simulated attack should not be known in the detection process. Therefore, the worst cases in which the mismatch (±0.5%) in frequency-scale modification (±4%) and frequency scale compensation is maximum were simulated. Consequently, the BERs obtained from ±3.5% frequency-scale compensation using Eq. 11 showed worse BER results; therefore, it was applied to obtain the amplitude envelopes of the subbands.

The averaged BERs are shown in Table 3. These results show that the maximum BERs averaged over 100 simulation runs for the mandatory attacks of 128-kbps MP3 coding and simulated DA/AD conversion and the five optional attacks, i.e., bandpass filtering, MP3 tandem coding, MPEG4AAC coding, a single echo addition, and ±4 % frequency scale modification, on stego audio are less than 10 %. These values satisfy the criteria. Additionally, although not recommended by the IHC criteria but provided for reference, Table 4 shows the maximum BERs among the 100 simulation runs. All maximum BERs, except for Gaussian noise addition, are also less than 10 %.

**Table 3.** Averaged BERs (%) across 100 simulation runs from mandatory and optional attacks.

| Track | Mandatory | | Optional | | | | | | |
| | MP3 coding | DA/AD | Bandpass filtering | MP3 tandem | MPEG4 AAC | A single echo | Frequency −4 % | shift +4 % | Gaussian noise |
|---|---|---|---|---|---|---|---|---|---|
| 27 | 0.000 | 0.000 | 0.000 | 0.000 | 0.028 | 0.044 | 0.594 | 0.006 | 0.000 |
| 32 | 1.911 | 0.000 | 0.333 | 1.728 | 1.994 | 0.033 | 1.806 | 1.272 | 6.244 |
| 35 | 4.594 | 5.367 | 0.000 | 4.539 | 3.694 | 0.794 | 2.539 | 3.467 | 50.69 |
| 40 | 3.689 | 4.106 | 2.206 | 5.483 | 6.389 | 1.817 | 7.522 | 3.983 | 9.261 |
| 65 | 0.000 | 0.450 | 0.000 | 0.056 | 3.333 | 0.000 | 0.000 | 0.000 | 7.406 |
| 66 | 0.194 | 0.000 | 0.000 | 0.056 | 2.756 | 0.000 | 1.217 | 0.000 | 0.556 |
| 69 | 0.000 | 0.000 | 0.000 | 0.072 | 2.172 | 0.044 | 0.572 | 0.567 | 0.200 |
| 70 | 0.200 | 0.000 | 0.000 | 0.289 | 0.628 | 0.000 | 0.917 | 0.094 | 0.039 |
| Maximum | 4.594 | 5.367 | 2.206 | 5.483 | 6.389 | 1.817 | 7.522 | 3.983 | 50.69 |
| Average | 1.324 | 1.240 | 0.317 | 1.528 | 2.624 | 0.342 | 1.900 | 1.174 | 9.299 |

**Table 4.** Maximum BERs (%) across 100 simulation runs from mandatory and optional attacks.

| Track | Mandatory | | Optional | | | | | | |
| | MP3 coding | DA/AD | Bandpass filtering | MP3 tandem | MPEG4 AAC | A single echo | Frequency −4 % | shift +4 % | Gaussian noise |
|---|---|---|---|---|---|---|---|---|---|
| 27 | 0.000 | 0.000 | 0.000 | 0.000 | 0.556 | 1.111 | 1.111 | 0.556 | 0.000 |
| 32 | 2.222 | 0.000 | 0.556 | 2.222 | 3.333 | 0.556 | 4.444 | 2.222 | 10.56 |
| 35 | 5.000 | 6.111 | 0.000 | 5.556 | 4.444 | 3.889 | 3.889 | 6.111 | 55.00 |
| 40 | 3.889 | 5.556 | 3.333 | 7.778 | 7.222 | 5.556 | 8.333 | 5.556 | 12.78 |
| 65 | 0.000 | 1.111 | 0.000 | 0.556 | 3.889 | 0.000 | 0.000 | 0.000 | 8.889 |
| 66 | 0.556 | 0.000 | 0.000 | 0.556 | 3.333 | 0.000 | 2.222 | 0.000 | 0.556 |
| 69 | 0.000 | 0.000 | 0.000 | 1.111 | 3.333 | 1.111 | 1.667 | 1.111 | 0.556 |
| 70 | 0.556 | 0.000 | 0.000 | 1.111 | 1.111 | 0.000 | 1.111 | 0.556 | 0.556 |

# 4  Discussion

The robustness of the AM-based watermarking system to pitch-invariant time-scale modification and speed change, i.e., time- and frequency-scale modifications, has been not confirmed. However, the present scale compensation technique can also be applied to both the frequency scale and time scale. Therefore, payload extraction with a small BER may be achieved from the stego audio modified in time and frequency.

If the frame synchronization process attempts a total of 13 searches, i.e., from $-6$ to $+6$ in 1% steps, the computational cost will be 13 times higher than that of no active search condition. An efficient search algorithm should be developed to reduce the computational loads.

The current AM-based watermarking system can satisfy, or will satisfy, all criteria proposed by the IHC, except for the attack of Gaussian noise addition. The power level of the additive Gaussian noise is determined relative to the power of the entire host signal, i.e., signal-to-noise ratio (SNR) of 36 dB. Therefore, small power segments of the stego signal exhibit a low SNR. Payload extraction from such low SNR segments of the stego audio is very challenging. Adaptive decision of watermarking intensity taking the signal power level into account should be reconsidered.

# 5  Summary

An audio watermarking system based on amplitude modulation was evaluated according to the IHC evaluation criteria. In contrast to the previous methods [10,11], the detection of frame synchronization to the stego signals of the frequency-scale modification attack is conducted by compensating the frequency scale from $-6$ to $+6\,\%$ in 1 % steps in the time-frequency domain. The maximum amplitude of AM collected from the subband group for synchronization is observed at the frequency-scale compensation that corresponds to the amount of frequency-scale modification. The results of a computer simulation showed that the quality degradation caused by the watermarking was tolerable. Moreover, the detectability of the watermark under mandatory attack tests (simulated DA/AD conversion and MP3 coding) and optional attack tests (bandpass filtering, tandem MP3 coding, MPEG4AAC coding, a single echo addition, and $\pm 4\,\%$ frequency-scale modification) was sufficiently maintained.

# References

1. EBU Committee: Sound quality assessment material recordings for subjective tests. http://tech.ebu.ch/webdav/site/tech/shared/tech/tech3253.pdf
2. Glasberg, B.R., Moore, B.C.J.: Derivation of auditory filter shapes from notched-noise data. Hear. Res. **47**, 103–138 (1990)
3. IHC Committee: IHC evaluation criteria Version 3 (2014). http://www.ieice.org/iss/emm/ihc/IHC_criteriaVer3.pdf

4. IHC Committee: IHC evaluation criteria Version 4 (2015). http://www.ieice.org/iss/emm/ihc/IHC_criteriaVer4.pdf
5. Kabal, P.: An examination and interpretation of ITU-R BS.1387: Perceptual evaluation of audio quality. TSP Lab Technical report, Department Electrical & Computer Engineering, McGill University, pp. 1–89 (2002)
6. Lin, Y., Abdulla, W.: A secure and robust audio watermarking scheme using multiple scrambling and adaptive synchronization. In: Proceedings of Information, Communications and Signal Processing, pp. 1–5. IEEE (2007)
7. Lin, Y., Abdulla, W., Ma, Y.: Audio watermarking detection resistant to time and pitch scale modification. In: Proceedings of Signal Processing and Communications, ICSpPC 2007, pp. 1379–1382. IEEE(2007)
8. Moore, B.C.J.: An Introduction to the Psychology of Hearing, 6th edn. Brill, Boston (2013)
9. Nishimura, A.: Subjective and objective quality evaluation for audio watermarking based on sinusoidal amplitude modulation. In: Proceedings of the 19th International Congress on Acoustics, pp. 1–9. No. ELE-04-009 (2007)
10. Nishimura, A.: Audio watermarking based on subband amplitude modulation. Acoust. Sci. Technol. **31**(5), 328–336 (2010)
11. Nishimura, A.: Audio watermarking based on amplitude modulation and modulation masking. In: Proceeding of the 1st International Workshop on Information Hiding and Its Criteria for Evaluation, pp. 49–55. ACM (2014)
12. Tachibana, R.: Improving audio watermark robustness using stretched patterns against geometric distortion. In: Chen, Y.-C., Chang, L.-W., Hsu, C.-T. (eds.) PCM 2002. LNCS, vol. 2532, pp. 647–654. Springer, Heidelberg (2002)

# Audio Watermarking Using Different Wavelet Filters

Toshiki Ito[1], Hyunho Kang[1(✉)], Keiichi Iwamura[1], Kitahiro Kaneda[2], and Isao Echizen[3]

[1] Department of Electrical Engineering, Tokyo University of Science, 6-3-1 Niijuku, Katsushika-ku, Tokyo 125-8585, Japan
itou@sec.ee.kagu.tus.ac.jp, {kang,iwamura}@ee.kagu.tus.ac.jp
[2] Osaka Prefecture University, Osaka, Japan
[3] National Institute of Informatics, Tokyo 101-8430, Japan
iechizen@nii.ac.jp

**Abstract.** Various digital watermarking methods have recently been developed. Among them, the frequency component is often used in watermark embedding. The discrete wavelet transform is a general frequency conversion technique that has been adopted in some watermarking methods. We found that different wavelet filters provide different watermarking performances based on the wavelet transform. In recent years, the Information Hiding and its Criteria for evaluation (IHC) Committee of Japan has developed evaluation criteria for information hiding. In this study, we developed a new audio watermarking method that satisfies the IHC evaluation criteria.

**Keywords:** Audio watermarking · IHC evaluation criteria · Discrete wavelet transform

## 1 Introduction

With the expansion of the information technology (IT) society, digital content such as pictures, music, and movies are utilized widely. This has allowed for the convenient storage and distribution of content. On the other hand, copyright protection technology has become necessary owing to the increase in piracy. Watermarking technology is one solution to this problem. In some existing watermarking schemes, a watermark is embedded in the frequency domain [1–3]; typical frequency conversions include the discrete cosine transform, discrete Fourier transform, and discrete wavelet transform (DWT). The discrete wavelet transform converts a signal to high-frequency and low-frequency components without losing timing information and is used by some watermarking schemes [4]. The discrete wavelet transform uses two band-pass filters, and the calculated results change depending on the filters. In other words, the performance of a watermarking scheme based on the discrete wavelet transform depends on the kind of filter. Therefore, we propose new audio watermarking method focusing this difference and choosing a suitable filter for improving the performance.

© Springer International Publishing Switzerland 2016
Y.-Q. Shi et al. (Eds.): IWDW 2015, LNCS 9569, pp. 312–320, 2016.
DOI: 10.1007/978-3-319-31960-5_26

The Information Hiding and its Criteria for evaluation (IHC) Committee is an organization that develops evaluation standards for watermarking techniques and holds watermark competitions. Particularly for audio watermarking, the complexity and sensitivity of the human auditory system mean that the criteria for audio watermarking are strict. In the FIT2013 contest, only one method [5] satisfied the second version standard. Recently, a method has been reported that satisfies the watermark criteria for audio [6]. In this study, our goal was to develop a watermarking method that satisfies the latest criteria.

This paper is organized as follows. In Sect. 2, we briefly summarize the IHC criteria. In Sect. 3, we explain our proposed method and the technologies used. In Sect. 4, we present the experimental results of the proposed method, which were evaluated based on the latest IHC standard. Section 5 concludes the paper.

## 2    Summaries of the IHC Criteria

The evaluation criteria were set to the sound sources used, the number of bits embedded, the signal processing attacks, and minimum required sound quality. The specified sound sources were eight SQAM tracks. Their format was set to a 44,100 kHz sampling frequency, two channels, and 60-s length. The watermarking capacity was set to 90 bits per 15 s. The IHC committee adopted the objective difference grade (ODG) for evaluation of the sound quality. As criteria, the lowest value of the ODG was set to $-2.5$, and the arithmetic mean of eight ODGs between the original signal and stego signal (i.e., the payload is embedded, and the MP3 is then compressed and decompressed as the degraded signal) should be more than $-2.0$. The watermark must be extracted after some signal processing attacks for evaluation of the tolerance. As mandatory attacks, MP3 coding, a series of attacks that mimic DA and AD conversions, and three of the seven optional attacks should be applied to the stego signal. Moreover, a 60 s stego signal should be randomly cropped into 45 s, and a 180-bit watermark must be extracted correctly more than 90 % of the time.

## 3    Proposed Watermarking Scheme

In our method, the watermark is embedded in the frequency domain, which is obtained with the discrete wavelet transform. When the audio signal is converted to the frequency component, we use two different wavelet filters to obtain two different wavelet components. The watermark bit is expressed by comparing the sizes of these components. Because of the aspects of the human auditory system, the watermark is embedded in the high-frequency components.

### 3.1    Discrete Wavelet Transform

The wavelet transform is one type of frequency conversion. Compared with the Fourier transform and cosine transform, the wavelet transform is characterized

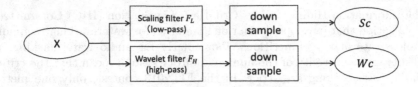

**Fig. 1.** DWT using wavelet and scaling filters.

by no loss of the timing information. The wavelet coefficients, $Wc = \{w(T), 1 \leq T \leq (M-1)/2 + L\}$, represent the high-frequency component, and the scaling coefficients, $Sc = \{s(T), 1 \leq T \leq (M-1)/2 + L\}$, represent the low-frequency component, where M is the length of the time domain signal and $L$ is the length of the low-pass filter, $F_L = \{f_L(k), 1 \leq k \leq L\}$, and the high-pass filter, $F_H = \{f_H(k), 1 \leq k \leq L\}$. They are obtained by performing a wavelet transform on the time domain signal, $X = \{x(t), 1 \leq t \leq M\}$, as shown in Fig. 1. In this research, we used the discrete wavelet transform function in the Wavelet Toolbox from Matlab [7]. This function can select the types and lengths of wavelet filters.

### 3.2    Wavelet and Scaling Filters

The filters used in the wavelet transform have some conditions. First, the wavelet and scaling filters have orthonormality between the original filter and integer multiple shifted filter. The relationship between the wavelet filter and scaling filter is represented as follows:

$$f_H(k) = (-1)^{k-1} f_L(L - k + 1), k = 1, 2, ..., L \tag{1}$$

### 3.3    Adjusting the Wavelet Coefficients

To embed a watermark, the relationship between the magnitudes of two wavelet coefficients, $Wc_1$ and $Wc_2$, from the two wavelet filters, $F_{H1}$ and $F_{H2}$, must be controlled. If you simply change one component and obtain the time domain signal by performing an inverse wavelet transform, another wavelet component also changes at the same time. This causes the relationship between the magnitudes of $Wc_1$ and $Wc_2$ to become unclear. In this study, we adjusted the wavelet coefficients by using wavelet filters. The difference between the two wavelet coefficients, $Wc_d = Wc_1 - Wc_2$, is adjusted by adding the difference between the two filters, $F_d = F_{H1} - F_{H2}$, to the time domain. With this operation, $Wc_1$ at the corresponding location is increased and $Wc_2$ is decreased. As shown in Fig. 2, the corresponding location is $(a+L)/2$ when $F_d$ of length $L$ is added in the time domain signal $x(a)$ to $x(a + L), 1 \leq a \leq M - L$. The value of $\alpha$, defined as the amount of change in $Wc_d$, varies depending on the kind of filter. In addition, when adding $F_d$ by $n$ times, the amount of change is proportional to the value of $n$.

(A) Time domain signal

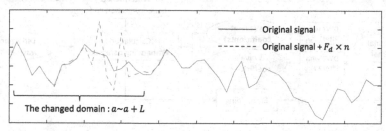

(B) Difference of wavelet coefficient

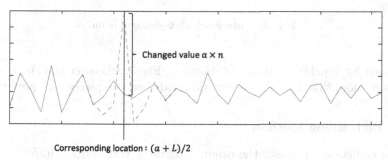

**Fig. 2.** The magnitude relationship of two wavelet coefficients.

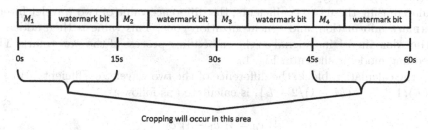

**Fig. 3.** Cropping part in the stego signal.

## 3.4 Measure Against Synchronous Difference

In the latest evaluation standard, de-synchronous attacks such as DA/AD conversion and random cropping must be considered. These two kinds of attacks need different countermeasures. The linear speed change conversion included in the mimic DA/AD conversion expands the sound data length. As a countermeasure, when the watermark is extracted from expanded sound data, several samples are eliminated at equal intervals, and the sound data are returned to the original length. In addition, synchronization code is inserted every 15 s to handle de-synchronous events due to random cropping. The synchronization code is generated by a sufficiently long M-sequence signal, $M_b = \{M_1, M_2, M_3, M_4\}$, and inserted every 15 s in the time domain. In the extraction process, $M_b$ is shared

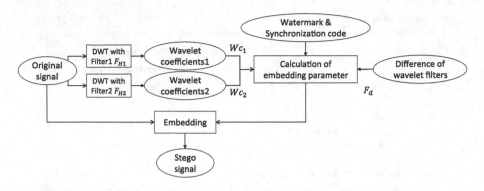

**Fig. 4.** Watermark embedding scheme.

and used for synchronization. As shown in Fig. 3, wherever the stego signal is cropped, more than two synchronization codes can be picked out perfectly.

### 3.5  Embedding Method

In the embedding process, the original signal is transformed into two wavelet coefficients, $Wc_1 = \{w_1(T), 1 \leq T \leq (M-1)/2 + L\}$ and $Wc_2 = \{w_2(T), 1 \leq T \leq (M-1)/2 + L\}$ by DWT with two wavelet filters. The embedding value is calculated using these two coefficients, the difference value of two wavelet filters, watermark information, and synchronization code. This value is then added in the time domain original signal as the embedding process of the watermark. The embedding model is shown in Fig. 4.

In the calculation block, the difference of the two wavelet coefficients, $Wc_d = \{w_d(T), 1 \leq T \leq (M-1)/2 + L\}$, is calculated as follows:

$$Wc_d = Wc_1 - Wc_2 \tag{2}$$

Several samples from the difference of wavelet coefficients, $Wc_d$, are used for embedding. The embedding area, $Wc_{emb}(s) = \{w_{emb}(s), 1 \leq s \leq ((M-1)/2 + L)/(L/2)\}$, is defined as samples picked up every $L/2$ length from $Wc_d$ as per the following equation and Fig. 5, where $L$ is the length of the filters and $s$ is the index.

$$w_{emb}(s) = w_d(sL/2) \tag{3}$$

Watermark and synchronization code are expressed using $Wc_{emb}$. As shown in Fig. 6, the watermark bits are embedded in $N$ samples repeatedly. In the extract process, the detected data with more than $N/2$ times in one region is judged a watermark bit. $N$ is adjusted by the length of the embedded audio data and the amount of the embedded watermark information (N=200 in this study).

As mentioned in Sect. 3.3, $Wc_{emb}$ is adjusted by adding the difference of the wavelet filters, $F_d = F_{H1} - F_{H2}$, to the original signal, $X = \{x(t), 1 \leq t \leq M\}$.

Difference of wavelet coefficient

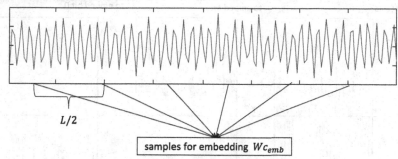

Fig. 5. Selected wavelet coefficients from embedding.

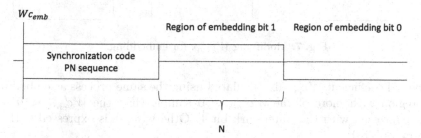

Fig. 6. The arrangement of the embedded data.

Corresponding to the watermark and synchronization code, $w_{emb}(s)$ is adjusted as per the following equation and obtain stego signal, $X' = \{x'(t), 1 \leq t \leq M\}$.

– To embed bit 1

   if $w_{emb}(s) \leq \gamma$ :

$$x'((s-1)L+j) = x((s-1)L+j) + f_d(j)(\gamma - w_{emb}(s))/\alpha \quad (0 \leq j < L) \quad (4)$$

– To embed bit 0

if $w_{emb}(s) \geq -\gamma$ :

$$x'((s-1)L+j) = x((s-1)L+j) + f_d(j)(w_{emb}(s) - \gamma)/\alpha \quad (0 \leq j < L), \quad (5)$$

where $\gamma$ is the embedding strength and $\alpha$ is the filter intervention mentioned in Sect. 3.3. By this process, $Wc_{emb}$ is adjusted as shown in Fig. 7.

### 3.6 Extraction Method

The wavelet transform is applied to the stego signal $X'$ with the same filters used in embedding to obtain the wavelet coefficients $Wc'_1$ and $Wc'_2$. Then, the

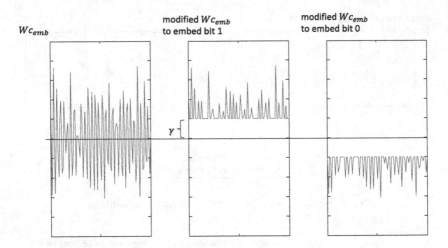

**Fig. 7.** Modifying $Wc_{emb}$ for embedding.

embedded coefficient $Wc'_{emb}$ is calculated using the same process as embedding. The region with more of the $Wc'_{emb} \geq 0$ sample than the $Wc'_{emb} < 0$ sample is expressed with the watermark bit 1. Otherwise, it is expressed with the watermark bit 0.

### 3.7   Decision of Parameter

This method uses the parameter $\gamma$ as the watermark embedding strength. If a strong $\gamma$ is set, the difference $Wc'_{emb}$ between different bits and the attack resistance are increased. On the other hand, the sound quality is lowered because of the increased change in the sound data. Because of the characteristics of the human auditory system, even a slight change can be sensitively perceived in a small-energy region. In contrast, slight changes are hardly perceived in large-energy regions. Thus, we can set $\gamma$ to correspond to the amount of energy and aim for both a high attack resistance and high sound quality.

## 4   Experimental Result

In this research, we carried out an evaluation experiment by using the Wavelet Toolbox of MATLAB. The wavelet functions of MATLAB can select the length and type of wavelet filter. We chose the Symlets and coiflets filters for the wavelet filters to embed with a length of 24. The embedding parameter was strictly adjusted to satisfy both the sound quality and robustness criteria. The used audio signals were the eight SQAM tracks specified by the IHC criteria.

### 4.1   Sound Quality Evaluation

According to the IHC criteria, the ODG between the original signal to stego signal and original signal to MP3 coded stego signal should be measured. Table 1

lists the results of the sound quality evaluation. The minimum ODG for the stego
signal was −1.640 of track 35, and the average ODG for the MP3 stego signal
was −1.997. These results satisfied the sound quality criterion.

**Table 1.** Sound quality evaluation

| Track.No | Stego singal | MP3 stego signal |
|----------|-------------|------------------|
| 27 | −0.715 | −1.213 |
| 32 | −1.055 | −2.629 |
| 35 | −1.640 | −2.739 |
| 40 | −0.775 | −2.457 |
| 65 | −1.166 | −2.609 |
| 66 | −0.769 | −1.465 |
| 69 | −0.705 | −1.461 |
| 70 | −0.972 | −1.406 |
| Minimum | −1.640 | −2.739 |
| Average | −0.975 | −1.997 |

**Table 2.** Bit error rate[%]

| | Mandatory | | Optional | | |
|----------|------------|-------|----------------|-------------------|---------------|
| Track.No | MP3 cording | AD/DA | Gaussian noise | MP3 128 kbps tandem | A single echo |
| 27 | 0.560 | 0.000 | 0.000 | 0.556 | 0.000 |
| 32 | 5.000 | 3.889 | 3.900 | 4.444 | 4.444 |
| 35 | 0.000 | 0.556 | 0.000 | 0.000 | 0.000 |
| 40 | 3.890 | 3.889 | 3.439 | 3.889 | 2.778 |
| 65 | 0.560 | 0.000 | 0.217 | 0.556 | 0.000 |
| 66 | 0.000 | 0.556 | 0.000 | 0.000 | 0.000 |
| 69 | 0.000 | 0.000 | 0.000 | 0.000 | 0.000 |
| 70 | 0.000 | 0.000 | 0.094 | 0.556 | 0.000 |

## 4.2 Robustness Evaluation

As optional attacks, we chose Gaussian noise addition, a single echo addition,
and MP3 tandem coding. Table 2 lists the bit correct rate for each attack to
represent the evaluated robustness. In consideration of the randomness of the
cropping region, we carried out the experiment 100 times under each condition;
the average values are given in the table. We achieved a bit error rate less than
10 % under all conditions and satisfied the robustness criterion.

## 5    Conclusion

In this paper, we propose an audio watermarking method that evaluates the difference between two wavelet filters based on IHC criteria. We set the embedding parameters strictly and achieved sufficient sound quality to satisfy the criteria. For the robustness, we carried out an extraction experiment after MP3 coding, DA/AD conversion, Gaussian noise addition, MP3 tandem cording, and echo addition with random cropping. An adequate number of experiments were carried out, and we achieved a high bit correct rate under all conditions. For future work, we will focus on finding a suitable combination of wavelet filters, consider the use of original wavelet filters, and further improve the performance.

## References

1. Cox, I.J., Kilian, J., Leighton, F.T., Shamoon, T.: Secure spread spectrum: watermarking for multimedia. IEEE Trans. Image Process. **6**(12), 1673–1687 (1997)
2. Chen, Q., Xiang, S., Luo, X.: Reversible watermarking for audio authentication based on integer DCT and expansion embedding. In: Shi, Y.Q., Kim, H.-J., Pérez-González, F. (eds.) IWDW 2012. LNCS, vol. 7809, pp. 395–409. Springer, Heidelberg (2013)
3. Huang, X., Ono, N., Echizen, I., Nishimura, A.: Reversible audio information hiding based on integer DCT coefficients with adaptive hiding locations. In: Shi, Y.Q., Kim, H.-J., Pérez-González, F. (eds.) IWDW 2013. LNCS, vol. 8389, pp. 376–390. Springer, Heidelberg (2014)
4. Lei, B., Soon, I.Y., Li, Z.: A robust audio watermarking scheme based on lifting wavelet transform and singular value decomposition. In: Shi, Y.Q., Kim, H.-J., Perez-Gonzalez, F. (eds.) IWDW 2011. LNCS, vol. 7128, pp. 86–96. Springer, Heidelberg (2012)
5. Ono, E.: Robust audio information hiding based on stereo phase difference in time-frequency domain. In: IIHMSP, pp. 260–263 (2014)
6. Nishimura, A.: Audio watermarking based on amplitude modulation and modulation masking. In: IWIHC 2014 Proceedings of the 1st International Workshop on Information Hiding and its Criteria for Evaluation, pp. 45–55 (2014)
7. MathWorks Wavelet Toolbox. https://mathworks.com/help/wavelet/index.html

# Reversible Data Hiding

# A Commutative Encryption and Reversible Watermarking for Fingerprint Image

Vaibhav B. Joshi$^{(\boxtimes)}$, Dhruv Gupta, and Mehul S. Raval

Institute of Engineering and Technology, Ahmedabad University, Ahmedabad, India
vaibhav.joshi@ahduni.edu.in

**Abstract.** In this work, authors propose a novel scheme with commutative encryption and reversible watermarking for a fingerprint image. Due to commutative property one can embed and extract watermark in either plain or encrypted fingerprint image, irrespective of order in which encryption or watermarking is applied. The encryption and the watermarking keys are shared using secret key sharing mechanism. The biometric database consists of encrypted and watermarked fingerprint images. After successful authentication, watermarking is inverted to get back the plain fingerprint. The proposed scheme protects many of the vulnerable points of a biometric authentication system. Also native biometric authentication accuracy remains unaffected due to reversible watermarking. As per best of our knowledge, this is the first scheme to include homomorphism between encryption and reversible watermarking. Advantages of the proposed method compared to existing techniques are; (1) higher embedding capacity; (2) better peak signal to noise ratio for the decrypted marked image; (3) use of an optimal key length to preserve security while lowering computational cost; (4) simpler cryptographic key management; (5) smaller side information.

**Keywords:** Commutative · Encryption · Fingerprint · Reversible watermarking

## 1 Introduction

In $21^{st}$ century, due to rapid growth in technology and digitization, human identification and authentication poses the key challenge. Classical authentication mechanisms (ID cards, passwords) are no longer full proof in this era. Hence, biometric features are broadly used for the human identification and authentication. Many developing countries like India [4] use biometric features for the human identification. Therefore, security of the biometric authentication systems is a major concern [8]. Among biometric traits like iris, palm print, retina, signature; fingerprint has been the longest serving, most successful and popular trait for human identification [13]. Therefore, the fingerprint is chosen as a modality in the present work. The authors [8] discussed several vulnerable points in a generic biometric authentication system. These vulnerabilities are shown in Fig. 1. Most biometric recognition systems are deceived by manipulating;

© Springer International Publishing Switzerland 2016
Y.-Q. Shi et al. (Eds.): IWDW 2015, LNCS 9569, pp. 323–336, 2016.
DOI: 10.1007/978-3-319-31960-5_27

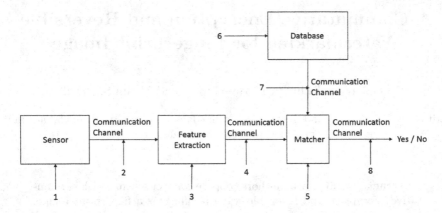

**Fig. 1.** Vulnerable points in a biometric authentication system [8].

(1) system database; (vulnerable point 6) (2) communication channel (vulnerable point 2 and 7).

Watermarking is one of the solution to secure these vulnerable points. Many researchers combined watermarking and biometrics for enhancing the security. In [10] authors proposed chaotic watermarking and steganography [14] to protect biometric data. In the communication channel, encryption and watermarking keys provide security and robustness to the biometrics. Authors in [16] used fragile watermarking to check integrity of the database. The authors used singular value decomposition (SVD) and least significant bit (LSB) plane for watermark embedding. In [11] block based fragile watermarking is used for detecting and localizing tampered parts of a fingerprint. These fragile techniques protect vulnerable point 6 (cf. Fig. 1). Authors in [5,7] proposed biometric sample dependent watermark generation and embedding to protect vulnerable point 2. They calculated features from the sample and used them as watermark. At the feature extractor, watermark and the sample features are matched to check the sample integrity.

All the watermarking methods discussed above embed and extract watermark disjointly in the plain or in the encrypted domain. They secure any one vulnerable point of a biometric authentication system. On the other hand reversible data hiding in encrypted images [6,12,17–19] embeds watermark in encrypted image and extract it from both; encrypted as well as decrypted image. Methods of data hiding in an encrypted image are broadly classified as separable [17,19] and non-separable [6,12,18]. In non-separable class, data can be extracted only after the image is decrypted. Thus, authentication always follows the image decryption step. In separable class, data is extracted either from the encrypted or the decrypted image for authentication. Hence, separable reversible data hiding in encrypted images secures two vulnerable points (i.e. point 6 and 7 cf. Fig. 1).

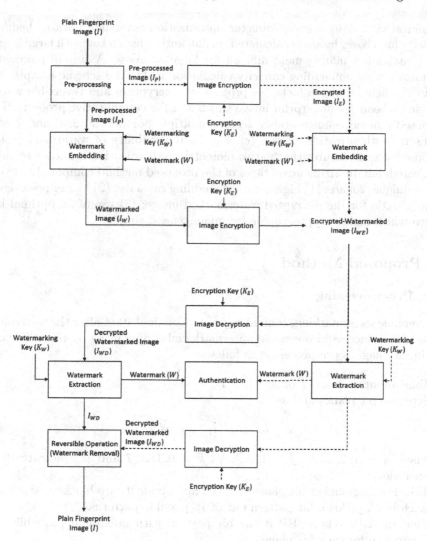

**Fig. 2.** Basic block diagram incorporating commutative property between encryption and reversible watermarking. (Arrow type indicate possible combinations for watermark embedding and extraction)

From above discussion it is clear that any of the existing data hiding techniques cannot secure vulnerable point 2, 6 and 7 simultaneously. This is possible if watermark is embedded or extracted from either the plain or the encrypted domain. In other words security of the multiple vulnerable points is achieved by incorporating commutative property [15] between encryption and reversible watermarking functions as shown in Fig. 2.

For natural images a commutative reversible data hiding and encryption is proposed in [20]. Author in [20] uses properties of exclusive-OR to incorporate commutativity. Also using parameter optimization reversible data embedding capacity for a cover image is calculated. In [20] author uses a key with large length which makes key management difficult for large database. A step of parameter optimization for embedding capacity calculation makes the scheme complex.

In the light of above facts, we propose an encryption and reversible watermarking scheme for fingerprint image which satisfies commutative property. The proposed scheme simultaneously secures multiple points Viz. 2, 6 and 7 of a biometric authentication system (cf. Fig. 1). Reversibility of watermark in the proposed scheme ensures that native biometric authentication accuracy remains unaffected. Summarizing advantages of the proposed method compared to existing technique [20] are: (1) higher data embedding capacity; (2) higher peak signal to noise ratio for the decrypted watermarked image; (3) use of an optimal key length which makes cryptographic key management simple.

## 2    Proposed Method

### 2.1    Pre-processing

In reversible watermarking, content regains its original state after the watermark removal. For successful reversible watermark embedding using proposed scheme, the input image is pre-processed as follows:

1. Take an input image $I$ of size $X \times Y$.
2. Separate bit planes of $I$ as:

$$b_{i,j,k} = \lfloor I_{i,j,k} \rfloor mod\ 2 \qquad (1)$$

   where, $i = 1, 2, ..., X$, $j = 1, 2, ..., Y$, $k = 0, 1, ..., 7$ and $\lfloor\ \rfloor$ indicates floor operation.
3. Take least significant bit plane ($LSBP$) and divide it into blocks of size $2 \times 2$. Each block yields a bit pattern out of 16 possible patterns.
4. Find the BP. Where, BP is the bit pattern with maximum probability of occurrence for each bit plane.
5. Perform lossless compression of the LSBP using the following rules: For each block, if the bit pattern equals BP then corresponding location map bit equals 1 otherwise it is 0. Each bit in location map points to the blocks with or without bit pattern BP. Hence size of location map with given $2 \times 2$ block is 25 % of LSBP.
6. Generate bit difference by Ex-ORing BP with pattern not equal to BP. The size of bit difference is proportional to the probability of 1s in location map. Here, the location map and watermark along with auxiliary data occupies 25 % and 5 % of LSBP respectively. Remaining 70 % is occupied by bit difference. Therefore, location map with probability of 1s less than 0.7 is placed in the LSBP to generate compressed LSBP as shown in Fig. 3. For other case location map is to be shared between watermark embedder and extractor.
7. Actual payload is zero padded (if required) to match size of the LSBP.

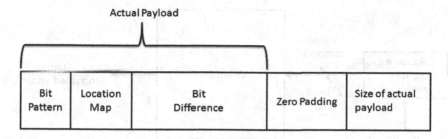

**Fig. 3.** Format of compressed LSB plane.

8. Recombine all bit planes as in Eq. 2 to generate the pre-processed image $I_P$.

$$I_{P(i,j)} = \sum_{k=0}^{7} (b_{i,j,k} \cdot 2^k) \qquad (2)$$

Note that under the consideration of sharing the location map, if all 16 bit pattern are equally probable then also one can get at least 6 % space of LSBP for watermark embedding.

## 2.2   Image Encryption

Due to commutative property in the proposed method, one can apply encryption on the pre-processed image $I_P$ or on the watermarked image $I_W$, as shown in Fig. 2.
 The image encryption process is shown in Fig. 4 and steps are as follows.

1. Take input image $I_P$ or $I_W$.
2. Using bit plane slicing, generate 8 bit planes $(P_i)$ from the input image.
3. Divide each bit plane into vector $(V)$ of dimension $N \times 1$, such that $N$ is a integer factor of $(X \times Y)$. Therefore, $\lfloor (X \times Y)/N \rfloor$ vectors are generated from each bit plane.
 where, $\lfloor \ \rfloor$ is the floor operation.
4. Using an encryption key $(K_E)$, generate $2^N$ integers randomly from the interval $[0, 2^N)$ in a non-repetitive manner. Divide them into sets of the even and the odd numbers.
5. Take a $2^N \times 1$ multiplexer and apply odd numbers to input lines with odd indices. Similarly, even numbers are applied to input lines with even indices.
6. Apply vector $V$ to selection lines of the multiplexer.
7. Convert output of the multiplexer into binary to generate encrypted vector $(V_c)$.
8. Repeat steps 6 and 7 for all the $(X \times Y)/N$ vectors in all the bit planes.
9. Combine all $V_c$ vectors to get the encrypted bit planes $(P_{ic})$.
10. Recombine all the eight encrypted bit planes to get the encrypted image $I_E$ or the encrypted watermarked image $I_{WE}$.

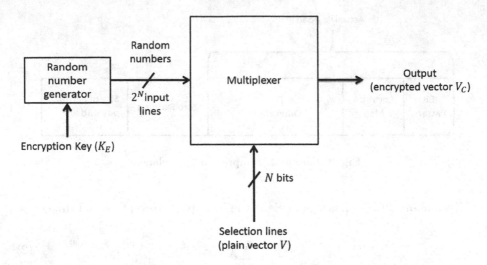

**Fig. 4.** Basic block diagram of encryption process.

## 2.3   Image Decryption

The steps for the image decryption process are as follows:

1. Use bit plane slicing to generate 8 bit planes from $I_{WE}$.
2. Divide each bit plane into vectors ($V_{WE}$).
3. Next, generate $2^N$ random integers using $K_E$ and divide them into sets of even and odd numbers.
4. Apply the odd numbers to the multiplexer's input lines with the odd indices and the even numbers to input lines with the even indices.
5. Convert $V_{WE}$ into decimal and match it with the random numbers applied to input lines of the multiplexer.
6. Index of the input line for which number matches $V_{WE}$ is converted into binary to get the decrypted vectors ($V_{WD}$).
7. Combine all $V_{WD}$ to get the decrypted bit planes.
8. Recombine all the eight decrypted bit planes to get the decrypted watermarked image $I_{WD}$.

## 2.4   Watermark Embedding

The steps for watermark embedding process are as follows:

1. Take an encrypted image $I_E$ or pre-processed image $I_P$.
2. Use bit plane slicing to generate 8 bit planes.
3. Divide LSBP into $(X \times Y)/N$ vectors, to get $V_P$ or $V_E$, each with dimension $N \times 1$.

4. Using watermarking key $(K_W)$ select the $V_P$ or $V_E$ between starting and ending point of zero padding block of Fig. 3. Note that watermarking key contains the starting and ending point of zero padding block of Fig. 3. The starting and ending point for watermarking key is:

$$SP = (\lceil SP_A/N \rceil) \times N$$
$$EP = (\lfloor EP_A/N \rfloor) \times N \tag{3}$$

where, $SP$ and $EP$ indicates the starting and ending point of a watermarking key respectively, $SP_A$ and $EP_A$ indicates the actual starting and ending point of a zero padded block.

5. Replace LSB of the $V_P$ or $V_E$ by watermark bit to get the watermarked vector $(V_W)$.
6. Combine all the $V_W$ vectors to get watermarked LSBP.
7. Recombine watermarked LSBP with all other bit planes to generate encrypted watermarked image $I_{WE}$ or watermarked image $I_W$.

## 2.5   Watermark Extraction

The proposed method can extract watermark from encrypted watermarked image $(I_{WE})$ as well as decrypted watermarked image $(I_{WD})$. The watermarking key $(K_W)$ and embedded watermark is shared with watermark extractor for authentication.

The watermark extraction process is as follows:

1. Take an image $I_{WE}$ or $I_{WD}$.
2. Using bit plane slicing generate 8 bit planes.
3. Divide the LSBP into vectors of dimension $N \times 1$.
4. Using $K_W$ select vector $V_{WE}$ or $V_{WD}$ from the LSBP.
5. Extract LSB of the vector to get the watermark bit.
6. Compare embedded and extracted watermark bit and if they do not match than corresponding vector is declared unauthentic.
7. Repeat steps 5 and 6 for all vectors selected by $K_W$.
8. Even if a *single* vector is found to be tampered then the image is declared unauthentic.

## 2.6   Reversible Operation

1. Get the decrypted watermarked image $I_{WD}$.
2. Perform bit plane slicing on $I_{WD}$ as in Eq. 1.
3. From the LSBP, extract the bit pattern, actual payload size and bit difference.
4. Get location map either from LSBP or from shared memory.
5. Using bit pattern, location map and bit difference, regenerate original LSBP.
6. Combine all MSBs and the original LSBP as per Eq. 2 to generate the original fingerprint image $I$.

## 2.7  Commutativity

Functions of watermark embedding and image encryption can be defined as maps, $\Omega$ and $E$ respectively.

$$\Omega : \mathbb{R}^{X \times Y} \times \{0,1\}^{2 \log_2(XY)} \times \{0,1\}^{f(I)} \to \mathbb{R}^{X \times Y}$$
$$E : \mathbb{R}^{X \times Y} \times \{0,1\}^{2^{N-1}} \to \mathbb{R}^{X \times Y}$$

where $X \times Y$ is the size of image and $f(I)$ is function on image $I$ defining size of watermark. $\Omega$ and $E$ is said to be commutative if $\Omega \circ E = E \circ \Omega$. This is visualized with the help of Fig. 5.

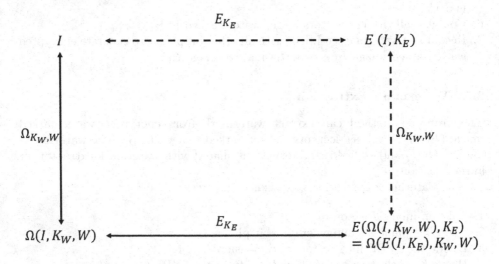

**Fig. 5.** Diagram of commutative property in $\Omega$ and $E$

In the proposed method watermark bit is embedded in the LSB of the plain vector $V_P$ or encrypted vector $V_E$. The encryption keeps these LSB's intact as even and odd indices of the multiplexer's input lines are mapped to even and odd set of random numbers respectively (cf. step 5, Sect. 2.2). Thus the watermark bits remains unaltered and commutative property is achieved. The commutative property allows to embed/extract watermark in both; the encrypted as well as the decrypted image. In other words, one can use any of the two paths (--→ or →) to get a watermarked encrypted image, or watermark extraction and authentication (cf. Fig. 2).

## 2.8  Security Analysis

The encryption key $K_E$ generates random integers in the interval $[0, 2^N)$ in a non-repetitive manner to form input of a multiplexer with size $2^N \times 1$. Total possible combinations of numbers generated this way are $(2^N)!$. Hence, probability $P_b$ of the successful brute force attack is $1/(2^N)!$. The method in [20] use the encryption key with length equal to one half of image size. Therefore, $P_b$ for this method is $\dfrac{1}{2^{\left(8 \times \lceil \frac{X \times Y}{2} \rceil\right)}}$.

For an encryption algorithm, large key size increases security as $P_b$ reduces at the same time key management and storage becomes a major overhead in private key encryption with a large user-base. Therefore, key size should be optimum to provide adequate security. Our proposal uses a key size which balances the security and memory requirements.

## 3   Experimental Results

### 3.1   Comparison with Existing Method [20]

The commutative encryption and data hiding was proposed by Zhang [20]. In this method author mask the gray level values of an image using pseudo-randomly generated bits which also act as an encryption key. The author used parameter optimization criterion to approximately balance embedding capacity and the distortion.

Next, we elaborate the data hiding operations applied by Zhang to understand its limitations. The data hider performs bit plane slicing on the plain or the encrypted image. Take two neighbouring bits in a bit plane and performs the exclusive-or operation on them.

$$x_n(t) = b_{n,1}(t) \oplus b_{n,2}(t) \tag{4}$$

where $t = 0, 1, 2, \ldots, 7$ indicates particular bit plane.

Permute $x_n(t)$ using data hiding key to get $x_p(t)$. Calculate the rate of zeros $(\rho(t))$ and find out optimal allowable bit alteration rate $(\Delta(t)) \in [0, (\rho(t) - 1/2)]$ for every $x_p(t)$. Find $x_p(t)$ for which $\Delta(t) > 0$ and equally divide it into $M$ number of sub-sequences with length $L$.

The limitation for the data hider while selecting the secret data for embedding are as follows: for a given $\rho(t)$ and $\Delta(t)$, the probability of 0 and 1 in the data should be $(\rho(t) - \Delta(t))/\rho(t)$ and $\Delta(t)/\rho(t)$, respectively. This limitation does not allow hider to use any data as it has to be chosen from a restrictive sub-space.

Embed the data in place of zeros in every subsequence; that remain as it is or flipped to one depending on the data. So, to keep the track of original 1s and embedded 1s data hider uses auxiliary data, which may contain zero to indicate original 1s and one to indicate embedded 1s.

According to Eqs. 28 and 31 in [20], the data carrying capacity $(\beta_E)$ for every sub-sequences is approximated as:

$$\beta_E \approx L \cdot \rho(t) \cdot H\left(\frac{\Delta(t)}{\rho(t)}\right) \tag{5}$$

and the size of auxiliary data $(\beta_A)$ is approximated as:

$$\beta_A \approx L \cdot \left(1 - \rho(t) + \Delta(t)\right) \cdot H\left(\frac{\Delta(t)}{1 - \rho(t) + \Delta(t)}\right) \tag{6}$$

Under the condition of $\beta_E > \beta_A$ the data hider can easily embed the auxiliary data along with the secret data into a cover image. This assumption holds true in the paper proposed by Zhang. However this may not be true for many natural images. For example: according to Table I and Table II in [20], $\rho(2) = 0.51$, $\lambda = 0.0003$ and $\Delta(t) = 0.011$ are given for lena image. Using these values, Eqs. 5 and 6, we obtain $\beta_E = 0.076$ and $\beta_A = 0.076$.

For every bit plane in which data is embedded, a vector $c(t)$ is generated which carry auxiliary data, $\rho(t)$, $\Delta(t)$ and supplementary information for image recovery. These $c(t)$s are inserted at the beginning of $x_p(0)$.

Therefore, image(s) for which $\beta_E \approx \beta_A$ and $\Delta(0) = 0$, data hider is forced to share auxiliary data and $c(t)$ via secondary channel or memory for data extraction and reversible operations.

Under the constraint that data hider needs secondary channel for sharing the auxiliary data, Table 1 shows the comparison of proposed method with Zhang [20] for natural images. PSNR and embedding capacity for Zhang [20] is directly taken from the paper.

**Table 1.** Comparison of proposed method with Zhang [20]

| Comparison | Proposed | | Zhang [20] | |
|---|---|---|---|---|
| Encryption key size | $2^N$ | | $2^{\left(8 \times \lceil \frac{X \times Y}{2} \rceil\right)}$ | |
| Image | PSNR (dB) | Capacity (bits) | PSNR (dB) | Capacity (bits) |
| lena | 51.16 | $2.18 \times 10^3$ | 48.6 | $1.60 \times 10^3$ |
| baboon | 51.13 | $2.10 \times 10^3$ | 40.2 | $2.00 \times 10^3$ |
| man | 51.15 | $8.81 \times 10^3$ | 41 | $7.00 \times 10^3$ |

Compared to natural images histogram of the fingerprint images is restricted to the specific intensity range [9] as shown in Fig. 6. Due to this property of histogram, 1s occurs with probability less than 0.7 and therefore location map is not shared separately. Hence, proposed method is more secure for fingerprint images.

## 3.2   Results on Fingerprint Images

The proposed method is evaluated using 500 fingerprint from FVC 2000 [1], FVC 2002 [2] and FVC 2004 [3] databases. For experiments 8 bit fingerprint image $I$ with 500 dpi resolution and size $X = Y = 512$ is selected. $2^8 \times 1$ multiplexer is used for image encryption and decryption. Hence random numbers are generated from the range $[0, 255]$ and the $P_b$ is 1/256! which tends to zero. Figure 7a and b

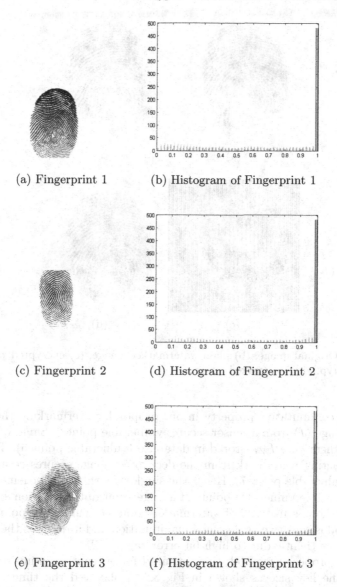

(a) Fingerprint 1          (b) Histogram of Fingerprint 1

(c) Fingerprint 2          (d) Histogram of Fingerprint 2

(e) Fingerprint 3          (f) Histogram of Fingerprint 3

**Fig. 6.** Fingerprint images and their respective histograms.

show the original finger print image and it's watermarked version. While Fig. 7c and d shows encrypted and decrypted versions of the watermarked image.

The watermarking method is reversible in nature, thus native fingerprint authentication accuracy remains unaffected. This means there is no change in the receiver operation characteristics (ROC) of the fingerprint authentication system.

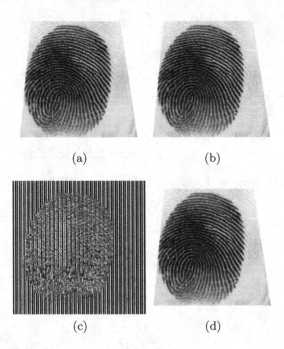

**Fig. 7.** (a) Original image, (b) plain watermarked image, (c) encrypted watermarked and (d) decrypted watermarked image.

Due to commutative property in our proposal, watermarking the plain fingerprint image ($I$) from a sensor secures vulnerable point 2. Same watermark is used to authenticate $I_{WE}$ stored in database (vulnerable point 6). The flexibility of extracting watermark from the decrypted image secures communication channel (vulnerable point 7). Hence the single watermarking scheme is used for securing multiple vulnerable points of a fingerprint authentication system.

Table 2 shows sensitivity of watermark at different vulnerable points. It shows that method is sensitive against any manipulation and it declares the fingerprint image as unauthentic due to high bit error rate (BER).

For the proposed method, time required for encryption is inversely proportional to the key size as shown in Fig. 8. As observed the time required for

**Table 2.** BER at different vulnerable point under different attacks

| Attacks | BER at vulnerable point 2 | BER at vulnerable point 6 | BER at vulnerable point 7 |
|---|---|---|---|
| Histogram equalization | 0.49 | 0.49 | 0.48 |
| Laplaceian filtering ($\alpha = 0.2$) | 0.49 | 0.52 | 0.51 |
| Average filtering ($3 \times 3$) | 0.50 | 0.51 | 0.50 |
| Gaussian noise ($\mu = 0$ and $\sigma = 0.01$) | 0.51 | 0.49 | 0.49 |

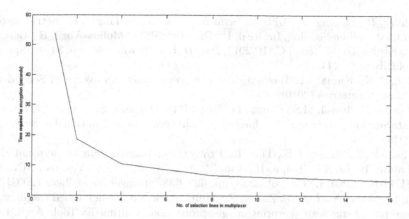

**Fig. 8.** Time required for encryption w.r.t number of selection lines $(N)$ in the multiplexer.

encryption does not change significantly after $N = 8$. Also $P_b = \frac{1}{2^8!} = \frac{1}{256!} \cong 1.2 \times 10^{-507}$. Therefore, as an optimal solution between the security and memory requirement we have selected an encryption key length $N = 8$.

## 4   Conclusion

In this work, we propose a novel scheme with encryption and reversible watermarking, satisfying commutative property. By introducing commutative property, proposed method secure multiple vulnerable points (i.e. 2, 6 and 7) of fingerprint authentication system. As reflected from Table 1, proposed method provides higher PSNR and higher embedding capacity than [20]. The proposed method has lower memory requirement for the key storage and management, and close to zero probability of a successful brute force attack.

## References

1. Fingerprint database: Fvc 2000 (2000). http://bias.csr.unibo.it/fvc2000/databases.asp
2. Fingerprint database: Fvc 2002 (2002). http://bias.csr.unibo.it/fvc2002/databases.asp
3. Fingerprint database: Fvc 2004 (2004). http://bias.csr.unibo.it/fvc2004/databases.asp
4. Unique identification authority of india - uidai (2012). http://uidai.gov.in/
5. Bartlow, N., Kalka, N., Cukic, B., Ross, A.: Protecting IRIS images through asymmetric digital watermarking. In: 2007 IEEE Workshop on Automatic Identification Advanced Technologies, pp. 192–197. IEEE (2007)
6. Hong, W., Chen, T.S., Wu, H.Y.: An improved reversible data hiding in encrypted images using side match. IEEE Signal Process. Lett. **19**(4), 199–202 (2012)

7. Huber, R., Stögner, H., Uhl, A.: Semi-fragile watermarking in biometric systems: template self-embedding. In: Real, P., Diaz-Pernil, D., Molina-Abril, H., Berciano, A., Kropatsch, W. (eds.) CAIP 2011, Part II. LNCS, vol. 6855, pp. 34–41. Springer, Heidelberg (2011)

8. Jain, A.K., Kumar, A.: Biometrics of next generation: An overview. Second Generation Biometrics (2010)

9. Joshi, V.B., Raval, M.S., Gupta, D., Rege, P.P., Parulkar, S.: A multiple reversible watermarking technique for fingerprint authentication. Multimedia Syst., 1–12 (2015)

10. Khan, M.K., Zhang, J.-S., Tian, L.: Protecting biometric data for personal identification. In: Li, S.Z., Lai, J.-H., Tan, T., Feng, G.-C., Wang, Y. (eds.) SINOBIOMETRICS 2004. LNCS, vol. 3338, pp. 629–638. Springer, Heidelberg (2004)

11. Li, C., Wang, Y., Ma, B., Zhang, Z.: Multi-block dependency based fragile watermarking scheme for fingerprint images protection. Multimedia Tools Appl. **64**(3), 757–776 (2013)

12. Ma, K., Zhang, W., Zhao, X., Yu, N., Li, F.: Reversible data hiding in encrypted images by reserving room before encryption. IEEE Trans. Inf. Forensics Secur. **8**(3), 553–562 (2013)

13. NSTC, Committee on Technology, Committee on Homeland, National Security, Subcommittee on Biometrics: Fingerprint recognition (2006). http://www.biometrics.gov/documents/fingerprintrec.pdf

14. Raval, M.S.: A secure steganographic technique for blind steganalysis resistance. In: Seventh International Conference on Advances in Pattern Recognition, 2009. ICAPR 2009, pp. 25–28. IEEE (2009)

15. Schmidt, G.: Relational mathematics, no. 132 in encyclopedia of mathematics and its applications (2010)

16. Wang, D.S., Li, J.P., Wen, X.Y.: Biometric image integrity authentication based on SVD and fragile watermarking. In: Congress on Image and Signal Processing, 2008. CISP 2008. vol. 5, pp. 679–682. IEEE (2008)

17. Zhang, W., Ma, K., Yu, N.: Reversibility improved data hiding in encrypted images. Sign. Process. **94**, 118–127 (2014)

18. Zhang, X.: Reversible data hiding in encrypted image. Sign. Process. Lett. IEEE **18**(4), 255–258 (2011)

19. Zhang, X.: Separable reversible data hiding in encrypted image. IEEE Trans. Inf. Forensics Secur. **7**(2), 826–832 (2012)

20. Zhang, X.: Commutative reversible data hiding and encryption. Secur. Commun. Netw. **6**(11), 1396–1403 (2013)

# Distortion-Free Robust Reversible Watermarking by Modifying and Recording IWT Means of Image Blocks

Shijun Xiang[✉] and Yi Wang

School of Information Science and Technology, Jinan University,
Guangzhou 510632, China
xiangshijun@gmail.com, wangyi9112@yeah.net

**Abstract.** This paper presents a novel distortion-free robust reversible watermarking scheme by modifying and recording the mean information of the integer wavelet transform (IWT) middle-frequency of the image blocks sized $8 \times 8$. The proposed method utilizes multiple watermarking by embedding the watermark with the robust watermarking method at first and a following reversible watermarking method to embed the mean information used to recover the cover image. The cover image is first divided into non-overlapping blocks sized $8 \times 8$ and applied 5/3 IWT to transform the blocks. One watermark bit is embedding into the HL and LH sub-bands of a block by modifying their mean values. The mean values are calculated by randomly choosing 10 coefficients instead of all the 16 coefficients so that the mean value has one decimal place at most and can be reversibly embedded for the recovery of the original cover image. Experimental results have shown the proposed method is blind, and provides better performance in the invisibility and the robustness against JPEG/JPEG2000 and noise attacks.

**Keywords:** Distortion-free robust reversible watermarking · Mean value · Integer wavelet transform (IWT) · Robustness

## 1 Introduction

Recently, reversible watermarking has aroused peoples interesting, which enables embed data into images and allow extraction of the original image and the embedded data [1]. Reversible watermarking is very useful in medical image system, military image and law enforcement [2]. It plays an important role in protecting the copyright of digital media [3]. Although there are so many reversible watermarking methods, but most of them can't resist any type of attacks. As a result, the original image or the embedded data can't be recovered after attack [4].

In some cases, the embedded data is expected to be robust to some attacks like image compression and some inevitable random noise. To this end, researchers pay more attention on robust reversible watermarking method. Robust reversible

© Springer International Publishing Switzerland 2016
Y.-Q. Shi et al. (Eds.): IWDW 2015, LNCS 9569, pp. 337–349, 2016.
DOI: 10.1007/978-3-319-31960-5_28

watermarking is that the original image and the embedded data can be recovered correctly when the watermarked image remains intact, and the embedded data can still be extracted without error even the watermarked image suffered some attacks [5]. Until now, a few robust reversible watermarking methods have been proposed, which can be classified into two groups:

- Blind watermarking scheme: In [5,6], Vleeschouwer et al. proposed a blind extraction scheme based on the patchwork theory and modulo-256 by using the gray-scale histogram rotation. This work is robust against JPEG compression, but the watermarked image has lower visible quality due to the salt-and-pepper noise is caused. Besides, the capacity is low. To handle the salt-and-pepper noise problem, Zou et al. proposed a scheme by shifting the absolute mean values of the integer wavelet transform (IWT) coefficients in a chosen sub-band [7], and Ni et al. proposed scheme by modifying the histogram of a robust statistical quantity in the spatial domain [8]. Since the embedding process may introduce the error bits, the error correction coding (ECC) has been used. Besides, these two methods suffered from the unstable robustness and incomplete reversibility according to [9]. In [10], Zeng et al. enhanced the scheme of Ni et al. by introducing two thresholds and a new embedding mechanism. This method is blind extraction and can avoid the error bits, but the threshold value changes with different cover images.
- Non-blind watermarking scheme: In [11], a non-blind extraction scheme based on wavelet-domain statistical quantity histogram shifting and clustering (WSQH-SC) is proposed. A pixel adjustment is presented at first to avoid the overflow and underflow, and a location map is used to record the changed pixels. This method achieved good robustness against JPEG, JPEG2000 and additive Gaussian noise, but this method is not blind since the locations of the changed pixels need to be saved as a part of side information and transmitted to the receiver side in order to recover the original image. In [12], the Slant-let transform (SLT) is applied to image blocks and then modifying the mean values of the HL and LH sub-band coefficients to embed the watermark bits. Due to the coefficients and the mean values are fractional with more decimal places, the mean information is taken as side information to be send to the receiver side for the recovery of the original cover image.

In [13], Coltuc et al. proposed a general framework for robust reversible watermarking by multiple watermarking. The scheme embeds the watermark with a robust watermarking method at first and then a reversible watermarking method is adopted to embed the information used to recover the original cover image into the watermarked image. Supposing $o$ and $w$ is the original image and the robust watermarked image, respectively. The embedding distortion, $d = o - w$, is compressed and embedded into the robust watermarked image with the reversible watermarking method. At the receiver side, if there is no attacks, the watermark and the difference $d$ can be extracted, the robust watermarked image can be recovered, then the original image $o$ can be recovered by:$o = d + w$. If the watermarked image goes through JPEG compression, the robust watermark can still be extracted. This framework is very instructive and achieves higher capacity and good robustness against JPEG compression.

Inspired by the work of Coltuc *et al.* [13], in this paper we develop a robust reversible watermarking method in the IWT domain. The main idea of the scheme includes the following 4 aspects: (1) choose IWT to get integer coefficients, (2) modify the mean values of the middle-frequency sub-bands coefficients to embed the watermark bit, (3) calculate the mean value by 10 of the 16 coefficients instead of all the 16 coefficients so that the mean value has at most one decimal place, (4) embed the mean information with reversible watermarking method so that the original cover image can be recovered. If the overflow or underflow happened, a location map and a pixel adjustment operation are introduced, and the location map need to be deeply compressed and embedded into the image. The proposed method is blind and without any side information, the watermark and the original image can be recovered perfectly if the watermarked image remains intact. When the watermarked image suffer some extent of attacks (such as JPEG/JPEG2000 or random noise), the watermark is also detectable. Comparing with recent robust reversible watermarking schemes, the proposed method is not only blind, but provides higher capacity, stronger robustness and better invisibility.

The rest of the paper is organized as follows. The foundation work is introduced in Sect. 2. The proposed algorithm is described in Sect. 3. Experimental results are presented in Sect. 4. Section 5 concludes this paper.

## 2  Algorithm's Principle

This section will introduce the foundation works of the proposed robust reversible watermarking scheme. Firstly, how to modify the statistic quantity of IWT domain to embed the watermark bit is introduced, then how to record the original statistic quantity by using reversible watermarking method is briefly described.

### 2.1  Modification of Block Mean Values

Given an $8 \times 8$ image block, we utilize 5/3 IWT to obtain the IWT-coefficients block. The coefficients of 5/3 wavelet filter are given in Table 1. There are 16 coefficients in HL and LH sub-bands in total. Their mean values are denoted by $\mu_{HL}$ and $\mu_{LH}$, respectively. For blind extraction, $\mu_{HL}$ and $\mu_{LH}$ are calculated by 10 randomly chosen of the 16 coefficients in each sub-band. As a result, they could be integer or fractional with one decimal place. The difference of $\mu_{HL}$ and $\mu_{LH}$, denoted by $A$, as the robust statistic quantity:

$$A = \mu_{HL} - \mu_{LH}, \tag{1}$$

It's clear that the difference $A$ could be an integer or a fractional with one decimal place. As an example, the distribution of all $A$ values of image Lena

**Table 1.** 5/3 Filter coefficients

|   | Analysis filter coefficients | | Synthesis filter coefficients | |
|---|---|---|---|---|
| n | Low-pass filter $h_L(n)$ | High-pass filter $h_H(n)$ | Low-pass filter $g_L(n)$ | High-pass filter $g_H(n)$ |
| 0 | 6/8 | 1 | 1 | 6/8 |
| ±1 | 2/8 | −1/2 | 1/2 | −2/8 |
| ±2 | −1/8 | 0 | 0 | −1/8 |

is shown in Fig. 1(a). We can see that the distribution is Laplacian-like distribution and the mean value is close to 0. The results of other images are similar.

For a block, a watermark bit can be embedded by modifying the difference value $A$ of $\mu_{HL}$ and $\mu_{LH}$. Here we choose the middle-frequency sub-bands is to achieve the trade-off between robustness and invisibility. The main idea of the bit embedding is that keep the difference value $A$ is beyond a pre-defined threshold $T$ to embed the watermark bit '1' and beyond $-T$ to embed the watermark bit '0'. Figure 1(b) shows the distribution of the modified difference values of Lena.

If the watermark bit is '1', then modify $\mu_{HL}$ and $\mu_{LH}$ to make sure $A = \mu_{HL} - \mu_{LH} \geq T$. If the watermark bit is '0', modify $\mu_{HL}$ and $\mu_{LH}$ to make sure $A = \mu_{HL} - \mu_{LH} \leq -T$. $T$ is a pre-defined positive integer threshold value. Since the bit-1-zone and bit-0-zone are separated by the robust zone $(-T, T)$, we can extract the watermark bit by identifying the difference value $A$. When the watermarked image remains intact, the watermark can be recovered correctly (see Fig. 1(b)). Even the watermarked image is attacked, the watermark is also able to be detected if the bit-0-zone and bit-1-zone are not overlapped. Figure 1(c) shows the distribution of the watermarked image after a JPEG compression operation.

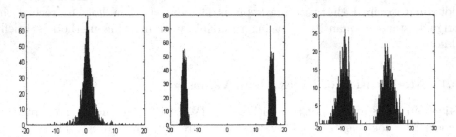

(a)Distribution of $A$ values of Lena (b)Distribution after embedding (c)Distribution after an attack

**Fig. 1.** Distribution of $A$ values of Lena.

The watermarking rules are as follows.
For the watermark bit '1': if $A = \mu_{HL} - \mu_{LH} < T$, let

$$\mu_{HL}^{new} = \mu_{HL} + round((T - A)/2);$$
$$\mu_{LH}^{new} = \mu_{LH} - round((T - A)/2),$$

$$(2)$$

Otherwise, if $A = \mu_{HL} - \mu_{LH} \geq T$, keep $\mu_{HL}$ and $\mu_{LH}$ unchanged.
For the watermark bit '0': if if $A = \mu_{HL} - \mu_{LH} > -T$, let

$$
\begin{aligned}
\mu_{HL}^{new} &= \mu_{HL} - round((T + A)/2); \\
\mu_{LH}^{new} &= \mu_{LH} + round((T + A)/2),
\end{aligned}
\tag{3}
$$

Otherwise, if $A = \mu_{HL} - \mu_{LH} \leq -T$, there is no operation.

$HL^{(k)}(i,j)$ and $LH^{(k)}(i,j)$ denotes the IWT coefficient of the point $(i,j)$ in the $k$th block's HL and LH sub-band respectively, and the modification of the mean values is done by ($M$ is a matrix using for selecting 10 of 16 coefficients):

$$
HL^{(k)}(i,j) = \begin{cases}
HL^{(k)}(i,j) + round((T - A)/2) * M(i,j), & \text{if } w_k = 1 \text{ and } A < T \\
HL^{(k)}(i,j) - round((T + A)/2) * M(i,j), & \text{if } w_k = 0 \text{ and } A > -T \\
HL^{(k)}(i,j), & \text{otherwise},
\end{cases}
\tag{4}
$$

$$
LH^{(k)}(i,j) = \begin{cases}
LH^{(k)}(i,j) - round((T - A)/2) * M(i,j), & \text{if } w_k = 1 \text{ and } A < T \\
LH^{(k)}(i,j) + round((T + A)/2) * M(i,j), & \text{if } w_k = 0 \text{ and } A > -T \\
LH^{(k)}(i,j), & \text{otherwise},
\end{cases}
\tag{5}
$$

At the receiver side, the bit-1-zone is redefined as $[0, +\infty)$ and bit-0-zone is $(-\infty, 0)$, and the watermark bit is extracted by:

$$
w_i^{'} = \begin{cases}
1, & \text{if } A^{'} \geq 0 \\
0, & \text{otherwise},
\end{cases}
\tag{6}
$$

The above operation can embed a watermark bit into a image block. In referring to (2) and (3), the difference value $A$ should be saved so that the original cover image could be recovered at the receiver side.

## 2.2 Recording of Block Mean Values

Due to the use of IWT, the coefficients are integers. By choosing 10 of the 16 coefficients to calculate the mean values of the sub-band, the mean values ($\mu_{HL}$ and $\mu_{LH}$) and the difference ($A$) could be an integer or only has one decimal place. So if we expand the difference $A$ 10 times, the new difference $A1$ will be an integer and can be changed into a string of binary bits $B$, then we can embed the binary bits into the watermarked image with the reversible watermarking method.

According to robust reversible watermarking scheme in [13], any reversible watermarking methods can be used as the second stage of embedding, but the distortion of the second stage of the reversible watermarking should be as lower as possible. In our method, we choose the reversible watermarking method proposed in [14]. For better description, the low distortion transform is introduced as below.

Let $n, w$, and $nw$ be the north, west, and north-west neighbors of pixel $x$, and $b$ is the watermark bit, the estimate of x is $\hat{x} = n + w - nw$, and $p = x - \hat{x}$,

$p_b = p + b$. The marked pixel is $x^{new} = x + \lfloor \frac{p_b}{4} \rfloor$, and $n^{new} = n - \lfloor \frac{p_{b+3}}{4} \rfloor$, $w^{new} = w - \lfloor \frac{p_{b+1}}{4} \rfloor$, $nw^{new} = nw + \lfloor \frac{p_{b+2}}{4} \rfloor$. $\lfloor \alpha \rfloor$ is the maximum integer not exceeding.

The transform is reversible. Suppose X, N, W, NW are the transformed pixels. The inverse transform are as follows: $\hat{X} = N + W - NW = \hat{x} - \lfloor \frac{p_{b+3}}{4} \rfloor - \lfloor \frac{p_{b+1}}{4} \rfloor - \lfloor \frac{p_{b+2}}{4} \rfloor$. $P = X - \hat{X} = x - \hat{x} + \lfloor \frac{p_b}{4} \rfloor + \lfloor \frac{p_{b+3}}{4} \rfloor + \lfloor \frac{p_{b+1}}{4} \rfloor + \lfloor \frac{p_{b+2}}{4} \rfloor = 2p + b$.

Then the embedded bit can be obtained by: $b = (X - \hat{X}) - 2 \times \lfloor \frac{(X - \hat{X})}{2} \rfloor, p = (X - \hat{X} - b)/2, p_b = p + b$.

Then the original pixels can be recovered by: $x = X - \lfloor \frac{p_b}{4} \rfloor, n = N + \lfloor \frac{p_{b+3}}{4} \rfloor, w = W + \lfloor \frac{p_{b+1}}{4} \rfloor, nw = NW - \lfloor \frac{p_{b+2}}{4} \rfloor$.

Table 2 gives the range of the difference $A$ of some images. It's obviously that most of them are within [-1024,1024] after expand 10 times. So we can replace the absolute value of $A1$ with 10 binary bits and one bit for sign bit, $A1$ is 10 times of the difference $A$, so 11 bits are totally enough for replacing a difference $A$. Since the reversible watermarking method can embed a bit into 4 pixels, so one $8 \times 8$ block is capable of embedding the 11 bits of the difference information.

**Table 2.** The range of difference value

| Image | Lena | Baboon | Boat | Barbara | Angkor | Large |
|-------|------|--------|------|---------|--------|-------|
| Range of $A$ | $[-34.7,25.8]$ | $[-43.1,43.6]$ | $[-21.2,23]$ | $[-46.3,55.2]$ | $[-31.7,33.1]$ | $[-16.1,17.3]$ |

## 2.3  Prevention of Overflow/Underflow

For an 8-bit gray-scale image, the permitted range is [0,255]. The watermark embedding process may cause overflow or underflow, to avoid the overflow or underflow, a location map and a pixel adjustment operation are introduced. The location map is used to record the position of the pixels, mark '1' if the pixel is overflow or underflow, and '0' if the pixel is normal. The location map is deeply compressed and embedded into the watermarked image with any reversible watermarking method after the pixel adjustment is done.

The pixel adjustment is done by, $T'$ is an integer bigger than $2T$:

$$x_{(i,j)} = \begin{cases} x_{(i,j)} + T', & \text{if } x_{(i,j)} < 0 \\ x_{(i,j)} - T', & \text{if } x_{(i,j)} > 255 \end{cases} \tag{7}$$

The inverse transform is done by:

$$x_{(i,j)} = \begin{cases} x_{(i,j)} - T', & \text{if } x_{(i,j)} < 125 \\ x_{(i,j)} + T', & \text{if } x_{(i,j)} > 125 \end{cases} \tag{8}$$

# 3   Proposed Algorithm

In our proposed robust reversible watermarking scheme, robust watermark based on robust statistic quantity is first embedded, and then the difference value of each block, $A = \mu_{HL} - \mu_{LH}$ is embedded by using the reversible watermarking scheme. Compared with the previous robust reversible watermarking schemes, the proposed method is blind and has a satisfactory robustness and visible quality, as described below.

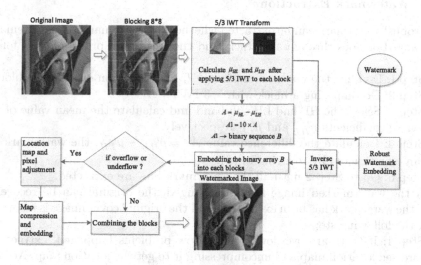

**Fig. 2.** Watermark embedding process.

## 3.1   Watermark Embedding

Figure 2 shows the proposed watermark embedding process. The robust watermark is embedded with the following five steps:

Step 1: Dividing the original cover image I into $8 \times 8$ non-overlapping blocks.

Step 2: Decomposing a block with 5/3 IWT.

Step 3: Select the HL and LH sub-bands of the block, and calculate their mean values, denoted by $\mu_{HL}$ and $\mu_{LH}$ respectively.

Step 4: Calculate the difference value $A = \mu_{HL} - \mu_{LH}$, and modify $\mu_{HL}$ and $\mu_{LH}$ to embed a robust watermark bit by referring to (4) and (5).

Step 5: Perform inverse 5/3 IWT to obtain the watermarked block. Go to Step 2 until all the blocks are marked to get the watermarked image $I_{w1}$.

In the embedding process of the robust watermark, the $A$ values of all the blocks should be saved and embedded into the image $I_{w1}$ reversibly. In this way, the original image can be recovered once the watermark was extracted. We use the following steps to embed all the $A$ values in reversible way:

Step 1: Expand a difference value $A$ ten times to get an integer $A1$, then change $A1$ into binary array $B$.

Step 2: Embedding the binary array $B$ into each blocks with the reversible watermarking technique. Repeat Step 1 until all the $A$ values are embedded to get image $I_{w2}$.

At last, a location map and pixel adjustment is taken if overflow or underflow occur.

## 3.2   Watermark Extraction

The robust watermark can be extracted whether the watermarked image remains unchanged or goes through an attack, and the extraction process are as follow steps:

Step 1: Dividing the watermarked image $I_w$ into $8 \times 8$ non-overlapping blocks.

Step 2: Decomposing a block with 5/3 IWT.

Step 3: Select the HL and LH sub-band and calculate the mean value of the chosen 10 coefficients $\mu'_{HL}$ and $\mu'_{LH}$ respectively.

Step 4: Calculate the difference value $A' = \mu'_{HL} - \mu'_{LH}$, the watermark bit $w'_i$ can be extracted by referring to (6).

Step 5: Go to Step 2 until all the watermark bits are extracted.

If the watermarked image keeps unchanged, the original can be recovered after the watermark has been extracted. And the original cover image is recovered with the following steps:

Step 1: If there are overflow or underflow problems happened, extract the compressed location map and uncompressing it to get the location map. According to the location map transform the changed pixels by referring to (6).

Step 2: Recover the binary array $B$ from each block and change the binary number into decimal number $\overline{A}$, then the difference value can be obtained by: $A' = \overline{A}/10$.

Step 3: Applying 5/3 IWT to the block, Select the HL and LH sub-band and calculate the mean value of the chosen 10 coefficients in each sub-band $\mu'_{HL}$ and $\mu'_{LH}$.

Step 4: According to the watermark bit $w'_i$, the mean value $\mu'_{HL}$ and $\mu'_{LH}$, the difference value $A'$, the threshold $T$, we can recover the original coefficients.

Step 5: Perform inverse 5/3 IWT to get the original block. Go to Step 2 until all the blocks are recovered. Combining the blocks to recover the original image.

## 4   Experimental Results

In this section, we take some experiments to evaluate the proposed method. In our experiments, some 8 bit grayscale images are chosen as example images, such as Lena, Boat, Barbara, and Baboon, *etc.*

The threshold $T$ has an effect on invisibility and robustness. Here, we choose 4 natural images and 4 synthetic aperture radar (SAR) images with the size of

(a1) Lena    (a2)Baboon    (a3) Boat    (a4)Barbara    (b1) Airport    (b2) Angkor    (b3) Large    (b4)Washsat

**Fig. 3.** Test images: (a) natural images; (b) SAR images.

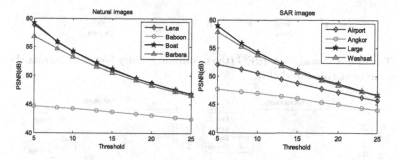

**Fig. 4.** PSNR values for different threshold values.

$512 \times 512$ (see Fig. 3) as data set [15]. The watermark is a fixed random sequence with 100 bits. The invisibility is evaluated by PSNR.

Figure 4 shows the relationship between the threshold $T$ and the PSNR values of the different images. The threshold is adjusted from 5 to 25. We can find that the PSNR values of the natural images are above 46 dB except the image Baboon, and the PSNR value of Baboon is lower than other 4 natural images when the threshold is low. The reason is that the Baboon image is more textural. The PSNR values of the SAR images are above 43 dB. Obviously, the higher the threshold T is, the lower the PSNR is.

To assess the effect of the threshold on robustness against JPEG compression, we utilize the ACDsee tool to compress the watermarked images at different quality factor (10, 20, 30,..., 100). Figure 5 shows the results that the robust watermark can be extracted correctly for different JPEG quality factors with different corresponding embedding thresholds. When $T$ is 5, all the 5 natural images can resist JPEG 90 compression. We can observe that the higher the threshold is, the better robustness is. In particularly, the SAR images achieved very good robustness. When the threshold is 25, the four images can resist JPEG compression with quality factor 40.

To make a comparison with other method, the surviving bit rate (bpp) is selected to evaluate the robustness against JPEG2000. The relationship between the surviving bit rate and the maximum compression ratio is: the surviving bit rate=8/(maximum compression ratio). So the lower the surviving bit rate, the better the robustness is. Figure 6 shows the relationship between the surviving bit rates and the threshold values. The watermark can be extracted correctly when the surviving bit rate is larger than it. We can observe that natural images

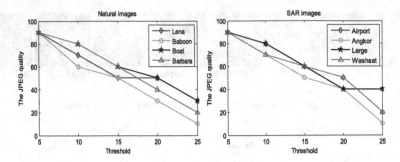

**Fig. 5.** The robustness against JPEG (the minimum quality factor to extract the watermark correctly at this threshold).

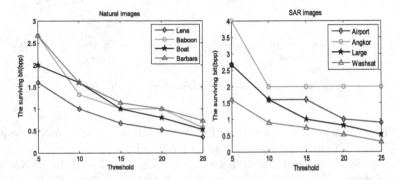

**Fig. 6.** The robustness against JPEG2000 (the minimum bpp to extract the watermark correctly at this threshold).

achieved very good robustness when the threshold value is 25, and all of the natural images achieve the robustness under 1 bpp.

Figure 7 shows the robustness against salt-and-pepper noise with different thresholds. It demonstrates that the robustness of these images against the maximum noise intensity at each threshold. Its clear that the robustness increases as the threshold increases while the invisibility drops at the same time. Its because that the lager the threshold is, the lager the robust zone is, so the robustness increases.

To make a comparison with the WSQH-SC mentioned in [11], we choose 50 natural images and 50 SAR images as the test images. The threshold in our method is 25 while $\lambda$ is 16 in the WSQH-SC method. The average robustness comparison results are shown in Table 3. We can see that our method achieved better robustness against JPEG/JPEG2000 with natural images and SAR images. Furthermore, our method is blind to extract the watermark while WSQH-SC is non-blind to some extent.

To make a comparison with Zeng et al.'s method [10], we take Lena, Baboon, Boat and Barbara, etc. as example images. The threshold in our method is 20. We evaluate the robustness by the minimum surviving bit rate (bpp) when the

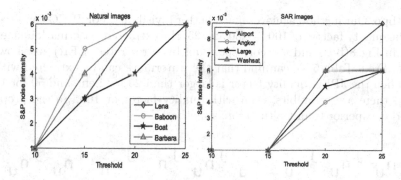

**Fig. 7.** The robustness against salt-and-pepper noise (the maximum noise intensity to extract the watermark correctly at this threshold).

**Table 3.** Comparison of robustness with WSQH-SC [11]

| Image | JPEG (quality factor) | | JPEG2000 (the surviving bit rate) | |
|---|---|---|---|---|
| | Proposed | WSQH-SC [11] | Proposed | WSQH-SC [11] |
| Natural | 30 | 40 | 0.53 | 1 |
| SAR | 20 | 40 | 0.8 | 1.14 |

BER is lower than 1 %. Table 4 shows that our method has better robustness at the same PSNR. The basic reason is that in our method the watermark is in the wavelet domain while Zeng *et al.*'s method embedding the watermark in the spatial domain.

**Table 4.** Comparison with Zeng *et al.*'s method [10]

| Image | Proposed | | | | Zeng *et al.*'s method [10] | | | |
|---|---|---|---|---|---|---|---|---|
| | PSNR (dB) | Capacity (B) | Robustness (bpp) | BER | PSNR (dB) | Capacity (B) | Robustness (bpp) | BER |
| Lena | 38.12 | 1100 | 0.57 | 0.91% | 38.07 | 2048 | 0.8 | 0.015% |
| Baboon | 38.15 | 430 | 1 | 0.93% | 38.05 | 850 | 1.6 | 0.243% |
| Boat | 38.07 | 1000 | 0.8 | 0.6% | 38.09 | 2048 | 1 | 0.182% |
| Barbara | 38.40 | 1000 | 1.14 | 0 | 38.07 | 2048 | 1.16 | 0.663% |
| Peppers | 38.13 | 950 | 0.57 | 0.95% | 38.12 | 2048 | 0.61 | 0.047% |
| Airplane | 38.12 | 1100 | 0.73 | 0.18% | 38.09 | 2048 | 0.8 | 0.013% |
| Goldhill | 38.10 | 1100 | 0.89 | 0 | 38.10 | 2048 | 1.08 | 0.157% |

To compare with Coltuc *et al.*'s method [13], we apply our method on the same test images Lena and Boat in size $512 \times 512$. The watermark is a binary image (a Logo with Jnu) with the size of $64 \times 64$ as shown in Fig. 8(a). The PSNR values of watermarked versions of Lena and Boat are 33.15 dB and 32.66 dB respectively while the threshold $T$ is 18. In [13], the PSNR values of the watermarked Lena and Boat are 24.63 dB at the 0.97 bpp and 22.62 dB at 0.93 bpp. Our method achieves much better invisibility. For JPEG compression with the quality factors of 100, 75, 50 and 25, the extracted watermark images are shown in Fig. 8(b-i), and the corresponding bit error rates (BER) are shown in Table 5. From Table 5 we can find that the watermark can be extracted without error when the JPEG quality factor is larger than 25 for Lena and 50 for Boat. In [13], there are error bits, even with quality factor at 100. So the proposed method is superior than Coltuc *et al.*'s method.

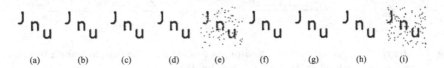

(a)        (b)        (c)        (d)        (e)        (f)        (g)        (h)        (i)

**Fig. 8.** The original watermark (a) and the extracted watermarks: (b) Lena-quality factor 100; (c) Lena-75; (d) Lena-50; (e) Lena-25; (f) Boat-100; (g) Boat-75; (h) Boat-50; (i) Boat-25.

**Table 5.** Comparison with Coltuc *et al.*'s method [13]

|  | Proposed | | | | Coltuc *et al.*'s method [13] | | | |
| --- | --- | --- | --- | --- | --- | --- | --- | --- |
| Quality factor | 100 | 75 | 50 | 25 | 100 | 75 | 50 | 25 |
| Lena | 0 | 0 | 0 | 2.51% | 0.12% | 0.3% | 0.53% | 2.17% |
| Boat | | 0 | 0 | 0.05% | 2.81% | 0.22% | 0.63% | 1.24% | 4.25% |

## 5    Conclusion

In this paper, we proposed a novel robust reversible watermarking method based on multiple watermarking. The robust watermarking based on shifting the mean value of the 5/3 integer wavelet transform coefficients is first adopted to embed the watermark, the reversible watermarking followed by the robust watermarking is taken to embed the difference values which is used to recover the original cover image. The original image can be recovered without error after the watermark extracted if the watermarked image keep intact, and the watermark can be extracted correctly even the watermarked image suffered some attacks such as JPEG/JPEG2000 or random noise. Compared to the method in [11], our method achieves better robustness, compared to the method in [10], our method achieves better robustness against JPEG2000 at the same PSNR, compared to the method in [13], our method achieves better image quality and better robustness against JPEG at the same capacity. Furthermore, the proposed method is very simple and can be applied in various images.

In the future research, we will combine the multiple robust reversible watermarking framework with the local feature of different kinds of images to improve the robustness with a higher image quality.

**Acknowledgments.** This work was supported by NSFC (No. 61272414).

# References

1. Shi, Y.Q., Ni, Z., Zou, D., Liang, C., Xuan, G.: Lossless data hiding: fundamentals, algorithms and applications. In: ISCAS, vol. 2, pp. 313–336. IEEE (2004)
2. Li, X., Yang, B., Zeng, T.: Efficient reversible watermarking based on adaptive prediction-error expansion and pixel selection. IEEE Trans. Image Process. **20**(12), 3524–3533 (2000)
3. Feng, J.B., Lin, I.C., Tsai, C.S., Chu, Y.P.: Reversible watermarking: current status and key issues. Int. J. Netw. Secur. **2**(3), 161–171 (2006)
4. Ni, Z., Shi, Y.Q., Ansari, N., Su, W., Sun, Q., Lin, X.: Robust lossless image data hiding. In: Mutimedia and Expo, ICME 2004, Taipei, Taiwan, 27–30 June, vol. 3, pp. 2199–2202 (2004)
5. De Vleeschouwer, C., Delaigle, J., Macq, B.: Circular interpretation of histogram for reversible watermarking. In: IEEE Workshop Multimedia, Signal Process, pp. 345–350 (2001)
6. De Vleeschouwer, C., Delaigle, J.E., Macq, B.: Circular interpretation of bijective transformations in lossless watermarking for media asset management. IEEE Trans. Multimedia **5**(1), 97–105 (2003)
7. Zou, D., Shi, Y., Ni, Z., Su, W.: A semi-fragile lossless digital watermarking scheme based on integer wavelet transform. IEEE Trans. Circ. Syst. Video Technol. **16**(10), 1294–1300 (2006)
8. Ni, Z., Shi, Y.Q., Ansari, N., Su, W., Sun, Q., Lin, X.: Robust lossless image data hiding designed for semi-fragile image authentication. IEEE Trans. Circ. Syst. Video Technol. **18**(4), 890–896 (2008)
9. An, L., Gao, X., Deng, C., Ji, F.: Robust lossless data hiding: analysis and evaluation. In: Proceedings of International Conference on High Perforance Computing and Simulation, pp. 512–516 (2010)
10. Zeng, X.T., Ping, L.D., Pan, X.Z.: A lossless robust data hiding scheme. Pattern Recogn. **43**(4), 1656–1667 (2010)
11. An, L., Gao, X., Li, X., Tao, D., Deng, C., Li, J.: Robust reversible watermarking via clustering and enhanced pixel-wise masking. IEEE Trans. Image Process. **21**(8), 3598–3611 (2012)
12. Mohammed, R.T., Khoo, B.E.: Robust reversible watermarking scheme based on wavelet-like transform. In: IEEE International Conference on Signal and Image Processing Applications, pp. 354–359(2013)
13. Coltuc, D., Chassery, J.M.: Distortion-free robust watermarking: a case study. In: Proceedings of SPIE: Security, Steganography, and Watermarking of Multimedia Contents IX, vol. 6505, pp. 588–595 (2007)
14. Coltuc, D.: Low distortion transform for reversible watermarking. IEEE Trans. Image Process. **21**(1), 412–417 (2012)
15. CVG-UGR Image Database. http://decsai.ugr.es/cvg/dbimagenes/index.php

# Reversible Data Hiding for Encrypted Audios by High Order Smoothness

Jing-Yong Qiu, Yu-Hsun Lin$^{(\boxtimes)}$, and Ja-Ling Wu

Department of GINM, National Taiwan University, Taipei, Taiwan
{hansqiu,lymanblue,wjl}@cmlab.csie.ntu.edu.tw

**Abstract.** This work presents a reversible data hiding method on encrypted audio files, where a data-hider, having no knowledge about the original content, tries to embed some additional data into the encrypted version of the content which was distributed from the content owner. A legal receiver, with the pre-negotiated decrypted key, can decrypt the encrypted content and get nearly the same version of the original medium. Moreover, if he/she has the pre-negotiated data-hiding key, the embedded data can be extracted, and therefore, the medium can be totally recovered. There are many kinds of media and some works targeting on hiding data into encrypted images have been proposed recently. Since human's auditory system is more sensitive than human's visual system, we apply a high order smoothness measurement to maintain the naturalness of a sound and let the content owner pre-calculate some necessary information for sound recovery, before encryption. With these two mechanisms, this work produces stego-audios of small quality degradation and has the capability to recover the original audios with zero error rate.

**Keywords:** Reversible data hiding · Encrypted audio · High order smoothness

## 1 Introduction

The technique of data hiding has been widely researched over the past few decades. It gives a way to enrich the multimedia with additional data for usages, like metadata recording, authentication, and covert communications. Within it, reversible data hiding aims at perfect recovering of the host media after the extraction of the additional data and is well applicable to biometric system or military communication, since any distortion or modification of the media is not allowed in these application scenarios. The concept of data reversibility was firstly brought up in Barton's patent [1] in 1997.

Given that the reversibility is a must, there are four additional goals when designing a good reversible data hiding method:

- Imperceptibility, or small degradation of the stego-signal quality.
- High capacity, or large embedding payloads.

© Springer International Publishing Switzerland 2016
Y.-Q. Shi et al. (Eds.): IWDW 2015, LNCS 9569, pp. 350–364, 2016.
DOI: 10.1007/978-3-319-31960-5_29

– Undetectability, or good concealment of the hidden stego-data.
– Efficiency, or small computational load.

A good design principle could reach a trade-off between two of the four goals. For example, larger embedding payloads obviously results in larger degradation of quality, or, a well-designed method with both high capacity and small degradation of quality usually takes much computational time.

Most of the existing reversible data hiding approaches are implemented in the plaintext domain, and they can be classified into three categories. The first one lies in *the spatial domain*. Works done in this domain usually have the advantages of being straightforward and having high efficiency. Most of them can be further classified into difference-expansion based methods [2–4] ([4] for audios) and histogram-modification based methods [5–7] ([7] for audios). The second category lies in *the spectral domain*. In [8], Huang created an embedding space in the high frequency part by transforming the original audio to the integer DCT (intDCT) domain for hiding extra payload data. The third one lies in *the compression domain*. In [9], Li embedded payload data into a compressed speech based on some properties of the coding bitstream.

Overall, in the plaintext domain the natural properties of the given media can be fully utilized for data hiding. But with the growing demands on privacy nowadays, data is very likely to be encrypted before any distribution or processing. Therefore, several hiding works designed and implemented in the ciphertext domain were newly presented [10–12]. In [10], Zhang proposed a new sketch scheme under which an effective method was designed to embed the additional data into an XOR-encrypted image. He first segmented the encrypted image into non-overlapping blocks, and then for each block, one bit '0' or '1' was embedded by flipping 3 LSBs of all encrypted pixels in group A or B, respectively. The groups A and B are mutually exclusive and are determined by the data-hiding key. Since the work is constructed based on a symmetric encryption system, Zhang's work keeps the advantage of efficiency as those works done in the spatial domain. In this paper, we deal with encrypted audios instead and propose a modified scheme as well as a reversible data hiding method with imperceptibility, efficiency, and acceptable capacity.

Human auditory system is more sensitive than the human visual system, so even a slight modification of audio signals can easily be perceived [7]. To narrow down the degradation of the stego-audio quality, we calculate a kind of smoothness threshold, defined as *NBI* (number of bits inverted), for each audio segment/frame. Obviously flipping more LSBs of all samples in an audio frame will make it less smooth, and then *NBI* is defined as the smallest value satisfying that the modified audio frame is less smooth than the original one. With a better smoothness measurement, *NBI* can be even smaller and caters for our data hiding work on audios.

In [10], Zhang defined

$$h = \sum_{u=2}^{s-1} \sum_{v=2}^{s-1} \left| p_{u,v} - \frac{p_{u-1,v} + p_{u,v-1} + p_{u+1,v} + p_{u,v+1}}{4} \right|, \tag{1}$$

as the measuring function for testing the spatial correlation of pixels in image blocks, where $p_{u,v}$ denotes the value of a pixel in position $(u,v)$ and $s$ denotes the block size. Lower $h$ function value implies higher correlation and local smoothness. The one-dimension version of Eq. (1) can be written as

$$\widetilde{h} = \sum_{l=2}^{f-1} \left| S_l - \frac{S_{l-1} + S_{l+1}}{2} \right|, \tag{2}$$

where $S_l$ denotes the value of the $l$-th sample in an audio frame and $f$ denotes the frame size. Both Eqs. (1) and (2) are second order smoothness measuring functions and are no longer good enough if audios are the target media. Therefore, a higher order version of $h$ (or $\widetilde{h}$) is considered in our scheme and the experimental result shows negligible degradation of stego-audios on a publicly available RWC Music Database [15].

## 2   Scheme and Algorithm

A modified version of the reversible data hiding scheme proposed by Zhang [10] for audios, is given in Fig. 1. Following similar idea, a content owner encrypts the original audio with an encryption key, and then a data-hider, having no knowledge of the content, embeds some additional data into the encrypted audio on the basis of a data-hiding key. If a receiver has the pre-negotiated encryption/decryption key, he/she can first decrypt the encrypted audio and get a data-embedded-but-decrypted version with high quality, which is listened much similar to the original audio. With the pre-negotiated data-hiding key, he/she can further recover the original audio and extract the additional embedded data. The main difference between [10] and our work is that, *NBI* information is pre-calculated by the data owner and then the data-hider embeds data with the help of this information for getting a surprisingly good performance. Again, this change is inspired by the fact that human's auditory system is more sensitive than its visual counterpart [7], and thus, audios usually ask for much higher *SNR* (signal-to-noise ratio) value than images when perceptual quality is of concern. Note that, in Fig. 1, the blocks with coarser borders are the newly proposed sub-procedures and a star symbol is adopted to differentiate the functional block of one sub-procedure from that of the original scheme [10], with similar name but conducting different works.

In most of the following discussions, a given audio is segmented into non-overlapped frames, and each frame is composed of $f$ samples. That is, the original audio can be represented as a sequence of audio frames $F_k$, where

$$F_k = [S_{k,0}, S_{k,1}, ..., S_{k,f-1}], \qquad k = 0, 1, 2, .... \tag{3}$$

In Eq. (3), $S_{k,l}$ $(0 \le l \le f-1)$ denotes the $l$-th sample of the $k$-th frame of the audio and it can be represented in binary form as

$$S_{k,l} = \sum_{u=0}^{t-1} b_{k,l,u} \cdot 2^u. \tag{4}$$

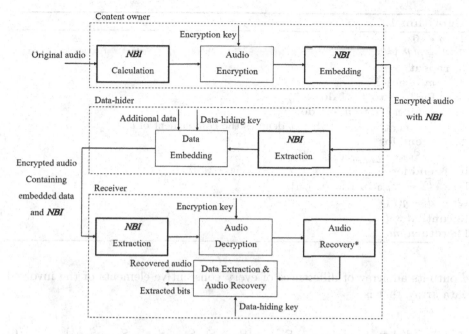

**Fig. 1.** A modified version of the scheme proposed by Zhang [10], in which (1) *NBI* information is transmitted from the content owner to the data-hider and then to the receiver, (2) some sub-procedures are newly proposed, and (3) the target media is changed from images to audios.

if a $t$-bit quantizer is used to quantize each audio sample. In other words, if $t = 16$, an audio sample value will lie in the range of [-32768 32767].

## 2.1 Content Owner Side

As illustrated in Fig. 1, the works done by the content owner can be divided into the following three steps.

***NBI* Calculation.** In this step, content owner calculates *NBI* information in advance which will be utilized by data-hider for data hiding. For each frame $F_k$, a corresponding integer $NBI_k$ between 1 and $t$ is determined by Algorithm 1.

The function $g$ is used to measure the smoothness and/or naturalness of an audio. Intuitively, the difference between two consecutive samples of a natural audio would be limited and Eq. (2) is a candidate for $g$ which can be further written in functional form as

$$h(A) = \frac{1}{2} sum(abs(d(d(A)))),  \tag{5}$$

where $A$ is an input audio frame (say $A = F_k$) or an array of audio samples, *abs* and *sum* respectively denote the summation and the absoluting operators, and

**Algorithm 1.**

1: $m \leftarrow 0$
2: $d \leftarrow g(F_k)$
3: **repeat**
4:     $m \leftarrow m + 1$
5:     **for** $l = 0$ **to** $f - 1$ **do**
6:         **for** $u = 0$ **to** $m - 1$ **do**
7:             $\widetilde{b}_{k,l,u} \leftarrow \overline{b_{k,l,u}}$ (where $\overline{b}$ denotes the complement of $b$)
8:         **end for**
9:         $\widetilde{S}_{k,l} \leftarrow \sum_{u=0}^{t-1} \widetilde{b}_{k,l,u} \cdot 2^u$
10:    **end for**
11:    $\widetilde{F}_k \leftarrow [\widetilde{S}_{k,0}, \widetilde{S}_{k,1}, ..., \widetilde{S}_{k,f-1}]$
12:    $\widetilde{d} \leftarrow g(\widetilde{F}_k)$
13: **until** $\widetilde{d} > d$
14: **return** $m$

$d$ outputs an array of differences of every consecutive elements of the involved data array, that is,

$$d(A \equiv [S_1, S_2, S_3, ..., S_n]) \equiv [S_2 - S_1, S_3 - S_2, ..., S_n - S_{n-1}]. \tag{6}$$

Moreover, we define

$$d^{(2)}(A) = d(d(A)),$$
$$d^{(n)}(A) = d(d^{(n-1)}(A)), \qquad n = 3, 4, 5.... \tag{7}$$

Omitting the scalar $1/2$ from Eq. 5, finally $g$ can be represented as

$$g(A) = sum(abs(d^{(2)}(A))). \tag{8}$$

The value of $g(F_K)$ is getting smaller as $F_k$ becomes smoother. For more discussions about the choice of $g$ function, please refer to Sect. 3.2 for the details.

In brief, what step 5 through step 11 did in Algorithm 1 is to invert all $m$ least significant bits of all samples of $F_k$. Figure 2 shows the results of this operation conducted on a sine wave, and it is clear from Fig. 2 that the fluctuation of the output waveforms becomes large as $m$ grows in value. For a given function $g$, the calculated $NBI_k$ with possible minimum value can help the data-hider do the embedding work with very good performance, that is, with very small quality degradation in the resulting stego-audio.

As shown in Fig. 1, an additional communication cost is a must for transmitting the $NBI$ information/sequence from the data owner side to the data-hider side, and the cost is inversely proportional to the frame size because as the frame size decreases the number of transmitted $NBI$ increases. However, one can embed the bits of $NBI_k$ into the encrypted audio frame $F_k$ to eliminate the cost (see Sect. 2.1 for details).

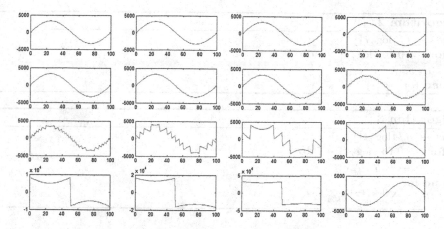

**Fig. 2.** Resulting waveforms of inverting $m$ ($1 \leq m \leq 16$) least significant bits of all 16-bits 100 samples of a sine wave. $m$ changes from 1 to 16 following the scan-line ordering (i.e., from left to right and from top to bottom).

**Audio Encryption.** For keeping the size of the cipher-text the same as that of the plain-text, a standard stream cipher is adopted to encrypt the target audio. The corresponding bit, $B_{k,l,u}$, of the cipher-text audio sample is determined by

$$B_{k,l,u} = b_{k,l,u} \otimes r_{k,l,u}, \qquad 0 \leq l \leq f - 1, 0 \leq u \leq t - 1, \qquad (9)$$

where $r_{k,l,u}$ is the encryption key and "$\otimes$" stands for the XOR operator.

**NBI Embedding.** The generated $NBI$ sequence can be embedded in the encrypted audio to eliminate the transmission cost. The size of one $NBI_k$ depends on the resolution of the audio quantizer, i.e. the number of bits per quantized sample. A $t$-bit quantizer results in $NBI_k$ valued from 1 to $t$, which costs $\lceil \log_2 t \rceil$ bits for storing. That is, $NBI_k$ can be represented in binary form as:

$$NBI_k = \sum_{u=0}^{\lceil \log_2 t \rceil - 1} c_{k,u} \cdot 2^u. \qquad (10)$$

For a normal setting, $\lceil \log_2 t \rceil$ is far less than the frame size $f$, and one method for embedding $\lceil \log_2 t \rceil$ bits of $NBI_k$ into the bitmap of $F_k$ is presented in Algorithm 2. In short, the most significant bits of some samples which are not close to each other in $F_k$ are overwritten by the bits of $NBI_k$. The less significant bits are prepared for data hiding and thus are not modified.

## 2.2 Data Hider Side

As illustrated in Fig. 1, the works done by the data-hider can be divided into the following two steps.

**NBI Extraction.** Data-hider first gets the $NBI$ sequence by reversely executing Algorithm 2, i.e. the Algorithm 3.

**Algorithm 2.**

$w \leftarrow \lfloor f / \lceil \log_2 t \rceil \rfloor$
for $l = 0$ to $\lceil \log_2 t \rceil - 1$ do
  $\widetilde{B}_{k,l \cdot w, t-1} \leftarrow c_{k,l}$
end for

**Algorithm 3.**

$w \leftarrow \lfloor f / \lceil \log_2 t \rceil \rfloor$
for $l = 0$ to $\lceil \log_2 t \rceil - 1$ do
  $c_{k,l} \leftarrow \widetilde{B}_{k,l \cdot w, t-1}$
end for
$NBI_k \leftarrow \sum_{u=0}^{\log_2 t - 1} c_{k,u} \cdot 2^u$

**Data Embedding.** With the *NBI* sequence and the pre-negotiated data-hiding key, data-hider embeds each bit of the stego-message into each frame of the encrypted audio by first dividing all samples within the frame, say $F_k$, into two mutually exclusive sets, say *Set-0* and *Set-1* according to the data-hiding key, and then executing Algorithm 4 to embed the stego-data.

**Algorithm 4.**

if the bit to be embedded is 0 **then**
  invert all $NBI_k$ least significant bits of all samples in *Set-0*
**else**
  invert all $NBI_k$ least significant bits of all samples in *Set-1*
**end if**

## 2.3  Receiver Side

As illustrated in Fig. 1, the works done by the receiver can be divided into the following four steps.

***NBI* Extraction.** Receiver first gets the *NBI* sequence as data-hider did.

**Audio Decryption.** With the encryption/decryption key $r_{l,u}$ sent from the content owner, receiver can recover the plain-text through the following operation:

$$b_{k,l,u} = B_{k,l,u} \otimes r_{k,l,u}. \tag{11}$$

As explained by Zhang in [10], the bits once inverted by data-hider in the cipher-text domain will remain inverted in the plain-text domain after decryption. That is,

$$b'_{k,l,u} = \overline{B_{k,l,u} \otimes r_{k,l,u}}$$
$$= \overline{\overline{b_{k,l,u} \otimes r_{k,l,u}} \otimes r_{k,l,u}}$$
$$= \overline{b_{k,l,u}}, \qquad u = 1, 2, ..., NBI_k, \qquad (12)$$

and the following equation holds:

$$b'_{k,l,u} + b_{k,l,u} = 1, \qquad u = 1, 2, ..., NBI_k. \qquad (13)$$

**Audio Recovery from the Corrupt Version Embedded with *NBI*.** Receiver recovers the audio from the *NBI*-corrupt version right after the above decryption step. The change of the value of one sample caused by *NBI* embedding could be $2^{t-1}$ or 0, since only the most significant bit is considered modified or not. From the high spatial correlation property of natural signals, Algorithm 5 is proposed.

---

**Algorithm 5.**

---

$w \leftarrow \lfloor f / \lceil \log_2 t \rceil \rfloor$
  **for** $l = 0$ **to** $\lceil \log_2 t \rceil - 1$ **do**
    $v_1 \leftarrow \sum_{u=0}^{t-2} b_{k,l \cdot w,u} \cdot 2^u$
    $v_2 \leftarrow 2^{t-1} + \sum_{u=0}^{t-2} b_{k,l \cdot w,u} \cdot 2^u$
    $interp \leftarrow (S_{k,l \cdot w-1} + S_{k,l \cdot w+1})/2$
    **if** $|v_1 - interp| \geq |v_2 - interp|$ **then**
      $b_{k,l \cdot w,t-1} \leftarrow 1$
    **else**
      $b_{k,l \cdot w,t-1} \leftarrow 0$
    **end if**
  **end for**

---

**Data Extraction and Audio Recovery.** With the pre-negotiated data-hiding key, the receiver can further extract the stego-message and recover the audio perfectly. Still, knowing of *NBI* information is a must. The corresponding data extraction and audio recovery processes are as follows.

The same as the data embedding process, the decrypted audio is segmented into non-overlapped frames and each frame is divided into two mutually exclusive sets *Set-0* and *Set-1* according to the data-hiding key. To extract the embedded stego-bit from a specific frame and jointly recover the original one, the spatial correlations of two modified versions of the frame are compared, as described in Algorithm 6.

---
**Algorithm 6.**

---
Given a frame $F_k$

$F_k^0 \leftarrow$ invert all $NBI_i$ least significant bits of all samples in *Set-0* of $F_k$
$F_k^1 \leftarrow$ invert all $NBI_i$ least significant bits of all samples in *Set-1* of $F_k$

**if** $g(F_k^0) > g(F_k^1)$ **then**
    **return** bit 1 and $F_k^1$
**else**
    **return** bit 0 and $F_k^0$
**end if**

---

As implied by the meaning of *NBI* or the calculation done in Algorithm 1, the frame with larger $g$-function value is exactly $\widetilde{F}_k$ in the step 11 of Algorithm 1 with $m$ being $NBI_k$ while the frame with smaller $g$-function value is the original audio frame created by the content owner. Note that there is no equal case between $g(F_k^0)$ and $g(F_k^1)$ in Algorithm 6, since $\widetilde{F}_k$ with $g(\widetilde{F}_k) > g(F_k)$ was figured out beforehand.

## 3    Experiment

### 3.1    Evaluation

A segmental signal-to-noise ratio (*segSNR*) testing tool [13] and a perceptual audio quality evaluation (PEAQ) software [14] are adopted to measure the objective quality degradation of the stego-audios. The latter is based on the ITU-R BS.1387 standard and outputs the objective difference grade (*ODG*) which is an impairment scale with "0" corresponding to "imperceptible", "-1" corresponding to "perceptible but not annoying", "-2" corresponding to "slightly annoying", etc.

### 3.2    Experimental Settings

We prepared 10 20-seconds single channel audio clips (c.f. Table 1), including speeches, pop songs, news, instrumental music, etc., as the host audios and a random sequence with '0', '1' as the stego-data to test our algorithms. Every host audio is of 44100 sampling rate and contains 16-bits samples.

Function $g$ and frame size $f$ are the two main factors to be adjusted. The former is decided based on the primitive goal of the scheme in Fig. 1: achieving small quality degradation of the stego-audio. Inverting some LSBs of samples can be viewed as an ideal method for data hiding since it provides small hints to the attacker who wants to unstego the audio illegally. Based on this method, smaller *NBI* implies smaller quality degradation and then the $g$ which produces smaller $NBI_k$ for each frame $F_k$ is the function we are going to choose. Considering the smoothness property of natural audios, Eq. (8) is a candidate, which calculates the sum of absolute values of the second derivatives of a discrete signal. Likewise,

**Table 1.** List of 10 testing audio clips (20s, mono, 16bits/sample, 44100 sampling rate) including both music and speech.

| Index | Tag | Brief description |
|---|---|---|
| 1 | Orchestra | Orchestra playing |
| 2 | Singing | Typical singing with background music |
| 3 | Piano | Monotonic piano playing |
| 4 | Soprano | Clip from movie "5 elemento" |
| 5 | Teaching | Sound-recording in class |
| 6 | Chinese | Chinese traditional music |
| 7 | News | SNG news programming |
| 8 | Twitch | Game Live streaming |
| 9 | Broadcast | Noisy news broadcasting |
| 10 | Pop song | Pop music with bass |

$$g_n(A) = sum(abs(d^{(n)}(A))) \tag{14}$$

calculates the sum of absolute values of the $n$-th derivatives of a discrete signal. In Eq. (14), more neighboring samples were taken as references when n increases.

As Fig. 3 shows, *NBI* tends to get smaller when $n$ grows. We take $n = 4$ here for both acceptable quality degradation (see Fig. 4) and computational efficiency. Fixing function $g$, the frame size $f$ can be further adjusted. Intuitively, the hiding capacity and/or embedding rate $EBR(bits/sample)$ will increase as $f$ decreases, that is,

$$EBR = k \cdot \frac{1}{f}, \tag{15}$$

where $k$ is the proportional constant and without loss of generality we can set $k = 1$ for the rest of our discussion.

However, if the length of *NBI* sequence grows, more communication costs and more information leakage will be introduced. We use *NBI* rate $NBIR(bits/sample)$ here to indicate the additional communication costs and we have

$$NBIR = \frac{4}{f} = 4 \cdot EBR, \tag{16}$$

since each *NBI* costs 4 bits. Of course, if Huffman coding is used to encode the *NBI* sequence, the above cost will be further reduced. For comparison purpose, the entropy, which is the theoretically optimal average code length of *NBI* is given in Table 2, for each test audio with $g_4$ and $f = 50$.

As shown in Fig. 4, the quality degradation of the stego-audio becomes larger as $f$ decreases. We take $f = 30$ here for providing acceptable quality degradation, efficiency and zero error rate.

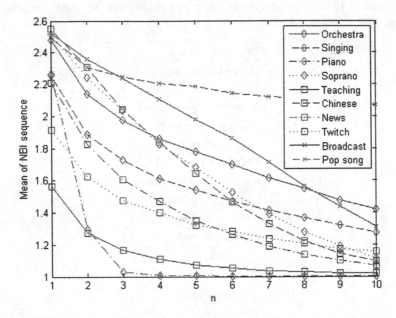

**Fig. 3.** Mean of *NBI* sequence of 10 test audios w.r.t. $n$ in Eq. (14), with frame size 50.

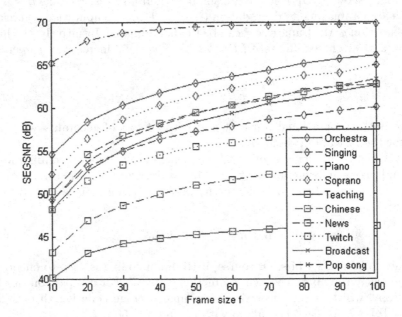

**Fig. 4.** Segmental signal-to-noise ratio w.r.t. Frame sizes on 10 testing audio clips (see Table 1) with function $g_4$ defined by Eq. (14).

**Table 2.** Some probabilities and entropy values of $NBI$ for each test audio, with $g = g_4$ and $f = 50$.

| Index | $P\{NBI = 1\}$ | $P\{NBI = 2\}$ | $P\{NDI - 3\}$ | Entropy(bits) |
|-------|------|------|------|------|
| 1 | 0.5502 | 0.2079 | 0.1272 | 1.8265 |
| 2 | 0.6403 | 0.1962 | 0.0998 | 1.5334 |
| 3 | 0.9906 | 0.0093 | 0 | 0.0765 |
| 4 | 0.5787 | 0.2027 | 0.1074 | 1.8007 |
| 5 | 0.9234 | 0.0539 | 0.0146 | 0.4871 |
| 6 | 0.5485 | 0.2115 | 0.1312 | 1.8014 |
| 7 | 0.6694 | 0.2239 | 0.0800 | 1.3197 |
| 8 | 0.7523 | 0.1450 | 0.0665 | 1.1865 |
| 9 | 0.5115 | 0.1930 | 0.1176 | 2.0694 |
| 10 | 0.5070 | 0.1858 | 0.1177 | 2.1624 |

### 3.3 Result

Given $g_4$ and $f = 30$, Table 3 shows the experimental results of the 10 test audios.

**Table 3.** Quality tests of the stego-audios corresponding to the 10 test audios given $g = g_4$ and $f = 30$. The error rate and embedding rate are shown together.

| Tag | $segSNR$(dB) | $ODG$ | Error rate | $EBR$(bps) |
|-----|------|------|------|------|
| Orchestra | 60.30 | 0.011 | 0 | 0.0333 |
| Singing | 54.91 | −0.063 | 0 | 0.0333 |
| Piano | 68.74 | −0.020 | 0 | 0.0333 |
| Soprano | 58.60 | −0.308 | 0 | 0.0333 |
| Teaching | 44.18 | −0.058 | 0 | 0.0333 |
| Chinese | 56.76 | −0.138 | 0 | 0.0333 |
| News | 48.62 | 0.069 | 0 | 0.0333 |
| Twitch | 53.36 | 0.017 | 0 | 0.0333 |
| Broadcast | 55.12 | −0.113 | 0 | 0.0333 |
| Pop song | 56.39 | −0.500 | 0 | 0.0333 |

### 3.4 Tests on Music Database

We further evaluate our method on a publicly available RWC Music Database [15] which contains 100 different types of audios (mono, 16 bits/sample, 44100 sampling rate were set). We find out that in some audios there could be small number of frames having no adequate *NBI* if the frame size is not large enough. For solving this problem and keeping acceptable capacity, we adopt a little additional trick in this situation (set *NBI* = 0). When data embedding, instead of inverting LSBs according to *NBI*, we invert fixed amount of LSBs to make samples be farther away from the origin. When data extraction, sum of distances between samples and their origins is calculated for comparison, and the one with a smaller value is indicated as the original frame.

For achieving zero error rate, we set $g_4$, $f = 50$ and invert 7 LSBs when *NBI* = 0. Figures 5 and 6 show the segSNR and the ODG results conducted on RWC database, respectively.

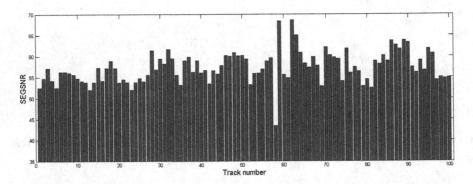

**Fig. 5.** Segmental signal-to-noise ratios of 100 audios in RWC Music Database.

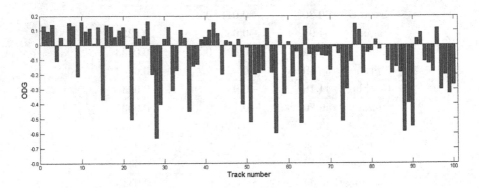

**Fig. 6.** Objective difference grades of 100 audios in RWC Music Database.

## 4    Conclusion

In this paper, a new reversible data hiding method for encrypted audios is proposed. With *NBI* information, data-hider having no knowledge of the original content can still embed the stego-data ideally into the encrypted audios. After decryption and recovery processes, the defects cause by the stego-data are nearly imperceptible (with average $ODG$ about -0.09 as shown in Fig. 6). If the receiver has the pre-negotiated data-hiding key, he/she can further recover the original audio and extract the stego-message without any error.

As mentioned above, the $NBI$ information plays an important role in the whole procedure. The value of $NBI_k$ changing with the naturalness of frame $F_k$ will limit the resulting quality degradation of $F_k$, or audio, to a small range. $NBI_k$ can be regarded as a feature of a signal segment while the entropy of the $NBI$ sequence can be regarded as a feature of the whole audio. The physical meaning and possible applications of the entropy of an $NBI$ sequence is worthy of further studying and is, of course, one of our future research directions.

The possibility for a legal receiver to extract the stego-data before conducting the decryption process is another interesting topic of our future work.

**Acknowledgments.** This work was supported in part by the Ministry of Science and Technology, National Taiwan University, and Intel Corporation under Grants MOST 103-2911-I-002-001, NTU-ICRP-104R7501, and NTU-ICRP-104R7501-1.

# References

1. Barton, J.M.: Method and apparatus for embedding authentication information within digital data. U.S. Patent 5646997 (1997)
2. Tian, J.: Reversible data embedding using a difference expansion. IEEE Trans. Circ. Syst. Video Technol. **13**(8), 90–93 (2003)
3. Thodi, D.M., Rodriguez, J.J.: Expansion embedding techniques for reversible watermarking. IEEE Trans. Image Process. **16**(3), 721–730 (2007)
4. Yan, D.Q., Wang, R.D.: Reversible data hiding for audio based on prediction error expansion. In: Intelligent Information Hiding and Multimedia Signal Processing, pp. 249–252 (2008)
5. Ni, Z.C., Shi, Y.Q., Ansari, N., Su, W.: Reversible data hiding. IEEE Trans. Circuits Syst. Video Technol. **16**(3), 354–362 (2006)
6. Tai, W.L., Yeh, C.M., Chang, C.C.: Reversible data hiding based on histogram modification of pixel differences. IEEE Trans. Circ. Syst. Video Technol. **19**(6), 906–910 (2009)
7. Wang, F., Xie, Z., Chen, Z.: High capacity reversible watermarking for audio by histogram shifting and predicted error expansion. Sci. World J. **2014**, Article ID 656251, 7 pages (2014)
8. Huang, X., Echizen, I., Nishimura, A.: A new approach of reversible acoustic steganography for tampering detection. In: Intelligent Information Hiding and Multimedia Signal Processing, pp. 538–542 (2010)
9. Li, M., Jiao, Y., Niu, X.: Reversible watermarking for compressed speech. In: Intelligent Information Hiding and Multimedia Signal Processing, pp. 197–201 (2008)
10. Zhang, X.: Reversible data hiding in encrypted images. IEEE Signal Process. Lett. **18**(4), 255–258 (2011)
11. Zhang, X.: Separable Reversible Data Hiding in Encrypted Image. IEEE Trans. Inf. Forensics Secur. **7**(2), 826–832 (2011)

12. Zhang, X., Qian, Z., Feng, G., Ren, Y.: Efficient reversible data hiding in encrypted images. J. Vis. Commun. Image Represent. **25**(2), 322–328 (2014)
13. VOICEBOX: Speech Processing Toolbox for MATLAB. http://www.ee.ic.ac.uk/hp/staff/dmb/voicebox/voicebox.html
14. Kabal, P.: An examination and interpretation of ITU-R BS.1387: Perceptual evaluation of audio quality, TSP Lab Technical Report, Dept. Electrical & Computer Engineering, McGill University, pp. 1–89 (2002)
15. Goto, M., Hashiguchi, H., Nishimura, T., Oka, R.: RWC music database: music genre database and musical instrument sound database. In: Proceedings of the 4th International Conference on Music Information Retrieval (ISMIR), pp. 229–230 (2003)

# Completely Separable Reversible Data Hiding in Encrypted Images

Dawen Xu[1,2](✉), Kai Chen[1], Rangding Wang[3], and Shubing Su[1]

[1] School of Electronics and Information Engineering,
Ningbo University of Technology, Ningbo 315016, China
xdw@nbut.edu.cn
[2] Shanghai Key Laboratory of Integrate Administration Technologies
for Information Security, Shanghai 200240, China
[3] CKC Software Lab, Ningbo University, Ningbo 315211, China

**Abstract.** As an emerging technology, reversible data hiding in encrypted images will be useful and popular in cloud computing due to its ability to preserve the confidentiality. In this paper, a novel framework of completely separable reversible data hiding in encrypted images is proposed. The cover image is first partitioned into non-overlapping blocks and specific encryption is applied to obtain the encrypted image. Then, image difference in the encrypted domain can be calculated based on the homomorphic property of the cryptosystem. The data-hider, who does not know the original image content, may reversibly embed secret data into image difference using a modified version of histogram shifting technique. Data extraction is completely separable from image decryption, i.e., data extraction can be done either in the encrypted domain or in the decrypted domain, so that it can be applied to different application scenarios. In addition, real reversibility is realized, that is, data extraction and image recovery are free of any error. Experimental results demonstrate the feasibility and efficiency of the proposed scheme.

**Keywords:** Image encryption · Reversible data hiding · Privacy protection · Histogram shifting · Homomorphic property

## 1 Introduction

With the rapid developments occurring in mobile internet and cloud storage, privacy and security of personal data has gained significant attention nowadays. The consumers would like to give the untrusted cloud server only an encrypted version of the data. The cloud service provider (who stores the data) is not authorized to access the original content (i.e., plaintext). However, in some scenarios, the cloud servers or database managers need to embed some additional messages directly into an encrypted data for tamper detection or ownership declaration purposes. For example, patient's information can be embedded into his/her encrypted medical image to avoid unwanted exposure of confidential information.

The capability of performing data hiding directly in encrypted images would avoid the leakage of image content, which can help address the security and privacy concerns

© Springer International Publishing Switzerland 2016
Y.-Q. Shi et al. (Eds.): IWDW 2015, LNCS 9569, pp. 365–377, 2016.
DOI: 10.1007/978-3-319-31960-5_30

with cloud computing. Data hiding in the encrypted version of image or video have been presented in recent years [1–3]. However, within these schemes [1–3], the host image/video is permanently distorted caused by data embedding. However, for a legal receiver, the original plaintext content should be recovered without any error after image decryption and data extraction. To solve this problem, reversible data hiding (RDH) in encrypted domain is preferred.

RDH techniques are gaining more attention for the last few years because of its increasing applications in some important and sensitive areas, i.e., military communication, healthcare, law-enforcement, and error concealment [4]. So far, three major approaches, i.e., lossless compression based [5], histogram modification based [6], difference expansion based [7], have already been developed for RDH. For more details of these methods and other RDH methods, refer to the latest review of recent research [8]. Although RDH techniques have been studied extensively, these techniques are suitable for unencrypted covers rather than encrypted covers. Nowadays, RDH in encrypted domain has emerged as a new and challenging research field [9]. In [10], Zhang divided the encrypted image into blocks, and each block carries one bit by flipping 3 Least Significant Bits (LSB) of each encrypted pixel in a set. Hong et al. [11] improved Zhang's method by adopting new smooth evaluation function and side-match mechanism to decrease the error rate of extracted bits. Later, several improved methods [12, 13] have also been proposed. Recently, Qian et al. [14] proposed a similar framework of RDH in an encrypted JPEG bitstream. However, in [10–14], the encrypted image containing hidden data should be first decrypted before data extraction.

To separate data extraction from image decryption, the method in [15] compressed the LSB of encrypted pixels to create a space for accommodating the additional data. Later, Zhang et al. [16] further proposed an improved scheme, in which a part of encrypted data is losslessly compressed using Low Density Parity Check (LDPC) code and used to carry the compressed data as well as the additional data. But the embedding capacity of these methods is relatively small and some errors occur during data extraction and/or image recovery. In order to achieve real reversibility, Ma et al. [17] provided a RDH idea in encrypted images by reserving room before encryption. Zhang et al. [18] proposed a reversibility improved RDH method in encrypted images. In [19], RDH in encrypted images based on interpolation technique is presented. However, in [17–19], prior to encrypting the image, room for data hiding should be vacated by shifting the histogram of estimating errors.

In this paper, we develop a more practical and reliable framework for reversible data hiding in encrypted domain. In contrast to the existing technologies discussed above, the new contribution of this paper is that the homomorphic property of the cryptosystem is exploited. Its advantages are mainly reflected in two aspects. First of all, room for data hiding does not need to be vacated before encryption, which is more reasonable compared with [17–19]. Second, completely separable and completely reversible can be achieved, which is more reliable than the methods in [10–16]. The rest of the paper is organized as follows. In Sect. 2, we describe the proposed scheme, which includes image encryption, data embedding in encrypted image, data extraction and original image recovery. Experimental results and analysis are presented in Sect. 3. Finally in Sect. 4, conclusion and future work are drawn.

## 2  Proposed Scheme

In this section, a RDH method in encrypted images is illustrated, which is made up of three parts, i.e., image encryption, data embedding in encrypted image, data extraction and image recovery. More precisely, the content owner encrypts the original image with encryption key to produce an encrypted image. Then, the data-hider without knowing the actual contents of the original images can embed some additional data into the encrypted image. Here, the data-hider can be a third party, e.g., a database manager or a cloud provider, who is not authorized to access the original content of the signal (i.e., plaintext). At the receiving end, maybe the content owner himself or an authorized third party can extract the hidden data either in encrypted or decrypted image. For illustrative purposes, the framework of the proposed scheme is given in Fig. 1.

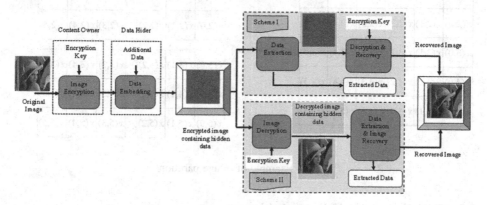

**Fig. 1.** The framework of proposed scheme

### 2.1  Image Encryption

Assume the original image $X$ is an 8 bit gray-scale image with its size $M \times N$ and pixels $x(i,j) \in [0, 255]$, $0 \leq i \leq M - 1$, $0 \leq j \leq N - 1$. The cover image is first divided into a number of non-overlapping blocks of size $3 \times 3$ as shown in Fig. 2. Then a pseudo-random matrix $C = \{c(p,q)|c(p,q) \in [0, 255], 0 \leq p \leq \lfloor \frac{M}{3} \rfloor + 1,$ $0 \leq q \leq \lfloor \frac{N}{3} \rfloor + 1\}$ is generated with the encryption key $En_{key}$. In order to encrypt the image $X$, the encryption matrix $R = \{r(i,j)|r(i,j) \in [0, 255]\}$ can be obtained via the following equation.

$$r(i,j) = c\left(\left\lfloor \frac{i}{3} \right\rfloor, \left\lfloor \frac{j}{3} \right\rfloor\right) \quad 0 \leq i \leq M - 1, \quad 0 \leq j \leq N - 1 \tag{1}$$

where $\lfloor i \rfloor$ denotes the greatest integer less than or equal to $i$. After getting the encryption matrix $R$, image encryption is done as follows.

$$S = E(X, R) = (x(i,j) + r(i,j)) \bmod 256 = s(i,j) \forall i = 0, 1, \ldots, M-1,$$
$$j = 0, 1, \ldots, N-1 \tag{2}$$

where $S$ is the encrypted image. The corresponding decryption can be accomplished in the following manner.

$$X = D(S, R) = (s(i,j) - r(i,j)) \bmod 256 = x(i,j)$$
$$\forall i = 0, 1, \ldots, M-1, \ j = 0, 1, \ldots, N-1 \tag{3}$$

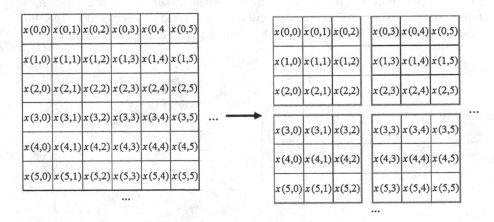

**Fig. 2.** Example of image partition

## 2.2 Data Embedding in Encrypted Image

After receiving the encrypted image, the data-hider can embed some additional information into it for the purpose of media notation or integrity authentication. Ni et al.'s histogram shifting-based algorithm [6] is an important work of RDH technique in terms of low distortion. However, the embedding capacity is not large enough since it highly dependents on the occurrence of the most frequent pixel value of the host image (i.e., peak points). Fortunately, there is a large probability that adjacent pixels in an image have similar pixel values. To enlarge the embedding capacity of the histogram-based scheme, the differences of adjacent pixels are exploited to hide secret data. The detailed procedure can be described as follows.

Step 1: Divide the encrypted image into non-overlapping $3 \times 3$ blocks, which is the same as Fig. 2. The center pixel in each block is selected as the basic pixel for prediction. If the width or height of the image is not a multiple of 3, then the edge block will be ignored during the data embedding process.

Step 2: Calculate the difference between the basic pixel and each pixel to form the prediction error. Here, the pixel located in coordinate $(i,j)$ is taken as the basic pixel for each block. Take $s(i, j+1)$ for example, the difference is calculated by using the following equation.

$$Diff(i,j+1) = (s(i,j+1) - s(i,j)) \bmod 256 \tag{4}$$

Although it should be noticed that $s(i,j+1)$ is encrypted pixel value, it is easy to prove the following equation.

$$(s(i,j+1) - s(i,j)) \bmod 256 = (x(i,j+1) - x(i,j)) \bmod 256 \tag{5}$$

*Proof:*

$$(s(i,j+1) - s(i,j)) \bmod 256 = ((x(i,j+1) + r(i,j+1)) \bmod 256 - (x(i,j) + r(i,j)) \bmod 256) \bmod 256$$
$$= ((x(i,j+1) + r(i,j+1)) - (x(i,j) + r(i,j))) \bmod 256$$
$\because r(i,j+1) = r(i,j)$    ( Refer to Eq. (1))
$\therefore (s(i,j+1) - s(i,j)) \bmod 256 = (x(i,j+1) - x(i,j)) \bmod 256$

Each block is sequentially processed in the same manner. After processing all blocks, the difference image is generated which has the same size as the original encrypted image.

Step 3: Generate the histogram of image difference which excludes the basic pixel in each block. In other words, eight differences are used in each block of $3 \times 3$ pixels. To demonstrate the distribution of the image difference, the histograms of some residual images are show in Fig. 3. It is clearly seen that the distribution is approximately symmetrical.

Step 4: Find the highest bin in the histogram. If the highest bin is located in the left side of the histogram, it can be denoted by $T_{pl}$. Data embedding is performed by modifying the histogram of the image difference. Specifically, for image difference $Diff(i,j+1)$, the embedding operation is formulated as

$$\overline{Diff}(i,j+1) = \begin{cases} Diff(i,j+1) + w & \text{if } Diff(i,j+1) = T_{pl} \\ Diff(i,j+1) + 1 & \text{if } Diff(i,j+1) \in [T_{pl}+1, T_{zl}-1] \end{cases} \tag{6}$$

where $\overline{Diff}(i,j+1)$ denotes the marked image difference, and $T_{zl}$ is the lowest bin. In addition, $w \in \{0, 1\}$ is the current to-be-embedded message bit.

Otherwise, if the highest bin is located in the right side of the histogram, it is denoted by $T_{pr}$. In this case, the image difference $Diff(i,j+1)$ can be modified as follows to hide message bit $w$:

$$\overline{Diff}(i,j+1) = \begin{cases} Diff(i,j+1) - w & \text{if } Diff(i,j+1) = T_{pr} \\ Diff(i,j+1) - 1 & \text{if } Diff(i,j+1) \in [T_{zr}+1, T_{pr}-1] \end{cases} \tag{7}$$

where $T_{zr}$ is the corresponding lowest bin of the histogram. Obviously, the capacity $C$ is equal to

$$C = \max\left(num\left(T_{pl}\right), num\left(T_{pr}\right)\right) \tag{8}$$

For example, if the highest bin is $T_{pl} = 0$ and the lowest bin is $T_{zl} = 125$, the first step is to empty +1 by shifting the bins between [1, 124] rightward by one level. Next, two cases should be addressed for one bit embedding. Similarly, if the highest bin is $T_{pr} = 255$ and the lowest bin is $T_{zr} = 128$, then the first step is to empty +254 by shifting the bins between [129, 254] leftward by one level.

According to the characteristic of modulus function, the following equation is established.

$$\begin{aligned} Diff(i,j+1) \pm 1 &= ((s(i,j+1) - s(i,j)) \bmod 256 \pm 1) \bmod 256 \\ &= ((s(i,j+1) \pm 1) \bmod 256 - s(i,j)) \bmod 256 \end{aligned} \tag{9}$$

From Eq. (9), the operation of $Diff(i,j+1) \pm 1$ can be accomplished by replacing $s(i,j+1)$ with $(s(i,j+1) \pm 1) \bmod 256$. Thus the marked and encrypted image $\tilde{S} = \{\tilde{s}(i,j) | \tilde{s}(i,j) \in [0, 255]\}$ of the proposed scheme is obtained.

However, ambiguities arise when non-boundary differences are changed from $T_{zl} - 1$ to $T_{zl}$ or from $T_{zr} + 1$ to $T_{zr}$ during the embedding process. The overlapping problem can be easily resolved using a location map $O_1$. It is a binary array with its every element corresponding to $T_{zl}$ and $T_{zr}$, 0 for genuine and 1 for pseudo.

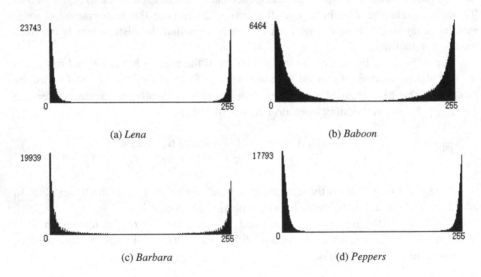

(a) Lena

(b) Baboon

(c) Barbara

(d) Peppers

**Fig. 3.** Histogram of image difference

## 2.3   Data Extraction and Original Image Recovery

In this scheme, data extraction and image decryption are completely separable. In other words, the hidden data can be extracted either in encrypted or decrypted domain, as shown in Fig. 1. We will first discuss the extraction in encrypted domain followed by decrypted domain.

(1)  Scheme I: Data Extraction in the Encrypted Domain

In the encrypted domain, the hidden data extraction can be accomplished by the following steps.

Step 1: Divide the encrypted image into non-overlapping $3 \times 3$ blocks, which is the same as Fig. 2. The center pixel in each block is selected as the basic pixel for prediction.

Step 2: Calculate the difference between the basic pixel and each pixel to form the prediction error. Similarly, take $\tilde{s}(i, j+1)$ for example, the difference is calculated by using the following equation.

$$\overline{Diff}(i, j+1) = (\tilde{s}(i, j+1) - \tilde{s}(i, j)) \bmod 256 \tag{10}$$

Step 3: Once the highest bin of the non-marked image difference, i.e., $T_{pl}$ or $T_{pr}$, is obtained, the hidden data $\tilde{w}$ can be extracted as

$$\tilde{w} = \begin{cases} 0 & \text{if } \overline{Diff}(i, j+1) = T_{pl} \text{ or } T_{pr} \\ 1 & \text{if } \overline{Diff}(i, j+1) = T_{pl} + 1 \text{ or } T_{pr} - 1 \end{cases} \tag{11}$$

Since the whole process is entirely operated in encrypted domain, it effectively avoids the leakage of original image content.

Step 4: If the highest bin of the non-marked image difference is $T_{pl}$, the mage difference can be further recovered using Eq. (12). Otherwise, Eq. (13) will be used.

$$Diff(i, j+1) = \begin{cases} \overline{Diff}(i, j) - 1 & \text{if } \overline{Diff}(i, j) \in [T_{pl}+1, T_{zl} - 1] \\ \overline{Diff}(i, j) & \text{otherwise} \end{cases} \tag{12}$$

$$Diff(i, j+1) = \begin{cases} \overline{Diff}(i, j) + 1 & \text{if } \overline{Diff}(i, j) \in [T_{zr}+1, T_{pr} - 1] \\ \overline{Diff}(i, j) & \text{otherwise} \end{cases} \tag{13}$$

Step 5: Decode the location map $O_1$ and restore the differences in marginal area, i.e., $T_{zl}$ or $T_{zr}$. Similarly, from Eq. (9), the operation of $\overline{Diff}(i, j+1) \pm 1$ can be accomplished by replacing $\tilde{s}(i, j+1)$ with $(\tilde{s}(i, j+1) \pm 1) \bmod 256$. Thus the encrypted image without the hidden data, i.e., $S = \{s(i, j) | s(i, j) \in [0, 255]\}$, is obtained. With the encryption key $En_{key}$, the original cover image can be completely restored by performing the decryption operation as Eq. (3).

(2)  Scheme II: Data Extraction in the Decrypted Domain

In scheme I, both data embedding and extraction are performed in encrypted domain. However, in some cases, users want to decrypt the image first and then extract the hidden data from the decrypted image when it is needed. The whole process of decryption and data extraction is comprised of the following steps.

Step 1: Image decryption can be accomplished according to the following equation.

$$\tilde{X} = (\tilde{s}(i, j) - r(i, j)) \bmod 256 = \tilde{x}(i, j) \quad \forall i = 0, 1, \ldots, M-1, \ j = 0, 1, \ldots, N-1 \tag{14}$$

Step 2: Divide the marked and decrypted image $\tilde{X} = \{\tilde{x}(i,j)|\tilde{x}(i,j) \in [0, 255]\}$ into non-overlapping $3 \times 3$ blocks, which is the same as Fig. 2. The center pixel in each block is selected as the basic pixel for prediction.

Step 3: Calculate the difference between the basic pixel and each pixel to form the prediction error. Similarly, take $\tilde{x}(i,j+1)$ for example, the difference can be calculated by using the following equation.

$$\overline{\overline{Diff}}(i,j+1) = (\tilde{x}(i,j+1) - \tilde{x}(i,j)) \bmod 256 \tag{15}$$

According to Eq. (5) which has been proved in Sect. 2.2, the following equation is established.

$$\overline{\overline{Diff}}(i,j+1) = \overline{Diff}(i,j+1) \tag{16}$$

Step 4: The hidden data $\tilde{w}$ can be extracted via the following equation.

$$\tilde{w} = \begin{cases} 0 & if \ \overline{\overline{Diff}}(i,j+1) = T_{pl} \ or \ T_{pr} \\ 1 & if \ \overline{\overline{Diff}}(i,j+1) = T_{pl} + 1 \ or \ T_{pr} - 1 \end{cases} \tag{17}$$

Step 5: According to the location of the highest bin, the image difference can be further recovered by using Eqs. (18) or (19).

$$Diff(i,j+1) = \begin{cases} \overline{\overline{Diff}}(i,j) - 1 & if \ \overline{\overline{Diff}}(i,j) \in [T_{pl}+1, T_{zl}-1] \\ \overline{\overline{Diff}}(i,j) & otherwise \end{cases} \tag{18}$$

$$Diff(i,j+1) = \begin{cases} \overline{\overline{Diff}}(i,j) + 1 & if \ \overline{\overline{Diff}}(i,j) \in [T_{zr}+1, \ T_{pr}-1] \\ \overline{\overline{Diff}}(i,j) & otherwise \end{cases} \tag{19}$$

Similarly, the operation of $\overline{\overline{Diff}}(i,j+1) \pm 1$ can be accomplished by replacing $\tilde{x}(i,j+1)$ with $(\tilde{x}(i,j+1) \pm 1) \bmod 256$. Therefore, the original image, i.e., $X = \{x(i,j)\}$, is successfully restored.

# 3   Experimental Results and Analysis

Four well-known standard gray images, i.e., *Lena, Baboon, Barbara, and Peppers* are considered for experimental purposes. The size of all images is $512 \times 512 \times 8$. The secret data is a binary sequence created by pseudo random number generator.

## 3.1   Security of Encryption Algorithm

For an image encryption scheme, the security depends on cryptographic security and perceptual security. Cryptographic security denotes the security against cryptographic attacks, which relies on the underlying cipher. In the proposed scheme, pseudo-random sequence $r(i,j)$ is used to encrypt image. Figure 4 illustrates the histogram of the original image. After encryption, the corresponding histogram is shown in Fig. 5. By comparing Figs. 4 and 5, it can be observed that the modified distribution appears to be uniform, which suggests that a statistical analysis would not be effective for evaluating the original image content.

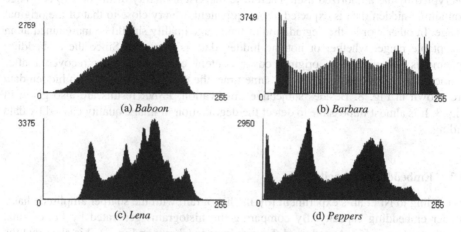

**Fig. 4.** Histogram of the original image

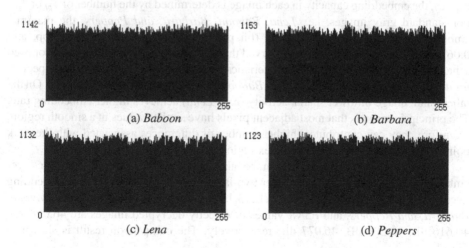

**Fig. 5.** Histogram of the corresponding encrypted image

Perceptual security refers to the encrypted image is unintelligible. The original images are given in Fig. 6, and their corresponding encrypted results are shown in Fig. 7. As can be seen, the visual information of the image is damaged, which means that there is no visual information available for the data-hider. In addition, *PSNR* (Peak Signal to Noise Ratio) values of four encrypted images are 9.529 dB, 9.515 dB,

7.865 dB, and 8.438 dB, respectively. Obviously, scrambling performance of the described encryption system is more than adequate.

## 3.2  Stego Image Quality

The encrypted image containing hidden data provided by the server should be decrypted by the authorized user. Therefore, the visual quality of the decrypted image containing hidden data is expected to be equivalent or very close to that of the original image. In other words, the degradation of the image quality should be maintained at an acceptable range, whether or not the hidden data is removed. Since the embedding scheme is reversible, the original cover content can be perfectly recovered after extraction of the hidden data. At the same time, the decrypted images with hidden data are shown in Fig. 8. Besides subjective observation, *PSNR* results are also given in Fig. 8. It is almost impossible to detect the degradation in image quality caused by data hiding.

## 3.3  Embedding Capacity

According to Ni et al.'s experiment [6], the histogram with the sharper amplitude has a higher embedding capacity. By comparing the histograms generated by the original images (shown in Fig. 4) and the difference images (shown in Fig. 3), it is clear that the histograms of the difference images change more dramatically in amplitude. According to Eq. (8), the embedding capacity in each image is determined by the number of $T_{pl}$ or $T_{pr}$. For standard gray images, i.e., *Lena, Baboon, Barbara, and Peppers*, the maximal embedding capacities are 0.0902 bpp (bit per pixel), 0.0242 bpp, 0.0752 bpp, and 0.0675 bpp, respectively. It can be observed that the embedding capacity of the proposed scheme depends strongly on the characteristics of the original cover image. As expected, for image of higher spatial activity (e.g., *Baboon*), low embedding rate is achieved. On the other hand, image of lower spatial activity (e.g., *Lena*) achieves higher embedding rate. The principal reason is that most adjacent pixels have similar values in a smooth region. Therefore, they can contribute a higher number of differences associated with the peak point compared with those in a complex region.

In addition, higher capacities can be also achieved by applying multiple-layer embedding strategy. For example, after two-layer embedding, the maximal embedding rates are 0.1732 bpp, 0.0482 bpp, 0.1243 bpp, and 0.1312 bpp for *Lena, Baboon, Barbara, and Peppers*, and *PSNR* values of directly decrypted images are 46.098 dB, 40.616 dB, 46.209 dB, 46.077 dB, respectively. The comparison result is shown in Fig. 9.

## 3.4  Comparison and Discussion

As mentioned in Sect. 1, the methods in [10–16] may introduce some errors on data extraction and/or image recovery, while the complete reversibility can be achieved in the proposed method. In addition, these methods are designed to carry relatively small

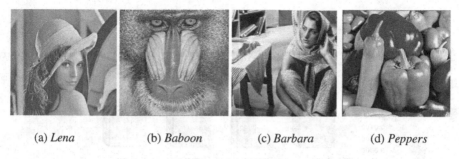

(a) *Lena*          (b) *Baboon*          (c) *Barbara*          (d) *Peppers*

**Fig. 6.** Original images

(a) *Lena*, PSNR= 9.529dB, (b) *Baboon*, PSNR= 9.515dB, (c) *Barbara*, PSNR= 7.865dB, (d) *Peppers*, PSNR= 8.438dB

**Fig. 7.** Encrypted images

(a) *Lena*, PSNR=51.342dB, (b) *Baboon*, PSNR= 41.007dB, (c) *Barbara*, PSNR= 51.649dB, (d) *Peppers*, PSNR=51.363dB

**Fig. 8.** Decrypted images containing hidden data

payloads. Take Zhang's method [10] and Hong et al.'s method [11] for example, the embedding rate is 0.0156 bpp associated with block size 8 × 8. If error correction mechanism is introduced, the actual embedding rate will be further decreased. It can be observed that our method achieves higher embedding rate. For methods in [17–19], completely error-free data extraction and image recovery can be obtained. However, end user has to cooperate with data hider, to vacate room before encryption. Moreover, the encryption algorithms are usually dedicated designed. Strictly speaking, it is not quite reasonable, as the embedding operations are always supposed to be accomplished not by the content owner but the service provided (i.e., data-hider).

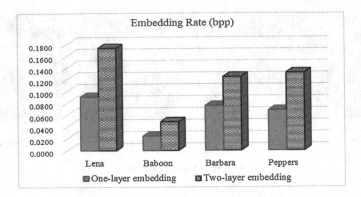

**Fig. 9.** Comparison result between one-layer embedding and two-layer embedding

## 4    Conclusions and Future Work

In this paper, an algorithm to reversibly embed secret data in encrypted images is presented, which consists of image encryption, data embedding and data extraction. The data-hider can embed the secret data into the encrypted image by modifying the histogram of image difference, even though he does not know the original image content. Since the embedding process is done on encrypted data, our scheme preserves the confidentiality of content. Data extraction is completely separable from image decryption, i.e., the additional data can be extracted either in encrypted domain or decrypted domain. Furthermore, this algorithm can achieve real reversibility, and high quality of marked and decrypted images. In future, considerable effort is needed to design more efficient reversible data hiding scheme that combines public-key encryption and somewhat homomorphic encryption [20].

**Acknowledgements.** This work is supported by the National Natural Science Foundation of China (61301247, 61170137, and 61300055), Public Welfare Technology Application Research Project of Zhejiang Province (2015C33237), Zhejiang Provincial Natural Science Foundation of China (LY13F020013, LZ15F020002), Ningbo Natural Science Foundation (2013A610059), Open Fund of Zhejiang Provincial Top Key Discipline (xkxl1405), Zhejiang Science and Technology Innovation Activities Project Foundation of College Students (2015R424015), and the Opening Project of Shanghai Key Laboratory of Integrate Administration Technologies for Information Security (AGK2013004).

## References

1. Subramanyam, A.V., Emmanuel, S., Kankanhalli, M.S.: Robust watermarking of compressed and encrypted JPEG2000 images. IEEE Trans. Multimedia **14**(3), 703–716 (2012)
2. Zheng, P., Huang, J.: Walsh-Hadamard transform in the homomorphic encrypted domain and its application in image watermarking. In: Kirchner, M., Ghosal, D. (eds.) IH 2012. LNCS, vol. 7692, pp. 240–254. Springer, Heidelberg (2013)

3. Xu, D.W., Wang, R.D., Shi, Y.Q.: Data hiding in encrypted H.264/AVC video streams by codeword substitution. IEEE Trans. Inf. Forensics Secur. **9**(4), 596–606 (2014)
4. Xu, D.W., Wang, R.D., Shi, Y.Q.: An improved reversible data hiding-based approach for intra-frame error concealment in H.264/AVC. J. Vis. Commun. Image Represent. **25**(2), 410–422 (2014)
5. Fridrich, J., Goljan, M., Du, R.: Lossless data embedding – new paradigm in digital watermarking. EURASIP J. Appl. Signal Process. **2002**(2), 185–196 (2002)
6. Ni, Z.C., Shi, Y.Q., Ansari, N., Su, W.: Reversible data hiding. IEEE Trans. Circ. Syst. Video Technol. **16**(3), 354–362 (2006)
7. Tian, J.: Reversible data embedding using a difference expansion. IEEE Trans. Circ. Syst. Video Technol. **13**(8), 890–896 (2003)
8. Khan, A., Siddiqa, A., Mubib, S., Malik, S.A.: A recent survey of reversible watermarking techniques. Inf. Sci. **279**, 251–272 (2014)
9. Xu, D.W., Wang, R.D.: Efficient reversible data hiding in encrypted H.264/AVC videos. J. Electron. Imaging **23**(5), 1–14 (2014)
10. Zhang, X.P.: Reversible data hiding in encrypted image. IEEE Signal Process. Lett. **18**(4), 255–258 (2011)
11. Hong, W., Chen, T.S., Wu, H.Y.: An improved reversible data hiding in encrypted images using side match. IEEE Signal Process. Lett. **19**(4), 199–202 (2012)
12. Liao, X., Shu, C.W.: Reversible data hiding in encrypted images based on absolute mean difference of multiple neighboring pixels. J. Vis. Commun. Image Represent. **28**, 21–27 (2015)
13. Wu, X.T., Sun, W.: High-capacity reversible data hiding in encrypted images by prediction error. Signal Process. **104**, 387–400 (2014)
14. Qian, Z.X., Zhang, X.P., Wang, S.Z.: Reversible data hiding in encrypted JPEG bitstream. IEEE Trans. Multimedia **16**(5), 1486–1491 (2014)
15. Zhang, X.P.: Separable reversible data hiding in encrypted image. IEEE Trans. Inf. Forensics Secur. **7**(2), 826–832 (2012)
16. Zhang, X.P., Qian, Z.X., Feng, G.R., Ren, Y.L.: Efficient reversible data hiding in encrypted images. J. Vis. Commun. Image Represent. **25**(2), 322–328 (2014)
17. Ma, K.D., Zhang, W.M., Zhao, X.F., et al.: Reversible data hiding in encrypted images by reserving room before encryption. IEEE Trans. Inf. Forensics Secur. **8**(3), 553–562 (2013)
18. Zhang, W.M., Ma, K.D., Yu, N.H.: Reversibility improved data hiding in encrypted images. Signal Process. **94**, 118–127 (2014)
19. Xu, D., Wang, R.: Reversible data hiding in encrypted images using interpolation and histogram shifting. In: Shi, Y.-Q., Kim, H.J., Pérez-González, F., Yang, C.-N. (eds.) IWDW 2014. LNCS, vol. 9023, pp. 230–242. Springer, Heidelberg (2015)
20. Cheon, J.H., Kim, J.: A hybrid scheme of public-key encryption and somewhat homomorphic encryption. IEEE Trans. Inf. Forensics Secur. **10**(5), 1051–1063 (2015)

# Optimal Histogram-Pair and Prediction-Error Based Reversible Data Hiding for Medical Images

Xuefeng Tong[1], Xin Wang[1(⊠)], Guorong Xuan[1], Shumeng Li[1], and Yun Q. Shi[2]

[1] Department of Computer Science, Tongji University, Shanghai, China
2014wangx@tongji.edu.cn
[2] ECE, New Jersey Institute of Technology, Newark, NJ, USA

**Abstract.** In recent years, with the development of application research on medical images and medical documents, it is urgent to embed data, such as patient's personal information, diagnostic information and verification information into medical images. Reversible data hiding for medical images is the technique of embedding medical data into medical images. However, most existed schemes of reversible data hiding for medical images could not achieve high performance and high payloads. This paper presents a reversible data hiding scheme for medical images based on histogram-pair and prediction-error. As the prediction-error histogram of medical images, compared with the gray level histogram of medical images, is more in line with quasi-Laplace distribution, histogram-pair and prediction-error based method could achieve high performance. We adjust the following four thresholds for optimal performance: embedding threshold, fluctuation threshold, left- and right-histogram shrinking thresholds. The left- and right-histogram shrinking thresholds are used not only to avoid underflow and/or overflow but also to achieve optimum performance. Compared to previous works, the proposed scheme has significant improvement in embedding capacity and marked image quality for medical images.

**Keywords:** Medical image · Reversible data hiding · Histogram-pair · Prediction-error

## 1 Introduction

With the rapid development of information technology, medical information, such as medical images and electronic patient records, is digitized and transmitted conveniently and quickly among patients, medical professionals and medical institutions through the Internet. With these benefits, there are some issues that need to be addressed. First of all, patients' privacies should be preserved in open networks [1]. Hence, embedding

This research is largely supported by Shanghai City Board of education scientific research innovation projects (12ZZ033) and National Natural Science Foundation of China (NSFC) on projects No. 90304017 and No. 61175014.

© Springer International Publishing Switzerland 2016
Y.-Q. Shi et al. (Eds.): IWDW 2015, LNCS 9569, pp. 378–391, 2016.
DOI: 10.1007/978-3-319-31960-5_31

patients' information data into medical images would be one of the effective methods for protecting privacies. Second, the cover image is supposed to be able to be recovered without any loss after the hidden information has been extracted in order to introduce any interference to diagnosis. To sum up, high quality, high capacity, authentication and reversibility are the main requirements for data hiding in medical images [1]. Therefore, it is important to develop an efficient reversible data hiding schemes to embedding data into medical images.

In the past two decades, a variety of reversible data hiding schemes have been proposed. Tian [2] proposed a technique of pixel-value difference expansion (DE) by performing arithmetic operations on pairs of pixel to explore hide-able spaces. Kim et al. [3] proposed an enhanced pixel-value difference expansion method achieving higher data hiding capacities by location map. With the DE-based schemes, data embedding capacity is limited to 0.5 bits per pixel (bpp) if the data hiding is done by once. Besides, Ni et al. [4] proposed a reversible data hiding method based on histogram shifting which shifts the part of the histogram between the maximum and minimum points to the right side by one unit to create a gap for hiding the data. This method enhanced the quality of marked image and has also been widely investigated and developed. And then Fallahpour and Sedaaghi [5] proposed an improved scheme which dividing the image into tiles and inserting data into the gap created by histogram shifting. This method successfully improved the data hiding capacity and enhanced the marked image quality and was applied into reversible data hiding for medical images [6]. Later, reversibly embedding data into prediction-error [7] is another effective scheme to largely boost embedding effectiveness in terms of the peak signal to noise ratio (PSNR) of the image with data hidden with respect to the original image versus data embedding rate. Xuan et al. [8] proposed a scheme to reversibly embed data into image prediction-errors by using histogram-pair method with the following four thresholds: embedding threshold, fluctuation threshold, left- and right- histogram shrinking thresholds. This scheme significantly improves the data hiding payload and marked image quality.

In this paper, we propose a reversible data hiding method based on histogram-pair and prediction-error for medical images. Compared with previous work [6], the proposed method achieves high data hiding capacity and high marked image quality.

The rest of this paper is organized as follows: Sect. 2 describes the proposed method. Experimental results and analysis are presented in Sect. 3. The conclusion is made in Sect. 4.

## 2 Proposed Method

The main idea of the reversible data hiding method based on optimal histogram-pair and prediction-error is to select histogram-pairs in the image prediction-error histogram and then shift the prediction-error of those pixels within the histogram-pair frequency range by one level, towards the minimum frequency level in the histogram-pair.

In this section, a simple example to explain the principle of histogram-pair in the first place and then the prediction-error is mentioned below. Next, we illustrate the four thresholds. After that, the optimal algorithm is presented. Finally, the data embedding and data extracting algorithm are presented in detail.

## 2.1 Histogram-Pair

We present a very simple example for the purpose of understanding the fundamental principle of histogram-pair reversible data hiding.

In Fig. 1(a), the original image containing only 9 pixels has 4 different gray values: $\{6, 7, 8, 9\}$. Its histogram is $[h(6), h(7), h(8), h(9)] = [4, 3, 1, 1]$. We suppose the data to be embedded are four bits: $[0, 1, 1, 0]$.

In Fig. 1(b), to avoid overflow or underflow after embedding data, histogram modification is executed. A pixel with gray value 9 is changed to 8. The information of this change called bookkeeping data will also be embedded into image in order to recover the original image reversibly as the hidden data are extracted late. So the histogram is changed to $[h(6), h(7), h(8), h(9)] = [4, 3, 2, 0]$.

In Fig. 1(c), we create a histogram-pair $[h(6), h(7)] = [4, 0]$ by shifting three pixels' gray values form 7 to 8 and two pixels' gray values from 8 to 9. Hence, the histogram is changed to $[h(6), h(7), h(8), h(9)] = [4, 0, 3, 2]$. The histogram-pair $[h(6), h(7)] = [4, 0]$ can be used to embed data.

In Fig. 1(d), four bits $[0, 1, 1, 0]$ are embedded into this histogram-pair and the histogram-pair $[h(6), h(7)] = [4, 0]$ changes to $[h(6), h(7)] = [2, 2]$. After four bits embedded, the histogram changes to $[h(6), h(7), h(8), h(9)] = [2, 2, 3, 2]$. It's worth pointing out that the bookkeeping data need to be embedded into the image for the image recovery late and this detail is not shown here.

| 6 | 7 | 6 | | 6 | 7 | 6 | | 6 | 8 | 6 | | 6 | 8 | 7 |
|---|---|---|---|---|---|---|---|---|---|---|---|---|---|---|
| 6 | 8 | 7 | | 6 | 8 | 7 | | 6 | 9 | 8 | | 7 | 9 | 8 |
| 7 | 6 | 9 | | 7 | 6 | 8 | | 8 | 6 | 9 | | 8 | 6 | 9 |
| (a) | | | | (b) | | | | (c) | | | | (d) | | |

Fig. 1. Simple example of data hiding by histogram-pair (a) original image, (b) histogram modification, (c) creation of histogram-pair, (d) after data embedded.

## 2.2 Prediction-Error

In the proposed method, we choose a pixel, x, for embedding a bit and consider its eight-neighbor, $x_1, x_2, x_3, x_4, x_5, x_6, x_7, x_8$, shown in Eq. 1. Because the fluctuation and prediction-error could not be calculated by the eight-neighbor in image edge part, in a $M \times H$ image, we scan those pixels, $(x, y)$, $2 \leq x \leq M-1$, $2 \leq y \leq H-1$, by raster order.

$$\begin{bmatrix} x_1 & x_4 & x_6 \\ x_2 & x & x_7 \\ x_3 & x_5 & x_8 \end{bmatrix} \tag{1}$$

The prediction-error, $P_E$, defined as Eq. 2. The average value of eight-neighbor, $\bar{x}$, could be seen as the prediction of the central pixel. The prediction-error is the difference between the pixel to be embedded and the average value of its eight-neighbor pixels. Due to the spatial correlation of the image pixels, this difference is normally rather small. The prediction-error histogram obeys quasi-Laplace distribution. For this reason, the prediction-error and histogram-pair based method is more suitable for reversible data hiding.

$$P_E = x - \bar{x} \text{ where } \bar{x} = \left\lfloor (1/12) \left( \sum_{i=1,3,6,8} x_i + \sum_{i=2,4,5,7} 2x_i \right) \right\rfloor \tag{2}$$

### 2.3  Four Thresholds

1. Fluctuation threshold, $T_F$

Before embedding data, we calculate the fluctuation F of each candidate pixel using Eq. 3 from its surrounding eight-neighbor and compare the fluctuation with the fluctuation threshold $T_F$. Then, All pixels in the image are divided into two parts. One part of pixels whose fluctuation is no less than the fluctuation threshold would be untouched. The other part of pixels can possibly be embedded. In this way, we could embed data in smooth areas of the original image to improve the quality of marked image.

$$F = (1/3) \left( \sum_{i=1,3,6,8} (x_i - \bar{x})^2 + \sum_{i=2,4,5,7} 2(x_i - \bar{x})^2 \right) \tag{3}$$

2. Embedding threshold, T

We select the embedding threshold T and generate a pair of thresholds, positive embedding threshold $T_P$ and negative embedding threshold $T_N$, by T. Next, the histogram-pair method is used to embed data. Different from previous works, the histogram-pairs are not chosen from the gray level histogram but the prediction-error histogram. Each pixel under consideration, which has satisfied the fluctuation threshold, is changed or not by comparing the positive or negative embedding threshold with the corresponding the positive or negative value of the pixel's prediction-error. All details are shown in Eq. 7.

3. Left- and Right-histogram shrinking thresholds, $T_L$, $T_R$

Before embedding data, left-histogram shrinking threshold $T_L$ is used to shrink the gray level at left histogram by $T_L$ to prevent underflow after data embedding. And right-histogram shrinking threshold $T_R$ is used to shrink the gray level at right histogram by $T_R$ to prevent overflow after data embedding. When shrinking the histogram, we record shrinking pixels as bookkeeping data for late recovering the original image reversibly. Because the bookkeeping data will be embedded into the host image, we must select the optimal shrinking gray values to enhance the pure payload and the quality of the marked image. The left-histogram shrinking cost of each gray value is calculated by the function, shown in Eq. 4. The right-histogram shrinking cost of each gray value is calculate by another function, shown in Eq. 5. In the two functions, $w_1$ and $w_2$ are two weight coefficients, x is the gray value and h(x) represents the number of pixels whose gray value equals to x. And then, some of the gray values with smaller shrinking costs are selected as left- and right-histogram shrinking gray values.

$$f_L(x) = w_1 \times (h(x) + h(x+1)) + w_2 \times \sum_{i=0}^{x} h(i), \ 0 \leq x < 255 \tag{4}$$

$$f_R(x) = w_1 \times (h(x-1) + h(x)) + w_2 \times \sum_{i=x}^{255} h(i), \ 0 < x \leq 255 \tag{5}$$

Note that some common test images, e.g., Lena, shown in Fig. 2, Barbara, and Airplane, have two ends of their histogram being zero, whereas medical images, e.g., Im3, shown in Fig. 3, with both sides of its histogram having peaks, shown in Fig. 4. Hence, reversible data hiding in medical images frequently may lead to underflow and/or overflow. Different from the previous works, in the proposed method the left- and right-histogram shrinking thresholds are adjusted not only to prevent underflow and/or overflow but also to achieve the optimal performance in reversible data hiding. The proposed scheme with left- and right-histogram shrinking thresholds is especially suitable for reversible data hiding in medical images.

**Fig. 2.** Lena (512 × 512)

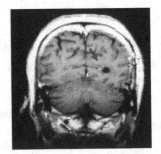

**Fig. 3.** Im3 (512 × 512)

## 2.4   Optimal Algorithm

Under the constraints of no underflow and/or overflow and the requirement of the given payloads, we adjust the four thresholds: embedding threshold T, fluctuation threshold

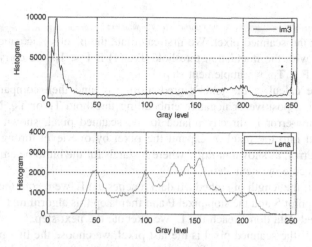

**Fig. 4.** Histogram of Im3 image and Lena image

$T_F$, left- and right-histogram shrinking thresholds $T_L$ and $T_R$, for optimal marked image quality, shown in Eq. 6.

$$[T, T_F, T_L, T_R] = \underset{\substack{neither\ underflow\ nor\ overflow \\ meeting\ embedding\ capacity}}{\arg\max} [PSNR(Payload)] \qquad (6)$$

## 2.5   Data Embedding Algorithm

First of all, we have the original image I of size M × H, each pixel grayscale value x ∈ [0, 255], and to be embedded data D (length L) and then select a set of four thresholds, T, $T_F$, $T_L$ and $T_R$. As mentioned before, we shrink the histogram of the original image towards the center by $T_L$ and $T_R$ and record the bookkeeping data before data embedding. Then, a pair of positive embedding threshold $T_P$ and negative embedding threshold $T_N$, as said in Sect. 2.3, are generated from T. For example, if the algorithm embeds data in T = 4, we scan the image and embed data into both $T_P = 4$ and $T_N = -4$ corresponding with the scanned pixel's prediction-error. If the data have not been completely embedded yet, after data embedded into $T_P = 4$ and $T_N = -4$, the next pair of $T_P = 3$ and $T_N = -3$ is generated. In this way, the data would be embedded in an order of {4, −4}, {3, −3}, {2, −2}, {1, −1}, {0} or {−4, 3}, {−3, 2}, {−2, 1}, {−1, 0}. In addition, It is not necessary that the data embedding algorithm has to end up at {0}. It can end up at any value in the sequence prior to 0 as long as the embedding capacity meets the requirement and the value is recorded as stop point S. With raster order scanning pixels, the data embedding algorithm is presented as follows:

Input: original image I, to be embedded data D (length L), four thresholds T, $T_F$, $T_L$ and $T_R$

Output: marked image I', stop point S, stop pixel P

Procedures:

- Step 1. For the scanned pixel, We first calculate the pixel's fluctuation F and then compare it with the fluctuation threshold $T_F$. (1) If $F < T_F$, we carry out the next step. (2) If $F \geq T_F$, we implement step 4.
- Step 2. We calculate the pixel's prediction-error and then compare it with the corresponding positive or negative embedding threshold $T_P$ or $T_N$. Next, because the prediction-error is directly related to the scanned pixel, shown in Eq. 2, we embed a bit into the pixel or expand the pixel by one level through altering the prediction-error, as shown in Eq. 7 where b stands for the bit to be embedded. After that, we execute the next step.
- Step 3. (1) If the length of embedded data reaches the L, we record the last $T_P$ or $T_N$ as the stop point S and the stop pixel P and then stop this algorithm. (2) If the length of embedded data don't reach the L, we execute the next step.
- Step 4. (1) If the scanned pixel is the last pixel, we choose the first pixel of a scan and select the next pair of positive and negative embedding thresholds $T_P$ and $T_N$ to embed data. Then, we implement Step 1. (2) If the scanned pixel is not the last pixel, we choose next pixel in raster order. Then, we implement Step 1.

$$P_E = \begin{cases} P_E - 1, & \text{if } P_E < T_N \\ P_E - b, & \text{if } P_E = T_N \\ P_E, & \text{if } T_N < P_E < T_P \\ P_E + b, & f\ P_E = T_P \\ P_E + 1, & \text{if } P_E > T_P \end{cases} \tag{7}$$

## 2.6   Data Extracting Algorithm

In data extracting, we recover the original image and extract data by stop point S, stop pixel P, marked image I', embedding threshold T and fluctuation threshold $T_F$. A set of $T_P$ and $T_N$ is derived from T and S. With reverse raster order scanning from stop pixel P, the data extracting algorithm is presented as follows.

Input: marked image I', embedding threshold T, fluctuation threshold $T_F$, stop point S, stop pixel P
Output: original image I, data D

Procedures:

- Step 1. We calculate the scanning pixel's fluctuation F and then compare F with fluctuation threshold $T_F$. (1) If $F < T_F$, we execute the next step. (2) If $F \geq T_F$, we implement step 4.
- Step 2. The pixel's prediction-error is calculated and compared with the positive embedding threshold $T_P$ and the negative embedding threshold $T_N$ generated from T, as shown in Eqs. 2 and 8 where b stands for the extracted bit. In this way, the bit is extracted and the pixel's value are recovered. After that, we execute the next step.

- Step 3. (1) If all of embedded data have been extracted, we stop data extracting algorithm. (2) If all of embedded data have not been extracted, we implement the next step.
- Step 4. (1) If the pixel is the first pixel which is also the last extracting pixel, we select the next pair of $T_P$ and $T_N$, by $T_P = T_P + 1$ and $T_N = T_N - 1$. We choose the last pixel which is the first extracting pixel and then execute step 1. (2) If the pixel is not the first pixel, we choose next pixel in reverse raster order and then execute step 1.

After extracting the embedded data D of the length L, reversibly, we use the bookkeeping data to recover the original image reversibly.

$$P_E = \begin{cases} P_E + 1, & & if\ P_E < T_N - 1 \\ P_E + 1, & b = 1 & if\ P_E = T_N - 1 \\ P_E, & b = 0 & if\ P_E = T_N \\ P_E, & & if\ T_N < P_E < T_P \\ P_E, & b = 0 & if\ P_E = T_P \\ P_E - 1, & b = 1 & if\ P_E = T_P + 1 \\ P_E - 1, & & if\ P_E > T_P + 1 \end{cases} \qquad (8)$$

## 3 Experimental Results and Analysis

We have implemented the proposed method and compared the performance of the proposed method with algorithms in [6] on a variety of medical images, shown in Fig. 5. The size of the original medical images is $512 \times 512$ with 8-bit depth.

The optimal four thresholds: T, $T_F$, $T_L$ and $T_R$ utilized, the resultant PSNR achieved on the ten test images by applying the optimal histogram-pair and prediction-error reversible data hiding method with various data embedding rates ranging from 0.01 bpp to 0.7 bpp are listed in Table 1. As said in Sect. 2.5, S is the stop value of the embedding threshold T. As the table shows, our presented method has high quality of ten marked images with embedding rate from 0.01 bpp to 0.7 bpp.

It is also observed that as low embedding rate is between 0.01 bpp and 0.1 bpp, $T_L$ and/or $T_R$ will not be all zero in most of ten medical images, therefore we have to shrink the histogram to avoid underflow and/or overflow. Whereas the $T_L$ and $T_R$ are all zero for Lena with data embedding rate not larger than 0.7 bpp, shown in [8]. Above all, overflow and/or underflow in reversible data hiding in medical images is more likely to occur compared with reversible data hiding into common images. Note that the proposed method with histogram shrinking not only avoids the problem but also works for optimal performance. It is suitable for reversible data hiding for medical images in particular.

The performance comparison on two medical images, Im5 and Im10, in terms of PSNR versus pure payload among the proposed method, and shifted histograms of whole, 4- and 16-tile versions [6], defined as WSH, TSH-4 and TSH-16, are shown in Figs. 6 and 7. Compared with Ni et al. [4] and Fallahpour et al. [6], the proposed method could significantly improve the data hiding capacity and the marked image quality.

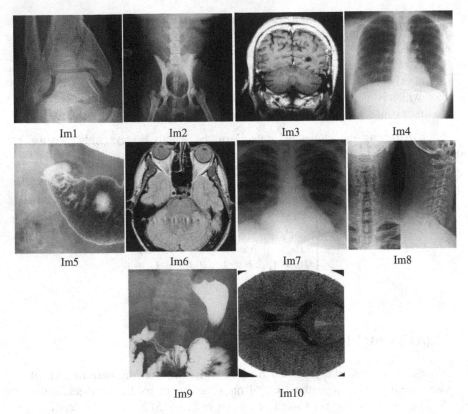

**Fig. 5.** Ten original medical images

**Table 1.** PSNR and optimal thresholds on ten test images with different payloads

Im1

| bpp | 0.01 | 0.02 | 0.03 | 0.04 | 0.05 | 0.1 | 0.2 | 0.3 | 0.4 | 0.5 | 0.6 | 0.7 |
|------|------|------|------|------|------|------|------|------|------|------|------|------|
| PSNR | 71.09 | 65.29 | 62.14 | 58.94 | 58.16 | 54.89 | 51.14 | 48.83 | 45.58 | 44.12 | 42.21 | 40.86 |
| T | 0 | 0 | 0 | −1 | −1 | −1 | −1 | −1 | −2 | −2 | −3 | 3 |
| $T_F$ | 1 | 12 | 20 | 9 | 12 | 32 | 90 | 435 | 671 | 527 | 286 | 705 |
| $T_L$ | 0 | 0 | 0 | 1 | 1 | 1 | 1 | 1 | 2 | 2 | 3 | 3 |
| $T_R$ | 0 | 0 | 0 | 0 | 0 | 0 | 0 | 0 | 0 | 0 | 0 | 0 |
| S | 0 | 0 | 0 | 0 | −1 | −1 | −1 | −1 | 0 | 0 | 0 | 0 |

Im2

| bpp | 0.01 | 0.02 | 0.03 | 0.04 | 0.05 | 0.1 | 0.2 | 0.3 | 0.4 | 0.5 | 0.6 | 0.7 |
|------|------|------|------|------|------|------|------|------|------|------|------|------|
| PSNR | 70.02 | 66.78 | 65.06 | 63.8 | 62.86 | 59.93 | 56.56 | 54.64 | 52.82 | 50.99 | 48.45 | 46.53 |
| T | 0 | 0 | 0 | 0 | 0 | 1 | −1 | −1 | −1 | −1 | 1 | −2 |
| $T_F$ | 1 | 4 | 4 | 4 | 4 | 5 | 5 | 8 | 16 | 44 | 78 | 205 |
| $T_L$ | 0 | 0 | 0 | 0 | 0 | 1 | 1 | 1 | 1 | 1 | 1 | 2 |
| $T_R$ | 0 | 0 | 0 | 0 | 0 | 0 | 0 | 0 | 0 | 0 | 0 | 0 |
| S | 0 | 0 | 0 | 0 | 0 | −1 | −1 | 0 | 0 | 0 | 0 | 1 |

*(Continued)*

**Table 1.** (*Continued*)

Im3

| bpp | 0.01 | 0.02 | 0.03 | 0.04 | 0.05 | 0.1 | 0.2 | 0.3 | 0.4 | 0.5 | 0.6 | 0.7 |
|---|---|---|---|---|---|---|---|---|---|---|---|---|
| PSNR | 70.68 | 67.1 | 65.24 | 58.7 | 58.67 | 57.42 | 55.34 | 53.76 | 52.34 | 50.97 | 48.03 | 46.71 |
| T | 0 | -1 | -1 | 0 | 0 | 0 | 0 | -1 | -1 | -1 | 1 | -2 |
| $T_F$ | 4 | 4 | 16 | 72 | 134 | 32 | 54 | 13 | 42 | 177 | 396 | 493 |
| $T_L$ | 0 | 1 | 1 | 0 | 0 | 0 | 0 | 1 | 1 | 1 | 1 | 2 |
| $T_R$ | 0 | 0 | 0 | 1 | 1 | 1 | 1 | 1 | 1 | 1 | 2 | 2 |
| S | 0 | -1 | -1 | 0 | 0 | 0 | 0 | -1 | -1 | 0 | -1 | -2 |

Im4

| bpp | 0.01 | 0.02 | 0.03 | 0.04 | 0.05 | 0.1 | 0.2 | 0.3 | 0.4 | 0.5 | 0.6 | 0.7 |
|---|---|---|---|---|---|---|---|---|---|---|---|---|
| PSNR | 71.08 | 68.03 | 66.36 | 65.12 | 64.16 | 60.97 | 57.92 | 56.14 | 54.73 | 53.56 | 52.6 | 51.75 |
| T | 0 | 0 | 0 | 0 | 0 | 0 | -1 | -1 | --1 | -1 | -1 | -1 |
| $T_F$ | 1 | 1 | 1 | 1 | 1 | 3 | 4 | 5 | 8 | 12 | 21 | 41 |
| $T_L$ | 0 | 0 | 0 | 0 | 0 | 0 | 0 | 0 | 0 | 0 | 0 | 0 |
| $T_R$ | 0 | 0 | 0 | 0 | 0 | 1 | 1 | 1 | 1 | 1 | 1 | 1 |
| S | 0 | 0 | 0 | 0 | 0 | 0 | -1 | 0 | -1 | 0 | -1 | -1 |

Im5

| bpp | 0.01 | 0.02 | 0.03 | 0.04 | 0.05 | 0.1 | 0.2 | 0.3 | 0.4 | 0.5 | 0.6 | 0.7 |
|---|---|---|---|---|---|---|---|---|---|---|---|---|
| PSNR | 70.35 | 66.75 | 64.74 | 63.22 | 62.06 | 58.53 | 54.94 | 52.72 | 51.16 | 49.82 | 47.75 | 46.71 |
| T | -1 | -1 | -1 | 1 | 1 | -2 | -2 | 1 | -1 | -1 | 1 | -2 |
| $T_F$ | 3 | 4 | 5 | 7 | 8 | 21 | 58 | 61 | 61 | 216 | 157 | 118 |
| $T_L$ | 0 | 0 | 0 | 0 | 0 | 0 | 0 | 0 | 0 | 0 | 0 | 0 |
| $T_R$ | 0 | 1 | 1 | 1 | 1 | 1 | 1 | 1 | 1 | 1 | 2 | 2 |
| S | 0 | 0 | -1 | -1 | -1 | -1 | 0 | -1 | 0 | -1 | -1 | 1 |

Im6

| bpp | 0.01 | 0.02 | 0.03 | 0.04 | 0.05 | 0.1 | 0.2 | 0.3 | 0.4 | 0.5 | 0.6 | 0.7 |
|---|---|---|---|---|---|---|---|---|---|---|---|---|
| PSNR | 68.52 | 65.82 | 64.19 | 62.89 | 61.97 | 58.84 | 55.05 | 52.81 | 50.38 | 48.88 | 47.55 | 46.12 |
| T | -3 | -3 | -2 | -2 | -2 | -2 | 1 | 1 | 1 | 1 | -2 | -2 |
| $T_F$ | 11 | 17 | 8 | 10 | 11 | 21 | 33 | 158 | 130 | 181 | 177 | 1010 |
| $T_L$ | 1 | 1 | 1 | 1 | 1 | 1 | 1 | 1 | 1 | 1 | 2 | 2 |
| $T_R$ | 0 | 0 | 0 | 0 | 0 | 1 | 1 | 1 | 2 | 2 | 2 | 2 |
| S | -3 | -3 | -2 | -2 | 1 | 1 | -1 | -1 | 0 | 0 | -1 | -1 |

Im7

| bpp | 0.01 | 0.02 | 0.03 | 0.04 | 0.05 | 0.1 | 0.2 | 0.3 | 0.4 | 0.5 | 0.6 | 0.7 |
|---|---|---|---|---|---|---|---|---|---|---|---|---|
| PSNR | 69.83 | 66.44 | 64.62 | 63.07 | 62.07 | 58.4 | 54.5 | 51.6 | 48.81 | 46.84 | 45.7 | 43.21 |
| T | -2 | 1 | -2 | -2 | -2 | 1 | -1 | -1 | -2 | 1 | -2 | -2 |
| $T_F$ | 4 | 4 | 7 | 9 | 10 | 12 | 20 | 56 | 30 | 136 | 115 | 85 |
| $T_L$ | 0 | 0 | 0 | 0 | 0 | 0 | 0 | 0 | 2 | 1 | 2 | 3 |
| $T_R$ | 0 | 0 | 0 | 0 | 0 | 0 | 0 | 0 | 2 | 2 | 2 | 2 |
| S | 1 | -1 | -2 | 1 | 1 | -1 | -1 | -1 | -1 | -1 | 0 | -2 |

Im8

| bpp | 0.01 | 0.02 | 0.03 | 0.04 | 0.05 | 0.1 | 0.2 | 0.3 | 0.4 | 0.5 | 0.6 | 0.7 |
|---|---|---|---|---|---|---|---|---|---|---|---|---|
| PSNR | 70.99 | 67.84 | 66.04 | 64.72 | 63.72 | 60.53 | 56.91 | 54.68 | 52.81 | 50.93 | 48.69 | 47.12 |
| T | -1 | 0 | -1 | -1 | -1 | -1 | -1 | -1 | -1 | -1 | -2 | -2 |
| $T_F$ | 1 | 2 | 2 | 3 | 4 | 6 | 9 | 16 | 33 | 116 | 70 | 178 |
| $T_L$ | 0 | 0 | 0 | 0 | 0 | 0 | 0 | 0 | 0 | 0 | 0 | 0 |
| $T_R$ | 0 | 0 | 0 | 0 | 0 | 0 | 0 | 0 | 0 | 0 | 0 | 1 |
| S | 0 | 0 | 0 | 0 | 0 | 0 | -1 | 0 | 0 | -1 | 0 | -2 |

Im9

| bpp | 0.01 | 0.02 | 0.03 | 0.04 | 0.05 | 0.1 | 0.2 | 0.3 | 0.4 | 0.5 | 0.6 | 0.7 |
|---|---|---|---|---|---|---|---|---|---|---|---|---|
| PSNR | 71.09 | 68.04 | 66.36 | 65.01 | 64.06 | 60.93 | 57.76 | 55.88 | 54.42 | 53.18 | 52.13 | 51.18 |
| T | 0 | 0 | 0 | 0 | 0 | -1 | -1 | -1 | -1 | -1 | -1 | -1 |

(*Continued*)

**Table 1.** (*Continued*)

| $T_F$ | 1 | 1 | 1 | 2 | 2 | 3 | 5 | 7 | 10 | 16 | 28 | 71 |
|---|---|---|---|---|---|---|---|---|---|---|---|---|
| $T_L$ | 0 | 0 | 0 | 0 | 0 | 0 | 0 | 0 | 0 | 0 | 0 | 0 |
| $T_R$ | 0 | 0 | 0 | 0 | 0 | 0 | 0 | 0 | 0 | 0 | 0 | 0 |
| S | 0 | 0 | 0 | 0 | 0 | −1 | −1 | −1 | −1 | −1 | 0 | −1 |
| Im10 | | | | | | | | | | | | |
| bpp | 0.01 | 0.02 | 0.03 | 0.04 | 0.05 | 0.1 | 0.2 | 0.3 | 0.4 | 0.5 | 0.6 | 0.7 |
| PSNR | 59.99 | 59.94 | 59.88 | 59.46 | 58.54 | 55.35 | 52.01 | 50.01 | 46.79 | 45.02 | 44.32 | 42.22 |
| T | 0 | 0 | 0 | 0 | 0 | −1 | −1 | −1 | −1 | −2 | −2 | −2 |
| $T_F$ | 12 | 2 | 6 | 22 | 41 | 25 | 141 | 354 | 1800 | 1000 | 760 | 3100 |
| $T_L$ | 0 | 0 | 0 | 0 | 0 | 1 | 1 | 1 | 2 | 2 | 2 | 3 |
| $T_R$ | 1 | 1 | 1 | 1 | 1 | 1 | 1 | 1 | 2 | 2 | 2 | 3 |
| S | 0 | 0 | 0 | 0 | 0 | −1 | 0 | 0 | −1 | −1 | 0 | 1 |

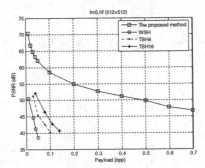

**Fig. 6.** Embedding for Im5

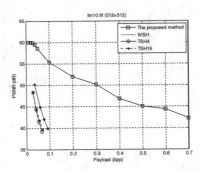

**Fig. 7.** Embedding for Im10

Different from shifting the histogram of the whole image and the histogram of the image sub-blocks method, our presented method selects histogram-pairs in prediction-error histogram and then shifts the histogram to embed data. The advantages of our presented method are illustrated as follows.

The histogram of prediction-error images obeys the quasi-Laplace distribution. Thus, it has the highest peak around zero prediction-error. A medical image, Im5,

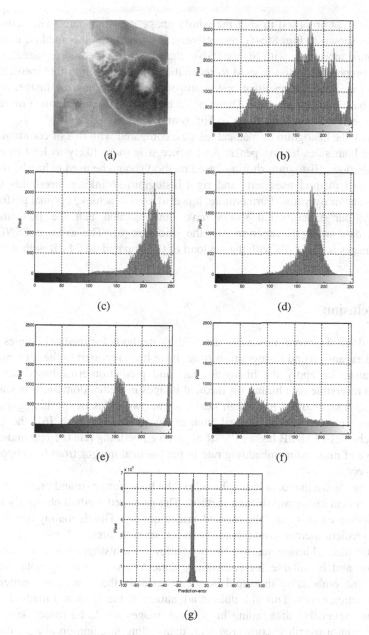

**Fig. 8.** Comparison of the histogram of the whole image, the histogram of the image sub-blocks and the prediction-error histogram (a) Im5, (b) The histogram of Im5, (c)(d)(e)(f) The histograms of the image sub-blocks in Im5, (g) The prediction-error histogram of Im5.

is shown in Fig. 8(a). Its histogram is shown in Fig. 8(b), which has peak value at gray level value 250. It is obvious that it will be difficult to apply the histogram-shifting method proposed in [4].

In [6], it was proposed to split the whole image into four parts. The histogram of each part is shown in Fig. 8(c–f), respectively. It is clear that this method is relatively easier to hide more data with higher PSNR than by using method reported in [4].

If the proposed method is used to reversibly embed data into this medical image, shown in Fig. 8(a), the resultant histogram of the prediction-error image, shown in Fig. 8(g), has a much high peak. Therefore, it is possible to embed much more data in the same medical image, as shown in Fig. 6 and Table 1.

Note that the histogram of medical images, compared with that of common images, has one or both sides having peaks. And hence it is more likely to lead to overflow and/or underflow. Histogram shifting based method should be used to handle this issue. The proposed method uses left- and right-histogram shrinking thresholds to avoid underflow and/or overflow. Furthermore, it is also used to achieve optimal performance.

Finally, our experimental works have demonstrated that the performance in reversible data hiding is superior than the prior art [6]. The average PSNR of ten marked images is 58.58 dB with the payload of 0.1 bpp and 46.24 dB with the payload of 0.7 bpp.

## 4 Conclusion

In spatial domain, several reversible data hiding methods for medical images, such as difference expansion and histogram shifting, have been reported in the literature [6, 9]. In this paper, we apply the histogram-pair and prediction-error based data hiding method to reversible data hiding for medical images in spatial domain. It is known that the medical images often have high peaks at the two sides of the histogram, which causes more challenge than normal images do. Compared with [6], the proposed method achieves 12.18 dB higher PSNR at given embedding rate 0.1 bpp and enhances the average of maximum embedding rate in ten medical images from 0.16 bpp to more than 0.7 bpp.

We have shown that data hiding based on the histogram-pair and prediction-error is much better than histogram shifting method. The proposed method obviously improves the data hiding capacity and the marked image quality. This is mainly due to the fact that the prediction-error could better exploit smooth areas of medical images to improve the marked image quality. The prediction-error histogram obeys quasi-Laplace distribution and is suitable for embedding data. When embedding data, fluctuation threshold and embedding threshold is not necessarily the smaller the better but the optimal solution exists. This is a unique advantage in the proposed method.

Besides, reversible data hiding in medical images would be more likely to cause underflow and/or overflow compared with data hiding in common images on account of medical images with both sides of its histogram having peaks. Left- and right-histogram shrinking thresholds are used not only for avoiding underflow and/or overflow but also for optimum performance.

**Acknowledgment.** The author would like to thank Mehdi Fallahpour for providing the ten medical images used in this study.

# References

1. Coatrieux, G., Maitre, H., Sankur, B., Rolland, Y., Collorec, R.: Relevance of watermarking in medical imaging. In: IEEE-EMBS Information Technology Applications in Biomedicine, Arlington, USA, pp. 250–255 (2000)
2. Tian, J.: Reversible data embedding using a difference expansion. IEEE Tarns. Circuits Syst. Video Technol. 13(8), 890–896 (2003)
3. Kim, H.J., Sachnev, V., Shi, Y.Q., Nam, J., Choo, H.G.: A novel difference expansion transform for reversible data embedding. IEEE Trans. Inf. Forensics Secur. 3(3), 456–465 (2008)
4. Ni, Z., Shi, Y.Q., Ansari, N., Su, W.: Reversible data hiding. IEEE Trans. Circuits Syst. Video Technol. 16(3), 354–362 (2006)
5. Fallahpour, M., Sedaaghi, M.H.: High capacity lossless data hiding based on histogram modification. IEICE Electron. Express 4(7), 205–210 (2007)
6. Fallahpour, M., Megias, D., Ghanbri, M.: Reversible and high-capacity data hiding in medical images. IET Image Process. 5(2), 190–197 (2011)
7. Thodi, D.M., Rodriguez, J.J.: Expansion embedding techniques for reversible watermarking. IEEE Trans. Image Process. 16(3), 721–730 (2007)
8. Xuan, G., Tong, X., Teng, J., Zhang, X., Shi, Y.Q.: Optimal histogram-pair and prediction-error based image reversible data hiding. In: Shi, Y.Q., Kim, H.-J., Pérez-González, F. (eds.) IWDW 2012. LNCS, vol. 7809, pp. 368–383. Springer, Heidelberg (2013)
9. Kumar, C.V., Natarajan, V., Muraledharan, S.S.: Difference expansion based reversible data hiding for medical images. In: IEEE International Conference on Communication and Signal Processing, pp. 720–723 (2014)

# Visual Cryptography

# Authenticated Secret Sharing Scheme Based on GMEMD

Wen-Chung Kuo[1]($\boxtimes$), Shao-Hung Kuo[2], Hong-Yi Chang[1],
and Lih-Chyau Wuu[1]

[1] Department of Computer Science and Information Engineering,
National Yunlin University of Science and Technology, Douliu, Taiwan
simonkuo@yuntech.edu.tw

[2] Graduate School of Engineering Science and Technology Doctoral Program,
National Yunlin University of Science and Technology, Douliu, Taiwan

**Abstract.** In secret image sharing schemes, all legal participants provide legitimate shared images and then they can extract the correct secret message. Recently, Wu et al. proposed a high quality data hiding secret sharing scheme with authentication ability. The major contribution of this scheme maintains good stego image quality while being able to verify secret message integrity. However, to ensure the process can work, the secret image's pixel values larger than 250 must be changed to 250 for Wu's scheme. Otherwise, extracting the secret image may fail. In other words, for a secret image, a few errors do not make the big difference but it could be distorted severely for some sensitive secrets. In order to improve this shortcoming, a secret image sharing scheme based on General Multi-Exploiting Modification Direction (GMEMD) data hiding technology will be proposed in this paper. According to simulation results and analysis, we can show that the stego image quality in Wu *et al.*'s scheme or our proposed scheme is larger than 43dB. We also demonstrate the authentication capability to find unauthorized participants. Furthermore, if all participants are legitimate, then the proposed scheme can extract the secret completely without any distortion.

**Keywords:** Image sharing scheme · General Multi-Exploiting Modification Direction (GMEMD) · Lagrange function · OPAP · Hash function

## 1 Introduction

Because of the rapid development of the mobile equipment and communication technology, digital information (such as images, music or video) being transmitted through Internet has become an inevitable phenomenon. In particular, image exchange always happen in social networks such as Facebook, Twitter, Instagram, etc. Therefore, how to protect the original image copyright or security has become an important issue. In general, the two common methodologies of cryptography and steganography are used to preserve image security. From the view of steganography, watermarking, the use of data hiding techniques to

© Springer International Publishing Switzerland 2016
Y.-Q. Shi et al. (Eds.): IWDW 2015, LNCS 9569, pp. 395–405, 2016.
DOI: 10.1007/978-3-319-31960-5_32

embed authentication information into the original image, is used to protect the image copyright and ownership. On the other hand, cryptography is also used to enhance the image's security. However, the information is transformed into meaningless collections of characters after encryption. This method is used for text files or communication protocols, but is not suitable for hiding images within other images. In order to solve this limitation, the visual secret sharing method (VSS) is commonly used. The VSS method was proposed by Naor and Shamir [8] in 1995. The concept of $(t, n)$VSS, where $2 \le t \le n$, is where a secret message is divided into $n$ parts and embedded into $n$ shared images. The secret message can only be recovered when $t$ or greater shared images are provided. The major contribution of VSS is the secret message can be decrypted by using the human visual system instead of using a computer.

Recently, many VSS-based authentication schemes which combine the advantages of VSS-scheme and authentication were proposed [2,4,6,7,9]. In 2008, Chang et al. proposed a stego sharing scheme with authentication (CHL-scheme [1]) to share the secret camouflage image validation mechanism. To improve stego image quality, Wu et al. (WKH-scheme [10]) proposed a high quality image sharing scheme with Optimal Pixel Adjustment Process (OPAP) in 2011. The major contribution of the WKH-scheme is maintaining good stego image quality and the ability to verify secret message integrity. To ensure the process succeeds, secret image pixel values larger than 250 must be changed to 250. Otherwise, the secret image may not be extracted. For a secret image, a few errors does not make the big difference but may distort some sensitive secrets. To improve this shortcoming where some pixel values must be changed to 250, a secret image sharing scheme with authentication based on GMEMD (General Multi-Exploiting Modification Direction) [5] data hiding technology will be proposed in this paper. According to our experimental results and analysis, there are three contributions from our proposed scheme. First, the stego image quality in our proposed scheme is larger than 43dB. Secondly, the authentication capability can find unauthorized participants. Finally, if all participants are legitimate, then the proposed scheme can extract the secret completely without any distortion.

The rest of paper is organized as follows: In Sect. 2, the WKH-scheme and GMEMD data hiding technique are reviewed briefly. In Sect. 3, the new Authenticated Secret Sharing Scheme is described. Experimental results and security analysis are provided in Sect. 4. Finally, the conclusion is given in Sect. 5.

## 2    Review of Schemes

In this section, there are two main related works reviewed. Section 2.1 describes the WKH-scheme which is a data hiding method based on VSS with addition of the OPAP method to improve the authentication ratio. Section 2.2 introduces the GMEMD data hiding technique which is based on EMD type method to increase embedding capacity.

## 2.1   WKH-scheme Review

In 2011, Wu *et al.* [10] presented a validation capability combined with high quality image sharing mechanism for data hiding. The major contribution of the WKH-scheme is they use OPAP, optimal pixel adjustment process, to enhance the PSNR (Peak Signal to Noise Ratio) value of the image. The WKH-scheme can improve the image quality of stego images by 9.29 % as compared with the Chang *et al.* scheme according to their experimental results. Here, we will review the hiding process of the WKH-scheme. For more details, we encourage the reader to refer [10].

| $X$ | $W$ |
|---|---|
| $X = (x_8 x_7 x_6 x_5 x_4 F_8 F_7 P_4)_2$ | $W = (w_8 w_7 w_6 w_5 w_4 F_6 F_5 P_3)_2$ |
| $V$ | $U$ |
| $V = (v_8 v_7 v_6 v_5 v_4 F_4 F_3 P_2)_2$ | $U = (u_8 u_7 u_6 u_5 u_4 F_2 F_1 P_1)_2$ |

**Fig. 1.** The embedding block of the WKH-scheme

## Algorithm 1. Hiding process of WKH-scheme:

**Input:** Secret image $S = (s_1, s_2, \ldots, s_{m \times m})$, $n$ original images $(I^{(1)}, I^{(2)}, \ldots, I^{(n)})$.
**Output:** $n$ secret sharing images.

Step 1.  Divide each original image $I^{(1)}, I^{(2)}, \ldots, I^{(n)}$ into $m \times m$ non-overlapping $2 \times 2$ blocks $B_i^j$, where $i = 1$ to $m \times m$ and $j = 1$ to $n$.

Step 2.  Choose $k$ pixel values. If the pixel $s_t$ value is less than 251 then maintain the original value, else the pixel value will adjust into 250 when it is greater than 250 for $t = 1, 2, \ldots, k$. Next, substitute these pixel values into the coefficient of Eq. (1).

$$f(x) = s_1 + s_2 x + \ldots + s_k x^{k-1} \bmod 251. \tag{1}$$

Step 3.  Substitute the different $X_j^i$ into the Eq. (1) to compute the secret sharing values $f(X_j^i)$ for $j = 1, \ldots, n$. Then transform them from integer to 8bit binary values.

Step 4.  Using the hash function, four pixel values of the previous block of the first 5 bits are used to produce a 4-digit verification code.

Step 5.  Use LSB replacement to embed the 8 bit secret sharing values from the Step 3 into the pixel location of 2-LSB position and 3-LSB position (such as $F_1, F_2, \ldots, F_8$), respectively (As seen in Fig. (1) F-location). Then use LSB replacement to hide the verification code into the 1-LSB position (such as $P_1, P_2, P_3, P_4$), as shown in Fig. (1) P-location.

Step 6.  Apply the OPAP process to each stego-block $B_i^j$.

Step 7.  Repeat Steps 2 to 6 until all pixels of the secret image are processed.

## 2.2   GMEMD Data Hiding Scheme Review

In 2012, a data hiding scheme with high embedding capacity based on GMEMD was proposed Kuo *et al.* [5]. There are three major contributions of this scheme. First, a new GMEMD extracting function was proposed. Second, the technique retains the original EMD feature to freely choose the pixel number of features. And third, we can embed the binary secret data directly. The GMEMD extraction function is

$$f_c(x_1, x_2, \ldots, x_n) = [\sum_{i=1}^{n} (x_i \cdot c_i)] \mod 2^{nk+1}, \tag{2}$$

where $x_i$ is the $i$-th pixel value for adjusting, $n$ is the number of values required for implementing the selected pixels, $k$ is how many bits are used to hide secret in the pixel values, and $c_i$ is for adjusting weights. It is defined as follows

$$c_i = \begin{cases} 1, & i = 1, \\ 2^k c_{i-1} + 1, i \neq 1 & and \quad i > 0. \end{cases} \tag{3}$$

In order to explain the embed process of GMEMD-scheme, we give the following example.

**Example 1:** Given an original $2 \times 2$ block with pixels $(10, 19, 5, 9)$ and a secret message of $(101010101)_2$, we get the stego pixels $(10, 20, 3, 8)$ by using the following steps of GMEMD scheme, where $n = 4$ and $k = 2$.

Step 1.  Compute the value $t = f_c(10, 19, 5, 9) = 463$ by Eq. (2).
Step 2.  Transform the secret messages from the binary values $s = (101010101)_2$
         to the decimal values $s = (341)_{10}$.
Step 3.  Compute the difference value $D = (341 - 463) \mod 2^9 = 390$.
Step 4.  $D > 2^8 = 256$, $D = 2^9 - 390 = (122)_{10} = (1322)_4$,
         when $d_3 = 1$, then $x_4' = 9 - 1 = 8$, $x_3 = 5 + 1 = 6$;
         when $d_2 = 3$, then $x_3' = 6 - 3 = 3$, $x_2 = 19 + 3 = 22$;
         when $d_1 = 2$, then $x_2' = 22 - 2 = 20$, $x_1' = 10 + 2 = 12$;
         when $d_0 = 2$, then $x_1 = 12 - 2 = 10$.

Finally, this gives the stego pixels $(10, 20, 3, 8)$.

## 3   Our Proposed Scheme

In the WKH-scheme, an inherent limitation is that higher hidden secret pixel values must be adjusted to 250; otherwise it will cause distortion after the embedding process. To improve this shortcoming, a new method will be proposed in this section. The image sharing flow chart is shown as Fig. 2 and the image sharing algorithm is described as following:

**Algorithm 2.(The hiding process of our proposed scheme)**
**Input:** Secret image $S = (s_1, s_2, \ldots, s_{m \times m})$, $n$ original images $(I^{(1)}, I^{(2)}, \ldots, I^{(n)})$.
**Output:** $n$ secret sharing images.

Step 1. Divide each original image $I^{(1)}, I^{(2)}, \ldots, I^{(n)}$ into $m \times m$ non-overlapping $2 \times 2$ blocks $B_i^j$, where $i = 1$ to $m \times m$ and $j = 1$ to $n$.

Step 2. Divide blocks from one $2 \times 2$ block to two $1 \times 2$ sub-blocks.

Step 3. Choose a random prime number from the range $[256, 511]$ and a set of $k$ pixel values $s_t$ for $t = 1, 2, \ldots, k$ to generate sharing function Eq. (4).

$$f(x) = s_1 + s_2 x + \ldots + s_k x^{k-1} \bmod p. \tag{4}$$

Plug in different values of $x$ according to the sharing images using Eq. (4) to calculate the shared secret value, and then convert the results into 9 binary bits.

Step 4. From Step 3, the 9 secret binary bits are divided two parts: 5-MSB and 4-LSB. Then, 5-MSB is embedded into the first sub-block of the two pixels using the GMEMD scheme. Likewise, a 1-bit verification code is generated for the 9-bit information with XOR operation and the 4-LSB bits are hidden in the second sub-block by using the GMEMD scheme with parameters $k = 2$ and $n = 2$.

In order to explain Algorithm 2, we give the following example.

**Example 2:** There four original sharing image pixels are $(121, 231, 103, 169)$ and the secret messages are 86 and 137. Then, we obtain the secret sharing image pixels $(124, 228, 105, 166)$ by using Algorithm 2 with modulus $p$ of 509.

Step 1. Get $f(x) = 86 + 173x \bmod 509$ with the secret message $(86, 137)$ and $p = 509$.

Step 2. Compute $f(x) = 86 + 173x \bmod 509 = (259)_{10} = (100000011)_2$. Therefore, 5-MSB is $(10000)_2$ and 4-LSB is $(0011)_2$.

Step 3. Divide the original image block into two sub-blocks $(121, 231)$ and $(103, 169)$.

Step 4. Embed $(10000)_2$ into $(121, 231)$ using the GMEMD scheme. Then, the stego pixels of first sub-group block are $(124, 228)$.

Step 5. Compute the verification code as $1 \oplus 0 \oplus 0 \oplus 0 \oplus 0 \oplus 0 \oplus 0 \oplus 1 \oplus 1 = 1$. Then, we obtain the stego pixels of the second sub-group block as $(105, 166)$ after the secret data $(00111)_2$ is embedded into $(103, 169)$ using the GMEMD scheme.

**Algorithm 3.** The secret extraction process of our proposed scheme
**Input:** $n$ secret sharing images $(I''^{(1)}, I''^{(2)}, \ldots, I''^{(n)})$.
**Output:** Secret image $S = (s_1, s_2, \ldots, s_{m \times m})$.

Step 1. Divide secret sharing images $(I''^{(1)}, I''^{(2)}, \ldots, I''^{(n)})$ into $m \times m$ non-overlapping $2 \times 2$ blocks $B_i^j$, where $i = 1$ to $m \times m$ and $j = 1$ to $n$.

Step 2. The $2 \times 2$ non-overlapping blocks are divided again into $1 \times 2$ sub-blocks. Then, each sub-block will get a 5-bit of information by using Eq. (2). Therefore, we concatenate these two 5-bits and get the 9-bit secret sharing value with 1-bit verification data.

Step 3. If the $10^{th}$ bit verification code is equal to the 9-bit secret sharing values, do mutual XOR operations, then these 9-bits will transform to decimal secret sharing values. Otherwise, reject it.

Step 4. With other verified secret sharing values by its $x$ value to using Lagrange Interpolation to get polynomial. Finally, from the polynomial coefficients we can get the secret sharing image's pixel values $s$.

Step 5. Get 9bits secret sharing value from the verified image's sub-blocks. Next, we combine secret sharing values and relative $x$ from other sharing images, then use the Lagrange Interpolation method to recover the secret sharing polynomial. Finally, from the polynomial coefficients, we obtain the secret image pixel values $s$.

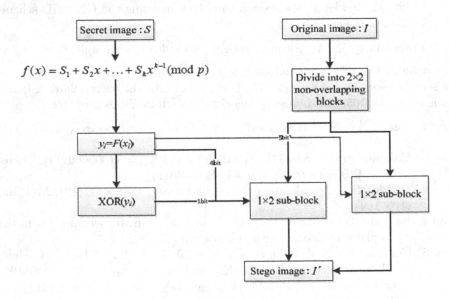

**Fig. 2.** The flow chart of proposed scheme

## 4   Simulation and Analysis

In this section, experimental results are given which shows our scheme can improve upon WKH-scheme's shortcoming effectively. The four $512 \times 512$ gray-level test images of "Lena", "Airplane", "Baboon" and "Pepper." The secret sharing images are the same as the original images, but the size is $256 \times 256$, as shown in Fig. 3. Here, we take the $(4, 4)$ secret sharing scheme as an simulation example, that is to say, there are four share images and we need all of four share images to reconstruct the original secret images. In general, we use PSNR (peak signal to noise ratio) factor to evaluate the stego image quality.

Therefore, whether the share image is similar to the original image is dependent on the PSNR. In other words, the share image approaches to the original image when PSNR is increasing. From the experimental result, the human visual system cannot detect embedded information as long as PSNR is greater than 30dB. The definition of PSNR is given as Eq. (5).

$$PSNR = 10\log_{10}(\frac{255^2}{MSE})dB, \tag{5}$$

where $MES$, as Eq. (6), is the mean square error of original images $I$ and the stego share images $I'$,

$$MSE = \frac{1}{MN}\sum_{i=0}M - 1\sum_{j=0}N - 1[I(i,j) - I'(i,j)]^2, \tag{6}$$

where $M, N$ is the image size, $I(i,j)$ and $I'(i,j)$ are the pixel values of share image and original image (cover image), respectively. In addition, to measure performance, we used the Detection Ratio (DR) to assess the ratio of the detected tampered blocks to the actual tampered blocks. DR is defined as follows:

$$DR = \frac{NTPD}{NTP}, \tag{7}$$

where $NTPD$ is the detected blocks of tampering and $NTP$ is the actual tampered blocks.

The simulation results after using our proposed method are shown as Fig. 4. According these results, we find the share image quality maintains PSNR is over 43dB. These results are similar to WKH-scheme and will easily to pass human eye inspection. It is noteworthy that the pixel values of the secret image do not need to be restricted to within 250 by using the proposed method.

For security, we consider steganalysis of shared stego image. In this paper, the common steganalysis method RS-steganalysis (Fridrich *et al.* [3] in 2001) will be used to test our proposed scheme. RS-Steganalysis uses the least significant bit of the stego image pixels to find statistical relationships. The shared stego image is divided into disjoint groups of adjacent pixels. Then, the discriminant function $f$ and flipping function $F$ are used to divide these groups $G$ into three categories: $R$, $S$ and $U$:

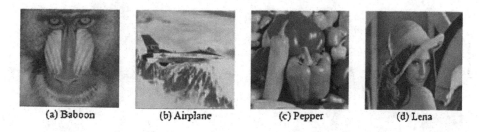

(a) Baboon          (b) Airplane          (c) Pepper          (d) Lena

**Fig. 3.** The original images

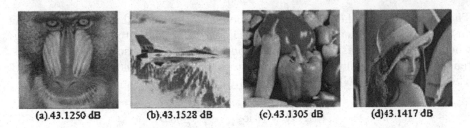

| (a).43.1250 dB | (b).43.1528 dB | (c).43.1305 dB | (d)43.1417 dB |

**Fig. 4.** The shared images

$$\text{Regular groups: } G \in R \leftrightarrow f(F(G)) > f(G),$$
$$\text{Singular groups: } G \in S \leftrightarrow f(F(G)) < f(G),$$
$$\text{Unusable groups: } G \in U \leftrightarrow f(F(G)) = f(G).$$

According to the relationships proposed by Fridrich *et al.*, the statistical characteristics are shown as Eq. (8).

$$R_M \cong R_{-M} \text{ and } S_M \cong S_{-M}, \tag{8}$$

where the $R_M$ and $S_M$ are the respective number of regular groups and singular groups under the positive mask $M = [1001]$. The regular and singular groups under the negative mask $-M = [-100-1]$ are named $R_{-M}$ and $S_{-M}$. The relationships between the groups is $R_M + S_M \leq 1$ and $R_{-M} + S_{-M} \leq 1$. The steganalysis results for our proposed scheme are as shown in Fig. 5. From the Fig. 5 (a)-(d), we can see that in these experimental results, $R_M \cong R_{-M}$ and $S_M \cong S_{-M}$.

Another tested feature is the image's authentication ability. The proposed method uses one authentication bit for verification. Figure 6(a) is the share image Lena that has been tampered with a block from share image Pepper. The detected result is shown in Fig. 6(b) with DR value of 0.5. This result is similar to the WKH-scheme. For the proposed method, if we want to get a high DR value, then more authentication information must be hidden in a block. However, the result is the image quality will decrease. From the Fig. 7(b), the tampered area extends to the full size of the share image. The DR value is maintained at 0.49 when our proposed scheme is used. According to the simulation results, we prove that the proposed method has the same authentication ability compared with the WKH-scheme since we can detect unauthorized participants.

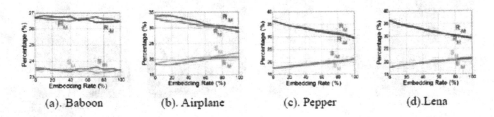

| (a). Baboon | (b). Airplane | (c). Pepper | (d).Lena |

**Fig. 5.** The RS steganalysis results

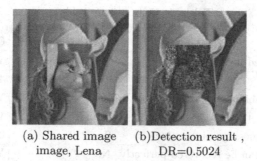

(a) Shared image     (b)Detection result ,
image, Lena          DR=0.5024

**Fig. 6.** Authentication characteristic

(a)The modified     (b) Detection result,
(a)shared image     (b) DR=0.489

**Fig. 7.** Authentication characteristic 2

A summation of the important characteristics of the proposed scheme in comparison to the WKH-scheme is given in Table 1. In the table, there are 5 important points to note:

1. Users can identify the sharing image because the PSNR value is at least 43dB for both schemes.
2. The image authentication ability and authentication bits in the WKH-scheme and our proposed scheme are 4 and 1, respectively.
3. The secret message pixel does not need to be restricted to within 250 with our proposed scheme. The values of the secret message pixels in the WKH-scheme are limited to 250. Therefore, the secret message can be extracted perfectly by using our proposed scheme. For the WKH-scheme, secret messages cannot be recovered when the pixel's value is bigger than 250.
4. In both schemes, the secret message is distributed to the share images using Shamir's method.
5. In the embedding process, the WKH-scheme uses LSB replacement to make optima hidden. Although the WKH-scheme has good embedding capacity and image quality of stego image, it is exposed by Regular Singular Steganalysis (RS-steganalysis). Since the secret image of the WKH-scheme is hidden by the LSB replacement without any protection mechanisms, it is easier to attack.

**Table 1.** Comparison Table

| Items | WKH-scheme [10] | Our scheme |
|---|---|---|
| Meaningful shared images | Yes | Yes |
| PSNR | 43.5dB | 43.2dB |
| Authentication ability | Yes | Yes |
| Authentication bit | 4-bit | 1-bit |
| Range of secret message pixel value | $0 \sim 250$ | $0 \sim 255$ |
| Secure message can be recovered perfectly | No | Yes |
| Data hiding method | Shamir Method | Shamir Method |
| Data embedding method | LSB replacement | GMEMD |
| Affected bits | 3bits | 2bits |
| Pass RS attack | No | Yes |

## 5　Conclusion

The major contribution of the proposed method is the secret image is not distorted as in the WKH-scheme which restricts the secret pixel value to under 250. As a result, the proposed method can detect and verify share images and maintain high image quality of stego image. Since the bit value of authentication information has the same DR value with the WKH-scheme. Furthermore, the proposed method can increase embedding capacity for number of bits in one pixel by using the GMEMD scheme to enhance the efficiency of authentication.

**Acknowledgments.** This work was supported in part by the Ministry of Science and Technology of the Republic of China under Contract No. MOST 104-2221-E-224-023.

## References

1. Chang, C.C., Hsieh, Y.P., Lin, C.H.: Sharing secrets in stego images with authentication. Pattern Recogn. **41**, 3130–3137 (2008)
2. Chang, C.C., Huynh, N.T., Le, H.D.: Lossless and unlimited multi-image sharing based on chinese remainder theorem and lagrange interpolation. Sig. Process. **99**, 159–170 (2014)
3. Fridrich, J., Goljan, M., Du, R.: Detecting LSB steganography in color and grayscale images. IEEE Comput. Soc. **8**(4), 22–28 (2001)
4. Guo, C., Chang, C.C., Qin, C.: A hierarchical threshold secret image sharing. Pattern Recogn. Lett. **33**, 83–91 (2012)
5. Kuo, W.C., Kuo, S.H., Wuu, L.C.: The high embedding steganographic method based on general Multi-EMD. In: 2012 International Conference on Information Security and Intelligent Control, pp. 286–289, August 2012
6. Lin, P.Y., Lee, J.S., Chang, C.C.: Distortion-free secret image sharing mechanism using modulus operator. Pattern Recogn. **42**, 886–895 (2009)

7. Lin, P.Y., Chan, C.S.: Invertible secret image sharing with steganography. Pattern Recogn. Lett. **31**, 1887–1893 (2010)
8. Naor, M., Shamir, A.: Visual cryptography. In: De Santis, A. (ed.) EUROCRYPT 1994. LNCS, vol. 950, pp. 1–12. Springer, Heidelberg (1995)
9. Ulutas, M., Ulutas, G., Nabiyev, V.V.: Invertible secret image sharing for gray level and dithered cover images. J. Syst. Softw. **86**, 485–500 (2013)
10. Wu, C.C., Kao, S.J., Hwang, M.S.: A high quality image sharing with steganography and adaptive authentication scheme. J. Syst. Softw. **84**, 2196–2207 (2011)

# Robust Content-Based Image Hash Functions Using Nested Lattice Codes

Thanh Xuan Nguyen[(✉)], Ricardo A. Parrao Hernandez,
and Brian M. Kurkoski

Japan Advanced Institute of Science and Technology, Nomi, Japan
{thanhnx,ricardo.parrao,kurkoski}@jaist.ac.jp

**Abstract.** This contribution improves content-based hash functions for image retrieval systems using nested lattice codes. Lattice codes are used to quantize image feature vectors to final hash values. The goal is to develop a nested lattice indexing scheme such that there is a proportional relationship between Euclidean distance and some metric distances (Hamming distance or, as in this paper, weighted Hamming distance and first difference distance) in order to increase the hash function's robustness. The proposed two-dimensional nested lattice code reduces the normalized mean squared error (NMSE) by 20 % compared to two-dimensional Gray code.

**Keywords:** Nested lattice codes · Nested lattice indexing · Image hash functions · Content-based

## 1 Introduction

Today, digital images are increasingly transmitted over the Internet and between mobile devices such as smartphones. It is easy to make an unauthorized copy and manipulate the content by using widely available image processing softwares. Therefore, image hash functions are used as an image authentication technique to protect data from distortion attacks that steal or alter data illegally. Cryptographic and content-based hash functions are two major data hashing techniques. Traditionally, data integrity issues are addressed by cryptographic hash functions, which are key-dependent and bit sensitive. This technique is usually applied to text message and file authentication, which requires all message bits to be unchanged [1]. In contrast, a content-based hash functions generates the hash value from the image features. This method is more suitable for multimedia files, which should be able to tolerate some minor modifications. In addition, the content-based approach can be applied to image retrieval systems [2]. Retrieval applications, such as online image search engines, require a response as quickly as possible to user queries. While sample-by-sample image comparison is computationally slow, robust content-based hash functions can compare numerous files in multimedia databases efficiently.

B.M. Kurkoski—This work was supported by JSPS Kakenhi Grant Number 26289119.

Y.-Q. Shi et al. (Eds.): IWDW 2015, LNCS 9569, pp. 406–417, 2016.
DOI: 10.1007/978-3-319-31960-5_33

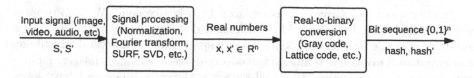

**Fig. 1.** A framework for hashing system.

A framework for hashing system is represented in Fig. 1. Consider an original input signal **s** and its modified signal **s′**. First, input signal **s** is pre-processed to real feature vectors **x** using signal processing techniques such as singular vector decomposition (SVD), speeded up robust features (SURF), Fourier transform and other signal processing operations. Then real feature vectors are converted to binary hash value *hash* using codes such as Gray code and Reed-Muller code or, as in this paper, lattice code. Similarly, modified signal **s′** is processed to feature vectors **x′**, then is converted to hash value *hash′*. In this research, we concentrate on improving the real-to-binary conversion.

Euclidean distance is widely known as a good measure of the similarity between features **x** and **x′** [3]. We let the Euclidean distance between **x** and **x′** be $d_E = ||\mathbf{x'} - \mathbf{x}||$, and let the metric distance between *hash* and *hash′* be $d_M = MetricDistance(hash, hash')$ where $d_M$ represents an arbitrary metric on hash values. By robustness, the greater the difference between two features, the greater the difference of their hash values that is desired [4]. If features **x** and **x′** are similar, then hash values *hash* and *hash′* should also be similar. If **x** and **x′** are very different, then *hash* and *hash′* should be also different. Then, we expect $d_E$ to be proportional to $d_M$, for a good hash scheme. Using the Euclidean distance between feature vectors allows us to study hashing schemes without considering specific signal processing schemes.

In fact, many hashing schemes have been proposed, but finding a proportional relationship remains a challenge. In 2000, Venkatesan and Ramarathnam [4] used randomized signal processing strategies and message authentication code (MAC) from cryptography for a non-reversible compression of images into random binary strings. As a result, it minimizes the probability that two hash values may collide and is robust against image changes due to compression, geometric distortions, and other attacks. From another perspective, in 2011, Parrao et al. [5] used image normalization and SVD as the first signal processing stage, then apply Gray code to obtain the binary hash sequence in image hash functions. According to his paper, the robustness of the hash functions was increased against rotation, scaling and JPEG attacks. Faloutsos in 1988 [6], Zhu et al. in 2010 [7] also used Gray code as the discrete-binary conversion stage of image hashing to improve clustering of similar records. In 2012, Yuenan et al. proposed hash functions based on random Gabor filtering and dithered lattice vector quantization (LVQ). A four-dimensional lattice is used for quantization, but codewords are normalized by a Gray code at the end. Basically, their approach can be considered as using Gabor filtering and a combination of a Gray code and a lattice.

In this paper, the Gray code is replaced by a lattice code. We also propose weighted Hamming distance and first difference distance as new metric distances. A lattice is a code over an $n$-dimensional real space and it has several advantages compared to Gray code. While Gray code requires a scalar quantizer, lattices employ vector quantization. It is well-known that vector quantizers have lower quantization error than scalar quantizers [9,10], therefore a lattice code is more suitable for quantization. The goal of this research is to find a hash-value encoding scheme such that the metric distance between hash values is proportional to their Euclidean distance. However, it is impossible to achieve a purely linear relationship, so our objective is to minimize the mean squared error of linear predictor function from metric distance to Euclidean distance among images using lattice codes.

The outline of the remainder of this paper is as follows. Section 2 gives background of lattice codes, Gray codes, Hamming distance, weighted Hamming distance, first difference distance and Euclidean distance metrics. Section 3 gives the proposed lattice coding method, evaluation method and the best choice of nested lattice code. Section 4 shows simulation results and performance comparison of Gray code and nested lattice code. Section 5 is the conclusion and future work.

## 2    Background

### 2.1    Lattices and Nested Lattice Codes

A lattice $\Lambda$ is a linear additive subgroup of $\mathbb{R}^n$. Lattices form effective structures for various geometric, coding and quantization problems. Some well-known lattices are $A_2, D_4, E_8$ [9]. In $n$ dimensions, a lattice point $\mathbf{x} \in \Lambda$ is an integral, linear combination of the basis vectors:

$$\mathbf{x} = G \cdot \mathbf{b} = \sum_{i=1}^{n} \mathbf{g}_i b_i, \tag{1}$$

where $\mathbf{b} \in \mathbb{Z}^n$ is a vector of integers, $G = \begin{bmatrix} \mathbf{g_1} \ \mathbf{g_2} \ \cdots \ \mathbf{g_n} \end{bmatrix}$ is an $n$-by-$n$ generator matrix and $\mathbf{g_i}$ are $n$-dimensional basis column vectors, for $i \in \{1, 2 \ldots n\}$. The corresponding fundamental volume is $V(\Lambda) = \det(\Lambda) = |\det(G)|$. A lattice $\Lambda$ with expansion factor $k$ forms itself a lattice. We define $k\Lambda$ as a nested lattice with factor $k$.

### 2.2    Lattice Quantizer

A lattice quantizer maps an $n$-dimensional input vector $\mathbf{y} = (y_1, y_2, \ldots, y_n)$ to a lattice point $\mathbf{x}^* \in \Lambda$ closest to $\mathbf{y}$, or more formally,

$$\mathbf{x}^* = \arg\min_{\mathbf{x} \in \Lambda} ||\mathbf{y} - \mathbf{x}||^2, \tag{2}$$

where $|| \cdot ||^2$ denotes squared Euclidean distance. And, we define quantization error vector $\mathbf{e}$:

$$\mathbf{e} = \mathbf{y} - \mathbf{x}^*. \tag{3}$$

## 2.3   Voronoi Region

The Voronoi region [12] $V(\mathbf{x})$ consists of all points of $\mathbb{R}^n$ which are at least as close to $\mathbf{x}$ as to any other lattice point, given by:

$$V(\mathbf{x}) = \{\mathbf{z} \in \mathbb{R}^n : ||\mathbf{z} - \mathbf{x}||^2 < ||\mathbf{z} - \mathbf{y}||^2, \text{ for all } \mathbf{y} \in \Lambda, \mathbf{y} \neq \mathbf{x}\}. \qquad (4)$$

Let $V_{r\Lambda}(\mathbf{a})$, integer $r$, vector $\mathbf{a} \in \mathbb{R}^n$, denote the Voronoi region for $r\Lambda$, shifted by vector $\mathbf{a}$. A Voronoi code $C_{r\Lambda}(\mathbf{a})$ consists of every lattice $\Lambda$ point which is placed inside the Voronoi region $V_{r\Lambda}(\mathbf{a})$:

$$C_{r\Lambda}(\mathbf{a}) = \Lambda \cap V_{r\Lambda}(\mathbf{a}). \qquad (5)$$

Figure 2 depicts 16 lattice points inside a solid line Voronoi region $V_{4\Lambda}(\mathbf{a})$ which is enlarged 4 times from $V_{r\Lambda}(\mathbf{0})$, then translated by vector $\mathbf{a}$.

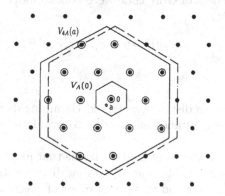

**Fig. 2.** Voronoi region $V_{4\Lambda}(\mathbf{a})$.

## 2.4   Gray Code and Gray Indexing

A Gray code is a binary code where two consecutive codewords differ by only one bit. Gray codes are widely used to reduce the number of bit errors in digital communication systems [13]. Gray codes are also known as reflected binary code. This section describes a recursive construction which encode binary sequences to Gray codes. Figure 3 depicts the algorithm to recursively generate Gray codes from binary sequences for two next levels from level one.

In this sub-section, we introduce $m \times n$ bits Gray code to index an $n$-dimensional real input datapoint $(x_1, \ldots, x_n)$ for $x_i \in [0, 2^m], i = \{1, \ldots, n\}$, uniformly distributed. Firstly, input $(x_1, \ldots, x_n)$ is quantized to integer vector by rounding to the nearest integer component-wise:

$$(y_1, \ldots, y_n) = Q_{Integer}(x_1, \ldots, x_n). \qquad (6)$$

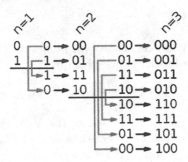

**Fig. 3.** The steps of the reflect and prefix method to generate Gray sequences.

Then, integer vector $(y_1, \ldots, y_n)$ is translated into binary sequences $(b_1, \ldots, b_n)$, then level $m$ Gray code encode $(b_1, \ldots, b_n)$ to binary Gray sequence $(c_1, \ldots, c_n)$. Finally, those $n$ sequences of Gray code were concatenated to an unique binary hash sequence.

$$GrayHash = c_1, \ldots, c_n. \tag{7}$$

## 2.5   Metrics

This paper uses Hamming distance, weighted Hamming distance, first difference distance and Euclidean distance as metrics to evaluate the normalized mean squared error.

Hamming distance is the number of positions that must be changed to transform one string to another [14]. The Hamming distance $d_H(\mathbf{x}, \mathbf{y})$ between two $n$-dimensional bit vectors $\mathbf{x}$ and $\mathbf{y}$ is the number of positions where they differ:

$$d_H(\mathbf{x}, \mathbf{y}) = \sum_{i=1}^{n} d_H(x_i, y_i), \tag{8}$$

where

$$d_H(x_i, y_i) = \begin{cases} 0 & \text{if } x_i = y_i \\ 1 & \text{if } x_i \neq y_i \end{cases}, \text{ for } i = 1, \ldots, n. \tag{9}$$

We propose a weighted Hamming distance measure which assigns weights exponentially to every group of bits of sequences of $n$-dimensional and $m$ levels:

$$d_{WH}(\mathbf{x}, \mathbf{y}) = \sum_{i=1}^{m \cdot n} w_i d_H(x_i, y_i), \tag{10}$$

where

$$w_i = 2^{\lfloor i/n \rfloor}, \text{ for } i = 1, \ldots, m \cdot n. \tag{11}$$

The purpose of weighted Hamming distance is explained in Sect. 3.

In this paper, we also propose the concept of first difference distance which reflects the similarity between bit sequences. Two bit sequences will be compared from the last element to the first element, the index of the first different element will be marked as first difference distance. In $n$-dimensional space, consider two binary sequences: $\mathbf{x} = \{(x_1,\ldots,x_n)^{(1)},\ldots,(x_1,\ldots,x_n)^{(n)}\}$ and $\mathbf{y} = \{(y_1,\ldots,y_n)^{(1)},\ldots,(y_1,\ldots,y_n)^{(n)}\}$, first difference distance is the index of the first group of $n$ bits, that they are different. More formally, For $i \in [0,n], i \in \mathbb{Z}$,

$$d_{FD}(\mathbf{x},\mathbf{y}) = i \Leftrightarrow \begin{cases} (x_1,\ldots,x_n)^{(n-i)} \neq (y_1,\ldots,y_n)^{(n-i)} \\ (x_1,\ldots,x_n)^{(n-j)} = (y_1,\ldots,y_n)^{(n-j)} \end{cases} \tag{12}$$

$\forall j \in [0,(i-1)], j \in \mathbb{Z}$.

Euclidean distance is the distance between two points in Euclidean space. For $n$-dimensional space, Euclidean distance from $\mathbf{x}$ to $\mathbf{y}$ is defined as:

$$d_E = \|\mathbf{y} - \mathbf{x}\| = \sqrt{\sum_{i=1}^{n}(y_i - x_i)^2}. \tag{13}$$

## 3  Proposed Algorithm

A hash scheme maps real numbers to bits. A good hash scheme will preserve distance as well as possible. That is, the Euclidean distance between two points in the real space should be proportional to the metric distance between the hash values of those two points. Our indexing scheme quantizes points into nested lattice points in multiple levels. If two points are far from each other, they tend to be quantized to different lattice points in high levels. In contrast, if two points are close together in Euclidean space, they should be quantized to same lattice points in high levels, and quantized to different lattice points only at low levels. To preserve distance, the higher the level, the higher the weight the bits groups should be assigned. On the other hand, consider from the highest level of nested lattice to the lowest level, the index of the first different position also represents the difference between two bit sequences. That is the idea for applying weighted Hamming distance in order to assign weights exponentially to every group of bits of codewords.

### 3.1  Nested Lattice Indexing

We indexed $n$-dimensional real points using $m$ levels nested lattice in $n$-dimensional space. Consider an $n$-dimensional real input datapoint $\mathbf{x} \in [0, 2^{m-1}]^n$, uniformly distributed. We define a lattice $\Lambda_{2^i}$ by a $n$-by-$n$ generator matrix $G_{\Lambda_{2^i}}$:

$$G_{\Lambda_{2^i}} = 2^i G_\Lambda = 2^i \begin{bmatrix} \mathbf{g_1} & \mathbf{g_2} & \cdots & \mathbf{g_n} \end{bmatrix}, \text{ for } i \in \{0, 1 \ldots (m-1)\}. \tag{14}$$

We also define a shift vector **a** as below.

$$\mathbf{a} = [a_1, \ldots, a_n]. \tag{15}$$

The best choice of shift vector **a** is explained in detail in Sect. 3.3.

An algorithm for finding a hash value *LatticeHash* from a real input vector **x** is given in three main steps.

Step 1: We shift the real input **x** by vector $2^i\mathbf{a}$ at the corresponding level $2^i$ or more formally,

$$\mathbf{y}^{(i)} = \mathbf{x} - 2^i\mathbf{a}, \text{ for } i \in \{0, 1 \ldots (m-1)\}. \tag{16}$$

Step 2: Datapoint $\mathbf{y}^{(i)}$ is quantized to lattice point $\mathbf{z}^{(i)}$ by $\Lambda_{2^i}$:

$$\mathbf{z}^i = Q_{\Lambda_{2^i}}(\mathbf{y}^{(i)}), \text{ for } i \in \{0, 1 \ldots (m-1)\}. \tag{17}$$

Next, we calculate the vector $b^{(i)}$, which is the integer representation of the lattice point $\mathbf{z}^{(i)}$.

$$\mathbf{b}^{(i)} = G_{\Lambda_{2^i}}^{-1}\mathbf{z}^{(i)}, \text{ for } i \in \{0, 1 \ldots (m-1)\}. \tag{18}$$

After that, the vector $\mathbf{b}^i$ is indexed inside Voronoi region $V_{2\Lambda_{2^i}}(\mathbf{0})$ which is generated by magnifying current fundamental region two times. In other words, we indexed the coset representatives of quotient group $\Lambda_{2^{i+1}}/\Lambda_{2^i}$. For instance, in two-dimensional lattice $A_2$, the coset includes $(0, 0), (0, 1), (1, 0), (1, 1)$. Particularly,

$$index^{(i)} = \mathbf{b}^{(i)} \mod 2, \text{ for } i \in \{0, 1 \ldots (m-1)\}. \tag{19}$$

Step 3: Finally, $m$ $n$-bit $l_i$ binary sequences corresponding to $m$ levels nested lattice $2^0, 2^1, \ldots, 2^{m-1}$ are concatenated into a binary hash sequence:

$$LatticeHash = index^{(1)}, index^{(2)}, \ldots, index^{(m)}. \tag{20}$$

## 3.2    Evaluation Method Based on Normalized Mean Squared Error

In this section, we consider two input distribution cases and introduce normalized mean squared error (NMSE) as a robustness measure.

For the hashing system input, we consider two distributions for the original feature vectors **x** and the modified vectors **x**′. In both cases, original vectors **x** are uniformly distributed, but modified vectors **x**′ are different.

Case $(a)$: **x** and **x**′ are both uniformly distributed. Then we apply lattice indexing scheme and Gray indexing scheme and compare their performance.

Case $(b)$: **x** is uniform and **x**′ is obtained by adding Gaussian noise to **x**, as: $\mathbf{x}' = \mathbf{x} + \mathbf{N}(0, \sigma^2)$. In this case, we change the Gaussian variance, then analyzing how the noise variance affects the indexing scheme's performance.

NMSE is used to compare the robustness between indexing schemes. After generating **x** and **x**′ according to the two mentioned cases, input vectors are decoded to binary sequences. Then, the Euclidean distance $d_E$ and other metric distances ($d_H$ or, as in this paper, $d_{WH}$ and $d_{FD}$) between every pairs $(\mathbf{x}, \mathbf{x}')$ are computed. Recall the target is calculating $d_E$ from some metric distances $d_M$, so we use least mean squared error technique to fit $d_E$ and $d_M$ by a linear predictor function $d'_E = \alpha d_M + \beta$, where $\alpha$ and $\beta$ are coefficients with least mean squared error. Then, we define the NMSE between estimated $d'_E$ and sample's $d_E$ for $n$-dimensional space and $N$ pairs of $d'_E$ and $d_E$ as:

$$NMSE = \frac{1}{n} MSE = \frac{1}{nN} \sum_{i=1}^{N} ||d'_{Ei} - d_{Ei}||. \tag{21}$$

NMSE is dimensionless. The smaller the NMSE, the better the linearity the indexing scheme can achieve and the more robust the indexing scheme is.

### 3.3 The Best Choice for Shift Vector a

There are infinite choices for the shift vector $\mathbf{a}$, this sub-section explains how to choose the optimized one. Firstly, we introduce the concept of inefficiently indexed regions (IIR) which consist of distinct points in Euclidean space with zero Hamming distances between indexed codewords. A set consists of $k$ regions $R_1, \ldots, R_k$ are IIR if and only if there exist pairs of $(\mathbf{x}, \mathbf{x}')$ such that:

$$\mathbf{x} \in R_i, \mathbf{x}' \in R_j, d_E(\mathbf{x}, \mathbf{x}') > 0, d_{WH}(\mathbf{x}, \mathbf{x}') = \mathbf{0}, \text{ for } i, j \in \{1, \ldots, k\}, i \neq j. \tag{22}$$

For instance, as shown in Fig. 4, $A$ and $A'$ are relatively IIR together, similarly with $B, B'$ and $C, C'$. All pairs which have one element from $A$ (hash value 01), the other from $A'$ (also hash value 01) are indexed to the same codeword with Hamming distance equal zero, but they have large Euclidean distance. In short, IIRs increase the MSE.

Consider a two-dimensional lattice $\Lambda$ and a Voronoi region $V_{2\Lambda}(\mathbf{a})$. According to the proposed rules in Sect. 3.1, all points in $V_{2\Lambda}(\mathbf{a})$ are indexed as shown in Figs. 4 and 5 where $\mathbf{a} = \mathbf{0}$ and $\mathbf{a} = 2/3(\mathbf{g_1}) + 1/3(\mathbf{g_2})$ respectively. Comparing these two cases, while 75 % of $V_{2\Lambda}(\mathbf{0})$ area is IIR, $V_{2\Lambda}(2/3(\mathbf{g_1}) + 1/3(\mathbf{g_2}))$ has only 25 %. The objective is to estimate the Euclidean distance between two points from Hamming distance between those two points with as low MSE as possible. We believe that minimizing MSE is equivalent to minimizing the area of IIRs by choosing vector $a$. As we can see, when moving vector $\mathbf{a}$, $V_{2\Lambda}(2/3(\mathbf{g_1}) + 1/3(\mathbf{g_2}))$ is the best choice to achieve minimum percentage of ineffective regions. In this research, for two-dimensional space, we used $V_{2\Lambda}(2/3(\mathbf{g_1}) + 1/3(\mathbf{g_2}))$. The centroid of $V_{2\Lambda}(2/3(\mathbf{g_1}) + 1/3(\mathbf{g_2}))$ is the lattice's deep hole [9], which is the point of the plane furthest from the lattice.

## 4 Simulation of Two-Dimensional Indexing Schemes

A two-dimensional nested lattice and a Gray indexing scheme were implemented and simulations were ran with the two input distribution cases

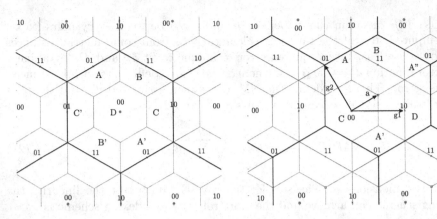

**Fig. 4.** Voronoi region $V_{2\Lambda}(\mathbf{0})$.

**Fig. 5.** Voronoi region $V_{2\Lambda}(\mathbf{a})$, where $\mathbf{a} = 2/3(\mathbf{g_1}) + 1/3(\mathbf{g_2})$.

**Table 1.** Case $(a)$: Nested lattice and Gray indexing scheme simulation information.

| Indexing scheme | Metric distance | NMSE |
|---|---|---|
| Gray code | $d_E$ vs. $d_H$ | 113.7115 |
| Lattice code | $d_E$ vs. $d_{WH}$ | 106.8708 |
| Lattice code | $d_E$ vs. $d_{FD}$ | 91.7450 |

which are described in Sect. 3.2. For fair comparison, we used: dimension $n = 2$, fundamental volume equal to one ($V(\Lambda) = 1$), level $m = 7$ means 14 bits per hash value, $10^4$ two-dimensional real input data points (or vectors) $\mathbf{x} \in [0, 2^{m-1}]^2$ uniformly distributed in Case $(a)$ and $10^4$ additional two-dimensional Gaussian noise vectors $\mathbf{N}(0, \sigma^2)$ in Case $(b)$. Particularly, these two indexing schemes are based on two corresponding quantizers, therefore quantization error depends on the lattice (and is slightly better for the hexagonal lattice). The density of points relates the possible number of hash values to the quantization error, and that is why we fairly compared lattice and Gray quantizer with fundamental volume equal to one.

When the input vectors $\mathbf{x}$ and $\mathbf{x}'$ are uniformly distributed, as in Case $(a)$ in Sect. 3.2, the $(d_E, d_H)$ for every sample pairs in the dataset, along with its linear predictor function for Gray indexing are shown in Fig. 6. Similarly, the $(d_E, d_{WH})$ and $(d_E, d_{FD})$ for every possible pairs, along with their linear predictor functions for nested lattice indexing are shown in Figs. 7 and 8, respectively. Table 1 depicts the NMSE and other details about this comparison simulation. The smaller the NMSE, the better the linearity the indexing scheme can achieve.

When the input $\mathbf{x}$ is uniformly distributed and $\mathbf{x}'$ is Gaussian distributed, as in Case $(b)$ in Sect. 3.2, we adjust noise intensity by changing Gaussian variance $\sigma^2$. The $(d_E, d_H)$, $(d_E, d_{FD})$ between original vectors $\mathbf{x}$ and noisy vectors $\mathbf{x}'$ are computed and fitted by linear predictor functions. Figure 9 represents the

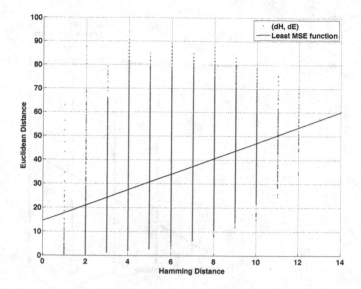

**Fig. 6.** Case ($a$): The Hamming distance versus the Euclidean distances of Gray indexing.

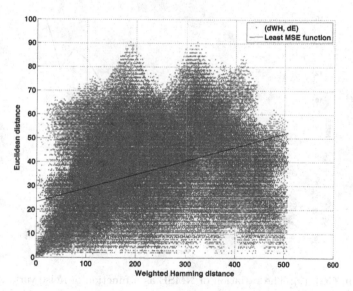

**Fig. 7.** Case ($a$): The weighted Hamming distance versus the Euclidean distances of nested lattice indexing.

variation of NMSE values of linear predictor functions as a function of noise variance $\sigma^2$ for two-dimensional Gray indexing and lattice indexing.

We observe that, nested lattice indexing generally have better performance than Gray indexing. In Case ($a$), the combination of nested lattice indexing and

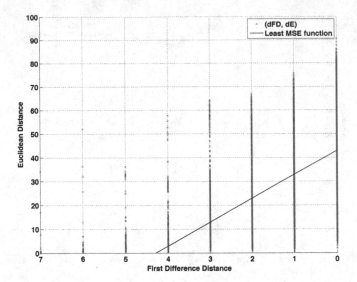

**Fig. 8.** Case $(a)$: The first difference distance versus the Euclidean distances of nested lattice indexing.

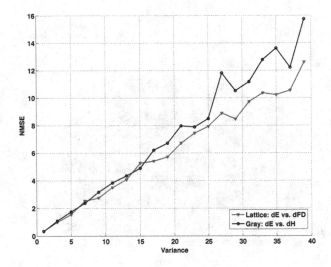

**Fig. 9.** Case $(b)$: The variation of NMSE as a function of noise variance.

first difference distance reduces approximately 20 % NMSE compared to Gray indexing. In Case $(b)$, on average, nested lattice indexing have smaller NMSE than Gray indexing.

# 5    Conclusion

In this paper, we developed a nested lattice indexing scheme that is suitable for content-based hash functions to increase the robustness. In addition, weighted Hamming distance, first difference distance and a coset lattice with shift vector $\mathbf{a} = 2/3(\mathbf{g_1}) + 1/3(\mathbf{g_2})$ were proposed to efficiently reflect the Euclidean distance. As a result, the NMSE of nested lattice indexing scheme was reduced 20 % compared to Gray indexing scheme. As future work, we will apply higher dimensional lattices with the expectation of a better relationship between metric distance and Euclidean distance. To demonstrate the effectiveness of lattice-based hashing, we plan to apply it to image's speeded up robust features (SURF) [11] to quantize and index SURF-based feature vectors to final hash values.

# References

1. Menezes, A.J., Van Oorschot, P.C., Vanstone, S.A.: Handbook of Applied Cryptography. CRC Press, Boca Raton (1996)
2. Huang, C.-L., Huang, D.-H.: A content-based image retrieval system. Image Vis. Comput. **16**(3), 149–163 (1998)
3. Agrawal, R., Faloutsos, C., Swami, A.: Efficient similarity search in sequence databases. In: Lomet, D.B. (ed.) FODO 1993. LNCS, vol. 730, pp. 69–84. Springer, Heidelberg (1993)
4. Venkatesan, R., et al.: Robust image hashing. In: Proceedings, 2000 International Conference on Image Processing, vol. 3. IEEE (2000)
5. Hernandez, R.A.P., Miyatake, M.N., Kurkoski, B.M.: Robust image hashing using image normalization and SVD decomposition. In: 2011 IEEE 54th Midwest Symposium on MWSCAS. IEEE (2011)
6. Faloutsos, C.: Gray codes for partial match and range queries. IEEE Trans. Softw. Eng. **14**(10), 1381–1393 (1988)
7. Guopu, Z., et al.: Fragility analysis of adaptive quantization-based image hashing. IEEE Trans. Inf. Forensics Secur. **5**(1), 133–147 (2010)
8. Li, Y., et al.: Robust image hashing based on random Gabor filtering and dithered lattice vector quantization. IEEE Trans. Image Process. **21**, 1963–1980 (2012)
9. Conway, J.H., Sloane, N.J.A.: Sphere Packings, Lattices and Groups, 3rd edn. Springer, New York (1999)
10. Gray, R.M.: Vector quantization. IEEE ASSP Mag. **1**(2), 4–29 (1984)
11. Bay, H., Tuytelaars, T., Van Gool, L.: SURF: speeded up robust features. In: Leonardis, A., Bischof, H., Pinz, A. (eds.) ECCV 2006, Part I. LNCS, vol. 3951, pp. 404–417. Springer, Heidelberg (2006)
12. Conway, J.H., Sloane, N.J.A.: A fast encoding method for lattice codes and quantizers. IEEE Trans. Inf. Theory **IT-29**, 820–824 (1983)
13. Gray, F.: Pulse code communication. U.S. Patent, 17 March 1953
14. Hamming, R.W.: Error detecting and error correcting codes. Bell Syst. Tech. J. **29**(2), 147–160 (1950)

# An Improved Aspect Ratio Invariant Visual Cryptography Scheme with Flexible Pixel Expansion

Wen Wang[1]([✉]), Feng Liu[1], Weiqi Yan[2], Gang Shen[3], and Teng Guo[4]

[1] State Key Laboratory of Information Security Institute of Information Engineering, Chinese Academy of Sciences, Beijing, China
wangwen@iie.ac.cn
[2] Auckland University of Technology, Auckland, New Zealand
[3] Zhengzhou Information Science and Technology Institute, Zhengzhou, China
[4] School of Information Science and Technology, University of International Relations, Beijing, China

**Abstract.** In traditional visual cryptography scheme (VCS), each pixel of secret image is encrypted into $m(\geqslant 1)$ subpixels in the share images. Unfortunately, recovered image will be distorted when the pixel expansion is not a square number. In order to reveal the information of the secret image faithfully, aspect ratio of the recovered image should be kept invariant in VCS. In this paper, we investigate the encryption process of traditional VCS and find that it is able to be divided into mapping stage and size invariant VCS (SIVCS) stage. By improving algorithms of these two stages respectively, we propose a novel construction of aspect ratio invariant VCS (ARIVCS) with flexible pixel expansion. Experimental results show the effectiveness of our scheme that it avoids the defects found in previous research works such as the details distortion problem, thin line problems and blurry edge problem. Meanwhile, our scheme eliminates the jaggy phenomenon to a certain extent when the pixel expansion is large which contributes to improving the visual quality of ARIVCS significantly.

**Keywords:** Visual cryptography · Flexible · Jaggy phenomenon

## 1 Introduction

The concept of visual cryptography schemes (VCS) was first proposed by Naor and Shamir [1]. Its basic idea is to split a secret image into several meaningless shares which consist of only black and white pixels. In decoding phase, secret information is able to be visually recovered without complicated mathematical computation. Due to its easy and rapid decryption mode, VCS has attracted many researchers' attention during the past twenty years. More comprehensive knowledge on VCS is able to be found in publication [2].

A traditional $(k, n)$-VCS has to satisfy the conditions that any $k$ out of $n$ shares recover the secret image while any less than $k$ shares get nothing. Each secret pixel

© Springer International Publishing Switzerland 2016
Y.-Q. Shi et al. (Eds.): IWDW 2015, LNCS 9569, pp. 418–432, 2016.
DOI: 10.1007/978-3-319-31960-5_34

is mapped into $m$ subpixels (called pixel expansion) in the share images. Hence, the size of the recovered image is $m$-times bigger than that of the secret image. When the pixel expansion is large, it is inconvenient for storage and transmission of the shares which affects the applications of VCS seriously. In order to reduce the pixel expansion, size invariant VCS (SIVCS) using probabilistic method is proposed [3]. Different from traditional VCS, the secret pixels are recovered with a certain probability in SIVCS. The pixel expansion is reduced in the price of visual quality. Then, a bunch of articles [5–12] are published subsequently for the sake of enhancing the visual quality of SIVCS. In recent years, new constructions of SIVCS based on random grid method [13–18] also contribute to the improvement of visual quality.

Meanwhile, when the pixel expansion $m$ ($> 1$) is not a square number, aspect ratio of the recovered image is distorted which will cause information loss in the case that shape of the secret image also represents a certain of information. To deal with the pixel expansion and distortion problems, a flexible VCS without distortion was proposed [19] by simulating the concept of fountains. Pixels in the secret image are compared to the injection nozzles, and they are evenly distributed in the pool which has the same size with share images. All the injection nozzles (secret pixels) spray water (subpixels) simultaneously and fill up the pool (share images). The scheme not only preserves the aspect ratio invariant but also generates shares with optional pixel expansion. However, the scheme can't allocate identical number of subpixels to every secret pixel and details of the recovered image are slightly distorted. Then another aspect ratio invariant VCS (ARIVCS) was proposed [20] utilizing image filtering and resizing methods. When the secret image is black and white, Yang's scheme first converts it into grayscale image with a low-pass filter. Then they resize and halftone the grayscale image to a particular shape on purpose that the handled image can generate aspect ratio invariant shares using deterministic VCS (DVCS). From the experimental results, we find that the scheme achieves fine visual quality when the secret image is natural. But details of the recovered image is blurry when the secret image consists of obvious outlines. What's more, compared with [19], Yang's scheme only directs in the distortion problem of DVCS with a certain pixel expansion. Other research works on the same goal are able to be found in [22–24]. In order to recover the details of secret images well and achieve optional pixel expansion, an improved ARIVCS is proposed [21]. Since pixels near the contour of the secret image are more important than the normal pixels in the recovery of the details. So they first detect the edge pixels and map these pixels in advance. The scheme performs very well when the secret images consist of apparent contour. But when the secret images are natural or the secret images take black color as background, Li's scheme loses details seriously especially when the pixel expansion is small.

In this paper, we investigate the encryption process of DVCS and find that it is able to be divided into the mapping and SIVCS stage. The image distortion problem is always caused by the mapping stage while the SIVCS stage determines the security and contrast conditions of DVCS. Based on this observation, we propose a new construction method of ARIVCS. Compared to the well-known

ARIVCSs [19–21], our scheme avoids all the defects such as the details distortion problem, thin line problems, and blurry edge problem. Meanwhile, our scheme also eliminates the jaggy phenomenon to a certain extent when the pixel expansion is large.

The rest of this paper is organized as follows. In Sect. 2, we introduce the preliminaries of the traditional VCS, and give a brief description of the distortion problem. In Sect. 3, we present our design concept and propose a new construction method of ARIVCS. In Sect. 4, we will compare the experimental results of our scheme and some well-known schemes. Finally, this paper is concluded in Sect. 5.

## 2 Preliminaries

### 2.1 Definitions of Traditional VCS

According to the previous papers, there are two methods to accomplish a $(k,n)$-VCS: deterministic VCS and probabilistic VCS. Actually, probabilistic VCS with no pixel expansion is also known as the size invariant VCS. To elaborate the concepts of VCS, we give the formal definitions of these two schemes as follows:

**Definition 1** (Deterministic VCS [1]). A $(k, n)$-VCS consists of two collections of $n \times m$ Boolean matrices $C_0$ and $C_1$. To share a white (resp. black) pixel, the dealer randomly chooses a matrix in $C_0$ (resp. $C_1$). These two collections of matrices must satisfy the following contrast and security conditions:

1. (Contrast) For any matrix S in $C_0$ (resp. $C_1$), the vector $v$ derived from the OR operation of any $k$ out of $n$ rows satisfies $w(v) \leq l$ (resp. $w(v) \geq h$), where $0 \leq l < h \leq m$.
2. (Security) For any subset $\{i_1, i_2, \ldots, i_t\} \subset \{1, 2, \ldots, n\}$ with $t < k$ , the two collections of $t \times m$ matrices, obtained by restricting each $n \times m$ matrix in $C_0$ and $C_1$ to the rows $\{i_1, i_2, \ldots, i_t\}$, contain the same matrices with the same frequencies.

**Note:** in the above definition, $m$ is called the pixel expansion of DVCS. It means that each pixel in the secret image is represented as an $m$-pixel block in the share images. $\alpha = \frac{h-l}{m}$ is defined as the contrast of DVCS. The recovered secret image with larger contrast usually has better visual quality. Particularly, the collections $C_0$ and $C_1$ are able to be constructed from the column permutation of a pair of basis matrices $B_0$ and $B_1$.

**Definition 2** (Size Invariant VCS [5]). A $(k, n)$-SIVCS consists of two collections of $n \times 1$ Boolean matrices $C_0$ and $C_1$. In order to share a white pixel (resp. black), one matrix in $C_0$ (resp. $C_1$) is randomly chosen, and each row of the matrix is distributed to the corresponding share image. Accordingly, these two collections of $n \times 1$ Boolean matrices should satisfy the following conditions:

1. (Contrast) For the collection $C_0$ (resp. $C_1$), the OR operation of any $k$ out of $n$ rows generates a collection $M_0$ (resp. $M_1$) consists of 0 s and 1 s. We denote the probability that 1 s appear in the collection $M_0$ (resp. $M_1$) as $p_w$ (resp. $p_b$). Then there must be a relation $p_w < p_b$.

2. (Security) For any subset $\{i_1, i_2, \ldots, i_r\} \subset \{1, 2, \ldots, n\}$ with $r < k$, the probability of $p_w$ and $p_b$ are equal.

For a $(k, n)$-SIVCS, when $k$ or more shares are overlapped, a white (resp. black) pixel in the secret image is recovered to a black pixel with the probability $p_w$ (resp. $p_b$). The secret image is only recovered in an overall view. For purpose of improving the visual quality of SIVCS, F. Liu et al. [12] proposed another typical construction as follows:

**Construction 1** $((k, n)$-Multi-pixel encryption size invariant VCS [12]). $C_0$ and $C_1$ are the two collections of DVCS under *Definition* 1, $m$ is the pixel expansion of the matrix. The secret image is divided into $p \times q$ blocks of $r \times s$ pixels. The block is denoted as $B_{r \times s, b}$, where $b$ is the number of black pixels. The following steps encrypt a block $B_{r \times s, b}$ at a time which satisfies $m|(r \times s)$ and $m|b$. $((r \times s)$ and $b$ are multiple of m).

1. For $p = 0$ to $\frac{I_H}{s} - 1$, where $I_H$ is the height of the secret image.
2. For $q = 0$ to $\frac{I_W}{r} - 1$, where $I_W$ is the width of the secret image.
3. /*Encrypt the black and white pixels in block $B_{r \times s, b}$ separately.*/
4. For $i = 0$ to $\frac{b}{m} - 1$
5. Select $m$ black pixels that has not been encrypted in order, choose a matrix in $C_1$ randomly and encrypt these pixels with the chosen matrix.
6. For $j = 0$ to $\frac{r \times s - b}{m} - 1$
7. Select $m$ white pixels that has not been encrypted in order, choose a matrix in $C_0$ randomly and encrypt these pixels with the chosen matrix.

The scheme divides secret image into several blocks and encrypts the black and white pixels separately in one block. This method not only improves visual quality of the recovered image, but also avoids the thin line problems which make a significant contribution to SIVCS.

## 2.2 The Distortion Problem of VCS

In traditional VCS with pixel expansion $m > 1$, each pixel of the secret image is expanded into a block of $m$ pixels. Generally, $m$ is not a square number, and then it's hard to keep aspect ratio of the recovered image invariant.

Figure 1 shows an example of $(2, 2)$-DVCS with pixel expansion $m = 2$. Since the number 2 is not a square number, we can only arrange the two subpixels in two ways: horizontal or vertical. The example in Fig. 1 adopts the horizontal way. But when the shape of a picture also represents an important information, the drawbacks are apparent. Hence, for the sake of revealing secret information faithfully, the secret image should be recovered without any distortions.

A simple solution to this problem is that we append extra pixels to expand the pixel expansion into a square number. Taking the $(2, 2)$-DVCS in Fig. 1 for instance, in order to make up a square number 4, we append extra pixel expansion and the size of the recovered image is doubled again. This method

(a) Secret image

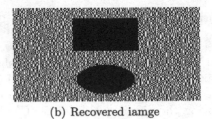

(b) Recovered iamge

**Fig. 1.** A $(2, 2)$-DVCS with pixel expansion $m = 2$. (a) the original image with size $100 \times 100$, (b) the recovered image with size $200 \times 100$.

is an acceptable solution when the extra pixel expansion is negligible to the whole pixel expansion.

In order to reduce the pixel expansion and deal with the distortion problem, F. Liu et al. [19] first proposed an aspect ration invariant VCS with flexible pixel expansion. In the scheme, the pixel expansion of the recovered image is optional, and it is not confined to be equal to the pixel expansion of a $(k, n)$-DVCS. Hence, we denote $m_s$ as the size expansion which refers to the size of the recovered image is $m_s$ times of the size of the secret image. $m$ still represents the pixel expansion of $(k, n)$-DVCS. For $(k, n)$-DVCS, the minimum pixel expansion $m$ is a constant integer. But the size expansion $m_s$ in flexible ARIVCS is a real number. Then C.N. Yang et al. [20] also proposed an ARIVCS using image filtering and resizing methods. Actually, the scheme only attempts to deal with the distortion problem of DVCS with a certain pixel expansion. Subsequently, [21] extended the resizing step to achieve optional size expansion which is also suitable for [20]. However, when we inspect visual quality of the recovered images, some undesirable drawbacks still exist in the previous schemes. In the following section, we will analyze the typical schemes and propose a new one without distortion, which avoids the drawbacks existed in the previous schemes.

## 3 The Proposed ARIVCS

### 3.1 Design Concept

As depicted in *Definition* 1, traditional DVCS encrypts a secret pixel by a matrix chosen from collections $C_0$ or $C_1$. But when we investigate the encryption process of DVCS in another way, we divide it into two stages. The first stage is to map a secret pixel into $m$ subpixels which have identical color. Through this stage, we obtain a mapped image and its size is $m$ times of the size of the secret image. Then the next stage is to encrypt $m$ black (resp. white) pixels of the mapped image with a matrix chosen from the relevant collection $C_1$ (resp. $C_0$). The second stage is a SIVCS in essence which encrypts $m$-pixels at a time. The encryption process of DVCS with two stages is shown in Fig. 2.

From Fig. 2, the distortion problem of DVCS is mainly caused by the mapping stage. While the SIVCS stage determines the contrast and security conditions

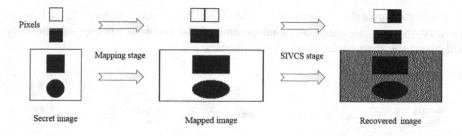

**Fig. 2.** The encryption process of DVCS with pixel expansion greater than 1.

of DVCS. Hence, to keep the aspect ratio of the recovered image invariant, much more efforts should be paid to the mapping stage so as to generating a mapped image which preserves its original aspect ratio. For traditional DVCS, the color of a pixel in the mapped image is only determined by the color of one secret pixel (See the pixels encryption process from upper part of Fig. 2). Therefore, the mapping stage of DVCS is the nearest neighbor interpolation method in image scaling field. But it is widely known that the nearest neighbor interpolation leads to undesirable jaggies when the picture is enlarged. Moreover, the nearest neighbor interpolation loses information of the secret image largely in the case of image shrinking.

In order to reduce the information loss and eliminate unwanted jaggies in the mapping stage, the color of one pixel in the mapped image is determined by more secret pixels. This is a widely considered problem in image scaling field. Here, we adopt the bicubic interpolation method in the mapping because each pixel in the mapped image is generated by sixteen secret pixels. However, when we apply the bicubic interpolation in the mapping, no matter the secret image is binary or gray-scale, it usually generates gray-scale image and blurs the image edge. Therefore, we adopt the image sharpening algorithm as a subsequent one to highlight the contour of resized image. In this paper, we apply the unsharp masking (USM) as a typical image sharpening algorithm. Finally, we utilize halftone technology to convert the grayscale image to binary one. Generally, halftone error diffusion method is appropriate for natural images while threshold method is more suitable for images having apparent contour.

As for the SIVCS stage, it determines contrast and security conditions of the whole scheme. Hence, it is very important to select a proper SIVCS which balances these two aspects well. F. Liu et al. [12] presents a SIVCS (*Construction* 1 of our paper). The scheme divides secret image into several blocks and encrypts the black and white pixels separately in one block. The security condition of the scheme relies on the size of block. By choosing a proper size of block, their scheme achieves fine visual quality without leaking any important information. Moreover, their scheme avoids the thin line problems existing in VCS. For the sake of improving visual quality of our scheme, we apply Liu's scheme in the SIVCS stage.

Figure 3 shows the design of our ARIVCS. By selecting proper algorithms in these two stages, we enhance visual quality of the recovered image significantly and avoid the drawbacks in previous schemes.

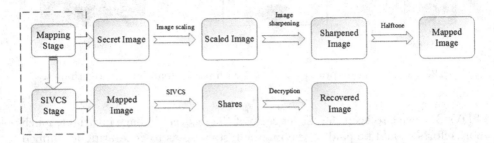

**Fig. 3.** The design of the proposed ARIVCS.

## 3.2 The Proposed Scheme

**Construction 2**

**Input:** The secret image $I$ with size $x \times y$; the size expansion $m_s$.
**Output:** Share images $S_1, S_2, \ldots, S_n$ without distortion.
**Step 1.** Apply the bicubic interpolation to the secret image and generate a resized image $I_{scale}$ with size $\sqrt{m_s}x \times \sqrt{m_s}y$.
**Step 2.** Enhance the out lines of image $I_{scale}$ by the unsharp masking algorithm. The generated image is denoted as $I_{sharpen}$.
**Step 3.** Generate the mapped image $I_{mapped}$ from image $I_{sharpen}$ utilizing halftone technology. Specifically, we use halftone error diffusion method for natural images and adopt threshold method for images with apparent outlines. The size of the binary image $I_{mapped}$ is $\sqrt{m_s}x \times \sqrt{m_s}y$.
**Step 4.** Apply the $(k, n)$-SIVCS presented in *Construction 1* to the mapped image $I_{mapped}$, and generate $n$ share images $S_1, S_2, \ldots, S_n$ with size $\sqrt{m_s}x \times \sqrt{m_s}y$.

**Note.** Since the mapping stage only aims at generating a mapped image with fine visual quality. The contrast and security conditions of the scheme are determined by the SIVCS in *Construction 1*. For the sake of security, conditions that $m|(r \times s)$ and $m|b$ should be satisfied in *Construction 1*. When we divide the mapped images into blocks with size $r \times s$, some blocks may not satisfy the condition $m|b$. To deal with this problem, an algorithm is presented [12] to modify the secret image. Here, according to the requirement of our scheme, we propose an adapted algorithm to adjust the mapped image.

## Algorithm 1.

---

**Input:** The grayscale image $I_{sharpen}$ and the binary image $I_{mapped}$ with size $\sqrt{m_s}x \times \sqrt{m_s}y$; the block size $r \times s$ which satisfies $m|(r \times s)$.

**Output:** Modified image so that each block of the images satisfies that the number of black pixels is a multiple of $m$.

1. Divide the image $I_{mapped}$ and $I_{sharpen}$ into $\frac{I_W}{r} \times \frac{I_H}{s}$ blocks and initial the error matrix $E[\frac{I_W}{r}][\frac{I_H}{s}]$ by setting all its entries to 0, where $I_H$ and $I_W$ are the height and width of the mapped image respectively.
2. For $p = 0$ to $\frac{I_H}{s} - 1$.
3. For $q = 0$ to $\frac{I_W}{r} - 1$.
4. /*Suppose the position of the block $B_{r \times s,b}$ in image $I_{mapped}$ is $(p,q)$. $b$ is the number of black pixels in the block $B_{r \times s,b}$.*/
5. $b \leftarrow b \bmod m$.
6. If $b - E[q][p] < m - b$
7. Select the block in image $I_{sharpen}$ with the same position $(p,q)$. Since the image $I_{sharpen}$ is grayscale, we set the grayscale value of the pixels in $I_{sharpen}$ as the weight of the pixels in $I_{mapped}$ which have the same position in the block. Then choose $b$ black pixels that have the maximum weight from the block $B_{r \times s,b}$ and covert them into white pixels.
8. $E[q+1][p] \leftarrow E[q+1][p] + \frac{3}{8}(E[q][p] - b)$.
9. $E[q+1][p+1] \leftarrow E[q+1][p+1] + \frac{1}{4}(E[q][p] - b)$.
10. $E[q][p+1] \leftarrow E[q][p+1] + \frac{3}{8}(E[q][p] - b)$.
11. Else
12. Select the block in image $I_{sharpen}$ with the same position $(p,q)$. Set the grayscale value of the pixels in $I_{sharpen}$ as the weight of the pixels in $I_{mapped}$ which have the same position in the block. Then choose $m - b$ white pixels that have the minimum weight from the block $B_{r \times s,b}$ and covert them into black pixels.
13. $E[q+1][p] \leftarrow E[q+1][p] + \frac{3}{8}(E[q][p] + m - b)$.
14. $E[q+1][p+1] \leftarrow E[q+1][p+1] + \frac{1}{4}(E[q][p] + m - b)$.
15. $E[q][p+1] \leftarrow E[q][p+1] + \frac{3}{8}(E[q][p] + m - b)$.

---

**Remark.** This algorithm will convert $b \bmod m$ black pixels to white pixels or covert $m - (b \bmod m)$ white pixels to black pixels according to the weight get from image $I_{sharpen}$. Hence the number of black pixels in block $B_{r \times s,b}$ of the mapped image is a multiple of $m$. Then the conditions of *Construction* 1 are satisfied and the mapped image after modification can be encrypted by the SIVCS directly.

## 4  Experimental Results

### 4.1  Comparisons Between Our Scheme and Typical ARIVCSs [19–21]

According to the analysis before, [20] is only designed to deal with the distortion problem of DVCS with a certain pixel expansion. But we can extend the resizing step of [20] to achieve optional size expansion by the method used in [21]. Then all of the three ARIVCSs [19–21] achieve flexible size expansion. To illustrate the effectiveness of our proposed scheme in *Construction* 2, we conduct experiments in two cases: (i) the size expansion $m_s \leqslant 1$, (ii) the size expansion $m_s > 1$. Moreover, in order to show comprehensive visual effects and reveal problems of the schemes, we use three images shown as in Fig. 4. A $512 \times 512$ black and white image "Ruler" which consists of regular thin lines; a natural image "Lena" with resolution $512 \times 512$; and a $400 \times 400$ image "Background" having different background colors.

(a)                          (b)                          (c)

**Fig. 4.** The three original images used in the experiments: (a) $512 \times 512$ "Ruler", (b) $512 \times 512$ "Lena", (c) $400 \times 400$ "Background"

**Experiment 1.** We will construct (2, 2)-ARIVCSs with the schemes in *Construction* 2 and [19–21]. Actually, [19] provides a primary scheme and an improved scheme. In order to achieve better visual quality, we adopt the improved scheme. Meanwhile, for our scheme, parameters of the USM algorithm in Step 2 are set as follows: $amount = 160$, $radius = 1.5$, and $threshold = 0$. Moreover, we adopt the halftone error diffusion method in Step 3 and the size of the block in *Construction* 1 is $2 \times 2$. Since the collections of DVCS are utilized in all of the four schemes, we construct a (2, 2)-DVCS from the basis matrices $B_0 = \begin{pmatrix} 1 & 0 \\ 1 & 0 \end{pmatrix}$ and $B_1 = \begin{pmatrix} 1 & 0 \\ 0 & 1 \end{pmatrix}$. Then the experiment is conducted in two cases $m_s = 0.49$ and $m_s = 6.25$.

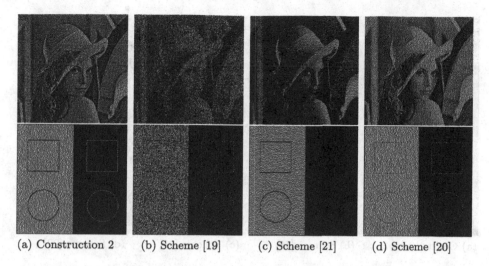

(a) Construction 2    (b) Scheme [19]    (c) Scheme [21]    (d) Scheme [20]

**Fig. 5.** ARIVCSs with size expansion $m_s = 0.49$, the resolutions of the recovered "Lena" and "Background" are $358 \times 358$ and $280 \times 280$ respectively.

**Table 1.** Comparisons on the values of SSIM and MSSIM in the case $m_s = 0.49$ (By comparing the recovered images with two standard images $I_N$ and $I_B$ which are generated by the nearest neighbor interpolation and bicubic interpolation respectively).

| | | Comparison with Standard image $I_N$ | | Comparison with Standard image $I_B$ | |
|---|---|---|---|---|---|
| | | SSIM | MSSIM | SSIM | MSSIM |
| "Lena" | Scheme [19] | 0.09745 | 0.03162 | 0.13891 | 0.03412 |
| | Scheme [21] | 0.07560 | 0.02393 | 0.12285 | 0.02870 |
| | Scheme [20] | 0.18664 | 0.05166 | 0.26241 | 0.07629 |
| | Construction 2 | 0.19140 | 0.11360 | 0.26768 | 0.16554 |
| "Background" | Scheme [19] | 0.23236 | 0.01820 | 0.23611 | 0.02503 |
| | Scheme [21] | 0.43630 | 0.02645 | 0.44197 | 0.02911 |
| | Scheme [20] | 0.43890 | 0.02296 | 0.44278 | 0.02786 |
| | Construction 2 | 0.44478 | 0.06537 | 0.44903 | 0.07655 |

Figures 5 and 6 are experimental results of the four schemes in the cases $m_s \leqslant 1$ and $m_s > 1$. In order to reveal the problems existed in the typical ARIVCSs, we use two secret images in each case. Particularly, when $m_s > 1$, the recovered images are so large that we only extract part of the recovered images and show the details.

From the experimental results, we obtain obvious comparisons on visual quality of the proposed ARIVCSs. Scheme [19] can't reveal the secret images well when the size expansion $m_s \leqslant 1$. Because their scheme can't allocate the same number of subpixels to the secret pixels, and details of the recovered images are slightly distorted. For scheme [21], it loses the details seriously when the

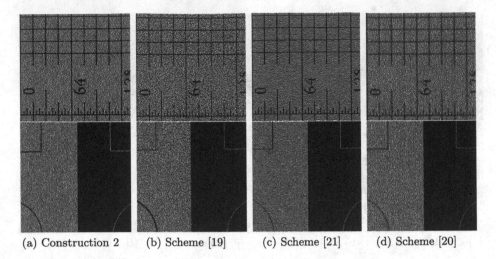

(a) Construction 2     (b) Scheme [19]     (c) Scheme [21]     (d) Scheme [20]

**Fig. 6.** ARIVCSs with size expansion $m_s = 6.25$, the recovered "Ruler" is $1280 \times 1280$, the recovered "Background" is $1000 \times 1000$. To show details of the recovered images, we extract $350 \times 350$ pixels from the recovered images.

**Table 2.** Comparisons on the values of SSIM and MSSIM in the case $m_s = 6.25$ (By comparing the recovered images with two standard images $I_N$ and $I_B$ which are generated by the nearest neighbor interpolation and bicubic interpolation respectively).

| | | Comparison with Standard image $I_N$ | | Comparison with Standard image $I_B$ | |
|---|---|---|---|---|---|
| | | SSIM | MSSIM | SSIM | MSSIM |
| "Ruler" | Scheme [19] | 0.16342 | 0.06777 | 0.16025 | 0.07617 |
| | Scheme [21] | 0.19051 | 0.08196 | 0.17086 | 0.07663 |
| | Scheme [20] | 0.09491 | 0.02257 | 0.12023 | 0.03410 |
| | Construction 2 | 0.18453 | 0.06579 | 0.20860 | 0.09088 |
| "Background" | Scheme [19] | 0.40245 | 0.02162 | 0.40400 | 0.01956 |
| | Scheme [21] | 0.44834 | 0.01767 | 0.45049 | 0.01892 |
| | Scheme [20] | 0.44192 | 0.01155 | 0.44578 | 0.01487 |
| | Construction 2 | 0.44750 | 0.02562 | 0.44910 | 0.02479 |

secret image is natural or contains black background which is demonstrated in the images (c) of Fig. 5. Meanwhile, by observations on the recovered images (c) in Fig. 6, we find that the recovered thin lines have distinct thickness while the thickness of these lines are identical in the secret image. This is a typical kind of thin line problem defined in [12]. Moreover, we observe from the experimental results that scheme [20] recovers the secret images with fine visual quality when size expansion $m_s \leqslant 1$. However, the scheme makes the edges of the secret images blurry when the size expansion $m_s > 1$. The image (d) in Fig. 6 illustrates this problem in details.

In this paper, we also apply the evaluation criteria proposed by Z. Wang et al. [4] to assess visual quality. Z. Wang et al. developed a measure of structural similarity (SSIM) which has been be used globally or locally. When calculating the value of SSIM locally, the mean SSIM (MSSIM) is suggested to evaluate the overall image quality. Since our visual system always concentrates on the local of a image, the value of MSSIM is more accurate than the value of global SSIM. Generally, the values of SSIM and MSSIM range from 0 to 1. Bigger value usually means the better visual quality.

Considering that the recovered images have too much noise, we adopt the global SSIM and MSSIM to evaluate visual quality of the recovered images together. Nevertheless, Wang's method only examines two pictures with the same size. Hence, we generate two standard images that have the same size with the recovered images by two kinds of image scaling methods, the nearest neighbor interpolation and bicubic interpolation. But it is widely known that the visual quality of the image generated by the bicubic interpolation is better than image produced by the nearest neighbor interpolation. Therefore, when evaluating visual quality of the recovered images, we mainly use standard image generated by the bicubic interpolation. The standard image generated by the nearest neighbor interpolation is utilized as an extra reference to our assessment. Then the $7 \times 7$ circular-symmetric Gaussian weighting function with standard deviation of 1.5 samples is used to figure the value of MSSIM.

The values of SSIM and MSSIM are shown in Tables 1 and 2. From the values of SSIM and MSSIM compared with standard image $I_B$ in Table 1. For image "Lena", the values of the schemes [19, 21] are smaller than the other two schemes. But for image "Background", the MSSIM values of [19–21] are nearly the same. When $m_s > 1$, we see from the last column of Table 2 that the values of [20] are the smallest, the values of [19, 21] are roughly identical, and the values of our scheme are the largest. The results from Tables 1 and 2 correspond to the visual effects shown in Figs. 5 and 6 accurately. Hence, the effectiveness of our scheme is verified by visual effects of the recovered images and the evaluation results of SSIM and MSSIM. Compared to the previous ARIVCSs, our scheme avoids the defects found in [19–21] and achieves better visual quality both in the cases $m_s \leqslant 1$ and $m_s > 1$.

### 4.2 Comparisons on the Jaggy Phenomenon

In image scaling, smooth straight lines or curves are usually mapped into stairlike lines which is called the jaggy phenomenon. According to the analysis in former section, encryption process of DVCS is divided into two stages. Based on this investigation, the encryption process of [19, 21] is able to be divided into the mapping and SIVCS stage as well. Similar to DVCS, the mapping stages of [19, 21] are the nearest neighbor interpolation which will lead to undesirable jaggies when the pixel expansion is large. Nevertheless, our scheme adopts the bicubic interpolation in the mapping stage. As a result, the jaggy phenomenon is eliminated to a certain extent in our ARIVCS.

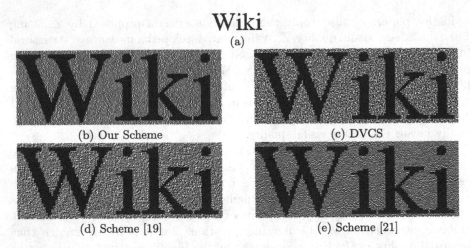

Fig. 7. (a) is the secret image "Jag" with size $109 \times 40$. (b)-(e) are the recovered images of our scheme, DVCS, scheme [19,21] with resolution $436 \times 160$.

Experiment 2. We use a secret image "Jag" to examine the jaggy phenomenon of our ARIVCS and some typical schemes. Different from *Experiment* 1, we use the threshold method in *Step 3*. Here we construct (2, 2)-ARIVCSs with size expansion $m_s = 16$ using the basis matrices $B_0 = \begin{pmatrix} 1 & 0 \\ 1 & 0 \end{pmatrix}$ and $B_1 = \begin{pmatrix} 1 & 0 \\ 0 & 1 \end{pmatrix}$. Meanwhile, we construct a (2, 2)-DVCS with pixel expansion $m = 16$ by concatenating the basis matrices $B_0$ and $B_1$.

From the experimental results Fig. 7, we see apparent comparisons on visual effects. Since the mapping of DVCS and schemes [19,21] is the nearest neighbor interpolation, lines in the secret image are recovered into the "stairway" shape. While our scheme eliminates undesirable jaggies and provides a more comfortable visual effects which is a significant improvement on the visual quality of ARIVCS.

## 5    Conclusions

In this paper, we investigate the encryption process of DVCS and find that the process can be divided into mapping stage and SIVCS stage. The mapping stage is the key point to keep aspect ratio invariant while the SIVCS stage determines contrast and security conditions of the scheme. By improving the algorithms of these two stages, we propose an improved ARIVCS which avoids all the defects such as the details distortion problem, thin line problems, and the blurry edge problem found in [19–21]. Moreover, our scheme can eliminate the jaggy phenomenon when the pixel expansion is large which contributes to improving the visual quality of ARIVCS significantly.

Moreover, the security and visual quality of [12] depend on the size of blocks. Smaller size leads to higher security but reduces visual quality of the recovered image. Hence we should select a proper size of blocks which balances the security and visual quality. In order to further improve visual quality of ARIVCS, new size invariant VCS with better visual quality will be studied in the future.

**Acknowledgments.** Many thanks to the anonymous reviewers for their valuable comments to improve our work. This work was supported by the Strategic Priority Research Program of the Chinese Academy of Sciences No. Y2W0012102 and the IIE Cryptography Research Project No. Y5X0061102.

# References

1. Naor, M., Shamir, A.: Visual cryptography. In: De Santis, A. (ed.) EUROCRYPT 1994. LNCS, vol. 950, pp. 1–12. Springer, Heidelberg (1995)
2. Liu, F., Yan, W.Q.: Visual Cryptography for Image Processing and Security - Theory, Methods, and Applications, pp. 1-143. Springer, Switzerland (2014). ISBN 978-3-319-09643-8
3. Kuwakado, H., Tanaka, H.: Image size invariant visual cryptography. IEICE Trans. Fund. Electron. Commun. Comput. Sci. **82**(10), 2172–2177 (1999)
4. Wang, Z., Bovik, A.C., Sheikh, H.R., Simoncelli, E.P.: Image quality assessment: from error visibility to structural similarity. IEEE Trans. Image Process. **13**(4), 600–612 (2004)
5. Yang, C.N.: New visual secret sharing schemes using probabilistic method. Pattern Recogn. Lett. **25**, 481–494 (2004)
6. Hou, Y.C., Tu, S.F.: Visual cryptography techniques for color images without pixel expansion. J. Inf. Technol. Soc. **1**, 95–110 (2004). (in Chinese)
7. Hou, Y.C., Tu, S.F.: A visual cryptographic technique for chromatic images using multi-pixel encoding method. J. Res. Pract. Inf. Technol. **37**(72), 179–192 (2005)
8. Cimato, S., De Prisco, R., De Santis, A.: Probabilistic visual cryptography schemes. Comput. J. **49**(1), 97–107 (2006)
9. Tu, S.F., Hou, Y.C.: Design of visual cryptographic methods with smoothlooking decoded images of invariant size for grey-level images. The Imaging Sci. J. **55**(2), 90–101 (2007)
10. Chen, Y.F., Chan, Y.K., Huang, C.C., Tsai, M.H., Chu, Y.P.: A multiple-level visual secret-sharing scheme without image size expansion. Inf. Sci. **177**(21), 4696–4710 (2007)
11. Lin, S.J., Chen, S.K., Lin, J.C.: Flip visual cryptography (FVC) with perfect security, conditionally-optimal contrast, and no expansion. J. Vis. Commun. Image Represent. **21**(8), 900–916 (2010)
12. Liu, F., Guo, T., Wu, C.K., Qian, L.: Improving the visual quality of size invariant visual cryptography scheme. J. Vis. Commun. Image Represent. **23**(2), 331–342 (2012)
13. Chen, T.H., Tsao, K.H.: Threshold visual secret sharing by random grids. J. Syst. Softw. **84**(7), 1197–1208 (2011)
14. Guo, T., Liu, F., Wu, C.K.: Threshold visual secret sharing by random grids with improved contrast. J. Syst. Softw. **86**(8), 2094–2109 (2013)
15. Lee, Y.S., Wang, B.J., Chen, T.H.: Quality-improved threshold visual secret sharing scheme by random grids. IET Image Process. **7**(2), 137–143 (2013)

16. Wu, X.T., Liu, T., Sun, W.: Improving the visual quality of random grid-based visual secret sharing via error diffusion. J. Vis. Commun. Image Represent. **24**(5), 552–566 (2013)

17. De Prisco, R., De Santis, A.: On the relation of random grid and deterministic visual cryptography. IEEE Trans. Inf. Forensics Secur. **9**(4), 653–665 (2014)

18. Shyu, S.J.: Visual cryptograms of random grids for threshold access structures. Theoret. Comput. Sci. **565**, 30–49 (2015)

19. Liu, F., Guo, T., Wu, C.K., Yang, C.-N.: Flexible visual cryptography scheme without distortion. In: Shi, Y.Q., Kim, H.-J., Perez-Gonzalez, F. (eds.) IWDW 2011. LNCS, vol. 7128, pp. 211–227. Springer, Heidelberg (2012)

20. Yang, C.N., Chen, P.W., Shih, H.W., Kim, C.: Aspect ratio invariant visual cryptography by image filtering and resizing. Pers. Ubiquit. Comput. **17**(5), 843–850 (2013)

21. Li, P., Ma, P.J., Li, D.: Aspect ratio invariant visual cryptography scheme with optional size expansion. In: Eighth International Conference on Intelligent Information Hiding and Multimedia Signal Processing (IIH-MSP), pp. 219–222. IEEE (2012)

22. Yang, C.N., Chen, T.S.: Aspect ratio invariant visual secret sharing schemes with minimum pixel expansion. Pattern Recogn. Lett. **26**(2), 193–206 (2005)

23. Yang, C.N., Chen, T.S.: Reduce shadow size in aspect ratio invariant visual secret sharing schemes using a square block-wise operation. Pattern Recogn. **39**(7), 1300–1314 (2006)

24. Yang, C.N., Lin, C.Y.: Almost-aspect-ratio-invariant visual cryptography without adding extra subpixels. Inf. Sci. **312**, 131–151 (2015)

# A New Construction of Tagged Visual Cryptography Scheme

Yawei Ren[1,3,4(✉)], Feng Liu[1], Dongdai Lin[1], Rongquan Feng[2],
and Wen Wang[1,4]

[1] State Key Laboratory of Information Security,
Institute of Information Engineering, Chinese Academy of Sciences,
Beijing 100093, China
renyawei@iie.ac.cn
[2] School of Mathematical Sciences, Peking University, Beijing 100871, China
[3] School of Information Management,
Beijing Information Science and Technology University, Beijing 100192, China
[4] University of Chinese Academy of Sciences, Beijing 100190, China

**Abstract.** Tagged visual cryptography scheme (TaVCS) is a new type of
visual cryptography scheme, in which an additional tag image is revealed
visually by folding up each share. A TaVCS not only carries augmented
information in each share, but also provides user-friendly interface to
identify each share. In this paper, we present a novel method to construct
$(k, n)$-TaVCS. It can adjust visual quality of both the reconstructed
secret image and the recovered tag image flexibly. Meanwhile, the proposed method provides better visual quality of both the reconstructed
secret image and the recovered tag image under certain condition. Experimental results and theoretical analysis demonstrate the effectiveness of
the proposed method.

**Keywords:** Visual cryptography · Secret sharing · Tagged visual
cryptography

## 1 Introduction

Visual cryptography scheme (VCS), firstly proposed by Naor and Shamir in [1],
is a branch of secret sharing. In a deterministic $(k, n)$-VCS, a secret image is
encoded into $n$ shares by expanding a secret pixel into $m$ subpixels. With any $k$
or more shares being stacked, the secret image can be reconstructed by human
visual system without complex computation, while fewer than $k$ shares cannot
recover the secret image.

The value of $m$ is referred to as the pixel expansion, which determines the
share size. Because larger pixel expansion causes inconvenient carrying of the
shares and distortion problem of the secret image, many researches tried to
reduce the pixel expansion [2–5]. The probabilistic VCSs [6,7] were proposed,
in which the generated shares are non-expansible. With no code book and pixel
expansion, some VCSs based on random grid (RG-based VCSs) were proposed

© Springer International Publishing Switzerland 2016
Y.-Q. Shi et al. (Eds.): IWDW 2015, LNCS 9569, pp. 433–445, 2016.
DOI: 10.1007/978-3-319-31960-5_35

in [8–10]. For reducing the suspicion to the meaningless shares, extended VCSs [11–16] were devised, in which the secret image is encoded into several meaningful shares.

Tagged VCS (TaVCS), as a new type of VCS, has the ability of managing the shares as well as extended VCS, which attaches an additional tag to each share such that it is recovered by folding up each tagged-share. A TaVCS not only carries augmented information in each share, but also supplies user-friendly interface to identify the shares. Wang and Hsu proposed a $(k,n)$-TaVCS in [17]. Their scheme firstly constructs $n$ interim shares from the secret image by using deterministic VCS or probabilistic VCS, then generates the final tagged-shares by embedding $n$ tag images into $n$ interim shares. Since each tagged-share is constructed by modifying white pixels in the interim share by black, the output tagged-share is darker than the original. Because of the darker shares, reduced visual quality of both the reconstructed secret image and the recovered tag image is provided in Wang and Hsu's scheme. Ou et al. proposed $(k,n)$ RG-based TaVCS in [18], in which each share is non-expansible and code book is not required in the encryption phase. Their scheme firstly constructs $n$ interim shares from $n$ tag images by using the $(2,2)$ RG-based VCS, then modifies $n$ interim shares into $n$ final tagged-shares according to the secret image. Comparing to Wang and Hsu's scheme, better visual quality of both the reconstructed secret image and the recovered tag image is provided in $(n,n)$ RG-based TaVCS and visual quality of the recovered secret image is reduced in some $(k,n)$ cases $(k < n)$.

In this paper, we present a novel method to construct $(k,n)$-TaVCS, which is based on the deterministic VCS or the probabilistic VCS. The proposed method can adjust visual quality of both the reconstructed secret image and the recovered tag image flexibly. Meanwhile, the proposed method provides better visual quality of both the reconstructed secret image and the recovered tag image under certain condition. Experimental results and theoretical analysis demonstrate the effectiveness of the proposed scheme.

The remainder of the paper is organized as follows: the deterministic $(k,n)$-VCS, the probabilistic $(k,n)$-VCS and $(k,n)$-TaVCS are reviewed in Sect. 2. We present the proposed $(k,n)$-TaVCS and make theoretical analysis in Sect. 3. Experimental results are shown in Sect. 4. At last, we make short conclusions about this paper in Sect. 5.

## 2   Preliminaries

### 2.1   $(k,n)$-VCS

In the deterministic $(k,n)$-VCS, white (resp. black) pixel is denoted as 0 (resp. 1) and each secret pixel is encoded into $n \times m$ subpixels. The decoding operation is "OR", which is denoted as $\otimes$. The deterministic $(k,n)$-VCS can be represented as two collections $C_0$ and $C_1$ of $n \times m$ Boolean matrices. When sharing a white (resp. black) pixel, the dealer chooses a $n \times m$ Boolean matrix from $C_0$ (resp. $C_1$) randomly and distributes a row of the matrix to the relative share. Particularly, the collections $C_0$ and $C_1$ are able to be constructed from the column permutation of a pair of basis matrices $B_0$ and $B_1$. The hamming weight of the vector $v$ is denoted as $H(v)$ and the $i$-th row of the matrix $M$ is denoted as $M(i, :)$. The deterministic $(k, n)$-VCS is considered to be valid if the following two conditions are satisfied.

1. (Contrast condition) For any $M \in C_0$ (resp. $C_1$), $H(M(i_1, :) \otimes M(i_2, :) \otimes \cdots M(i_k, :)) \leq l$(resp. $H(M(i_1, :) \otimes M(i_2, :) \otimes \cdots M(i_k, :)) \geq h$), where $1 \leq i_1 < i_2 < \cdots < i_k \leq n$, $1 \leq l < h \leq m$.
2. (Security condition) For any subset $\{i_1, i_2, \cdots, i_q\}$ of $\{1, 2, \cdots, n\}$ with $q < k$, the two collections of $q \times m$ matrices obtained by restricting each matrix in $C_0$ and $C_1$ to the $i_1, i_2, \cdots, i_q$ rows are indistinguishable in the sense that they contain the same matrices with the same frequencies.

Different from the deterministic $(k, n)$-VCS, each secret pixel is encoded into $n \times 1$ subpixels in the probabilistic $(k, n)$-VCS. The probabilistic $(k, n)$-VCS is represented as two collections $C_0$ and $C_1$ of $n \times 1$ Boolean matrices. When sharing a white (resp. black) pixel, the dealer randomly chooses a $n \times 1$ Boolean matrix from $C_0$ (resp. $C_1$) and randomly chooses a row of the matrix to the relative share. For any matrix $M \in C_0$ (resp. $C_1$), $L(M) = M(i_1, 1) \otimes M(i_2, 1) \otimes \cdots M(i_t, 1)$, $1 \leq i_1 < i_2 < \cdots < i_t \leq n$, $1 \leq t \leq n$. These values $L(M)$ construct the set $\lambda(resp. \gamma)$. Denote $p(0, t)$ and $p(1, t)$ as the appearance probabilities of the "1" (black pixel) in the set $\lambda$ and $\gamma$, respectively. The probabilistic $(k, n)$-VCS can be considered valid if the following two conditions are satisfied.

1. (Contrast condition) When $t = k$, the two sets $\lambda$ and $\gamma$ satisfy that $p(0, k) \leq p_l$, $p(1, k) \geq p_h$, $0 \leq p_l < p_h \leq 1$.
2. (Security condition) When $t = q$, $q < k$, the two sets $\lambda$ and $\gamma$ satisfy that $p(0, q) = p(1, q)$.

As a measurement, contrast is used to evaluate the visual quality of the reconstructed secret image. There are some different definitions of contrast, which are presented in [1,2,19,20]. Herein, we adopt a relative appropriate definition of contrast [19] in this paper.

**Definition 1.** *Denote* $S(0)(resp. S(1))$ *as the area of all the white (resp. black) pixels in secret image* $S$. $R[S(0)](resp. R[S(1)])$ *is the corresponding area of all the white (resp. black) pixels in the reconstructed secret image. The white pixel density of* $R[S(0)](resp. R[S(1)])$ *is denoted as* $D(R[S(0)])$ *(resp.* $D(R[S(1)])$*). Define* $\alpha_S$ *as contrast of the reconstructed secret image,* $\alpha_S = \frac{D(R[S(0)]) - D(R[S(1)])}{1 + D(R[S(1)])}$.

With the above definition, we get $\alpha_S = \frac{h-l}{2m-h}$ in the deterministic $(k, n)$-VCS and $\alpha_S = \frac{p_h - p_l}{2 - p_h}$ in the probabilistic $(k, n)$-VCS. Generally, the reconstructed secret image is visually recognizable as the original secret image when $\alpha > 0$. According to Definition 1, $D(R[S(0)]) > D(R[S(1)])$ means that $\alpha > 0$.

## 2.2  $(k, n)$-TaVCS

In $(k, n)$-TaVCS, a secret image and $n$ tag images are encoded into $n$ tagged shares. The secret image is reconstructed visually by stacking any $k$ or more tagged shares, while no information of the secret image is disclosed from fewer than $k$ tagged-shares. Meanwhile, each tag image is revealed visually by folding up each single tagged share. We give the formal definition of $(k, n)$-TaVCS [18] as follows.

**Definition 2.** *[18] Let $S$ be the secret image and let $T_1, T_2, \cdots, T_n$ be the $n$ tag images. $SH_1, SH_2, \cdots, SH_n$ are $n$ shares generated by $(k, n)$-TaVCS. A construction of $(k, n)$-TaVCS is considered valid if the following conditions are met.*

1. *The stacked result $SH_{x_1 \otimes x_2 \otimes \cdots \otimes x_t} = SH_{x_1} \otimes SH_{x_2} \otimes \cdots \otimes SH_{x_t}$ by $t(t < k)$ shares gives no clue about the secret image. The folded up result of every share does not reveal the secret and every share can not disclose any information about the associated tag image without folding up.*
2. *The stacked result $SH_{x_1 \otimes x_2 \otimes \cdots \otimes x_t} = SH_{x_1} \otimes SH_{x_2} \otimes \cdots \otimes SH_{x_t}$ by $t(t \geq k)$ shares reconstructs the secret image visually:*

$$D(SH_{x_1 \otimes x_2 \otimes \cdots \otimes x_t}[S(0)]) > D(SH_{x_1 \otimes x_2 \otimes \cdots \otimes x_t}[S(1)]).$$

3. *The folded up result of every share reveals the tag image visually:*

$$D(FR(SH_y)[T_y(0)]) > D(FR(SH_y)[T_y(1)]), 1 \leq y \leq n,$$

*where $FR(SH_y)$ denotes the folded up result of share $SH_y$.*

## 2.3  Analysis on the Previous $(k, n)$-TaVCSs

In Wang and Hsu's method, two steps are adopted in their work to construct tagged-shares: (1) interim shares generating procedure, where $n$ interim shares are constructed from the secret image by using deterministic VCS or probabilistic VCS, and (2) tag images stamping procedure, where $n$ tagged-shares are constructed by embedding $n$ tag images into $n$ interim shares. Since each tagged-share is constructed by modifying white pixels in the interim share by black, the output tagged-share is darker than the original. Because of the darker shares, visual quality of both the reconstructed secret image and the recovered tag image is reduced.

Two stages are contained in Ou et al.'s RG-based TaVCS: (1) interim shares generation procedure, where $n$ interim shares are constructed from $n$ tag images by using the $(2, 2)$ RG-based VCS, and (2) interim shares modification procedure, where $n$ tagged-shares are constructed by modifying interim shares according to the secret image. Comparing to Wang and Hsu's scheme, better visual quality of both the reconstructed secret image and the recovered tag image is provided in $(n, n)$ RG-based TaVCS and visual quality of the recovered secret image is reduced in some $(k, n)$ cases $(k < n)$.

# 3    Proposed $(k,n)$-TaVCS

In this section, we propose a new construction of $(k,n)$-TaVCS for sharing a binary secret image and $n$ binary tag images simultaneously.

## 3.1    Encryption Process of Proposed $(k,n)$-TaVCS

Figure 1 illustrates the encryption process of the proposed $(k,n)$-TaVCS. The secret encryption code books $C_0^S$ and $C_1^S$, are used to encipher white and black secret pixels in secret image $S$, respectively. The previous constructions of the deterministic $(k,n)$-VCS or the probabilistic $(k,n)$-VCS can be used as the secret encryption code books. The tag encryption code books $C_0^T$ and $C_1^T$, are used to encipher white and black tag pixels in tag image $T_l, 1 \leq l \leq n$. The code books of the deterministic $(2,2)$-VCS or the probabilistic $(2,2)$-VCS having same white-pixel density with $C_0^S$ and $C_1^S$ can be used as $C_0^T$ and $C_1^T$. According to the input probability $r$, the encryption process generates a bit $d$. The value of $d$ determines whether a pair of secret pixels being symmetric around the middle line of the secret image or a tag pixel will be encrypted. Detailed encryption procedure of the proposed $(k,n)$-TaVCS is described as follows.

**The encryption algorithm of proposed $(k,n)$-TaVCS**

**Input:** A binary secret image $S$ with $L \times N$ pixels, $n$ binary tag images $T_1, T_2, \cdots, T_n$ with $L \times \frac{N}{2}$ pixels and a probability $r$ $(0 < r < 1)$.

**Output:** $n$ tagged shares $SH_1, SH_2, \cdots, SH_n$.

**Step 1:** Generate $n$ tagged shares $SH_1, SH_2, \cdots, SH_n$ by **Step 2-Step 10** when $1 \leq i \leq L, 1 \leq j \leq \frac{N}{2}$.

**Step 2:** Generate a bit $d$, which is 0 with prob.$r$ or 1 with prob.$1 - r$.

**Step 3: If** $d$ is equal to 0

**Step 4: If** $S(i,j) = 0$, **then** choose one matrix randomly from $C_0^S$ and $\forall 1 \leq l \leq n$, distribute the $l$-th row of the matrix to $SH_l(i, (j-1)m + 1 : jm)$.

**Step 5: If** $S(i,j) = 1$, **then** choose one matrix randomly from $C_1^S$ and $\forall 1 \leq l \leq n$, distribute the $l$-th row of the matrix to $SH_l(i, (j-1)m + 1 : jm)$.

**Step 6:** Use **Step 4** or **Step 5** to encrypt the secret pixel $S(i, N + 1 - j)$, too.

**Step 7: Else if** $d$ is equal to 1

**Step 8: If** $T_l(i,j) = 0$, **then** choose one matrix randomly from $C_0^T$ and $\forall 1 \leq l \leq n$, distribute the two rows of the matrix to $SH_l(i, (j-1)m + 1 : jm)$ and $SH_l(i, (N+1-j)m : (N-j)m + 1)$, respectively.

**Step 9: If** $T_l(i,j) = 1$, **then** choose one matrix randomly from $C_1^T$ and $\forall 1 \leq l \leq n$, distribute the two rows of the matrix to $SH_l(i, (j-1)m + 1 : jm)$ and $SH_l(i, (N+1-j)m : (N-j)m + 1)$, respectively.

**Step 10: End if**

**Remark:** in the above encryption algorithm, $m$ represents the pixel expansion of the deterministic $(k,n)$-VCS. For the probabilistic $(k,n)$-VCS, the pixel expansion $m = 1$. For succinct expression, we denote $(k,n)$-TaDVCS and $(k,n)$-TaPVCS as $(k,n)$-TaVCS based on the deterministic VCS and the probabilistic VCS, respectively.

## 3.2  Theoretical Analysis

Furthermore, we prove that the proposed method is a valid construction of $(k, n)$-TaVCS by Theorem 1, which satisfies security condition and contrast condition. Contrast of the reconstructed secret image and contrast of the revealed tag image are given in Theorems 2 and 3, respectively.

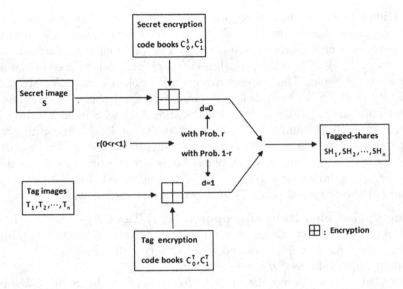

**Fig. 1.** Encryption progress of the proposed $(k, n)$-TaVCS

**Lemma 1.** *The proposed $(k, n)$-TaVCS is secure.*

*Proof.* The proposed scheme is composed of secret image encryption process and tag images encryption process. The secret image encryption process adopts the construction of $(k, n)$-VCS. The tag images encryption process adopts the code books of $(2, 2)$-VCS to encrypt tag pixels, despite secret pixels. The construction of $(k, n)$-VCS has been proved that it satisfies the security condition. Hence, the proposed $(k, n)$-TaVCS satisfies the security condition of the corresponding $(k, n)$-VCS. In addition, each tag image is revealed only by folding up each tagged-share. The folded up result of each tagged-share discloses no information of the secret image. Thus, the proposed $(k, n)$-TaVCS is proved to hold security property.

Herein, we consider two schemes: (a) the conventional $(k, n)$-VCS, which encodes the secret image into $n$ noise-like shares by using the code books $C_0^S$ and $C_1^S$ and (b) the tagged-shares generation scheme, which conceals $n$ tag images into $n$ tagged-shares by using the code books $C_0^T$ and $C_1^T$. Let notations $p_0$ (resp. $p_1$) and $\bar{p}_0$ (resp. $\bar{p}_1$) represent the white-pixel density in the white (resp. black) area of the reconstructed secret image in scheme (a) and of the recovered tag image in scheme (b), respectively. Let notation $p$ denote the white pixel density of the tagged-shares generated by the proposed method.

**Lemma 2.** *The stacked result* $SH_{x_1 \otimes x_2 \otimes \cdots \otimes x_t} = SH_{x_1} \otimes SH_{x_2} \otimes \cdots \otimes SH_{x_t}$ *by* $t(t \geq k)$ *shares reconstructs the secret image visually:*

$$D(SH_{x_1 \otimes x_2 \otimes \cdots \otimes x_t}[S(0)]) > D(SH_{x_1 \otimes x_2 \otimes \cdots \otimes x_t}[S(1)]).$$

*Proof.* $D(SH_{x_1 \otimes x_2 \otimes \cdots \otimes x_t}[S(0)])$ (resp. $D(SH_{x_1 \otimes x_2 \otimes \cdots \otimes x_t}[S(1)])$) consists of two conditions: (a) encrypting as white pixels based on the secret encryption code books $C_0^S$ (resp. $C_1^S$), and (b) encrypting as white pixels determined by $p$, the white-pixel density of the tagged-shares. The ratios of the two conditions are $r$ and $1 - r$. Thus, white-pixel density is $rp_0$ (resp. $rp_1$) and $(1 - r)p^t$ for condition (a) and condition (b), respectively. Then, we get

$$D(SH_{x_1 \otimes x_2 \otimes \cdots \otimes x_t}[S(0)]) = rp_0 + (1 - r)p^t \tag{1}$$

$$D(SH_{x_1 \otimes x_2 \otimes \cdots \otimes x_t}[S(1)]) = rp_1 + (1 - r)p^t \tag{2}$$

Since the code books of $(k, n)$-VCS satisfy the contrast condition, we obtain $p_0 > p_1$. Then, we get

$$D(SH_{x_1 \otimes x_2 \otimes \cdots \otimes x_t}[S(0)]) > D(SH_{x_1 \otimes x_2 \otimes \cdots \otimes x_t}[S(1)]).$$

**Lemma 3.** *The folded up result of every share reveals the tag image visually:*

$$D(FR(SH_y)[T_y(0)]) > D(FR(SH_y)[T_y(1)]), 1 \leq y \leq n.$$

*Proof.* $D(FR(SH_y)[T_y(0)])(resp. D(FR(SH_y)[T_y(1)]))$ $(1 \leq y \leq n)$ is composed of two parts: (a) encrypting as white pixels based on the tag encryption code books $C_0^T$ (resp. $C_1^T$), and (b) encrypting as white pixels determined by $p$, the white-pixel density of the tagged-shares. The ratios of the two parts are $1 - r$ and $r$. Hence, white-pixel density is $(1 - r)\overline{p}_0$(resp. $(1 - r)\overline{p}_1$) and $rp^2$ for part (a) and part (b), respectively. Then, we get

$$D(FR(SH_y)[T_y(0)]) = (1 - r)\overline{p}_0 + rp^2 \tag{3}$$

$$D(FR(SH_y)[T_y(1)]) = (1 - r)\overline{p}_1 + rp^2 \tag{4}$$

Since the code books of $(2, 2)$-VCS satisfies the contrast condition, we get $\overline{p}_0 > \overline{p}_1$. Then, $D(FR(SH_y)[T_y(0)]) > D(FR(SH_y)[T_y(1)])(1 \leq y \leq n)$ is obtained.

**Theorem 1.** *The proposed method is a valid construction of $(k, n)$-TaVCS, if the following conditions are met.*

1. *The stacked result $SH_{x_1 \otimes x_2 \otimes \cdots \otimes x_t} = SH_{x_1} \otimes SH_{x_2} \otimes \cdots \otimes SH_{x_t}$ by $t(t < k)$ shares gives no clue about the secret image. The folded up result of every share does not reveal the secret and every share can not disclose any information about the associated tag image without folding up.*

2. *The stacked result $SH_{x_1 \otimes x_2 \otimes \cdots \otimes x_t} = SH_{x_1} \otimes SH_{x_2} \otimes \cdots \otimes SH_{x_t}$ by $t(t \geq k)$ shares reconstructs the secret image visually:*

$$D(SH_{x_1 \otimes x_2 \otimes \cdots \otimes x_t}[S(0)]) > D(SH_{x_1 \otimes x_2 \otimes \cdots \otimes x_t}[S(1)]).$$

3. *The folded up result of every share reveals the tag image visually:*

$$D(FR(SH_y)[T_y(0)]) > D(FR(SH_y)[T_y(1)]), 1 \leq y \leq n,$$

*where $FR(SH_y)$ denotes the folded up result of share $SH_y$.*

*Proof.* Lemmas 1–3 have been proved respectively, which guarantee that the proposed method satisfies the three conditions. Therefore, the proposed method is a valid construction of $(k, n)$-TaVCS.

**Theorem 2.** *Contrast of the reconstructed secret image by the proposed $(k, n)$-TaVCS is $\alpha_S = \frac{r(p_0 - p_1)}{1 + rp_1 + (1-r)p^t}$, where $t \geq k$.*

*Proof.* From Lemma 2, we get $D(SH_{x_1 \otimes x_2 \otimes \cdots \otimes x_t}[S(0)]) = rp_0 + (1-r)p^t$ and $D(SH_{x_1 \otimes x_2 \otimes \cdots \otimes x_t}[S(1)]) = rp_1 + (1-r)p^t$.

Hence, the contrast of the reconstructed secret image by the proposed scheme is represented by

$$\alpha_S = \frac{D(SH_{x_1 \otimes x_2 \otimes \cdots \otimes x_t}[S(0)]) - D(SH_{x_1 \otimes x_2 \otimes \cdots \otimes x_t}[S(1)])}{1 + D(SH_{x_1 \otimes x_2 \otimes \cdots \otimes x_t}[S(1)])} = \frac{r(p_0 - p_1)}{1 + rp_1 + (1-r)p^t}.$$

**Theorem 3.** *Contrast of the recovered tag image by the proposed $(k, n)$-TaVCS is $\alpha_T = \frac{(1-r)(\overline{p}_0 - \overline{p}_1)}{1 + (1-r)\overline{p}_1 + rp^2}$.*

*Proof.* According to Lemma 3, $D(FR(SH_y)[T_y(0)]) = (1-r)\overline{p}_0 + rp^2$ and $D(FR(SH_y)[T_y(1)]) = (1-r)\overline{p}_1 + rp^2$ are obtained.

Thus, the contrast of the recovered tag image by the proposed scheme is

$$\alpha_T = \frac{D(FR(SH_y)[T_y(0)]) - D(FR(SH_y)[T_y(1)])}{1 + D(FR(SH_y)[T_y(1)])} = \frac{(1-r)(\overline{p}_0 - \overline{p}_1)}{1 + (1-r)\overline{p}_1 + rp^2}.$$

According to $\frac{\partial \alpha_S}{\partial r} = \frac{(p_0 - p_1)(1 + p^t)}{(1 + rp_1 + (1-r)p^t)^2} > 0$ and $\frac{\partial \alpha_T}{\partial p} = \frac{(\overline{p}_1 - \overline{p}_0)(p^2 + 1)}{(1 + (1-r)\overline{p}_1 + rp^2)^2} < 0$, contrast $\alpha_S$ increases and contrast $\alpha_T$ decreases with increment $r$, where $0 < r < 1$. As the ratio $r \to 0$, we get $\alpha_S \to 0$ and $\alpha_T \to \frac{\overline{p}_0 - \overline{p}_1}{1 + \overline{p}_1}$. While the ratio $r \to 1$, we get $\alpha_S \to \frac{p_0 - p_1}{1 + p_1}$ and $\alpha_T \to 0$. The above results show that $\alpha_S$ and $\alpha_T$ cannot achieve the optimal value simultaneously. Hence, the ratio r can be adjusted to make a trade off in the visual quality of the reconstructed secret image and of the recovered tag image. While the ratio $r = 0.5$, both the reconstructed secret image and the recovered tag image obtain their respective medium visual quality. Compared with the previous $(k, n)$-TaVCSs, better visual quality of both the reconstructed secret image and the recovered tag image is obtained when the ratio $r = 0.5$. Experimental results in next section demonstrate the above conclusion.

## 4   Experimental Results

Firstly, we give the simulation results of some $(k, n)$-TaVCSs by using the proposed method. Secondly, we show the experimental results of visual performance comparison of some $(k, n)$-TaVCSs among the proposed method and the related methods.

## 4.1   Simulation Results of the Proposed Method

The first experiment is a $(2,3)$-TaDVCS by using the proposed method. Herein, the basis matrices $B_0 = \begin{pmatrix} 1\,0\,0 \\ 1\,0\,0 \\ 1\,0\,0 \end{pmatrix}$ and $B_1 = \begin{pmatrix} 1\,0\,0 \\ 0\,1\,0 \\ 0\,0\,1 \end{pmatrix}$ are adopted to construct $(2,3)$-DVCS. $(2,2)$-DVCS is constructed by the basis matrices $B_0 = \begin{pmatrix} 1\,0\,0 \\ 1\,0\,0 \end{pmatrix}$ and $B_1 = \begin{pmatrix} 1\,0\,0 \\ 0\,1\,0 \end{pmatrix}$. Figure 2 shows the experimental results of a $(2,3)$-TaDVCS by the proposed method $(r = 0.5)$. The $256 \times 256$ secret image is shown in Fig. 2(a). Three $256 \times 128$ tag images are shown in Fig. 2(b)–(d). Three tagged-shares are exhibited in Fig. 2(e)–(g). The reconstructed secret images by stacking any two tagged-shares are shown in Fig. 2(h)–(j). The reconstructed secret image by stacking all three tagged-shares is shown in Fig. 2(k). Figure 2(l)–(n) show the recovered tag images by folding up each tagged-share.

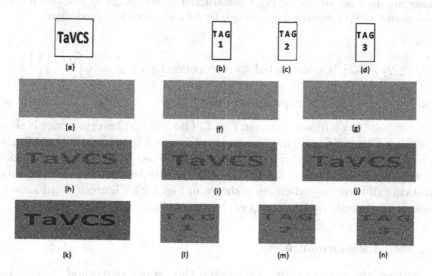

**Fig. 2.** A $(2,3)$-TaDVCS by the proposed method $(r = 0.5)$. (a) secret image, (b)–(d) three tag images, (e)–(g) three tagged-shares, (h)–(j) reconstructed secret images by stacking any two tagged-shares, (k) reconstructed secret image by stacking all three tagged-shares, (l)–(n) recovered tag images by folding up each tagged-share.

The second experiment is a $(3,3)$-TaPVCS by using the proposed method. In the proposed scheme, we adopt the collections $C_0 = \left\{ \begin{bmatrix} 0 \\ 0 \\ 0 \end{bmatrix}, \begin{bmatrix} 1 \\ 1 \\ 0 \end{bmatrix}, \begin{bmatrix} 0 \\ 1 \\ 1 \end{bmatrix}, \begin{bmatrix} 1 \\ 0 \\ 1 \end{bmatrix} \right\}$ and $C_1 = \left\{ \begin{bmatrix} 1 \\ 1 \\ 1 \end{bmatrix}, \begin{bmatrix} 0 \\ 0 \\ 1 \end{bmatrix}, \begin{bmatrix} 0 \\ 1 \\ 0 \end{bmatrix}, \begin{bmatrix} 1 \\ 0 \\ 0 \end{bmatrix} \right\}$ to construct $(3,3)$-PVCS. Mean-

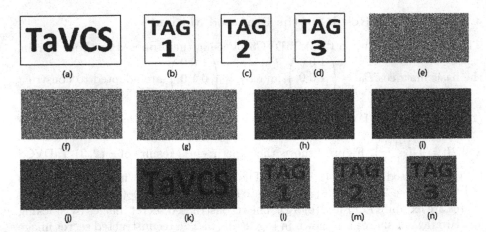

**Fig. 3.** A $(3, 3)$-TaPVCS by the proposed method ($r = 0.6$). (a) secret image, (b)–(d) three tag images, (e)–(g) three tagged-shares, (h)–(j) reconstructed secret images by stacking any two tagged-shares, (k) reconstructed secret image by stacking all three tagged-shares, (l)–(n) recovered tag images by folding up each tagged-share.

while, $(2, 2)$-PVCS is constructed by the collections $C_0 = \left\{ \begin{bmatrix} 0 \\ 0 \end{bmatrix}, \begin{bmatrix} 1 \\ 1 \end{bmatrix} \right\}$ and $C_1 = \left\{ \begin{bmatrix} 1 \\ 0 \end{bmatrix}, \begin{bmatrix} 0 \\ 1 \end{bmatrix} \right\}$. The experimental results of a $(3, 3)$-TaPVCS by the proposed method ($r = 0.6$) are shown in Fig. 3. The $256 \times 512$ secret image is shown in Fig. 3(a). Three $256 \times 256$ tag images are shown in Fig. 3(b)–(d). Three tagged-shares are exhibited in Fig. 3(e)–(g). The reconstructed secret images by stacking any two tagged-shares are shown in Fig. 3(h)–(j). The reconstructed secret image by stacking all three tagged-shares is shown in Fig. 3(k). Figure 3(l)–(n) show the recovered tag images by folding up each tagged-share.

### 4.2 Visual Performance

We compare the visual quality among the the proposed method, Wang-Hsu's $(k, n)$-TaPVCS and Ou et al.'s RG-based $(k, n)$-TaVCS as follows. Herein, the probabilistic VCS by Yang's work [7] is adopted in Wang and Hsu's method and the proposed method, where the corresponding code books are obtained from [7]. Ou et al.'s construction method is based on Chen and Tsao's method [9]. Experimental contrast is used for evaluating the visual quality.

Table 1 shows the comparison of contrast of reconstructed secret image among the proposed method ($r = 0.5$), Wang-Hsu's method and Ou et al.'s method. For the $(2, 4), (3, 4)$ cases, the largest contrast of reconstructed secret image is provided by the proposed method ($r = 0.5$) among three methods. For the $(3, 3), (4, 4)$ cases, larger contrast of reconstructed secret image is provided by the proposed method ($r = 0.5$) while comparing to Wang-Hsu's method.

**Table 1.** Comparison of contrast (%) of reconstructed secret image among the proposed method ($r = 0.5$) and the related methods, where $t$ is the number of stacked shares.

| $(k, n)$ | $t$ | Schemes | | |
|---|---|---|---|---|
| | | Our scheme($r = 0.5$) | Scheme [17] | Scheme [18] |
| $(2, 3)$ | $t = 2$ | 13.86 | 17.09 | 14.22 |
| | $t = 3$ | 23.58 | 21.28 | 24.98 |
| $(2, 4)$ | $t = 2$ | 13.66 | 17.18 | 7.34 |
| | $t = 3$ | 22.98 | 21.72 | 11.82 |
| | $t = 4$ | 23.84 | 16.97 | 12.60 |
| $(3, 3)$ | $t = 3$ | 12.13 | 10.31 | 25.18 |
| $(3, 4)$ | $t = 3$ | 7.19 | 6.36 | 5.97 |
| | $t = 4$ | 15.95 | 10.70 | 12.52 |
| $(4, 4)$ | $t = 4$ | 5.57 | 4.01 | 12.50 |

**Table 2.** Comparison of contrast (%) of recovered tag image among the proposed method ($r = 0.5$) and the related methods.

| $(k, n)$ | Schemes | | |
|---|---|---|---|
| | Our scheme ($r = 0.5$) | Scheme [17] | Scheme [18] |
| $(2, 3)$ | 21.88 | 14.04 | 14.01 |
| $(2, 4)$ | 22.67 | 14.00 | 22.64 |
| $(3, 3)$ | 21.63 | 13.84 | 14.36 |
| $(3, 4)$ | 21.96 | 14.06 | 22.50 |
| $(4, 4)$ | 22.54 | 14.09 | 21.92 |

Experimental contrast of the recovered tag image by folding up each tagged-share is illustrated in Table 2. For all mentioned cases, larger contrast of recovered tag image is provided by the proposed method ($r = 0.5$) while comparing to Wang-Hsu's method. Meanwhile, contrast of recovered tag image by the proposed method ($r = 0.5$) for all mentioned cases is larger than or approximate to the value of contrast obtained from Ou et al.'s method.

Experimental results of visual quality comparison of the $(2, 4)$-TaVCS among the proposed method ($r = 0.5$) and the related methods are demonstrated in Fig. 4. According to experimental results, the proposed method ($r = 0.5$) provides better visual quality of both the reconstructed secret image and the recovered tag image.

## 5    Conclusions

In this paper, we propose a novel method to construct a $(k, n)$-TaVCS. The proposed method is proved to be a valid construction of $(k, n)$-TaVCS by theoretical

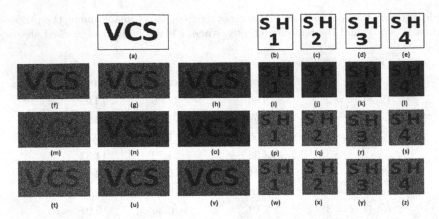

**Fig. 4.** Comparison of visual quality for the $(2,4)$-TaVCS among Wang and Hsu's method, Ou et al.'s method and the proposed method ($r = 0.5$): (a) the $256 \times 512$ secret image, (b)–(e) the four $256 \times 256$ tag images, (f)–(h) reconstructed secret images by superimposing two, three and four shares from Wang-Hsu's method, (i)–(l) recovered tag images by Wang-Hsu's method, (m)–(o) reconstructed secret images by superimposing two, three and four shares from Ou et al.'s method, (p)–(s) recovered tag images by Ou et al.'s method, (t)–(v) reconstructed secret images by superimposing two, three and four shares from the proposed method ($r = 0.5$), (w)–(z) recovered tag images by the proposed method ($r = 0.5$).

analysis and experiment results. The proposed method can not only adjust visual quality of both the reconstructed secret image and the recovered tagged image flexibly, but also provide better visual quality of both the reconstructed secret image and the recovered tag image under certain condition. Devising a TaVCS with better property will be the future work.

**Acknowledgments.** Many thanks to the anonymous reviewers for their valuable comments. This work was supported by the "Strategic Priority Research Program" of the Chinese Academy of Sciences grant No. Y2W0012102 and the IIE's Project grant No. Y5X0061102.

# References

1. Naor, M., Shamir, A.: Visual Cryptography. In: De Santis, A. (ed.) EUROCRYPT 1994. LNCS, vol. 950, pp. 1–12. Springer, Heidelberg (1995)
2. Eisen, P.A., Stinson, D.R.: Threshold visual cryptography schemes with specified whiteness levels of reconstructed pixels. Des. Codes Crypt. **25**, 15–61 (2002)
3. Koga, H.: A general formula of the $(t,n)$-Threshold visual secret sharing scheme. In: Zheng, Y. (ed.) ASIACRYPT 2002. LNCS, vol. 2501, pp. 328–345. Springer, Heidelberg (2002)
4. Blundo, C., Cimato, S., De Santis, A.: Visual cryptography schemes with optimal pixel expansion. Theoret. Comput. Sci. **369**, 169–182 (2006)

5. Shyu, S.J., Chen, M.C.: Optimum pixel expansions for threshold visual secret sharing schemes. IEEE Trans. Inf. Forensics Secur. **6**, 960 969 (2011)
6. Ito, R., Kuwakado, H., Tanaka, H.: Image size invariant visual cryptography. IEICE Fundam. Electron. Commun. Comput. Sci. **82**(10), 2172–2177 (1999)
7. Yang, C.N.: New visual secret sharing schemes using probabilistic method. Pattern Recogn. Lett. **25**, 481–494 (2004)
8. Shyu, S.J.: Image encryption by random grids. Pattern Recogn. **40**, 1014–1031 (2007)
9. Chen, T.H., Tsao, K.H.: Threshold visual secret sharing by random grids. J. Syst. Softw. **84**, 1197–1208 (2011)
10. Wu, X.T., Sun, W.: Generalized random grid and its applications in visual cryptography. IEEE Trans. Inf. Forensics Secur. **8**(9), 1541–1553 (2013)
11. Ateniese, G., Blundo, C., De Santis, A., Stinson, D.R.: Extended capabilities for visual cryptography. Theor. Comput. Sci. **250**(1–2), 143–161 (2001)
12. Wang, D., Yi, F., Li, X.: On general construction for extended visual cryptography schemes. Pattern Recogn. **42**, 3071–3082 (2009)
13. Liu, F., Wu, C.K.: Embedded extended visual cryptography schemes. IEEE Trans. Inf. Forensics Secur. **6**(2), 307–322 (2011)
14. Guo, T., Liu, F., Wu, C.K.: K out of k extended visual cryptography scheme by random grids. Signal Proc. **94**, 90–101 (2014)
15. Yang, C.N., Yang, Y.Y.: New extended visual cryptography schemes with clearer shadow images. Inf. Sci. **271**, 246–263 (2014)
16. Yan, X.H., Wang, S., Niu, X.M., Yang, C.N.: Generalized random grids-based threshold visual cryptography with meaningful shares. Signal Proc. **109**, 317–333 (2015)
17. Wang, R.Z., Hsu, S.F.: Tagged visual cryptography. IEEE Signal Proc Lett. **18**(11), 627–630 (2011)
18. Ou, D., Wu, X., Dai, L., Sun, W.: Improved tagged visual cryptograms by using random grids. In: Shi, Y.Q., Kim, H.-J., Pérez-González, F. (eds.) IWDW 2013. LNCS, vol. 8389, pp. 79–94. Springer, Heidelberg (2014)
19. Verheul, E.R., Van Tilborg, H.C.A.: Constructions and properties of k out of n visual secret sharing scheme. Des. Codes Crypt. **1**, 179–196 (1997)
20. Liu, F., Wu, C.K., Lin, X.J.: A new definition of the contrast of visual cryptography scheme. Inform. Process. Lett. **110**, 241–246 (2010)

# Author Index

Printed in the United States
By Bookmasters